W9-BGH-452

Contents

+ = white stands slightly better   les blancs ont jeu un peu meilleur   Weiss steht etwas besser   wit staat er iets beter voor vit står nagot bättre   il bianco sta un po' meglio   el blanco está algo mejor белые стоят немного лучше

= + black stands slightly better   les noirs ont jeu un peu meilleur   Schwarz steht etwas besser   zwart staat er iets beter voor svart står nagot bättre   il nero sta un po' meglio el nero está algo mejor   черные стояат немного лучше

± white has the upper hand   les blancs ont le meilleur jeu   Weiss steht besser   wit staat beter   vit står bättre   il bianco sta meglio   el blanco está mejor   белые стоят лучше

∓ black has the upper hand   les noirs ont le meilleur jeu   Schwarz steht besser zwart staat beter   svart står bättre   il nero sta meglio   el negro está mejor черные стоят лучше

+ − white has a decisive advantage   les blancs ont un avantage décisif   Weiss hat entscheidenden vorteil   wit heeft een beslissend voordeel   vit har avgörande fördel il bianco è in vantaggio decisivo   el blanco tiene una ventaja decisiva   белые имеют решающее преимущество

− + black has a decisive advantage   les noirs ont un avantage décisif   Schwarz hat entscheidenden vorteil   zwart heeft een beslissend voordeel   svart har avgörande fördel   il nero è in vantaggio decisivo el negro tiene una ventaja decisiva   черные имеют решающее преимущество

= the game is even   le jeu est égal   das Spiel ist ausgeglichen   de stellingen zÿn gelÿkwaardig   spelet är jamnt   giuoco pari   el juego está equilibrado   игра равна

≈ approximately equal   plus où moins égal ungefähr gleich   ongeveer gelÿkwaardig narmelsevis jämnt   piu o meno eguale más o menos igual   приблизительно равно

∝ the position is unclear   le jeu est incertain das Spiel ist unklar   de posities zÿn onduidelÿk   ställningen är oklar   il giuoco è poco chiaro   la posición no es clara неясная позиция

! a very good move   un tres bon coup ein sehr guter Zug   een zeer goede zet ett bra drag   una buona mossa   una jugada muy buena   очень хороший ход

!! an excellent move   un excellent coup ein ausgezeichneter Zug   een uitstekende zet   ett utmärkt drag   una mossa ottima una jugada excelente   отличный ход

? a mistake   un coup faible   ein schwacher Zug   een fout   ett dåligt drag   una mossa debole   una mala jugada   плохой ход

?? a blunder   une grave erreur   ein grober Fehler   een ernstige fout   ett grovt fel un grave errore   un gran error   грубая ошибка

!? a move deserving attention   un coup qui mérite l'attention   ein beachtenswerter Zug   een zet die de aandacht verdient ett drag som fortjäner uppmärksamhet una mossa degna di considerazione   una jugada que merece atención   ход, заслуживающий внимания

?! a dubious move   un coup d'une valeur douteuse   ein Zug von zweifelhaftem wert   een dubieuze zet   ett tvivelaktigt drag   una mossa dubbia   una jugada de dudoso valor   ход, имеющий сомнительную ценность

Δ with the idea . . .   avec l'idée . . .   mit der Idee . . .   met het idee om . . .   med idén . . .   con l'idea . . .   con idea . . . с идеей...

N a novelty   une innovation   eine Neuerung   een nieuwtje   en nyhet   un'innovazione   una novedad   новинка

4

The New Chess Player
Le Nouveau Joueur d'Échecs
Der neue Schachspieler
De Nieuwe Schaakspeler
Den nye Schackspelaren
Il Nuovo Giocatore di Scacchi
El Nuevo Ajedrecista
Новый Шахматист

7

1979
C

PITMAN PUBLISHING LIMITED
39 Parker Street, London WC2B 5PB

Associated Companies
Copp Clark Limited, Toronto
Fearon-Pitman Publishers Inc., Belmont, California
Pitman Publishing New Zealand Ltd., Wellington
Pitman Publishing Pty Ltd., Melbourne

Distributed in Italy by
Edizioni Scolastiche APE SpA
Via Tanaro 14, 20128 Milano

Distributed in Federal Republic of
Germany, DDR, Austria and
Switzerland by
Joachin Beyer Verlag, Langgasse 29,
Postfach 1148 860, Hollfeld, Federal
Republic of Germany.

© The Chess Player Ltd 1980

First published in Great Britain 1980

Printed and bound in England by
Billing & Son Ltd., Guildford

ISBN 0 273 01412 9

Contributors

A. Adorjan	GM	H. Kasparov	IM
B. Balogh		R. Keene	GM
J. Banas		A. Kotov	GM
G. Botterill	IM	M. Madler	
W. Browne	GM	R. Maric	IM
M. Ciamarra		S. Mechkarov	
V. Ciocaltea	GM	E. Mednis	IM
J. Fedorowicz		C. Meleghegyi	
A. Foldi		A. Miles	GM
T. Georgadze	GM	J. Nunn	GM
F. Gheorghiu	GM	E. Paoli	IM
A. Gipslis	GM	K. Pytel	IM
E. Gufeld	GM	S. Samarian	
E. Haag	IM	W. Schmidt	GM
P. Hardicsay		R. Snyder	
W. Hartston	IM	J. Speelman	IM
K. Honfi	IM	I. Szabo	
B. Ivanovic	GM	M. Tal	GM
A. Kapengut		J. Tompa	
		V. Vaisman	IM
		G. Vegh	
		L. Vogt	GM

Journals

Ajedrez, British Chess Magazine, Butlleti D'Escacs, Ceskoslovensky Sach, Chess, Chess Bulletin (Canada), Chess in Australia, Chess Life and Review, Deutsche Schachblatter, Deutsche Schachzeitung, Europe Echecs, Fernschach, Jaque, Jaque Mate, Le Courrier Des Echecs, L'Italia Scacchistica, Magyar Sakkelet, Modern Chess Theory, Revista Romana de Sah, Rochade, Sahovski Glasnik, Scacco, Schaakbulletin, Schach, Schach-Echo, Schack nytt, Schakend Nederland, Shahmat, Shakhmatna Mis'l, Skakbladet, South African Chessplayer, Suomen Shakki, Szachy, Tidskrift fur Schack, 64 Шахматы Шахматный Бюллетень Шахматы в СССР

Bulletins

1979: Alicante, Amsterdam, Bagneux, Berne, Biel, Bled, Bogota, Brisbane, Bucharest, Budapest, Cape Town, Clare Benedict, Coka, Dortmund, Esbjerg, Jakarta, Jugoslavia Junior Final, Karlovac, Kecskemet 2, London, Lublin, Manila, Netherlands Final, Oslo, Polanica Zdroj, Prague, Quebec, Queensland, Riga, Rio, Rzeszow, Spartakiad, Sochi, Sofia, Tilburg, Timman - Polugaevsky, Trstenik, Tuzla, Vrsac, Waddinxveen, Zagreb.

Combinations

1	Iannaccone	– Toth
5	Csom	– Tompa
43	Liebert	– A.Schneider
56	Botterill	– Boersma
85	Gulko	– Sveshnikov
88	Stefanov	– Stanclu
99	Botterill	– Kraidman
113	Portisch	– Balashov
125	Zaichik	– Gipslis
125	Gheorghiu	– Adorjan
140	Spassky	– Sigurjonsson
158	Vaganian	– Hubner
183	Plachetka	– Basagic
185	Portisch	– Torre
191	Romanishin	– Grunfeld
202	Zaichik	– Mik.Tseitlin

203	Nunn	– Pedersen
212	Maric	– Cvetkovic
226	Ostaszewski	– Stankovic
241	Hardicsay	– Stull
243	Ljubojevic	– Ribli
256	Ivanovic	– Prevoznik
260	Plaskett	– Lombardy
271	Velimirovic	– Cvetkovic
275	Tseshkovsky	– Polugaevsky
278	Telesijevic	– Honfi
285	Chase	– A.Smith
288	Beljavsky	– Gheorghiu
292	Vitolins	– Georgadze
304	Karpov	– Larsen
322	Gipslis	– Ruderfer
329	Mark.Tseitlin	– Vilela
345	Bohm	– Bagirov
349	Vorotnikov	– Sturua
358	Prokopovic	– Verus

Novelties

4	Denker	– Gheorghiu
12	Szabo	– Horvath
15	Godes	– Karasev
18	Govbinder	– Kapengut
25	Polugaevsky	– Veingold
41	Tomaszewski	– Barczay
55	Diesen	– Matulovic
81	Nikolic	– Azmajparashvili
114	Portisch	– Ljubojevic
116	Vaiser	– Sturua
139	Chechelian	– Andrianov
152	Tal	– Ubilava
163	Farago	– Kirov
164	Portisch	– Vadasz
185	Portisch	– Torre
203	Franzen	– Banas

208	Sveshnikov	– Hartston
216	Savage	– Gheorghiu
217	Romanishin	– Sturua
220	P.Whitehead	– Lindsay
225	Ljubojevic	– Adorjan
228	Vrabec	– Hardicsay
233	Klovan	– Gurgenidze
234	Zuckerman	– Day
236	Ciocaltea	– Banas
255	Shakarov	– Nasybullin
283	Ljubojevic	– Miles
288	Beljavsky	– Gheorghiu
300	Klovsky	– Bobolovich
313	Chiburdanidze	– Psahis
336	Tal	– Portisch
337	Westerinen	– Botterill
340	Grunfeld	– Mednis
366	Klaman	– Karasev

Theory

1 b3

1 b3 e5 1...d5 2 &b2
a) 2...&g4!? 3 c4 d4 4 h3 &h5 5
g4!? &g6 6 &g2 &c6 7 b4 a6 8 &a4
&d7 9 b5 &d8 10 &f3 f6 11 &xd4
e5 12 &b3 h5 13 g5 fxg5∞ Baljon-
van der Sterren, Amsterdam 1979;
5 g3;
b) 2...&g4!? 3 h3 &h5 4 &f3 (4 g3
+=) 4...&xf3?! 5 exf3 e6 6 g3 a5 7
a4 &e7 8 f4 &d7 9 &g2 h5 10 0-0
&f5 11 c4 c6 12 cxd5 cxd5 13 &e1
&c5= Yap-Dorfman, Manila 1979;
c) 2...c5 3 e3 &c6 4 &f3 (4 &b5 Δ
f4, &f3) 4...&f6 5 &b5 &d7 6 0-0
e6 7 d3 &e7 8 &xc6 &xc6 9 &e5 0-0
10 &xc6 bxc6 11 &e2 &d7 12 e4
&c7 13 f4 &ae8= Psahis-Mohring,
Sochi 1979;
d) 2...&f5!? 3 &f3 e6 4 g3 &f6 5 &g2
&d6 6 0-0 &e7 7 d3 h6 8 c4 c6 9 cxd5
cxd5 10 &c3 &c6 11 &b5 &b8 12
&a3 &d7 13 &d2 += Mascarinas-
Shaw, Queensland 1979
e) 2...&f6 3 e3 &g4 4 &f3 e6 5 h3
&h5 6 &e2 &d6 7 0-0 &bd7 8 d3 0-0
9 &bd2 c6 10 e4 &c7 11 c4 dxe4
12 &xe4 &xe4 13 dxe4 &xf3 14
&xf3 &e5∓ Hammer-Hoen, Lucerne
1979

2 &b2 &c6
a) 2...d6 3 e3 &c6 4 &b5 a6 5 &xc6+
bxc6 6 f4 exf4 7 &f3 d5 8 &xf4 &d6
9 &a4 &d7 10 &f3 &f6 11 0-0 0-0
12 &c3 &e8 13 &ae1 h6 14 &h4 +=
Planinc-Bielczyk, Polanica Zdroj
1979;
b) 2...d6 3 c4 &f6 4 &f3 g6 5 e3
&g7 6 &e2 0-0 7 0-0 &e8 8 d3 &bd7
9 &bd2 c6 10 &e1 &c7 11 &c2 b6

12 d4 &b7= Monnard-Cordes, Berne
1979
3 e3 &f6
a) 3...a6!? N 4 &f3 e4 5 &d4 &xd4
6 &xd4 &g5 7 c4 b6 8 d3 f5 9 g3
&b7 10 &g2 0-0-0 11 0-0 &e8 12 &d2
&h6 13 &c2 += Schussler-Nicevski,
Lublin 1979;
b) 3...d5!? 4 &b5 &d6 5 &f3 (5 f4!)
5...&e7 6 d4 exd4!? (6...e4 7 &e5
&g5!) 7 &xd4 &d7 8 &f3 &b4+ 9 &d2
&f6 10 0-0-0 &a3 11 &f4 0-0 12 &f5
&xf5 13 &xf5 &e5 14 &f3 &eg4 15
&hf1 c6∓ Nicolac-Toth, Berne 1979
4 &b5
4 c4 &e7 5 g3 d5 6 a3 d4 7 exd4
&xd4 8 d3 &g4 9 f3 &f5 10 &d2
&d7 11 &e4 0-0-0∓ Bozanovic-
Ivanovic, Jugoslavia 1979
4...d6 5 d4
5 &f3 &d7 6 0-0 &e7 7 &e2 0-0 8 c4
&e8 9 &c3 &f8 10 d3 h6= Larsen-
Andersson, Teesside 1972
5...exd4 6 exd4 &d7 7 &f3 &e7+
8 &e2 g6? 9 0-0 &g7 10 &e1 &e6
11 d5! &xd5 12 &a6 +− Nicolac-
Weber, Berne 1979

English

1 c4 e5 2 &c3 &f6
a) 2...&c6 3 &f3 f5 4 d4 e4 5 &g5
&f6 6 e3 d6 7 b4 h6 8 &h3 g5 9
&g1 &d7 10 h4 gxh4 11 b5 &e7 12
&xh4 += Rajkovic-Lein, Vrsac 1979;
5...&b4!;
b) 2...d6 3 g3 c6 4 d4 &f6 5 &g2
&e7 6 e4 0-0 7 &ge2 &e6 8 b3 &c8
9 0-0 &h3 10 &a3 &xg2 11 &xg2
&c7 12 &c1 += Dorfman-Shaw,
Manila 1979
3 &f3
3 g3 c6 4 d4 exd4 5 &xd4 d5 6 &f3
&e7 7 cxd5 cxd5 8 &g2 &c6 9 &a4

7

0-0 10 ♗e3!? ♘g4 11 ♗d4! ♘xd4 12 ♘xd4 ♘f6 Hort-Kavalek, Waddinxveen 1979, 13 ♕b3! +=

3...♘c6 4 e3

a) 4 d4 exd4 5 ♘xd4 ♗b4 6 ♘xc6 ♗xc3+ 7 bxc3 bxc6 8 ♗g5 N h6 9 ♗h4 c5 10 f3 ♕e7 11 e4 ♕e5 12 ♕c2 d6 13 ♗d3 += Joksic-Bergstrom, Biel 1979; 7...dxc6! 8 ♕xd8+ ♔xd8 9 ♗g5 ♔e7 10 e3 ♗e6=;

b) 4 g3 ♗b4 5 ♘d5 e4 6 ♘h4 0-0 7 ♗g2 ♗c5 8 0-0 ♖e8 9 d3 exd3 10 ♕xd3 ♘e5 11 ♕c2 c6 12 ♗e3! N (12 ♘c3 ♘xc4 13 ♘a4 ♗f8 14 ♕xc4 b5∓ Smyslov-Mecking, Petropolis 1973) 12...cxd5 13 ♗xc5 d6 14 ♗d4 dxc4 15 ♖fd1 ♕e7 16 ♖d2!± Smejkal-Mecking, Rio de Janeiro 1979

4...♗e7

4...♗b4 5 ♕c2 ♗xc3 6 ♕xc3 ♕e7 7 a3 a5 8 ♗e2 (8 b4± Keene-Tisdall, Orense 1977) 8...0-0 9 0-0 d5 10 d3 ♖d8 11 cxd5 ♘xd5 12 ♕c2 a4 13 ♗d2 ♗e6 14 ♖fe1 += Hort-Sosonko, Waddinxveen 1979

5 d4

5 a3 0-0 6 ♕c2 d5 7 cxd5 ♘xd5 8 ♘xd5 ♕xd5 9 ♗c4 ♕d6 10 b4 ♗f6 11 ♖b1 g6 12 d3 ♗f5 13 ♘d2 += Smyslov-Kapengut, Spartakiad 1979 **exd4 6 ♘xd4 0-0 7 ♗e2 d5 8 cxd5 ♘b4 9 ♗f3 ♘bxd5 10 ♘xd5 ♘xd5 11 0-0 ♗f6=** Miles-Timman, Bled 1979

1 c4 c5 2 ♘f3 ♘f6 3 ♘c3

3 g3 d5 4 cxd5 ♘xd5 5 ♗g2 ♘c6 6 d4 cxd4 7 ♘xd4 ♘db4 8 ♘xc6 ♕xd1+ 9 ♔xd1 ♘xc6 10 ♗xc6+ bxc6 11 ♘c3 e5 12 ♗e3 ♗b4= Timman-Polugaevsky (7) 1979

3...d5

a) 3...♘c6 4 g3 d5 5 cxd5 ♘xd5 6 ♗g2 g6 7 0-0 ♗g7 8 ♘g5 e6 9 ♘ge4 b6 10 ♕a4 (10 d3 0-0 11 ♗g5 f6 12

♗d2 ♘de7 13 a3 f5 14 ♘g5 h6 15 ♘h3 ♗b7= Smyslov-Miles, Tilburg 1977) 10...♗d7 11 ♘xd5 exd5 12 ♘c3 ♘e7 13 ♕f4 ♗c6 14 b4 0-0 15 bxc5 d4! =+ Timman-Polugaevsky (3) 1979;

b) 3...♘c6 4 d4 exd4 5 ♘xd4 e6 6 g3 ♗c5 7 ♘b3 ♗b4 8 ♗g2 d5 9 0-0 (9 cxd5 ♘xd5 10 a3 ♗xc3+ 11 bxc3 0-0 12 ♕c2 ♕c7 13 c4 ♘e5 14 ♘d2 b5 15 c5 ♗b7 =+ Korchnoi-Spassky, Belgrade 1977) 9...dxc4 10 ♘d2 0-0 11 ♘xc4 ♕e7 12 ♗e3 (12 ♗d2 ♖d8 13 ♕c1 ♗d7 14 a3 ♗c5 15 ♗g5 h6 16 ♗xf6 ♕xf6 17 ♘e4 ♕e7 18 e3 += G.Garcia-Hubner) 12...♖d8 13 ♕b3 ♘d5 14 ♖fd1 N (14 ♗d2 ♘d4 15 ♘xd5 exd5 16 ♕xb4 ♘xe2+ 17 ♔h1 ♕xb4 18 ♗xb4 dxc4= Stean-Sosonko, Amsterdam 1978) 14...♘xe3 15 ♖xd8 ♘xd8 16 ♘xe3 ♗xc3 17 ♕xc3 ♗d7 18 ♖d1 ♗c6= Timman-Polugaevsky (5) 1979;

c) 3...e6 4 g3 b6 5 ♗g2 ♗b7
1) 6 d4 cxd4 7 ♕xd4 ♗e7 8 0-0 d6 9 b3 ♘bd7 10 e4 a6 11 ♗a3 ♕b8= Portisch-Andersson, Milan 1975;
2) 6 0-0 ♗e7 7 d4;
3) 6 0-0 ♘c6 7 e4 ♕b8 8 d4 cxd4 9 ♘xd4 ♘xd4 10 ♕xd4 ♗d6= Smejkal-Larsen, Biel 1976
4) 6 0-0 d5 7 cxd5 ♘xd5 8 d4 ♘xc3 (8...♗e7) 9 bxc3 ♘d7 10 ♖e1 cxd4 11 cxd4 ♗b4 12 ♗g5! f6 13 ♗d2 ♗xd2 14 ♕xd2 ♖c8 15 ♕d3!± Karpov-Hort, Waddinxveen 1979

Diagram

4 cxd5 ♘xd5 5 e4

5 g3 ♘c6 6 ♗g2 ♘c7 7 0-0 e5 8 d3 ♗e7 9 ♘d2 ♗d7 10 ♘c4 0-0!? 11 ♗xc6 ♗xc6 12 ♘xe5 ♗e8
a) 13 e4?! b5 14 ♗e3 f6 15 ♘f3 ♗h5

8

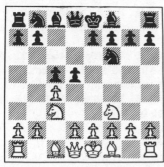

16 h3 ♕d7 17 g4 ♗xg4!? 18 hxg4 ♕xg4+∞ Libernosh-Haag, Budapest 1976;

b) 13 e4?! ♗f6 14 ♘g4 ♗d4 15 ♘e3 ♗c6

1) 16 ♘f5?! ♘e6 17 ♘d5 ♖e8 18 ♘xd4 ♘xd4 19 ♘e3 ♕d7 20 f3 ♖ad8 =+ Petrosian-Vaganian, Moscow 1976;

2) 16 ♕e2 ♕d7 17 ♗d2 ♖ad8 18 ♖ad1 ♖fe8 19 f4 f5= Suba-Georgadze, Decin 1977;

c) 13 ♕b3!? b6 14 ♗e3 ♔h8! 15 ♖fd1 f6 16 ♘f3 ♗f7 17 ♕a4 ♘d5 18 ♘xd5 ♗xd5 =+ Commons-Gheorghiu, Lone Pine 1975; 17 ♕c2;

c) 13 ♕b3!? ♘e6

d) 13 ♗e3 ♘d5?! 14 ♘xd5 ♕xd5 15 f4 f6 16 ♘f3 ♗f7 17 ♗f2 += Vukic-Witkowski, Vukovar 1976;

e) 13 ♗e3 ♘d5?! 14 ♕b3! ♘xe3 15 fxe3 ♗g5 16 ♘d5± Dorfman-Timoshenko, Leningrad 1975;

f) 13 ♗e3 ♘e6 14 ♕b3 b6?! 15 ♕d5! ♕c8 16 f4 ♗f6 17 f5 ♘c7 18 ♕e4± Smejkal-Portisch, Biel 1976;

g) 13 ♗e3 ♘e6 14 ♕b3 ♗f6

1) 15 f4 ♗xe5 16 fxe5 ♗c6 17 ♕c4 ♕c7 18 ♘d5 ♕xe5 19 ♘e7+ ♔h8 20 ♕c1 Sahovic-Joksic, Jugoslavia 1976, 20...♘d4 21 ♘xc6 bxc6 22 ♖f2 ♖ab8 23 b3 ♖fe8=;

2) 15 ♘f3 ♗c6 16 ♘e4 ♗d4?! 17 ♗xd4 ♘xd4 18 ♘xd4 cxd4 19 ♖ac1

♖e8 20 ♖c2 ♕d7 21 ♕c4 ♖e5 22 f4 ♖h5 23 f5± Sznapik-Ostos, Caracas 1976; 16...♗e7! 17 ♘e5?! ♗d5 18 ♕a4 f6 19 ♘c4 Ftacnik-Gilksman, Stary-Smokovec 1976, 19...f5 20 ♘c3 f4!∓; 17 ♖ac1 b6 18 ♘e5 ♗d5 19 ♕a4 ♔h8 20 ♘c3 ♗b7 21 ♘c6 ♕d6 22 ♘xe7 += Joksic; 17...♗d5 18 ♕a4 b5!∞;

3) 15 ♘g4 ♗d4 16 ♗xd4 cxd4 17 ♘e4 ♗c6 18 ♘e5 ♗d5 19 ♕b4! f6 20 ♘f3± Geller-Timoshenko, Rostov-on-Don 1976; 17...♕a5!≈;

h) 13 ♗e3 ♘e6 14 ♖c1 ♗f6 15 ♘c4 N (15 ♘f3 ♗c6 16 a3 ♕e7 17 ♕c2 ♗d4 18 ♘a4 ♖ac8 =+ Mochalov-Kapengut, Minsk 1974) 15...♗c6 16 ♘e4 ♗d4 17 ♗xd4 cxd4 18 ♘e5 ♗d5 19 ♕a4 ♖e8!∓ Govrinder-Kapengut, Spartakiad 1979

5...♘b4 6 ♗c4

6 ♗b5+ ♘8c6 7 d4 cxd4 8 a3 dxc3 9 ♕xd8+ ♔xd8 10 axb4 cxb2 (10...c2 N 11 ♗xc6 bxc6 12 ♘d4 ♗d7 13 ♘xc2 e5 14 ♗e3 ♔c7 15 ♖xa7+ ♖xa7 16 ♗xa7 ♗xb4+ 17 ♘xb4 ♖a8 18 ♘a6+ ♔b7 19 ♗c5 ½-½ Ree-Langeweg, Netherlands Final 1979) 11 ♗xb2 f6!? 12 e5! (12 ♗xc6 bxc6 13 e5 ♗e6 14 0-0 ♗d5 15 ♖fd1 ♔c7 16 b5∞ Juferov-Cgin, Spartakiad 1979) 12...♗d7 13 ♗c4 ♖c8 14 ♖d1 ♔c7 15 e6 ♗e8 16 b5 ♘a5 17 ♗e2 ♔b8 18 0-0± Timman-Bohm, Netherlands Final 1979

Diagram

6...♗e6!? 7 ♗xe6 ♘d3+ 8 ♔f1 fxe6 9 ♘g5 ♕b6! N 10 ♕e2?
a) 10 ♕f3 c4 11 b3 h6 12 bxc4 ♘e5 13 ♕h3 hxg5!; 11...♘a6 12 bxc4 ♘xc5∞;
b) 10 b3 ♘d7 Δ ♘7e5
10...c4 11 b3 h6 12 ♘f3 ♘c6 13 bxc4

0-0-0! 14 g3 g5 15 ♔g2 ♕c5! ∓/−+
Polugaevsky-Tal, Riga 1979

1 c4 ♞f6 2 ♞f3 b6 3 g3 ♝b7 4 ♝g2 g6 5 b3 ♝g7 6 ♝b2 0-0 7 0-0 c5 8 ♞c3 ♞a6
8...d5 9 ♘xd5 ♘xd5 10 ♝xg7 ♔xg7 11 cxd5 ♕xd5 12 d4! cxd4 13 ♕xd4+ ♕xd4 14 ♘xd4 ♝xg2 15 ♔xg2± Andersson-Robatsch, Munich 1979
9 d4
9 e3 d5 10 ♘e5?! ♕b8 11 f4 dxc4 12 bxc4 ♝xg2 13 ♔xg2 ♘d7! =+ Pfleger-Larsen, London 1977; 10 ♘xd5 ♘xd5 11 ♝xg7 ♔xg7 12 cxd5 ♕xd5 13 d4 ♖fd8 14 dxc5 ♘xc5= Smyslov-Karpov, USSR Final 1976

9...d5 10 dxc5
10 cxd5 ♘xd5 11 e3?! ♘xc3 12 ♝xc3 ♖c8 13 ♕e2 cxd4 14 ♝xd4 ♝xd4

15 ♘xd4 ♝xg2 16 ♔xg2 ♕d5+ 17 ♔g1 ♘c5 =+ Timman-Larsen, Bugojno 1978
10...♝xc5 11 ♞xd5 ♞xd5 12 ♝xg7 ♔xg7 13 cxd5 ♕xd5 14 ♕xd5
½-½ Miles-Timman, Amsterdam 1978
14...♝xd5 15 ♖fd1 ♖fd8 16 ♖ac1 ♕f6 17 b4
17 ♘d4
17...♞e6 18 a3?!
18 ♖xd5! ♖xd5 19 ♘e1 ♖ad8 20 ♝xd5 ♖xd5 21 ♘d3=
18...♝xf3! =+ Ivkov-Timman, Bled 1979

Slav

1 d4 d5 2 c4 c6 3 ♞f3 ♞f6 4 ♞c3 dxc4
4...e6 5 ♝g5 dxc4 6 e4 b5 7 e5 h6 8 ♝h4 g5 9 ♘xg5 hxg5 10 ♝xg5 ♘bd7 11 g3 b4 12 ♘e4 ♘xe4 13 ♝xd8 ♔xd8 14 ♕f3 (14 ♝g2 f5 15 exf6 ♘dxf6 16 ♝xe4! N ♘xe4 17 ♕f3 a5 18 ♕xe4 +− Knaak-Borkowski, Polanica Zdroj 1979; 16 ♕e2 ♘d6 17 ♕e5 ♝e7 18 ♝xc6 ♖b8 19 ♕a5+ ♖b6 20 ♝g2 ♖h5 ∓− Radchenko) 14...f5 15 exf6 ♘dxf6 16 ♝xc4 ♝e7 17 0-0-0 ♘d6 (≈ Taimanov) 18 ♝d3 ♔c7 19 h4 a5 20 g4 ♘d5 21 g5 ♖f8 22 ♕g3 ♘f4∞ Spassov-Borkowski, Polanica Zdroj 1979
5 a4 ♝f5
a) 5...♘a6 6 e4 ♝g4 7 ♝xc4 e6 8 ♝e3 ♝b4 9 ♕c2 ♝xf3 10 gxf3 0-0 N (10...♕a5 11 0-0 ♝e7 12 ♔h1 ♘b4 13 ♕e2 h6 14 f4 ♕h5 15 f3 g5 16 e5 ♘fd5 17 ♝xd5!± Gligoric-Green, Hastings 1961) 11 0-0 c5 12 d5 ♝xc3 13 bxc3 exd5 14 ♖fd1 ♕c8 15 exd5 ♕h3 16 ♖ab1 ♕xf3 17 ♝e2 ♕h3 18 ♖xb7± Hubner-Smyslov, Tilburg 1979;
b) 5...♘a6 6 e3 ♝g4 7 ♝xc4 e6 8

10

0-0 ♞b4 9 ♕e2 (9 h3 ♝h5 10 ♕e2 ♝d6?! 11 ♖fd1 ♕c7 12 e4 ♞fd7 13 ♝e3 0-0 14 ♖ac1 ♖fe8 15 ♝b3 += Beljavsky-Vasjukov, Frunze 1979) 9... ♝e7 10 ♖d1 0-0 11 h3 ♝h5 12 g4 ♝g6 13 ♞e5 c5 14 ♞xg6 hxg6 15 d5 exd5 16 g5 ♝d6 17 gxf6 dxc4 18 ♕xc4 gxf6 19 ♞e4 ♝h2+ 20 ♔xh2 ♕xd1 21 ♝d2± Botterill-Boersma, London 1979

6 ♞e5
a) 6 e3 e6 7 ♝xc4 ♝b4 8 0-0 0-0 9 ♕e2 ♞e4 10 ♝d3 ♝xc3 11 bxc3 ♞xc3 12 ♕c2 ♝xd3 13 ♕xd3 ♞d5 14 ♖b1 N (14 ♝a3 ♖e8 15 ♖ab1 b6 16 ♞e5 ♞f6 17 ♕c3 ♞fd7 18 ♞c4 c5 19 ♞d6 ♖f8 20 ♖fd1± Najdorf-Trifunovic, Prague 1946) 14...a5! 15 ♝a3 ♞b4 16 ♝xb4 axb4 17 ♖xb4 ♞a6 18 ♖b3 += Ivkov-Hebert, Rio de Janeiro 1979;
b) 6 ♞h4 ♝c8 7 ♞f3 ♝f5 8 ♞h4 ♝c8 9 e4 e5 10 ♝xc4 exd5 11 e5 ♝e7!? N (11...♞d5 12 ♕xd4 ♝e6 13 ♞f3 ♝e7 14 0-0 0-0 15 ♞e4 ♞f4 16 ♞d6 ♝xd6 17 ♝xf4 ♝e7 18 ♕c3 += Forintos-Sokolov, Wijk aan Zee II 1970) 12 exf6 ♝xf6 13 ♕e2+ ♔f8 14 ♞e4 ♝xh4 15 ♕h5 ♝e6 16 ♝xe6 fxe6 17 0-0 ±/+− Rogers-Jamieson, Brisbane 1979
6...♞bd7 6...♞a6 7 f3 ♞d7 8 ♞xc4 e5

9 dxe5 ♕h4+ 10 g3 ♕xc4 11 e4 ♕e6 N (11...♕c5 12 exf5 ♕xe5+ 13 ♞e4 ♞f6∝ Kotov) 12 ♝xa6 ♝h3 13 ♝xb7 ♖d8 14 ♕e2 ♞c5∓ Cvetkovic-Meduna, Prague 1979
7 ♞xc4 ♕c7 8 g3 e5 9 dxe5 ♞xe5 10 ♝f4 ♞fd7 11 ♝g2 ♝e6 12 ♞xe5 ♞xe5 13 0-0 f6 N
13...♝e7 14 ♕c2 ♖d8 15 ♖fd1 0-0 16 ♞b5 ♖xd1+ 17 ♖xd1 ♕a5 18 ♞d4 ♝c8 19 b4! ♕c7 20 b5± Alekhine-Euwe 1935
14 ♕c2 ♝d6 15 ♞e4 0-0 16 a5 a6 17 ♖fd1 ♖ad8 18 ♝e3 ♞c4 19 ♝c5± Timman-Hebert, Rio de Janeiro 1979

Queens Gambit

1 d4 d5 2 c4 e6 3 ♞f3
3 ♞c3 ♞f6 4 ♞f3 c5 5 cxd5 ♞xd5 6 e4 ♞xc3 7 bxc3 cxd4 8 cxd4 ♞c6 9 ♝c4 b5 10 ♝d3 N ♝b4+ 11 ♝d2 (11 ♔f1!? a6 12 ♝b2 0-0 13 h4 Δ ♖h3-g3∝) 11...a6 12 a4 ♖b8 13 axb5 axb5 14 0-0 ♝xd2 15 ♕xd2 0-0 16 ♕c3 ♕d6 17 ♖fc1 ♝d7 18 ♕c5± Keene-Bjerring, Clare Benedict 1979
3...♞f6 4 g3 c5 5 cxd5 exd5 6 ♝g2 ♞c6 7 0-0 ♝e7 8 ♞c3 0-0 9 ♝g5 c4
a) 9...♝e6 10 dxc5 ♝xc5 11 ♝xf6 (11 ♖c1 ♝b6 12 b3! N ± Browne-Strauss, Lone Pine 1979) 11...♕xf6 12 ♞xd5 ♕xb2 13 ♞c7 ♖ad8 14 ♕c1 ♕xc1 15 ♖axc1 b6! (15...♝b6 16 ♞xe6 fxe6 17 ♖c4 ♖d6 18 h4 h6 19 ♖e4 ♖fd8 20 e3 += Dementiev-Kuindzhi, USSR 1977) 16 ♞xe6 fxe6 17 ♝h3! N (17 ♖c4 ♞d4 18 ♞xd4 ♖xd4 19 ♖xd4 ♝xd4 20 e3 ½-½ Petrosian-Spassky (16) 1969) 17... ♖f6! 18 ♞g5 ♞d4 Sosonko-Hort, Waddinxveen 1979 19 ♖fe1! +=;
b) 9...cxd4 10 ♞xd4 h6 11 ♝e3 ♖e8

1) 12 ♘xc6 bxc6 13 ♕a4 ♗d7 14 ♕c2 += Vadasz-Nunn, Budapest 1978
2) 12 ♖c1 ♗f8 13 ♘xc6 bxc6 14 ♗d4!? (14 ♘a4 ♕a5 15 b3 ♕b5 16 ♕c2 ♗d7 17 ♘c3 ♕b4 18 ♖cd1 ♕g4= Timman-Gligoric, Buenos Aires 1978) 14...♘h7!? 15 ♘a4 ♗g4 16 ♖e1 ♕d7 17 ♗c5! += Nikolac-Nunn, Dortmund 1979
3) 12 ♕a4 ♗d7 13 ♖ad1 ♘b4 14 ♕b3 a5 15 a4 ♗g4 (15...♗f8 16 ♘c2 ♗e6 17 ♗d4 ♘e4 18 ♘xb4 axb4 19 ♘b5 ♕a5 20 ♗xe4 dxe4 21 ♕e3± Vaganian-Nunn, Buenos Aires 1978) 16 ♘c2! N (16 h3 ♗d7 17 ♘c2 ♕c8 18 ♘xb4 axb4 19 ♘xd5 ♘xd5 20 ♕xd5 ♗xa4 21 ♖c1 ♗c6 22 ♕b3 ♕f5= Quinteros-Ivkov, Bled 1979) 16...♕c7 17 ♖c1! ♘xc2 18 ♖xc2 ♖ac8 19 ♖fc1 ♕c4 20 ♕xc4 ♖xc4 21 ♘xd5 +− Polugaevsky-Timman (8) 1979

10 ♘e5 ♗e6 11 f4
a) 11 ♘xc6 bxc6 12 b3 ♕a5 13 ♘a4 ♖fd8 14 e3 c5!? 15 ♗xf6 gxf6 16 dxc5 ♗xc5 17 ♕h5 ♖ac8 18 ♖fd1 ♗f8 19 ♖ac1 ♕b4 20 ♗xd5 ♖xd5∓ Polugaevsky-Pfleger, Buenos Aires 1978; 14...♖ac8 15 ♗xf6 gxf6 16 ♕h5 c5 17 dxc5 ♗xc5 Stean-Dankert, Munich 1979 18 ♘xc5 ♖xc5 19 ♕h6 +=;
b) 11 e3 ♘d7! 12 ♗xe7 ♘xe7 13 b3

♘xe5 14 dxe5 ♕a5= Polugaevsky-Pfleger, Montilla 1975;
c) 11 ♘xc4 dxc4 12 ♗xf6 ♗xf6 13 d5 ♗d7 14 dxc6 ♗xc6 15 ♗xc6 bxc6 16 ♕c2 += Flohr-Maroczy, London 1932
11...♘xe5 12 dxe5 d4 13 ♘b5 13 exf6 gxf6 14 ♗h6 dxc3 15 bxc3 ♕b6+ 16 ♔h1 ♖fd8 17 ♕c2 Rubinstein-Perlis, St. Petersburg 1909, 17...f5! 18 ♖ab1 ♕e3= Lasker
13...♕b6 14 a4
14 ♘xd4? ♖fd8! 15 e3 ♘g4! 16 ♗xe7 ♘xe3 17 ♗xd8 ♖xd8∓
14...d3+ 15 ♔h1 ♗g4! 16 ♗f3 ♗xf3 17 ♖xf3 a6 18 ♘c3 ♕xb2 19 exf6 ♗b4!∓ Ribli-Marjanovic, Bled 1979

Benko

1 d4 ♘f6 2 c4 c5 3 d5 b5 4 cxb5 a6 5 bxa6
a) 5 ♘c3 axb5 6 e4 b4 7 ♘b5 d6 8 ♗f4 g5 9 ♗xg5 (9 ♗e3 ♗b7 10 f3 ♖a5 11 ♗xg5 ♗g7 12 a4 0-0 13 ♘e2 ♘e8 14 ♕d2 f5≈ Kovacevic-Bukal, Zagreb 1979) 9...♘xe4 10 ♗f4 ♗g7? 11 ♕e2 ♘f6 12 ♘xd6+ ♔f8 13 ♘xc8 ♕xc8 14 d6 ♘c6 15 dxe7+ +− Kolpakov-Egin, Spartakiad 1979; 10...♘f6; 10...♘bd7? 11 ♕e2!;
b) 5 f3 d6 6 e4 g6 7 ♘c3 ♗g7 8 a4 0-0 9 ♖a3 e6 10 ♗c4 axb5 11 ♗xb5 ♘a6 12 ♘ge2 ♘b4 13 dxe6 fxe6 14 0-0 += Duric-Tassi, Berne 1979; 5...axb5!;
c) 5 e3 e6 6 ♘c3 exd5 7 ♘xd5 ♗b7 8 ♘xf6+ ♕xf6 9 ♘f3 ♗e7 N 10 ♕b3 0-0 11 bxa6 ♗xf3 12 gxf3 ♕xf3 13 ♖g1 ♗h4 14 ♕c2 ♘xa6∓ Portisch-Vaganian, Kecskemet 2 1979; 9...♗d6? 10 ♗d2! ♕xb2 11 ♖c1 ♕f6 12 ♗c3 ♗xf3 13 gxf3 ♗e5 14 ♗xe5 ♕xe5 15 ♗g2± Bagirov-Shereshevski, USSR 1975;

d) 5 e3 g6 6 ♘c3 d6? 7 a4 ♗g7 8 ♕b3 ♘bd7 9 ♘f3 0-0 10 ♖a3 axb5 11 ♗xb5 ♘e8 12 0-0 ♘c7 13 ♗c6 ♖b8 14 ♘b5± Donner-Miles, Amsterdam 1977;

e) 5 e3 g6 6 ♘c3 ♗g7 7 a4?! 0-0
1) 8 ♕b3 e6! 9 b6? ♗b7 10 dxe6 fxe6 11 a5 ♘g4! 12 ♘f3 ♘c6! =+ Schussler-Borik, Dortmund 1979;
2) 8 ♘f3 e6! 9 bxa6 ♘xa6 10 ♗c4 ♘b4 11 0-0 exd5 12 ♘xd5 ♘fxd5 13 ♗xd5 ♖b8 14 ♖a3 ♗a6 15 ♖e1 c4∓ Reinhardt-Szmetan, Argentina 1977;
3) 8 ♘f3 e6! 9 ♖a3 ♗b7 10 ♗c4 Baumbach-Stankov, Primorsko 1973, 10...exd5=;

f) 5 e3 g6 6 ♘c3 ♗g7 7 e4 d6 8 ♘f3 0-0 9 a4 e6!? 10 dxe6 fxe6
1) 11 e5!? ♘g4! 12 ♕xd6 ♘xe5! 13 ♕xd8 ♘xf3+ 14 gxf3 ♖xd8 15 ♗e3 ♗b7! 16 ♗c4 axb5 17 ♘xb5 ♗xf3= Farago-Filipowicz, Polanica Zdroj 1977;
2) 11 ♗g5 N h6 12 ♗d2 d5 13 e5 ♘fd7 14 h4?! ♗b7 15 ♕c2 ♖xf3! 16 gxf3 ♘xe5∓ Toth-Borik, Berne 1979;

g) 5 e3 g6 6 ♘c3 ♗g7 7 ♘f3 d6 8 a4 0-0 9 ♖a3
1) 9...axb5 N 10 ♗xb5 ♘a6 11 0-0 ♘b4 12 h3 ♗f5 13 ♘e1 ♕c8 14 ♕f3 ♗h6 15 ♖a1 ♗d7 16 ♗c4± dc Lange Bjerring, Clare Benedict 1979;
2) 9...♘bd7 10 e4 ♕c7? 11 ♗e2 axb5 12 ♘xb5 ♕b8 13 ♕c2 ♗a6 14 0-0 ♖c8 15 ♗d2 ♘e8 16 ♖b3± Razuvaev-Tukmakov, USSR Final 1977;
3) 9...e6 10 ♗c4 axb5 11 ♘xb5 exd5 12 ♗xd5 ♘xd5 13 ♕xd5 ♖a6 14 0-0 += Inkiov-Szmetan, Buenos Aires Olympiad 1978

Diagram

5...♗xa6 6 ♘c3

6 g3 d6 7 ♗g2 g6 8 b3 ♗g7 9 ♗b2 0-0 10 ♘h3 ♘bd7 11 0-0 ♕b8 12 ♗c3 ♖a7 13 ♖e1
a) 13...♖b7 N 14 ♕d2 ♘b6 15 ♘f4 ♖c8 16 h4 h5 17 ♕c2 ♘bd7∞ Giffard-Malek, Rzeszow 1979;
b) 13...♖c8 14 ♘a3 ♗xe2!? 15 ♖xe2 ♖xa3= Vaiser-Kozlov, USSR 1979; 15 ♕xe2 ♖xa3 16 ♕b2 ♖a7 17 ♖xe7±
6...g6 7 ♘f3 d6 8 e4 ♗xf1 9 ♔xf1 ♗g7 10 g3 0-0 11 ♔g2 ♘bd7 12 h3
a) 12 ♖e1 ♘g4 13 ♖e2 ♕a5 14 ♗g5 ♖fe8 15 ♖c1 ♕a6 16 b3 ♘ge5 17 ♘xe5 ♘xe5 18 ♘a4 ♖ab8≈ Gavrikov-Tseshkovsky, Spartakiad 1979;
b) 12 ♕e2 ♕c7 13 ♖d1 ♖fb8 14 h3 ♕b7 15 ♖e1 ♘e8 16 ♕c2 ♕b8∓ Belle-Csonkica, Lublin 1979
12...♕a5 13 ♗d2 ♖fb8 14 ♕c2 ♘e8 15 ♖hb1 ♖b7 16 a4 ♕a6 17 ♘d1 ♖ab8= Gligoric-Tseshkovsky, Bled 1979

1 d4 ♘f6 2 c4 c5 3 d5 b5 4 cxb5 a6 5 bxa6 ♗xa6 6 ♘c3 g6 7 ♘f3 d6 8 g3 ♗g7 9 ♗g2 0-0 10 0-0 ♘bd7 11 ♖e1 11 ♕c2 ♕a5 12 ♖d1 ♖fb8 13 ♗d2 ♘g4 14 b3 ♕a3 15 ♖ab1 ♗c8 16 ♘a4 ♘df6 17 ♘e1 ♘xf2 18 ♔xf2 ♘g4+ 19 ♔f1 ♘xh2+ 20 ♔g1 ♘g4∞ Kakageldiev-Vaganian, Spartakiad 1979

13

11...Ɲb6!
11...Ⱳb6; 11...Ⱳa5
12 Ɲd2
12 e4!? Ɲfd7 13 Ⱳc2
a) 13...Ɲc4 14 Ɽd1 Ⱳa5 15 Ɲd2
Ɲa3! 16 bxa3 Ⱳxc3 17 Ⱳxc3 Ɓxc3∓
Averkin-Miles, Dubna 1976;
b) 13...Ⱳc7 N 14 b3 Ɽfb8 15 Ɓb2
Ɲc8 16 Ɲa4 Ɓxb2 17 Ɲxb2 f6∞
Allanepesova-Samaganova, Spartakiad
1979

12...Ⱳd7 N
a) 12...Ⱳc7 13 Ɲf1 Ɲg4 14 Ⱳc2 Ɲc4
15 h3 Ɲge5 16 Ɽd1 Ⱳa5 17 a3 Ɽfb8
18 Ɽa2 Ⱳb6 19 f4 Ɲd7 20 Ⱨh2
Ⱳb3! 21 Ɓe4 Ⱳxc2 22 Ɓxc2 Ɲxb2!
23 Ɓxb2 Ɲc4∓ Averkin-Alburt, Odessa
1974;
b) 12...Ɽa7 N 13 h3 Ⱳa8 14 e4 Ɲfd7
15 f4 Ɽb8 16 Ⱳc2 Ɲc4 17 Ɲf3 Ⱳb7
18 b3 Ⱳb4 19 e5± Kakageldiev-
Peshina, Spartakiad 1979
13 Ɽb1
13 Ⱳc2 Ɓb7 Δ Ɲa4
13...Ⱳb7
13...Ɓb7
14 b4!
Δ b5
**14...Ɲfd7 15 bxc5 Ɲxc5 16 Ɓb2 Ⱳd7
17 Ɲce4 Ɲba4 18 Ɓxg7 Ⱨxg7 19
Ɲxc5 Ɲxc5∓** Unzicker-Miles, Cape
Town 1979

Nimzo-Indian

**1 d4 Ɲf6 2 c4 e6 3 Ɲc3 Ɓb4 4 Ⱳc2
c5 5 dxc5 0-0**
5...Ɓxc5 6 e3 b6 7 Ɲf3 Ɓb7 8 Ɓe2
0-0 9 0-0 Ɲc6 10 a3 Ɽc8 11 Ɽd1
Ⱳc7 12 b4 Ɓe7 13 Ɓb2 +=
Kozlovskaya-Miles, Rio de Janeiro
1979
6 Ɲf3
a) 6 a3 Ɓxc5 7 Ɓf4 Ɲc6 8 Ɲf3 b6
9 e3 Ɓb7 10 Ɓe2 Ɓe7 11 Ɽd1 Ɽc8
12 0-0 Ɲa5! =+ Soos-Hubner,
Lucerne 1979;
b) 6 Ɓe3 Ⱳe7 (6...b6!? 7 cxb6 d5∞
Bronstein) 7 Ɲf3 Ɲa6 N (7...Ɓxc5 8
Ɓg5 Ⱳd8 9 e3 Ɲc6 10 a3 Ɓe7 11
Ɓe2 += Bronstein-Averbakh, USSR
Final 1963) 8 g3 Ɓxc5 9 Ɓg5 h6 10
Ɓxf6 Ⱳxf6 11 Ɓg2 Ɽd8 12 0-0 Ɓe7
13 Ɽad1 d6 14 a3 Ɲc7 15 Ɲd4 +=
Barle-Gligoric, Bled 1979

6...Ɲa6 7 e3
7 a3 Ɓxc3+ 8 Ⱳxc3 Ɲxc5 9 Ⱳc2!?
N (9 Ɓf4; 9 Ɲd2; 9 g3; 9 e3) 9...a5
10 e3 b6 11 Ɓe2 Ɓb7 12 0-0 Ɓe4
13 Ⱳc3 Ɓg6 14 Ɲd2 a4 15 f3 d5 16
b4 axb3 17 Ɲxb3 += Kovacs-
Goldenberg, Bagneux 1979
7...Ɲxc5 8 Ɓd2 b6
8...d5 9 Ɓe2 dxc4 10 Ɓxc4 Ɓd7 11
a3 Ɓxc3 12 Ɓxc3 Ɽc8 13 Ⱳe2 Ɲce4=

14

Bagirov-Padevsky, Vrnjacka Banja 1974
9 ♗e2 ♗b7 10 0-0 a5!? N
10...♘ce4 11 ♘xe4 ♗xe4 12 ♗d3 ♗xd3 13 ♕xd3 ♗xd2 14 ♕xd2 d5= Petrosian-Tal 1959
11 ♖fd1 ♕e7 12 b3 ♖ac8 13 ♕b2 ♘ce4 14 ♘xe4 ♘xe4 15 a3 ♘xd2 16 ♘xd2 ♗c5 =+ Ivkov-Larsen, Bled 1979

Queen's Indian

1 d4 ♘f6 2 c4 e6 3 ♘f3 b6 4 ♗f4
a) 4 g3 ♗a6
1) 5 ♕a4 c6 6 ♘c3 b5 7 cxb5 cxb5 8 ♘xb5 ♕b6 9 ♘c3 ♗b4 10 ♗g2 0-0 11 ♕c2 ♘c6 12 0-0 ♖ac8 13 ♗g5 ♗xc3 14 bxc3 ♘xd4= Hamman-Sigurjonsson, Lucerne 1979;
2) 5 ♕a4 ♘e4?! N 6 ♗g2 ♘d6?! 7 c5! bxc5 8 dxc5 ♘b7 9 c6 dxc6 10 ♘c3 ♗d6 11 0-0 0-0 12 ♖d1 ♕e8 13 ♘d4 += Unzicker-Korchnoi, Cape Town 1979;
3) 5 b3 ♗b4+ 6 ♗d2 ♗e7 7 ♗g2 (7 ♘c3 0-0 8 ♗g2 c6 9 0-0 d5 10 ♘e5 ♘fd7 11 ♘xd7 ♕xd7 12 cxd5 cxd5 13 ♗e3 ♘c6 14 ♕d2 ♖ac8= Sahovic-Barle, Bled 1979) 7...c6 8 0-0 (8 ♗g5 d5 9 ♘bd2 ♘bd7 10 0-0 0-0 11 ♕c2 ♖c8 12 e4 c5 13 exd5 exd5 14 ♖ad1 dxc4 15 ♘xc4± Lein-Stean, Amsterdam 1979) 8...0-0 (8...d5 9 ♘e5 ♘fd7 10 ♘xd7 ♘xd7 11 ♗c3 ♖c8 12 ♘d2 0-0 13 ♖e1 f5= Gralka-Giffard, Rzeszow 1979) 9 ♗c3 d5 10 ♘bd2 ♘bd7 11 ♖e1 c5 12 ♗b2 ♖c8 13 ♖c1 dxc4 14 ♘xc4 ♗b7= Sahovic-Parma, Bled 1979;
b) 4 a3 c5 5 d5 ♗a6 6 ♕c2 exd5 7 cxd5 g6! 8 ♘c3 d6 9 g3 ♗g7 10 ♗g2 0-0 11 a4 ♗b7 12 ♘d2 ♘a6 13 0-0 ♘b4 14 ♕b3 ♕e7 =+ Marjanovic-

Timman, Bled 1979; 5 e3! += Gheorghiu-Ree, Lone Pine 1979;
c) 4 a3 ♗b7 5 ♘c3 d5 6 cxd5 ♘xd5
1) 7 ♘xd5 ♕xd5 8 ♗f4 ♗d6 9 ♗xd6 cxd6 10 e3 ♘d7 11 ♖c1 0-0 12 ♖c7 ♖fc8 13 ♗c4 ♕a5+ 14 b4 ♗xf3 15 ♕xf3 ♕xa3∓ Sarkisian-Makarichev, Spartakiad 1979;
2) 7 e3 ♗e7 8 ♗b5+ c6 9 ♗d3 0-0 10 e4 ♘xc3 11 bxc3 c5 12 h4!? N (12 0-0 += Dzhindzhihashvili-Miles, Amsterdam 1978) 12...cxd4 13 cxd4 ♘c6 14 e5 (△ ♗xh7+) 14...♘a5 15 ♗e3 g6 16 h5 ♖c8 Timman-Polugaevsky (1) 1979, 17 hxg6 fxg6 18 ♕b1!±
4...♗b7
4...♗b4+ N 5 ♘bd2 ♗b7 6 e3 0-0 7 ♗d3 d6 8 0-0 ♗xd2 9 ♘xd2 h6 10 ♕e2 ♕e7 11 ♗g3 c5 12 dxc5 bxc5 13 ♖fd1 += Bukic-Djuric, Tuzla 1979

5 e3 ♗b4+
a) 5...♗e7 6 h3 0-0 7 ♘c3 d5 8 ♗e2 a6 9 cxd5 ♘xd5 10 ♘xd5 ♗xd5 11 0-0 ♗d6 12 ♗xd6 ♕xd6 13 ♕c2 f5 14 ♖ad1 += Damljanovic-Bozanovic, Jugoslavia 1979;
b) 5...c5 6 d5!? (6 ♘c3) 6...exd5 7 ♘c3 dxc4 8 ♘b5 ♘a6 9 ♗xc4 ♗e7 (9...d5!?) 10 ♘d6+ ♗xd6 11 ♗xd6 b5 12 ♕b3 bxc4 13 ♕xb7 ♕c8∞ Rastianis-Fokin, Spartakiad 1979
6 ♘fd2

6 ♘bd2 ♗e7! 7 h3 0-0 8 ♗d3 c5 9 0-0 cxd4 10 ♘xd4 ♘c6 11 ♘xc6 ♗xc6 12 ♘f3 ♗b7 13 ♕e2 d5 14 ♖fd1 h6= Bukic-Diesen, Tuzla 1979
6...0-0 7 a3
7 ♗d3 d5! 8 0-0 c5 =+ Miles-Andersson, Buenos Aires Olympiad 1978
7...♗e7 8 ♘c3 c5
8...d5 9 cxd5 exd5 (9...♘xd5 10 ♘xd5 ♗xd5 11 ♕c2 c5 12 dxc5 ♗xc5 13 ♘e4 ♘d7 14 ♖ad1 ♕c8= Miles-Unzicker, Durban 1979) 10 ♗e2 c5 11 dxc5 bxc5 12 ♗f3 ♘c6 13 ♖c1 ♕d7 14 0-0 ♘d8 15 ♘b3 ♘e6 16 ♗e5 += Miles-Jelen, Bled 1979
9 d5 exd5 10 cxd5 ♗xd5
10...d6 11 e4 ♘a6 12 ♗e2 ♘c7 13 0-0 ♘e8 14 ♕c2 += Orestes-Eslon, Alicante 1979
11 ♘xd5 ♘xd5 12 ♕f3 ♘c7 13 ♕b7! d6 14 ♘e4 ♕d7
14...♘d7 15 0-0-0 ♖c8 16 ♘xd6 ♗xd6 17 ♗xd6 ♖e8 18 ♗e2 c4! =+/∓ Miles-Alexandria, Rio de Janeiro 1979, 18 ♗c4; 18 ♗g3
15 0-0-0 ♘e6 N
15...♕c6 16 ♘xd6 ♕xb7 17 ♘xb7 ♘e6 18 ♗g3± Miles-Timman, Wijk aan Zee 1979
16 ♕xd7 ♘xd7 18 ♗g3!± Miles-Lein, Cape Town 1979

Grunfeld

1 d4 ♘f6 2 c4 g6 3 ♘c3 d5 4 cxd5 ♘xd5 5 e4 ♘xc3 6 bxc3 ♗g7 7 ♘f3
7 ♗c4 0-0 8 ♘e2 c5 (8...♘c6 9 0-0 b6 10 ♗e3 ♗b7 11 f4! e6 12 f5 ♘a5 13 ♗d3 exf5 14 exf5 ♖e8 15 ♕d2 ♗e4 16 ♗g5± Spassky-Hubner, Tilburg 1979) 9 ♗e3 ♘c6 10 0-0
a) 10...♗g4 11 f3 ♘a5 12 ♗d5 ♗d7 13 ♗g5!? ♗b5∝ Spassky-Timman,

Montreal 1979;
b) 10...♗g4 11 d5 N ♘a5 12 ♗d3 c4 13 ♗c2 ♗xc3 14 ♖b1 ♗g7 15 f3 ♗d7 16 f4 b5 17 e5 a6 18 ♘c3∝ Polugaevsky-Timman (6) 1979;
c) 10...♘a5 11 ♗d3 b6 12 ♖c1 cxd4 13 cxd4 e6 14 ♕d2 ♗b7 15 h4 ♕d7 (15...♘c6 16 ♗b5 ♖c8 17 h5 a6 18 ♗xc6 ♖xc6 19 f3 ♕d7 20 ♗h6± Knaak-Jansa, Polanica Zdroj 1979) 16 ♗h6 ♖ac8 17 ♗xg7 ♔xg7 18 ♕g5 ♕d8= Razuvaev-Jansa, Polanica Zdroj 1979
7...c5 8 ♗e2
a) 8 ♗e3 ♘c6 9 ♖c1 cxd4 10 cxd4 0-0 11 d5! ♘a5 12 ♗e2 e6 13 d6! e5 14 ♖c7 ♗e6 15 ♘g5± Miles-Rodriguez, Riga 1979;
b) 8 ♗e3 0-0 9 ♖c1 ♗g4 10 ♗e2 ♕a5 11 ♕d2 ♖d8 12 d5 ♕a4 13 c4 += Miles-Khadilkar, Rio de Janeiro 1979
8...0-0
8...♘c6?! 9 d5!? ♗xc3+ 10 ♗d2 ♗xa1 11 ♕xa1 ♘d4 12 ♘xd4 cxd4 13 ♕xd4 f6 14 ♗c4 ♕b6 15 ♕d3± Hess-Vallifuoco, Berne 1979

9 0-0 cxd4
a) 9...♕a5 10 ♗g5 ♖e8 11 ♕b3 ♘d7 12 ♗c4 e6 13 e5 a6 14 a4 ♕b6 15 ♕a2± Alexandria-Hund, Rio de Janeiro 1979;
b) 9...♗g4 10 ♗e3 ♕a5 11 ♕b3 cxd4

12 cxd4 ♘c6 13 ♖ad1 ♕b4 14 h3
♗xf3 15 ♗xf3 ♕xb3 16 axb3 ♖fd8∓
Meinsohn-Wittmann, Berne 1979;
c) 9...b6 10 ♗g5 cxd4 N 11 cxd4
♗b7 12 ♕d3 ♘c6 13 ♖ad1 ♕d7 14
d5 ♘a5 15 ♘d4 ♖ac8 16 ♕g3±
Meinsohn-Feller, Berne 1979
**10 cxd4 ♘c6 11 ♗e3 ♗g4 12 d5 ♗xf3
13 ♗xf3 ♘b4!?**
13...♘e5 14 ♗e2 ♕a5 15 ♕b3 b6 16
♖ac1 ♖ac8 17 a4 ♘d7 18 ♗b5 +=
Keene-Bachtiar, Manila 1979
**14 ♖b1 ♘xa2 15 ♖xb7 a5 16 ♕d2
♘c3 17 ♗d4 ♗xd4 18 ♕xd4 +=**
Chandler-J.Littlewood, British Final
1979

**1 d4 ♘f6 2 c4 g6 3 ♘c3 d5 4 ♘f3 ♗g7
5 ♗g5 ♘e4**
5...dxc4!? 6 e4 c5 (6...0-0?! N 7 ♗xc4
♗g4 8 ♗e2 ♘fd7 9 d5 ♘b6 10 ♕b3
c6 11 ♖d1 cxd5 12 exd5 h6 13
♗e3 ♘8d7 14 0-0± Haik-Popovic,
Zagreb 1979) 7 d5 b5 8 e5 b4 9 exf6
exf6 10 ♕e2+ ♔f8 11 ♗e3 bxc3 12
♗xc5+ ♔g8 13 bxc3 ♗b7!? N (13...
♘d7 14 ♗e7 ♕e8 15 ♗b4!±) 14 ♖d1
♘a6? (14...♘d7!) 15 ♗e3 ♘c7 16
♕b2!± Hartston-Castro, Esbjerg 1979
**6 cxd5 ♘xg5 7 ♘xg5 c6 8 ♕d2 cxd5
9 ♕e3+ ♔f8 10 ♕f4 ♗f6 11 h4 h6**
11...♔g7 12 e4 dxe4 13 0-0-0 ♕d6
N (13...h6 14 ♘gxe4 ♗e6 15 d5 ♗f5
16 ♘xf6 ♕xf6 17 g4 ♗d7 18 ♕g3!±
Taimanov-Liberzon, Suhumi 1972) 14
♕xd6 cxd6 15 ♘gxe4 ♗e7 16 ♘d5
♗f5 17 ♗d3± Sinevskin-Chalinkia,
Spartakiad 1979

Diagram

12 ♘f3 ♕g7 13 0-0-0 ♗e6
13...c5 N 14 e3 ♘c6 15 g4 ♗e6 16
♗b5 cxd4 17 exd4 ♕b8 18 ♕xb8

♖axb8 19 ♖hg1 ♖bc8= Cebalo-
Vujakovic, Zagreb 1979 **14 e3**
14 g4 c5 15 ♗g2 N (15 e3 ♘c6 16
♗d3 cxd4 17 exd4 ♕b8= Sakovic-
Gutman, USSR 1967) 15...♘c6 16
g5 ♗xd4 17 ♘xd4 cxd4 18 ♘b5 ♖c8
19 ♔b1 ♕b6 20 ♘d6± Rodriguez-
Popovic, Zagreb 1979
**14...♘d7 15 ♗d3 c6 16 g4 ♕b8! 17
♖dg1 h5 N**
17...♗e7 18 ♘e5 ♗d6 19 ♘xd7 ♗xf4
20 ♘xb8 ♗xb8=; 18 ♕xb8 ♖axb8 19
♔d2 ♗d6= Spassky-Stein, USSR Final
1963
18 ♕xb8 ♖axb8 19 gxh5 ♖xh5=
Sahovic-Torre, Amsterdam 1979

King's Indian

**1 d4 ♘f6 2 c4 g6 3 ♘c3 ♗g7 4 g3 0-0
5 ♗g2 d6 6 ♘f3 ♘c6 7 0-0 a6 8 b3**
8 ♘d5!? ♘d7 9 ♗e3 b5 10 cxb5
axb5 11 ♖c1 ♗b7 12 ♘xc7! ♕xc7
13 d5 ♘db8 14 dxc6 ♘xc6 15 ♘d4
♗xd4 16 ♕xd4! ♘xd4 17 ♖xc7 ♗xg2
18 ♔xg2 ♘f5 19 ♗a7!± Romanishin-
Adorjan, Amsterdam 1978; 8...♗g4!=
Portisch-Timman, Montreal 1979
**8...♖b8 9 ♗b2 b5 10 cxb5 axb5 11
♖c1**
11 ♘e1 ♘a5 12 ♖c1 c5 13 e4 ♘d7
14 ♘c2 e6 15 ♗a1 b4∓ Romanishin-
Tseshkovsky, USSR Final 1978

11...♘a5 12 ♕c2 ♗b7 13 ♖fd1 ♕d7 14 e4! b4 15 e5!± Romanishin-Grunfeld, Riga 1979

1 d4 ♘f6 2 c4 g6 3 ♘c3 ♗g7 4 e4 d6 5 ♗e2 0-0 6 ♗g5 c5 7 d5 h6 8 ♗f4 e6 9 dxe6 ♗xe6 10 ♗xd6 ♖e8 11 ♘f3 ♘c6 12 0-0 ♕a5?! 12...♘d4!= **13 ♘d2!** N
13 e5 ♘d7 14 ♘d5 ♗xd5 15 ♕xd5 ♖ac8 16 a3 ♘dxe5= Popov-Cebalo, Zagreb 1973
13...♖ed8 14 ♗f4 ♘d4
14...♘e8 N 15 ♘d5! ♗xb2 16 ♘b3 ♕a3 17 ♗xh6 ♗xd5 18 cxd5 ♗xa1 19 ♕xa1 ♘d4 20 ♘xd4 cxd4 21 ♕xd4 ±/+− Ivkov-Torre, Rio de Janeiro 1979

15 ♘d5 ♗xd5 N
15...♘xd5 16 cxd5 ♘xe2+ 17 ♕xe2 ♗d7 18 ♘b3? ♕b4 19 ♖fc1 ♗b5 20 ♕e3 b6 21 ♖c2 ♗a4∓ Uhlmann-Ghitescu, Bucharest 1979; 18 ♘c4!± Uhlmann-Peev, Bucharest 1979
16 cxd5 ♘xe2+ 17 ♕xe2 ♕b4 18 a3! ♕xb2 19 ♖ab1± Uhlmann-Sznapik, Berlin 1979

1 d4 ♘f6 2 c4 g6 3 ♘c3 ♗g7 4 e4 d6 5 ♘f3 0-0 6 ♗e2 e5 7 0-0 ♘bd7
7...♘c6 8 d5 ♘e7 9 b4 ♘h5
a) 10 c5 ♘f4 11 ♗xf4 exf4 12 ♖c1

♗g4 13 ♘d2 ♗xe2 14 ♕xe2 g5 15 ♕h5!? ♘g6≈ Speelman-Biyiasis, Hastings 1978/79;
b) 10 g3 a5!? N 11 ♗a3 f5 12 bxa5 ♘f6 13 ♘d2 ♘h6 14 ♗f3 ♗xd2 15 ♕xd2 fxe4 16 ♘xe4± Sosonko-Van der Wiel, Netherlands Final 1979;
c) 10 g3 f5 11 ♘d2 (11 ♘g5) ♘f6 12 c5 f4 13 ♘c4 ♗h3 N (13...g5 14 ♗a3 ♗h3 15 ♖e1 ♖f7 16 b5 ♘c8! 17 ♗b2 ♖e7= Sosonko-Uhlmann, Amsterdam 1975) 14 ♖e1 ♘c8 15 a4 h5! 16 ♕d3 ♘g4 17 ♘d1 ♘h6 18 ♖a3 ♗g4 =+ Sosonko-Kavalek, Waddinxveen, 1979
8 d5
8 ♗e3 a5 9 ♕c2 ♘g4 10 ♗g5 f6 11 ♗d2 c6!? (11...exd4 12 ♘xd4 ♘c5 13 ♘b3 ♘xb3 14 axb3 f5= R.Byrne-Vukevic, USA 1969) 12 ♖ad1 ♕e7 13 h3 ♘h6 14 ♖fe1 ♘f7 15 ♗e3± Miles-P.Littlewood, British Final 1979

8...♘c5 9 ♕c2 a5 10 ♗g5 h6
10...♕d7!? 11 ♘d2 h6 12 ♗e3 b6 13 b3 ♘g4 14 ♗xg4 ♕xg4 15 a3 f5 16 f3± Csonkics-Kowalska, Lublin 1979
11 ♗e3 b6 12 ♘d2 ♗g4 N
a) 12...♘g4 13 ♗xg4 ♗xg4 14 a3 ♘a6 15 ♖ab1 ♗d7 16 b4 += Smyslov-Suetin, Sochi 1974;
b) 12...♘fd7!?
c) 12...♘e8 13 f3 f5 14 exf5 gxf5 15

18

f4 += Polugaevsky-Browne, Mar del Plata 1971
13 f3 Bd7 14 b3 Nh5 15 a3 Nf4 16 Rfe1 Qg5 17 Bf1 Ncd3!∓ Keene-Torre, Manila 1979

Trompovsky Attack

1 d4 Nf6 2 Bg5 Ne4
a) 2...c5 3 Nc3 cxd4 4 Qxd4 Nc6 5 Qh4 d6 (5...e6 6 e4 Be7 7 0-0-0 a6 8 f4 b5 9 e5 b4 10 exf6 gxf6 11 Ne4 fxg5 12 fxg5 Qa5 13 Kb1± Vaganian-Knaak, Tallinn 1979) 6 0-0-0 Bd7 N (6...Qa5 7 e4 Bd7 8 Bc4 h6 9 Bxf6 gxf6 10 Nd5 Rg8 11 Ne2 Rg4 12 Qh5 Ne5α Tseitlin-Taborov, Daugavpils 1978) 7 e4 Rc8 8 Bd3 e6 9 f4 Be7 10 Qe1 Qa5 11 Kb1 h6 12 Bh4 g5 13 Bg3 Nh5 14 f5 Nxg3 15 hxg3 Bf6 16 Nb5± Nei-Yurtaev, Spartakiad 1979;
b) 2...d6 3 Nc3 Nbd7 4 Nf3 h6 5 Bxf6 exf6 6 e3 f5 7 Bd3 Nf6 8 Ne2 g6 9 h4 Nh5 10 c3 Bg7 11 Qc2 0-0= Basagic-Kolarov, Sofia 1979;
c) 2...c6!? N 3 Bxf6 exf6 4 c4 Bb4+ 5 Nd2 d5 6 e3 0-0 7 a3 Be7 8 Ngf3 a5 9 b3 Bf5 10 cxd5 cxd5 11 Nh4 Be6 =+ Kokimidis-Georgiev, Sofia 1979;
d) 2...g6 3 Bxf6 exf6 4 e3 f5 5 Ne2 d6 6 c4 Bg7 7 Nbc3 Nd7 8 Nf4 Nf6 9 h4 h5 10 g3 c6 11 Bg2 0-0= Krizsanne-Vreeken, Budapest 1979;
e) 2...d5 3 Bxf6 exf6 4 e3 Bf5 5 Ne2 N Bd6 6 Ng3 Bg6 7 Bd3 Qd7 8 c3 Nc6 9 Qc2 Ne7 10 Nd2 0-0 11 Bxg6 fxg6 12 e4 += Klimova-Sikora, Lublin 1979;
f) 2...e6 3 e4 h6 4 Bxf6 Qxf6 5 Nf3
1) 5...d5 6 Nbd2 b6 N 7 c3 Bb7 8 Qa4+ Nc6 9 Bb5 Bxb5 10 Qxb5+ c6 11 Qe2 Qd8 12 exd5 cxd5 13 Ne5

+= Cvitan-Vujacic, Jugoslav Junior Final 1979;
2) 5...b6 6 Nbd2 Bb7 7 Bd3 d6 8 Qe2 g6 N (8...Qd8 9 h4 a6 10 0-0-0 Nd7 11 g4 g6 12 c3 Bg7 13 Kb1 Qe7= Kiarner-Ornstein, Tallinn 1977; 8...g5!?) 9 e5 Qe7 10 h4 Bg7 11 h5 g5 12 0-0-0 Nc6 13 exd6 Qxd6 14 c3 += Palatnik-Kayumov, Spartakiad 1979
3 Bh4 c5
a) 3...c6 4 f3 N Qa5+ 5 Nd2 Qh5 6 Nxe4 Qxh4+ 7 g3 Qh5 8 Bg2 d5= Mkrtichan-Kartanaite, Spartakiad 1979;
b) 3...c6 4 Nd2 d5 5 Nxe4 dxe4 6 c3 h6 N (6...Bf5 7 e3 Qb6 8 Qc2 e6 9 h3 c5 10 g4 Bg6 11 Ne2 Nc6 12 Bg2 cxd4 13 exd4 Rc8 14 Bxe4 Qb5 15 a3 Na5 16 0-0 Nc4 17 a4 Qd7 18 Ng3± Bronstein-Tseitlin, Odessa 1976) 7 e3 Bf5 8 Qb3 Qc8 9 h3 e6 10 g4 Bh7 11 Ne2 Bd6 12 Ng3 Be7 13 c4 Nd7= Zvorikina-Mkrtichan, Spartakiad 1979;
c) 3...d5 4 f3 (4 Nd2 Bf5=) 4...g5 5 fxe4 gxh4 6 exd5 Qxd5 7 Nc3 Qa5 8 e3 N (8 Nf3 h3 9 g3 Bh6 10 Qd3 Nc6 11 Qb5 Qxb5 12 Nxb5 Nb4= Diaz-Smyslov, Biel 1976) 8...Bh6 9 Qf3 Nd7 10 Nh3 c6 11 Bc4 Nf6 12 0-0 Bg4 13 Qf2 Bxh3 14 gxh3 0-0-0= Vaganian-Smejkal, Rio de Janeiro 1979

Diagram

4 f3 Nf6
4...g5 5 fxe4 gxh4 6 e3 Nc6 7 Nc3 Bh6 (7...e6 8 Qh5 cxd4 9 exd4 Qf6 10 e5 Qg6 11 Qxg6 hxg6 12 Nf3 d5 13 Bb5 += Tseitlin-Egin, Spartakiad 1979) 8 d5 Ne5 9 Qh5 Bg7 10 Nf3 d6 11 Bb5+ Bd7 12 0-0 Bxb5 13

&xe5!± Korzubov-Levit, Spartakiad 1979
5 d5 N
5 dxc5 ♕a5+ N 6 ♔d2 ♕xc5 7 ♘c3 e6 8 e4 a6 9 f4 d6 10 0-0-0 ♗e7 11 ♘f3 ♘bd7 12 ♗d3 b5 13 e5 dxe5 14 fxe5 ♘xe5 15 ♘xe5 ♕xe5 16 ♗e4 ♖a7 17 ♗c6+ ♔f8∞ Vaganian-Popov, Kecskemet 2 1979
5...d6 6 e4 g6 7 ♘c3 ♗g7 8 f4 0-0 9 ♘f3 ♕b6 10 ♖b1 e6 11 ♘d2 exd5 12 ♗xf6 ♗xf6 13 ♘xd5 ♕d8= Vaganian-Slupkin, Spartakiad 1979

Sicilian

1 e4 c5 2 ♘f3 ♘c6 3 d4 cxd4 4 ♘xd4 e5 5 ♘b5 a6 6 ♘d6+
6 ♘5c3 ♘f6 7 ♗g5 ♗c5 8 ♗c4 h6 9 ♗h4 N (9 ♗xf6 ♕xf6 10 0-0 0-0 11 ♘d2 d6 12 ♘d5 ♕h4 13 f3 ♔h8= Foguelman-Rossetto, Mar del Plata 1958) 9...b5 10 ♗d5 ♗b7 11 ♘d2 ♕e7 12 ♘b3 ♗b6= Borkowski-Bielczyk, Polanica Zdroj 1979 **6... ♗xd6 7 ♕xd6 ♕f6 8 ♕d1** 8 ♕a3 ♘ge7! 9 ♗e3?
a) 9...d5! 10 ♗c5 ♘d4 11 ♗xe7 ♕f4! 12 ♔d1 ♕xf2 13 ♗d3 dxe4 14 ♖f1 ♗g4+ 15 ♔c1 ♕e3+ −+ Kliner-Soltis, Corresp 1973;
b) 9...d5! 10 exd5 ♘xd5 11 ♗c5

♕g6 12 ♕d3 ♕xd3 13 ♗xd3 ♘db4 =+;
c) 9...♘d4 N 10 ♗xd4 exd4 11 ♗d3 0-0 12 0-0 ♘g6 13 ♘d2 b5 14 g3 d5 15 f4 += Vitolins-Manatov, Spartakiad 1979
8...♕g6 9 ♘c3 ♘ge7 10 h4 h5 11 ♗g5 b5
11...d5!
12 a3 d6 13 ♕d2 ♗b7 14 0-0-0 ♖d8 15 f4± Vujacic-Sinanovic, Jugoslavia 1979

1 e4 c5 2 ♘f3 d6 3 d4 cxd4 4 ♘xd4 ♘f6 5 ♘c3 g6 6 ♗e3 ♗g7 7 f3 0-0 8 ♕d2 ♘c6 9 ♗c4
a) 9 0-0-0 d5 10 ♘xc6 bxc6 11 exd5 ♘xd5 12 ♗d4 e5 13 ♗c5 ♗e6 14 ♘e4! ♖e8 15 h4 f5 16 ♘g5 ♗h6 17 ♗e2 ♗xg5 N 18 hxg5 ♘f4≈ Poupinel-Lecroq, Corresp 1975/79;
b) 9 0-0-0 ♘xd4 10 ♗xd4 ♗e6 11 ♔b1 ♕c7 12 g4 ♖fc8 13 g5! N (13 h4 ♕a5 14 ♗xf6 ♗xf6 15 ♘d5 ♕xd2 16 ♘xf6+ ♔g7!=) 13...♘h5 14 ♘b5 ♕d8 15 ♗xg7 ♘xg7 16 ♘d4 ♖c5 17 h4 ♖ac8 18 ♖c1 ♕b6 19 ♘xe6 fxe6 20 ♗h3± Hort-Sosonko, Tilburg 1979
9...♗d7 10 h4 ♖c8 11 ♗b3 h5 12 0-0-0 ♘e5 13 ♗g5
a) 13 ♔b1 ♘c4 14 ♗xc4 ♖xc4 15 ♘b3 ♕c7 16 ♗d4 ♗c6 17 ♕e2 (17 ♖he1 △ e5) 17...b5 18 e5 ♘d5! 19 exd6 ♕xd6 20 ♘xd5 ♗xd5 21 ♗xg7 ♔xg7 22 ♕e3 N (22 ♕d2 e6 23 ♘d4 ♖fc8 24 g4 ♖h8 25 ♘xb5 ♕b4 26 ♘a3 ♗xf3!= Kaplan-Miles, Hastings 1976/77) 22...e6 23 ♕xa7 ♖a4 24 ♕e3 ♖fa8 25 a3 ♕g3∓ Tseshkovsky-Miles, Riga 1979;
b) 13 ♗h6? ♗xh6 14 ♕xh6 ♖xc3 15 bxc3 ♕c7 16 g4 ♕xc3 17 ♔b1 a5 18 a3 N a4∓ Chi-Miles, Bled 1979;
c) 13 g4!? hxg4 14 h5 ♘xh5 15 ♗h6∞

20

13...♖c5

13...♘h7 14 ♗h6 ♗xh6 15 ♕xh6 ♖xc3 16 bxc3 ♕a5 17 ♔b1! ♕xc3 18 ♘e2 ♕c5 19 g4 +− Geller-Kuzmin, USSR Final 1978; 17...♖c8!∞

14 ♖he1 N

a) 14 ♔b1 b5 15 ♖he1 a5 16 f4 ♘c4 17 ♗xc4 bxc4 18 e5 ♕b6! 19 exf6 ♖b8!∓ Barczay-Sosonko, Wijk aan Zee 1977;

b) 14 g4 hxg4 15 ♗xf6 ♗xf6 16 h5 g5 17 ♘d5 e6 18 ♘xf6+ ♕xf6 =+ Georgadze-Miles, Dortmund 1979; 17...♖xd5!?∞; 15 f4 ♘c4 16 ♕e2 b5 17 e5 dxe5 18 ♘dxb5 ♘xb2!∓ Westerinen-Mestel, Esbjerg 1979;

c) 14 f4 ♘c4 15 ♕d3 b5 16 e5 ♘g4 N (16...dxe5 17 ♗xf6 ♗xf6 18 ♘dxb5 ♘xb2?!∞ Klovan-Gufeld, Otborochny 1978) 17 ♘e4 ♖d5 18 ♘xd6 ♘cxe5 19 fxe5 ♘xe5 20 ♗xd5 ♘xd3+ 21 ♖xd3 ♕b6 22 ♗xe7 ♗xd4∓ Ljubojevic-Miles, Riga 1979

14...b5 15 f4 ♘c4 16 ♗xc4 bxc4

16...♖xc4!? 17 e5 b4 18 ♘e4!±

17 ♗xf6 ♗xf6 18 e5 ♗g7

18...dxe5 19 fxe5±

19 e6!± Karpov-Sosonko, Tilburg 1979

1 e4 c5 2 ♘f3 ♘c6 3 d4 cxd4 4 ♘xd4 g6 5 c4

5 ♘c3 ♗g7 6 ♗e3 ♘f6

a) 7 ♘xc6 bxc6 8 e5

1) 8...♘d5 9 ♘xd5 cxd5 10 ♕xd5 ♖b8 11 ♗c4! e6 12 ♕c5 ♗b7 13 0-0? N ♖c8 14 ♕b4 ♗xe5 =+ Duckstein-Karlsson, Lucerne 1979; 13 0-0-0 ♖c8 14 ♕b4 ♕c7 15 ♗g5± Muratov-Veresov, Novgorod 1961;

2) 8...♘g8 9 ♗d4 f6 10 exf6? N ♘xf6 11 ♗c4 d5 12 ♗d3 ♕d6 13 ♕e2 0-0∓ Hoen-Kagan, Lucerne 1979;

b) 7 ♗c4 0-0 8 ♗b3

1) 8...d6 9 h3 a6 N 10 0-0 ♘a5 11 ♕d2 b5 12 ♗h6 ♗b7 13 ♗xg7 ♔xg7 14 ♖fe1 ♖c8= Pritchett-Soos, Clare Benedict 1979;

2) 8...a5 9 a4 ♘g4 10 ♕xg4 ♘xd4 11 ♕h4 N ♘xb3 12 cxb3 ♖a6 13 0-0 d6 14 ♘d5 ♖e8 15 b4 axb4 16 a5 ♖c6 17 ♘xb4 ♖c4∓ Borkowski-Pokojowczyk, Polanica Zdroj 1979

5...♗g7 6 ♗e3 ♘f6

a) 6...♘h6 7 ♗e2 d6 8 ♕d2 ♘g4 9 ♗xg4 ♗xg4 10 ♘c3 0-0 11 0-0 ♖c8 12 b3 ♕a5 13 ♖ac1 a6 14 f3 N ♗d7 15 ♖fd1 ♘xd4 16 ♗xd4 ♗xd4 17 ♕xd4 += Fernandez-Martin, Alicante 1979;

b) 6...d6 7 ♘c3 ♘h6

1) 8 h3!? N f5 9 exf5 ♘xf5 10 ♘xf5 ♗xf5 11 ♕d2 ♕a5 12 ♖c1 0-0 13 ♗e2 ♖ac8 14 0-0 += Chi-Larsen, Bled 1979;

2) 8 ♗e2 0-0 9 0-0 f5 10 exf5 gxf5 11 ♘xc6 N bxc6 12 ♕d2 ♘g4 13 ♗xg4 fxg4= Csom-Popov, Kecskemet 2 1979; 11 f4! ♗d7 12 ♕d2 ♘g4 13 ♗xg4 fxg4 14 ♘d5!± Szabo-Larsen, Vinkovci 1970

Diagram

7 ♘c3 ♘g4

7...0-0 8 ♗e2 b6 9 0-0 ♗b7

21

a) 10 Rc1!? Nxd4 11 Bxd4 Nh6 12 f4 Nxe4 13 Nxe4 Bxe4 14 Rc3 f5 15 b4 e6 16 Rh3∝ Liberzon-Rantanen, Lucerne 1979;
b) 10 f3 Nh5 11 Ndb5 a6 12 Na3 Rb8 13 Rb1 e5!? 14 Nc2 Nf4= Suba-Honfi, Kecskemet 2 1979

8 Qxg4 Bxd4 9 Qd1 Be6 10 Qd2
a) 10 Be2 Bxc3+ 11 bxc3 Qc7 N 12 0-0 b6 13 Bd4 f6 14 Re1 Bb7 15 Bf1 += Imanaliev-Lanka, Spartakiad 1979;
b) 10 Rc1 d6 11 Bd3 Bd7 12 0-0 0-0 13 Qd2 Nc5 14 Bb1 Na4 15 Nd1 Nc5 16 Re1± Spartakiad 1979

10...Qa5
a) 10...b6 11 Rc1 Bb7 12 Bd3 0-0 13 h4 Nc5 14 Bb1 e5!? 15 Rd1 Qe7 16 h5± Van der Sterren-Hernandez, Amsterdam 1979;
b) 10...d6 11 Be2 Bd7 12 0-0 Qa5 13 f4? Bc6 14 f5 Nc5 15 f6 exf6 16 Rac1 0-0∓ Ardiansah-Averbakh, Jakarta 1979

11 Rc1 d6 12 Be2 Bd7 13 b3 Bc6 14 f3 f5 15 exf5 gxf5 16 0-0 0-0=
Maninang-Keene, Manila 1979

1 e4 c5 2 Nf3 Nc6 3 d4 cxd4 4 Nxd4 Nf6 5 Nc3 e5 6 Ndb5 d6 7 Bg5
7 Nd5 Nxd5 8 exd5
a) 8...Ne7 9 c3 Ng6 10 Qa4 Bd7

11 Qb4 Bf5 12 Qc4 Qe7 13 g4 Bc8 14 Bd3 a6 15 Nc7 Rb8= Bozic-Darmanovic, Jugoslavia 1979;
b) 8...Nb8 9 c4 Be7 10 c5! 0-0 11 Be3 Na6 12 cxd6 Bxd6 13 Bc4 Bb4+ 14 Nc3 Bxc3+ 15 bxc3 Qd6 16 0-0± Messing-Lin Veuzhe, Coka 1979;
c) 8...Nb8 9 c4 a6 10 Nc3 Be7 11 Be2 0-0 12 0-0 f5 13 f4 Bf6 14 Qc2 Nd7 15 Kh1 g6 16 g3 += Tal-Tseshkovsky, Riga 1979;
2) 10 Nc3 Nd7 11 Be2 g6 12 0-0 Bg7 13 Ne4 Qe7 14 Qa4 f5 15 Bg5 Qf8 16 f4± Gufeld-Ivanovic, Sochi 1979

7...a6 8 Na3 b5 9 Bxf6
9 Nd5 Be7
a) 10 Bxf6 Bxf6 11 c3 0-0
1) 12 Be2 Bg5 13 0-0 Ne7 14 Nxe7+ Qxe7 15 Nc2 Bb7 16 Bd3 Rad8 =+ Carvajal-Alexandria, Rio de Janeiro 1979;
2) 12 Nc2 Rb8 13 h4! N g6 14 g3 Be6 15 Nce3 Bg7 16 h5 Ne7 17 hxg6 hxg6 18 Nxe7+ Qxe7 20 Qf3± Nunn-Wirthensohn, Clare Benedict 1979;
3) 12 Nc2 Bg5! 13 Bd3 Bd7 14 0-0 g6 15 Nce3 Kh8 16 Qe2 f5 17 exf5 gxf5 18 f3 Ra7 =+ Marggraff-Schneider, Biel 1979;
4) 12 Nc2 Bg5! 13 a4 bxa4 14 Rxa4

♔h8 15 ♗e2 ♗b7 16 0-0 ♘e7 17 ♗c4 f5 18 exf5 ♖xf5 19 ♖b4 ♗c6 20 ♘xe7 ♕xe7 21 ♗d5 += Karpov-Yurtaev, Spartakiad 1979;
b) 10 ♘xe7 ♕xe7 11 ♗d3 0-0 12 0-0 h6 13 ♗h4 ♗b7 14 c3 ♕e6 ½-½ Grunfeld-Adorjan, Riga 1979;
c) 10 ♘xe7 ♘xe7 11 ♗xf6 gxf6
1) 12 ♕f3 f5 13 exf5 ♗xf5 14 ♗d3 ♗e6 15 0-0 d5 16 ♖fd1 f5? 17 ♕h5+ ♗f7 18 ♕h6 e4 19 ♘xb5!± Tringov-Georgadze, Primorsko 1977; 14...♗xd3 15 ♕xd3 d5 16 c3 ♕b6 17 0-0 f5!? 18 ♖ae1 e4 19 ♕e3± Gipslis-Jasnikowski, Hradec Kralove 1977/78;
c) 12 c4!? ♗b7 13 ♗d3!? bxc4 14 ♘xc4 d5= Ljubojevic-Tseshkovsky, Riga 1979;
3) 12 c4!? ♗b7 13 cxb5 ♗xe4 14 ♕a4 d5 15 bxa6+ ♔f8 16 ♕b4 N (16 h4 ♖g8 17 f3 ♗f5 18 g4 ♗c8 19 0-0-0 ♕b6 20 ♔b1 ♔g7∓ Izvozchikov-Sveshnikov, Riga 1975) 16...♖g8 17 f3 ♗f5 18 g4 ♗c8 19 0-0-0 ♗xa6 20 ♔b1 ♔g7 =+ Ljubojevic-Adorjan, Riga 1979

9...gxf6 10 ♘d5 f5 11 ♗d3
a) 11 c3 ♗g7 12 exf5 ♗xf5 13 ♘c2 0-0 14 ♘ce3 ♗e6 15 ♗d3 f5 16 ♕h5 b4 17 ♖d1 bxc3 18 bxc3 e4= Shamkovich-Van der Wiel, Amsterdam 1979;
b) 11 exf5 ♗xf5 12 ♗d3 e4 13 ♕e2 ♘d4 14 ♕e3 ♗g7 15 f3 ♘xf3+ 16 gxf3 ♕h4+ 17 ♔d2 ♔f8 18 ♗xe4 ♗xe4 19 ♕xe4± Matulovic-Vukic, Vrsac 1979;
c) 11 ♘xb5!? axb5 12 ♗xb5 ♗d7 13 exf5 ♖b8 14 a4 ♕g5
1) 15 g4 ♕h4 16 ♕d3 ♗h6 17 c3 0-0 18 ♕g3 ♗g5 19 b4 ♔h8 20 ♕xh4 ♗xh4 21 0-0-0± Bronstein-Vukic, Vrsac 1979;
2) 15 0-0! N ♖g8 16 g3 ♔d8 17

♖a3 ♖b7? 18 ♕e1 +– Panuskin-Kajumov, USSR 1979
11...♗e6 12 ♕h5
a) 12 c4 ♕a5+ 13 ♔f1 ♗xd5 14 cxd5 fxe4 15 ♗xe4 ♘e7 16 ♘c2 ♖c8 17 h4 ♕c7 18 ♘e3 ♗h6 19 ♘f5 ♘xf5 20 ♗xf5 ♕c4+∓ Kupreichik-Yurtaev, Spartakiad 1979;
b) 12 0-0 ♗g7 13 c4 ♗xd5 14 cxd5 fxe4 15 ♗xb5 axb5 16 dxc6 0-0 17 ♘xb5± Maninang-Jamieson, Queensland 1979

12...♖g8! N
12...♗g7 13 0-0 f4
a) 14 ♔h1 0-0 15 g4!? ♔h8 16 ♖g1 ♘e7 17 ♘xe7 ♕xe7 18 ♘b1 ♖g8 19 ♘d2± Wedberg-Wirthensohn, Lucerne 1979;
b) 14 ♘b1 0-0 15 a4 b4
1) 16 c4 ♔h8 17 ♘d2 ♖g8 18 ♘f3 ♗f6 20 h3 ♖g6 21 ♔h1 ♕f8= Psahis-Panchenko, Sochi 1979;
2) 16 ♘d2 f5 17 ♗c4 ♘a5 18 b3 ♘xc4 19 bxc4 ♖c8 20 ♖ab1 a5 21 exf5 ♗xf5 22 ♖bc1 ♗d7= Ivanovic-Sveshnikov, Sochi 1979
13 f4!?
a) 13 0-0? f4!
1) 14 h3 ♖g5?! 15 ♘c7+ ♔d7 16 ♘xe6 fxe6= Sax-Rohland, Canadian Open 1978;
2) 14 h3 ♖g6! △ ♖h6, ♖c8, ♕g5∓;

3) 14 c3? ♗g4 15 ♕xh7 ♖g6 16 f3
♗e6 17 ♖f2 ♖h6 18 ♕g8 ♖c8 −+
Zuckerman-Day, Quebec 1979;
b) 13 c3!? f4 14 ♗e2 ♖xg2 15 ♕xh7
♖g6 16 ♕h5 b4 17 ♘c4 bxc3 18 bxc3
♘a5 19 ♘xf4 exf4 20 ♕xa5 ♕xa5
21 ♘xa5 d5! 22 ♗f3 d4!∓ Nurmi-
Day, Toronto 1978;
c) 13 g3!? ♘d4 14 c3 fxe4 15 ♗xe4
♗g4 16 ♕xh7 ♖g7 17 ♕h6 ♘f3+ 18
♔f1 ♖g5 19 ♘f6+ ♕xf6! 20 ♕xf6
♘d2+ 21 ♔g2 ♘e4 22 ♕h8 ♖h5∓
13...♖xg2 14 ♘e3 ♕a5+
14...♖g6 15 exf5 ♖h6∝
**15 ♔f1 ♖g7 16 exf5 ♕b4! 17 fxe6
♕xf4+ 18 ♔e2 ♘d4+** = Hubner-Sax,
Rio de Janeiro 1979

**1 e4 c5 2 ♘f3 d6 3 d4 cxd4 4 ♘xd4
♘f6 5 ♘c3 a6 6 ♗e2 e5 7 ♘b3 ♗e7
8 0-0 0-0**
a) 8...♗e6 9 a4 0-0 10 ♗e3
1) 10...♘bd7 11 a5 ♖c8 12 ♕d2 ♕c7
13 ♖fc1 ♕c6 14 ♗f3 ♖fd8 15 ♘d5
♗xd5 16 exd5 ♕c4! 17 ♕d3! ♕xd3
18 cxd3 += Mednis-Bouaziz, Riga
1979; 12...♖xc3!?∝;
2) 10...♘c6 11 ♔h1 ♖c8 12 f4 ♘b4
13 ♗f3 d5= Mednis-Ljubojevic, Riga
1979;
b) 8...♗e6 9 f4 ♕c7 10 ♔h1 ♘bd7 11
a4 0-0 12 f5 ♗c4 13 ♗g5 h6 14 ♗h4
♖fc8= Ljubojevic-Ribli, Riga 1979
9 f4
9 ♗g5 ♗e6 10 f4 exf4 11 ♗xf4 ♘c6
12 ♔h1
a) 12...d5? 13 e5 ♘e4? Karpov-
Najdorf, Hastings 1971/72, 14 ♗d3!±;
b) 12...♖e8 13 ♕e1 ♘d7 14 ♖d1 ♘de5
15 ♘d5 ♗f8 16 ♕f2 ♘d7 17 ♗g3 ♘ce5
18 ♗h4 ♕c8 19 c3 b5 20 ♗g5±
Karpov-Kavalek, Waddinxveen 1979
9...b5
9...♕c7 10 a4 ♗e6 11 f5 ♗c4 12 a5

♘bd7 13 ♗e3 ♖fc8!? N 14 ♔h1 ♗xe2
15 ♕xe2 d5 16 exd5 ♗b4 17 ♗d2
♗xc3 18 ♗xc3 ♘xd5 =+ Sigurjonsson-
Portisch, Buenos Aires Olympiad
1978

10 a4
a) 10 fxe5 dxe5 11 ♕xd8 ♖xd8 12
♗g5 ♗e6 13 a4 b4 14 ♗xf6 ♗xf6 15
♘d5 ♗xd5 16 exd5 ♖a7= Klovan-
Gutman, USSR 1978;
b) 10 a3 ♗b7 11 ♗d3 ♘bd7 12 ♔h1
♖c8 13 fxe5 ♘xe5 14 ♗f4
1) 14...♘g6 15 ♗g3 d5? 16 exd5 ♘xd5
17 ♗e4!± Klovan-Zaichik, Sochi
1978;
2) 14...♘c4 15 ♗xc4 ♖xc4 16 ♘d2
♖c8 17 ♕e2 ♖e8 =+ Gufeld
**10...b4 11 ♘d5 ♘xd5 12 ♕xd5 ♕b6+
13 ♔h1 ♗b7 14 a5 ♕c7 15 ♕d3 ♘d7
16 ♗d2 ♘c5 17 ♘xc5 dxc5 18 ♕f3**
18 ♕g3! ♗xe4 19 fxe5 ♗xc2 20
♖ac1 b3 21 ♗c4∝
18...♖ad8 19 ♗e3 f5!∓ Larsen-
Romanishin, Riga 1979

**1 e4 c5 2 ♘f3 d6 3 d4 cxd4 4 ♘xd4
♘f6 5 ♘c3 a6 6 ♗g5 e6 7 f4 b5 8 e5
dxe5 9 fxe5 ♕c7 10 exf6**
10 ♕e2 ♘fd7 11 0-0-0 ♗b7
a) 12 ♘xe6 fxe6 13 ♕g4 ♕xe5 14
♗d3 ♗e7 15 ♗xe7 ♔xe7 16 ♖he1
h5 N 17 ♕b4+ ♕c5 18 ♕h4+ ♘f6 19

24

♕g3 ♔f8 Wittmann-van der Vliet, Clare Benedict 1979, 20 ♖xe6!∝;
b) 12 ♕g4 ♕xe5 13 ♘xb5 axb5 14 ♖he1 h5! 15 ♕h4 ♕c5 16 ♕g3 ♗e7!? 17 ♗xe7 ♕xe7 18 ♘f5! +– Speelman-van Dop, Clare Benedict 1979
10...♕e5+ 11 ♗e2 ♕xg5 12 0-0 ♕e5 13 ♘f3! N
13 ♗f3 ♖a7 14 ♘c6 ♘xc6 15 ♗xc6+ ♗d7 16 ♗xd7+ ♖xd7 17 ♕f3 ♗d6!=+ Mariotti-Ribli, Manila 1976
13...♗c5+ 14 ♔h1 ♕xf6 15 ♘e4 ♕e7 16 ♘fg5 0-0 17 ♘xf7! ♖xf7 18 ♖xf7 ♔xf7 19 ♗h5+ ♔g8 20 ♘xc5 ♘d7? 21 ♘xe6!± Beljavsky-Polugaevsky, Spartakiad 1979, 20...♖a7∝

1 e4 c5 2 ♘f3 d6 3 d4 cxd4 4 ♘xd4 ♘f6 5 ♘c3 a6 6 ♗g5 e6 7 f4 ♕b6 8 ♕d2
8 ♘b3 ♗e7
a) 9 ♕e2 ♕c7 10 g3 ♘bd7 11 0-0-0 h6 12 ♗h4 b5 13 ♗g2 ♖b8 14 ♖he1 b4 15 ♘d5! += Torre-Rodriguez, Manila 1979;
b) 9 ♕f3 ♕c7 10 0-0-0 ♘bd7 11 ♗d3 b5 12 a3 ♗b7 13 ♖he1
1) 13...0-0-0 14 ♕e2 ♘c5! 15 ♘xc5 dxc5 16 e5 c4! =+ Bronstein-Portisch, Rio de Janeiro 1979;
2) 13...♘c5 14 ♕h3 0-0-0 15 ♘xc5 dxc5 16 e5 ♘d5= Spassky-Portisch, Tilburg 1979
8...♕xb2 9 ♖b1 ♕a3 10 f5 ♘c6 11 fxe6 fxe6 12 ♘xc6 bxc6 13 e5 dxe5 14 ♗xf6 gxf6 15 ♘e4
15 ♗e2 ♕d6 16 ♕e3 N ♕d4 17 ♕f3 ♗b4!∝ Hubner-Portisch, Rio de Janeiro, 1979
15...♗e7 16 ♗e2 h5 17 ♖b3
17 0-0 f5 18 ♖b3 ♕a4 19 c4 fxe4 20 ♔h1 ♗d7 21 ♕c3!?∝ Hubner-Hort (5) 1979; 21 ♕c2 Δ ♕xe4

17...♕a4 18 ♘xf6+!?
18 c4 f5 19 ♘d6+ ♗xd6 20 ♕xd6 ♕a5+ 21 ♔f2 ♖a7 22 ♖b8? ♔f7 23 ♖d1 ♔f6 24 c5 ♖d7 –+ Matulovic-Stean, Vrsac 1979
18...♗xf6 19 c4 ♗h4+
19...♖a7!? 20 0-0 ♖f7 21 ♖b8 0-0; 21 ♕d6 c5 Δ ♕d7
20 g3 ♗e7 21 0-0 ♖a7
21...♗d7 22 ♖b7 c5 N 23 ♗d1 ♕c6 24 ♗f3 ♕d6 25 ♕c2! e4 26 ♖d1 +– Nunn-Macaulay, British Final 1979
22 ♖b8 ♖c7 23 ♕d3
23 ♗d3; 23 ♔h1!?
23...♗c5+ 24 ♔h1 ♕e7 25 ♕g6 ♕d6 26 ♕f6 ♖e8 27 ♗xh5 ♖ce7 28 ♖d1+ ♗xd4 29 ♖xd4+ = Hund-Fischdick, Rio de Janeiro 1979 (Vitolins-Gavrikov, USSR 1977!)

1 e4 c5 2 ♘f3 d6 3 d4 cxd4 4 ♘xd4 ♘f6 5 ♘c3 a6 6 ♗g5 e6 7 f4 ♗e7
7...♘bd7 8 ♕f3 ♕c7 9 0-0-0 b5?! 10 ♗xb5 axb5
a) 11 ♘dxb5 ♕b8! 12 e5 ♖a5!∓ Balashov-Polugaevsky, Manila 1976;
b) 11 e5! ♖a5! 12 ♘dxb5 ♖xb5 13 ♘xb5 ♕b8∝;
c) 11 e5! ♕b7 N 12 ♘dxb5 dxe5 13 fxe5 ♖xa2 14 ♔b1 ♖a5 15 exf6 ♕xf3 16 ♘c7+! ♔d8 17 fxg7+ ♔xc7 18 gxh8♕ ♕a8 19 ♗d8+! +– Maninang-

Bachtiar, Manila 1979, Poletschuk-Foigel, 13 USSR Corresp Final 1978/79 **8 ♕f3**

a) 8 ♕e2 ♕c7 9 0-0-0 ♘bd7 10 g4 0-0 N 11 ♗h4 ♘c5 12 g5 ♘fd7 13 ♕e3 b5 14 a3 ♖e8 15 ♗g3 ♗f8 16 ♗e2 ♘b6 =+ Bordonada-Bachtiar, Manila 1979;

b) 8 ♕e2 h6 9 ♗xf6 ♗xf6 10 0-0-0 ♘d7 11 f5 ♕e7 N 12 ♕h5 0-0 13 fxe6 fxe6 14 ♗c4 ♘e5 15 ♗b3 ♔h7 16 ♔b1 ♗d7= Beshan-Eolian, Spartakiad 1979

8...♕c7 9 0-0-0 ♘bd7 10 g4 b5 11 ♗xf6 ♘xf6 12 g5 ♘d7 13 f5 ♗xg5+ 14 ♔b1 ♘e5 15 ♕h5 ♕e7

15...♕d8 16 ♖g1 ♗f6 17 fxe6 0-0 18 ♗h3 g6 19 ♘d5! (19 ♕e2 ♔h8 20 ♖gf1? ♗g7 21 ♕g2 ♘c4∓ Matulovic-Quinteros, Wijk aan Zee 1974) 19... ♔h8 20 ♕e2 fxe6 21 ♗xe6 ♖e8 22 ♗xc8 ♖xc8 23 h4!± Mecking-Quinteros, Manila 1976

16 ♖g1 N

16 ♘xe6 ♗xe6 17 fxe6 g6 18 exf7+ ♔xf7 19 ♕e2 ♔g7 20 ♘d5 ♕d8 21 ♗h3 ♖a7 22 ♖hf1 ♖e8= Browne-Najdorf, Mar del Plata 1971; 21 h4!? Gligoric

16...♗e3?

16...♗f6 17 fxe6 ♗xe6 18 ♘xe6 g6 19 ♘c7+ ♕xc7 20 ♘d5 ♕d8 21 ♕h6±

17 ♖xg7 ♕f8 18 ♖g3 ♕h6 19 ♕e2 ♗f4 20 ♖h3 ♕g5 21 ♖h5 ♕g4 22 ♗h3 +− Hubner-Westermeier, BRD 1979

Caro Kann

1 e4 c6 2 d4 d5 3 ♘d2

3 e5 ♗f5 4 ♘c3 e6 5 g4 ♗g6 6 ♘ge2

a) 6...f6 7 ♘f4 fxe5 N 8 ♘xg6 hxg6 9 dxe5 ♗c5 10 ♗f4 ♕b6 11 ♕d2 Balashov-Bellon, Karlovac 1979, 11... ♕xb2 12 ♖b1 ♕a3 13 ♖b3 ♕a5∞; 8 dxe5 ♗f7 9 h4 +=;

b) 6...c5 7 ♗e3 ♘c6 8 dxc5 ♘xe5 9 ♘d4 h5 10 ♗b5+ ♘d7 11 ♕e2 ♗e7 12 f4!± Efimov-Machulsky, USSR 1979;

c) 6...c5 7 h4 cxd4 8 ♘xd4 h5 9 ♗b5+ ♘d7 10 ♗g5 ♕c7 11 ♕e2 ♗b4 12 ♖h3 a6 13 0-0-0 axb5 14 ♘xd5!± Kupreichik-Roizman, USSR 1979

3...dxe4 4 ♘xe4 ♘f6

4...♗f5 5 ♘g3 ♗g6 6 h4 h6 7 h5 ♗h7 8 ♘f3 ♘d7 9 ♗d3 ♗xd3 10 ♕xd3 ♘gf6 (10...♕c7) 11 ♗f4 ♕a5+

a) 12 c3 e6 13 a4 c5 14 0-0 ♖c8 15 ♖fe1 c4 16 ♕c2 ♗e7 17 ♘e5 0-0 18 ♘f5± Gaprindashvili-Nikolac, Amsterdam 1979;

b) 12 ♗d2 ♕c7 13 0-0-0 e6 14 ♕e2 c5 15 ♔b1 0-0-0 16 c4 ♗d6 17 ♘e4 ♘xe4 18 ♕xe4 ♘f6 19 ♕e2 += Kavalek-Karpov, Waddinxveen 1979

5 ♘xf6+

a) 5 ♘g3 c5 6 ♘f3 ♘c6 7 ♗e3 ♘d5 8 dxc5 N ♕a5+ 9 ♗d2 ♕xc5 10 ♗d3 g6 11 ♘e4 ♕b6 12 c4 ♘db4 13 ♗c3 f6 14 ♗b1 ♗g7 15 a3 ♘a6 16 b4± Castro-Bellon, Alicante 1979;

b) 5 ♘g3 g6 N 6 ♘f3 ♗g7 7 ♗e2 0-0 8 0-0 ♕b6 9 b3 ♗g4 10 ♗b2 a5 11 a4 ♘bd7 12 h3 ♗xf3 13 ♗xf3 += Karpov-Larsen, Tilburg 1979

26

5...gxf6

5...exf6
a) 6 ♗e2 ♗d6 7 ♘f3 0-0 8 ♘e2 ♕c7 9 h3 ♗e6 10 0-0 ♘d7 11 b3 b5 12 ♗b2 ♘b6 13 ♘c3 ♖ad8= van Riemsdijk-Bohm, Amsterdam 1979;
b) 6 ♗c4 ♘d7 7 ♘e2 ♗d6 8 0-0 ♕c7 9 ♘g3 0-0 10 ♕h5 ♘b6 11 ♗d3 g6 12 ♕h4!± Barczay-Ciric, Warsaw 1979;
c) 6 ♗c4 ♗d6 7 ♕e2+ ♗e7 8 ♘f3 0-0 9 0-0 ♗d6 10 ♖e1 ♘d7 11 ♗d3 ♘b6 12 c3 ♗g4= Ligterink-Lein, Amsterdam 1979

6 ♗c4

a) 6 ♘f3 ♗f5 7 ♗e2 ♕c7 8 0-0 ♘d7 9 c4 0-0-0 10 ♗e3 e6 11 ♕a4 ♕b8 12 b4 ♖g8 13 ♔h1± Kavalek-Larsen, Tilburg 1979;
b) 6 ♗f4 ♗f5 7 ♘f3 ♕d5 8 ♗e3 ♗e4 9 ♗e2 e6 10 ♕d2 ♗xf3 11 ♗xf3 ♕b5 12 0-0-0 ♘d7 13 ♖he1 += Martin-Bellon, Alicante 1979;
c) 6 ♘e2 h5 7 h4 ♗g4 8 ♕d3 e5!? 9 ♗e3 ♘a6 10 a3 ♕a5+! 11 ♗d2 ♕b6∓ Mihaljcisin-Speelman, Frunze 1979

6...♗f5 7 ♗f4

7 c3 e6 8 ♕f3 ♘d7 9 ♘e2 h5!= Ivanovic-Bronstein, Tallinn 1979

7...♕b6 N **8 ♗b3 a5 9 a4 ♗g7 10 ♘f3 0-0 11 0-0 ♘a6 12 ♖e1 e6 13 ♘h4 ♗g6 14 ♗e3 ♕c7=** Lau-Keene, Clare Benedict 1979

Scandinavian

1 e4 d5 2 exd5 ♕xd5 2...♘f6
a) 3 ♘c3 ♘xd5 4 ♗c4 e6 5 ♘ge2 ♗e7 6 0-0 0-0 7 d4 c6 8 ♖e1 ♘d7 9 ♘e4 b6 10 c3 ♗b7 11 ♘f4 c5= Hug-Haas, Berne 1979;
b) 3 d4 ♘xd5 4 c4 ♘f6 5 ♘c3 ♗g4 6 ♗e2 ♗xe2 7 ♘gxe2 e6 8 0-0 ♗e7 9 ♗f4 0-0 10 ♕b3 ♕c8 11 d5 ♘a6= Kurajica-Bronstein, Vrsac 1979;
c) 3 ♗b5+ ♗d7 4 ♗c4 b5 5 ♗b3 (5 ♗e2 ♘xd5 6 d4 e6 7 ♘f3 ♗d6 8 0-0 ♗c6 9 a4! b4 10 c4 bxc3 11 bxc3 0-0 12 c4 ♘f4 13 ♗xf4 ♗xf4 14 ♘c3 ♕f6 15 ♗d3 ♘d7 16 ♗e4± Matulovic-Bronstein, Hamburg 1965) 5...♗g4 6 f3 ♗c8
1) 7 ♕e2 a6 8 a4 b4 9 ♕c4 ♕d6 10 d3 e6 11 ♗f4 e5 12 ♗g5 ♗b7∞ Keres-Lutikov, Tallinn 1964
2) 7 a4 b4 8 ♘e2 ♘xd5 9 c4 ♘f6 10 d4 a5 11 0-0 e6 12 ♗e3 += Zuravlev-Hribovsek, Corresp 1966;
3) 7 ♘c3 N b4 8 ♘e4 ♘xd5 9 d4 e6 10 ♘e2 ♗e7 11 0-0 0-0 12 c4 ♘b6 13 ♗e3 ♘c6 14 ♕d3 ♗a6 15 ♗c2 f5 16 b3! += Sellos-Haas, Berne 1979

3 ♘c3 ♕a5

3...♕d6 4 d4 ♘f6
a) 5 ♗g5 c6 6 ♗c4 ♗g4 7 f3 ♗f5 8 ♘ge2 e6 9 ♕d2 ♗e7 Turiscev-Gubricki, USSR 1968 10 0-0-0±
b) 5 ♘f3 N a6 6 ♗e3 ♘c6 7 ♕d2 ♗g4 8 ♘g5 e5 9 d5 ♘b4 10 f3 ♗f5 11 ♘ge4± Karpov-Lutikov, Spartakiad 1979

4 d4

4 ♘f3 ♘f6 5 d3 N ♗g4 6 h3 ♗h5 7 ♗e2 c6 8 0-0 ♘bd7 9 ♘d2 ♗g6 10 ♘c4 += Shaw-Rogers, Manila 1979

4...♘f6 5 ♘f3

5 ♗c4 c6 6 ♗d2 N (6 ♘f3 ♗f5 7 ♘e5 e6 8 0-0 += Parma-Germek, Bled

27

1961) 6...♗f5 7 ♘f3 ♕c7 8 ♘e5 e6
9 g4!? ♗e4 10 f3 ♗d5 11 ♗d3 ♘bd7
12 ♕e2 ♘xe5 13 dxe5 ♘d7 14 ♘xd5
cxd5 15 f4 0-0-0 =+ Rogers-Lein,
Queensland 1979

5...♗f5
a) 5...♗g4 6 h3 ♗h5 7 g4 ♗g6 8 ♘e5
e6 N (8...c6 9 h4±) 9 h4 ♗b4 10
♗d2 ♕b6 11 ♗g2 0-0= Voronova-
Agabagyan, Spartakiad 1979; 9 ♘c4!
+=;
b) 5...c6 6 ♘e5 ♗f5
1) 7 ♗d3 ♗xd3 8 ♕xd3 e6 9 ♗d2
♘bd7 10 ♕e2 ♗e7 11 0-0-0 ♘xe5
12 dxe5 ♘d7 13 f4 += Marjanovic-
Janicijevski, Vrsac 1979;
2) 7 g4 ♗e6 8 ♘c4 ♕c7 9 ♘e3 ♘bd7
10 g5 ♘d5 11 ♘cxd5 ♗xd5 12 ♘xd5
cxd5 13 c3 e6= Matanovic-
Janicijevski, Vrsac 1979
6 ♗d3
6 ♗d2 N c6 7 ♗c4 e6 8 ♗b3 ♕c7 9
♕e2 ♘bd7 10 h3 0-0-0 11 0-0-0
♗d6 12 ♘h4 ♗g6 13 ♘xg6 hxg6 14
♔b1 ♗f4 15 ♕f3 ♗xd2 ½-½ Matanovic-
Sahovic, Vrsac 1979
6...e6 7 ♗xf5 N
7 0-0 ♘bd7 8 ♖e1 ♗b4 9 ♗f4 0-0 10
♘e5 ♗xc3 11 bxc3 ♗xd3 12 ♕xd3
♖ad8 13 ♖ab1 ♘d5 14 ♗d2 ♘xe5
15 ♖xe5 ♕xa2 −+ Danstrup-Larsen,
Denmark 1979

**7...♕xf5 8 ♘e5 h5!? 9 0-0 ♘bd7 10
♕e2 a6**
10...♘xe5=
11 f4 ♖d8 12 ♖f3 ♘b6 13 ♖g3 ♘bd5=
Barle-Larsen, Bled 1979

Vienna

1 e4 e5 2 ♘c3 ♘f6 3 f4
3 ♗c4 ♘c6 4 d3
a) 4...♘a5 5 ♘f3 ♘xc4 6 dxc4 ♗b4 7
♗d2 ♗xc3 8 ♗xc3 d6 9 ♕e2 b6 10
0-0-0 ♕e7 11 ♘h4 g6 12 g3 ♗b7 13
f3 0-0-0= Tseitlin-Luczak, Lublin
1979;
b) 4...♗b4 5 ♗g5 h6! 6 ♗xf6 ♗xc3+!
7 bxc3 ♕xf6 8 ♘e2 d6 9 0-0 ♗e6 N
10 ♗b5 0-0 11 f4 exf4 12 ♖xf4 ♕g5
13 ♗xc6 bxc6 =+ Lieb-Unzicker,
Munich 1979; 10 ♗b3=;
c) 4...♗b4 5 ♘e2 d5 6 exd5 ♘xd5
7 0-0 ♗e6 8 ♘e4 N (8 ♗xd5 ♗xd5 9
f4 0-0 10 a3 ♗e7 11 ♗e3 f5= Nielsen-
Hulak, 5th World Corresp Final)
8...♗e7 9 f4 exf4 10 ♘xd5 ♗xd5 11
♗xf4 0-0 12 ♘2c3 ♗e6 13 ♕d2 h6 =+
Janosevic-Toth, Biel 1979
3...d5 4 fxe5 ♘xe4 5 ♘f3
5 d3 ♘xc3 6 bxc3 d4 7 ♘f3
a) 7...dxc3! Euwe 8 d4 ♗e6 9 ♕d3 c6
10 ♕xc3 ♗e7 11 ♗e2 ♘d7 12 ♗e3
♘b6= Kasprzyk-Jackson, Lublin 1979;
b) 7...♘c6!? 8 cxd4 ♘xd4 9 c3 ♘xf3+
10 ♕xf3 ♗e6 11 d4 ♕d5 12 ♕g3 c5≈
5...♗e7
5...♗g4 6 ♕e2 ♘c5? (6...♘xc3 7 dxc3
Δ ♗f4, 0-0-0, c4 +=) 7 d4 ♗xf3? (7...
♘e6 8 ♗e3 += Larsen) 8 ♕xf3 ♘e6 N
(8...♕h4+ 9 g3 ♕xd4 10 ♗e3 ♕xe5
11 0-0-0 c6 12 ♘xd5!± Spielmann-
Flamberg, Mannheim 1914) 9 ♗e3
c6 10 ♗d3 ♗e7 11 0-0 0-0 12 ♕h3
g6 13 ♖xf7!! +− Berg-Dobosz, Esbjerg
1979; 6...♘g5!≈

28

6 d4
a) 6 ♕e2 ♘xc3 7 dxc3 0-0 8 ♗f4 c5
9 0-0-0 ♕a5! N 10 ♔b1 ♘c6 =+
Janosevic-Baretic, Jugoslavia 1977;
b) 6 ♕e2 f5 7 d3 ♘c5
1) 8 ♗e3 ♘e6 9 d4 c6 10 ♕d2 0-0 11
♗e2 ♗d7 12 0-0 ♗e8 13 ♗d3 ♗g6=
Sikora-Ciechocinska, Lublin 1979;
2) 8 g3! Keres d4 9 ♘d1 ♘e6 10 ♗g2
0-0 11 ♘f2 c5 12 h4± Westerinen-
Lengyel, Saint-Feliu 1973
6...♘c6 7 ♗d3 f5 8 exf6 ♘xf6
8...♗xf6!
9 0-0 ♗g4 10 ♗e3 N 0-0 11 h3 ♗h5
12 ♕e1 h6 13 g4!? ♗e8 14 ♕g3 ♘h7=
Yap-Rodriguez, Manila 1979

Spanish

1 e4 e5 2 ♘f3 ♘c6 3 ♗b5 a6 4 ♗a4
♘f6 5 0-0 ♘xe4 6 d4 b5 7 ♗b3 d5 8
dxe5
8 ♘xe5 ♘xe5 9 dxe5 c6 10 c3 ♗c5 11
♘d2 ♘xd2 12 ♗xd2 0-0 13 ♕h5
a) 13...g6 14 ♕h6 f6 15 exf6 ♕xf6 16
♗e3 ♗xe3 17 fxe3 ♕e7 18 ♖xf8+ ♕xf8
19 ♕h4 += Spassky-Keres 1965;
b) 13...f6 14 exf6 g6 15 ♕e5 ♕d6 16
♕g5 ♖xf6 17 ♖ae1 += Holmov-Petran,
Budapest 1 1979
8...♗e6 9 ♕e2
a) 9 ♗e3 ♗e7 10 ♘bd2 ♘xd2 11

♕xd2 ♕d7 12 a4 0-0 13 ♖fd1 ♖ad8
14 axb5 axb5 15 c3 ♕c8 16 ♕d3
♕b7= Grushevskin-Hermlin, Spartakiad 1979;
b) 9 ♗e3 ♘a5 10 ♘d4 ♕d7 11 ♕e1
♘xb3 12 axb3 ♗e7 13 b4 c5 14 ♘xe6
fxe6 15 f3 d4≈ Kupreichik-Slupskin,
Spartakiad 1979;
c) 9 ♘bd2 ♘c5 10 c3 d4 11 ♘g5 dxc3
(11...♕xg5! 12 ♕f3 0-0-0!?∞) 12
♘xe6 fxe6 13 bxc3 ♕d3 14 ♘f3 (14
c4!?∞) 14...♕xd1 15 ♗xd1 ♗e7 16
♗e3 ♘d3 17 a4 += Liu Vendze-Popov,
Coka 1979;
d) 9 c3 ♗e7 10 ♘bd2 0-0 11 ♗c2 f5
12 ♘b3 ♕d7 13 ♘fd4 ♘xd4 (13...
♘a5!? 14 ♘xe6 ♕xe6 15 ♘d4 ♕xe5
16 f3 ♗d6 17 g3 f4!= Boleslavsky-
Zagorovsky, USSR 1954) 14 ♘xd4
c5 15 ♘xe6 (15 ♘e2 ♖ad8 16 ♘f4
♕c6 17 a4 ♗c8= Fischer-Unzicker,
Santa Monica 1966) 15...♕xe6 16
f3 ♘g5 17 a4 ♖ad8?! (17...c4 18
axb5 ♕b6+ 19 ♔h1 ♕b5= Korchnoi)
18 axb5 axb5 19 ♕e2 N (19 ♗xg5
♗xg5 20 f4 ♗e7 21 ♔h1 ♔h8 22 ♕e2
c4 23 g4! g6 24 gxf5 gxf5 25 ♖g1
♗c5 26 ♖g2± Shamkovich-Suetin,
Moscow 1962) 19...c4? (19...♕b6)
20 ♗e3 b4 21 ♕d2 b3 22 ♗d1±
Beljavsky-Tarjan, Bogota 1979

9...♗e7

29

9...♗c5 10 ♗e3 (10 c3 0-0 11 ♗e3 ♗g4 12 ♖d1 ♘e7 13 ♘bd2 ♘xd2 14 ♖xd2 ♗xe3 15 ♕xe3 ♗xf3 16 ♕xf3 += Mesing-Zakic, Coka 1979) 10...♗xe3 11 ♕xe3 ♘a5 12 ♘bd2 ♘xd2 13 ♘xd2 0-0 14 c3 ♘c4 15 ♘xc4 bxc4 16 ♗c2 += Ilijin-Kajari, Coka 1979

10 ♖d1

10 c4!? bxc4

a) 11 ♗a4 ♗d7 12 ♘c3 ♘c5 13 e6 fxe6 14 ♗xc6 ♗xc6 15 ♘e5 ♕d6 16 ♕h5+ g6 17 ♘xg6 hxg6 18 ♕xh8+ ♔d7 19 ♕g7 d4 =+ Abroshin-Radchenko, Corresp 1954;

b) 11 ♗xc4 N dxc4 12 ♕xe4 ♕d5 13 ♕f4 0-0-0!?∝ Panchenko-Haritonov, Sochi 1979

10...0-0

a) 10...♘a5

1) 11 ♘d4! c5 12 ♘f5! ♗xf5 13 ♗xd5 ♘g5 14 h4!± Korchnoi;

2) 11 c3 ♘xb3 12 axb3 0-0 13 ♘d4 ♕d7 14 f3 ♘c5 15 ♗e3 f6= Gusenov-Levit, Spartakiad 1979;

b) 10...♘c5 11 ♗e3 0-0 12 c4 bxc4 13 ♗xc4 ♘a5 14 ♗xd5 ♗xd5 15 ♘c3 ♗xf3 16 ♕xf3 ♕e8 17 b4 ♘d7 18 bxa5 ♘xe5 (+= Korchnoi)

1) 19 ♕g3 ♘g6= Vyboril-Sapundzhiev, Corresp 1973/75;

2) 19 ♕f5 ♘g6 20 ♖ac1 ♗a3 21 ♖b1 ♕c6 22 ♘d5 ♖ab8= Hubner-Korchnoi (5) 1973;

3) 19 ♕b7 N ♘c4 20 ♗d4 ♗d6 21 ♖e1 ♕d7 22 ♕d5 ♘a3= Jansa- Stoica, Bagneux 1979

11 c4 bxc4 12 ♗xc4 ♗c5

12...♘a5?! 13 ♗d3 ♘c5 14 ♗c2 ♘c4 N (14...♘c6 15 ♘c3 d4 16 h3 ♖b8 17 ♗e3 ♖b4 18 b3 dxe3 19 ♖xd8 exf2+ 20 ♔xf2± Bogolanovic-Ilievski, Jugoslav Final 1965) 15 ♘c3 c6 16 ♘d4 ♕d7 17 b3 ♘b6 18 h3± Lijan Tjin Lon-Popov, Coka 1979

13 ♗e3 ♗xe3 14 ♕xe3 ♕b8 15 ♗b3 ♘a5!? 16 ♘e1

16 ♘bd2 ♕a7! 17 ♘d4!? ♘xd2 18 ♕xd2 ♕b6 19 ♗c2 N (19 ♕e2 c5 20 ♘xe6 fxe6 21 ♗c2 c4 22 b3 Janosevic-Haag, Birmingham 1975, 22...♖ac8∓) 19...c5 20 ♘f5 ♗xf5 21 ♗xf5 ♖ad8 22 ♖e1 ♘c6 =+ Jansa-Stean, Vrsac 1979

16...♘xb3 17 axb3 f5! 18 exf6

a) 18 ♘d2 c5 19 ♘xe4 fxe4 20 ♕xc5 ♕xe5∓;

b) 18 f3 f4 19 ♕d4 c5 20 ♕d3 ♘g5∓;

c) 18 ♘d3 d4! 19 ♕xd4 ♖d8 20 ♕e3 ♕b6 21 ♖a3 ♖d4 22 ♖f1 ♖ad8 23 ♘f4 ♘xf2∓ Ude-Kuuskmaa, Corresp 1978/79

18...♖xf6 19 f3

19 ♘f3? ♗g4! 20 ♖xd5 ♗xf3 21 gxf3 c6 22 ♖h5 ♖g6+ 23 ♔h1 ♕f4! 0-1, Preinfalk-Kuuskmaa, Corresp 1978/79

19...♘d6 20 ♘d2 ♖h6 21 ♘f1!

a) 21 ♖dc1 c5!

1) 22 ♕xc5 ♘e4! 23 fxe4 ♕xh2+ 24 ♔f1 ♕f4+ 25 ♘ef3 dxe4 26 ♕d4 ♖f8 27 ♔f2 ♗g4 28 ♖c4 ♖d6∓ Cording-Kuuskmaa, Evrard-Delannoy Cup 1978/79;

2) 22 ♘f1! c4 23 bxc4 dxc4 24 ♘g3 a5 25 ♕c5 ♘b7 26 ♕e3 ♘d6 27 ♕c5 a4 28 ♖d1 ♗f7 29 ♖d2 ♘b7 30 ♕e3 ♕c7 =+/∓ Sakharov-Yim, IX World

Corresp   Final/Bobkow-Kuuskmaa,
Corresp 1978/79;
b) 21 ♖dc1 ♗f7! 22 ♖dc1 ♘f5 23
♕c5 ♕b6 24 ♘d3 ♘d4 =+

1 e4 e5 2 ♘f3 ♘c6 3 ♗b5 a6 4 ♗a4
♘f6 5 0-0 ♗e7 6 ♖e1 b5 7 ♗b3 d6
8 c3 0-0 9 h3 ♗b7 10 d4 ♖e8 11
♘bd2
a) 11 ♘g5 ♖f8 12 f4?! exf4 13 ♗xf4
♘a5 14 ♗c2 ♘d5! =+ Ljubojevic-
Gligoric (5) 1979;
b) 11 dxe5 ♘xe5 12 ♘xe5 dxe5 13
♕f3 c5 14 ♘d2 c4 15 ♗c2 ♕c7 16
♘f1 ♖ad8 17 ♘g3 += Tseitlin-
Vasjukov, Spartakiad 1979

11...♗f8 12 a3 N
12 ♗c2 ♘b8 (12...g6)
a) 13 a4 ♘bd7 14 b4 ♘b6 15 a5 ♘bd7
16 ♗b2 ♖c8 17 ♕b1 c5 18 bxc5 dxc5
19 dxe5 ♘xe5 20 c4± Klovan-
Seredenko, Spartakiad 1979; 14 ♗d3
c6 15 b3 ♕c7 16 ♗b2 g6 17 ♕c2 ♗g7
18 c4 bxa4= Semonova-Zatulovskaya,
Spartakiad 1979;
b) 13 b3 ♘bd7 14 d5 c6 15 c4 ♕c7 16
a4 ♖ec8 17 ♖a2 bxc4 18 bxc4 a5 19
♗d3   +=   Karpov-Romanishin,
Spartakiad 1979; 15...♘b6 16 ♗b2
♘fd7 17 dxc6 ♗xc6 18 cxb5 axb5 19
♘f1 ♘c5 20 ♘g3 f6 =+ Klovan-Geller,
Spartakiad 1979

12...h6
12...g6 13 ♗a2 ♗g7 14 b4 ♘b8 15
dxe5 dxe5 16 ♘g5 ♖f8 17 ♕c2 ♘bd7
18 c4± Ivanovic-Zaitsev, Sochi 1979
13 ♗c2 ♘b8 14 b4 ♘bd7 15 ♗b2
c5!? 16 bxc5 dxc5 17 dxe5 ♘h5 18
c4± Tal-Romanishin, Riga 1979

1 e4 e5 2 ♘f3 ♘c6 3 ♗b5 a6 4 ♗a4
♘f6 5 0-0 ♗e7 6 ♖e1 b5 7 ♗b3 d6 8
c3 0-0 9 h3 ♘a5 10 ♗c2 c5 11 d4

11...♘d7 (Keres) 12 ♘bd2 cxd4 13
cxd4
a) 13...♗f6 14 ♘f1 ♘c6 15 ♗e3 exd4
16 ♘xd4 ♘de5
1) 17 a4 N bxa4 18 ♖xa4 ♗d7 19
♘g3 ♘a5 20 ♖a2 ♘ec4= Ardiansah-
Dorfman, Jakarta 1979;
2) 17 ♘g3 g6 18 a4 ♖b8 19 axb5
♘xd4 20 ♗xd4 ♖xb5= Minic-Ciocaltea,
Reggio Emilia 1968/69;
b) 13...♘c6 14 ♘f1 ♗f6 15 d5 ♘b4
16 ♗b1 a5
1) 17 ♕e2 N ♖b8 18 g4 ♘c5 19
♘g3 g6 20 ♔g2 ♗d7 21 ♗e3 ♘ba6 22
g5± Vujacic-Bozanovic, Jugoslavia
1979;
2) 17 a3 ♘a6 18 ♗d3 ♖b8 19 ♕e2
♕b6   20   ♗e3   ♘dc5=   Bouaziz-
Reshevsky, Sousse 1967;
c) 13...♘c6 14 ♘b3! a5
1) 15 ♗e3 a4 16 ♘c1 exd4 17 ♘xd4

31

♘xd4 18 ♗xd4 ♗f6 19 ♘e2 ♗b7 20 ♕d2 ♖e8 21 ♘c3 ♗c6= Tal-Larsen, Biel 1976; 15...♗a6
2) 15 ♗d3 ♖b8 16 ♕e2 ♗a6 17 ♗d2!± Tal-Reshevsky, Amsterdam 1964;
3) 15 ♗d3 a4 16 ♗xb5 ♕b6 17 ♗xc6 ♕xc6 18 ♘bd2± Matulovic-Ciocaltea, Lugano 1968;
4) 15 ♗d3 ♗a6 16 d5 ♘b4 17 ♗f1 a4 18 ♘bd4! (18 a3 ♘xd5 19 ♕xd5 axb3 20 ♗xb5 ♘f6! 21 ♕d3 ♗xb5 22 ♕xb5 ♕b8= Matulovic-Lengyel, Maribor 1967) 18...exd4 19 a3 ♘c2?! N (19...♗f6? 20 axb4 ♕b6 21 b3 axb3 22 ♕xb3 ♘e5 23 ♘xe5 dxe5 24 ♖a5± Shamkovich-Benjamin, USA 1976; 19...♘c5!? 20 ♘xd4 ♗f6 21 ♗e3 ♗xd4 22 ♗xd4 ♘b3 23 axb4 ♘xa1 24 ♕g4! f6 25 ♖xa1±) 20 ♕xc2 ♗f6 21 ♗f4 ♖c8 22 ♕d2 ♘c5 23 ♖ad1 ♖e8 24 ♘xd4± Lau-Toschkov, Oslo 1979;

11...♗b7 12 ♘bd2 cxd4 13 cxd4 ♖c8 14 d5 ♘h5 15 ♘f1 (15 b4!? ♕c7 16 ♘b3 ♘c4 17 ♗d3 ♘f4 18 ♗xf4 exf4 19 ♖c1± Velimirovic-Hennings, Havana 1971) 15...♘c4 16 b3 ♘b6 17 ♘e3 g6 18 ♗d2 ♘d7 19 a4 bxa4 N (19...♖a8 20 b4 ♘b6 21 axb5 axb5 22 ♗d3 ♕d7 23 ♖a5± Stein-Kluger, Kislovodsk 1964) 20 ♖xa4 ♘g7 21 ♕b1 ♖a8 22 b4 ♘b6 23 ♖a5± Jansa-Sellos, Bagneux 1979
11...♕c7 12 ♘bd2 cxd4
12...♘c6 13 d5 ♘d8 14 ♘f1 (14 a4 ♖b8 15 ♘f1 N ♘e8 16 ♘3h2 f6 17 f4 exf4 18 ♗xf4 ♘f7 19 axb5 axb5 20 b3 ♘e5= Maninang-Shaw, Queensland 1979) 14...♘e8 15 ♘g3 g6 16 ♗h6 ♘g7 17 ♕d2 f6 18 a4 ♖b8 19 axb5 axb5 20 b4 ♘f7= Bachtiar-Shaw, Manila 1979
13 cxd4 ♘c6
a) 13...♗b7 14 ♘f1 ♖ac8 15 ♗d3

1) 15...♘d7 16 d5 f5 17 ♘e3 (Fischer) 17...f4 18 ♘f5 ♗d8 19 ♗d2 ♘c4 20 ♖c1 ♕b8 21 ♗xc4 bxc4 22 ♗b4 ♘c5 23 ♘d2 ♖xf5! 24 ♗xc5 Judovich-Berta, Corresp 1978/79, 24...♖f8 25 ♗a3 +=;
2) 15...d5 16 dxe5 ♘xe4 17 ♘g3 f5 18 exf6 ♗xf6 19 ♘xe4 dxe4 20 ♗xe4 ♖fd8 21 ♕e2 ♖e8 22 ♕d3?! N (22 ♘d2≈ Geller-Keres, Amsterdam 1956) 22...♖xe4! 23 ♖xe4 ♖d8 24 ♖d4 ♗xd4 25 ♘xd4 Sellos-Honfi, Trstenik 1979, 25...♕e5!∓;
b) 13...♖d8 14 ♘f1 exd4 15 ♗g5? h6! 16 ♗h4 ♘c4 17 ♕xd4 ♘e5!∓ Westerinen-Szabo, Helsinki 1979

14 a3
a) 14 ♘b3 a5 15 ♗e3 a4 16 ♘bd2 ♘b4 17 ♗b1 ♗d7 18 a3 ♘c6 19 ♗d3 ♘a5 20 ♕e2 ♕b8 21 ♖ac1 (21 ♘h2!? N ♗d8 22 f4 ♖e8 23 ♘hf3 += Grunfeld-H.Olafsson, Lucerne, 1979) 21...♖e8 22 ♖c2 h6 (22...♗d8 23 dxe5 dxe5 24 ♖ec1 h6 25 ♖c3 b4 26 axb4 ♕xb4 27 ♖1c2 ♗b6= Matanovic-Smejkal, Banja Luka 1979) 23 ♖d1 += Gufeld-Vasjukov, USSR 1979;
b) 14 d5 ♘b4 15 ♗b1 a5 16 ♘f1 ♗d7 17 ♗d2 ♖fc8 18 ♘e3 N ♘a6 19 ♘h2 ♘c5 20 ♕f3 g6 21 ♘hg4± Golovein-Shivaeva, Spartakiad 1979
14...♕a7 N 15 ♘b3 ♗d8 16 d5

32

16 Be3 Bb6 17 Qd2 a5 18 Qc3 Bb7
19 dxe5 Nxe5 20 Nxe5 Rfc8 21 Nc6
Rxc6 22 Qd2 += Jansa-Pytel,
Bagneux 1979
**16...Be7 17 Qe2 Bd7 18 Bd2 Be8
19 Na5±** Timoshenko-Filip, Polanica
Zdroj 1979

**1 e4 e5 2 Nf3 Nc6 3 Bb5 a6 4 Ba4
Nf6 5 0-0 Be7 6 Re1 b5 7 Bb3 d6 8
c3 0-0 9 h3 h6 10 d4 Re8 11 Nbd2
Bf8 12 Bc2** 12 Nf1 Bd7 13 Ng3 Na5
14 Bc2 c5 15 b3 Nc6
a) 16 d5 Ne7 17 Be3 Kh8 18 Qd2
Qc8 19 c4 += Gufeld-Augustin, Sochi
1979;
b) 16 Bb2 b4 17 dxe5 bxc3 18 exf6
N (18 Bxc3 dxe5 19 Bd3 Nd4 20
Nd2 ½-½ Tringov-Matanovic, Ljubljana
1969) 18...cxb2 19 fxg7 Bxg7 20 Rb1
Be6 21 Nh5 Bh8 22 Qd2 Kh7 23
Rxb2± Barczay-Augustin, Sochi 1979

12...Bb7
12...Bd7 13 Bd3 Qb8 14 b3 g6 15
Bb2 Bg7 16 d5 Nd8 17 c4! += Savon-
Geller, Lvov 1978
13 d5!
13 a3 Nb8 14 b4 Nbd7 15 Bb2 c5!
16 bxc5 exd4! 17 cxd4 dxc5 18
d5 Bd6=
**13...Nb8 14 b3 c6 15 c4 Nbd7 16
Nf1 Qc7 17 Be3 Rec8 18 Rc1 Qd8**

19 Ng3 += Karpov-Balashov, Munich
1979

**1 e4 e5 2 Nf3 Nc6 3 Bb5 Nf6 4 0-0
Nxe4 5 d4 Be7 6 dxe5**
6 Qe2 Nd6 7 Bxc6 bxc6 8 dxe5
a) 8...Nf5 9 Qe4! g6 10 Nc3 0-0 11
Rd1 Rb8 12 Qa4± Tseshkovsky-
Mihalchishin, USSR Final 1978;
b) 8...Nb7 9 Nc3 0-0 10 Re1 Nc5
11 Be3 Ne6 12 Rad1! f6 13 Nd4 Nxd4
14 Bxd4 fxe5 15 Bxe5 Nf6 16 Qc4+±;
10...d5 11 exd6 Bxd6 12 Bg5 Qd7
Balashov-Smyslov, Leningrad 1977,
13 Ne4 c5! 14 Rad1 Qc6 15 Qd2
Bf5=; 15 Nxd6 cxd6 16 Be7 Re8 17
Qd3! h6 18 Bxd6 Rxe1+! 19 Nxe1
Bg4 20 f3 Rd8 21 fxg4 Rxd6 22 Qe2
Re6=
6...0-0 7 Qd5
7 Be3 a6 8 Bc4 d6 9 Nd5 Bf5 10
Nd4 Nxd4 11 Qxd4 dxe5 12 Qxe5
Nd6 13 Nc3!? Bxc2 14 Rac1 Bg6 15
Rfd1 +=/∞ Romanishin-Knezevic,
Leningrad 1977
7...Nc5 8 Be3 a6!?
8...Ne6 9 Nc3 a6 10 Bc4 d6 11 exd6
Qxd6=

9 Bxc5 axb5 10 Bxe7
10 Nbd2 b4
a) 11 Rfe1 Bxc5 12 Qxc5 Ra5 13
Qe3 Qe7 14 Nb3 Ra6!=;

33

b) 11 ♘b3?! ♗xc5 12 ♕xc5 ♖e8 13 ♖fe1 b6 14 ♕c4 ♗b7 15 ♕f4 h6 16 h4 ♘e7! 17 h5 ♗xf3 18 ♕xf3 ♘c6 =+ Makarichev-Vladimirov, Lvov 1975
10...♕xe7 11 ♘c3 b4 12 ♘b5 ♖a5 13 a4 b6!? N
a) 13...♘a7? 14 ♕c4 c6 15 ♘d6 c5 16 ♕g4 ♕e6 17 ♘f5 g6 18 ♘h6+ ♔g7 19 ♕h4±; 14...♘xb5 15 axb5 ♖xa1 16 ♖xa1 c5∞;
b) 13...bxa3 14 ♖xa3 ♖xa3 15 bxa3±
14 ♖fe1 ♘d8 15 ♕c4 ♘e6 16 c3 bxc3 17 b4 += Lanka-Asanov, Spartakiad 1979

Alekhine

1 e4 ♘f6 2 e5 ♘d5 3 d4
a) 3 c4 ♘b6 4 c5 ♘d5 5 d4 b6 6 cxb6 axb6 7 ♘c3 ♗b7 8 ♘f3 e6 9 ♗c4 ♘xc3 10 bxc3 d5= Groszpeter-Vaganian, Kecskemet 2 1979;
b) 3 ♘c3 ♘xc3 4 dxc3 d6 5 ♗c4 (5 ♘f3 dxe5 6 ♕xd8+ ♔xd8 7 ♘xe5 ♔e8 8 ♗c4 e6 9 ♗f4 ♗d6 10 0-0-0 ♘d7 11 ♖he1 N ♘xe5 12 ♗xe5 ♗xe5 13 ♖xe5 ♗d7= Szumilo-Malek, Rzeszow 1979) 5...c6!? 6 ♗f4 d5 7 ♗d3 g6 8 h4 ♗g7 9 ♕e2 ♘a6 10 h5 ♘c5 11 0-0-0 ♘xd3+ 12 ♖xd3 += Hubner-Hammer, Lucerne 1979
3...d6 4 ♘f3 ♗g4 5 ♗e2 e6
5...c6 6 0-0 ♗xf3 7 ♗xf3 dxe5 8 dxe5 e6 9 ♕e2 ♘d7 10 c4 ♘e7 11 ♗g4 ♕c7 12 f4 += Chandler-Fernandez, Alicante 1979
6 0-0 ♗e7 7 c4
7 h3 ♗h5 8 c4 ♘b6 9 ♘c3 0-0 10 ♗e3 d5
a) 11 c5 ♗xf3 12 ♗xf3 ♘c4 13 b3 ♘xe3 14 fxe3 ♘c6 15 ♖c1 ♕d7 16 ♕d3 ♔h8 17 ♗g4 ♗g5∓ Westerinen-Bagirov, BRD 1979;
b) 11 cxd5 ♘xd5 12 ♕b3 ♘b6 13

♖fd1 c6 14 a4 a5! N 15 d5 ♘xd5 16 ♕xb7 ♘d7= Matanovic-Vukic, Banja Luka 1979

7...♘b6 8 ♘c3
8 exd6 cxd6 9 b3 (9 ♘bd2 0-0 10 b3 ♘c6 11 ♗b2 ♗f5!? N 12 a3 a5 13 ♖e1 ♗f6 14 ♘f1 ♗g6 15 ♖c1± Tseshkovsky-Larsen, Bled 1979) 9...0-0 10 ♘c3 (10 ♗b2 ♘c6 11 ♘bd2 a5 12 a3 ♘d7 13 ♖e1 d5 14 ♘f1 dxc4 15 bxc4 ♗f6 16 ♘g3± Kagan-Hammer, Lucerne 1979) 10...♘c6 11 ♗e3 ♗f6 12 ♘e4 ♗e7 13 d5 exd5 14 cxd5 ♘b4 15 ♗xb6 ♕xb6 16 a3 ♘a6= Tal-Bagirov, Spartakiad 1979
8...0-0 9 ♗e3
9 h3 ♗h5 10 ♗e3 d5 11 c5 ♗xf3 12 gxf3 ♘c8 13 f4 f5!? 14 ♗d3 ♘c6 15 a3 ♖f7 16 ♔h2 ♗f8 17 ♘e2 ♕h4 18 ♕d2 ♘8e7 19 ♘g1 △ ♘f3± Janetschek-Dankert, Berne 1979
9...d5 10 c5 ♗xf3 11 gxf3
11 ♗xf3 ♘c4 12 ♗f4 ♘c6! 13 b3 ♘4a5=
11...♘c8 12 f4
12 b4 a6 13 f4 ♕d7 14 ♗d3 ♗d8 15 a4 c6 16 ♘e2 f5? 17 ♔h1 ♖f7 18 ♘g1± Matanovic-Vukic, Jugoslavia Final 1978
12...♗h4!?
12...♘c6 13 b4 ♗h4 14 b5 ♘a5 15 ♗d3 g6 16 ♕g4± Dorfman-Bagirov, USSR

34

1978
13 &d3 f5?
13...g6 14 ♕g4± Bagirov
14 exf6 g6
14...&xf6 15 f5±
15 f7+ ♛h8 16 ♕g4 ♛f6 17 ♛g2
Δ ♔h3!
17...♛e7 18 ♖ae1± Van der Wiel-
Bohm, Netherlands Final 1979

Pirc

1 e4 d6 2 d4 ♞f6 3 ♞c3 g6 4 f4
a) 4 &c4 &g7 5 ♕e2 c6 6 e5 dxe5 7
dxe5 ♞d5 8 &d2 ♞d7 9 f4 ♞7b6
10 &b3 ♞xc3 11 &xc3 ♞d5 12 &d2
&e6 13 ♞f3 += Short-Ludgate,
British Final 1979;
b) 4 g3 &g7 5 &g2 0-0 6 ♞ge2 e5 7
0-0 c6 8 h3 a5 9 &e3 ♞fd7 10 ♕d2
♖e8 11 ♖ad1 ♕c7 12 f4 exd4 13
&xd4 += Lein-Donner, Amsterdam
1979
4...&g7 5 ♞f3 0-0 5...c5 6 &b5+ &d7
7 e5 ♞g4
a) 8 e6 &xb5 9 exf7+ ♔d7 10 ♞xb5
♕a5+ 11 ♞c3 cxd4 12 ♞xd4 &xd4
13 ♕xd4 ♞c6 14 ♕e4 ♕b6!? 15 ♕f3
h5 16 h3 ♞h6 17 ♞d5 ♕b5 18 c3
♞f5∝ Lutikov-Podgaets, USSR 1979;
b) 8 &xd7+ ♕xd7 9 d5 dxe5 10 h3
e4 11 ♞xe4 ♞f6 12 ♞xf6+ &xf6 13
0-0 0-0
1) 14 ♞e5 ♕d6 15 c4 ♞d7 16 ♞g4
&d4+ 17 &e3 Dvoretsky-Gljanec,
USSR 1979, 17...&xe3+ 18 ♞xe3
f5=;
2) 14 c4 N e6 15 ♞e5 ♕d6 16 &e3
exd5 17 cxd5 ♖d8 18 ♞g4 &g7≈
Dolmatov-van Wijgerden, Amsterdam
1979
6 &d3
6 &e3 b6 7 &d3 c5 8 d5 e6 9 dxe6
fxe6 10 0-0 d5 11 e5 ♞g4 12 &d2

♞h6 13 ♞b5 ♞f7 14 c4 += Martin-
Chandler, Alicante 1979

6...♞c6
6...♞a6 7 0-0 c5 8 d5 b6 9 ♕e1 ♞b4
10 ♕h4 b5 11 a3 ♞xd3 12 cxd3 b4
13 axb4 cxb4 14 ♞d1 &g4 15 &e3
+= Ligterink-Torre, Amsterdam 1979
7 e5
7 0-0 e5 8 dxe5 dxe5 9 f5 ♞b4 10
fxg6 hxg6 11 &g5 ♞xd3 12 cxd3 ♕d7
13 ♕b3!?∝ Van der Wiel-Timman,
Netherlands Final 1979
7...dxe5 8 fxe5
8 dxe5 ♞d5 9 &d2 ♞b6 10 ♕e2 ♞b4
11 &e4 f5 12 &d3 &e6= Reznicek-
Felkomk, Prague 1979
8...♞h5
a) 8...♞d5? 9 ♞xd5 ♕xd5 10 c3 &e6
11 ♕e2 ♖ad8 12 &f4 ♕d7 13 0-0±
Veroci-Miles, Rio de Janeiro 1979;
b) 8...♞g4 9 &e4 f6 10 h3 ♞h6 11
exf6 exf6
1) 12 &e3 ♞f5 13 &f2 ♞h6 14 0-0
♞e3 =+ Unzicker-Donner, Bamberg
1968;
2) 12 0-0 ♕e7 13 ♞e2=;
3) 12 &f4 N ♞e7 13 ♕d2 ♞hf5 14
0-0-0 ♞d6 15 d5 ♞xe4 16 ♞xe4
c6! 17 d6 ♞d5∝ Timman-Donner,
Netherlands Final 1979
9 &e2 &g4 10 &e3
10 d5!? N &xf3 11 &xf3 ♞xe5 12

35

♗xh5 gxh5 13 ♕xh5 ♕d6 14 0-0 ♕g6 15 ♕xg6 hxg6= Bengtsson-Polihroniade, Budapest 1979

10...f6 11 exf6
11 e6 f5 12 ♕d2!? N f4 13 ♗f2 ♗xf3

14 ♗xf3 ♘xd4∓ Honfi-Horton, Corresp 1979/80
11...♗xf6!? 12 ♘e4 ♗xf3 13 ♘xf6+ ♘xf6 14 ♗xf3 e5 15 dxe5 ♘xe5 16 0-0± Timman-Kuzmin, Bled 1979

Riga Interzonal 5.ix-10.x.79

				1	2	3	4	5	6	7	8	9	0	1	2	3	4	5	6	7	8	
1	Tal	GM	2615	x	1	½	½	1	1	½	1	1	1	1	½	1	½	1	½	1	1	14
2	Polugaevsky	GM	2625	0	x	½	½	½	1	1	1	1	0	½	1	½	1	½	½	1	1	11½
3	Adorjan	GM	2525	½	½	x	½	0	0	1	½	1	1	½	½	1	½	1	1	1	½	11
4	Ribli	GM	2595	½	½	½	x	1	0	0	½	1	½	½	1	1	1	½	½	1	1	11
5	Gheorghiu	GM	2540	0	½	1	0	x	½	½	1	½	½	½	½	1	1	1	1	0	1	10½
6	Romanishin	GM	2560	0	0	1	1	½	x	1	0	½	½	1	1	½	½	½	1	1	½	10½
7	Larsen	GM	2620	½	0	0	1	½	0	x	0	1	½	½	1	½	1	1	1	½	1	10
8	Kuzmin	GM	2565	0	0	½	½	0	1	1	x	1	½	½	½	½	1	½	½	0	1	9
9	Miles	GM	2560	0	0	0	0	½	½	0	0	x	1	½	½	1	1	1	1	1	1	9
10	Tseshkovsky	GM	2560	0	1	0	½	½	½	½	½	0	x	0	½	½	1	1	1	1	½	9
11	Tarjan	GM	2525	0	½	½	½	½	0	½	½	½	1	x	0	1	0	1	0	½	1	8
12	Grunfeld	IM	2430	½	0	½	0	½	0	0	½	½	½	1	x	0	1	1	0	½	1	7½
13	Ljubojevic	GM	2590	0	½	0	0	0	½	½	½	0	½	0	1	x	½	½	1	1	0	6½
14	S.Bouaziz	IM	2420	½	0	½	0	0	½	0	0	0	0	1	0	½	x	0	½	1	1	5½
15	Mednis	IM	2510	0	½	0	½	0	½	0	½	0	0	0	0	½	1	x	½	½	1	5½
16	van Riemsdijk	IM	2435	½	½	0	½	0	0	0	½	0	0	1	1	0	½	½	x	½	0	5½
17	Trois	IM	2415	0	0	0	0	1	0	½	1	0	0	½	½	0	0	½	½	x	½	5
18	R.Rodriguez	IM	2370	0	0	½	0	0	½	0	0	0	½	0	0	1	0	0	1	½	x	4

Rio de Janeiro Interzonal
23.ix.-20.x.79

				1	2	3	4	5	6	7	8	9	0	1	2	3	4	5	6	7	8	
1	Hubner	GM	2595	x	½	½	½	½	1	1	½	1	1	0	½	½	½	½	1	1	1	11½
2	Petrosian	GM	2610	½	x	½	½	1	½	½	1	½	½	½	½	1	½	1	1	½	1	11½
3	Portisch	GM	2640	½	½	x	½	1	0	1	1	0	½	½	1	1	1	1	1	1	0	11½
4	Timman	GM	2625	½	½	½	x	½	½	0	1	1	½	1	1	½	1	½	½	½	1	11
5	Ivkov	GM	2525	½	0	0	½	x	1	½	½	1	1	½	½	½	½	½	½	½	1	9½
6	Sunye		2375	0	½	1	½	0	x	1	0	0	½	1	1	½	1	1	½	½	½	9½
7	Balashov	GM	2600	0	½	0	1	½	0	x	1	½	½	½	½	½	½	1	½	½	1	9
8	Sax	GM	2590	½	0	0	0	½	1	0	x	1	½	½	1	0	1	0	1	1	1	9
9	Torre	GM	2520	0	½	1	0	0	1	½	0	x	0	½	½	1	½	1	1	1	½	9
10	Shamkovich	GM	2495	0	½	½	½	0	½	½	½	1	x	1	½	1	1	0	0	½	½	8½
11	Smejkal	GM	2550	1	½	½	0	½	0	½	½	½	0	x	½	1	0	½	1	1	½	8½
12	Vaganian	GM	2570	½	½	0	0	½	0	½	0	½	½	½	x	0	1	1	1	½	1	8
13	Guil.Garcia	GM	2490	½	0	0	½	½	½	½	1	0	0	0	1	x	1	0	½	1	½	7½
14	Velimirovic	GM	2515	½	½	0	0	½	0	½	0	½	0	1	0	0	x	1	1	1	1	7½
15	Harandi	IM	2410	½	0	0	½	½	0	0	1	0	1	½	0	1	0	x	0	½	1	6½
16	L.Bronstein	IM	2420	0	0	0	½	½	½	½	0	0	1	0	0	½	0	1	x	½	1	6
17	Hebert	IM	2365	0	½	0	½	½	½	½	0	0	½	0	½	0	0	½	½	x	0	4½
18	Kagan	IM	2445	0	0	1	0	0	½	0	0	½	½	½	0	½	0	0	0	1	x	4½
19	Mecking	GM	2615					½						?								

	Frunze 1979	1	2	3	4	5	6	7	8	9	0	1	2	3	4	5	6	7	8	
1	Dolmatov	x	0	½	1	½	0	1	0	½	1	½	½	1	½	1	1	1	1	11
2	Makarichev	1	x	½	½	0	½	½	½	½	½	½	½	1	½	1	½	1	1	10½
3	Razuvaev	½	½	x	½	½	½	½	½	½	½	½	½	1	½	1	1	1	½	10½
4	Anikaev	0	½	½	x	½	½	1	1	½	½	½	½	0	1	½	1	1	½	10
5	Lerner	½	1	½	½	x	1	½	0	½	½	1	1	0	1	½	½	0	1	10
6	Jusupov	1	½	½	½	0	x	½	½	1	½	1	½	½	0	½	½	½	1	9½
7	Grigorian	0	½	½	0	½	½	x	½	1	1	0	½	0	½	½	1	1	1	9
8	Ivanov	1	½	½	0	1	½	½	x	0	½	0	½	1	0	½	1	1	½	9
9	Tukmakov	½	½	½	½	½	0	0	1	x	½	½	1	1	1	0	0	1	½	9
10	Kochiev	0	½	½	½	½	½	0	½	½	x	½	½	0	1	½	1	1	1	9
11	Timoshenko	½	½	½	½	0	0	1	1	½	½	x	0	½	½	1	1	½	½	9
12	Bagirov	½	½	½	½	0	½	½	½	0	½	1	x	½	0	½	½	1	1	8½
13	Psahis	0	0	0	1	1	½	1	0	0	1	½	½	x	1	½	½	1	0	8½
14	Mihalchishin	½	½	½	0	0	1	½	1	0	0	½	1	0	x	0	1	1	½	8
15	Yurtaev	0	0	0	½	½	½	½	½	1	½	0	½	½	1	x	0	0	½	6½
16	Vitolins	0	½	0	0	½	½	0	0	1	0	0	½	½	0	1	x	0	½	5
17	Lputian	0	0	0	0	1	½	0	0	0	0	½	0	0	0	1	1	x	1	5
18	Sideif-Zade	0	0	½	½	0	0	0	½	½	0	½	0	1	½	½	½	0	x	5

	USSR Final 30.xi.-26.xii.79	1	2	3	4	5	6	7	8	9	0	1	2	3	4	5	6	7	8	
1	Geller	x	½	½	½	½	½	½	½	1	1	1	½	1	½	½	½	1	1	11½
2	Jusupov	½	x	½	0	1	1	½	1	½	½	½	½	1	½	1	1	½	0	10½
3	Balashov	½	½	x	½	½	½	½	½	½	½	½	½	1	½	½	½	1	1	10
4	Kasparov	½	1	½	x	1	1	½	1	0	0	½	½	½	1	½	1	0	½	10
5	Georgadze	½	0	½	0	x	1	½	1	½	0	1	½	0	1	1	½	½	1	9½
6	Kupreichik	½	0	½	0	0	x	0	1	1	½	1	1	1	½	½	0	1	1	9½
7	Makarichev	½	½	½	½	½	1	x	0	1	0	½	½	½	1	½	½	½	1	9½
8	Vaganian	½	0	½	0	0	0	1	x	1	½	0	½	1	½	1	1	1	½	9
9	Lerner	0	½	½	1	½	0	0	0	x	1	½	½	½	1	½	1	½	½	8½
10	Beljavsky	0	½	½	1	1	½	1	½	0	x	½	0	0	0	0	1	1	½	8
11	Razuvaev	0	½	½	½	0	0	½	1	½	½	x	½	½	1	½	½	½	½	8
12	Rashkovsky	½	½	½	½	½	0	½	½	½	1	½	x	½	0	½	½	½	½	8
13	Romanishin	0	0	0	½	1	0	½	0	½	1	½	½	x	1	1	½	0	1	8
14	Dolmatov	½	½	½	0	0	½	0	½	0	1	0	1	0	x	½	1	1	½	7½
15	Tal	½	0	½	½	0	½	½	0	½	1	½	½	0	½	x	0	1	1	7½
16	Sveshnikov	½	0	½	0	½	1	½	0	0	0	½	½	½	0	1	x	1	½	7
17	Anikaev	0	½	0	1	½	0	½	0	½	0	½	½	1	0	0	0	x	½	5½
18	Tseshkovsky	0	1	0	½	0	0	0	½	½	½	½	½	0	½	0	½	½	x	5½

Bulgaria Final 22-23.xii.79

Ermenkov GM 2495 11   Georgiev   IM 2440 00

Novi Sad x.79

#				1	2	3	4	5	6	7	8	9	0	1	2	3	4	
1	Gheorghiu	GM	2540	x	½	½	½	½	1	½	1	1	½	1	1	1	1	10
2	Sveshnikov	GM	2545	½	x	½	½	½	1	1	0	1	½	½	1	1	1	9
3	Geller	GM	2550	½	½	x	½	½	½	1	½	½	1	1	1	1	½	9
4	Gligoric	GM	2560	½	½	½	x	0	0	½	1	0	1	1	1	1	1	8
5	Kurajica	GM	2515	½	½	½	1	x	1	½	½	½	½	½	½	½	½	7½
6	Beljavsky	GM	2595	0	0	½	1	0	x	0	½	½	1	1	1	1	1	7½
7	Knaak	GM	2565	½	0	0	½	½	1	x	0	1	1	½	½	½	1	7
8	Popovic	IM	2410	0	1	½	0	½	½	1	x	½	½	0	½	½	1	6½
9	Browne	GM	2540	0	0	½	1	½	½	0	½	x	0	½	½	1	1	6
10	Farago	GM	2510	½	½	0	0	½	0	0	½	1	x	½	½	1	1	6
11	Rajkovic	GM	2460	0	½	0	0	½	0	½	1	½	½	x	½	0	1	5
12	Buljovcic	IM	2430	0	0	0	0	½	0	½	½	½	½	½	x	½	0	3½
13	Bojkovic		2410	0	0	0	0	½	0	½	½	0	0	1	½	x	½	3½
14	Deze	IM	2415	0	0	½	0	½	0	0	0	0	0	0	1	½	x	2½

Category 11 (2503)   GM=8½   IM=6

Buenos Aires xi-xii.79

#				1	2	3	4	5	6	7	8	9	0	1	2	3	4	
1	Larsen	GM	2620	x	1	½	½	1	½	1	1	1	1	1	½	1	1	11
2	Andersson	GM	2560	0	x	½	½	½	½	½	1	½	½	1	½	1	1	8
3	Miles	GM	2560	½	½	x	½	½	½	½	0	1	½	1	½	1	1	8
4	Najdorf	GM	2515	½	½	½	x	½	½	½	½	½	½	1	½	1	1	8
5	Spassky	GM	2640	0	½	½	½	x	½	½	½	½	½	1	1	1	1	8
6	Gheorghiu	GM	2540	½	½	½	½	½	x	0	1	½	½	1	½	½	1	7½
7	Ivkov	GM	2525	0	½	½	½	½	1	x	1	½	½	0	½	1	1	7½
8	Quinteros	GM	2545	0	0	1	½	½	0	0	x	½	1	½	½	1	1	6½
9	Panno	GM	2545	0	½	0	½	½	½	½	½	x	0	½	½	1	1	6
10	Petrosian	GM	2610	0	½	½	½	½	½	½	0	1	x	½	½	0	1	6
11	Franco		2360	0	0	0	0	0	0	1	½	½	½	x	1	1	½	5
12	Lombardy	GM	2520	½	½	½	½	0	½	½	½	½	½	0	x	½	0	5
13	Tempone			0	0	0	0	0	½	0	0	0	1	0	½	x	1	3
14	Rubinetti	IM	2430	0	0	0	0	0	0	0	0	0	0	½	1	0	x	1½

Trencianske Teplice
17.xi.7.xii-79

				1	2	3	4	5	6	7	8	9	0	1	2	3	4	5	
1	Smejkal	GM	2560	x	0	½	1	½	½	1	1	0	½	1	1	1	1	1	10
2	Ftacnik	IM	2430	1	x	½	0	1	1	½	1	1	½	½	1	½	½	½	9½
3	Hort	GM	2600	½	½	x	1	½	1	½	0	½	1	½	½	½	1	1	9
4	Dobosz	IM	2380	½	1	0	x	½	½	½	½	½	0	1	1	1	1	½	8
5	Holmov	GM	2550	½	0	½	½	x	½	½	½	½	½	1	½	½	1	1	8
6	Ambroz		2320	½	0	0	½	½	x	½	½	1	½	½	½	½	1	1	8
7	Uhlmann	GM	2530	0	½	½	½	½	½	x	½	1	1	0	0	1	0	1	7
8	Vogt	GM	2500	0	0	1	½	½	½	½	x	0	½	½	½	1	1	½	7
9	Rogulj	IM	2440	1	0	½	½	½	0	0	1	x	1	½	½	0	1	0	6½
10	Prandstetter	IM	2385	½	½	0	1	½	½	0	½	0	x	½	½	½	½	1	6½
11.	Barczay	GM	2470	0	½	½	0	0	½	1	½	½	½	x	½	½	½	1	6½
12	Jansa	GM	2435	0	0	½	0	½	½	1	½	½	½	½	x	½	½	½	6
13	Plachetta	GM	2445	0	½	½	0	½	½	0	0	1	½	½	½	x	½	1	5½
14	Sikora		2430	0	½	0	0	0	0	1	0	0	½	½	½	½	x	1	4½
15	Vokac		2330	0	½	0	½	0	0	0	½	1	0	0	½	½	0	x	3½

Category 9 (2457) GM=10 IM=7

Sochi 1979

				1	2	3	4	5	6	7	8	9	0	1	2	3	4	5	6	
1	Rashkovsky	IM	2500	x	½	½	1	½	1	½	1	½	1	½	½	1	1	½	½	10½
2	Sveshnikov	GM	2545	½	x	½	½	½	1	½	½	1	½	½	½	½	1	1	1	10
3	Psahis		2480	½	½	x	½	1	½	½	1	0	½	1	½	1	½	1	½	9½
4	Haritonov			0	½	½	x	½	½	½	1	1	½	½	1	½	½	1	1	9½
5	Antoshin	GM	2440	½	½	0	½	x	½	½	½	1	1	1	0	1	½	0	1	8½
6	Gufeld	GM	2530	0	0	½	½	½	x	1	1	½	½	1	½	½	½	½	1	8½
7	Kirov	GM	2420	½	½	½	½	½	0	x	½	½	1	½	½	½	½	½	1	8
8	Panchenko	IM	2485	0	½	0	0	½	0	½	x	½	½	1	½	½	1	1	1	7½
9	Sustin			½	0	1	0	0	½	½	½	x	½	½	½	1	½	½	1	7½
10	I.Zaitsev	GM	2505	0	½	½	½	0	½	0	½	½	x	0	½	½	1	1	1	7
11	B.Ivanovic	GM	2460	½	½	0	½	0	0	½	0	½	1	x	1	0	1	½	1	7
12	Hartston	IM	2485	½	½	½	0	1	½	½	½	½	½	0	x	½	½	½	½	7
13	Augustin	IM	2430	0	½	0	½	0	½	½	½	0	½	1	½	x	½	0	1	6
14	Ghitescu	IM	2400	0	0	½	½	½	½	½	0	½	0	0	½	½	x	1	1	6
15	Barczay	GM	2470	½	0	0	0	1	½	½	0	½	0	½	½	1	0	x	½	5½
16	Mohring	IM	2400	½	0	½	0	0	0	0	0	0	0	0	½	0	0	½	x	2

(Category 8 (2444) GM=11 IM=8

Berlin 11-29.xi.79

				1	2	3	4	5	6	7	8	9	0	1	2	3	4	5	
1	Csom	GM	2510	x	½	½	½	1	0	1	1	½	½	1	½	1	½	1	9½
2	Smyslov	GM	2560	½	x	½	1	½	½	1	½	½	½	½	1	1	½	1	9½
3	Bagirov	GM	2545	½	½	x	½	½	1	½	1	½	½	½	½	½	1	1	9
4	Suba	GM	2435	½	0	½	x	½	1	½	½	½	1	½	½	½	1	½	8
5	Vogt	GM	2500	0	½	½	½	x	1	1	½	½	½	½	½	½	½	1	8
6	A.Rodriguez	GM	2465	1	½	0	0	0	x	0	½	½	½	½	1	1	1	1	7½
7	Bonsch	IM	2460	0	0	½	½	0	1	x	1	1	½	½	½	1	½	0	7
8	Plachetka	GM	2445	0	½	0	½	½	½	0	x	½	½	½	½	1	1	1	7
9	L.Popov	IM	2430	½	½	½	½	½	½	0	½	x	½	1	½	0	½	1	7
10	Uhlmann	GM	2530	½	½	½	0	½	½	½	½	½	x	½	½	½	1	½	7
11	Espig	IM	2450	0	½	½	½	½	½	½	½	0	½	x	½	½	½	½	6
12	Malich	GM	2530	½	0	½	½	½	0	½	½	½	½	½	x	0	½	1	6
13	Pahtz		2400	0	0	½	½	½	0	0	0	1	½	½	1	x	0	½	5
14	Sznapik	IM	2435	½	½	0	0	½	0	½	0	½	0	½	½	1	x	½	5
15	Casper		2355	0	0	0	½	0	0	1	0	0	½	½	0	½	½	x	3½
16	Knaak	GM	2565	½	0	½		0								½	½		2

Polanica Zdroj 5-23.viii.79

				1	2	3	4	5	6	7	8	9	0	1	2	3	4	5	6	
1	Razuvaev	GM	2470	x	½	1	½	½	½	½	1	½	½	½	1	½	½	1	1	10
2	Filip	GM	2475	½	x	½	½	½	½	½	½	½	1	½	½	½	1	1	1	9½
3	Knaak	GM	2565	0	½	x	1	1	½	1	½	0	½	1	½	½	1	0	1	9
4	Jansa	GM	2495	½	½	0	x	½	½	1	½	½	½	½	1	½	½	1	1	9
5	Farago	GM	2510	½	½	0	½	x	½	½	½	½	½	1	1	0	1	1	1	9
6	Bielczyk		2410	½	½	½	½	½	x	½	1	½	½	½	1	½	½	½	½	8½
7	Arnason	FM	2410	½	½	0	0	½	½	x	½	½	½	½	1	1	½	1	1	8½
8	Timoshenko	IM	2530	0	½	½	½	½	0	½	x	½	0	½	1	1	1	1	1	8½
9	Spassov	GM	2470	½	½	1	½	½	½	½	½	x	½	½	0	½	½	½	1	8
10	J.Adamski	IM	2415	½	0	½	½	½	½	½	1	½	x	½	½	½	½	½	1	8
11	Spiridonov	GM	2440	½	½	0	½	0	½	½	½	½	½	x	½	1	½	1	1	8
12	Planinc	GM	2445	0	½	½	0	0	0	0	0	1	½	½	x	1	1	1	0	6
13	Schinzel	IM	2400	½	½	½	½	1	½	0	0	½	½	0	0	x	1	0	0	5½
14	Pokojowczyk	IM	2365	½	0	0	½	0	½	½	0	½	½	½	0	0	x	½	1	5
15	Kruszynski		2285	0	0	1	0	0	½	0	0	½	½	0	0	1	½	x	0	4
16	Borkowski		2395	0	0	0	0	0	½	0	0	0	0	0	1	1	0	1	x	3½

Category 8 (2442)   GM = 11   IM = 8   FM = 6

41

Netherlands 1979

			1	2	3	4	5	6	7	8	
Timman	GM	2625	1	½	½	½	1	½	½	0	4½
Polugaevsky	GM	2625	0	½	½	½	0	½	½	1	3½

Budapest 20.x.-4.xi.79

			1	2	3	4	5	6	
Adorjan	GM	2525	½	0	0	1	1	½	3
Ribli	GM	2595	½	1	1	0	0	½	3

Cologne 1979

			1	2	3	4	5	6	
Hubner	GM	2595	1	½	0	½	1	½	3½
Hort	GM	2600	0	½	1	½	0	½	2

Linares 1979

				1	2	3	4	5	6	7	8	9	0	1	2	
1	Christiansen	GM	2475	x	0	½	1	1	½	1	1	½	½	1	1	8
2	Korchnoi	GM	2695	1	x	0	1	1	½	0	½	½	1	1	1	7½
3	Rivas		2365	½	1	x	0	0	1	½	1	1	1	1	½	7½
4	Castro	IM	2430	0	0	1	x	½	½	½	1	1	1	1	1	7½
5	Eslon	IM	2380	0	0	1	½	x	½	½	0	½	½	1	1	5½
6	Sahovic	GM	2520	½	½	0	½	½	x	½	1	½	½	0	½	5
7	Marovic	GM	2470	0	1	½	½	½	½	x	0	½	½	½	½	5
8	Calvo	IM	2425	0	½	0	0	1	0	1	x	0	½	1	1	5
9	Ermenkov	GM	2495	½	½	0	0	½	½	½	1	x	½	0	½	4½
10	Knezevic	GM	2500	½	0	0	0	½	½	½	½	½	x	½	½	4
11	Bellon	GM	2395	0	0	0	0	0	1	½	0	1	½	x	½	3½
12	Visier		2360	0	0	½	0	0	½	½	0	½	½	½	x	3

Category 9   GM=7½

Tilburg xi.79

			1	2	3	4	5	6	7	8	9	0	1	2	
Karpov	GM	2705	x	½	½	½	1	½	½	1	1	½	½	1	7½
Romanishin	GM	2560	½	x	½	½	½	½	1	0	1	½	1	1	7
Portisch	GM	2640	½	½	x	½	1	½	0	½	½	1	½	1	6½
Sax	GM	2590	½	½	½	x	0	1	1	½	½	0	½	1	6
Larsen	GM	2620	0	½	0	1	x	½	1	0	1	½	1	0	5½
Spassky	GM	2640	½	½	½	0	½	x	½	½	½	1	½	½	5½
Timman	GM	2625	½	0	1	0	0	½	x	1	½	½	½	1	5½
Sosonko	GM	2535	0	1	½	½	1	½	0	x	0	1	½	½	5½
Hort	GM	2600	0	0	½	½	0	½	½	1	x	½	½	1	5
Hubner	GM	2595	½	½	0	1	½	0	½	0	½	x	½	1	5
Kavalek	GM	2590	½	0	½	½	0	½	½	½	½	½	x	½	4½
Smyslov	GM	2560	0	0	0	0	1	½	0	½	0	0	½	x	2½

Category 15 (2605)

Eksjo 1979
(1-2) Schneider IM 2420, Ornstein IM 2445 7½; (3) Karlsson 2375 7; (4) Wedberg IM 2425 6; (5) J. Nun IM 2400? 4½; (6) G.Andersson 2255 3½; (7) Jasznikowski 2310 3; (8-9) Trincardi 2235, Danner 2335 2½; (10) Akvist 2325 1.

Prague vii-viii.79   Category 4 (2339) IM = 10½
(1-2) Ftacnik IM 2430, Hausner 2365 10½; (3-4) Danik, Meduna IM 2405 9½; (5-6) Ekstrom 2385, Renman 9; (7) Cvetkovic 2385 8½; (8) Mrdja 2340 7½; (9-11) Bjorck, Mihaljcisin IM 2420, Votruba 7; (12) Hardicsay 2340 6½; (13) B.Lengyel 2350 6; (14) Reznicek 5½; (15) Vrabek 4½; (16) Stull 2270 2½.

Athens vii-viii.79
(1) Urzica 2385 8½; (2) Varasdy 2380 8; (3-5) Birnboim IM 2460, Zichichi IM 2360, Georgiev IM 2440 7; (6) Skalkotas 2370 6½; (7) Trikaliotis 2255 5½; (8-10) Pedersen 2330?, Tsomis, Grigoriou IM 2230 3½; (11-12) Balaskas 2220, Kalosskambris 2205 3.

Nis 1979
(1-2) Seirawan IM 2485, Kuligowski 2495 9½; (3) Tringov GM 2460 8½; (4) Jansa GM 2495 8; (5) Dukic 2370 7½; (6) Bukic GM 2495 7; (7-9) Marjanovic GM 2505, Pavlovic 2340, Ermenkov GM 2495 6½; (10-11) Golubovic, Ilic 2440 5; (12) Ciric GM 2440, Maksimovic 2265 4½; (14) Civkovic 2½.

Krosno 2-15.ix.79   Category 4 (2334) IM = 7   FM = 5½

(1) Kojder 7; (2-3) Gazik 2460, Bielczyk IM 2410 6½; (4-5) Beckenmayer, Szymczak IM 2355 5½; (6-8) Gromek 2325, Lind 2355, Skrobek IM 2370 5; (9) Lipski 2310 4; (10) Przewoznik 2240 3; (11) Antosik 2450 2.

Slupsk 26.viii.-6.ix.79
Category 8 (2428)   GM = 7½
IM = 5½   FM = 4
(1) Timoshenko IM 2530 7½; (2) Petkevich 2445 6½; (3-4) Spiridonov GM 2440, Borkowski 2395 5½; (5-7) Bilek GM 2460, J.Adamski IM 2415, Dobosz IM 2380 5; (8-9) Arnason IM 2410, Schinzel IM 2400 4; (10-11) Schmidt GM 2430, Doda IM 2400 3½.

Rzeszow 13-25.x.79
(1) J.Adamski IM 2415 8½; Danner 2335 7½; (3-5) Witkowski IM 2330, Dizdar 2395, Marszalek 2340 6½; (6) Giffard 2330 6; (7) Tonchev IM 2460 5½; (8-10) Szajna 2265, Mihaljcisin IM 2420, Gralka 2345 4½; (11) Szumilo 2290 4; (12) Malek 2.

New York xi.79 Category 8 GM = 8
(1) Dzindzihashvili GM 2595 7½; (2-4) Soltis IM 2445, Shamkovich GM 2495, Bisguier GM 2445 7; (5-6) Zaltsman IM 2470, Fedorovicz IM 2405 6; (7-9) Biyiasas GM 2485, Gild.Garcia IM 2410, Zapata IM 2375 5; (10) La Rota 2310 4½; (11) Valvo 2460 3½; (12) Ostos IM 2360 2½.

33 Bulgaria Final 8-25.xi.79
(1-2) Ermenkov GM 2495, K.Georgiev IM 2440 9½; (3-4) Velikov IM 2440,

Grigorov IM 2350 8½; (5-6) Donchev 2400, Lukov IM 2385 8; (7-8) V.Antonov FM 2360, Kirov GM 2420 7½; (9-11) Inkiov IM 2460, Prodanov 2375, Spassov GM 2470 7; (12) Semkov 2330 5½; (13) Peev IM 2435 5; (14) Danailov 2285 3½; (15) G.Georgiev 3; (16) Radulov GM 2485 2½/5.

Stip 25.xi.-10.xii.79
Category 7 (2408)   GM = 10
IM = 7½   FM = 6
(1) Hulak GM 2450 10½; (2) Tatai IM 2475 8½; (3-5) Tringov GM 2460, Matulovic GM 2510, L.Popov IM 2430 7½; (6-8) Filipowicz IM 2375, Ivanovic GM 2460, Kovacevic GM 2500 7; (9-10) Gruchacz FM 2355, R.Nicevski IM 2380 6½; (11-12) Banas IM 2395, Trois IM 2415 5½; (13) Trkaljanov 3; (14) Zaharijev 2300 1½.

Kiel Category 7   GM = 8½   IM = 6½
(1) Vadasz GM 2490; (2-3) Schmidt GM 2430, Schussler IM 2460 7; (4) Ghinda IM 2455 6½; (5-8) Ciocaltea GM 2430, Parma GM 2530, Soos IM 2430, Schneider IM 2420 6; (9) Wockenfuss 2385 4½; (10) Eising 2390 4; (11) Neumann 2210 3; (12) Marxen 2½.

Malmo 26.xi.-8.xii.79
Category 8   GM = 8½   IM = 7
(1) Karlsson IM 2375 7½; (2-5) Nemet GM 2470, Schmidt GM 2430, Ornstein IM 2445; Seirawan IM 2485 7; (6) Schussler IM 2460 6½; (7) Westerinen GM 2465 5½; (8-9) Stean GM 2540, Niklasson IM 2385 4½; (10) Kaisauri IM 2405 3½; (11-12) Hoi IM 2355, Wedberg IM 2425 3.

Albena 1-13.ix.79   Category 7 (2420)
GM = 8½   IM = 6½   FM = 5
(1) Ermenkov GM 2495 7½; (2-4) Inkiov IM 2460, Pinter IM 2445, Velikov IM 2440 7; (5) Georgiev IM 2440 6; (6-8) Bellin IM 2425, Lukov IM 2385, Spassov GM 2470 5½; (9) Padevsky GM 2410 5; (10) Biriescu 2390 4; (11) S.Ivanov 2380 3½; (12) Durao IM 2300 2½.

Ramat Hasharon 2-14.x.79
Category 5   IM = 7½
(1-2) Balshan FM 2430, Murei 2430 8; (3) Kraidman GM 2445 7½; (4) Zilber 2410 7; (5-6) Basman 2405, Gelfer 2300 6½; (7) Lederman IM 2415 6; (8-9) Lipnowski 2390, Grinberg 2400 4½; (10) E.Pedersen 2330 4; (11) Afek 3½; (12) J.Cuellar 2215 0.

Brisbane Category 7 (2401)
GM = 8   IM = 6
(1) Lein GM 2535 7½; (2) Keene GM 2465 6½; (3) I.Rogers 2390 6; (4-5) Robatsch GM 2435, Maninang 2310 5; (6-8) Jamieson IM 2425, Mascarinas IM 2395, Aridijansah IM 2380 4½; (9-10) Fuller 2380, Suradiradja GM 2340 4; (11) Shaw 2355 3½.

Primorsko 14-28.ix.79
IM = 9   FM = 7½
(1) Peev IM 2435 11; (2) Meduna IM 2405 9½; (3-5) Grigorov IM 2350, Toshkov, Kiarner 9; (6-8) Foisor 2310, Dobosz IM 2380, J.Adamski IM 2415 8; (9-11) Rigo 2385, Machulsky 2390, Sokolov 2420 7½; (12-13) Donchev 2400, Danailov 6½; (14) Onat IM 2365 5½; (15) Joksic 2370 5; (16) Manolov 2310 2½.

Cienfuegos 23.v.-9.vi.79
(1) Ortega 2350 9; (2) J.C.Diaz IM 2370 8½; (3-4) Lukov IM 2385, Huerta 2300 7½; (5-7) Ochoa 2350, Lima 2275, Andreas 2340 7; (8) Verduga IM 2325 6½; (9-10) M.Gonzalez 2285, Frey IM 2405 6; (11-13) Cobo IM 2395, Veliz 2335, Trujillo 2290 5½; (14) Junco 2285 2½.

Timisoara 16-29.vi.79
Category 6 (2395)   IM = 6½
(1) Knezevic GM 2500 8; (2-3) Martinovic IM 2410, Marasescu 7; (4) Ciocaltea GM 2430 6½; (5-6) Bilek GM 2460, Lukacs IM 2420 5½; (7-8) Biriescu 2390, Arapovic 2420 5; (9-11) Deze IM 2415, Neamtu 2375, Ilijin 2325 4½; (12) Ungureanu IM 2405 3.

Satu Mare 5-17.vii.79
Category 5 (2372)   IM = 7
(1) Ciocaltea GM 2430 8½; (2-3) Ungureanu IM 2405, Sindik 2330 7½; (4) Biriescu 2390 7; (5) Bukal IM 2405 6½; (6) Banas 2395 5½; (7-8) Ilijin 2325, I.Szabo 2360 5; (9-10) Rajna IM 2370, Preissman 2355 4; (11) I.Fischer 2395 3½; (12) F. Lengyel 2305 2.

Gausdal 12-20.viii.79   9 Rd SS
(1) Romanishin GM 2560 7; (2) L.Karlsson 2375 6½; (3-7) Keene GM 2465, W.Morris 2345, Ornstein IM 2445, Wibe IM 2425, Kaiszauri IM 2405 6; (8-13) Sigurjonsson GM 2490, Schussler IM 2460, Fedorowicz 2405, Ofstad 2220, Rantanen IM 2460, Petursson IM 2420 5½; (14-20) Robatsch GM 2435, Dobosz IM 2380, ...5; (50)

Malgrat de Mar 5-14.x.79
Category 7 (2408)
GM = 7   IM = 5   FM = 4
(1-3) Tatai IM 2475, Gufeld GM 2530, Chiburdanidze 2380 6; (4-5) Barczay GM 2470, Ochoa FM 2350 5; (6) A.Rodriguez GM 2465 4½; (7) Pomar GM 2435 4; (8) Gonz.Mestres 2330 3½; (9) Martin 2370 3; (10) J.P. Dominguez 2275 2.

Barcinona 5-14.x.79
Category 4 (2338)   IM = 6½   FM = 5
(1) O.Rodriguez GM 2495 6½; (2-3) Westerinen GM 2465, J.L.Fernandez FM 2340 6; (4-5) Kristiansen IM 2365, Rivas 2365 5½; (6-7) Vehi, van Baarle 2325 3½; (8-9) H.Perez, Pares 2285 3; (10) Garcia Conesa 2345 2½.

Bonn 11-21.viii.79
Category 7 (2420)
GM = 7   IM = 5½   FM = 4
(1) Hort GM 2600 7; (2) Sahovic GM 2520 6; (3-5) Hecht GM 2490, Bohm IM 2410, van Riemsdijk 2435 5½; (6) Reefschlager IM 2370 4½; (7-8) Gerusel 2425, Behling 2375 3½; (3) Borngasser 2370 3; (10) Weber 1. Stean GM 2540 1½/3.

Sydney 1979   Category 3
IM = 7   FM = 6
(1-2) Keene GM 2465, I.Rogers 2390 7½; (3-4) Fuller FM 2380, Mascarinas IM 2395 5½; (5-8) Shaw 2355, Hay 2350, C.Morris, Laird 2245 4½; (9-10) Kerr, Maninang 2310 4; (11) C.Purdy IM 2250 3.

Graz xi.79   Category 8
GM = 9½   IM = 7
(1) Ree IM 2480 8; (2-6) Ligterink IM 2440, Darga GM 2505, Bellin IM

45

2425, Pytel IM 2425, Dur 2385 7½; (7) Damjanovic GM 2420 7; (8) Zaitsev GM 2505 6½; (9-10) Lengyel GM 2455, Watzka 2330 6; (11-12) Wittmann 2360, Pribyl IM 2420 5½; (13) Duckstein IM 2420 5; (14) Schinzel 2400 4.

London/Bristol x.79
A: (1) Schmid GM 2520 2½; (2) Korchnoi GM 2695 2; (3) Byrne GM 2535 1; (4) Stean GM 2540 ½.
B: (1) Browne GM 2540 2½; (2-3) Nunn GM 2500, Hort GM 2600 1½; (4) Pfleger GM 2545 ½.
Final Schmid 1 Browne 0

Ramsgate 29.x.-8.xi.79
A: Category 4 (2337)
IM = 6½ FM = 5
(1) Plaskett 2410 7; (2) Niklasson IM 2385 6½; (3-5) Hebden 2230, Iskov IM 2370, Langeweg IM 2440 5½; (6) Boersma 2350 5; (7) Nicholson 2310 4; (8) Macdonald-Ross 2265 8; (3) Kaiszauri IM 2405 2½; (10) Josephs 0.
B: Category 4
IM = 6½ FM = 5
(1) Wedberg IM 2425 8½; (2) Kouatly IM 2335 7; (3-5) Basman 2405, Povah 2325, v.d.Sterren IM 2400 5; (6-7) Boudre, Cuartas IM 2425 4; (8-9) Pigott 2370, v.d. Weide 2290 3; (10) Erdogan ½.

New York xi.79 Category 5
IM = 9½ FM = 7
(1)Alburt GM 2515 13; (2) Kaufman 2390 11; (3) Benjamin 2320 8½; (4) J.Watson IM 2375 8; (5) Zlotnikov 2435 7½; (6-7) Bonin 2260, Blocker 2435 6½; (8-11) Kudrin 2360, Taylor 2445, Wilder 2255, Coudari IM 2320

6; (12) Pavlovich 5½; (13-14) Litvinchuk, Weeramantry 2240 5; (15) van Tilbury 2350 4½.

Singapore xii.79 Asian Team Final
A: (1) Philippines 22/28; (2) China 19½; (3) Indonesia 18; (4) Australia 14; (5) Singapore A 11; (6) Hongkong 10; (7) Thailand 9; (8) Sri Lanka 6½.
B: (1) Bangladesh 22½; (2) Singapore B 19½; (3) Malaysia 19½; (4) United Arab Emirates 18½; (5) Japan 12; (6) Brunei 11½;. (7) Papua New Guinea 8; (8) Kuwait 1½.

Prague 1-15.xii.79 Category 3
IM = 8½ FM = 7
(1-2) Kristiansen IM 2355, Mohring IM 2400 8; (3) Neckor 2355 7½; (4-6) Choleva, Lanc IM 2395, Voboril 7; (7) Blatny 2325 6; (8-9) Witkowski IM 2330, Mrdja 2340 5½; (10-11) Zinn IM 2325, Jankovec 2380 5; (12-13) Scajna, Siroky 2305 3½.

Stary Smokovec 27.x.-7.xi.79
Category 8 (2413)
GM = 8 IM = 6½ FM = 5
(1-2) Plachetka GM 2445, Vogt GM 2500 7½; (3) Mnatsakanian IM 2425 7; (4-5) Adamski IM 2415, Knezevic GM 2500 6½; (6-7) Cvetkovic 2385, Gonsior 2390 5½; (8) Mohring IM 2400 5; (9) Banas IM 2395 4½; (10) Novak 2340 4; (11) Franzen 2300 3½; (12) Gazic 2460 3.

Bern (Mitropa Cup) 8-17.x.79
(1) Jugoslavia 19½; (2) Switzerland 15; (3-4) BRD, Austria 12½; (5) Italy 11½; (6) France 8; (7) Luxemburg 5.

Virovitica ix-x.79   Category 5   IM=8½
(1) Kovacevic GM 2500 10; (2) Nemet GM 2470 9; (3) Rukavina IM 2420 8½; (4-6) Minic IM 2395, Ftacnik IM 2430, T.Horvath IM 2410 8; (7-8) Pytel IM 2425, Klaric 2360 7; (9) Maroja 2205 6½; (10) Diesen IM 2460 6; (11) Arapovic 2420 5; (12) Frank 4; (13) Zoric 2½; (14) Paidoussis 2220 1½.

Vrsac 7-24.ix.79   Category 9 (2462)
(1) Stean GM 2540 10½; (2) Rajkovic GM 2460 10; (3) Sahovic GM 2520 9½; (4) Kurajica GM 2515 9; (5-7) Bronstein GM 2555, Matanovic GM 2495, Jansa GM 2495 8½; (8) Marjanovic GM 2505 8; (9) Lein GM 2535 7½; (10) Matulovic GM 2510 7; (11) Kapelan 2335 5½; (12-13) Vukic GM 2485, Janicijevski 5; (14) Grubisic 1½. L.Szabo GM 2515 1/8.

Hungary Final 27.xi.-16.xii.79
(1) Pinter 10½; (2-4) Farago, Hazai, Lukacs 9½; (5-6) Vadasz, Forintos 8½; (7-8) Csom, F.Portisch 7½; (9-10) Karolyi, Groszpeter 6; (11) Halasz 5½; (12) Rigo 5; (13) P.Petran 4½; (14) A.Schneider 4; (15) Orso 3.

Ribnica 1979   IM = 8
(1-5) Lau 2440, Cuartas IM 2425, T.Horvath IM 2410, Mestrovic IM 2465, Osterman 2335 8; (6) Jelen 2420 7½; (7-8) Bukal IM 2405, Cebalo IM 2450 7; (9-10) L.Bronstein IM 2420, Bertok IM 2390 6½; (11) Holzl 2425 6; (12) Basman 2405 5½; (13) Ilic 3½; (14) Zilverski 1½.

Brighton 13-19.xii.79
Category 3 (2324)
IM = 6½   FM = 5½
(1) Speelman IM 2470 8½; (2) Goodman 2340 6½; (3) Whiteley 2370 5½; (4) Chandler IM 2380 5; (5) Blackstock 2340 4½; (6-8) Wells, Denman, Cummings 2265 3½; (9) Fedorowicz IM 2405 3; (10) MacDonald-Ross 2265 1½.

Narvik 27.viii.-4.ix.79   IM = 6
(1) Rantanen IM 2460 7; (2) Fedorowicz IM 2405 6½; (3-4) Binham 2345, L.D.Evans 2375 6; (5-6) Johannessen IM 2390, Pytel IM 2425 5½; (7) Johnsen 2260 4½; (8-9) Lundin IM 2355, Heiberg 2250 4; (10) S.Jensen 2260 3; (11) ? Kristensen 1½; (12) Berglund ½.

Buenos Aires 1979
(1-2) Korchnoi GM 2695, Ljubojevic GM 2590 10½; (3) Browne GM 2540 9; (4-5) Miles GM 2560, Liberzon GM 2515 7½; (6-8) Najdorf GM 2515, Quinteros GM 2545, Rubinetti IM 2430 7; (9) del Corral GM 6; (10) Emma IM 2435 5½; (11) Trois IM 2415 5; (12-13) Schweber IM 2450, Szmetan IM 2400 3; (14) Bernat IM 2410 2½.

47

1 b3

1 Iannaccone-Toth Naples 79

1 ♘f3 ♞f6 2 b3 d5 3 e3 ♝g4 4 ♗b2
♞bd7 5 d4 e6 6 ♗e2 ♝b4+ 7 c3 ♝e7
8 c4 0-0 9 ♘c3 c6 10 0-0 ♝h5 11
h3 ♜c8 12 g4?! ♝g6 13 ♞h4 ♝d6 14
♞xg6 hxg6 15 ♛g2 g5! 16 ♜h1 16
f4 ♘h7 =+ ♝h7 17 ♛d3 ♜e8 18 h4
gxh4 19 f4 ♞hf8 20 g5?! 20 ♜af1!
♞g6 21 ♝h5 ♞df8 22 ♞e2 c5! 23
♜ad1 ♛e7 24 dxc5 ♜xc5 25 ♛f2
e5 =+ 26 b4?! 26 f5 ♛xg5! ♜xc4
27 ♛xd5 ♜c2 28 ♝xg6 ♞xg6 29 f5?
29 ♛xd6

**29...♞f4! −+ 30 exf4 exf4 31 ♜d2
♛e3+ 32 ♚e1 ♜xd2 33 ♛xd2 ♝xb4
34 ♛xb4 ♛xe2 mate 0-1 Paoli**

2 Yap-Dorfman
Manila 79

1 b3 d5 2 ♗b2 ♝g4 3 h3 ♝h5 4 ♞f3
♝xf3 5 exf3 5 gxf3!?∞ e6 6 g3 a5
7 a4?! 7 a3 ♞e7 8 f4 ♞d7 9 ♝g2 h5
10 0-0 ♞f5 11 c4?! c6 12 cxd5 cxd5
13 ♜e1 ♝c5 14 d4 ♝b4∓ 15 ♝c3
15 ♘xd5 ♝xe1 16 ♛xe1 0-0 17 ♝f3
♘f6 −+ ♞f6 16 ♛d3 0-0 17 ♞a3
♝xc3 18 ♛xc3 ♜c8 19 ♛d3 ♛b6 20
♞b5 ♜c6 21 ♝f3 ♜fc8 22 g4 hxg4
23 hxg4 ♞h4 24 ♝h1 ♛d8 25 g5
25 ♛g3 ♘e4 26 ♝xe4 dxe4 27 ♜xe4

♛d5 28 ♜ae1 ♜c1 −+ ♞e8 26 ♛g3
♞f5 27 ♛h2 ♛b6? 27...g6? 28 ♘a7!;
27...♜c2! **28 ♜ad1** △ ♜d3-h3 ♞c7
29 ♝f3! △ ♚g2, ♜h1 ♞xb5 30 axb5
♛xb5 31 ♝g4 ♛xb3 32 ♝xf5 exf5
33 ♚g2! ♜c2 34 ♛h4 34 ♜h1? ♜xf2+!
35 ♚xf2 ♜c2+ ♛b2 35 ♜b1 ♛xd4
36 ♜xb7 △ ♜be7 g6 37 ♜be7 ♜f8
38 ♜7e5 +− ♛xe5 39 fxe5 ♜c4 40
♛h6 ♜g4+ 41 ♛f3 1-0 Keene

3 Britton-Botterill
England 79

1 b3 e5 2 c4 ♞f6 3 ♗b2 ♞c6 4 d3
g6 5 ♞f3 d6 6 g3 ♝g7 7 ♝g2 0-0 8
♞c3 ♞d4 9 0-0 ♞xf3+ 10 ♝xf3 c6
11 d4 ♛e7 12 e4 ♝h3 13 ♜e1 ♞d7
14 d5 c5 15 ♝g4! ♝xg4 16 ♛xg4 f5
17 ♛h3 a6 18 ♜e2 ♜f7 19 ♝c1 ♜b8
20 ♜b1 20 a4≈ b5 21 cxb5 axb5
22 b4 cxb4 23 ♜xb4 ♞c5 24 ♝e3
♞d3 24...♞xe4 25 ♞xe4 fxe4 26
♜eb2± △ a4; 24...♛c7!? **25 ♜xb5
♜c8 26 ♜b3 ♛f8! 27 ♛f1 ♝h6 28
♛d1 f4! 29 ♝b6** 29 ♛xd3 fxe3∓

**29...fxg3! 30 ♛xd3 ♜f3 31 ♝e3 gxh2+
32 ♚xh2 ♝f4+?** 32...♛f6 −+ **33 ♚g1**
33 ♚g2?? ♛h6 34 ♚xf3 ♛h3 mate
♛f6 34 ♛f1? 34 ♛a6!∞ **♛h4 35 ♚e1
♝xe3 −+ 36 ♛d1 ♛h1+ 37 ♚c2** 37
♜e1 ♛xe1+ −+; 37 ♜e1 ♛h5 −+
♛c1 mate 0-1 Botterill

1 c4 b6

4 Denker-Gheorghiu Chicago 79
1 c4 c5 2 ♘c3 b6 2...g6! **3 ♘f3 ♗f6**
4 e3 g6 5 ♗e2 ♗g7 6 d4 0-0 7 0-0
♗a6 7...♗b7 8 d5! **8 ♕a4!** N 8 ♖b1
△ a3∞; 8 d5 **♗b7 9 ♖d1 e6! 10 a3**
♕e7 11 ♗d2 ♖fd8 12 ♖ab1 d6 13
b4 ♘c7! =+ **14 ♕c2 ♖ac8 15 ♗e1**
cxd4! 16 exd4 e5 17 dxe5 17 d5 b5!∓
dxe5 18 ♖xd8+ ♖xd8 19 ♖d1 ♖c8!∓
20 ♕d2 △ ♕d6∞ **♘ce8 21 ♕e3 e4!**
22 ♘b5 a6 23 ♘bd4 ♘g4! 24 ♕g5
♕xg5 25 ♘xg5 ♘e5! 26 c5! ♗f6!!∓
26...h6!? 27 c6!!∞ **27 ♘h3 bxc5 28**
bxc5 ♖xc5 29 ♖b1 ♗c8 30 ♘b3 ♖c2
31 ♗d1! ♖a2 32 ♘c1!! ♖xa3 32...
♖b2 33 ♖xb2 ♘f3+ △ ♗xb2= **33 ♗b4**
♖xh3∓ 34 gxh3 ♗xh3 35 ♗e2 h5 36
♖b3! ♗e6 37 ♖a3 ♘c7! 38 ♗d6 ♘b5!
39 ♖xa6 39 ♗xb5? axb5 −+ **♘xd6**
40 ♖xd6 ♗g5! 41 ♖d1 h4 42 ♗a6
♘f3+ 43 ♔h1 ♗f4 44 ♗b7 f5 45 h3
♔g7 46 ♘e2 ♗e5! 47 ♗d5! ♗c8 48
♗b7! ♗e6 49 ♗d5 ♗d7! 50 ♗xe4
♗a4!∓ 51 ♗xf3 ♗xd1 52 ♔g2?! 52
♘d4!! =+ **♗c2! 53 ♗c6 ♔f6 54 f4**
♗d6! 55 ♔f3 ♗c5 56 ♘c3 ♗d4 57
♘d5+! ♔e6 58 ♘e3! ♗d3! 59 ♘g2
59 ♗e8 ♗xe3 60 ♔xe3 ♗f1∓ **♔d6!!**
60 ♗b7 60 ♗e8?? ♗e4 mate **♗f6 61**
♘e3 ♔c5! 62 ♗d5 ♔d4 63 ♗f7 ♗e4+
64 ♔e2 g5!∓ 65 fxg5 ♗xg5 66 ♘d1
♗g2 67 ♗g6 67 ♗e6 ♗xh3 −+ **f4**
68 ♗f5 f3+ 69 ♔f2 ♗f4 −+ 70 ♗g4
♗g3+ 71 ♔g1 ♔d3 72 ♘f2+ ♔e3 73
♘d1+ ♔e2 74 ♘c3+ ♔e1 75 ♘e4 ♗f4!
76 ♗e6 ♗e3+ 77 ♔h2 f2 0-1 78 ♘xf2
♔xf2 △ ♗f4 mate **Gheorghiu**

5 Csom-Tompa Kecskemet 79
1 ♘f3 ♘f6 2 c4 e6 3 ♘c3 b6 4 g3
♗b7 5 ♗g2 c5 6 0-0 ♗e7 7 b3 0-0
8 ♗b2 d5 9 cxd5 9 e3 dxc4 10 bxc4

♘c6 11 ♕e2 ♖c8 12 ♖fd1 ♘a5 13
d3 a6 14 ♖ab1 ♕c7 15 ♗a1 ♘d7 16
♗h3 ♗f6= Csom-Nunn, Buenos Aires
78 **♘xd5 10 ♘xd5** 10 ♖ac1 ♘d7 11
♘xd5 ♗xd5 12 d4 ♗f6 13 ♕d2 ♖ac8
14 ♖fd1 ♕e7 15 ♗a3 ♖fd8 16 ♕e3
♕d6 17 dxc5 bxc5 18 ♖d2 h6 19
♗b2 ♗xb2 20 ♖xb2 ♘b6= Smyslov-
Ribli, Leningrad 77; 10 d4 ♘d7 11
♖c1 ♘xc3 12 ♗xc3 ♗f6 13 ♕d2 ♖c8
14 ♖fd1 ♕e7 15 ♕b2 ½-½ Gheorghiu-
Ribli, Leningrad 77 **♗xd5 11 ♕c2**
11 d4 ♗f6 12 ♕d3 ♘d7 13 ♖ad1 cxd4
14 ♗xd4 ♖c8 15 e4 ♗b7 16 ♗a1
♖c7 17 e5 ♗e7 18 ♘d2 ♗xg2 19 ♔xg2
♘xe5! 20 ♕xd8 ♖xd8 21 ♗xe5 ♖cd7
22 ♘c3 ♗f6∓ Jansa-Adorjan, Budapest
78 **♘d7 12 ♖ac1 ♖c8 13 ♔b1 ♗f6**
14 ♖fd1 ♗xb2 14...♕e7?! 15 ♗a3 △
d4, b4 **15 ♕xb2 ♕f6?!** 15...♖c7 △
♕a8= **16 d4! += ♖fd8 17 ♖d2 ♗xf3**
17...♖c7 18 ♕b1 +=; 17...cxd4 18
♘xd4 ♖xc1+ 19 ♕xc1± **18 ♗xf3**
cxd4 19 ♖xc8 ♖xc8 20 ♖xd4?! 20
♕xd4 ♕xd4 21 ♖xd4 ♘f8 22 ♗b7
♖c7 23 ♗a6 f6 +=; 21...♖c7?! 22
♗c6 ♘f8 23 ♖d6 △ b4-b5± **♘e5!=**
21 ♗b7 21 ♕d2 ♘xf3+ 22 exf3 h6
♘g4! 22 e3? 22 f3?! ♖c1+ 23 ♕xc1
♕xd4+ 24 ♔h1 ♕d1!! 25 ♕xd1 ♘f2+
26 ♔g2 ♘xd1 (△ ♘c3) 27 a4 eb
+=; 22 ♗f3 ♘e5= **♖c1+ 23 ♔g2**

23...♘xe3+! 24 ♔h3 24 fxe3 ♕f1 mate
**♖c2 25 ♕a1 e5! −+ 26 ♖h4 ♕xf2
27 ♔h1 g5 28 ♖e4 ♕f5+ 29 g4 ♕f2
0-1 Tompa**

6 Szmetan-Prundeanu
Poiana Brasov 78
**1 c4 c5 2 ♘f3 e6 3 g3 b6 4 ♗g2
♗b7 5 0-0 ♘f6 6 ♘c3 ♗e7 7 d4 cxd4
8 ♕xd4 0-0 9 e4** 9 ♖d1 d6 10 ♘g5!?;
9 b3 d6 10 ♗b2 ♘bd7 11 ♖fd1 a6
12 ♕e3 △ ♘d4± **d6 10 b3 a6 11
♗b2 ♕c7 12 ♖fd1 ♘bd7 13 ♖ac1
♖fd8 14 ♕e3 ♖ac8 15 ♘d4 ♗f8 16
h3 g6 17 f4?** 17 ♔h1 e5 18 ♘de2
d5! △ ♗c5 **19 fxe5 ♗c5 20 ♘d4 ♕xe5
21 ♘xd5 ♗xd5 22 cxd5 ♘xd5 23
♕h6 ♘5f6 24 b4?!** 24 ♖xc5 ♕xc5!
−+; 24 ♔h2 ♗f8 **25 ♕d2 ♕xg3 25
♘c6!? ♘e5! 27 ♗xe5 ♖xd2 28 ♗xg3
♖xc6! 29 ♖xc6 ♖xd1+ 30 ♔h2 ♘d7
−+ 31 ♖c8 ♔g7 32 a3 ♗d6! 33 ♗xd6
♖xd6 34 a4?!** 34 ♖a8 **♖d4 35 ♖c7
♘e5 36 ♖a7 ♖xb4 37 ♖xa6 ♘d3** △
♘c5 **38 a5 bxa5 39 ♖xa5 ♘f4! 40
♗f3 ♖b3 41 ♗g4 h5 42 ♗d7 ♖e3 43
e5 ♘d3 44 e6 fxe6 45 ♖a3 e5 0-1
Vaisman**

7 Kirov-Schinzel Lodz 79
**1 ♘f3 ♘f6 2 g3 b6 3 ♗g2 ♗b7 4 0-0
c5 5 c4 g6 6 b3 ♗g7 7 ♗b2 0-0 8 ♘c3
♘e4 9 d4 ♘xc3 10 ♗xc3 ♘c6=** 11 e3
cxd4 **12 exd4?!** 12 ♘xd4= **d5 =+ 13
♘e5 ♘xe5 14 dxe5 ♕c7! 15 ♗xd5
♖fd8 16 ♕f3 ♗xd5 17 cxd5 ♖ac8
18 ♖ac1 ♗xe5 19 ♗b2 ♕d6 20 ♗xe5
♕xe5 21 ♖ce1 ♕d6 22 ♖e2 ♖c5 23
♖fe1 ♖d7**

Diagram

24 ♖e5? 24 ♖d2 e6 25 dxe6!! ♕xd2
26 exd7 ♕xe1+ 27 ♔g2 +− **♕f8!**

**25 ♕e3 ♖xd5 26 ♕h6+ ♔g8 27 ♖xd5
♕xd5 28 ♖c1 ♖d8 29 ♖c7 ♕f3! 30
♖c1 ♕e2 31 a4 ♖d1+ −+ 32 ♔g2?
♕f1+ 0-1 Pytel**

8 Rind-Regan USA 79
1 ♘f3 b6 2 g3 2 c4 ♗b7 3 ♘c3 e6 4
e4 ♗b4 5 ♗d3!? +=; 2 e4 ♗b7 3 ♘c3
e6 4 d4 ♗b4 5 ♗d3 ♘f6 6 ♕e2 d5
7 exd5 ♘xd5 8 ♗d2 ♘xc3! 9 bxc3
♗e7= Kagan-Sahovic, Biel 76; 4 a3
♘f6 5 e5 ♘d5 6 ♘xd5 ♗xd5 7 b4
c5 8 b5 d6∝ Shamkovich-Regan,
Lone Pine 77 **♗b7 3 ♗g2 g6** 3...♘f6
4 c4 e6 5 0-0 c5; 3...f5!? **4 c4** 4 d4
♘f6 5 0-0 c5 6 ♘c3! cxd4 7 ♕xd4
♗g7 8 e4 d6 9 e5! += Bernstein-
Alekine, Paris 40 **♗g7 5 0-0** 5 d4 ♘f6
6 ♕c2 e6 7 ♘c3 d5 8 cxd5 exd5 9
♗g5 0-0 10 0-0 += Vaganian-Smyslov,
USSR 76; 6...♗e4!= **♘f6 6 ♘c3** 6 d4
0-0 7 ♕c2! ♗e4 8 ♕b3 ♘c6! 9 ♘bd2
d5 10 ♕c3 ♘a5 11 cxd5 ♗xd5 12
b4 ♘c6 13 b5? ♘xd4!∓ Karpov-
Matanovic, Skopje 76; 11 c5 +=
Matanovic **0-0 7 d3** 7 b3 △ ♗b2, d4,
♖e1, e4 **d5!** 7...c5 8 e4 △ h3, ♗e3
+= **8 cxd5** 8 ♘e5 c6∝ **♘xd5 9 ♗d2
c5** 9...♘xc3 10 ♗xc3 ♗xc3?! 11
bxc3 c5 12 ♕d2 +=; 10...c5 11 ♗xg7
♔xg7 12 ♕d2 +=; 10 bxc3!? △ ♖b1,
a4 **10 ♕a4** 10 ♕c1 ♘c6 11 ♘xd5
♕xd5 12 ♗h6 e5!? 13 ♗xg7 ♔xg7 14

Ðd2 ♕d7 ∝/+= ♞c6 11 ♖ac1 e6
11...Ðd4! (Δ Ðxc3, Ðxe2+) 12 Ðxd4
♗xd4 13 ♕b3 Ðxc3! 14 ♗xc3 ♗xg2
15 ♔xg2 ♕d7= 12 a3 ♕e7!? 13 ♖c2
+= ♖fd8 14 ♖fc1 ♞d4?! 14...Ðc7
15 ♞xd4 ♗xd4 16 b4! ♖ac8? 16...
Ðxc3 17 ♗xc3 ♗xg2 18 ♔xg2 ♕b7+
19 ♔g1 ♖ac8 += 17 ♞xd5 17 ♕xa7?
♖a8? 18 Ðxd5; 17...♗xc3 18 ♗xd5
♗xd2 19 ♕xb7 ♕xb7 20 ♗xb7 ♗xc1
21 ♗xc8 ♗xa3 −+; 18 ♗xc3? ♖a8
♗xd5 18 ♗xd5 ♖xd5 19 e3 ♗f6 20
d4! ♕d8 21 bxc5 bxc5 22 ♗b4 e5
23 ♖xc5 ♖dxc5 24 ♖xc5 ♖xc5 25
♗xc5 exd4 26 exd4 a5 27 d5 +−
♞g7 27...♕xd5?? 28 ♕e8+ ♔g7 29
♕f8 mate 28 ♞c6 ♕b8 29 d6 29
♗b6! h5 30 h4 30 ♗b6 ♕b1+ 31 ♔g2
♕d3 32 d7 g5 33 ♗f8+! 1-0 Ciamarra

9 Speelman-Savon Frunze 79
1 c4 ♞f6 2 ♞f3 b6 3 d3!? g6 4 g3
♗g7 5 ♗g2 0-0 6 0-0 ♗b7 7 ♗g5 h6
7...c5 8 ♗d2 d5 8...c5? 9 ♕c1 ♔h7?!
10 Ðg5+! 9 ♕c1 ♔h7 10 cxd5 ♞xd5
11 d4!? 11 Ðc3 c5 =/+= ♞d7 11...
Ða6?! 12 e4 Ðf6 13 Ðc3 Ðxe4 14
Ðxe4 ♗xe4 15 ♕c4? ♕d5!∓; 15
Ðg5+! hxg5 16 ♗xe4 12 e4!? ♞5f6
13 ♞c3 c5 13...Ðxe4! 14 Ðxe4 ♗xe4
15 Ðg5+ hxg5 16 ♗xe4 ♖c8 17 ♗xg5
♗xd4 ∝/=+ 14 d5 ♞a6 15 ♖d1 ♞g4
16 ♕c2 b5 17 h3 ♞ge5 18 ♞xe5 ♗xe5
18...Ðxe5 19 f4 Ðc4 20 e5 f6 ∝/±
Nunn 19 ♗e3 b4 20 ♞e2! ♗d6 20...c4
21 Ðd4! 21 f4± f6 22 ♔h1 ♗b5 23
h4 ♔g7 24 ♞g1 ♕e8 25 ♞f3 g5!?
26 ♔g1 26 hxg5 hxg5 27 e5 ♕g6
27 ♔f2 ♞b6!

Diagram

28 hxg5 hxg5? Zeitnot 28...fxg5!
29 ♗h3 Ðc4 30 ♗f5 ♖xf5!; 29 ♖ac1!

gxf4 30 gxf4 ♗xf4 31 ♗xf4 ♖xf4 32
♕xc5 ∝/+−; 30...♖xf4!? 29 ♗h3 +−
♞c4 30 ♗f5 ♞xe3 31 ♔xe3 gxf4+
31...♕h6 32 fxg5 fxg5 33 ♖h1 ♕f6
34 ♖h7+ ♔g8 35 ♖ah1 Δ ♗e6+ 32
gxf4 ♕g3 32...♕h6 33 ♖g1+ ♔f7 34
♗g6+ ♔g7 35 ♗e8+!; 32...♗xf4+ 33
♔xf4 ♕h6+ 34 ♔g3 +− 33 e5! fxe5
34 ♖g1 exf4+ 35 ♕d2 ♖h8 36 ♖xg3+
fxg3 37 ♕e4 ♕f8 38 ♗g6 ♔g7 39
♕g4 1-0 Speelman

10 Lein-Korchnoi
South Africa 79
1 c4 ♞f6 2 ♞f3 b6 3 g3 ♗b7 4 ♗g2
e5!? 5 d3 ♗b4+ 6 ♗d2 6 Ðbd2 ♗xd2+
7 ♕xd2 0-0 8 0-0 d6 9 ♞c3 ♞bd7 10
e4?! ♞c5 11 ♞h4 ♞e6 12 ♞e2 12 f4
exf4 13 gxf4 Ðxe4 −+ ♞h5 Δ f5
13 ♞f5 13 d4; 13 ♕e3 Δ ♗h3, Ðg2,
f4 g6 14 ♞e3 ♕g5 15 ♖ad1 f5 16 exf5
♗xg2 17 ♞xg2 ♕xf5∓ 18 ♔h1 ♕g4
19 ♞h4 g5 20 ♞g2 ♖f6 21 ♞g1 ♞hg7
22 ♞e3 ♕h5 23 ♕e2 ♕g6 24 ♞d5 ♖f7
25 ♕e4 ♕xe4+ 26 dxe4 ♖af8 27 ♔g2
♞d4 28 ♖d2 ♞ge6 29 h3 h5 30 ♖e1
g4 31 h4 −+ a6 32 ♞e3 ♞c5 33
♞d5 c6 34 ♞c3 34 Ðxb6 ♖b7 35
b4 ♖xb6 36 bxc5 dxc5; 34...a5 35
b3 ♖b8 36 Ða4 ♖xa4 37 bxa4 ♖b4
b5 35 cxb5 axb5 36 b4 ♞ce6 37 ♖e3
♖a8 38 ♞ge2 c5 39 bxc5 dxc5 40
♞d5 c4 0-1 Miles

1 c4 c5

11 Portisch-Hubner Montreal 79
**1 c4 ♘f6 2 ♘c3 c5 3 ♘f3 d5 4 cxd5
♘xd5 5 d4 cxd4?!** 5...g6 **6 ♕xd4
♘xc3 7 ♕xc3 ♘c6 8 e4 ♗g4** 8...e6!?
9 ♗b5 ♕b6 10 ♗xc6+ ♕xc6 11 ♕xc6+
bxc6 12 0-0 += Olafsson-Shaw,
Manila 79 **9 ♗b5 ♖c8 10 ♗e3!** N
10 0-0?! a6 11 ♗xc6+ ♖xc6 12 ♕e3
+=/= Korchnoi-Ljubojevic, Jugoslavia
79 ♗xf3 **11 gxf3 a6 12 ♖d1 ♕c7 13
♗xc6+ ♕xc6 14 ♕d4 f6 15 0-0 e5?**
15...♕e6 16 ♕a7 b5 17 ♖d5 ♔f7 18
♖fd1±; 16 ♔g2!? ♔f7 17 ♖c1 ♖xc1
18 ♖xc1 △ ♖c7 **16 ♕a7 ♗e7 17 ♖c1
♕d7 18 ♖xc8+ ♕xc8 19 ♖c1 ♕d7
20 ♕a8+ +−** 20 ♕b8+? ♗d8 21 ♖c8
♔e7 22 ♗c5+ ♔e6 23 ♗b6? ♗c7!
**♗d8 21 ♖c8 ♕f7 22 ♗b6 ♗xb6 23
♖xh8 ♕g6** 23...♗xf2+ 24 ♔g2! △ ♕g8+
**24 ♕e8+ ♕xe8 25 ♖xe8 ♗d4 26
b4 ♗c3 27 a3 ♗b2 28 a4 ♗a3 29
♖b8 ♗xb4 30 ♖xb7 ♗c3 31 ♔f1 h5
32 ♔e2 a5 33 f4! exf4 34 ♔f3 f5
35 ♖b6+ ♔g5 36 ♖b5 g6 37 e5 ♗d2
38 h4+ ♔h6 39 ♖b7 1-0 Keene**

12 Szabo-Horvath Hungary 79
**1 ♘f3 c5 2 c4 ♘f6 3 ♘c3 d5 4 cxd5
♘xd5 5 e4 ♘b4** 5...♘xc3!? **6 ♗b5+
♘8c6 7 d4!** 7 a3 ♘d3+ 8 ♔e2 ♘f4+!
9 ♔xf1 ♘e6 =+ **cxd4 8 a3 dxc3 9
♕xd8+ ♔xd8 10 axb4 cxb2!? 11
♗xb2 e5 12 ♗xc6!** N 12 0-0-0+ ♔c7
13 ♗xc6 bxc6 14 ♗xe5+ ♔b7 15 ♗c3
♗e7= **bxc6 13 ♘xe5 ♗xb4+** 13...♗e6
14 ♘xc6+ ♔c7 15 ♖c1 ♔b7 16 0-0±;
13...♔e8 14 0-0 ♗xb4 15 ♘xc6 ♗c5
16 ♖fc1 ♗b6 17 ♗xg7± **14 ♔e2 ♔c7**
14...♔e8 15 ♘xc6± **15 ♖hc1 ♗b7 16
♗xc6! ♗xc6 17 ♖a6 ♔b7 18 ♖axc6
♗a5 19 ♗xg7 ♖hg8 20 ♗h6! ♗ae8?!**
20...♖xg2 21 ♖f6 ♖xh2 22 ♖xf7+

♕a6 23 ♗e3± **21 ♕f3 ♖e7 22 ♗e3
♖e6 23 ♖xe6 fxe6 24 g3 ♖d8 25
♖b1+ ♗b6 26 ♕f4 ♔c6 27 ♗xb6 axb6
28 ♔e5 ♖d2 29 f4! 1-0 Meleghegyi**

**13 L.Lengyel-Mik.Tseitlin
Trnava 79**
**1 ♘f3 ♘f6 2 c4 c5 3 ♘c3 d5 4 cxd5
♘xd5 5 e4** 5 g3 += **♘b4 6 ♗b5+**
6 ♗c4!? ♗e6 7 ♗xe6 ♘d3+ 8 ♔f1
fxe6 9 ♘g5 ♘c6 10 ♘xe6 ♕d7 11
♘xc5! += Timman-Stean, Amsterdam
78 **♘8c6 7 d4!?** 7 a3; 7 0-0 **cxd4 8
a3 dxc3** 8...♕b6!?; 8...♗d7!? 9 axb4
dxc3∞ **9 ♕xd8+ ♕xd8 10 axb4 e5**
10...♗d7 11 bxc3 g6 12 0-0 ♗g7 13
♖a3 ♖c8 14 ♖d1± Stean-Browne,
Buenos Aires 78; 10...♘xb4 11 ♔e2!
+=; 10...g6?! 11 bxc3 ♗g7 12 ♖a3!
♗d7 13 0-0 ♖c8 14 ♖d1 += Csom-
Stean, Las Palmas 78; 10...cxb2!?
11 ♗xb2 e5! 12 0-0-0+ ♔c7 13 ♗xc6
bxc6 14 ♗xe5+ ♔b7 15 ♗c3 ♗e7!=
Miles-Schmidt, Buenos Aires 78 **11
bxc3** 11 ♗xc6 ♗xb4!∞ **f6 12 ♗xc6?!**
12 ♗e3 += ♔c7 13 ♗c4! △ ♗d5, b5
bxc6 13 ♗e3 ♔c7 14 ♘d2 14 ♖xa7+
♖xa7 15 ♗xa7 ♗a6 16 ♔d2 ♗e7∞
♗e6 15 0-0?! 15 ♖xa7+ ♖xa7 16
♗xa7 ♗xb4! 17 cxb4 ♖a8 18 ♔e2
♔b7 =+ 16 ♖a5 a6 17 ♖fa1 ♗d6
18 c4 ♖hb8 19 ♖5a4 ♔c7 20 c5 ♗e7
△ ♖b5, ♖ab8 **21 ♖c1 ♖b5 22 ♘c4
♗xc4 23 ♖xc4 a5 24 g3 ♔b7 25 bxa5
♖axa5 26 ♖xa5 ♖xa5 27 ♖c2 ♖a4
f3 g6 29 g4 ♔c7 30 ♔f2 ♖a5 31
♔e2 ♕d7 32 ♖b2 ♔c7 33 ♖c2 ♖a3
34 ♗c1 ♖b3 35 ♗e3 ♖a3 36 ♗c1 ♖a1
37 g5!? fxg5 38 ♗b2 ♖h1 39 ♗xe5+
♕d7 40 ♖d2+ ♔e6 41 ♗d6 h5 42
♔e3 ♗f6 ½-½ Gufeld**

14 Azmajparashvili-Savon USSR 79
1 ♘f3 ♘f6 2 c4 g6 3 g3 ♗g7 4 ♗g2

c5 5 0-0 d5 5...0-0 6 d4 +=; 5...♘c6
6 cxd5 ♘xd5 7 ♘c3 ♘xc3?! 7...♘c6;
7...0-0 8 dxc3! += 0-0? 8...♛c7 +=
9 ♛xd8 ♖xd8 10 ♗e3± ♘a6 11 ♖fd1
♖e8 11...♗d7 12 ♘e5! ♗xe5 13 ♗xb7
♘c7 14 ♗xa8 ♘xa8 15 ♗xc5 ♔f8
16 ♗xa7± 12 ♘d2! ♖b8 13 ♘e4 b6
14 ♗f4 ♖b7 14...e5 15 ♗g5±

15 ♘d2 +- ♖c7 16 ♗xc7 ♘xc7 17
♗c6 ♖f8 18 a4 ♗a6 19 a5! ♗e5 19...
♗xe2 20 ♖e1 +- 20 ♘f3 ♗d6 21 ♖d2
f6 22 axb6 axb6 23 e4 b5 24 e5!
fxe5 25 ♘g5 b4 26 ♘e4 bxc3 27 bxc3
♗b5 28 ♗xb5 ♘xb5 29 ♖a5 1-0 Gufeld

15 Godes-Karasev USSR 79
1 ♘f3 ♘f6 2 c4 c5 3 ♘c3 d5 4 cxd5
♘xd5 5 g3 5 e4 ♘b4 6 ♗c4 ♘d3+
7 ♔e2 ♘f4+ 8 ♔f1 += ♘c6 6 ♗g2 ♘c7
7 a3 e5 8 b4! cxb4 8...f6 9 bxc5 ♘e6
10 e3 ♗xc5 11 0-0 0-0 12 ♛c2 f5∞
Espig-M.Tseitlin, Trnava 79 9 axb4
b5!? N 9...♗xb4 10 ♘xe5! ♘xe5 11
♛a4+± 10 0-0 ♗xb4 11 ♘g5?! 11
♗b2 0-0 12 ♖c1∞ ♗d7 12 ♘xf7
♔xf7 13 ♗xc6 ♗xc6 14 ♛b3+ ♘e6
14...♘d5 15 e4 += 15 ♛xb4 a5 15...
♘g5 16 ♛h4 16 ♛b3 a4 =+ 16...b4
17 ♘a4 17 ♛b4 ♛d4 18 ♗a3 ♛xb4
19 ♗xb4 ♘d4 20 f4 e4 21 ♖a2!
♖hd8 22 ♔f2 h5 23 ♖b1 ♛e6?! 24
♖ab2 ♖d7 25 h3 g6 26 d3 exd3 27

exd3 ♛f7 28 ♘e4 ♗xe4 29 dxe4
♘c6 30 ♖c1? 30 ♖c2! ♘xb4 31 ♖xb4
♖b7 32 ♔e3 a3 33 ♖a1 a2 Zeitnot
34 ♔d4 34 ♖bb2 ♖c7 35 ♔f2∞ ♖a3
35 ♖b2 35 g4!? ♖xg3 36 ♖bxa2 ♖d7+
37 ♔c5 ♖xh3 38 ♖a7 ♖c3+ 39 ♔xb5
♖cc7 40 ♖xc7+ ♖xc7 41 ♖h1! ½-½
Gufeld

16 Zivkovic-Ivanovic
Jugoslavia 79
1 c4 ♘f6 2 ♘c3 c5 3 g3 d5 4 cxd5
♘xd5 5 ♗g2 ♘c7 6 a3 e5 7 ♘f3 ♘c6
8 b4!? f6! 8...cxb4 9 axb4 ♗xb4 10
♘xe5!± 9 bxc5 ♗xc5 10 0-0 0-0 11
♗b2 ♛h8 12 d3 a6 13 e3 ♗g4 14
h3 ♗h5 15 g4 ♗f7 16 ♘e2 ♗a7 17
d4 exd4 18 ♘fxd4 18 ♘exd4!? ♘e5
19 ♛c2 ♘d5 20 ♖ac1 ♖ac8 21 ♛f5!
♖xc1 22 ♖xc1 ♖e8 △ ♘g6 23 ♛c2
h5!? 24 g5? 24 gxh5!? ♗xh5 25
♛b3 ♘b6! 26 ♗xb7 ♛d7 27 ♗g2 ♖b8∞
fxg5∓ 25 ♘f3 ♗xf3+ 26 ♗xf3 ♘xe3!
27 fxe3 27 ♛c3 ♘f5 ♖xe3 -+ 28
♖d1 28 ♔g2 ♖xf3! 29 ♔xf3 ♗d5+
30 ♔g3 ♛d6+ -+ ♖xf3+ 29 ♗d4
♗xd4+ 30 ♘xd4 ♖g3+ 31 ♔f2 31
♔h2 ♛b8! h4 32 ♛c5 ♛f6+ 33 ♘f5
♗e6 0-1 Ivanovic

17 Saharov-Zilberstein USSR 79
1 c4 ♘f6 2 ♘f3 c5 3 ♘c3 d5 4 cxd5
♘xd5 5 g3 5 e4 ♘b4 6 ♗b5+ ♘8c6
7 d4!?∞ Csom-Stean, Las Palmas 78
♘c6 6 ♗g2 ♘c7 7 0-0 e5 8 b3 8 d3
♗e7 9 ♘d2 △ ♘c4, f4 ♗e7 9 ♗b2 0-0
10 ♖c1 △ ♘a4 f6 11 e3?! 11 ♘e1!?
△ ♘d3, f4 ♗g4!= 12 h3 ♗h5 13 g4
♗g6 14 d4!? cxd4 15 exd4 exd4 16
♘e2 d3 17 ♘f4 ♗e4 18 ♖c4 f5 19
gxf5 ♗xf5 20 ♘d4 ♘xd4 21 ♖xd4
♛e8 =+ 22 ♘xd3 ♗f6 23 ♖f4 ♗xb2
23...♗xd3 24 ♖xf6! ♗xf1 25 ♖xf8+
=+ 24 ♘xb2 ♘e6 25 ♖f3 25 ♛d5

Rd8∓ Rd8 26 Qc1 Nd4 27 Qc4+
Kh8 28 Re3 Qg6 29 Qc7 b5∓ 30
Qxa7?

30...Be4! 31 f3 31 Rxe4 Nf3+ 32
Kh1 Qxe4 –+ Rxf3! 32 Rxe4 Qxe4
33 Bxf3 Nxf3+ 34 Kf2 Nd2 34...
Nh4 –+ 35 Rd1 Rf8+ 36 Kg1 Nf3+
37 Kg2 Nh4+ 0-1 Gufeld

18 Govbinder-Kapengut Moscow 79
1 Nf3 Nf6 2 c4 c5 3 Nc3 d5 4 cxd5
Nxd5 5 g3 Nc6 6 Bg2 Nc7 7 0-0 e5
8 d3 Be7 9 Nd2 Bd7 10 Nc4 0-0!?
11 Bxc6 Bxc6 12 Nxe5 Be8 13 Be3
Ne6 14 Rc1 14 Qb3 b6?! 15 Qd5!
Qc8 16 f4 Bf6 17 f5 Nc7 18 Qe4
Bxe5 19 Qxe5 f6 20 Qe4 Bf7 21
Bf4 Qd8 22 Bxc7± Smejkal-Portisch,
Biel 76; 14...Bf6 15 f4?! Bxe5 16
fxe5 Bc6 17 Qc4 Qc7 18 Nd5 Qxe5
19 Ne7+ Kh8 20 Qc1 Sahovic-Joksic
76, 20...Nd4!? 21 Nxc6 bxc6 22
Rf2 Rab8 23 b3 Rfe8 =+; 15 Nf3
Bc6 16 Ne4 (1) 16...Bd4?! 17 Bxd4
Nxd4 18 Nxd4 cxd4 19 Rac1 Rc8
20 Rc2 Qd7 (2) 16...Be7! 17 Ne5?!
Bd5 18 Qa4 f6 19 Nc4 Ftacnik-
Gliksman, Stary Smokovec 76, 19...
b6!∓; 17 Rac1 b6 18 Ne5 Bd5 19
Qa4 Jansa-Joksic, Vratsa 75, 19...f6!
20 Nc4 Bb7 =+; 17...Bd5!? 18 Qa4
b5 19 Qxb5 Rb8 20 Qa6 Rxb2 21

a4 Qb8; 19 Qa6 Qb6 20 Qxb6 axb6
21 a3 Rfd8 Δ h6, f5; 15 Ng4!? Bd4
16 Bxd4 cxd4 17 Ne4 Lerner-
Timoshenko, Rostov 76; 17...Qa5! (Δ
h5) 18 h4 Bc6 19 Rfc1 Kh8 =+ Bf6
15 Nc4 15 Nf3 Bc6 17 a3 Qe7 18
Qc2 Bd4 18 Na4 Rac8 19 b4? Bxe3
20 fxe3 cxb4 21 axb4 Ng5∓
Mochalov-Kapengut, Minsk 74 Bc6
16 Ne4 Bd4 17 Bxd4 cxd4 18 Ne5
Bd5 19 Qa4 Re8! 19...f6?! 20 Nd7
Bc6? 21 Rxc6 Qxd7 22 Ra6! +– 20
Nf3 Qb6 21 Rc2 Rad8 22 Rfc1 h6!
Δ Ng5 23 h4 Kh8! N 23...f5?! 24
Ned2 Nf4?! 25 Nc4!± Dorfman-
Kapengut, Tbilisi 76 24 Ned2

24...Nf4! –+ 25 gxf4 Qg6+ 26 Kf1
26 Kh2 Rxe2 27 Ne4 Rxe4 –+ Qg4
27 Ne4 f5 28 Ng3 28 Nd6!? Bxf3
29 Nxe8 Qg2+ 30 Ke1 Qg1+ 31 Kd2
Qxf2 32 Re1 Qe3+ 33 Kd1 Qxd3+
34 Kc1 Qe3+ 35 Rd2 Rc8+ 36 Kd1
d3! –+ Qh3+ 29 Kg1 Rxe2! 0-1
Kapengut

19 Coppini-Marovic Rome 79
1 Nf3 Nf6 2 c4 c5 3 Nc3 d5 4 cxd5
Nxd5 5 g3 Nc6 5...g6 6 Bg2 Nc7 7
0-0 7 Qa4!? e5 8 d3 Be7 9 Nd2 Bd7
10 Nc4 0-0!? 10...f6 11 f4!? b5 12
Ne3 exf4 13 Rxf4 0-0 14 Ned5 Ne6
15 Rf2 Rb8 16 Bd2 Ne5 17 Rc1

🜚f7 18 ♘xe7+ ♕xe7 19 b4 c4 20 ♘d5 ♕d8 21 ♗c3 ♘g4 ½-½ Portisch-Karpov, Milan 75; 13 gxf4!? 0-0 14 ♘ed5 += **11 ♗xc6 ♗xc6 12 ♘xe5 ♗e8 13 ♗e3!? ♘e6!? 14 ♖c1** 14 ♕b3!? ♗f6 15 f4 ♗xe5 16 fxe5 ♗c6∝ 17 ♕d2 ♕d7 18 ♗f4 ♖ad8 19 ♕e3 b6 20 ♘e4 20 a3!? ♕d5 21 b3 a5!? h4 a4 23 h5 axb3 24 axb3 ♕d4!? 25 ♕xd4 ♘xd4 26 ♘c3 b5= 27 ♗e3 ♘xb3 28 ♖b1 c4 29 dxc4 bxc4 30 ♖f4 ♗d5 31 ♘xd5 ♖xd5 32 ♖xc4 ♘d2 33 ♗xd2 ♖xd2 34 ♖e4 ♖e8 35 e6!? f5! 36 ♖e5 ♖d6 37 ♖f1 ♖dxe6 38 ♖xe6 ♖xe6 39 ♖xf5 ♖xe2 40 ♖f2 ♖e5 41 g4 ♖e4 42 ♖g2 ♔f7 ½-½ **Schmidt**

20 Foldi-Lukacs Hungary 79
1 ♘f3 ♘f6 2 c4 c5 3 ♘c3 e6 4 g3 d5 5 cxd5 ♘xd5 6 ♗g2 ♘c6 7 0-0 ♗e7 8 ♘xd5 exd5 9 d4 0-0 10 dxc5 ♗xc5 11 b3 ♗f5 12 ♗b2 ♗e4! 13 ♖c1 ♕e7 14 ♕d2 ♗b6 14...f6 **15 ♖fd1 ♖fe8** 15...♖ad8 16 ♘d4 ♘xd4 17 ♗xd4 ♗xd4 18 ♕xd4 ♗xg2 19 ♔xg2 ♕xe2 20 ♕xa7 +=; 16...♘e5!?∝ **16 ♕f4!? ♖ad8 17 e3 h6 18 ♘d4 ♗xd4! 19 ♗xd4 ♕a3!? 20 ♗a1! ♗xg2** 20...♕xa2 21 ♕g4! **21 ♔xg2 ♕xa2 22 ♕g4 d4!** 22...g5? 23 ♕h5; 22...g6 23 ♕h4 **23 exd4 ♖d5 24 ♕f3 ♕a5** 24...♖ed8 25 ♖c5! += **25 b4 ♕d8 26 b5! ♘xd4** 26...♖xb5? 27 d5! ♘e5 28 ♗xe5 ♖xe5 29 d6 +− **27 ♗xd4 ♖xd4 28 ♖xd4 ♕xd4 29 ♖c7 ♕e4 30 ♖xb7 ♕xf3+ 31 ♔xf3 ♖e5= 32 ♔f4 f6 33 h4 h5 34 g4 hxg4 35 ♔xg4 ♔h7 36 f4 ♖d5 37 ♔f3 ½-½ Foldi**

21 Pytel-Honfi Trstenik 79
1 d4 ♘f6 2 c4 c5 3 ♘f3 cxd4 4 ♘xd4 ♘c6 5 ♘c3 e6 6 ♘db5 d6 7 ♗f4 e5 8 ♗g5 a6 9 ♗xf6 gxf6 10 ♘a3 f5 11 g3 ♗e6 12 ♗g2 ♗g7 13 ♕d2 0-0 14 ♘d5 14 ♖d1 e4 15 ♕xd6? ♗xc3+ 16 bxc3 ♕a5∓ **e4 15 0-0 ♖c8?!** 15... b5!? 16 cxb5 ♘d4 17 ♘dc3 axb5 18 ♘axb5 ♘xb5 19 ♘xb5 ♕b6∝ **16 ♖ac1 ♗xd5 17 cxd5 ♕a5 18 ♕xa5 ♘xa5 19 ♖xc8** 19 b4 ♖xc1 20 ♖xc1 ♗b2 21 ♖c7 ♗xa3 22 bxa5 ♖e8 23 f4 (23 ♖xb7 ♖e5) exf3 24 ♗xf3 ♖b8= **♖xc8 20 b4 ♘c4 21 ♖c1 b5 22 ♖c2 ♘b6 23 ♖c6 ♖b8 24 ♖xd6 ♗f8 25 ♖c6 ♘xd5 26 ♘c2 ♖a8= 27 g4 fxg4 28 ♗xe4 ♘xb4 29 ♘xb4 ♗xb4 30 ♖h6 ♖e8 31 ♗d3 ♖e6 32 ♖h4**

32...♗c5?! += 32...♔f8 33 ♖xg4 ♗d6 34 e3 h6= **33 ♗xh7+ ♔f8 34 ♗d3 ♖f6 35 e3 ♖d6 36 ♗c2 a5! 37 ♖h5!** 37 ♖xg4? ♖d2 38 ♗b3 a4 39 ♗xa4 bxa4 =+ **♖c6 38 ♗d3 b4 39 ♗b5?!** 39 ♖g5! += **♖c7 40 ♗a4 ♗b6 41 ♖d5 ♔e7 42 ♔g2 ♖c5 43 ♖d7+ ♔e6 ½-½ Honfi**

22 Ubilava-Gipslis USSR 79
1 ♘f3 ♘f6 2 c4 c5 3 d4 cxd4 4 ♘xd4 e5?! 5 ♘b5 d5 N **6 cxd5 ♗c5** 6... ♘xd5?? 7 ♕xd5 +− **7 e3 0-0 8 ♘5c3 e4 9 ♗e2 ♖e8 10 a3 ♘bd7** 10...b4!? **11 b4 ♗f8 12 ♗b2 ♘b6 13 ♘d2 ♗f5 14 ♘b3 ♘fxd5 15 ♘xd5 ♘xd5 16 0-0 ♘b6 17 ♗b5 ♗d7?! 18 ♗xd7 ♕xd7 19 ♕xd7 ♘xd7 20 ♖ac1± ♘e5 21**

♗xe5 ♖xe5 22 ♖fd1 ♖e7 23 ♖d5 g6 24 g4! +− ♖ae8 25 h3 ♗g7 26 ♖c4 a6 27 a4 ♗e5 28 ♘c5 28 ♖xe4? ♗h2+ −+ ♗b8 29 ♖d7 f5 30 ♖xb7 1-0 Georgadze

23 Kraidman-Botterill England 79
1 d4 ♘f6 2 c4 e6 3 ♘f3 c5 4 g3 cxd4 5 ♘xd4 d5 6 ♗g2 e5 7 ♘f3 7 ♘c2 d4 8 f4 ♗d6 9 0-0 ♕b6 10 ♕d3 ♘c6 11 b4 e4 12 ♗xe4 ♘xb4 13 ♘xb4 ♗xb4 14 ♘d2 0-0 =+ Alcock-Botterill, British Final 79 d4 8 0-0 ♘c6 9 e3 ♗c5! 10 exd4 exd4 11 ♖e1+ 11 ♘bd2 0-0 12 ♘b3 ♕b6 13 ♗f4 ♖e8 14 ♘xc5 ♕xc5 15 ♘d2 h6 16 ♘b3 ♕xc4 17 ♖c1 ♕a4 =+ Knezevic-Kasparov, Banja Luka 79; 13 ♖e1 ♗f5 14 ♗g5 ♘d7 15 ♘h4 ♗e6 16 ♕h5 ♘ce5 17 h3 ♖fe8 18 ♘xc5 ♕xc5 19 b3 ♘d3! 20 ♖ed1 ♘xf2∓ Birnboim-Povah, England 79 ♗e6 12 ♘bd2 12 ♘g5?! 0-0 13 ♘xe6 fxe6 14 ♖xe6 ♕d7 0-0 13 ♘b3 ♕b6 14 ♘e5!? 14 ♗f4; 14 ♗g5 ♗b4! 15 ♘xc6 15 ♗d2 ♗xd2 16 ♕xd2 ♘xe5 17 ♖xe5 ♗xc4 18 ♕xd4 ♗xb3 −+; 18 ♘xd4 ♖ad8 −+ ♗xe1!? 15...bxc6 16 ♗d2 ♗xd2 17 ♕xd2 ♗xc4 18 ♕xd4 ♗xb3 19 ♕xb6 axb6 20 axb3 ≈/+= 16 ♘cxd4! 16 ♘e7+ ♔h8 17 ♕xe1 ♖fe8∓ ♗b4 17 ♘xe6 ♕xe6 18 ♗xb7 ♖ad8 19 ♕f1 ♖d7 20 ♗f3? 20 ♗g2! ♖c7 21 ♗e3!; 20...♕e5!? 21 ♗h3! ♖dd8∞ ♖c8 21 ♗e2 ♖e8 22 ♗e3 ♘g4∓ 23 ♗xg4 ♕xg4 24 a3 ♗e7 25 h3 ♕g6 26 c5

Diagram

26...♖d3! −+ 27 ♘a5 ♖xe3 28 fxe3 ♕xg3+ 29 ♔h1 ♗xc5 30 ♖d1 30 ♘c4; 30 ♖e1 ♖e4 △ ♖h4 ♖xe3 31 ♘c6 ♕h4 32 ♖d8+ ♗f8 33 ♖d4 ♖xh3+

34 ♔g1 ♖h1+ 0-1 Botterill

24 Vladimirov-Kapengut
Moscow 79
1 d4 ♘f6 2 ♘f3 e6 3 g3 c5 4 c4 cxd4 5 ♘xd4 d5 6 ♗g2 e5 7 ♘f3 d4 8 0-0 ♘c6 9 e3 ♗c5!? 10 exd4 exd4 11 ♖e1+ 11 b4!? ♘xb4 12 ♘bd2 d3 13 ♘b3 ♗e7 14 ♘fd4 ♗g4! 15 ♕d2 0-0 16 ♗b2 ♕d7 17 ♖fe1 ♖ac8 18 a3 ♘a6 19 ♕xd3 ♘c5 20 ♘xc5 ♕xc5= Rashkovsky-Alburt, Daugavpils 78; 11 ♘bd2 0-0 12 ♘b3 ♕b6 13 ♗f4 ♖e8 14 ♘xc5 ♕xc5 15 ♘d2 h6 16 ♘b3 ♕xc4 17 ♖c1 ♕a4 18 ♘c5 ♕xa2 19 ♕d2 ♗f5 20 ♖a1 ♕c4 21 ♖fc1 ♕b5 22 ♘xb7!∞ Knezevic-Kasparov, Banja Luka 79 ♗e6 12 ♘g5 0-0 13 ♘xe6 13 ♖xe6?! fxe6 14 ♘xe6 ♕b6 15 ♘xf8 ♖xf8 16 ♕b3 ♘g4 17 ♕xb6 ♗xb6 18 ♗d5+ ♔h8 19 ♗f4 d3∓ Alburt-Palatnik, Kiev 78 fxe6 14 ♘d2 14 ♖xe6? d3 15 ♗xc6 bxc6 16 ♗e3 ♗d4 17 ♘c3 ♕d7 18 ♕xd3 ♕xe6∓ Nenashev-Kasparov, USSR 78; 14 a3 a5 15 b3 e5 16 ♖a2 ♕d6 17 ♘d2 d3∓ Litiuskaya-Chekhova, USSR 78 d3! 15 ♘b3 ♗d4! N 16 ♗e3! 16 ♘xd4 ♕xd4 17 ♗xc6 bxc6 18 ♗e3 ♕xc4 19 b3 ♕b5= ♗xb2 17 ♖b1 ♗c3 18 ♗d2 18 ♖f1 ♘e5∞ ♗d4 18...♗xd2 19 ♕xd2 ♘g4?! 20 f4 e5 21 h3 exf4 22 ♗d5+

♔h8 23 hxg4 fxg3 24 ♕g2 +–; 19...
♕d6= **19 ♗e3 ♗c3 ½-½ Kapengut**

25 Polugaevsky-Veingold
Moscow 79
1 ♘f3 ♘f6 2 c4 c5 3 d4 cxd4 4 ♘xd4
e6 5 g3 d5 6 ♗g2 e5 7 ♘f3 d4 8 0-0
♘c6 9 e3 ♗e7 10 exd4 exd4 11 ♗f4
0-0 12 ♘e5 ♘xe5 13 ♗xe5 ♗c5 14
♘d2 ♘g4?! 14...♖e8 (1) 15 ♗xf6 ♕xf6
16 ♖e1 ♖xe1+ 17 ♕xe1 ♗d7! 18
♘e4 ♕b6 19 ♘xc5 ♕xc5 20 ♕d2=
Zilberstein-Kapengut, Odessa 72; 16
♘e4 ♕e5 (16...♕b6 17 b4!? ♗xb4
18 ♖b1 ♗f5 19 c5 ♕c7 20 ♕xd4 ♗xe4
21 ♗xe4 ♗xc5 22 ♕d3 ♖ad8=) 17
♘xc5 Rashkovsky-Balashov, Moscow
76; 17 ♕a4! ♗f5 18 ♖ae1 ♔f8 19
b4!±; (2) 15 ♖e1 ♘g4 16 ♗f4 ♖xe1+
17 ♕xe1 d3 18 ♘e4 ♗d4 19 h3 ♘e5
20 ♖d1! ♗xb2 21 ♖d2 ♘xc4= Alburt-
Furman, Erevan 75 **15 ♗f4** 15 ♘f3
d3 Keres-Furman, Tallinn 65; 16
♗c3 ♕b6 17 ♕d2 ♘e3?! 18 b4! ♘xf1
19 ♕g5!± **♘e3?!** 15...♗d6 16 ♗xd6
♕xd6 17 ♘e4 ♕h6 18 h3 ♘f6 19
♕xd4 ♘xe4 20 ♕xe4 ♗xh3 21 ♗xh3
♕xh3 22 ♕xb7± Grunberg-Knaak,
DDR 73 **16 fxe3 dxe3 17 ♕h5!** N
17 ♔h1 exd2 18 ♕xd2 ♕xd2 19 ♗xd2
½-½ Alburt-Gipslis, Lublin 72 **♗d4**
18 ♘b3! e2+ **19 ♖f2 ♗xf2+ 20 ♔xf2**
♗e6 20...♕f6 21 ♖e1 +– **21 ♕xe2**
♖c8 22 ♖d1 ♕f6 23 ♕e5 +– ♕xe5
24 ♗xe5 b6 25 ♘d4 ♗xc4 26 ♗d6
♖fe8 27 ♗b7 ♖cd8 28 ♗c6 ♖xd6
29 ♗xe8 ♗xa2 1-0 Kapengut

26 Andersson-Robatsch Munich 79
1 ♘f3 ♘f6 2 c4 c5 3 g3 b6 4 ♗g2
♗b7 5 0-0 g6 6 b3 ♗g7 7 ♗b2 0-0
8 ♘c3 d5 8...d6! 9 d4 cxd4 10 ♘xd4
♗xg2 11 ♔xg2 d5! 12 cxd5 ♘xd5
13 ♘db5 ♘xc3 14 ♕xd8 ♖fxd8 15

♗xc3 ♗xc3 16 ♘xc3 ♘c6= Alburt-
Polugaevsky, USSR 74 **9 ♘xd5 ♘xd5**
10 ♗xg7 ♔xg7 11 cxd5 ♕xd5 12 d4
cxd4 13 ♕xd4+ ♕xd4 14 ♘xd4
♗xg2 15 ♔xg2

15...a6 15...♘d7 16 ♖ac1 ♖fc8 17
♖fd1 ♔f6! 18 ♘b5 ♖xc1 19 ♖xc1
♘c5 20 b4 ♘e6 21 ♖c6 += Portisch-
Pachman, Sarajevo 63 **16 ♖ac1** 16
♖fc1 ♖a7 17 ♖c2 ♖d8 18 e3 ♔f8 19
♖ac1 ♔e8 20 g4! h6 21 h4 ♖ad7
22 f4 a5 23 ♔f3 ♖d6 24 h5!±
Andersson-Hort, Niksic 78 **♖a7 17**
♖c2 ♖d8 18 e3 e5? 19 ♘f3 f6 20
g4! ♖d6 21 ♖fc1 ♘d7 22 ♖c6 ♖xc6
23 ♖xc6 ♔f7 +– 24 ♘d2 ♔e7 25
♘e4 ♖b7 26 b4 ♖b8 27 ♘c3 f5 27...
♖b7 28 ♘d5+ ♔f7 +– **28 ♘d5+ ♔f7**
29 ♔g3 h5 30 gxf5 gxf5 31 ♖d6 ♖b7
32 ♔h4 ♔g7 33 ♔xh5 1-0 Samarian

1 c4 e5

27 Godes-Smetanin USSR 79
1 c4 e5 2 ♘c3 ♘c6 3 ♘f3 ♘f6 4 d3
4 e3; 4 g3 d5 5 cxd5 ♘xd5 6 g3 ♗e7
7 ♗g2 ♘b6 8 0-0 0-0 9 a4 a5 10
♘b5 f5!? 11 ♕b3+ ♔h8 12 ♖d1 12
♗e3 f4! 13 gxf4 exf4 14 ♗xb6 cxb6
15 d4 ♗f6 **♗f6 13 ♗e3 ♘b4!** 13...♘d5?
14 ♘xe5 ♘xe3 15 ♘xc6 bxc6 16
fxe3 ♗g5 17 d4± **14 ♗c5 ♖e8 15**

e4 ♞a6 16 ♕c3 16 ♗a3!

16...♞xa4! 17 ♖xa4 ♗d7 18 ♗e3 ♗xb5̄
19 ♖xa5 c6 20 ♖aa1 f4 21 gxf4
exf4 22 ♗d4 ♗xd4 23 ♞xd4 ♕g5
24 ♔h1? ♞c7 25 ♗f3 ♖ad8 =+ 26
♞f5 ♖d7 27 d4 ♕f6 △ ♘e6, g6 28
♗g4 ♖xe4 28...g6 29 e5! 29 d5 ♕xc3
30 bxc3 ♖xd5∓ 31 ♞d6 ♖a4 32 ♞xb7
♖xd1+ 33 ♖xd1 ♞d5 34 ♖c1 g5 35
♞d6 ♗d3 36 ♞f7+ ♔g7 37 ♞xg5
♔f6 38 ♞f3 c5 39 ♞e1 ♗e4+ 0-1
Gufeld

28 Keene-Hammar Cleveland 79
1 c4 e5 2 ♞c3 ♞f6 3 ♞f3 ♞c6 4 d3
d5 5 cxd5 ♞xd5 6 g3 ♗e6 7 ♗g2 ♗e7
8 0-0 0-0 9 a3 a5 10 ♗d2 ♞xc3?!
10...♘b6; 10...f6 11 bxc3 += ♕d7
11...a4!? 12 ♕a4 ♖ab8 12...♘d4?
13 ♕xd7 ♘xe2+ 14 ♔h1 ♗xd7 15
♖fe1 13 ♖fb1 b5?! 13...f6 14 ♖xb5
♖xb5 15 ♕xb5 ♖b8 16 ♕a4 16 ♕a6
♖b6 17 ♕a8+ ♖b8 18 ♕a6 ♖a6=
♗b3? 16...♘d4! 17 ♕xd7 ♘xf3+
18 ♗xf3 ♗xd7 17 ♕e4 ♕e6 17...f5
18 ♘xe5!; 17...♗d5 18 ♘xe5! +-
18 ♞g5 ♗xg5 19 ♗xg5 ♞d8 20 c4
f6 21 ♗d2 a4 22 ♕e3 ♕b6 23 ♗d5+
♔h8 24 ♕xb6 cxb6 25 f4 exf4 26
♗xf4 ♖c8 27 ♗g2 g5? 27...♘e6 28
♗e3 ♘c5 29 d4 ♘e6 30 c5 bxc5 31
dxc5 ♘xc5? 32 ♖c1 +- 28 ♗e3 1-0
28...♖b8 29 ♗d4 ♔g7 30 ♖f1 Keene

29 Larsen-Portisch Montreal 79
1 c4 e5 2 ♞c3 ♞f6 3 ♞f3 ♞c6 4 d3
d6 5 g3 g6 6 ♗g2 ♗g7 7 ♖b1 a5 8
a3 ♞d4! 9 b4 9 0-0 0-0 10 ♘xd4 exd4
11 ♘b5 ♘g4 12 h3 ♘xf2! 13 ♖xf2
c6 axb4 10 axb4 c6 11 b5 0-0 12 bxc6
bxc6 13 ♞xd4 exd4 14 ♞e4 14 ♗xc6?
♖a6 -+ ♞xe4 15 ♗xe4 ♖a6= 15...d5
16 cxd5 cxd5 17 ♗g2 ♖e8 18 0-0
♗g4= 16 0-0 ♗g4 17 ♗f4 f5!? 18 ♗g2
g5 19 ♗d2 f4 20 ♖b7 ♕c8 21 ♕b1
♗e5 21...♗xe2? 22 ♖e1 f3 23 ♗xg5
22 gxf4?! 22 ♗f3 ♗xf3 23 exf3=
gxf4 23 ♔h1 △ ♖g1 ♖a1! 24 ♕xa1
♕xb7 25 ♗e4 ♔h8 25...♗xe2!? 26
♖g1+ ♔h8 27 f3?! d5! 28 cxd5 cxd5
29 ♕a5 ♗g7 30 ♗xd5 ♗xf3+ -+
26 ♖g1 ♗xe2 27 ♕e1 27 f3 d5! ♗h5
28 c5 Zeitnot ♖g8 28...dxc5? 29
♖g5 +- 29 ♖xg8+ ♔xg8 30 cxd6
♗xd6 31 ♕c1 f3 32 ♗xc6 32 ♕xc6=
♕c7 33 ♕c4+ ♗f7 34 ♕b5 ♗f4 35
♗b4 ♕c8 △ ♕h3 36 ♕c5 ♗h6 37
♗xf3 ♕h3 38 ♗g2? 38 ♗e2! △ ♕xd4
♕xd3 39 ♕c8+ ♔g7 0-1 time 40
♕f8+ ♔g6 41 ♕d6+ = Keene

30 Godes-Ljubomirov USSR 79
1 c4 ♞f6 2 ♞c3 e5 3 ♞f3 ♞c6 4 d3
g6 5 a3 a5 6 g3 ♗g7 7 ♗g2 0-0 8
0-0 d6 9 ♖b1 ♗f5 9...♗d7 10 b4 axb4
11 axb4 ♕c8 12 ♗g5 ♗h3∞; 9...♖e8
10 b4 axb4 11 axb4 e4! 10 b4 axb4
11 axb4 ♕c8 12 b5 ♞e7 13 ♖fe1
13 ♗g5?! h6 14 ♕b3 += ♞d7 15 ♗e3
♗e6 16 ♞d5 ♞f5 17 ♞h4! ♕d8 18
♞xf5 ♗xf5 19 ♞c3! ♖b8 20 ♗a7!
♖a8 21 ♖a1 ♕c8 22 ♕b4 ♖e8±
23 ♗e3 ♖xa1 24 ♖xa1 ♞f6 25 b6!
c5 26 ♕b3 e4 27 ♖a7 ♗h3 28 ♗xe4
♞xe4 29 dxe4 ♕c6 29...f5 30 f3
30 f3 f5 31 ♕b5! ♕c8 32 ♞d5 fxe4
33 ♖xb7 ♕d8 34 ♖xg7+! ♔xg7 35
♕b2+ 1-0 Gufeld

31 Seirawan-Barbero Skien 79

1 c4 e5 2 ♘c3 ♞f6 3 ♘f3 ♞c6 4 e3 ♝b4 4...♝e7 **5 ♕c2 ♝xc3 6 ♕xc3 ♕e7 7 a3 a5** 7...d5 8 cxd5 ♘xd5 9 ♕b3 ♘b6 10 d3 += **8 b4! axb4** 8...d6 9 ♝b2 ♝g4 10 b5 ♝xf3 11 gxf3 ♘d4 12 0-0-0! ♘xf3 12 ♝g2± Keene-Tisdall, Orense 77; 12...♘e6 13 ♖g1 Δ ♝h3 += **9 axb4 ♖xa1 10 ♕xa1 e4** 10...♕xb4 11 ♘xe5; 10...♘xb4 11 ♕xe5 **11 b5 exf3** 11...♘b4 12 ♘d4 **12 bxc6 bxc6 13 gxf3 0-0 14 ♝b2±♝e8 15 ♝d3 ♕h4 16 ♝e2 c5 17 ♕a8! ♞d6 18 ♖g1 f6 19 ♕d5+ ♔h8 20 ♕xc5 ♕xh2 21 ♖g3!** 21 ♖xg7 ♔xg7 22 ♕g5+ ♔h8? 23 ♝xf6+ ♖xf6 24 ♕xf6+ ♔g8 25 c5 ♘f7 26 ♝c4; 22...♔f7 23 ♕xf6+ ♔e8! −+ **h5? 22 ♖xg7!! ♔xg7 23 ♕g5+ ♔f7 24 ♕xf6+ ♔e8 25 ♝g6+ ♞f7 26 ♝e5!! 1-0** 26...♔h3 27 ♝xc7 Δ ♕d8 mate **Keene**

32 Timman-Karpov
Montreal 79

1 c4 ♞f6 2 ♘c3 e5 3 ♘f3 ♞c6 4 e3 ♝e7!? 5 d4 exd4 6 ♘xd4 0-0 7 ♘xc6 bxc6 8 ♝e2 d5 9 0-0 ♝d6 10 b3 10 cxd5 cxd5 11 b3 **♕e7 11 ♝b2?! dxc4!** 11...♖d8 12 cxd5 ♕e5 13 g3 += Keene-Jansson, Haifa 76 **12 bxc4?!** 12 ♕d4!?; 12 ♝xc4 ♘g4 13 g3 ♘xh2 14 ♔xh2 ♕h4+ = **♖b8 13 ♕c1 ♞g4** N 13...♖e8 14 c5 ♝xc5 15 ♘a4 ♝d6∓ Sande-Svenneby, corr 77 **14 g3** 14 h3 ♕e5 **♖e8** Δ 15...♘xh2 16 ♔xh2 ♕h4+ 17 ♔g1 ♝xg3 18 fxg3 ♕xg3+ 19 ♔h1 ♖e6 −+ **15 ♞d1 ♝xh2 16 c5 ♞xf1 17 cxd6 ♞xg3! −+ 18 fxg3 ♕xd6 19 ♔f2 ♕h6 20 ♝d4 ♕h2+ 21 ♔e1 ♕xg3+ 22 ♔d2 ♕g2 23 ♝b2 ♝a6 24 ♞d3 ♝xd3 25 ♔xd3 ♖bd8** Δ ♕e4+ **26 ♝f1 ♕e4+ 27 ♔c3 c5! 28 ♝xc5 ♕c6 29 ♔b3 ♖b8+ 30 ♔a3 ♖e5 31 ♝b4 ♕b6 0-1 Keene**

33 Karpov-Hubner
Montreal 79

1 c4 e5 2 ♘c3 ♞f6 3 ♘f3 ♞c6 4 g3 ♝b4 5 ♞d5 ♝c5 5...♘xd5 6 cxd5 ♘d4 7 ♘xd4 exd4 8 ♕c2 += **6 ♝g2 d6 7 0-0 0-0 8 d3 h6 9 e3 a5 10 ♞c3 ♞e7 11 h3 c6 12 b3 ♖e8 13 ♝b2 ♝b6 14 ♖e1 ♝d7 15 ♔h2 ♞g6** Δ d5 **16 ♞d2 ♝e6** 16...♕c7!? **17 ♞a4 ♝c7 18 d4** += **♖b8 19 ♖c1 b5?!** 19...h5!? Δ h4 **20 dxe5 ♞xe5 21 ♝xe5 dxe5 22 ♞c5 ♝d6 23 cxb5** 23 ♘xe6 ♖xe6 24 ♝xc6 ♝a3 **cxb5 24 ♕e2 ♕e7** 24...♝f5 25 ♝c6 **25 ♞xe6 ♕xe6 26 ♖c6 ♖ec8 27 ♖d1 ♖xc6 28 ♝xc6 b4** 28...e4!? 29 ♝xb5 h5 30 ♝c4 ♕e7! Δ h4; 30...♕e5? 31 ♝xf7+ ♔xf7 32 ♘c4 +− **29 ♖c1 ♝e7 30 ♕c4 ♕d6 31 ♞e4 ♞xe4 32 ♝xe4±** g6 33 ♔g2 ♔g7 34 ♝d5 f5 34...♖f8 35 e4 Δ ♕c7 **35 e4 f4 36 ♕d3 ♖b6 37 ♖c8 fxg3 38 fxg3 ♕d7?** Zeitnot

39 ♕c4?? 39 ♖g8+ ♔h7 40 ♖xg6!! ♔xg6 41 ♝f7+ +−; 40...♖xg6 41 ♝g8+ +− **♖f6! 40 ♖c7 ♕d6 41 h4 ♖f8 42 ♖a7 h5 43 ♝c6 ♕xc6 44 ♝xc6 ♖c8 45 ♖a6 ♝c5 46 g4 hxg4 47 ♔g3 ♖f8 48 ♖xa5 ♝f2+ 49 ♔xg4 ♖f4+ 50 ♔h3 ♖xh4+ 51 ♔g2 ♝d4 52 a4 bxa3 53 ♖xa3 ♖g4+ ½-½ Keene**

34 Grodzensky-Godes USSR 79

1 c4 ♘f6 2 ♘c3 e5 3 ♘f3 ♘c6 4
g3 ♗b4 4...g6?! 5 d4 exd4 6 ♘xd4
♗g7 7 ♘xc6 bxc6 8 ♗g2 += 5 ♗g2
5 ♘d5 ♘xd5 6 cxd5 ♘d4 7 ♘xd4
exd4 8 ♕c2! += ♗xc3 5...0-0 6 bxc3
0-0 7 0-0 ♖e8 8 d3 b6!? 9 ♘d2 ♗b7
10 ♘e4 ♘xe4 11 ♗xe4 ♘a5 12 ♗xb7
♘xb7 13 e4 c6 14 f4 += 14 ♕f3
♖c8 15 ♗d2 ♘c5 △ d5 exf4 15 ♗xf4
d5 16 cxd5 cxd5 17 exd5 ♕xd5
18 ♕f3 ♕d7! 18...♕xf3 19 ♖xf3 +=
19 ♖ae1 ♘c5 20 ♗d6?! ♘e6 21 ♗a3
♖ac8? 21...♖ad8! =+ 22 d4 h6 23
h4 ♘c7 24 ♕b7! ♖xe1 25 ♖xe1
♕g4 26 ♔g2 ♖e8 27 ♖xe8+ ♘xe8
28 ♗e7 ♕e2+ 29 ♔g1 ♕d1+ 30 ♔g2
♕c2+ 31 ♔h3 ♕f5+ 32 ♔g2= ♕e6
32...♔h7 33 ♕c6 33 ♕xa7 g6 34 ♔f2
♔h7 35 d5 ♕f5+ 36 ♔e2 ♕c2+ 37
♔f1 ♕d1+ 38 ♔f2 ♕d2+ 39 ♔f1
♕d3+ 40 ♔f2 ♘g7 41 ♗f8 ½-½ Gufeld

35 Ubilava-Vitolins USSR 79

1 c4 e5 2 ♘c3 ♘f6 3 ♘f3 ♘c6 4 g3
♘d4!? 4...♗b4 5 ♗g2 5 ♘xe5!? ♕e7
6 f4 d6 7 ♘d3 ♗f5 8 ♔f2!∞ ♘xf3+
6 ♗xf3 ♗b4 7 0-0 0-0 8 d3 ♖e8 9
a3 ♗xc3 10 bxc3 e4!= 11 ♗g2 h6 12
♕c2 ♕e7 13 ♗d2?! b6 14 a4 a5 15
♗e3 ♗b7 16 ♗d4 ♘h7 16...d6 17
♗xf6 ♕xf6 18 dxe4 ♕e6 =+ 17 ♕d2
♗c6 18 ♕f4 exd3 19 exd3 ♘g5 20 h4
♘e6 21 ♕d2 ♗xg2 22 ♔xg2 d5 22...
♕d6 23 ♗e3 ♕c6 24 ♔g1 d5 27 cxd5
♕xd5 =+ 23 cxd5 ♘xd4 24 cxd4
♕d7 25 ♔g1 ♕xd5 26 ♕f4 c6 27
♕c7 ♕xd4 28 ♕xc6 ♖ac8 29 ♕b7
♖c2 30 ♖c1 ♖ee2 31 ♖xc2 ♖xc2
32 ♕a8+ ♔h2 33 ♕f3 33 ♕e4+?
♕xe4 34 dxe4 ♖c4 35 ♖b1 ♖b4 -+
♕xa4 34 ♕xf7 ♖c5 35 ♖e1 ♕d4 36
♖e7 36 ♖e8 ♕d5 ♕g4 37 ♖d7 ♖e5
38 ♖d8 1-0 Georgadze

36 Kasparov-Mnatsakanian
USSR 79

1 c4 e5 2 ♘c3 ♘c6 3 g3 g6 4 ♗g2
♗g7 5 d3 d6 6 ♖b1 ♗e6 7 b4 ♕d7 8
b5 ♘d8 9 ♘d5!? 9 ♘f3 ♗h3 10 0-0
♗xg2 11 ♔xg2 ♘e7= c6 9...♘e7 10
♘xe7 ♕xe7 11 ♘f3 += 10 bxc6 bxc6
11 ♘c3 ♘e7 12 ♗a3 f5 13 ♕b3 0-0
14 ♘f3 ♘f7 15 0-0 ♕c8 16 ♗b2!
16 ♘d2 ♖b8 17 ♕a4 e4!∞ ♖b8 16...
♕a6 17 ♗a1 e4 18 dxe4 ♗xc4 19
♕b7 fxe4 20 ♘d2! ∝/+= 17 ♕a3
♕c7 18 ♗a1 ♖xb1 19 ♖xb1 ♖b8 20
♖xb8+ ♕xb8 21 ♘d2 += ♗f6 22
♘b3 e4?! 22...♕b6 23 ♕a4 += 23
♘d5?! 23 dxe4! ♗xc4 24 exf5 gxf5
25 ♘a5 ♗xe2 26 ♕c1! +=/± cxd5
23...♘xd5 24 cxd5 ♗xa1 25 dxe6
♘e5 26 ♘xa1 ♕b1+ 27 ♗f1 ♕xa1
28 ♕xd6 +- 24 ♗xf6 dxc4! 25 ♗xe7
cxb3 26 axb3 exd3 27 exd3 ♗xb3?!
27...♕c7! 28 ♗f6 ♘e5 29 b4 h6!≈
28 h3! += ♕b6 29 ♕c1 ♗e6 29...♕c5
30 ♕b2 ♕c2?! 31 ♕a3± 30 ♗f6 ♕c5
31 ♕f4 ♗d5? Zeitnot 31...♗d7 32
d4 ♕c7 33 ♕e3 += 32 ♕a4! +- ♔f8
33 ♕d7 1-0 Kasparov

37 Lein-Unzicker
South Africa 79

1 c4 e5 2 ♘c3 ♘c6 3 g3 g6 4 ♗g2
♗g7 5 e3 ♘ge7 6 ♘ge2 d6 7 0-0
7 ♖b1 △ b4 0-0 8 d3 ♗d7 8...♗e6 9
♘d5 9 ♖b1 ♕c8 10 ♖e1 ♖e8 11
♘d5 ♘xd5 12 cxd5 ♘e7 13 ♗d2 c6
14 ♘c3 ♗f5 15 dxc6 bxc6 16 ♕c2
♕a6 17 ♗f1 ♕c8 18 ♘e4 ♕d7 19 b4
+= ♖ed8 20 ♗g2 h6 21 ♖ec1 ♗e6
22 ♕a4 a6 23 ♕c2 ♗d5 24 ♗f1 ♗e6
25 ♗g2 ♗d5 26 ♗f1 ♗e6 27 ♗e1 ♖dc8
28 ♗g2 ♗d5 29 a4 f5 30 ♘d2 ♗xg2
31 ♔xg2 d5 32 ♘f3 e4 33 ♘d2 g5
34 ♕d1 ♖a7 35 ♘b3 ♘g6 △ ♘e5-f3
36 d4 f4 37 ♕h5 ♔h7 37...f3+ 38

♔h1 ♘f4!? 39 ♗d2 **38 ♚h1 ♖f8 39
♖c3 ♘e7 40 ♘c5 ♛c8 41 gxf4 gxf4
42 ♗d2 fxe3 43 fxe3 ♖f2 44 ♘b3
♖b7 45 ♖cc1 ♛f5 46 ♛xf5+ ♘xf5
47 ♖f1 ♖xd2!?∝ 48 ♘xd2 ♘xe3 49
♖fc1 ♘f5 50 ♖xc6 ♘xd4 51 ♖xa6
e3 52 ♘f1 e2 53 b5 ♘xb5** 53...exf1♛+
54 ♖xf1 △ ♖b1 +−; 53...♘f3 54 ♖e6
**54 axb5 ♖xb5 55 ♖e1 exf1♛+ 56
♖xf1 ♖b7 57 ♖d6 d4**

**58 ♖e1 ♚g8 59 ♖f1 ♚h7 60 ♖f5
♖e7 61 h4 ♖e5 62 ♖xe5 ♗xe5 63
♖d5 ♗g3 64 h5 ♗f2 65 ♚g2 ♗e3 66
♚f3 ♚g7 67 ♖f5 ♚g8 68 ♚e4 ♚g7
69 ♖f3 ♚g8 70 ♚d5 ♚g7 71 ♚e5
♚g8 72 ♚e6 ♗g5 73 ♚d7 ♚g7 74
♚e8 ♗f6 75 ♖f5 ♗g5 76 ♖f7+ ♚g8
77 ♖d7 ♗f6 78 ♖d5 ♚g7 79 ♖d6
♗e5 80 ♖g6+ ♚h7 81 ♖g2 d3** 81...
♗f4 82 ♚f7 d3 83 ♖g7+ ♚h8 84
♚g6! d2 85 ♖e7 d1♛ 86 ♖e8 mate
82 ♖d2 82 ♚f7? ♗c3 ♚g7 83 ♖xd3
**♚f6 84 ♖d5 ♚e6 85 ♖b5 ♗f4 86
♖b6+ ♚f5 87 ♚f7 ♗e3 88 ♖b5+ ♚e4
89 ♚g6 ♗c1 90 ♖b1 ♗d2 91 ♖d1
♗g5** 91...♗e3 92 ♖e1 △ ♖xe3+; 91...
♗f4 92 ♖e1+ **92 ♖e1+ ♚d5 93 ♖g1
♗e3** 93...♗f4 94 ♖f1 **94 ♖d1+ ♚c6
95 ♖d8 △ ♖h8, ♖xh6 1-0 Miles**

38 Grokhotov-Poliantsev USSR 79
1 c4 e5 2 ♘c3 ♘f6 3 ♘f3 d6 4 d4

e4!? 4...♘bd7 5 ♗g5 ♗e7 6 e3 0-0
7 ♛c2 +=; 5 e4 += **5 ♘g5** 5 ♘d2 ♗f5
6 e3 c6 7 ♗e2 d5 8 ♛b3 += **♗f5 6
g4 ♗xg4 7 ♗g2** 7 ♘gxe4 ♘xe4 8 ♘xe4
♗e7 9 ♘g3 c6= **♘c6!? 8 ♘gxe4 ♘xe4
9 ♗xe4 ♛d7** 9...g6!? **10 ♖g1 ♗f5
11 ♗h1?!** 11 ♗f3!? ♗g6 12 h4 +=
♗g6= 12 ♗e3 ♗e7 13 ♛b3?! 13 ♛a4
0-0 14 0-0-0 ♚h8= **♖b8 14 ♗xc6?!**
14 0-0-0∝ **♛xc6 15 d5 ♛d7 16 ♗xa7
♖a8 17 ♗d4** 17 ♛xb7?! 0-0 18 ♗d4
♖fb8 19 ♛c6 ♛c8! 20 ♘b5 ♖b7∝
0-0∝ 18 ♘d1?! 18 ♘e4!? **c5?!** 18...
♖fe8 19 ♛c3 ♗f8 20 h4?! f5! =+
**19 dxc6 bxc6 20 ♛c3 f6 21 ♛g3!?
♖fe8?!** 21...d5 **22 h4 d5 23 h5?!**
23 c5!? **♗b4+ 24 ♗c3** 24 ♚f1?! ♗xh5
25 ♗xf6 ♗xe2+∝ **♗xc3+ 25 ♘xc3
♗xh5 26 cxd5 cxd5 27 0-0-0 +=
♗xe2 28 ♖xd5 ♛f7 29 ♖c5** △ ♖c7
**♖ac8 30 ♖xc8 ♖xc8 31 b3 ♗h5
32 ♚b2 ♗g6 33 ♖d1 h5 34 ♚h3**
34 ♖d4 **♖c7 35 ♖d8+ ½-½ Gufeld**

39 I.Szabo-Biro Zamardi 79
**1 c4 e5 2 ♘c3 ♘f6 3 g3 c6 4 ♘f3
e4 5 ♘d4 ♛b6 6 ♘b3 a5 7 d3** N 7
♘a4!? ♛b4 8 ♘d4!; 7 d4?! **a4 8
♗e3!** 8 ♘d2 e3! 9 fxe3 ♘g4 10 ♘de4
♘xe3 11 ♛d2 ♘xf1∝ ½-½! Hofland-
Sosonko, Netherlands Final /8 **♛b4
9 ♘d2 d5?** 9...♛xb2? 10 ♗d4! (△
♘b5) c5 11 ♗xf6 gxf6 12 ♘dxe4
△ 13 ♖b1 ♛a3 14 ♘b5 ♛xa2 15
♘ec3 +−; 10...♛a3 11 dxe4±; 9...a3
10 ♖b1 axb2 11 ♛c2 exd3 (11...d5?
12 cxd5 cxd5 13 ♘xd5! +−) 12
exd3±; 9...exd3!? 10 exd3 ♛xb2
11 ♗d4 ♛a3 12 ♗g2∝ **10 ♗g2?!** 10
a3! ♛xb2? 11 ♗d4 +−; 10...♛a5 11
cxd5 cxd5 12 dxe4 ♘xe4 13 ♘dxe4
dxe4 14 ♗g2 ±/+−; 12...dxe4 13
♘c4 +− **♘g4 11 cxd5 ♘xe3 12 fxe3
♛xb2 13 ♖c1 exd3 14 exd3 ♗c5**

61

14...♗b4 15 ♖c2 ♕a3 16 ♘db1 ♗xc3+
17 ♘xc3±; 14...♗e7 15 ♘c4 ♕b4
16 a3! ♕c5 17 ♘e4 ♕a7 18 ♘ed6+
♗xd6 19 ♘xd6+ ♔d7 20 ♘c4 ±/+−;
19...♔e7 20 ♘xc8+ ♖xc8 21 ♕f3
±/+−; 16...♕b3 17 ♕xb3 axb3 18
♘b6 ♖xa3 19 ♘b1! +− 15 d4 ♗a7
16 0-0 0-0 17 ♔h1 cxd5 18 ♘xd5
♘c6 19 ♘de4? 19 ♖c2! ♕b5 20
♘c7 ±/+−; 20...♕a3 21 ♘c4 +−
f5 20 ♘d6 ♕xa2 20...♕a3 21 ♘b5
♕b2 22 ♖b1 ♕xa2 23 ♘dc7 ♗e6 24
d5 +− 21 ♖xc6?! 21 ♘c7! ♗e6 22
d5 +− bxc6 22 ♘e7+ ♔h8 23 ♗xc6
♗a6 24 ♗d5 ♕a3? 24...♕e2!∝ 25
♘g6+! hxg6 26 ♖f4 ♕xe3 27 ♖h4+
♕h6 28 ♖xh6+ gxh6 29 ♕xa4 ♖ab8
29...♗e2 30 ♗xa8 ♖xa8 31 ♘f7+!
♔g7 32 ♘e5 +− 30 ♕xa6 ♗xd4 31
♕d3 Zeitnot ♗g7 32 ♕c4 ♔h7 33
♕g2 ♖b2+ 34 ♔g1 ♖b1+ 35 ♔g2 ♖b2+
36 ♔h3 g5 37 ♘xf5 h5 38 ♘xg7
g4+ 39 ♔h4 ♖xh2+ 40 ♔g5 ♕xg7
41 ♕c7+ 1-0 Adorjan/I.Szabo

1 c4 ♘f6

40 Korchnoi-Diesen
Lone Pine 79
1 c4 ♘f6 2 ♘c3 e6 3 e4 c5 4 e5 ♘g8
5 d4 cxd4 6 ♕xd4 ♘c6 7 ♕e4 ♗b4!?
7...d6; 7...f5 8 ♕e2 a6 9 ♘f3 ♕b6∝
8 ♗d2 8 ♘f3 d6! d6! 9 exd6 9 ♘f3
dxe5 10 ♘xe5 ♘f6 11 ♘xc6? ♕xd2+!
−+; 9 f4 f5! =+; 9 ♕g4! dxe5 10
♕xg7 ♕f6 11 ♕g3! ♘h6 12 0-0-0
♘f5 13 ♘e4! ♗xd2+ 14 ♖xd2 ♕e7
15 ♕c3±; 14...♘xg3?! 15 ♘xf6+ ♔e7
16 hxg3 ♔xf6 17 ♘f3±; 9...♘xe5
10 ♕xg7 ♕f6 11 ♕xf6 ♘xf6 12 f4 ♘g6
13 ♘f3 ♗g7 ∝/+=; 11 ♕g3! += ♘f6
10 ♕h4 ♗xd6 10...♕xd6 11 0-0-0±
11 0-0-0 ♗d7 12 ♘f3 ±/+= h6 12...
0-0 13 ♗g5 ♗e7 14 ♘e4 ♘xe4 15

♗xe7 ♕xe7 16 ♕xe4 Δ ♗d3, h4±
13 ♘b5 ♗e7 14 ♗d3? 14 ♘c3! ♘d5?!
15 ♘d6+ ♗xd6 16 ♕xd8+ ♔xd8
17 cxd5± exd5 18 ♗xg7 ♗f4+ 19 ♔b1
♗f5+ 20 ♗d3; 15...♔f8? 16 ♗xg7+!
♔xg7 17 ♕g3+ ♔h7 18 ♘xf7 +−;
16...♔g8 17 ♕g3; 14...0-0 15 ♕g3±
♘b4!∓ 14...0-0 15 ♕h3 (Δ g4) e5?!
16 ♗f5 ♗xf5 17 ♕xf5 ♕c8 18 ♕xc8
♖axc8 19 ♖he1 ±/+− 15 ♗xb4 ♗xb4
16 ♗c2 16 a3 ♗e7; 16 ♕d4 0-0 Δ ♕a5
♕b8?! 16...♕a5! Δ 0-0, ♖ac8, ♖fd8
∓/−+ 17 ♕d4 0-0 17...♗xb5!? 18
cxb5 0-0 19 ♔b1 ♖d8 =+ 18 ♘d6
♗xd6 19 ♕xd6 ♕xd6 20 ♖xd6 ♗c6
=+ 21 ♘e5? Zeitnot 21 ♖hd1 ♘g4;
21 h3!? ♗e4? 21...♗xg2! 22 ♖g1
♗e4 ∓/−+ 22 f3 ♗xc2 23 ♔xc2 ♖fd8
24 ♖hd1 ♖xd6 25 ♖xd6 ♖c8 26
♔d3= ♔f8 27 b4 ♔e7 28 ♖d4 ♖c7
29 h4 g5 30 a3 ♘h5 31 hxg5 hxg5
32 ♔c3 f6 33 ♘g4 b6 34 ♘e3 ♘f4
35 ♖d2 35 g3?? ♘e2+ ♖d7 ½-½
Ciamarra

41 Tomaszewski-Barczay
Kecskemet 79
1 c4 ♘f6 2 ♘c3 e6 3 e4 c5 4 e5 ♘g8
5 d4 cxd4 6 ♕xd4 ♘c6 7 ♕e4 f6!?
N 7...f5; 7...d6; 7...♗b4 8 f4 ♘h6!
9 ♗d2 9 ♗d3! f5 10 ♕f3 += f5 10
♕e2 a6!? 11 ♘f3 b5 12 cxb5 axb5
13 ♘xb5 ♗a6∝ 14 ♕d1 14 ♕f2 ♕b8
15 a4 ♘g4 17 ♕g1 ♗xb5 18 ♗xb5
♕xb5 19 axb5 ♖xa1+ −+ ♕b6 15
♕b3 ♖b8 16 ♘d6+ ♗xd6 17 ♕xb6
♖xb6 18 ♗xa6 18 exd6 ♗xf1 19
♔xf1 ♖xb2! 20 ♘c3 ♖c2 21 ♗xg7
♖g8 22 ♗xh6 ♖gxg2 23 ♖g1 ♖gf2+
24 ♔e1 ♖xf3∓; 23 ♘h4 ♖gf2+ 24
♔g1 ♘d4 −+ ♗c5 19 ♖c1 ♖xa6 20
♖xc5 ♖xa2 21 ♖c2 ♔e7 =+ 22 ♔e2
♖b8 23 ♖b1 ♘f7 24 h4 ♘b4 25
♖c4? 25 ♗xb4!? ♖xb4 26 g3 ♖b3

62

27 ♔f2 ♘h6 =+ ♞d5 26 b4 d6∓ 27
b5 dxe5 28 fxe5 h5 29 ♖b3 ♔d7
30 ♔d3 ♖ba8 31 ♔d4 ♞b6 32 ♖cb4?
32 ♖c6!? ♖8a4+ 33 ♔d3 ♘d5 =+
♚c7 33 ♔d3 ♖d8+ 34 ♖d4 ♞xe5+!
35 ♚c3? 35 ♘xe5 ♖xd2+ 36 ♔xd2
♖xd4+ −+; 35 ♔e3 ♘ec4+ −+ ♖xd4
36 ♞xd4 ♞d5 mate 0-1 Tompa

42 Korchnoi-Unzicker
South Africa 79

1 c4 ♞f6 2 ♞c3 e6 3 e4 d5 4 cxd5
4 e5 ♘fd7 5 cxd5 exd5 5 e5 ♞e4
6 ♞f3 ♞c6 7 ♗b5 ♞xc3 7...♗e7 8
♕a4!? 8 dxc3 ♗e7 9 ♞d4 ♗d7 10
♞xc6 bxc6 11 ♗d3 0-0 12 ♕c2 h6
13 ♗e3 f5? 13...f6 += 14 f4± △ g4
c5 15 c4 d4 16 ♗d2 ♗e6 17 0-0-0
♕d7 18 ♖df1 ♖f7 19 g4 ♖af8 20
gxf5 ♗xf5 21 ♖hg1 ♗xd3 22 ♕xd3
♕f5 23 ♚c2 g5!? 24 h4 ♔h7 25
hxg5 hxg5 26 ♖g2 ♔g6 26...gxf4?
27 ♖h1+ +− 27 ♖h1 ♖h7 28 ♖xh7
♚xh7 29 fxg5 ♔g6 30 ♖h2 ♕xd3+
31 ♚xd3 ♔f5 32 b4! cxb4 32...♔xe5
33 ♖e2+ ♔d6 34 bxc5+ ♔d7 35 c6+
♔d8 36 ♖xe7 △ ♗b4+ +− 33 ♖f2+
♔e6 33...♔xe5 34 ♖e2+ ♔d6 35
♖xe7! 34 ♖xf8 ♗xf8 35 ♚xd4 c5+
36 ♚e4 a5 37 ♗e3 a4 38 g6 a3 38...
b3 39 axb3 axb3 40 ♗c1 +− 39 g7!
♗xg7 40 ♗xc5 ♗xe5 41 ♗xb4 ♗b2
42 ♔d3 ♚e5 43 ♗c5 ♗c1 44 ♚c3 ♚e4
45 ♚b4 ♔d3 46 ♔b5 ♚c2 47 ♗d6
♗e3 48 ♗xa3 ♔b1 49 ♗c5 1-0 Miles

43 Liebert-A.Schneider
Prievidza 79

1 c4 ♞f6 2 ♞f3 g6 3 ♞c3 d5 4 cxd5
♞xd5 5 ♕a4+ 5 e4!? ♘xc3 6 dxc3
+= ♗d7 6 ♕c2 6 ♕h4!? ♞b4 7 ♕b1
c5 8 a3 ♞4c6 9 b4?! 9 e3 △ d3, ♗e2=
♗f5?! 10 d3 10 e4!? ♗g4 11 bxc5
♕d7 12 ♗b2 ♗g7 13 ♘d5! += ♗g7

11 ♗b2 ♞d7! 12 ♞e4 0-0 −+ 13 ♗xg7
♔xg7 14 ♞g3 ♗g4 15 ♞d2 ♖c8 16
b5 ♞a5 −+ 17 h3 ♗e6 18 e3 c4! 19
dxc4 ♞e5! 20 f4 ♞exc4 21 ♗xc4
♗xc4 22 ♕b2+ f6 23 a4 ♕b6 24
♔f2 ♖fd8 25 ♖he1 ♖d3 26 ♖a?

26...♗b3!! 27 ♞xb3 27 ♖xb? ♖xd2+
28 ♕xd2 ♘xb3 −+; 27. ♙xb3?!
28 ♘xb3 ♖cc3 29 ♘d4 e5 3 ♙a5! +=
♞c4 28 ♕c1 ♞xe3! 29 ♙3 29
♕xc8? ♘g4+ −+ ♖c2+ 30 ♔ ♖cc3
31 ♞f1 ♕d6! 32 ♞c5 ♕xc5 ♕xd3
♖xa3 34 ♕xa3 ♕xa3+ 35 ♙3 ♚c5
0-1 Hardicsay

44 Ftacnik-Hardicsay Prague
1 ♞f3 ♞f6 2 c4 g6 3 ♞c3 d ♙4 cxd5
♞xd5 5 e4!? ♞xc3 5...♘b6?! 6 d4
♗g4!? 7 ♗b5+? c6 8 ♗e2 ♗g7 9 ♗e3
♗xf3! 10 ♗xf3 ♘c4 =+; 7 ♗e2 ♗g7
8 ♗e3 0-0 9 ♘e5! += 6 dxc3! ♕xd1+
7 ♔xd1 f6 △ e5, ♗e6= 8 e5 N 8 ♗c4
e5 9 ♗e3 ♘d7 △ ♗c5= ♞c6! 9 exf6
9 ♗f4 ♗g4 10 exf6 0-0-0+!∓; 9 ♗b5!?
♗g4!= exf6 10 ♗f4 10 ♗c4 ♗g4 11
♖e1+ ♘e5! =+ ♗d6 11 ♗xd6 cxd6=
12 ♗c4 ♗g4! 13 ♖e1+ ♔d7 13...♘e5!?
14 ♗d5 0-0-0 15 ♖e3= 14 h3!? ♗xf3
15 gxf3 ♖ae8 16 ♖e3! g5 16...f5!
17 f4 ♖e4 18 ♖xe4 fxe4 19 ♔e2 ♘e7
20 ♖d1 ♔c6 △ d5 =+ 17 ♔d2 a6 18
f4! gxf4 19 ♖xe8 19 ♖f3 ♘e5 20

☐xf4 ♘xc4+ 21 ☐xc4 ☐hg8= **☒xe8
20 ☒g1 ♞e5 21 ♗d5**

21...♞g6! 22 h4 22 ♗xb7 ☐b8 23
♗xa6 ☐xb2+∓; 22 ♗f7 ☐e7 23 ♗xg6
hxg6 24 ☐xg6 f3!= **☒e5! 23 ♗f3**
23 ♗xb7? ☐b5∓ **d5 24 h5 ♞h4 25
☒g7+ ♚c6 26 ♗d1 h6 27 ☒g4 ♞f5
28 ☒xf4 ♚c7!** △ ♘d6= **29 ♗g4** 29
♗f3! ♚d8 △ ♚e7= **♞d6 30 ♗f3 f5
31 ☒d4 ♞e4+ 32 ♗xe4 fxe4 33 c4**
Zeitnot **☒xh5 34 cxd5 ♚d6 35 ☒xe4
☒xd5+ 36 ♚c3** =/=+ 36 ♚e3?? ☐e5
−+ ½-½ **Hardicsay**

45 Angantysson-Quinteros
USA 79

**1 ♞f3 ♞f6 2 c4 g6 3 g3 ♗g7 4 ♗g2
0-0 5 0-0 d6 6 ♞c3 ♞c6 7 ☒b1** 7 d4;
7 d3 **d5!?= 8 cxd5 ♞xd5 9 ♞xd5
♛xd5 10 b3 ♗f5 11 d3 ♛d7 12 ♗b2
e5** 12...♗xb2 13 ☐xb2 ♗h3= **13 b4
☒fe8 14 b5 ♞d8 15 ♛b3 a6 16 a4
axb5 17 axb5 c5?!** 17...♗h3 18 ☐fc1±
**18 ♞d2!± ♗h3 19 ♗xh3 ♛xh3 20
♛d5! ♞e6 21 ♛xb7 ☒ab8 22 ♚c6!
☒ec8 23 ♛e4 ♞c7 24 ♗xe5 ☒e8 25
♗xc7! +− ☒xe4 26 ♞xe4 ☒b7 27
b6 ♗f8 28 ☒fc1 ♛e6 29 ♞xc5 ♗xc5
30 ☒xc5 ♛a2 31 ☒bc1 h5 32 ♗e5 ♚h7
33 ☒c8 g5 34 ☒1c6** △ ☐h8 mate **f6
35 ☒8c7+ ☒xc7 36 bxc7 +− 1-0
Gheorghiu**

46 Godes-Soloviev USSR 79

1 c4 ♞f6 2 g3 g6 2...c6; 2...e5 **3 ♗g2
d5 4 cxd5 ♞xd5 5 ♞c3** 5 e4 += **♞b6!?**
5...♘xc3 += **6 h4!?** 6 ♞f3 ♗g7 7 0-0
0-0 8 d4 ♞c6 9 e3 e5 10 d5 ♞a5 11
e4 c6 12 ♗g5 += **h5?!** 6...h6 **7 d4
♗g7 8 d5** 8 ♞f3?! **0-0** 8...c6 9 e4 0-0
10 ♞ge2 += **9 ♗g5 ♞c4 10 ♛b3 ♞d6
11 e4 c6 12 ♞ge2 cxd5 13 ♞xd5
♞c6 14 0-0± ♚h7?!** 15 ☒ad1 △ e5
**f6 16 ♗e3 ♗g4 17 f3 ♗e6 18 f4 +−
1-0 Gufeld**

Queen's Pawn

47 Romanishin-Miles Riga 79

**1 d4 ♞f6 2 ♞f3 e6 3 g3 b5 4 ♗g2
♗b7 5 0-0 c5 6 ♗g5!?** 6 c3 ♗e7 6...
cxd4 7 ♞xd4 ♗xg2 8 ♚xg2 a6 +=/=
**7 dxc5 ♗xc5 8 ♞c3 a6 9 e4 h6!?
10 ♗xf6 gxf6!?** 10...♛xf6 11 e5 +=
11 e5 f5 12 ♞e2 ♞c6 13 ♞f4 △ ♘h5
h5 14 h4 14 ♛e2 h4!? **♛c7 15 ♛e2
0-0-0 16 c3** 16 b4!? (△ c4/a4) 16...
♞d4!? **☒dg8 17 ♚h2 d6** 17...☐g4∝;
17...f6∝ **18 ♞d3 ♗xe5 19 ♞fxe5
♗xg2 20 ♚xg2** 20 ♞xf7 ♗xf1 21
♛xe6+ ♚d7 22 ♞xc5 ♛xe6 23 ♞xe6
♗c4! 24 ♞eg5 ♗xf7 25 ♞xf7 ☐h7
26 ♞xd6+ ♚c7 27 ♞xf5 ☐f7∓; 22
♛xd7+ ♚xd7 23 ♞xc5+ dxc5 24
♞xh8 ♗c4! −+ **dxe5**

21 a4! 21 ♘xe5 ♗d6 =+/∓ **♗d6α 22 axb5 axb5 23 ♖fd1** 23 ♘b4!? **♕b7+** 23...♖d8!? **24 ♕h2 e4 25 ♘b4α ⊥-⊥** 25...♗c7 26 ♘a6 f4!? 27 ♗xc7 ♔xc7 28 ♕d2 fxg3+ 29 fxg3 ♖d8 30 ♕f4+ ♔c8 31 ♕e5; 31 ♖d4!? α/±; 26... ♕b6! 27 ♘xc7 ♔xc7 28 ♕d2 ♖d8 α/=+; 25...♗xb4? 26 cxb4 ♖d8 27 ♖dc1+ Δ ♖a5, ♖c5∓ **Miles/Speelman**

48 Cibulka-Hardicsay
Prievidza 79

1 d4 g6 2 ♘f3 ♗g7 3 c3 d6 4 ♗f4 ♘d7! Δ e5 **5 e3 e5 6 ♗g3** 6 dxe5 dxe5 7 ♗g5 f6 8 ♗h4 ♘h6!∓ Terebesi-Hardicsay, Hungary 78 **♘h6! 7 ♗c4** 7 h3! ♕e7 =+ **♘f5! 8 0-0 ♕e7** 8...h5?! **9 e4 ♘xg3 10 hxg3 0-0 11 ♘bd2 exd4 12 cxd4 c5! 13 dxc5 dxc5 14 ♕c2!** **♘b6 15 ♗b3 ♗d7 16 ♘c4 ♘xc4 17 ♗xc4 ♗c6 18 ♗d5! ♗xd5 19 exd5 b5 20 ♖ad1 ♕d6 21 b3 h6 22 ♖fe1 ♖fe8 23 ♕d3 a6 24 ♖xe8+ ♖xe8 25 ♕f1 ♖d8 26 ♕c2 ♖c8 27 ♕g1 c4! -+ 28 bxc4 bxc4 29 ♕e4 c3 30 ♘e1 ♕e5! 31 ♕xe5 ♗xe5 32 ♕f1 ♕f8 33 ♕e2 ♖b8 34 ♖c1 ♕e7 35 f4 ♗f6 36 ♘c2 ♕d6 37 ♕d3 ♕xd5 38 g4 ♕c5 39 ♘e3 ♖d8+ 40 ♕e4 ♖d4+! 41 ♕f3 ♖d2 0-1** 42 ♖c2 ♗d4 43 ♔e4 h5! -+ **Hardicsay**

49 Puschmann-Honfi Budapest 79

1 d4 ♘f6 2 ♘f3 g6 3 ♗f4 ♗g7 4 e3 d6 5 h3 0-0 6 ♗c4 b6 7 0-0 c5 8 c3 8 dxc5?! bxc5 9 ♗d5? ♘xd5 10 ♕xd5 ♕b6∓; 8 ♕e2!? **♗a6 9 ♘bd2?!** 9 ♗xa6 ♘xa6 10 ♕e2 ♕c8 11 ♘bd2 ♕b7 12 a4= **♗xc4 10 ♘xc4 b5! 11 ♘cd2 ♘c6 12 a4?!** 12 dxc5 dxc5 13 e4 **b4 13 ♗g3** 13 dxc5? bxc3 14 bxc3 ♘d5 15 cxd6 ♘xc3 16 dxe7 ♕xe7 17 ♕e1 ♘b4 -+; 13 cxb4?! ♘xb4 14 dxc5 dxc5 =+ **bxc3 14**

bxc3 **♕a5! 15 ♘b3 ♕xc3 16 ♖c1 ♕b4 17 dxc5 d5 =+ 18 ♘bd4 ♘a5 19 ♘e5 ♖fc8!** 19...♘c4? 20 ♘dc6 ♕xc5 21 ♕d4! += **20 ♘d3 ♕b7 21 ♖b1 ♕d7 22 ♕c2 ♘e4 23 ♗h2 ♘c4 -+ 24 c6 ♕e8 25 ♖b5 ♘a3 26 ♕a2 ♘xb5 27 axb5 e5 28 ♘e2 ♕e6 29 f3 ♘d6 30 ♘c5 ♕e7 31 ♕xd5 ♘xb5 32 ♘b7** a6 33 ♖c1 ♖c7 34 f4 ♕a3 35 ♕e4 ♖e8 36 fxe5 ♖ce7 37 ♕f3 ♗xe5 38 ♗xe5 ♖xe5 39 c7 ♖c8 40 ♕f6 ♕xe3+ 41 ♕h1 ♕xe2 42 ♘d8 ♖f5 0-1 **Honfi**

1 d4 d5 2 c4 dxc4

50 Kaufman-J.Whitehead USA 79

1 d4 d5 2 c4 dxc4 3 e4 e5 3...♘f6 4 e5 ♘d5 5 ♗xc4 ♘c6 (5...♘b6!? Δ ♘c6, ♗f5) 6 ♘e2 ♘b6 7 ♗d3 ♗e6 8 ♘bc3 ♕d7 9 ♘e4± Korchnoi-Suetin, Budva 67; 5...e6 6 ♘f3 ♗e7 7 0-0 +=; 3...c5 4 d5!? ♘f6 5 ♘c3 b5 6 e5 b4 7 exf6 bxc3 8 bxc3 ♘d7≈ **4 ♘f3 exd4** 4...♗b4+ 5 ♗d2 ♗xd2+ 6 ♕xd2 exd4 7 ♕xd4 ♕xd4 8 ♘xd4 ♗d7 9 ♗xc4 ♘c6 10 ♘xc6 ♗xc6 11 ♘c3 += Bagirov-Matulovic, Titovo Uzice 78; 5 ♘c3 exd4 6 ♕xd4 ♕xd4 7 ♘xd4 c6 8 ♗xc4 ♘e7 9 ♗e3 0-0 10 0-0-0 +=; 7...♘f6 8 f3 ♗d7 9 ♗xc4 ♘c6 10 ♘xc6 ♗xc6 11 ♗g5 += **5 ♗xc4** 5 ♕xd4 ♕xd4 6 ♘xd4 ♗c5 7 ♘b5 ♘a6 8 ♗xc4 (8 ♗f4 ♗e6!) c6 9 ♘5a3 (9 ♘5c3 ♘b4 10 ♘a3 ♘f6 11 0-0 b5 =+) b5 10 ♗b3 ♘f6= **♘c6** 5...♘b4+ 6 ♘bd2 ♘c6 7 a3 ♗xd2+ 8 ♕xd2?! ♗g4! 9 ♕f4 ♗h5∓; 7 0-0 ♗e6 8 ♗xe6 fxe6 9 ♘b3 (9 ♘c4 ♘f6 10 a3 ♗e7=) ♕d7 10 ♘bxd4 ♘xd4 11 ♕xd4 ♕xd4≈; 6 ♗d2 ♗xd2 7 ♘bxd2 ♘c6 (7...♘h6!?α) 8 0-0 ♘f6 9 e5 ♘g4 (9...♘d5 10 ♕b3 ♘ce7 11 ♘xd4 0-0 12 ♖ad1± Bagirov-Petrushin, USSR 77) 10 h3 ♘h6 11 ♘b3 +=; 8...♕f6!?

Romanishin **6 0-0 ♗c5?!** 6...♗e6 7 ♘xe6 fxe6 8 ♕b3 ♕d7 9 ♕xb7 ♖b8 10 ♕a6 ♘f6 11 ♘bd2 ♗e7 12 a3 0-0 13 b4 △ ♗b2, ♘b3, ♖ad1± **7 ♘g5 ♘h6 8 ♘xf7! ♘xf7 9 ♗xf7+ ♔xf7 10 ♕h5+ g6** 10...♔g8 11 ♕xc5 ♕e7!? 12 ♕xe7 ♘xe7 13 ♗f4 +=; 12 ♕b5 ♕xe4; 12 ♕c2 ♘b4 **11 ♕xc5 ♕e7 12 ♕c2** +=/± **♖d8?!** 12...♖e8 13 ♕b3+ ♗e6 14 ♕xb7?? ♘b4 15 ♘a3 ♖eb8 −+; 13 ♘d2 ♘b4 14 ♕d1 c5 15 f4 △ f5 +=; 12...♗e6!? 13 f4 ♘b4 14 ♕d1 ♕c5 ∞/±; 14 ♕f2 ♕c5!? (△ ♔g7, ♖af8-f7, ♖hf8) 15 f4± **13 ♘d2 ♘b4** 13...♗e6 **14 ♕d1 d3 15 ♘f3! ♖e8 16 ♘g5+ ♔g7 17 ♗d2 ♗c2** 17...h6 18 ♗c3+ ♔g8 19 ♕b3+ ♔f8 20 ♗xb4 c5 21 ♗xc5 +− **18 ♗c3+ ♔g8 19 ♕xd3** +− **♕xg5** 19...♘xa1 20 ♕d4 **20 ♕xc2 b6** 20...♗h3 21 ♕b3+ **21 f4 ♕c5+ 22 ♔h1 ♕c4 23 f5 ♖xe4 24 fxg6 hxg6 25 ♕d2** △ ♕d8+ **♗h3 26 ♕h6** 26 gxh3? ♖e2 27 ♕xe2 ♕xe2 28 ♖cd1 ♕h5∓ **♗xg2+ 27 ♔g1 1-0 Ciamarra/A.Smith**

51 Botterill-Muir
British Final 79

1 d4 d5 2 c4 dxc4 3 ♘f3 ♘f6 4 ♕a4+ ♘bd7 4...c6; 4...♘c6!? 5 ♘c3 ♘d5 6 ♕xc4? ♘db4 7 ♕b3 e5!∓ Botterill-Miles, Telex 79; 6 e4! ♘b6 7 ♕d1 ♗g4 8 d5 ♘e5 9 ♗f4∞ **5 ♘c3 e6 6 e4 ♗e7** 6...c5 7 d5 exd5 8 e5!± **7 ♕xc4 0-0 8 e5?!** 8 ♗e2 ♘b6 8...♘d5!? 9 ♘xd5 exd5 10 ♕xd5 ♖e8 11 ♔d1∞ **9 exf6 ♘xc4 10 fxe7 ♕xe7 11 ♗xc4 b6 12 0-0 ♗b7 13 ♗e2 c5 14 ♗g5 f6?!** 14...♕c7≈ **15 ♗e3 cxd4 16 ♗xd4 ♖ac8 17 ♗d1 ♔h8 18 ♗b3 e5?** 18...♗a6!? △ ♗c4 **19 ♘e6 ♖fe8 20 f4± exf4 21 ♗xf4 ♕b4 22 ♖ad1 h5?! 23 ♖d4 ♕a5 24 ♗g3! b5 25 ♖h4 b4 26 ♘d5 g6**

27 ♘df4 27 ♘xf6! ♖xe6 28 ♗xe6 ♕b6+ 29 ♗f2 ♕xe6 30 ♗d4 +− **♗e4? 27...♔h7 28 ♗f2± 28 ♘xh5 +− gxh5 29 ♖xe4 ♖c6 30 ♖fe1 ♕b6+ 31 ♗f2 ♕b8 32 ♗d4 ♕c8 33 ♗xf6+ ♔h7 34 ♘g5+ ♔g6 35 ♖xe8 ♕g4 36 ♖g8+ ♔f5 37 ♘f3 ♕f4 38 ♗g5 ♕c7 39 ♖e5+ ♔g4 40 ♗d2+ 1-0 Botterill**

52 Ravikumar-Botterill England 79

1 d4 ♘f6 2 ♘f3 d5 3 c4 dxc4 4 e3 e6 5 ♗xc4 c5 6 0-0 a6 7 a4 ♘c6 8 ♘c3 ♗e7 9 ♕e2 ♕c7 10 ♖d1 0-0 11 e4? 11 b3 ♗d7 12 ♗b2 ♖ac8 13 d5! += Botvinnik-Euwe, Groningen 46; 11 b3 ♗d7 12 ♗b2 cxd4 13 exd4 ♘a5 14 ♘e5≈ Botvinnik **♘g4∓ 12 dxc5** 12 d5 ♘d4; 12 ♗e3 cxd4 13 ♗xd4 ♘xd4 14 ♖xd4 ♗c5 **♗xc5 13 ♗e3 ♘xe3 14 fxe3 b6** 14...♘e5∓ **15 ♔h1 ♗b7 16 ♖ac1 ♘e5 17 ♗a2 ♘g4 18 b4! ♗xe3 19 ♘d5 ♕xc1 20 ♖xc1 ♗xc1 21 ♘xb6 ♖ad8** △ ♖d1+ **22 ♗b3 ♗e3 23 a5**

Diagram

23...♖d3 24 ♗c2 ♖a3 25 g3 25 h3 ♖a1+ 26 ♘e1 ♗f2 27 ♕xg4 ♗xe1 28 ♔h2 ♗xb4 −+ **♖a1+** 25...♗xb6 26 axb6 ♖e3! 27 ♕f1 f5 −+ **26 ♔g2 ♖a2 27 ♕c4** 27 ♔h3 ♗xe4 28 ♔xg4 ♗xb6 29 axb6 ♖xc2 −+ **♖xc2+ 28**

♛xc2 ♗xb6 29 ♕e2 ♗a7 30 ♘d2 f5
31 b5 fxe4! 32 ♕xg4 e3+ 33 ♘e4
e2 0-1 Botterill

53 Spassov-Marszalek Warsaw 79

1 d4 d5 2 c4 dxc4 3 ♘f3 ♘f6 4 e3
♗g4 5 ♗xc4 e6 6 0-0 6 h3! ♘bd7 7
h3 ♗h5 8 ♘c3 ♗d6 9 ♗e2 0-0 9...
♗g6!? 10 e4 e5 11 d5 11 dxe5! +=
♗g6! 12 ♘d2 12 ♗g5 ♗e7! △ ♘xd5
♗b4 12...a6!? 13 ♗f3 c6 14 dxc6 bxc6
15 ♕a4 ♕a5! 16 ♕c2 ♗xc3 16...♘c5!?
17 ♘c4 ♕c7∞ 17 bxc3 ♘b6 18 a4!
♘bd5 19 ♗a3 ♖fd8 20 ♖fc1 ♕a6
21 g3 ♖ab8 22 ♗g2 ♖d7 23 a5! ♘c7
24 ♘b3± ♘e6 25 f3 h5 26 h4 ♕d3?!
27 ♕xd3 ♖xd3 28 ♖ab1 ♘d7 29
♖f2 c5 30 ♗f1 ♖d6 31 ♗c4 +- ♔h7
32 ♖d1! ♖xd1 33 ♖xd1 ♘df8 34
♖d6 ♖c8 35 a6 ♖c7 36 ♘a5 ♘d7
37 ♗d5 ♘f6 38 ♗b7 ♘e8 39 ♖d5
f6 40 ♘c6 ♗f7 41 ♘xa7 1-0 Pytel

54 Unzicker-Miles
South Africa 79

1 d4 d5 2 c4 dxc4 3 ♘f3 ♘f6 4 e3
♗g4 5 ♗xc4 e6 6 ♘c3 ♘bd7 7 0-0
♗d6 8 h3 ♗h5 9 e4 e5 10 ♗e3 0-0
11 ♗e2 ♖e8 12 d5 ♗g6 12...♘c5 13
♕c2 △ b4; 12...♘c5 13 ♕d2 13 ♘d2
♗c5 14 ♗xc5 ♘xc5 15 ♗b5! 15 ♗f3?
c6! =+ Hubner-Miles, Buenos Aires
78 ♖e7 16 ♖e1

16...♖c8 16...c6!? 17 dxc6 bxc6 18
♗xc6 ♖c8 19 ♗d5 ♖d7 20 ♕f3!
♘cxe4 21 ♗xe4 ♖xd2 22 ♗xg6 hxg6=;
20 f3 ♘d3; 19...♘d3 20 ♖e3 ♘xb2
(1) 21 ♕b1 ♖xc3; (2) 21 ♕b3 ♖b8;
(3) 21 ♕c1 ♘a4; (4) 21 ♕c2 ♘xd5;
19 ♗b5 a6 △ ♖d7 17 b4 c6? 17...♘cd7
18 bxc5 18 dxc6 bxc6 △ ♖d7; 18
♗f1 ♘a6 cxb5 19 ♘b3! 19 ♘xb5
♖xc5 20 a4 f6 21 ♘a3 ♖ec7 b4 20
d6! ♖d7 20...bxc3 21 dxe7 ♕xe7
22 f3 21 ♘d5 ♘xe4 21...♘xd5 22
♕xd5 ♕e8 23 a3 +- 22 ♘e7+ ♖xe7
23 dxe7 ♕xe7 24 ♕d5! ♘c3 24...
♘xc5 25 ♖ac1! b6 26 ♖xe5 +-;
24...♕h4 25 g3 25 ♕xe5 ♕xe5 26
♖xe5 ♔f8 26...♗b1 27 ♖e3 △ ♖xc3
27 a3! bxa3 27...♗c2 28 axb4 ♗xb3
29 ♖e3 +- 28 ♖xa3 f6 29 ♖e3 ♘b5
30 ♖a5 a6 31 ♖a1 ♗f7 32 ♖d1! △
♖d7 ♗xb3 32...♖c7?? 33 ♖d8+ +-
33 ♖xb3 ♖xc5 34 ♖d7 b6 35 ♖g3
g5 36 ♖xh7 ♘d6 36...♖c7 37 ♖xc7
♘xc7 38 ♖c3 ♘d5 39 ♖d3 △ ♖d7
37 ♖d3 ♖c6 38 ♖d7 ♘e4 39 ♖a7
39 f3 ♖c1+ 40 ♖d1; 39...♘c5 40
♖7d6 ♖c1+ 40 ♔h2 ♖h1+ 41 ♔xh1
♘xf2+ 42 ♔g1 ♘xd3 43 ♖xa6 ♔f7
44 ♖xb6 ♔g6 45 ♔f1 ♔f5 46 ♔e2
♘e5 47 ♖b4 ♘g6 48 ♖a4 ♘e7 49
♖c4 ♘g6 50 ♔e3 ♘h4 51 g3 ♘g6 52
♖c5+ ♔e6 53 ♔e4 ♘e7 54 ♖a5 ♔f7
55 ♖a7 ♔e6 56 h4 ♘c8 57 ♖a6+ ♘d6+

58 ♖xd6+ ♛xd6 59 hxg5 ♛e6 60
gxf6 ♛xf6 61 ♛f4 ♛g6 62 ♛g4 ♛f6
63 ♛h5 1-0 Miles

55 Diesen-Matulovic Bajmok 78
**1 d4 d5 2 c4 dxc4 3 ♘f3 ♘f6 4 e3
♗g4 5 ♗xc4 e6 6 h3 ♗h5 7 ♘c3** 7 g4
♗g6 8 ♘e5 ♘bd7 9 ♘xg6 hxg6 10
♕f3 c5 11 0-0 cxd4 12 exd4 ♗e7
13 ♘c3 ♘b6 14 ♗b5+ ♔f8 15 ♗e3 +=
Hort-Miles, IBM 78 **♘bd7 8 ♗e2 ♗d6
9 0-0 0-0 10 e4 e5 11 dxe5** 11 d5
♗g6!; 11 ♗e3 ♖e8= **♘xe5 12 ♘d4**
12 ♘xe5 ♗xe2 13 ♕xe2 ♗xe5 14
♗g5 ♕e8=; 12 ♗g5 ♗xf3 13 ♗xf3 h6!=
♗g6?! 12...♗xe2 13 ♕xe2 ♘g6 14
♘f5 ♗e5 15 f4 ♗xc3 16 bxc3 ♖e8
17 e5 ♘d5 18 ♕f3 +=; 12...♘c5!=
Byrne 13 **♗g5 ♗e7 14 f3!** N 14 ♘f5
♗xf5 15 exf5 c6 16 ♕xd8 ♖fxd8 17
♖ad1 ♖xd1 18 ♖xd1 ♖d8= Smyslov-
Matulovic, Palma 70; 16 ♕c2!? △
♖ad1 += **♗c5** 14...c6?? 15 f4; 14...h6
15 ♗e3 **15 ♗e3 ♘c6 16 ♘c2± ♛e7
17 ♛c1 ♖ad8 18 ♗xc5 ♕xc5+ 19
♛e3 ♕xe3+?!** 19...♘d4 20 ♔h1?!
♘h5! 21 f4 ♘g3 22 ♕xg3 ♘xe2 23
♘xe2 ♕xc2∓; 20 ♘xd4 ♕xd4 21
♕xd4 ♖xd4 22 ♖fd1 ♖fd8 23 ♖xd4
♖xd4 24 ♖d1 △ ♔f2-e3±; 22 ♘b5?!
♖d2 23 ♗c4 c6 24 ♘xa7? ♖a8 **20
♘xe3 ♘d4 21 ♗c4 c6 22 a4!** △ a5-a6
♖fe8 22...♘e8 23 f4!± **23 ♖ad1 a6
24 a5 c5 25 ♘a4! ♘c6 26 ♘xc5 ♘xa5
27 b4 ♖c8** 27...♘xc4 28 ♘xc4 ♖b8
29 e5 ♘h5 30 ♘d6 +-; 28...b5 29
♘d6 **28 ♖c1** 28 ♗a2!? **♘xc4 29 ♘xc4
♖c6 30 ♘a5 ♖b6 31 ♖c4 h6** 31...♖e7
32 ♖d1 h6± **32 ♖d1 ♘h5?!** 32...♘h7
△ f5 **33 ♘axb7 ♖eb8 34 ♖d7 ♘f4
35 h4 ♘e6 36 ♘xe6 ♖xe6 37 ♖d8+!
♖xd8** 37...♖e8 38 ♖xe8+ ♖xe8 39
♘d6 ♖d8 40 ♖c6 ♖a8 41 ♔f2 △ ♔e3-
d4±; 39...♖f8 40 ♖c6 ♖b8 41 ♖xa6

♖xb4 42 ♖a8+ ♔h7 43 ♖f8; 39
♘c5 ♖c8 40 ♖d4 ♖a8 41 ♖d6 a5
42 b5 +-; 40...♖c6 41 ♖d8+ ♔h7 42
♖a8 +-; 40...a5!∞ **38 ♘xd8 ♖b6 39
♘c6 f6** 39...♗h7 40 ♘e7+ ♔f8 41
♘d5 +- **40 ♘e7+ ♛h7 41 ♘d5 ♖b8
42 ♖c7 ♛g8 43 ♘e7+ ♛h7 44 ♘d5
♛g8 45 ♛f2! ♛f8 46 ♖c6 ♗f7 47
♖b6! ♖d8!** 47...♖xb6 48 ♘xb6 ♔e7
49 ♔e3 +- **48 ♖xa6 ♗xd5 49 exd5
♖xd5 50 ♖a8+ ♛f7 51 ♖a7+ ♛f8 52
♖a2** △ ♖b2, b5, ♔e3 **♖d4 53 ♖b2
♛e7 54 b5 ♛d7 55 g4 f5?** 55...h5 56
♔e3 ♖a4 **56 ♛e3 ♖a4 57 b6 +-
♛c8 58 b7+ ♛b8 59 gxf5 ♖a3+** 59...
♖xh4 60 ♖g1 +- **60 ♛e4 ♖a4+ 61
♛e5 ♖a3 62 ♖g2! ♖e3+ 63 ♛f4 ♖e7
64 f6!! gxf6 65 ♖b2 ♖e5 66 ♖b6 ♖a5
67 ♖xf6 ♛xb7 68 ♖xh6 ♛c7 69
♖e6 ♛d7 70 ♖e5 ♖a8 71 h5 ♖f8+
72 ♛e3 ♛d6 73 f4 ♖h8 74 ♛f3 ♖h7
75 ♛g4 ♖g7+ 76 ♛f5 ♖f7+ 77 ♛g5
♖g7+ 78 ♛f6 1-0 Ciamarra**

1 d4 d5 2 c4 c6

56 Botterill-Boersma London 79
**1 d4 d5 2 c4 c6 3 ♘f3 ♘f6 4 ♘c3
dxc4 5 a4 ♘a6 6 e3** 6 e4 ♗g4 7 ♗xc4
♗xf3 8 ♕xf3 ♕xd4 9 ♗xa6 bxa6
10 0-0± **♗g4 7 ♗xc4 e6 8 0-0 ♘b4
9 ♛e2 ♗e7 10 ♖d1 0-0 11 h3 ♗h5
12 g4 ♗g6 13 ♘e5** 13 e4!? c5 14
♘xg6 hxg6 15 d5!? exd5 16 g5!?
16 ♘xd5 ♘fxd5 17 ♗xd5 ♘xd5
18 e4 ♗f6 19 ♖xd5 ♕b6≈; 17 e4!?
♗d6! 16...♘h5 17 ♘xd5 ♘xd5 18
♗xd5±; 16...♘e8 17 ♘xd5 ♘d6 =+
17 gxf6 dxc4 18 ♕xc4 gxf6 18...
♖e8!?; 18...♕d7!?

Diagram

19 ♘e4! ♗h2+ 20 ♛xh2 ♕xd1 21

♗d2! ♕f3 21...♕xa1 22 ♘xf6+ ♔g7 23 ♗c3 +− **22 ♗c3 ♖fc8! 23 ♘xf6+ ♔f8 24 ♖f1** 24 ♕h4!? ♘d5∞ ♖c6? 24...♕f5! **25** ♕h4 ♘d5 ∞/=+ **25 ♘d7+ ♔e8 26 ♘e5** +− ♕d5 **27 ♕h4 ♖d8 28 ♕h8+ ♔e7 29 ♘xc6+ ♕xc6 30 ♕h4+ ♔d7 31 ♖d1+ 1-0 Botterill**

57 Polugaevsky-Larsen Riga 79

1 ♘f3 ♘f6 2 c4 c6 3 d4 d5 4 ♘c3 dxc4 5 a4 ♘a6 5...♗f5 **6 e4 ♗g4 7 ♗xc4 e6 8 ♗e3 ♗b4 9 ♕d3** 9 ♕c2 ♗xf3 10 gxf3 ♕a5 11 0-0 0-0 += Gligoric-Green, Hastings 60/61; 9 ♗d3 ♗xf3 **10 gxf3 ♘c7 11 ♖g1 ♘h5** 11...g6 **12 ♔e2** 12 0-0-0 **g6 13 d5?! ♗d6** 13...exd5 14 exd5 ♕e7! **14 dxc6 bxc6 15 ♕d4! 0-0** 15...e5 16 ♕d2 ♔e7 **16 ♖gd1! ♗xh2** 16...♗e7?! 17 ♕xd8 ♖fxd8 18 ♖xd8+ ♗xd8 19 ♖d1 Δ ♗xa7; 16...♗f4?! 17 ♕xd8 ♖fxd8 18 ♖xd8+ ♖xd8 19 ♖d1! **17 ♕xd8 ♖fxd8 18 ♖xd8+ ♖xd8 19 ♗xa7 ♗e5 20 a5 ♘f4+ 21 ♔f1 ♖d2**

Diagram

22 ♘d1!± ♘a8 22...♗d4 23 ♗b8! **23 ♗e3 ♖d7 24 a6 ♔f8 25 ♘c3 g5 26 ♘a4 ♗d4 27 ♖d1 e5 28 ♘c5! ♖d8** 28...♖d6 29 ♘b3 ♖h6 30 ♔g1 **29 ♘b3** +− **♗b6 30 ♖xd8+ ♗xd8 31 a7** Δ ♗a6-b7 **♗b6 32 ♗xb6 ♘xb6 33**

♘a5! ♔e7 34 ♘xc6+ ♕d6 35 ♘b4! ♘e6 35...♔c7 36 ♘d5+ ♘fxd5 37 ♗xd5 **36 ♘d5 ♘a8 37 ♘f6 h6 38 ♗d5 ♘ec7 39 ♘e8+! 1-0** 39...♘xe8 40 ♗xa8 ♘c7 41 ♗d5 +− **Miles/ Speelman**

58 Bisguier-Kohalmi USA 79

1 d4 d5 2 c4 e6 3 ♘c3 c6 4 ♘f3 4 ♕b3 f5!? 5 e3 ♘f6 6 ♗d3 ♗d6 7 f4 ♘e4 8 ♘f3 ♘d7 9 0-0 ♘df6 10 c5 ♗c7 11 ♕c2 h6 12 b4 a6 13 ♘e2 += Taimanov-Shamkovich, USSR Final 54 **dxc4 5 a4** 5 g3 Gheorghiu ♗b4 6 a4!? c5 7 ♗g2 ♘c6 8 ♗e3 ♘f6 9 dxc5 ♕xd1+ 10 ♖xd1 ♘g4!=; 5 e4; 5 e3 ♗b4 5...c5? 6 d5! ♘f6 7 e4 exd5 8 e5!± Glass-Grunfeld 31 **6 e3** 6 e4 b5 7 ♗d2 a5! 8 axb5 ♗xc3 9 ♗xc3 cxb5 10 ♘d2 ♘f6 11 b3= Gheorghiu **b5 7 ♗d2** 7 g3 ♗b7 8 ♗g2 ♘d7 9 0-0 a6 10 ♕c2=; 7 ♗e2?! a6 8 0-0 ♗b7 9 ♕c2 ♘f6 10 e4 0-0 =+ **a5** 7...♗b7 8 b3 a5 9 bxc4 ♗xc3! 10 ♗xc3 b4 11 ♗b2 ♘f6 12 ♗d3 c5 13 0-0 ♘bd7 14 ♖e1 ♖c8 15 ♖c1 ♕c7? 16 d5!± Knaak-Karasev, Lublin 74; 15...0-0! ∞/+=; 7...♕e7 8 axb5 ♗xc3 9 ♗xc3 cxb5 10 d5 ♘f6 11 dxe6! fxe6 12 ♘d4 0-0 13 ♘xb5 ♘e4 14 ♗xc4! ♘xf2 15 ♕h5!± Euwe **8 axb5 ♗xc3 9 ♗xc3 cxb5 10 b3! ♗b7 11 bxc4** 11 d5!?∞ **b4 12 ♗b2**

12 ♗d2? ♘f6 13 ♗d3 ♘bd7 14 0-0
0-0 15 ♕c2 ♕c7 16 e4 e5!∓ Plater-
Trifunovic, Hilversum 47; 13 ♘e5
♘bd7 ♘f6 13 ♗d3 ♗e4 13...♘bd7 14
0-0 0-0 15 ♕c2 ♕c7 16 e4±; 14 ♕c2
♕c7 15 e4! ♘g8 16 0-0 ♘e7
e5 ♗xf3 18 gxf3 g6 19 d5±
Landau-Noteboom, Triberg 31;
14...0-0 15 e4 e5!? +=; 13...♘e4?
14 ♕a4+! 14 ♘e5 14 ♗xe4 ♘xe4
15 ♕c2 f5 16 d5 0-0 17 ♘d4 ♘dc5!
∝/+=; 16 0-0 0-0 17 ♖fd1 Ogaard-
Mestel, Esbjerg 78; 16 ♘e5!? +=
Pachman; 15...♘f6 Polugaevsky 0-0
15 0-0 ♘bd7 16 ♗xe4 ♘xe4 17 ♘c6
17 f3? ♘xe5 ♕c7 17...♕b6 18 d5
18 d5± ♘df6 19 f3 ♘c5 20 e4 20
♗e5! ♕b6 21 ♕d4± ♖a6! 21 ♗xf6
21 ♗e5 ♕b6 22 ♗d4 ♘fd7∝ gxf6
22 ♕d4!? ♖xc6! 23 dxc6 ♕xc6 23...
♘b3 24 ♕xf6 ♕b6+ 25 ♔h1 ♕d4?
26 ♕xd4 ♘xd4 27 ♖xa5 ♘xc6 28
♖b5 +−; 25...♘xa1 26 ♕g5 += 24
♕xf6 a4 25 ♖fd1 Δ ♖d5 ♖c8 26
♖d8+ ♖xd8 27 ♕xd8+ ♔g7 28 ♕g5+
♔f8 29 ♖d1 ♗b7 30 ♕h6+ ♔e7 31
♕xh7 b3 32 ♕h4+ ♔f8 33 ♕h8+ ♔e7
½-½ Ciamarra

59 Dorfman-Timoshenko
USSR Final 78

1 d4 d5 2 c4 c6 3 ♘f3 ♘f6 4 ♘c3
dxc4 5 a4 ♗f5 6 e3 e6 7 ♗xc4 ♗b4
8 0-0 0-0 9 ♕e2 9 ♘h4!? ♗g4 10 f3
♗h5 11 g4 ♗g6 12 ♘xg6 hxg6 13
♕b3 ♕b6 14 ♔h1 += Polugaevsky-
Timoshenko, USSR Final 78 ♘bd7
10 ♖d1?! 10 e4 ♗g6 11 ♗d3 ♗h5!∝
♗g6! 10...♗g4 11 e4 ♕e7 12 h3 ♗h5
13 g4 ♗g6 14 ♘h4 += 11 ♘e5 ♘xe5
12 dxe5 ♘d7 13 f4 ♕e7 =+ 14 ♘a2
♗a5 15 b4 ♗c7 16 ♗a3 ♘b6 17 ♗b3
♘d5∓ 18 ♗xd5 cxd5 19 ♘c3 ♖fc8
20 ♘b5! ♗d8 21 ♘d6 ♖c2 22 ♖d2

♖c3 Δ ♗b6 23 ♗b2 ♖b3 24 ♗d4
♖xb4 25 ♖b2 ♗a5?! 25...♖xb2 26
♗xb2 ♗b6 27 ♗d4 ♗c7 =+ 26 ♖xb4
♗xb4 27 ♕b5! a5 28 ♖c1! 28 ♕xb7?
♗d6 ♗xd6 29 exd6 ♕xd6 30 ♕xb7∝
♕f8 31 h3 h6 32 ♖c5 ♔h7 33 ♕c7
♕e8 34 ♖xa5 ♖c8 35 ♕b7 ♗e4=
36 ♖b5 f6 37 ♖c5 ♖b8 38 ♕c7 ♕g6
39 g4 ♖b1+ 40 ♔c1 ♖b3?! 41 ♕e7
♖b1 42 ♖xb1 ♗xb1 43 ♕xe6 ♕c2?
44 ♕f5+ ½-½ Gufeld

60 Laukach-Panchenko
Dubna 79

1 d4 ♘f6 2 c4 e6 3 ♘c3 d5 4 ♘f3
c6 5 e3 ♘bd7 6 ♗d3 dxc4 6...♗d6 7
e4! += 7 ♗xc4 b5 8 ♗d3 a6 9 e4 c5
10 d5 c4 10...e5 11 b3 c4!? 11 dxe6
fxe6! 12 ♗c2 ♗b7 12...♕c7 13 ♘g5!
13 0-0 ♕c7 13...♕b6 14 ♗e3 ♗c5 15
♗xc5 ♕xc5 16 ♕e1 0-0-0 17 b4!±
14 ♕e2 ♗d6 15 ♘g5 ♘c5 16 f4 e5!
17 a4 b4!? 17...h6 18 ♘d5 ♗xd5
19 exd5 0-0-0 =+ 20 fxe5 ♗xe5 21
♘f7 ♗xh2+ 22 ♔h1 ♖he8!∝ 23 ♕g4+
♖d7 24 ♗f5 24 d6!? ♗xd5 25 ♗xd7+
♘xd7 26 ♗f4 ♗xf4 27 ♖xf4 27 ♕xf4
♖e2 ♔b8!∓ 28 ♖d4 ♘f6 29 ♕xg7
♘h5 30 ♕g4 ♘g3+ 0-1 Gufeld

61 Dorfman-Sveshnikov
USSR Final 78

1 d4 d5 2 c4 e6 3 ♘f3 ♘f6 4 ♘c3 c6
5 e3 ♘bd7 6 ♗d3 6 ♕c2 dxc4 7 ♗xc4
b5 8 ♗d3 a6 8...♗b7 9 e4 b4 10
♘a4 c5 11 e5 ♘d5 12 0-0 cxd4 13
♖e1 g6∝ 9 e4 c5 10 d5 c4 11 dxe6
fxe6 12 ♗c2 ♕c7 12...♗b7 13 0-0
13 ♘g5!? ♗b7 14 ♕e2 ♗d6∝ 15
♘g5 ♘c5 16 f4 e5 17 fxe5 ♗xe5 18
♘f3 ♗xc3! 19 bxc3 0-0 20 e5!?
♖ae8 21 ♗e3 ♗xf3 21...♘g4? 22
♗xh7+! 22 ♕xf3 ♕xe5 23 ♗d4 ♕d6
24 ♖ad1∝ ♘d3 25 ♗xd3 cxd3 26

70

♛xd3 ♖e6= 27 c4! bxc4 28 ♛xc4 ♛c6
29 ♛xc6 ♖xc6 30 ♖c1 ½-½ Gufeld

62 Botterill-Petursson London 79

1 d4 d5 2 c4 c6 3 ♘f3 ♘f6 4 ♘c3
e6 5 e3 ♘bd7 6 ♗d3 dxc4 7 ♗xc4
b5 8 ♗d3 a6 9 e4 c5 10 d5 c4 11
dxe6 fxe6 11...cxd3 12 ♗c2 ♗b7
13 ♗g5? 13 ♕e2 Δ e5 ♛c7 14 ♕e2
♗c5 15 0-0 0-0 16 ♖ad1 ♘g4 17
h3 ♖xf3 18 hxg4 ♖h3?! 18...♖f7!∓
19 e5! ♖g3 19...♘xe5 20 ♗f4 ♖xc3
21 ♗xe5?? ♖xc2 −+; 21 bxc3 ♛c6
22 ♗e4 ♛xe4 23 ♛xe4 ♗xe4 24
♗xe5 ♗d3 25 ♖fe1 ♖f8 26 ♖d2 +=
20 ♘e4± ♖d3 21 ♗xd3 cxd3 22
♖xd3 ♛xe5 23 ♖xd7 ♗xe4 24 ♖e1
♖f8 25 ♗h4 ♛f4 26 ♛xe4 ♗xf2+ 27
♔h1 ♗xh4 28 ♛xf4 ♖xf4 29 ♖xe6
h6 30 ♔h2 ♖f2 31 ♖xa6 ♖xb2 32
♖d3 Δ ♖b3 ♗f6 33 ♔g3?! 33 ♖b3!
♗e5+ 34 ♔h3 ♖e2 35 ♖xb5 ♖e1
36 g5 h5 37 g3 ♖e3 38 ♔h4 +−;
34...♖xb3 35 axb3 b4 36 ♖b6 ♗c3
37 ♔g3 +− ♗e5+ 34 ♔f3 ♖b4 35
g3 ♖c4 36 ♖a5 ♗f6 37 ♖xb5 ♖a4
38 ♖d2 ♔h7 38...♗e7!? 39 ♖b7 ♗a3
40 ♖dd7 ♗f8 41 ♖d8/41 ♖a7 +−;
39...♗c5! 39 ♖e2! Δ ♖b3, a3 ♖a2
♔g6 40 ♖b3 ♖a7 41 a3 ♖f7 42 a4
♗d8+ 43 ♔g2 ♖a7 44 ♖a2 ♗a5 45
♖b5 ♖a6 46 ♔f3 ♔f6 47 ♔e4 ♔e6
48 ♔d4 ♔d6 49 ♖d5+ ♔e6 50 ♖e2+
♔f6 51 ♖f5+ ♔g6 52 ♖a2 ♖a7 53
♔c4 ♖a6 54 ♔b5 ♖a8 55 ♔c6 ♖a7
56 ♖xa5 ♖xa5 57 ♔b6 ♖e5 58 a5
♔g5 59 ♖a4 ♖e8 60 a6 ♖g8 61 a7
♖f8 62 ♔b7 ♖f7+ 63 ♔c6 ♖f8 64
♖b4! ♖f6+ 65 ♔b7 ♖f7+ 66 ♔a6
♖f6+ 67 ♖b6 ♖f8 68 ♖b8 ♖f6+
69 ♔b5 1-0 Botterill

63 Honfine-Kempe corr 78-79

1 ♘f3 d5 2 c4 c6 3 d4 ♘f6 4 ♘c3

e6 5 e3 ♘bd7 6 ♗d3 dxc4 7 ♗xc4
b5 8 ♗d3 a6 9 e4 c5 10 d5 e5 11
b3 c4 12 bxc4 ♗b4 13 ♗d2 bxc4
14 ♗c2 ♛a5 15 ♘e2 ♘xe4 16 ♗xe4
c3 17 ♘xc3 ♗xc3 18 0-0 ♗xd2 19
♘xd2 0-0 20 ♘c4 ♛b4 21 d6! N
♖a7 21...♗b7 22 ♖b1 ♛xc4 23 ♗xb7
♖b8 24 ♛d2 +=; 21...♖b8 22 ♗d5
♖e8 23 ♖e1 += 22 ♗d5 ♖d8?! 23
♖e1 ♛f8? 23...♘f6? 24 ♘xe5 ♛xd6
25 ♘c6 +−; 23...h6? 24 ♖b1 ♛c5
25 ♘xe5 ♘xe5 26 ♖xe5 ♛xd6? 27
♖e8+! +−; 23...♗b7 24 ♖b1 += 24
♛d3! ♘f6 25 ♖xe5 ♘xd5 26 ♖xd5
g6? 26...♗e6 27 ♛xh7 f6 28 ♛h8+
♔g8 29 ♖d4 +− 27 ♛d4 1-0 Honfi

64 Tal-Mihalchishin
USSR Final 78

1 ♘f3 d5 2 c4 e6 3 d4 ♘f6 4 ♘c3
c6 5 ♗g5 5 e3 += dxc4 5...h6 6 ♗h4
dxc4 7 e4 g5 8 ♗g3 b5 9 ♗e2 ♘bd7
10 0-0 b4 11 e5! += Mikenas-Klovan,
USSR 78 6 e4 b5 7 a4!? 7 e5 +=
♗b4!? 7...b4 8 ♘b1 h6 9 ♗xf6 ♛xf6
10 ♗xc4 ♛g6 11 ♘bd2 +=; 7...♛b6
8 axb5 8 e5∞ cxb5 9 e5 h6 10 ♗h4
10 exf6?! =+ g5 11 ♘xg5 11 exf6!?
gxh4 12 ♘e5∞ hxg5 12 ♗xg5 ♘bd7
13 ♛f3 ♖b8 14 exf6 ♗b7 −+ 15
♛g3 ♖g8! 16 ♗e2 ♛b6! 17 0-0 ♗d6
18 ♛h4 b4 18...♘f8!? =+ 19 ♘d1
19 ♘a4? ♛b5 ♛b5 20 f4 ♛d5 21
♗f3! ♛xd4+ 22 ♔h1 ♘c5?! 22...♗xf3!
Δ ♗c5 23 ♛h7 ♖f8 24 f5? 24 ♗xb7
♖xb7 25 ♘f2!∞ ♗xf3 25 ♖xf3 ♘b3!
26 ♖xb3 cxb3 27 ♘e3 ♛e4 28 ♛h5
♗c5∓ 29 fxe6 ♗xe3 30 ♖e1 ♖b5
31 ♛d1! ♖d5 32 ♛a1

Diagram

32...♖xg5? Zeitnot 32...fxe6!∓
33 ♛a4+ ♔d8 24 ♛d7 mate 1-0
Gufeld

65 Veingold-Ivanovic Tallinn 79

**1 d4 d5 2 c4 c6 3 ♘c3 ♘f6 4 ♗g5
e6 5 ♘f3 dxc4 6 e4 b5 7 a4 ♗b4 8
e5?!** 8 axb5 axb5 9 e5 h6 9 ♗h4
g5 **10 ♘xg5 hxg5?!** 10...♗xc3+!
11 bxc3 ♕a5 12 ♘xf7!?∝ **11 ♗xg5
♘bd7 12 exf6 ♘b6 13 ♗e2?!♘xa4
14 ♖xa4 bxa4 15 ♕xa4 ♕b6 16
0-0 ♗b7?!** 16...♗d7!? **17 d5! 0-0-0?**
17...♗xc3 18 bxc3 ♕b5 19 ♕a3!;
18...exd5 19 ♗g4!; 17...♕a5!? **18
dxe6± ♖dg8?!** 18...♗d6 **19 ♗f4
♕d4 20 ♗g3 +− a5 21 ♖d1 ♕xf6 22
♘d5! ♕d8 23 ♘xb4 ♕e8 24 ♕xa5
♖xg3 25 hxg3 fxe6 26 ♕e5 1-0
Ivanovic**

66 Ojanets-Monin USSR 79

**1 d4 d5 2 c4 e6 3 ♘c3 c6 4 ♘f3 ♘f6
5 ♗g5 dxc4 6 e4 b5 7 e5 h6 8 ♗h4
g5 9 ♘xg5 ♘d5?! 10 ♘xf7 ♕xh4
11 ♘xh8 ♗b4 12 ♕d2!?** 12 ♖c1
♕e4+ 13 ♗e2 ♘f4 14 ♕d2 ♘d3∝
c5 13 0-0-0 ♘c6 13...cxd4 14 ♕xd4
♕g5+ 15 f4 ♘xf4 16 ♘e4!± **14 dxc5
♘xe5 15 f4** 15 ♕e1 ♕g5+ 16 ♔b1
♕g7 17 f4 += **♗xc3 16 bxc3 ♕xf4
17 ♕xf4 ♘xf4 18 ♖d4 += ♘d5 19
♖e4 ♘c6 20 ♔b2 e5 21 ♗e2 ♗f5**

Diagram

---

22 ♖h4 22 ♗f3!? ♘xe4 23 ♗xe4 ♖d8
24 ♖d1 += **b4! 23 ♗xc4?!** 23 ♗f3!
bxc3+ 24 ♔a3 ♘db4 25 ♖xc4 **bxc3+
24 ♔a3** 24 ♔c1 ♖b8 25 ♗b3 ♘d4
♘db4 25 ♘f7 25 ♗b5!? += **♖b8
26 ♘d6+ ♕d7 27 ♗b5 ♘c2+ 28 ♔a4
♘2d4 29 ♗xc6+ ♕xc6 30 ♘xf5 ♕xc5!!
31 a3** 31 ♘xd4? exd4 =+ **♘xf5 32
♖h3 ♕c4 33 ♖c1∝ ♖b3 34 g4 ♘d4
35 ♖e3 ♘b5= 36 ♖e4+ = ♘d4 37
♖e3 ♘b5 ½-½ Gufeld**

67 Schmidt-Pinter Rome 79

**1 d4 ♘f6 2 c4 e6 3 ♘f3 d5 4 ♘c3
c6 5 ♗g5 dxc4 6 e4 b5 7 e5 h6 8
♗h4 g5 9 ♘xg5 hxg5 10 ♗xg5 ♘bd7
11 exf6 ♕a5!** 11...♗b7 12 g3 c5 13
d5 ♕b6 14 ♗g2 0-0-0 15 0-0 b4 +=
12 g3!? b4 12...♗a6 13 a3!; 12...♗b7
13 ♘e4 ♗a6 13...♕d5? 14 ♗g2 ♗b7
15 ♗f4! +− **14 ♗e2** 14 b3!? ♕d5!;
14 ♕f3 0-0-0=; 14 ♗g2 c3!∓ **0-0-0
15 0-0** 15 ♕c1 ♘b6 16 ♗e3 c3 17
♗xa6+ ♕xa6 18 ♔c2 e5!∝ Furman-
Zak, USSR 54 **♕f5 16 ♕c2** 16 f3?
♘c5 17 ♘xc5 ♖xd4! −+ Baturinsky-
Davinsky, USSR 46 **♘b6 17 f3?**
17 ♖ad1 c5 18 dxc5 ♗xc5 19 ♖xd8+
♖xd8 20 g4 ♕g6 21 ♖d1 ♗d4 Shashin-
Kochiev, USSR 72, 22 h4!± Korchnoi
c5!∓ 17...♖xd4?! **18 ♗e3 18 b3**
18 dxc5 ♗xc5+ 19 ♔h1 ♗b7 −+
♗b7! 19 h4 ♖xd4! 20 bxc4 ♗h6! −+

21 ♗xh6 ♖xh6 22 ♗d3 ♗xe4!? 23
♗xe4 ♕e5! 24 ♕g2?! 24 ♕f2!? ♖xf6
25 ♖ae1 ♕d6∓ ♘xc4 25 ♖fe1 ♖d2!
−+ 26 ♕h3 26 ♕xd2 ♘xd2 27 ♗b7+
♔xb7 28 ♖xe5 ♘xf3+ −+ ♕d4+ 27
♔h1 ♘e5! 28 ♕f1 ♘d3 29 ♗xd3
♖xh4+! 0-1 Schmidt/Pytel

68 Schinzel-Barczay Warsaw 2 79

1 c4 c6 2 d4 d5 3 ♘c3 ♘f6 4 ♘f3
e6 5 ♗g5 dxc4 6 e4 b5 7 e5 h6 8
♗h4 g5 9 ♘xg5 hxg5 9...♘d5 10
♘xf7 ∞/± 10 ♗xg5 ♘bd7 11 g3 ♗b7
12 ♗g2 ♕b6 13 exf6 0-0-0 14 0-0
♗h6!? N 14...♘e5∞ 15 h4 ♗xg5
16 hxg5 c5 17 dxc5 ♘xc5 18 ♕e2
♖d3! =+ 19 ♖ae1 b4 20 ♗xb7+ ♔xb7
21 ♘e4 ♖d4! 22 f3 22 ♘xc5?? ♖h1
mate ♘xe4 23 fxe4 ♕c7 24 ♕g2
♖g8 25 ♖d1 ♖xg5 26 ♖f3 ♖xd1
27 ♕xd1 ♖c5!? 28 ♖f2 c3 29 bxc3
♖xc3 30 ♕g4! ♔b7 31 ♕g5 ♔b6!=
32 ♔h3 a5 33 e5 ♕c6 34 ♕d2 ♔b5
35 ♖f4 ♔a4 36 ♔g4 ♔a3 37 ♖f2
♕c4+ 38 ♕f4 ♕xf4 39 gxf4 a4 40
f5 ♖c6 41 ♖d2 b3 42 axb3 exf5+
43 ♔xf5 axb3 44 ♖d6 ♖c7 45 e6
fxe6 46 ♖xe6 ½-½ Pytel

69 Korchnoi-Miles
South Africa 79

1 d4 d5 2 c4 c6 3 ♘f3 ♘f6 4 e3
♗f5 5 ♗d3 5 cxd5 cxd5 6 ♘c3 e6
7 ♗b5+ ♗xd3 5...e6 6 0-0 ♗xd3;
5...♗g6!? 6 ♕xd3 e6 7 0-0 ♘bd7 8
♘bd2 8 ♘c3 ♗b4 ♗e7 9 ♖d1 9 e4
dxc4 10 ♘xc4? ♘c5; 10 ♕xc4 0-0
10 e4 a5 10...dxe4 11 a4 ♕c7? 11...
dxe4 12 e5 ♘e8 12...dxc4 13 ♘xc4
♘d5 14 ♗g5 13 b3 f5? 13...♕d8
Δ ♘c7 14 exf6 ♖xf6 14...♗xf6 15
♗a3; 14...♘exf6 15 ♗b2 Δ ♖e1,
♘g5 15 ♘f1 ♘d6 16 ♘g3 ♖af8?!
16...♖e8 17 ♖e1 ♘f7? 18 ♘h5 ♖f5

18...♖g6 19 ♘f4 Δ ♘xe6 19 ♘g3!
19 ♖xe6 ♘fe5! 20 dxe5? ♘c5; 20
♘xe5 ♘xe5 22 ♖xe5? ♖xe5 23 dxe5
♕xe5; 21 dxe5! ♖f6 20 cxd5 cxd5

21 ♘h5! ♖f5 22 ♖xe6 ♖xh5 22...
♘fe5 23 ♘xe5 ♘xe5 24 dxe5; 23
dxe5 ♘c5 24 ♕xd5+ 23 ♖xe7 ♘d8
24 ♗a3 ♖xf3 +− 24...♘c6 25 ♖xd7
+− ♖xf3 26 ♕xf3 ♕xh2+ 27 ♔f1
♕h1+ 28 ♔e2 ♘xd4+ 29 ♔d3; 25...
♕xd7 26 ♗xf8 ♔xf8 +− 25 ♕xf3
♕xh2+ 26 ♔f1 ♘f6 27 ♖e8+ ♔f7
28 ♖f8+ ♔g6 29 g4 ♖g5 30 ♗c1
1-0 Miles

1 d4 d5 2 c4 e6

70 Gheorghiu-Alburt USA 79

1 c4 c5 2 ♘f3 ♘f6 3 ♘c3 e6 3...d5;
3...♘c6; 3...g6 4 e3 d5 5 d4 a6!
5...♘c6 6 cxd5 += 6 cxd5 exd5 7
dxc5 7 ♗e2!? c4!∞; 7 b3!∞ ♗xc5 8
♗e2 0-0 9 0-0 ♘c6 10 b3 ♕d6!? 10...
d4! 11 ♘a4 ♗a7 12 exd4 ♘xd4 13
♘xd4 ♗xd4 14 ♗b2 += 11 ♗b2 ♗g4
12 h3! ♗xf3 12...♗h5 13 ♘a4! ♗a7
14 ♗xf6!± 13 ♗xf3 ♖ad8 14 ♘e2!±
Δ ♘d4 ♘e5 15 ♘d4 ♖fe8 16 g3
♘e4 17 ♗g2! ♕g6 18 ♖c1 ♗b6 19
♕e2 Δ ♖fd1± ♘xf2!∞ 20 ♖xf2
♘d3 21 ♘f5! 21 ♕f3 ♗xb2 22 ♖xb2
♕g5! 23 ♕f4! ♕xf4 24 gxf4 ♖xe3

73

25 ♖d2 +=; 21 ♖cf1?! ♘xb2 22
♕xb2 ♖xe3∓; 21 ♖f4?! ♘xb2 Δ ♖xe3
d4!! 21...♘xc1 22 ♗xc1 d4 23 ♖f3!
dxe3 24 ♔h2!± **22 ♖f3! dxe3 23
♔h2! ♘xc1** 23...♘xb2 24 ♕xb2 ♖d2
25 ♖c8!! +−; 25 ♘e7+!! ♖xe7 26
♕xd2! +− **24 ♗xc1 ♖e5 25 ♗xe3!±
♖xf5 26 ♖xf5 ♗xe3?** Zeitnot 26...
♕xf5?! 27 ♗xb6±; 26...♖e8 **27 ♖e5!!
+− ♗g1+ 28 ♔xg1 f6 29 ♖d5 ♖e8
30 ♕g4! +− ♖e1+ 31 ♔h2 ♕xg4 32
hxg4 ♖e2 33 a4 b5 34 axb5 axb5
35 ♖xb5 ♔f7 36 ♖b7+ ♔g6 37 b4
♖b2 38 b5 h5 39 gxh5+ ♔xh5 40
b6 ♖b5 41 ♖b8! +− ♔g4 42 b7
1-0 Gheorghiu**

71 Petkevich-Luczak Lodz 79

**1 ♘f3 d5 2 d4 ♘f6 3 c4 e6 4 ♘c3
c5 5 e3 ♘c6 6 ♗d3 dxc4 7 ♗xc4
cxd4** 7...a6! **8 exd4 ♗e7 9 0-0 0-0
10 ♖e1 b6 11 a3 ♗b7 12 ♗a2 ♖c8
13 ♕d3 a6?!** 13...♖e8! Δ ♗f8, g6=
**14 ♗g5 b5 15 ♖ac1 ♖e8 16 ♗b1 g6
17 ♗a2 ♔g7** 17...♘a5 18 ♘e5; 17...
b4!? **18 ♕d2± ♘a5 19 ♘e5 ♘c4
20 ♗xc4! bxc4 21 ♕f4 ♕d6 22 ♖e3
♖ed8 23 ♖d1 ♖c7 24 g4 +− ♖dc8
25 ♗h6+ ♔g8 26 g5 ♘e8 27 ♕xf7+
♔h8 28 ♖h3!** Δ ♘xg6+ **1-0 Pytel**

72 R.Rodriguez-Ljubojevic Riga 79

**1 c4 c5 2 ♘f3 ♘f6 3 ♘c3 e6 4 e3 d5
5 cxd5** 5 d4 exd5 5...♘xd5 **6 d4
♘c6 7 ♗e2 ♘e4!? 8 0-0 ♗e7 9 h3?**
9 dxc5 **0-0 10 ♗d3?!** 10 dxc5 ♘xc3
11 bxc3 ♗xc5 12 c4= **♗f5 11 dxc5
♗xc5 12 ♘a4 ♗e7** 12...♗d6 Δ ♕d7
**13 b3 ♕d6 14 ♗b2 ♕g6∓ 15 ♘e1
♗xh3!?** 15...♖ad8 Δ d4∓ **16 f3**

Diagram

16...♖ad8? 16...♗h4! 17 ♕e2 ♘g3?

18 fxe4 ♗g4 19 exd5! ♗xe2 20 ♗xg6
♗xf1 21 ♗f5; 19...♕h5? 20 ♘f3;
17...♘g3 18 ♗xg6 ♘xe2+ 19 ♔h2
♗e6 −+; 18 ♕d2 ♗f5; 16...♕g5!?
17 ♕e2 17 ♕b1 ♗b4! **♘g3 18 ♗xg6
♘xe2+ 19 ♔f2 hxg6 20 gxh3 b5!
21 ♔xe2 bxa4 22 ♖c1 ♖c8** 22...♖d6
23 bxa4 ♖e6 **23 bxa4 ♖fe8 24 ♘d3
♗g5** 24...♗f6 **25 f4 ♗f6 26 ♗xf6 gxf6
27 ♕d2 ♘a5 28 ♘b4?** 28 ♖xc8 ♖xc8
29 ♘b4 f5?? 28...♘c4+ 29 ♔d3 ♖xe3+
30 ♔d4 ♖e4+ 31 ♔xd5 f5! −+ **29
♖xc8 ♖xc8 30 ♖c1 ♖e8?** 30...♖d8
**31 ♘xd5 ♖d8 32 ♖c8! ♖xc8 33 ♘e7+
♔g7 34 ♘xc8 a6 35 ♘d6 ♕f6 36 ♕c3
♕e6 37 ♔b4! +− ♘c6+ 38 ♔c5 ♕d7
39 ♘b7 ♘e7 40 ♘a5 f6 41 h4 ♕c7
42 ♘b3 ♕d7 43 ♘d4 ♘c8 44 ♘c6
♕e6 45 a5 ♘d6 46 ♘b8 ♘e4+ 47
♕c6 ♘c3 48 ♘xa6 ♕xa2 49 ♘c7+
♕e7 50 ♘d5+ ♕d8 51 a6 1-0 Miles/
Speelman**

73 Torre-Maninang Jakarta 79

**1 c4 c5 2 ♘f3 ♘f6 3 ♘c3 e6 4 e3
♘c6 5 d4 d5 6 cxd5 ♘xd5 7 ♗d3
cxd4 8 exd4 ♗e7 9 0-0 0-0 10 ♖e1
♘cb4?!** 10...♗f6; 10...♘f6; 10...♗d7!?
Pomar **11 ♗b1 ♘xc3 12 bxc3 ♘d5
13 c4 ♘f6** 13...♘c3? 14 ♗xh7+ **14
♘e5± g6 15 ♗h6 ♖e8 16 ♖e3 ♘d7
17 f4 ♘xe5?!** 17...♘f6 **18 fxe5 ♗g5
18...♗c5 19 ♖d3 Δ ♔h1± **19 ♗xg5**

♛xg5 20 ♖f3 ♛h4 21 ♕d2 ♖d8 22
♖f4 ♛h5 △ ♕xe5 23 ♗d3 ♗d7 24
♖af1 ♗e8 25 ♖1f3 ♛g5 26 h4 ♛h5
27 ♕f2 ♖d7 28 g4 ♛h6 29 g5 ♛g7
30 ♖f6 ♖ad8 31 ♖3f4 b6

32 h5?? 32 ♗f1 △ ♗g2±; 32 ♔f1 △
h5!± gxh5 33 ♕h4 h6 34 ♖xh6 ♖xd4
–+ **35 ♖g6** 35 ♗h7+ ♔f8 36 ♕g3
♖d3! 37 ♗xd3 ♖xd3 38 ♕xd3 ♕xg5+
39 ♔h1 ♗c6+ 40 ♖e4 ♗xe4+ 41 ♕xe4
♕xh6 –+ **fxg6 36 ♖xd4 ♕e7 37 ♖xd8
♕xd8 38 ♗f1 ♕d2 39 ♕g3 ♕d4+
40 ♔h2 h4 41 ♕e1 ♕f4+ 42 ♔h3 ♗c6
43 ♗e2 ♕e3+ 44 ♔xh4 ♗f3 0-1 Keene**

74 Mariotti-Toth
Rome 79
1 d4 ♘f6 2 ♘f3 d5 3 c4 e6 4 ♘c3
♗e7 5 e3 0-0 6 ♗d3 c5 7 0-0 ♘c6 8
a3 a6 9 b3 cxd4 10 exd4 b6 11
♗b2 ♗b7 12 ♘a4?! ♖c8 13 ♕e2
dxc4 14 bxc4 ♘a5 15 ♘e5 ♗xc4!
16 ♘xc4 16 ♗xc4 b5 17 ♗xb5 ♕d5
b5 17 ♘cb6 ♖b8! 17...♖c6 18 ♗xb5!
18 ♖ac1 18 ♗xb5 axb5 19 ♕xb5
♘d5 20 ♘xd5 ♕xd5! 21 ♕xd5 ♗xd5
22 ♘c3 ♖b3 23 ♗b4 ♗xb4 24 axb4
♖xb4 =+; 22 ♖ab1 ♗b3 23 ♘c5 ♗c2
–+ **bxa4 19 ♘xa4 a5 20 ♘c5 ♗a8
21 ♖fd1? 21 ♗a1! ♕d5 –+ 22 f3
♕h5 △ ♗d6 23 d5 ♗d6! 24 g4 0-1**
24...♕xh2+ –+ **Paoli**

75 Karpov-Spassky Montreal 79
1 d4 ♘f6 2 c4 e6 3 ♘f3 d5 4 ♘c3
♗e7 5 ♗f4 0-0 6 e3 c5 7 dxc5 ♘c6
8 ♕c2 ♕a5 9 a3 ♗xc5 10 ♖d1 ♗e7
11 ♘d2 ♗d7?! N 11...e5 12 ♗g5 d4
13 ♘b3 ♕d8! 14 ♗e2 g6!? 15 exd4
exd4 16 0-0 ♗f5 17 ♕c1 d3 18 ♗xd3
♗xd3 19 ♖fe1 ♖e8 20 ♖xe7!? ♘xe7
21 ♗xf6 **12 ♗e2?!** 12 ♘b3! ♕b6 13
cxd5 ♘xd5 14 ♘xd5 exd5 15 ♖xd5
♘b4 16 axb4 ♗xb4+ 17 ♔e2 ♖ac8
18 ♕d3! ♗e6 19 ♖b5; 18...♗a4 19
♘d4; 17...♗b5+ 18 ♖xb5 ♕xb5+ 19
♔f3±; 15...♗e6 16 ♖b5 ♕d8 17
♗d3±; 15...♘b4+ 16 ♘d2± **♖fc8 13
0-0 ♕d8 14 cxd5 exd5?!** 14...♘xd5!
**15 ♘f3 h6 16 ♘e5! ♗e6 17 ♘xc6
♖xc6** 17...bxc6? 18 ♗a6 +– **18 ♗f3
♕b6 19 ♗e5 ♘e4 20 ♕e2!** 20 ♗xe4
dxe4 21 ♕xe4 ♕xb2 22 ♘d5 ♗xd5
23 ♖xd5 ♕xa3 **♘xc3 21 ♗xc3 ♖d8
22 ♖d3 ♖cd6 23 ♖fd1 ♖6d7 24
♖1d2 ♕b5 25 ♕d1 b6 26 g3 ♗f8**
26...a5!? △ ♕c6 **27 ♗g2 ♗e7 28
♕h5** △ e4 a6 28...♕c6 **29 h3 ♕c6
30 ♔h2 ♕b5** 30...♗f8 **31 f4! f6 32
♕d1 ♕c6??** 32...a5! 33 g4 ♖d6 △ ♕d7
**33 g4 g5?! 34 ♔h1 a5 35 f5 ♗f7 36
e4 +– ♕g7 37 exd5 ♕c7 38 ♖e2 b5
39 ♖xe7 ♖xe7 40 d6 ♕c4 41 b3
1-0 Keene**

76 Stean-Nunn Geneva 79
1 c4 ♘f6 2 ♘f3 e6 3 ♘c3 c5 4 g3
d5 5 cxd5 exd5 6 d4 ♘c6 7 ♗g2
♗e7 8 0-0 0-0 9 ♗g5 9 dxc5 **cxd4
10 ♘xd4 h6 11 ♗e3 ♖e8 12 ♕a4!**
12 ♘b3 ♗e6 13 ♖c1 ♕d7!? 14 ♗c5
♖ad8 15 ♗xe7 ♕xe7 16 ♘d4 ♕b4
17 ♘xc6 bxc6∓ 18 ♘a4 ♗g4 19
f3 ♗f5 20 a3 ♕b5 21 ♔f2 ♘d7 22
b3 d4 23 ♖e1 c5 24 ♗f1 ♖e3 –+
Emerson-Nunn, London 79; 16 e3=;
14 ♘a4 +=; 12 ♖c1 ♗f8 13 ♘xc6

bxc6 14 ♗d4 ♘h7!? += Nikolac-Nunn, Dortmund 79 ♟a5 12...♗d7 13 ♖ad1 ♘b4 14 ♕b3 a5 15 a4 ♗f8 16 ♘c2!± Vaganian-Nunn, Buenos Aires 78 **13 ♖ad1** 13 ♘xd5? ♘xd5 14 ♗xd5 ♗d7 15 ♕d1 ♗h3 16 ♗g2 ♗xg2 17 ♔xg2 ♘c4 18 ♗c1 ♗f6 19 e3 ♕d5+ =+ H.Olafsson-Nunn, Groningen 74/5; 13 ♕c2 ♗g4 14 h3 ♗d7 15 ♖ad1 ♖c8 16 ♘f5 += Tal-Stean, Moscow 75 **♗d7** 13...♘c4 14 ♗c1 ♘b6 +=/± Stean-Pfleger, Munich 79 **14 ♕c2 ♖c8 15 ♕b1!?** 15 ♘f5 ♘c4!? **16 ♘xd5** 16 ♗c1 ♗g4 **♘xd5 17 ♗xd5 ♘xe3 18 fxe3 ♗f6 19 ♕d3** 19 ♗xb7 ♕e7! 20 ♗xc8 ♕xe3+ 21 ♔h1 ♗xc8 22 ♘f3 ♗h3∞; 22...♗a6∞ 19 e4 ♗g4!; 19 ♖xf6 ♕xf6 20 ♖f1 ♕e5 21 ♗xf7+ ♔h8 22 ♗xe8 ♕xe3+ 23 ♔g2 ♖xe8 24 ♕d3 ♕e5 += **♗h3**

20 ♘f5 ♗xf5 20...♗xf1? 21 ♘xh6+ gxh6 22 ♕g6+ ♔h8 23 ♗xf7 +−; 20...♔h8!? 21 ♗xf7?! ♖f8∞ **21 ♖xf5 ♕b6=** 22 ♗xf7+ 22 ♖xf6 ♕xf6 23 ♖f1 ♕xb2 24 ♗xf7+ ♔h8 25 ♗xe8 ♖xe8= ♠xf7 **23 ♖xf6+ gxf6!** 23... ♕xf6 24 ♖f1 +=; 23...♔xf6? 24 ♖f1+ ♔e7 25 ♕e4+ ♕e6 26 ♕xb7+ ♔d6 27 ♖d1+ ♔e5 28 ♕xg7+ +− **24 ♕h7+ ♔f8 25 ♕h8+ ♔f7 26 ♕h7+ ♔f8 27 ♕xh6+ ♔f7** 27...♔g8 28 ♖d4∞ **28 ♕h7+** 28 ♖d7+ ♔e6 29 ♕h3+ f5

♔f8 ½-½ Nunn

77 Botterill-Strauss England 79
1 d4 d5 2 c4 e6 3 ♘c3 c5 4 cxd5 exd5 5 ♘f3 ♘c6 6 g3 ♘f6 7 ♗g2 ♗e7 8 0-0 0-0 9 ♗g5 9 ♗f4!? cxd4 10 ♘xd4 h6 11 ♗e3 ♖e8 12 ♕a4 ♗d7 **13 ♕b3?** 13 ♖ad1 ♘a5 14 ♕c2 ♘c4 15 ♘xd5±; 13 ♖ad1 ♘b4 14 ♕b3 a5 15 a4! ♗f8 16 ♘c2 ♗e6 17 ♗d4± Vaganian-Nunn, Buenos Aires 78; 13 ♖ad1 ♖c8!?∞; 13 ♘xd5 ♘xd5 14 ♗xd5 ♘b4 15 ♕b3 ♘xd5 16 ♕xd5 ♗h3 17 ♕xd8 ♖axd8 18 ♖fe1 ♗f6 19 ♖ad1 ♗g4 20 ♖d2 ♗xd4 21 ♗xd4 ♖xe2=; 13 ♘xd5 ♘xd5 14 ♗xd5 ♘b4 15 ♗xf7+!? ♔xf7 16 ♕b3+ ♔f8 17 ♖ad1∞ **♘a5 14 ♕c2 ♖c8 15 ♖fd1 ♗b4 =+ 16 ♘f5?** ♖e5 17 ♘d4 17 ♗h3 ♗xc3! 18 bxc3 ♘e4 19 ♖xd5 ♖xd5 20 ♕xe4 ♗xf5 21 ♗xf5 ♖xc3∓ **♘c4 18 ♗f4 ♘xb2! 19 ♗xe5** 19 ♕xb2 ♗xc3 20 ♕xb7 ♖e7! +−; 20 ♕a3! =+ **♘xd1 20 ♖xd1 ♗xc3 21 ♕b3 ♕e8! 22 ♗xf6 ♘a4 23 ♕b1** 23 ♕xd5 ♗xd1 24 ♗xg7 ♖d8! 25 ♕c4 ♗xd4 26 ♗xd4 ♕xe2 27 ♕c3 ♖xd4! 28 ♕xd4 ♕e1+ 29 ♗f1 ♗e2 −+ **♗xd1 24 ♕xd1** 24 ♗xg7 ♗c2! −+ **♗b2!** 24...gxf6? 25 ♘f5 Δ ♘d6, Δ ♗d5, Δ e4, ♕g4+ **25 ♕d2 ♖c1+ 26 ♗f1 ♕e4!!** −+ Δ ♖xf1+, ♔h1 mate **27 ♘f3 ♖c2 28 ♕a5 ♗xf6 29 ♕xa7 d4 30 ♕a8+ ♔h7 31 ♔g2 ♕d5 32 a4 d3 33 ♕e8 d2 34 e4 ♕d8 35 ♕xd8 ♗xd8 36 ♗e2 ♗a5 37 ♘d4 ♖c1 38 ♘b3 ♗b4 0-1 Botterill**

78 Miles-Tarjan Riga 79
1 c4 c5 2 ♘f3 ♘f6 3 ♘c3 e6 4 g3 d5 5 cxd5 ♘xd5 6 ♗g2 ♘c6 7 0-0 ♗e7 8 d4 0-0 9 ♘xd5 9 e4 ♘b4! exd5 10 dxc5 ♗xc5 11 ♕c2!? ♗b6!? N 11...♗e7 12 ♗e3 += Stean-Langeweg, Amsterdam 78 **12 ♘g5 g6 13 ♕d1!?**

♗d4! 13...d4 14 ♘e4 +=/± **14 ♛b3
♗f6!** 14...h6?! **15 ♕xd5 ♞d4! 16
♔h1 ♞xe2 17 ♗e3!?** 17 ♕xd8 ♗xd8
18 ♗e3 +=; 17...♖xd8 18 ♘e4 ♘xc1!
19 ♘xf6+ ♔g7 20 ♘h5+ gxh5!=
♛xd5 **18 ♗xd5 ♗xb2 19 ♖ae1 ♞c3
20 ♗b3**

20...h6! 20...b6 21 ♗d4 ♗b7+ 22 f3
♖ad8 23 ♗f6±; 21...♗a6 22 ♘xf7!
♖xf7 23 ♖e7 ♖f8 24 ♖fe1! ♘d5 25
♗xb2 ♘xe7 26 ♖xe7 Δ ♖xa7, ♗a3;
23...♗xf1 24 ♖xf7 +−; 22...♗xf1?
23 ♘h6 mate **21 ♞xf7! ♖xf7 22 ♗d4!**
22 ♗c1?! ♗xc1 **♔f8** 22...♗h3? 23
♖e7! ♗xf1 24 ♖xf7 ♘d5 25 ♖g7+
Δ ♗xb2; 22...♗d7!? **23 ♗c5+ ♔g7
24 ♗d4+** 24 ♖e8? ♗g4 25 ♗d4+ ♔h7
26 ♗xf7 ♖xe8 27 ♗xc3 ♗f3+ 28 ♔g1
♖e2 =+/∓ **♔f8 25 ♗c5+ ♔g7 26
♗d4+ ½-½ Miles/Speelman**

79 Gutman-Azmajparashvili
USSR 79
**1 d4 d5 2 c4 e6 3 cxd5 exd5 4 ♘c3
♞f6 5 ♗g5 ♗e7 6 e3 0-0 7 ♗d3 ♖e8
8 ♕c2 ♞bd7 9 ♞ge2 c6 10 0-0 h6
11 ♗h4** 11 ♗f4 ♘h5 12 ♖ab1 ♘xf4
13 ♘xf4 ♗d6= **♞e4 13 ♗xe7 ♕xe7
13 ♗xe4?!** 13 b4! ♘df6 14 b5 c5 15
dxc5 ♘xc5 16 ♖ac1 b6 17 ♘d4
♗b7 18 a4 += Geller-Durao, Sochi
77 **dxe4 14 b4 ♛xb4 15 ♞xe4 ♕e7!?**

16 ♞c5 16 ♘ec3 ♘f6 17 ♘g3 h5 =+
♞xc5 17 dxc5 ♗g4! 18 ♞g3?! 18
♘d4 ♖ad8 Δ ♖d5∓ **♖ad8 19 e4?**
19 ♕a4 ♕g5 20 ♕xa7 h5!∓ **♖d4∓
20 f4?!** 20 f3? ♗e6 Δ ♖c4 −+ **h5!
21 f5 h4 22 f6!? ♕d8!** 22...gxf6 23
♘f5 ♗xf5 24 ♖xf5 ♕xe4 25 ♕xe4
♖exe4 26 ♖xf6 ♖e2 27 ♖f2 ♗xf2
28 ♔xf2 ♖c4 29 ♖b1 ♖xc5 30 ♖xb7
♖c2+ 31 ♔f3 ♖xa2 32 ♖c7 =+ **23
♞f5 ♗xf5 24 ♖xf5 ♖dxe4 25 ♖d1
♖e1+ 26 ♖xe1** 26 ♖f1 ♖xf1+ 27
♖xf1 ♕d4+ 28 ♕f2 ♕xf6 −+ **♖xe1+
27 ♔f2 ♖e6! 28 fxg7 ♕d4+ 29 ♔f1
♕a1+ 0-1 Georgadze**

80 Romanishin-Geller
USSR Final 78
**1 d4 d5 2 c4 e6 3 ♞f3 ♞f6 4 ♞c3
♗e7 5 ♗g5 h6 6 ♗xf6?! ♗xf6 7 e4?!**
7 e3 dxe4 8 ♞xe4 ♞c6 9 d5? 9 ♘xf6+
♕xf6 10 ♕d3!= **♞e5 10 ♗e2 0-0 11
♕b3 exd5 12 cxd5 c6! 13 ♖d1** 13
dxc6 ♘xf3+ 14 ♗xf3 ♕a5+ 15 ♔f1
♕a6 16 ♔g1 ♕xc6∓ **♞xf3 14 ♗xf3
♕a5+ 15 ♖d2 ♖e8!∓** 15...♗g5 =+
16 ♔d1 ♗e5 17 ♖e1 ♗f5 18 g4!?
18 ♘g3 ♗f4! 19 ♖de2 ♖xe2 20 ♖xe2
♕c5 −+ **♗g6 19 ♞c3 ♗xc3! 20 bxc3
cxd5 21 ♗xd5 ♕c7 22 f3 ♖xe1+**
22...♕c5 23 ♖f1∓ **23 ♔xe1 ♖e8+
24 ♔f1 b6 25 c4 ♕f4 26 ♖f2?!** 26
♕c3! h5! 27 ♕d4 ♕g5∓ **h5! 27 ♕d1
♖e3 28 ♔g2 ♕e5 29 f4 ♗e4+ 30
♔f1 ♗d3+** Zeitnot **31 ♔g2** 31 ♕xd3
♕a1+ −+ **♕d4** −+ **32 ♖f3 ♕b2+
33 ♖f2 ♕d4 34 ♖f3 hxg4 35 ♖xe3
♗e4+ 36 ♖xe4 ♕xd1 37 ♖e7 ♔h7
38 ♖xf7 ♕d3?!** 38...a5 −+ **39 ♖xa7
♔h6 40 ♖a8 g6 41 ♖h8+ ♔g7 42
♖g8+ ♔h7 43 ♖e8 b5! 44 ♗g8+
♔g7 45 cxb5 ♕xb5 46 ♖e5 ♕b2+
47 ♔g3 ♕xg8 48 ♖g5 ♔f7 49 ♖xg4
♕a3+ 50 ♔g2 ♕xa2+ 51 ♔g3 ♕b3+**

52 ♔g2 ♕c2+ 53 ♔g3 ♕d3+ 54 ♔f2 ♕d2+ 55 ♔f3 ♕d1+ 56 ♔g3 ♕e2 57 ♖g5 ♕e3+ 58 ♔g4 ♕f2 59 ♖e5 ♕g2+ 0-1 Gufeld

81 Nikolic-Azmajparashvili
Jugoslavia-USSR 79

1 c4 ♞f6 2 ♞c3 e6 3 ♞f3 d5 4 d4 ♗e7 5 ♗g5 0-0 6 e3 h6 7 ♗h4 b6 8 ♖c1 8 cxd5 ♞xd5 9 ♗xe7 ♕xe7 10 ♞xd5 exd5 11 ♖c1 ♗e6 12 ♕a4 c5 13 ♕a3 ♖c8 14 ♗b5 ♕b7! 15 dxc5 bxc5 16 ♖xc5 ♖xc5 17 ♕xc5 ♞a6 18 ♗xa6 ♕xa6≈ Timman-Geller, Hilversum 73; 11 ♕b3 ♗e6 12 ♖c1 ♖c8 13 ♗d3 c5 14 ♕a3 ♔f8 15 b3 a5! 16 ♞e5 ♞d7 17 ♞xd7 ♗xd7 18 0-0 cxd4 19 ♕xe7+ ♔xe7 20 exd4 ♖xc1 21 ♖xc1 ♖c8= Browne-Grefe, USA Final 75 **♗b7 9 ♗xf6 ♗xf6 10 cxd5 exd5 11 b4 c6!? 12 ♗d3 a5!?** N 12...♖e8 13 0-0 ♞d7 14 ♕b3 ♞f8 15 ♖fd1 ♖c8 16 ♗b1 ♞e6 17 a4 ♗a8 18 ♗a2 ♖c7 19 ♕b1 a5 Korchnoi-Spassky (11) 77 **13 b5 c5 14 0-0 ♞d7 15 ♗b1 ♖c8 16 dxc5 ♞xc5 17 ♞d4 ♞e4?!** 17...g6!= **18 ♞a4 ♕d6 19 ♗xe4! dxe4 20 ♞c6 += ♕e6 21 ♕b3! ♕xb3 22 axb3 ♗xc6 23 bxc6** 23 ♖xc6!± ♖xc6 24 bxc6 ♗d8 25 ♞c3 +− **♗d8 24 g3 b5= 25 ♞c3 ♖xc6 26 ♞xb5 ♖b6 27 ♖c5 ♗e7 28 ♖d5 ♖d8 29 ♖fd1 ♖xb5 31 ♖xd8+ ♗xd8 31 ♖xd8+ ♔h7 32 ♖a8 ♔g6 33 ♔g2 ½-½ Georgadze**

82 Gheorghiu-Rohde USA 79

1 d4 ♞f6 2 c4 e6 3 ♞f3 d5 3...c5; 3...b6; 3...♗b4+ **4 ♞c3 ♗e7 5 ♗g5** 5 ♗f4 0-0 6 e3 h6 7 ♗h4 ♞e4 7...b6; 7...c6 8 ♗xe7 ♕xe7 9 ♕b3 9 ♖c1 += ♞xc3 10 ♕xc3! += 10 bxc3 dxc4 11 ♗xc4 b6 12 0-0 ♗b7∞ **c6 11 ♗e2 ♞d7 12 0-0 dxc4 13 ♗xc4 b6 14 b4!**

+= ♗b7 15 ♗e2! a5 15...c5 16 dxc5 bxc5 17 b5± **16 a3 ♖a7! 17 ♖fc1 ♖fa8 18 ♖ab1! axb4 19 axb4 ♖a2 20 ♕e1!± e5 21 ♞xe5 ♞xe5 22 dxe5 ♕xe5 23 ♗f3!**

25...♕f5? Zeitnot 23...♕b5! 24 ♕f1!± **24 b5! +− ♖d8 25 bxc6 ♗xc6 26 ♖xc6 ♖dd2 27 e4! ♕f4 28 ♕e3 ♕e5 29 ♕c3 ♕g5 30 ♕e3 ♕a5 31 e5!** Δ e6 +− ♖a1 32 ♖c8+ ♔h7 33 ♖cc1 ♖aa2 34 e6 fxe6 35 ♕xe6 1-0 **Gheorghiu**

83 Larsen-Spassky Montreal 79

1 c4 e6 2 ♞c3 d5 3 d4 ♗e7 4 cxd5 exd5 5 ♗f4 c6 6 e3 ♗f5 7 ♗d3 7 g4!? ♗xd3 8 ♕xd3 ♞f6 9 ♞f3 ♞bd7 10 0-0** 10 h3 0-0 11 0-0-0!? **0-0 11 ♖ab1?! a5** 11...♞h5! **12 h3! += ♖e8 13 a3 a4 14 ♕c2 ♕a5 15 ♖fd1 ♗f8 16 ♞e5 ♖e7?** 16...♕a6! Larsen **17 b4 axb3 18 ♖xb3 ♞xe5** 18...♕a6 19 ♖db1 ♖a7 20 ♕b2± **19 dxe5 ♞d7** 19...♞e8 20 e4 dxe4 21 ♞xe4± **20 ♖xb7 ♕xa3 21 ♖c7 ♕c5?? 21...♞xe5 22 ♗xe5 ♖xe5 23 ♖xc6 +=/± 22 ♖xd5! +− cxd5 23 ♖xc5 ♞xc5 24 ♞xd5 ♖ea7 25 ♗g5 ♖a1+ 26 ♔h2 ♖8a2 27 ♕f5 ♞e6 28 ♗h4 ♖f1 29 f4 ♖c1 30 ♕g4 ♖c4** 30...♖cc2 31 f5 ♖xg2+ 32 ♕xg2 ♖xg2+ 33 ♔xg2 ♞c5 34 ♔f3 +− **31 ♞f6+ ♔h8 32**

♕h5 1-0 32...gxf6 33 ♕xf7 +– **Keene**

84 Averbakh-Bachtiar Manila 79
**1 c4 e6 2 ♘f3 d5 3 d4 ♘f6 4 ♘c3
♗e7 5 ♗f4 0-0 6 e3 a6?!** 6...c5! **7 cxd5
♘xd5** 7...exd5 **8 ♘xd5 exd5 9 ♗d3 +=
♗g4?** 10 ♕c2!± ♘c6 **11 ♗xh7+ ♔h8
12 ♘e5** 12 ♗f5 ♘xe5 **13 ♗xe5 ♗b4+
14 ♔f1 ♗d6 15 ♗xd6 ♕xd6 16 ♗d3**
16 ♗f5 ♖ae8 **17 ♖ac1 c6 18 h3 ♗c8
19 g3 ♖e6 20 ♔g2 ♘f6 21 ♕c5 ♕d8
22 b4 ♖e8 23 ♖ce1 ♔g8 24 a4 ♖h6
25 ♕c2 ♕g5** Δ ♕h5 **26 ♕e2 ♗f5 27
♗xf5 ♕xf5 28 ♕g4 ♕c2 29 ♖c1?**
29 a5 **♕d2** 29...♕xa4 30 ♕d7 **30 ♖hd1
♕xb4 31 ♕d7 ♕e7 32 ♕xe7 ♖xe7 33
a5 += ♖d6 34 ♖c3 ♔f8 35 ♖b3 ♔e8
36 ♖db1 ♖dd7 37 h4 ♔d8 38 g4
♔c8 39 ♔g3 ♖e6 40 ♖c3 ♖e4 41 h5
g6 42 hxg6** 42 h6 fxg6 **43 ♖h1 ♖g7
44 ♖h8+ ♔d7 45 ♔h4 g5+ 46 ♔h5
♖e6 47 ♖b3 ♔c7 48 ♖h6 ♖e8 49
♖g6 ♖f7 50 ♔xg5 ♖xf2 51 ♖g7+
♔c8 52 ♖gxb7 ♖g8+ 53 ♔h4 ♖h8+
54 ♔g3 ♖hh2 55 ♖b8+ ♔c7 56 ♖3b7+
♔d6 57 ♖d8+ ♔e6 58 ♖e8+ ♔d6 59
♖ee7 c5 60 ♖g7 1-0 Keene**

Catalan

**85 Gulko-Sveshnikov
USSR Final 79**
**1 d4 d5 2 c4 e6 3 ♘f3 ♘f6 4 g3
dxc4!? 5 ♗g2 a6 6 0-0 6 ♘e5 ♗b4+
7 ♘c3 ♘d5 8 ♗d2 b5 9 a4∝ ♘c6**
6...b5 7 ♘e5 ♘d5 8 e4 ♘f6 9 a4 +=
7 e3! 7 ♘c3 ♖b8 8 e4 ♗e7 9 d5 ♘b4
=+ **♗d7 8 ♘c3 ♘d5 9 ♘d2 ♘xc3 10
bxc3 b5 11 a4∝ ♖b8 12 ♕g4!? e5
13 ♕h5 ♗d6?!** 13...g6 **14 axb5 axb5
15 ♖a6! ♖b6 16 ♖xb6 cxb6 17 ♘e4±
♕e7 18 f4! exf4 19 exf4 0-0 20
♕d5! ♗b8 21 f5!** Δ ♗g5 **h6 22 f6
♕e6 23 ♕h5 ♕g4**

24 fxg7! +– **♕xh5 25 ♘f6+ ♔xg7
26 ♘xh5+ ♔h8 27 ♘f6 ♘e5 28 dxe5
♗e6 29 ♗f4 b4 30 cxb4 ♖d8 31 b5
♖c8 32 ♗c6 ♖d8 1-0 Gufeld**

86 Hubner-Karpov Montreal 79
**1 d4 ♘f6 2 c4 e6 3 g3 d5 4 ♗g2 ♗e7
5 ♘f3 0-0 6 0-0 dxc4 7 ♕c2 a6 8
a4 ♗d7!?** 8...c5 **9 ♕xc4** 9 ♘e5 ♗c6
**10 ♗g5 a5 11 ♘c3 ♘a6 12 ♖ac1 ♗d5
13 ♘xd5?!=** 13 ♕d3! ♘b4 14 ♕b1
h6 15 ♗f4 ♘h5? 16 ♗xc7! ♕xc7
17 ♘xd5 +–; 14...♗c6 15 e4±; 13...
c5 14 e4 ♗b3 15 ♘d2 cxd4 16 ♘xb3
dxc3 17 ♕xc3 ♘xe4!; 14 ♘xd5 ♘xd5
15 ♗xe7 ♕xe7 16 dxc5 ♘xc5 17
♕b5 += exd5 **14 ♕b5 ♘b4! 15 ♕xb7
♗d6 16 ♘e5 ♖b8 17 ♕a7 ½-½ Keene**

1 d4 d5 2 c4 ♗f5

87 Portisch-Larsen Montreal 79
**1 ♘f3 d5 2 d4 ♗f5 3 c4 e6 4 ♕b3
♘c6 5 c5** 5 ♕xb7? ♘b4 6 ♘a3 ♖b8 7
♕xa7 ♖a8 8 ♕b7 ♖xa3 Δ ♘c2+ **♖b8
6 ♗f4 h6! 7 e3 g5 8 ♗g3 ♗g7 9 ♘c3
a6?!** 9...♘ge7 10 ♘b5 ♖c8 **10 h4!
g4 11 ♘e5 ♘ge7** 11...♘xe5 12 dxe5
♘e7 13 0-0-0 Δ e4± **12 ♘xc6 ♘xc6
13 ♗e2 0-0 14 ♕d1** 14 0-0-0 b6!
e5?! 14...h5! 15 f3 e5 16 fxg4 exd4
17 gxf5 dxc3 18 bxc3 ♗xc3+ 19 ♔f2
♗xa1 20 ♕xa1 d4!; 16 dxe5 d4 17

exd4 gxf3 18 ♗xf3 ♕xd4 **15 dxe5
d4 16 exd4 ♗xd4** 16...♕xd4 17 ♕xd4
♘xd4 18 0-0-0 += **17 0-0 ♕d7 18 ♗c4
♗c2 19 ♕c1 ♖bd8 20 ♖e1 ♗h7 21
♗d5?** 21 ♘d5!± △ ♘f6+ ♕e7 21...
♘c2? 22 e6 +− **22 ♗e4 ♕xc5 23
♗xh7+** 23 ♕f4! **♔xh7 24 ♕f4 ♕b6**
24...h5 25 ♘e4 **25 ♖ad1 ♕xb2 26
♖xd4 ♕xc3 27 ♖de4 ♔h8 28 ♕xg4
♖d4?!** 28...♕c2!? **29 ♖xd4 ♕xe1+
30 ♔h2 ♕a1** 30...♗xe5!? 31 f4 ♕xg3+
32 ♕xg3 ♗xd4 33 f5 ♖e8 **31 ♖d7
♕xa2 32 ♖xc7 b5** 32...♕d5!? **33 f4
♕d5 34 ♖d7 ♕e4 35 ♕h5 ♔g8** 35...
b4 36 f5 b3 37 f6 b2 38 e6 b1♕ 39
fxg7+ △ ♗e5+ +− **36 ♖e7! ♕b4** 36...
♕d5 37 f5 ♕c5 38 ♕g4! ♕xe7 39
f6 +− **37 ♖a7 ♕c5 38 ♖xa6 b4 39
♕f3 ♕b5 40 ♖a7 ♖b8 41 f5 ♗xe5
42 f6 ♔h8** 42...h5 43 ♔h3! +− **43
♖xf7 △ ♕e4 ♖e8 44 ♕g4 ♗xg3+
45 ♔h3! 1-0** 45...♖g8 46 ♖f8 ♕d5
47 ♕g7 mate **Keene**

Dutch

88 Stefanov-Stanciu
Satu Mare 78

**1 c4 f5 2 ♘f3 ♘f6 3 g3 d6 4 d4 e6
5 ♗g2 ♗e7 6 0-0 0-0 7 b3** 7 ♘c3
♕e8 **8 ♖e1 ♘e4!?** 7...♕e8 **8 ♗b2
♗f6 9 ♕c2 ♘c6 10 ♖d1** 10 ♘bd2
♕e8 **11 ♘c3 ♗xc3 12 ♗xc3 e5= 13
d5** 13 dxe5 ♘e7 **14 ♖ac1 f4! 15**
gxf4?! exf4 16 ♘d4 ♗xd4! 17 ♖xd4
♕h5∓ **18 ♕d2 ♘g6 19 ♔h1 ♗h3 20**
♗xh3 20 ♖g1 ♕xh3 **21 ♖g1 ♖ae8
22 f3 ♖e7 23 ♕c2 ♖fe8 24 ♖d2 ♘h4!
−+ 25 ♗d4 ♘f5 26 ♗f2 g6** 26...♖xe2!
27 ♕d3 ♖f7?! 27...♖e3! **28 b4?** 28
♖g2

Diagram

28...**♖e3!!** 29 ♗xe3 29 ♕c2 ♖xe2!
♘g3+ 30 ♖xg3 fxg3 31 ♔g1 31 ♗g1
g2 mate **♕xh2+ 32 ♔f1 g2+ 0-1
Vaisman**

89 Ghinda-Stanciu Rumania 79

1 d4 f5 2 ♘c3 d5 2...♘f6 **3 ♗g5
c6 4 e3 ♕d6?** 4...♘d7 **5 ♗d3 e5 6**
dxe5 **♕xe5 7 ♘f3 ♕c7 8 ♘d4 ♕f7
9 ♕f3 g6 10 ♕g3 ♘f6 11 ♘db5! cxb5
12 ♘xb5 ♘c6** 12...♘a6 13 ♘d6+ ♗xd6
14 ♕xd6 **13 ♘c7+ ♔d7 14 ♘xa8
♗b4+ 15 c3 ♗d6 16 ♕h4 ♘g4 17 h3
♘ge5 18 ♗b5! h6 19 0-0-0 ♕e6 20
♗f6 g5?!** 21 ♗xg5 ♘g6 22 ♕a4! hxg5
**23 c4 dxc4 24 ♗xc6+ bxc6 25 ♕xa7+
♕e8 26 ♘c7+ ♔xc7 27 ♕xc7 ♘e7
28 ♖d8+ ♔f7 29 ♖xh8 1-0 Vaisman**

Benko Gambit

90 Unzicker-Miles
South Africa 79

**1 d4 ♘f6 2 c4 g6 3 g3 c5 4 d5 b5 5
cxb5 a6 6 bxa6 ♗g7 7 ♘c3 ♗xa6 8
♘f3 d6 9 ♗g2 ♘bd7 10 0-0 ♘b6
11 ♖e1 0-0 12 ♘d2 ♕d7** △ ♘a4 **13
♖b1** 13 ♕c2 ♕f5!? **14 e4** ♕xf2+!!; **
14** ♕xf5?! gxf5 **♕b7** 13...♖fb8; **
13...♗b7 14 e4 ♘a4 14 b4 ♘fd7 15
bxc5 ♘xc5 16 ♗b2 ♕d7 17 ♘ce4!
♘ba4!** 17...♗xb2? **18 ♘xc5 dxc5
19 ♖xb2 ♘xd5? 20 ♘b3!± 18 ♗xg7**

♛xg7 19 ♘xc5 ♞xc5 20 ♘b3 ♖fc8
21 ♖c1 21 ♘d4 ♝c4 22 ♘c6 ♝xa2
23 ♖b2 ♞xb3 22 axb3 22 ♛xb3
♖ab8 ♛g8! 23 ♝f3 ♛b5 24 ♖xc8+
♖xc8 25 e4 ♛b4 26 ♛g2? 26 ♝e2
♖c3 =+ 27 ♛a1 27 ♖e3 ♖xe3 28 fxe3
♛c3 29 ♔f2 ♝d3 30 b4 ♛b2+ 31 ♔g1
♝b5 =+ ♖xb3 28 ♖c1 ♖a3 29 ♛b1
♛d4! 30 ♖d1? ♛f6!∓ 31 ♝g4 h5
32 ♝h3

32...♝e2?? 32...♛f3+ 33 ♔g1 ♝d3
34 ♝g2=; 33...♖d3 34 ♖e1∝; 33...
♖a2!! −+ 33 ♖e1 ♝d3?= 34 e5! dxe5
35 ♛b8+ ♛g7 36 ♛xe5 ♛xe5 37 ♖xe5
♖a1 38 ♝d7 ♛f6 39 ♖e3 ♝c4 40 ♝c6
g5 40...♖d1 41 h4=; 40...♝f1+ 41
♔f3 g5∝ 41 f4! ♖a2+ 41...gxf4 42
♖f3! 42 ♔g1 ♖a1+ 43 ♔g2 g4 44
♖e5 ♖a2+ 45 ♔g1 ♖a1+ 46 ♔g2 ♖a2+
47 ♔g1 ♝e2 48 ♖xh5 ♝f3 49 ♝d7
♖g2+ ½-½ 50 ♔f1 ♖d2 51 ♖f5+ ♔g6
52 ♖g5+ ♔f6 53 ♝xg4 ♝xg4 54 ♖xg4
♖xh2= **Miles**

91 F.Portisch-Vaganian
Kecskemet 79

1 d4 ♞f6 2 c4 c5 3 d5 b5 4 cxb5
a6 5 e3 e6 6 ♞c3 exd5 7 ♞xd5 ♝b7
7...axb5 8 ♝xb5 ♝b7 9 ♝c4 ♝e7 10
♞e2 ♞xd5 11 ♝xd5 ♝xd5 12 ♛xd5±
Tukmakov-Bednarski, Decin 77 8
♞xf6+ ♛xf6 9 ♞f3 ♝e7 10 ♛b3?!

10 ♝e2 0-0 11 0-0 d5≈ 0-0 11 bxa6
11 ♝e2 axb5 12 ♛xb5 ♝a6 =+ ♝xf3
12 gxf3 ♛xf3 13 ♖g1 ♝h4∓ 14 ♔c2
♞xa6 15 ♛e2 ♛f6 16 ♖g4 ♞b4 17
♖f4 ♛e7 18 ♝g2 d5! 19 ♛f1 ♝g5 20
♖g4 ♝f6 21 a3 21 ♝d2 ♛e6 22 ♝f3
c4! 23 ♖b1 ♞d3 24 ♝d2 ♖ab8 25
b3 ♞e5 26 ♝b4 26 ♖g3 ♝h4 27 ♝g4
♛g6 −+ ♞xg4 27 ♝xg4 ♛e4 0-1
Tompa

92 Razuvaev-Tseshkovsky
USSR Final 78

1 d4 ♞f6 2 c4 c5 3 d5 b5 4 ♞f3
4 cxb5 a6 5 e3 g6 6 ♞c3 ♝g7 7 ♞f3
0-0 8 a4 += g6 5 cxb5 a6 6 e3 6 bxa6
♝xa6 7 ♞c3 Δ g3, ♝h3 ♝g7 7 ♞c3
0-0 8 a4 ♝b7! 8...d6 9 ♖a3! ♞bd7
10 e4!±; 9...e6 10 ♝c4 axb5 11
♞xb5 exd5 12 ♝xd5 += Inkiov-
Szmetan, Buenos Aires 78 9 e4 e6
10 ♝g5?! 10 ♖a3 exd5 11 exd5 h6
12 ♝xf6 12 ♝h4 g5 13 ♝g3 d6 =+
♛xf6 13 ♖c1?! 13 ♝e2 Δ 0-0 ♖e8+
14 ♝e2 axb5 15 axb5 15 ♞xb5 ♛xb2
Δ ♖xe2+! −+ ♛e7! =+ 16 ♛d2 16
♖c2 ♝xc3+ 17 ♖xc3 ♖a1!; 16 0-0?
♝xc3 17 bxc3 ♛xe2 18 ♖e1 ♛xd1
−+ d6! 17 0-0 ♝xc3 18 bxc3 ♛xe2
19 ♖ce1 ♛xb5 20 ♛xh6 ♞d7∓ 21
♞g5 ♞f8! 21...♞f6?! 22 ♞e6! 22 ♞e4
♖xe4! 23 ♖xe4 ♛d3! 24 ♖e3 24 ♖h4
♛c3 ♛xd5 Δ ♛xg2 mate 25 ♖g3
♞e6 26 h4 ♞g7 Zeitnot 27 ♔c1 ♖e8
28 ♖e1 ♖e4! −+ 29 ♖g5 ♛e6 30
♖xe4 ♛xe4 31 f3 ♛xh4 32 ♖g4 ♛e7
33 ♔f2 ♝c6 34 ♛d2 ♞f5 35 ♖g5
♛f6 36 ♖g4 ♔g7 37 ♖f4 ♛e7 38
c4 ♛e5 39 ♖g4 ♛f6 40 ♖f4 ♛e7 41
♖g4 ♞d4 42 ♖f4 f5 0-1 **Gufeld**

93 Hvenekilde-Borik
Cleveland 79

1 d4 ♞f6 2 c4 c5 3 d5 b5 4 cxb5 a6

5 g4!? ⧹b7?! 5...⧹xg4 6 e4 d6! 6 ⧹g2 e6 6...⧹xg4? 7 e4 ⧹f6 8 e5± 7 e4 exd5 8 exd5 d6 9 ⧹c3 ⧹e7 10 g5 ⧹fd7 11 ⧹f3 axb5 12 0-0 12 ⧹xb5 ⧹a6 0-0 13 ⧹e1 b4 14 ⧹e4 ⧹b6 15 ⧹h4 g6 16 f4 16 ⧹xc5? dxc5 17 d6 ⧹xg5! 18 ⧹xb7 ⧹a7! −+ ⧹xd5 17 b3 ⧹xe4 18 ⧹xe4 d5 19 ⧹e3 ⧹c6 20 ⧹h3 ⧹e8

21 ⧹f5 ⧹f8 21...gxf5? 22 ⧹h5 ⧹d6 23 ⧹xh7+ ⧹f8 24 ⧹b2 ⧹d4 25 ⧹xd4 cxd4 26 g6 fxg6 27 ⧹h8+ ⧹e7 28 ⧹h7+ ⧹e8 29 ⧹e1+ +− 22 ⧹b2 ⧹d7 22...gxf5 23 ⧹xh7 ⧹d4 24 ⧹h5 ⧹g7; 23 ⧹h5 h6 24 gxh6 +− 23 ⧹h6+ 23 ⧹e3!? d4 24 ⧹g4 ⧹g7 25 f5!? ⧹xh6 24 ⧹xh6 ⧹e3 25 ⧹c1 ⧹ae8 26 ⧹e5 26 ⧹xc5 ⧹g4! ⧹e2∓ 27 ⧹f3 ⧹8xe5! 28 fxe5 ⧹d4 29 ⧹f4 ⧹xe5 30 ⧹g4 ⧹e7 31 ⧹f1 ⧹xg5 32 ⧹h1 ⧹e4+ 33 ⧹xe4 dxe4 34 ⧹d1 e3 35 ⧹e1 e2 36 ⧹xe2 ⧹xe2 37 ⧹xe2 ⧹e5 0-1 Keene

Benoni

94 Balashov-Kagan Rio 79

1 d4 c5 2 d5 e5 3 e4 d6 4 ⧹c3 ⧹e7 5 f4 exf4 6 ⧹xf4 a6 7 ⧹f3 ⧹g4 8 e5! += ⧹b6 9 ⧹d2 ⧹xf3 10 gxf3 ⧹h4+ 10...dxe5 11 ⧹xe5 ⧹f6 12 d6± 11 ⧹g3 ⧹xg3+ 12 hxg3 dxe5 13 0-0-0± Δ ⧹h3, d6, d7+ ⧹d7 13...⧹f6 14 ⧹g5±

14 ⧹h3 0-0-0 15 ⧹g5 ⧹f6 16 ⧹e3 ⧹b8 17 ⧹xd7 ⧹xd7 18 ⧹e4 +− ⧹b6 19 ⧹xc5 ⧹a7 19...⧹d8 20 ⧹d7+ +− 20 ⧹xe5! ⧹xc5 21 ⧹xg7 ⧹e3+ 22 ⧹b1 ⧹xf3 23 ⧹xh8 ⧹xd5 24 ⧹df1 ⧹g4 25 ⧹xh7 ⧹f6 26 ⧹h4 ⧹g6 27 ⧹c4 1-0 Miles

95 Antoshin-Hartston Sochi 79

1 d4 ⧹f6 2 c4 c5 3 d5 e5 4 ⧹c3 d6 5 e4 ⧹e7 6 h3 6 ⧹f3; 6 g3!? 0-0 6...⧹bd7!? 7 g4 ⧹f8 7 g4 ⧹e8 Δ ⧹g5 8 ⧹f3 a6 9 a4 ⧹bd7 10 ⧹d3 g6 11 ⧹h6 ⧹g7 12 ⧹e2?! 12 ⧹e2!? Δ 0-0-0; 12 ⧹c2 Δ ⧹e2, ⧹ag1 ⧹f6 13 ⧹g3 ⧹h8 14 ⧹c2 ⧹d7 14...b6!? 15 a5 b5 16 axb6 ⧹xb6 17 ⧹d2 a5 18 ⧹c3 a4 19 ⧹a3?! 19 ⧹g1!? Δ ⧹1e2, f4 ⧹g8! 20 ⧹g1 f5!= 21 exf5 gxf5 22 ⧹xf5?! 22 gxf5 ⧹h6∞ ⧹xf5 23 ⧹xf5 ⧹xf5 24 gxf5 ⧹f6? 24...⧹h6! =+ 25 ⧹e2 ⧹a6 26 ⧹e4 ⧹d8 27 0-0!± ⧹f6 28 ⧹d3 ⧹c8 29 f4 e4!? 29...exf4? 30 ⧹xf4 +− 30 ⧹xe4 ⧹a7 31 ⧹g3?? 31 ⧹h2± ⧹g7! Δ ⧹xg3/⧹xe4 32 ⧹xf6 ⧹xf6 33 ⧹h2 ⧹b7!∓ 34 ⧹f2 ⧹b4! 35 ⧹a2 ⧹e8 36 ⧹c2 ⧹e3! 37 ⧹e2 ⧹e8 38 ⧹e4 ⧹bb3 −+ 39 ⧹xe3 39 ⧹c3 ⧹xe2+ 40 ⧹xe2 ⧹e3 −+ ⧹xe3 40 ⧹c3 a3! 41 ⧹d2 41 ⧹xa3 ⧹xc3 −+ ⧹d4! 41...axb2 42 ⧹a8!∓ 0-1 Hartston

96 J.Meyer-Costigan USA 79

1 d4 c5 2 d5 2 dxc5!? ⧹a5+ 3 ⧹c3 ⧹f6 4 ⧹f3 ⧹c6 5 ⧹d2 ⧹xc5 6 e4 d6 7 ⧹c4 ⧹g4 8 ⧹e3?! ⧹xe3 9 ⧹xe3 ⧹a5 10 ⧹c4 g6= K.Smith-Browne, San Antonio 72; 8 ⧹d2!? Δ h3 +=; 2 ⧹f3 cxd4 3 ⧹xd4 d5 4 g3?! e5 5 ⧹b3 ⧹c6 6 ⧹g2 ⧹e6 7 0-0 f5!∓ Tatai-Mariotti, Rome 77; 4 c4 ⧹f6=; 3 ⧹xd4 ⧹c6 4 ⧹d1 d5 5 g3 e5 =+ ⧹f6 3 ⧹c3 d6 4 e4 g6 5 ⧹f3 5 ⧹b5+ ⧹fd7 6 a4 ⧹g7 7 ⧹f3 ⧹a6 8 0-0 ⧹c7

9 ♗e2 0-0 10 ♗f4 f5! 11 exf5 ♖xf5
12 ♗g5! ♗xc3 13 bxc3 ♘xd5 14
♗d3 ♘xc3 15 ♕d2? ♖xf3 16 gxf3
♘e5 17 ♗c4+? e6! −+ Larsen-Browne,
USA 72; 15 ♕e1! ♖xf3 16 ♗c4+ ♖f7
17 ♗xf7+ ♔xf7 18 ♕xc3 ♘e5≈
Gerusel-Browne, Mannheim 75 ♗g7
6 h3 6 ♗b5+ ♗d7 7 a4 0-0 8 0-0
♘a6 9 ♗xa6 bxa6 10 ♘d2 ♖b8 =+
Dorfman-Tal, USSR 77; 9 ♖e1 ♘c7
10 ♗xd7 ♕xd7 11 h3 ♖ad8 12 ♗f4
+= Gheorghiu-Soos, Bucharest 61;
6 ♗e2 ♘a6 7 0-0 ♖b8 8 a4 +=; 7...♘c7
8 ♖e1 0-0 9 h3 +=; 6...0-0 7 0-0
♗g4 8 ♘d2 ♗xe2 9 ♕xe2 ♘a6 10
♘c4 ♘c7 11 a4 a6 12 a5 ♘d7 13
♘a4 ♘b5 14 c3 += Tukmakov-
Georgadze, Decin 77 **0-0 7 ♗e2 b5!
8 ♘xb5** 8 ♗xb5 ♘xe4! **♘xe4 9 0-0
♗b7 10 ♖e1 ♘d7** 10...a6 11 ♘a3 ♘bd7
12 ♗xa6?? ♖xa6 13 ♖xe4 ♖xa3;
12 ♗d3 ♘ef6 13 c4 ♖b8∞ **11 ♗d3
♘ef6 12 c4 ♘b6 13 ♗f4! ♗c8?!** 13...a6
14 ♘c3 ♗c8 △ e6 **14 a4 ♗d7 15 ♗f1
♘c8 16 a5 ♖b8 17 ♖a2 ♖e8 18 ♕d2**
△ ♗h6; 18 b4!? a6 19 bxc5 axb5
20 c6 △ cxb5±; 18...cxb4 19 ♘fd4
a6 20 ♘c6 ♗xc6 21 dxc6 axb5 22
cxb5 ∞/+= **a6 19 ♘c3 ♖b4 20 ♗h6
♗h8 21 ♗g5! ♘h5?** 21...♕c7 △ ♕b7
**22 ♖e4± ♗g7 23 g4 ♖f8 24 ♗d3 ♖b7
25 h4** △ h5 **f5 26 ♖e6!** ♘xe6 26...
fxg4 27 h5 ♘xh5 28 ♘xh7! ♗xe6
(28...♔xh7 29 ♗xg6+) 29 ♘xf8 ♗f5??
30 ♗xf5 gxf5 31 ♕g5+ ♗g7 32 ♘e6
+−; 29...♗f7 30 ♘xg6; 27...♗xe6!?
28 hxg6 hxg6 29 ♗xg7 ♗xg7 (29...
♗f7? 30 ♗xh8) 30 ♘xe6 ♕e8 31 ♘xf8
♔xf8 32 ♕g5± **27 dxe6 ♗c6 28
gxf5 gxf5 29 ♘f7! ♖xf7 30 exf7+
♔xf7 31 ♕g5 ♕g8 32 ♗xf5 ♗d7 33
♗e4 ♖b4?** Zeitnot; 33...♖b3! 34 ♗c2
♖b7 ∞/± **34 ♖a3 ♗f6 35 ♕xg8+ ♔xg8
36 ♘d5 ♖xb2 37 ♘xf6+ exf6 38**

♗d5+ **1-0** Ciamarra

**1 d4 ♘f6 2 c4 c5 3 d5 g6 4 ♘c3 ♗g7
5 e4 d6 6 ♗d3 0-0 7 ♘ge2 e6 8 0-0
exd5 9 cxd5 ♖e8 10 ♔h1 c4!? 11
♗c2 ♘a6 12 ♗g5 h6 13 ♗e3 ♗d7 14
♕d2 b5 15 a3 ♘c5 16 f3 h5?!** 16...
♔h7 **17 ♘d4 a6 18 ♖ae1 ♖c8 19 ♗h6±
♗xh6 20 ♕xh6 ♘h7 21 ♕e3 ♘f6 22
♕f4 ♕e7 23 ♕d2 ♕f8 24 f4! ♕h6
25 h3 ♖e7 26 ♕f2 ♘h7 27 e5 f5**

28 ♘c6?! 28 e6!? ♗e8 29 ♗xf5!?;
28 exd6! ♖xe1 29 ♖xe1 ±/+− △ ♖e7,
♘c6 **♗xc6 29 dxc6 ♕f8! 30 ♘d5 ♖xc6
31 exd6 ♖xe1 32 ♖xe1 ♕xd6 33 ♘e7+
♔f7 34 ♘xc6 ♕xc6 35 ♕e3 ♘f8**
35...♕e6!? 36 ♕c3 ♕c6 37 b3; 36...
♕d6 **36 ♕e7+ ♔g8 37 ♖d1! +− ♘ce6
38 ♖d6 ♕c8 39 ♗d1 c3 40 bxc3 ♕c4
41 ♗f3 h4 42 ♕xh4 ♕xc3 43 ♗d5
♕e3 44 ♖xa6 ♔g7 1-0 Miles/Speelman**

**1 d4 ♘f6 2 c4 e6 3 ♘c3 c5 4 d5 exd5
5 cxd5 g6 6 e4** 6 d6!? **d6 7 ♗d3 ♗g7
8 ♘ge2 0-0 9 ♘g3** N 9 0-0 b6!? (△
♗a6) **10 ♗g5!** h6 **11 ♗f4 ♗a6 12
♗xa6 ♘xa6 13 ♕d3 ♘c7** +=; 9...♖e8
10 h3 ♗d7!? 11 ♗g5 ♕c7 12 ♕d2
c4 13 ♗c2 b5≈ Spassky-Ljubojevic,
Manila 76; 9...a6 10 a4 ♕c7 · 11 h3

♘bd7 12 f4 ♖b8! 13 ♗e3 ♖e8 14 ♘g3 c4 15 ♗c2 ♘c5 16 ♗d4 b5 17 axb5 axb5 18 e5 dxe5 19 fxe5 ♖xe5! =+ Timman-Ljubojevic, IBM 75; 16 ♕f3!? b5 17 axb5 axb5 18 e5! +=; 15...b5?! 16 axb5 axb5 17 ♖a7 +=; 9...♘e8!? Matulovic **a6 10 a4 b6 11 0-0 ♕c7 12 h3** 12 ♖a3!? **♗bd7 13 ♗e3** 13 b3 ♘h5 14 ♘ge2 ♘e5∓ **c4! 14 ♗e2 ♖b8 15 f4** 15 ♕d2; 15 f3!? **♖b7** 15...b5 16 axb5 axb5 17 e5!? **16 ♗f3 ♘c5 17 e5 ♗e8 18 e6?** 18 exd6 ♘xd6 19 ♘ge4∝ **♗d3! 19 ♕d2 b5! 20 axb5 axb5 21 ♖ab1 b4 22 exf7+ ♖xf7 23 ♘d1 ♗xb2! ‒+ 24 ♘xb2 c3 25 ♕d3 cxb2 26 ♘e2 ♖e7 27 g4 ♗d7 28 ♘d4 ♕c3 29 ♕xc3 bxc3 30 ♘c2 ♗a4 1-0 Ciamarra**

99 Botterill-Kraidman London 79
1 d4 ♘f6 2 c4 c5 3 d5 d6 4 ♘c3 g6 5 e4 ♗g7 6 ♗e2 0-0 7 f4 a6 8 a4 e6 9 ♘f3 exd5 10 cxd5 ♖e8 10...♗g4! **11 e5!? dxe5 12 fxe5 ♘g4 13 0-0** 13 ♗g5 f6 =+ **♗xe5 14 ♗f4 ♘bd7 15 d6 ♘xf3+ 16 ♗xf3 ♗d4+!?** 16...♘e5 **17 ♔h1 ♘e5 18 ♗d5 ♗e6 19 ♗xe6 ♖xe6 20 ♘e4 h6!? 21 ♖c1! b6?** 21...♘d7 22 ♕f3 ♕e8 23 ♘c3 ∝/± **22 b4 ♖c8 23 bxc5 bxc5**

24 ♗xh6 ♕h4 25 ♕xd4! ♕xh6 25... cxd4 26 ♖xc8+ ♔h7 27 d7! +−

26 ♖xc5 ♘c6 27 ♖xc6 +− ♖d8 28 ♗f6+ ♕f8 29 h3 a5 30 ♕b6 ♖a8 31 d7 1-0 Botterill

100 Kosciuk-Meduna
Bialystok 79
1 d4 ♘f6 2 c4 c5 3 d5 e6 4 ♘c3 exd5 5 cxd5 d6 6 ♘f3 g6 7 ♘d2 ♘a6?! N 7...♗g7; 7...♘bd7 **8 ♘c4 ♘c7 9 a4 b6 10 ♗g5 ♗e7 11 ♗h6?! ♘g4 12 ♗f4 0-0 13 h3 ♘f6 14 e4 ♗a6 15 ♗d3 ♗xc4 16 ♗xc4 a6 17 0-0 ♘d7?!** 17... b5!? **18 ♗h6 ♖e8 19 f4 ♗f6 20 e5!± dxe5 21 f5** △ d6! **gxf5 22 ♖xf5** △ ♘e4! **e4 23 ♕g4+ ♔h8 24 ♖af1 ♖g8 25 ♕h5 ♕e7 26 ♗f4 ♘e8 27 d6! ♗xd6 28 ♘d5 ♗d4+ 29 ♔h1 ♕f8 30 ♗xd6 ♕xd6 31 ♖xf7 ♖g7 32 ♘e7! ♖xf7 33 ♖xf7 ♘f8 34 ♖xh7+! ♘xh7 35 ♕f7! +− b5 36 ♗d5 ♖d8** 36...♖f8 **37 ♗xe4! ♗g7 38 ♘g6+ ♕xg6 39 ♕xg6 ♖d1+ 40 ♔h2 1-0 Vaisman**

101 Toth-Nunn Geneva 79
1 d4 ♘f6 2 c4 c5 3 d5 e6 4 ♘c3 exd5 5 cxd5 d6 6 ♘f3 g6 7 ♘d2 ♗g7 8 e4 8 ♘c4 **0-0 9 ♗e2 ♖e8** 9...♘a6 **10 0-0 ♘bd7 11 a4 a6** 11...♘e5 **12 ♖a3 ♖b8 13 ♕c2!?** 13 ,a5 ♕c7 14 h3 b5?! 15 axb6 ♖xb6 16 ♕c2± Petrosian-Quinteros, Lone Pine 76; 13...♕e7 14 ♘c4 b5?! 15 axb6 ♘xb6 16 ♘a5 ♕c7 17 ♕c2± Bagirov-Jansa, Titovo Uzice 78 **♕c7?** 13...♘e5 += **14 a5± ♘e5** 14...b5 15 axb6 ♖xb6 16 ♘c4 △ ♗f4 +− **15 f4!?** 15 h3 g5 16 ♘f3 ♘xf3+ 17 ♗xf3 +=/± **♘eg4 16 ♘c4 ♘h5 17 e5?** 17 ♔h1!? ♕d8 18 ♗xg4 ♗xg4 19 e5 ♕h4 20 ♘e4 dxe5∝; 17 f5 gxf5! **dxe5 18 d6** 18 h3 exf4! 19 hxg4 ♗d4+ 20 ♖f2 f3! 21 d6 fxe2 −+ **♕d8 19 ♘d5 exf4** 19...e4 =+ **20 ♘xf4! 20 ♘e7+ ♖xe7 −+ ♗f5 =+** 20...♘xf4 21 ♗xg4 **21 ♕d1**

♘xf4 **21...♗d4+ 22 ♔h1 ♘f2+ 23 ♖xf2 ♗xf2 24 ♘xh5 gxh5 25 ♖f3;** 24...♗g4 25 ♘f4; 22...♕h4 23 ♘h3! △ ♗g5 **22 ♖xg4** 22 ♗xf4 ♗d4+ 23 ♔h1 ♘f2+ ♗xg4 **23 ♕xg4 ♘e2+ 24 ♔h1 f5 25 ♕f3 ♖e4 26 ♕d3 ♕h4?** 26... ♘d4 =+ **27 ♕d5+** 27 ♘d2 ♘xc1 28 ♕d5+ ♔h8 29 ♘xe4 ♕xe4 30 ♕xe4 dxe4 31 ♖xc1 ♗xb2 −+ **♔h8 28 ♖h3 ♖d4** 28...♘f4 29 ♖xh4 ♘xd5 30 ♖xe4 fxe4 31 ♗g5∝; 29 ♗xf4? ♕xf4 =+ **29 ♕e6! ♖e4** 29...♘f4! 30 ♗xf4 ♕xf4 =+; 30 ♖xh4 ♘xe6 31 ♖xd4 =+ **30 ♕d5 ♕f6?** 30...♖d4 **31 ♕xc5 ♕e6?** 31...♘xc1 32 ♖xc1 ♕e6∝ **32 ♕c7!± ♕g8** 32...♖c8 33 d7 ♖xc7 34 d8♕+ ♕g8 35 ♕xc7 ♖xc4 36 ♕xb7 ♖xc1 37 ♖xc1 ♘xc1 38 ♕xa6 +− **33 d7??** Zeitnot 33 ♘b6! ♘xc1 34 ♖xc1 ♖be8 35 ♖f3± **♖xc4 34 ♕d6 ♖c6 35 ♕d2 ♘xc1 36 ♖xc1 ♕d5! 37 ♕e1 ♖xc1 38 ♕xc1 ♕xd7 0-1 Nunn**

102 Dorfman-Keene Manila 79

1 d4 ♘f6 2 c4 g6 3 ♘c3 ♗g7 4 e4 d6 5 f3 0-0 6 ♗g5!? c5 6...♘c6 **7 d5 h6?!** 7...e6 **8 ♗e3 e6 9 ♕d2 exd5 10 cxd5** 10 exd5!? ♖e8 11 0-0-0∝ **♔h7 11 ♘ge2 ♘bd7 12 ♘g3 a6 13 a4 ♘e5 14 ♗e2 ♗d7 15 0-0 ♖b8?** 15...b5! 16 axb5 axb5 17 ♖xa8 ♕xa8 18 ♘xb5 ♗xb5 19 ♗xb5 ♖b8∝; 17 ♘xb5! ♗xb5 18 ♗xb5 ♕b6 19 ♗e2 += **16 h3!± b5 17 f4!** 17 axb5? ♗xb5! **♘c4 18 ♗xc4 bxc4 19 e5! ♘e8 20 f5 dxe5** 20...♗xe5 21 fxg6+ +− **21 ♗xc5 ♖g8 22 fxg6+ fxg6 23 ♖f7** +− **♕h4 24 ♘ge4 ♗f5 25 ♗f2?!** 25 ♗e7 ♕f4 26 ♕e2 ♗xe4 27 ♖xf4 ♗d3 28 ♕f2 exf4 29 d6 +− **♕d8 26 d6 ♖f8 27 ♖xf8 ♗xf8 28 ♖d1 ♘f6 29 ♕e2 ♘xe4 30 ♘xe4 ♗g7 31 d7 ♕c7! 32 ♘c5 ♖d8 33 ♕xc4 e4 34 ♕f7 ♔h8 35**

♘e6 ♗xe6 Zeitnot **36 ♕xe6 ♕c2**

37 ♖e1? 37 ♕e8+ ♔h7 38 ♕xd8 ♕xd1+ 39 ♔h2 ♗e5+ 40 g3 ♗xg3+!!=; 37 ♖d4! **♕xa4 38 ♕xg6 ♕xd7 39 ♕xa6 ♖e8 40 ♕c4?** 40 b4!± ♗xb2 **41 ♖xe4 ♖xe4 ½-½ Keene**

103 Kluger-Bilek Hungary 79

1 d4 ♘f6 2 c4 c5 3 ♘f3 e6 4 d5 exd5 5 cxd5 g6 6 ♘c3 ♗g7 7 d6!? 0-0 8 e3 b6 9 ♗c4 9 ♗e2 ♗b7 10 0-0 ♘c6 11 ♕d2 a6! 12 ♖b1 12 a4 ♘a5 13 ♗a2 c4 **b5 13 ♗e2 c4 14 b4!? cxb3 15 axb3 ♖c8 16 ♗b2 ♘a5 17 ♘d4** 17 ♗a1 ♕b6 **18 ♖fd1 ♖fe8** 18...♕xd6? **19 ♘cxb5 ♕d5 20 ♗f3 ♘xb3 21 ♗xd5 ♘xd2 22 ♗xb7** +− **19 ♖a1 ♘c6 20 ♗f3? ♘xd4 21 ♕xd4 ♕xd4 22 ♖xd4 ♘e4! 23 ♘xe4 ♗xd4 24 ♘f6+ ♗xf6 25 ♗xf6 ♗xf3 26 gxf3 ♖c6 27 ♗e7 f5 28 ♔g2 ♔f7 29 ♔g3 ♖a8! 30 b4 ♖c4 31 ♖b1 ♖ac8 32 h4 ♖c1 33 ♖b3 ♖8c3 34 ♖b2 ♖3c2 35 ♖b3 ♖g1+ 36 ♔f4 ♖xf2 37 ♖c3 ♖g4+ 38 ♔e5 ♖xf3 39 ♖c7 ♖xe3+ 40 ♔d5 ♖c4 0-1 Meleghegyi**

104 Kuzmin-Tal Riga 79

1 d4 ♘f6 2 c4 e6 3 g3 c5 4 d5 exd5 5 cxd5 d6 6 ♘c3 g6 7 ♗g2 ♗g7 8 ♘f3 0-0 9 0-0 ♖e8 10 h3!? 10 ♘d2!∝ **♘e4 11 ♘xe4 ♖xe4 12 ♗g5 ♕c7 13**

♘d2 ♖e8 14 ♘e4 ♖xe4! 15 ♗xe4 ♗xh3 16 ♗g2?! ♗xg2 17 ♕xg2 ♗xb2 =+ 18 ♖b1 ♗g7 19 ♕a4 ♘d7 20 ♖h1 a6 21 ♖h4 b5! 22 ♖xb5 ♘b6! 23 ♖xb6 ♕xb6 24 ♕d7 ♗e5 25 ♖xh7?? ♕xh7 26 ♕xf7+ ♗g7 27 ♗f6 ♕a7! −+ 1-0 Gheorghiu

105 Browne-Ostos USA 79

1 d4 ♘f6 2 ♘f3 g6 3 c4 ♗g7 4 ♘c3 c5 5 e4 0-0 6 ♗e2 d6 7 0-0 ♘a6 8 d5 ♘c7 9 ♗f4 a6 10 e5!± ♘h5 11 ♗e3! dxe5 11...f6 12 exd6 exd6 13 ♘d2 12 ♗xc5 ♘e8 13 ♖e1 ♘d6 14 ♕b3 ♗g4 15 h3! ♗xf3 16 ♗xf3 ♘f4 17 ♗b6 ♕c8 18 c5 ♘f5 19 ♗e2!± ♘xe2+ 20 ♗xe2 ♘d4 21 ♕c4 ♕d7 22 ♖ad1 ♕h8 23 ♗f1 e6 24 d6 g5 25 ♖e4 △ ♖xd4 ♘c6 26 b4 f5 27 ♖ee1 e4 28 a4 e5 29 b5 axb5 30 axb5 ♘d4 31 ♕d5! ♖fe8 32 ♖a1 ♗f6 33 ♖xa8 ♖xa8 34 ♗c4 ♖f8 35 ♖d1 g4 36 hxg4 ♕g7 37 d7 ♕g5 38 d8♕! +− ♗xd8 39 ♕xe5+ ♗f6 40 ♕d6 1-0 Gheorghiu

106 Petrosian-Guil.Garcia Rio 79

1 d4 ♘f6 2 c4 c5 3 d5 d6 4 ♘c3 g6 5 e4 ♗g7 6 ♘f3 0-0 7 ♗e2 e6 8 0-0 ♖e8 9 ♘d2 ♘a6 10 dxe6!? ♗xe6 11 ♘b3! 11 f4 ♗d7 △ ♗c6 ♕b6? 11...♗d7? 12 ♕xd6 ♘xe4 13 ♘xe4 ♖xe4 14 ♗f3 ♖e6 15 ♕d1 ♗c6=; 12 ♗f4±; 11...♘d7!? 12 ♕xd6 ♘b6 13 ♕xd8 ♖axd8= 12 ♗g5 ♕c6 13 ♘d2 ♘d7 14 f4 ♗xc3 15 bxc3 f6 16 ♗h4 ♗f7 17 ♗g4 ♖ad8 18 ♕f3 ♘ab8 19 a4 a5 20 ♕d3 ♕g7 21 ♖fb1 b6 22 ♗f3 ♕c7 23 ♘f1 ♘c6 24 ♘e3 ♘e7 25 ♖d1± ♘f8 26 ♗g3 ♕a7 27 ♖d2 ♘e6 28 ♖ad1

Diagram

28...g5!? 29 fxg5 ♘xg5 30 ♕f1 ♗g6

31 e5! +− ♘g8 31...fxe5 32 ♗xe5+ 32 ♗c6 ♘e4 33 ♗xe4 ♗xe4 34 exf6+ 34 ♖xd6 ♖xd6 35 ♖xd6 fxe5 36 ♘g4± ♘xf6 35 ♗h4 ♖f8 36 ♖f2 ♕e7 37 ♖e1 37 ♘g4 ♕xg4 38 ♗xe7 ♖xf2 39 ♗xd8 ♖xf1+ 40 ♖xf1 ∝/± ♕e5 38 ♖f4?! Zeitnot 38 ♗xf6+ ♖xf6 39 ♘g4 ♖xf2 40 ♕xf2 △ ♖xe4, ♕f6+ +−; 40 ♘xf2 ♖f8 41 ♖xe4 ♖xf2 42 ♖g4+ +− ♘h5 39 ♖g4+ ♗g6 40 ♘f5+! ♖xf5 41 ♕d3 ♘f4 41...♕xe1+!? 42 ♗xe1 ♖df8 43 h3 ∝/± 42 ♖xe5 ♘xd3 43 ♖xf5 ♖f8 44 ♖xf8 ♗xf8 45 ♗d8 ♘b2 46 ♗xb6 ♘xa4 47 ♗xa5 ♗e7 48 h4 ♘b2 49 h5 ♗xh5 50 ♖g7+ ♗f7 51 ♗d8+! ♗e6 52 ♖xh7 ♘xc4 53 ♖h6+ ♗d7 54 ♗h4 ♘e3 55 ♗g3 ♘f5 56 ♖h3 ♗e6 57 ♗f4 ♘e7 58 ♗f2 ♘d5 59 ♗h2 ♗g6 60 ♗e2 c4 61 ♗d2 ♗e4 62 ♖h6+ ♗f5 63 ♖h5+ ♗g4 64 ♖h8 ♗xg2 65 ♖g8+ ♗f3 66 ♗xd6 ♗f1 67 ♖f8+ ♗g2 68 ♖f5 ♘b6 1-0 69 ♗c5 ♘a4 70 ♖f2+ ♗g1 71 ♗e1 ♗h3 72 ♗d4 +− Miles

107 Diesen-Gheorghiu USA 79

1 d4 ♘f6 2 c4 c5 3 d5 g6 4 ♘c3 ♗g7 5 e4 d6 6 ♘f3 0-0 7 ♗f4 7 h3; 7 ♗e2 ♘h5! 7...a6 8 a4 ♕a5 += 8 ♗g5 h6 9 ♗e3 e5!= 10 ♘d2 ♘d7 11 g3 ♘df6 12 h3 12 ♗e2 ♗h3∝ ♗d7 13 a3 b6 14 ♗g2 ♘h7 15 ♗f3 ♘5f6 16 g4

10...♛h8!∓ Δ ♘g8 17 ♞f1 ♞g8 18 h4
♗f6! 19 g5 19 h5 ♗g5! hxg5 20 h5
♛g7! 21 hxg6 fxg6 22 ♞h2 22 ♘g3
♘h6∓ ♞h6 23 ♛e2 ♗e7 24 0-0-0
♞f7 25 ♞g4 ♖h8 26 ♖h2 ♞f6 26...a6
27 ♖dh1 ♛c7 28 ♘h6∝ 27 ♖xh8
♛xh8 28 ♞xf6 28 ♖h1?! ♘h5∓
♗xf6 29 ♖h1 ♛c8! 30 ♛f1 g4! 31
♗e2 ♗g5 32 ♞d1 ♛d8! Δ ♛f6 −+
33 ♛g2 ♞h6 34 ♚c2 ♛f6 35 ♛d2
♖f8 −+ 36 ♛h2 ♗f4 37 ♗xf4 ♛xf4+
38 ♞e3 38 ♛xf4 exf4! −+ ♛xh2
39 ♖xh2 ♖f4 40 ♛d3 ♞g8! 41 ♖g2
♞f6 42 ♚c2 ♖xe4 −+ 43 ♗d3 ♖f4
44 b4 ♞e4 45 ♗xe4 ♖xe4 46 ♚d3
♖d4+ 47 ♚e2 ♗f5! 48 bxc5 bxc5
49 f3 gxf3+ 0-1 50 ♚xf3 ♗e4+
Gheorghiu

Nimzo-Indian

108 Berta-Madler corr. 79
1 d4 ♞f6 2 c4 e6 3 ♘c3 ♗b4 4 ♛b3
c5 5 d5?! N b5! 5...♘e4 Δ ♛f6 6
dxe6 bxc4! 7 exf7+ ♛xf7 8 ♛c2 8
♛xc4+ d5 (Δ d4) 9 ♛b3 ♗e6 10 e3
d4 11 ♗c4 ♗xc4 12 ♛xc4+ ♛d5! −+
d5 9 a3 ♗a5 10 e3 ♖e8! 10...d4?!
11 ♗xc4+ ♚f8 12 exd4 cxd4 13
b4= 11 ♗d2 ♞c6 Δ ♘d4 12 ♞f3 ♛f8
13 0-0-0 ♗e6 14 ♗e2 ♖b8 14...d4?!
15 ♘b5! d3 16 ♗xd3 ♗xd2+ 17
♖xd2 cxd3 18 ♛xc5+ ♘e7 19 ♘c7∝

15 g4 d4! 16 exd4 cxd4 17 ♗e3 17
♗f4 d3 18 ♛a4 ♛b6 19 ♗xb8 dxe2
d3 18 ♗xd3! 18 ♛a4 ♛c8 19 ♗f1
♛b7 20 b4 ♘xb4 21 axb4 ♗xb4 −+
cxd3 19 ♖xd3 ♛c8 20 g5 ♗b3! 21 ♛e2
♞e4 22 ♞d2 ♞xc3 23 ♖xc3 23 bxc3
♘d4!! ♗xc3 24 bxc3 ♞d4! 25 ♛d3
♞e2+ 0-1 Madler

109 Richter-Snyder corr. 79
1 d4 ♞f6 2 c4 e6 3 ♘c3 ♗b4 4 ♛c2
d5 5 a3 ♗xc3+ 6 ♛xc3 ♞e4 7 ♛c2 c5
8 dxc5 ♞c6 9 cxd5 exd5 10 ♞f3 ♗f5
11 b4 0-0 11...♘g3 12 ♛b2 ♘xh1 13
♛xg7 ♖f8 14 ♗h6± 12 ♗b2 b6!?
12...d4= 13 b5 bxc5! 14 bxc6 ♛a5+
15 ♞d2 ♖ab8 16 ♖d1 d4 17 c7 ♛xc7
18 ♞xe4 ♗xe4 19 ♛d2 ♖fe8 20
f3 N 20 h4 ♖b6 21 ♖h3 ♛b7
Grigorian-Gulko, USSR 75 ♗c6 21
♖c1 ♛b6 22 ♗a1 ♗d5 22...♖e3? 23
♖xc5! ♛xc5 24 ♗xd4 23 ♛c2?!
23 e4 c4 24 e4 d3 24...c3 25 ♗d3
25 ♛c3 f6 26 ♛d4 ♛xd4 27 ♗xd4
♗xe4 28 ♛d2 ♗d5 29 h4 h5 30 ♖h3
♚f7 31 g4? hxg4 32 fxg4 ♖e4 33 ♗c3
♖xg4 −+ 34 ♖e1 ♖b3 35 a4 ♖a3 36
a5 ♗g2 37 h5 ♗xf1 38 ♖xf1 ♖g2+
0-1 Snyder

110 Keene-Janetschek
Cleveland 79
1 d4 ♞f6 2 c4 e6 3 ♘c3 ♗b4 4 e3
0-0 5 ♗d3 d5 6 a3 ♗xc3+ 7 bxc3
c5 8 cxd5 exd5 9 ♞e2 b6 10 0-0
♗a6 11 ♞g3 11 ♗xa6 ♘xa6 12 ♛d3
♘b8 13 ♘g3 ♘c6 14 f3 ♗xd3 12 ♛xd3
♞c6 13 f3 ♛d7 13...♖e8?! 14 ♗b2
cxd4 15 cxd4 ♖fc8! 15...♖ad8 16
e4 dxe4 17 fxe4 ♘xd4 18 ♖ad1 ♘e6
19 ♛b1± 16 e4 ♞e7 17 ♖ac1 ♖xc1
18 ♗xc1 h6 18...♘e8 19 e5 ♖c8 20
♗g5 19 e5 ♞e8 20 f4 f5 21 a4! g6
21...♛xa4 22 ♗a3± 22 ♗a3 ♖c8 23

87

a5 ♖c4

24 ♗xe7? 24 axb6 axb6 25 ♖b1 ♘c8 26 ♘f1 ♕a4 27 ♖d1 △ ♘e3±; 25... ♘c6 26 ♖xb6 ♖xd4 27 ♕a6 ♖c4 28 ♖b7 ♕d8 29 ♘f1!± ♕a5 30 ♕xa5 ♘xa5 31 ♖b8 ♔f7 32 e6+ +−; 27 ♕b5? ♘xe5 **♕xe7 25 axb6 axb6 26 ♖b1 ♕a7 27 ♘f1 ♕a5 28 ♘e3?** 28 ♕b3!= **♖c3 29 ♕d2?** 29 ♕e2! **♖b3! 30 ♕c1 ♖xb1 31 ♕xb1 ♕d2 32 ♕b3 ♘c7 33 ♘c2 ♕c1+ 34 ♔f2 ♕xf4+ 35 ♔e2 ♕e4+** 35...♕xh2 36 ♘e1! b5 37 ♕c3= **36 ♔f1 b5 37 ♕c3 ♘e6 38 ♕c8+ ♘f8 39 ♕c5 ♕d3+ 40 ♔e1 ♕c4 41 ♘b4?** 41 ♔d2!= **♘e6! 42 ♕xc4 dxc4?** 42...bxc4 43 ♘xd5 ♘xd4 44 ♔d2 ♔f7 45 ♔c3 ♘c6 46 ♔xc4 g5 =+ **43 d5 ♘c5 44 ♔d2 ♔f7** 44...♘d3 45 ♘xd3 cxd3 46 d6 ♔f7 47 d7 ♔e7 48 e6 g5 49 ♔xd3 f4 50 ♔d4 g4 51 ♔c5 f3 52 gxf3 gxf3 53 ♔c6 f2 54 ♔c7= **45 ♔e3 g5 46 ♔d4 ♘b3+ 47 ♔e3 ½-½** 47...♘c5 48 ♔d4=; 48 ♘c2!? △ ♘a3∝ **Keene**

111 Keene-Ardijansah Jakarta 79
1 d4 ♘f6 2 c4 e6 3 ♘c3 ♗b4 4 e3 c5 5 a3 ♗xc3+ 6 bxc3 0-0 6...b6 **7 ♗d3 d6 8 e4 ♘c6 9 ♘e2 e5 10 d5 ♘a5** 10...♘e7 11 h4 ♘e8 12 ♘g3 f5 13 exf5 ♘xf5 14 ♘e4 += **11 ♘g3 b6 12 0-0** 12 ♖b1!? **♖e8** 12...♗a6 13

♘f5 ♗xc4 14 ♗g5 += **13 ♖a2 ♘d7 14 ♘f5 ♘f8 15 ♘e3 ♘g6 16 g3 ♗h3 17 ♖e1 ♖b8 18 f3 h5 19 ♖f2 ♖b7 20 ♔h1** 20 f4? exf4 21 gxf4 ♘xf4! 22 ♖xf4 ♕g5+ −+ **♕f6 21 ♗d2 h4 22 ♖g1 ♗c8 23 ♗c2! h3?** 23...♔f8 24 ♕f1!± **♕e7 25 ♘f5 ♗xf5 26 exf5 ♘f8 27 g4 b5 28 cxb5 c4 29 g5 ♕xb5 30 ♕xh3** △ ♖g4-h4 +− **♕d7 31 ♖g4 ♖b2 32 ♗e4** 32 ♖h4 ♘g6! 33 ♖h7 △ ♖xg7+ +− **♘b3 33 ♗e3 ♖xf2 34 ♗xf2 1-0 Keene**

112 Vaisman-Kojder Krosno 78
1 d4 ♘f6 2 c4 e6 3 ♘c3 ♗b4 4 e3 0-0 5 ♗d3 c5 6 ♘e2!? d5 7 cxd5 cxd5 7...exd5 8 a3 ♗xc3+ 9 bxc3± **8 exd4 ♘xd5 9 0-0 ♘f6 10 ♗c2! ♘bd7 11 ♕d3 b6 12 ♗g5 ♗b7 13 ♖ad1 ♖c8 14 a3 ♗e7** 14...♗xc3 15 ♘xc3! △ ♕h3 **15 ♕h3 ♖e8** 15...h6 16 ♗xh6! **16 d5! exd5** 16...♗xd5 17 ♘f4!∝ **17 ♘d4 a6** 17...♗f8 18 ♘a4± **18 ♘f5 ♘f8 19 ♖fe1 ♖a8?** △ ♗c8 **20 ♖xe7!! ♖xe7 21 ♗xf6 gxf6 22 ♕h6 1-0** 22...♘e6 23 ♘xe7+ ♕xe7 24 ♕xh7+ ♔f8 25 ♕h8 mate **Vaisman**

113 Portisch-Balashov
Rio 79
1 d4 ♘f6 2 c4 e6 3 ♘c3 ♗b4 4 e3 0-0 5 ♗d3 c5 6 ♘f3 d5 7 0-0 dxc4 8 ♗xc4 ♘bd7 9 ♕e2 a6 10 a4 ♕c7 11 ♖a2! b5 11...♗a5? 12 dxc5 ♕xc5 13 b4 ♗xb4 14 ♘xb4 ♕xb4 15 ♗a3 +− **12 ♗d3 ♗a5** 12...bxa4!? **13 axb5 axb5 14 ♗xb5± ♗b7 15 ♖d1 ♖ab8 16 dxc5 ♗xf3 17 gxf3 ♘xc5 18 b4 ♘b3 19 ♖b1 ♕e5** 19...♘xc1? 20 ♖dxc1 +− **20 bxa5! ♖xb5** 20...♕xb5 21 ♕xb5 ♖xb5 22 ♘c3 ♖bb8 23 a5± **21 ♔h1 ♕b8 22 ♗a3 ♖c8 23 ♗d6 ♕b7 24 a6! ♕b6** 24...♕xa6? 25 ♖xb3 +−

25 ♗c7! ♕c6 26 a7 +− h6 27 ♗b8 ♘d7 28 ♖d6 ♕b7 29 ♖xd7 ♕xd7 30 a8♕ ♖bxb8 31 ♕e4 1-0 Miles

114 Portisch-Ljubojevic
Montreal 79
1 d4 ♘f6 2 c4 e6 3 ♘c3 ♗b4 4 e3 0-0 5 ♗d3 d5 6 ♘f3 c5 7 0-0 dxc4 8 ♗xc4 ♘bd7 9 ♕e2 9 ♗d3 **b6 10 d5 ♗xc3 11 dxe6 ♘e5 12 exf7+ ♔h8 13 bxc3 ♗g4 14 e4 ♕e7 15 ♖d1!?** N 15 ♖e1 b5! 16 ♗xb5 ♘h5 17 ♗g5 ♕e6 18 ♕e3 ♗xf3 19 gxf3 ♕xf7 20 ♗e2 h6 21 f4 ♘xf4 22 ♗xf4 ♕xf4 23 ♖ad1 += Gligoric-H.Olafsson, Lone Pine 79 **♘xc4 16 ♕xc4 ♕xe4 17 ♕xe4 ♘xe4 18 ♖d3** Δ ♘e5 **♗xf3! 19 ♖xf3 ♘f6 20 ♗g5 ♖xf7 21 ♖d1 ♖e8 22 ♔f1 ♔g8 23 ♗xf6 gxf6 24 ♖d6 ♔g7** 24... ♖e4 25 ♖dxf6 ♖xf6 26 ♖xf6 ♖a4 27 ♔e2 ♖xa2+ 28 ♔d3 **25 ♖f4 ♖fe7 26 g3 ♖e6 ½-½ Keene**

115 Rohde-Zaltsman USA 79
1 d4 ♘f6 2 c4 e6 3 ♘c3 ♗b4 4 e3 0-0 5 ♘f3 c5 6 ♗d3 d5 7 0-0 ♘c6 8 a3 ♗xc3 9 bxc3 dxc4 10 ♗xc4 ♕c7 11 ♕c2!? 11 ♗d3 e5 12 ♕c2 ♖e8 13 ♘xe5 ♘xe5 14 dxe5 ♕xe5 15 f3 ♗e6 16 e4 ♖ad8 17 ♗e2 b6=; 11 ♗b5!? ♗d7 12 a4 a6 13 ♗d3 e5 14 ♕c2 ♖fe8! 15 ♘xe5 ♘xe5 16 dxe5 ♕xe5=;

13 ♗e2!? ♖fd8 14 ♗a3 += Lerner-Zaichik, USSR 78; 11 ♗b2!? e5 12 h3 b6 13 ♕e2 e4!? 14 ♘d2 ♗f5 15 ♗a2 ♖fd8 16 ♖ad1 ♖ac8 17 f3 += Diesen-Hook, Georgetown 79 **e5 12 ♗a2** 12 ♗b5!? e4 13 ♘g5! ♕e7 14 f3 exf3 15 ♖xf3 h6 16 ♖xf6 hxg5 17 ♖f2± Beljavsky-Slucky, USSR 75; 12...cxd4 13 cxd4 exd4 14 ♘xd4 +=; 12 h3 **♗g4!** 12...e4?! 13 ♘d2 ♖e8 14 f3 exf3 15 ♘xf3 h6 16 e4! ♘xe4 17 ♘e5± Taimanov **13 dxe5 ♘xe5 14 ♗e1** Δ f3, c4, ♗b2; 14 ♘xe5 ♕xe5 15 ♗b1 ♖fe8 16 e4 ♖ad8 17 f3 ♗e6 18 f4 ♕h5 19 e5 ♗c4!≈ Korchnoi-Matanovic, USSR-Jugoslavia 56; 15 f3 ♗d7 Δ ♗b5 **♖ad8** 14...c4?! 15 f3 ♗e6 16 e4 ♕c5+ 17 ♕f2±; 14...b5!? Δ ♗e6 **15 f3 ♗d7** N 15...♗e6 16 c4 ♕a5?! 17 ♗b2 ♖d2 18 ♕c1± Portisch-Sosonko, Tilburg 78 **16 c4 b5!?** 16...♗c6 17 ♗b2± **17 ♗b2** 17 cxb5?! ♗xb5 18 ♖f2 ♖d7 Δ ♖fd8 =+ **♖fe8 18 e4 a6 19 cxb5 axb5 20 h3! c4!=** 20...♘h5? 21 f4 **21 ♖d1 ♗c6 22 ♗b1 ♘g6** 22...♖xd1 23 ♕xd1 ♘fd7 (Δ ♘c5) 24 ♗d4!? Δ ♕c1-c3/♖f2-d2, ♘c2 +=; 23...♖d8?? 24 ♗xe5 **23 ♖f2 ♕b6 24 ♖xd8 ♖xd8 ½-½ Ciamarra**

116 Vaiser-Sturua USSR 79
1 d4 ♘f6 2 c4 e6 3 ♘c3 ♗b4 4 e3 c5 5 ♗d3 0-0 6 ♘f3 6 d5 b5!? 7 dxe6 fxe6 8 cxb5 ♗b7∞ Korchnoi-Karpov, (7) 78 **d5 7 0-0 cxd4** 7...dxc4 8 ♗xc4 ♘bd7 9 ♕e2 += **8 exd4 dxc4 9 ♗xc4 b6 10 ♘e5** 10 ♗g5 ♗b7 11 ♖e1 ♗xc3 12 bxc3 ♘bd7 13 ♗d3 ♖c8 14 ♖c1 ♕c7 15 ♗h4! += Portisch-Browne, Tilburg 78 **♗b7 11 ♗g5 ♘c6!?** 11... ♘bd7 **12 ♗xf6 ♕xf6 13 ♘d7 ♕h4 14 ♘xf8**

Diagram

14...♖xf8 14...♘xd4!? 15 ♘e2? ♘f3+! 16 gxf3 ♗xf3 17 ♕d4 ♕h3 −+; 15 ♘d7! ♗d6 16 g3 ♕h3 17 ♗d5! exd5 18 ♕xd4 ♕d7 ∞/+= **15 ♕f3!** N 15 ♘e2 ♖d8 16 ♕b3 ♘xd4 17 ♘xd4 ♖xd4 18 ♕xb4 ♗xg2 19 ♕b5 g6 20 ♗e2 ♗h3 21 ♕e5= **♗a5!** 15...♖d8 **16 ♕d3 ♗xc3 17 bxc3 ♘xc4 18 ♕xc4 ♗xg2 19 ♘xg2** 19 ♖fe1 ♗d5 20 ♕d3 f5 21 c4 ♗e4 22 ♕g3 ♕h5 =+ **♕g4+ ½-½ Gufeld**

117 Gligoric-Browne
Novi Sad 79

1 d4 ♘f6 2 c4 e6 3 ♘c3 ♗b4 4 e3 0-0 5 ♗d3 c5 6 ♘f3 6 d5!? exd5 7 cxd5 ♘xd5 8 ♗xh7+ **d5 7 0-0 cxd4 8 exd4 dxc4 9 ♗xc4 b6 10 ♗g5 ♗b7 11 ♖c1** 11 ♖e1 ♘bd7 **12 ♖e1 ♖c8 13 ♗d3** 13 ♕b3!? ♕e7?! 14 ♗d5!! Browne-Ljubojevic, Tilburg 78 **♖e8** 13...♗xc3 14 bxc3 ♕c7 **14 ♕e2 ♗xc3 15 bxc3 ♕c7 16 ♗h4 ♘h5! 17 ♕e3 ♘df6! 18 ♘e5** N 18 ♗g3 ♘xg3 19 hxg3 ½-½ Portisch-Andersson, Buenos Aires 78 **♘d5 19 ♕f3 ♘df4 20 ♗e4 ♗xe4 21 ♖xe4 f6! =+ 22 ♘d3 ♘xd3 23 ♕xd3 f5! 24 ♖ee1! ♘f4 25 ♕f3 ♘d5** 25...♘g6 26 ♗g5 f4? 27 h4! h6 28 h5± **26 c4 b5** 26...♕f4?! 27 ♕e2 ♘b4 28 ♗g3 ♕xd4 29 ♖ed1 ♕f6 30 ♕a3! =+/∞ **27 c5 h6 28 h3 f4 29 ♖e5 ♕f7** 29...g5? 30 ♗xg5 hxg5 31

♖xg5+ ♔f8 32 ♕h5 ♕f7 33 ♕h6+ +− **30 ♖ce1 g5 31 ♗xg5 hxg5 32 ♖xg5+ ♔f8 33 ♖e4! ♖cd8 34 ♖g4 ♕h7?** 34...♔e7! 34 ♖gxf4 ♘xf4 36 ♖xf4 ♕h7 37 ♕a3 b4!∓ **35 ♖gxf4+?** 35 ♖exf4+! ♘xf4 36 ♕xf4+! ♔e7 37 c6! ♖c8 38 ♕g5+ ♔d6 39 ♕c5+ +−; 37... ♖h8 38 ♕c7+ ♔e8 39 ♖g7 +−; 37... ♕b1+ 38 ♔h2 ♖g8 39 ♕c7+ ♔f6 40 ♖f4+ +− **♘xf4 36 ♖xf4+ ♔e7 37 ♕a3 b4! 38 ♕xb4?! ♖b8 39 ♕a3?** 39 ♕a5! **♖d8!∓ 40 ♕g3 ♕c8 41 ♖g4** 41 ♕f3 ♕c7! 42 g3 ♖b1+ 43 ♔h2 ♕b7! 44 c6 ♕b5! 45 ♖f8 ♖xf8 46 ♕xf8+ ♔c7 47 ♕e7+ ♔xc6 48 ♕xe6+ ♔c7 49 d5?! ♖d1! 50 ♕e7+ ♔b6 51 ♕d6+ ♔b7 52 ♕e7+ ♔a6 53 ♕a3+ ♕a5 54 ♕d6+ ♔b5 55 ♕c6+ ♔b4; 41 ♖h4 ♖b1+ 42 ♔h2 ♕c7 43 f4 ♕d8! 44 ♕g6! ♖e1!; 41 ♔h2?! ♕c7 42 ♕e3 ♘d8! 43 g3 ♕c6! 44 ♖f7 ♖b1 −+ **♕c7 42 ♕d3** 42 f4? ♕d7 −+ **♖b2 43 a3 ♖f8! 44 f3 e5! 45 d5 ♕xc5+ 46 ♔h2 ♕b8 47 d6** 47 ♕e4 ♕d4! 48 ♕xd4 exd4 49 ♖xd4 ♖xf3 −+ **♖d8 48 d7 ♕c7!** 48...♖b7? 49 ♖g8! **49 ♕e4 ♖xd7 −+ 50 f4! ♖d8!** 50... exf4?? 51 ♖g8+ +− **51 f5 ♖b6 52 h4 a6 53 h5 ♕a7 54 ♖g6 ♖d4 55 ♕e2 ♕e7 56 g3 ♖xg6 57 hxg6 e4 58 ♕e3 ♕e5 59 ♔g2 ♕a8 60 ♕c3 e3 61 g7 ♕d5+ 62 ♔h2 ♖d2+ 63 ♔h3 ♕xf5+ 64 g4 ♕f3+ 65 ♔h4 ♖h2+ 66 ♔g5 ♕d5+ 67 ♔g6 ♕e6+ 68 ♔g5 ♕d5+ 69 ♔g6 ♕e6+ 70 ♔g5 ♕h6+ 71 ♔f5 ♖f2+ 72 ♔e4 ♕e6+ 0-1 Browne**

118 Botterill-Dunne Dublin 79
1 d4 ♘f6 2 c4 e6 3 ♘c3 ♗b4 4 e3 c5 5 ♘e2 d5 5...cxd4 6 exd4 d5 7 c5 ♘e4 8 ♗d2; 7 a3!? ♗e7 8 c5 **6 a3 ♗xc3+** 6...♗a5!? 7 dxc5 dxc4 8 ♕xd8+ ♔xd8 9 ♗d2 e5 10 ♘g3 ♗e6 11 ♘ce4

♗xd2+ 12 ♔xd2 ♘xe4+ 13 ♘xe4 ♔e7 14 ♖c1 ♖d8+ 15 ♔c3 ♗d5! =+ Ghitescu-Schneider, Roskilde 78; 10 ♘e4!? ♘c6 11 ♘2g3 ♘xe4? 12 ♘xe4± Hort-R.Garcia, Leipzig 73; 10 ♘e4!? ♘c6 11 ♘2g3 ♗xd2+ 12 ♘xd2 c3 13 bxc3∞ **7 ♘xc3 cxd4 8 exd4 dxc4 9 ♗xc4 ♘c6 10 ♗e3 0-0 11 0-0 b6 12 ♕d3** 12 ♕f3!? ♗b7 13 ♖ad1 h6! 13...♘e7 14 ♗g5 ♘g6 15 f4! h6 16 f5!± Botvinnik-Tolush, Moscow 65 **14 ♗a2** 14 f3!? Korchnoi-Karpov (5) 78 **♘e7 15 ♖fe1 ♖c8 16 f3 ♖e8 17 ♗f2 ♖c7 18 ♘e4 ♘fd5 19 ♗b1 ♘g6 20 ♗g3 ♖d7 21 ♗c2 ♘de7 22 ♗f2 ♕a8 23 ♘g3 ♖ed8 24 h4! += ♘f8 25 h5 ♘d5 26 ♘e2 a5?! 27 ♗h4 ♖c8 28 ♗b1 ♗a6 29 ♕d2 ♗b7 30 ♘g3 ♗c6 31 ♘e4 ♗a4 32 ♖c1 ♖dc7 33 ♖xc7 ♖xc7 34 g4 f6** 34...♕c8!? Δ ...♗c2 **35 ♗g3 ♖d7 36 ♖c1 ♕d8 37 ♗a2 ♗b5 38 ♘c3?! ♗c6 39 ♘e4 ♗b7 40 ♗b3 ♘e7 41 ♗f2 ♘c6 42 ♖d1** 42 ♗a4? ♘xd4 -+ **♘e5?! 43 ♕e3 ♘f7 44 ♘c3! ♗d5** 44...♘g5 45 d5!± **45 ♘xd5± exd5 46 ♖c1 ♖e7 47 ♕d3 ♘g5 48 ♕f5 ♖d7 49 ♗a4 ♖c7 50 ♖xc7 ♕xc7 51 ♕xd5+ ♘fe6 52 ♕a8+! ♔h7 53 ♕c6 ♕d8** 53...♘h3+ 54 ♔f1 ♕xc6 55 ♗xc6 ♘xf2 56 d5! +− **54 ♗c2+ ♔h8 55 ♕f1 ♘f4 56 ♗g3 ♘fe6 57 ♗f2 ♘f4 58 ♗b3 ♔h7 59 ♗g3 ♕xd4 60 ♗c2+ ♘d3 61 ♕c3 ♘xf3 62 ♗xd3+ 1-0 Botterill**

119 Mititelu-Suba Rumania 79
1 d4 ♘f6 2 c4 e6 3 ♘c3 ♗b4 4 e3 0-0 5 ♗d3 d5 6 cxd5 exd5 7 ♘e2 c6?! 8...c5 **8 ♘g3 ♖e8 9 0-0 ♘bd7 10 a3 ♗d6 11 ♘f5 ♗b8 12 f3 c5 13 ♘e2 a6 14 g4! h6 15 ♔h1 ♕c7 16 ♖f2 ♘f8 17 ♗d2 c4?! 18 ♗c2 ♘g6 19 ♕g1 b5 20 g5! hxg5 21 ♕xg5 ♘h7 22 ♕h5 ♘f6 23 ♕g5 ♘h7 24 ♕g2!**

♕c6 25 ♖g1 ♕f6 26 e4! ♗xf5 27 exf5 ♘e7 28 ♕h3 ♘c6 29 ♗h6 1-0 Vaisman

120 Vantilbury-Odendahl USA 79
1 d4 ♘f6 2 c4 e6 3 ♘c3 ♗b4 4 ♗g5 h6 4...c5 5 d5 d6 6 e3 ♗xc3+ 7 bxc3 e5 8 ♗d3 ♘bd7 9 f4! h6 10 ♗h4 ♖g8 11 ♘h3 += Cooper-Petrosian, Buenos Aires 78 **5 ♗h4 c5 6 d5 ♗xc3+** 6...b5 7 dxe6 fxe6 8 cxb5 d5! 9 e3 0-0 10 ♗d3 e5?! 11 ♘ge2 d4 12 exd4 exd4 13 a3 ♗a5 14 b4!± Vantilbury-Winston, New York 77; 10...d4 11 exd4 cxd4 12 a3 ♗a5 13 b4 dxc3 14 bxa5 ♗b7 15 ♘f3 ♕xa5 16 0-0 ♘bd7≈ Spassky-Unzicker, Bath 73; 6...d6 7 e3 g5 8 ♗g3 ♘e4 (1) 9 ♗d3?! ♘xc3 10 bxc3 ♗xc3+ 11 ♔e2 ♗xa1 12 ♕xa1 f6 (12...0-0 =+ MacDonald-Ross) 13 h4 ♔e7 14 ♘f3 g4∓ Kavalek; 11...♕f6 12 ♖b1 exd5 13 cxd5 ♘d7 14 ♘f3 ♘b6 15 ♕b3 g4 16 ♘d2 ♗e5 ½-½ Kouatly-Diesen, Groningen 79; (2) 9 ♕c2 ♕f6 10 ♖c1 exd5 11 cxd5 ♗f5 12 ♗d3 ♕g6! =+ Guil.Garcia; (3) 9 ♖c1!? ♕f6 10 ♘e2 exd5 11 ♕xd5 ♕e7 12 ♖d1 ♘c6 13 ♗xd6 ♕xd6 14 ♕xd6 ♗e6 15 a3 ♗a5 16 ♘g3 ♕xd6 17 ♖xd6 ♔e7 18 ♖d1 ♗xc3+ 19 bxc3 f5∞ Taylor-Diesen, USA 77 **7 bxc3 d6 8 e3 e5 9 f3** 9 ♗d3 e4! 10 ♗c2 ♘bd7 11 ♘e2 ♕e7 Bagirov-Kuzmin, USSR 77; 9 ♘f3 ♗f5! =+ **e4!?** 9...g5 10 ♗g3 e4 11 f4 ♕e7 12 ♗e2 ♖g8 13 ♘h3!? ♗xh3 14 gxh3 gxf4 15 ♗xf4 ♘bd7 16 ♖b1 ♘b6 17 a4± Timman-Smyslov, Teesside 75; 9...0-0 10 e4 ♘bd7 11 ♗d3 ♖e8= **10 f4 ♖g8 11 ♘h3 g5 12 fxg5 ♘g4 13 ♕d2!?** 13 ♗f2 hxg5 14 ♗e2 ♘e5 =+; 14 ♕c2 ♕e7 =+ **hxg5 14 ♗g3 ♕e7** =+ 14...f5!? Δ ♘xe3 **15 ♗e2 ♘e5 16 ♗f2 ♗f5?!** 16...f5!

17 ♕b3? f4 18 exf4 e3+ **17 ♕b3 b6 18 a4! ♘bd7 19 a5 f6 20 ♖hf1 ♕f7 21 ♗xe5** 21 ♖a2!? **♘xe5** 21...♕xe5? **22 ♘g4 22 axb6 axb6 23 ♖a4** 23 ♖xa8 ♖xa8 24 ♕xb6? ♖a2+ 25 ♔d1 ♘d3! −+ **23...♖a5! 24 ♖fa1 ♕a7 25 ♕b5!? ♖a8 26 ♖xa5 bxa5 27 g4?** 27 ♗d1∝ **♗g6 28 ♕b1 ♖b8 29 ♕a2 ♕e7!∓ 30 ♘d1** 30 ♕xa5 ♖b2+ 31 ♔d1 ♖b1+! −+ **♖h8 31 ♕xa5 ♕xa5 32 ♖xa5 ♖xh2 33 ♖a7+ ♕f8 34 ♕e1 ♘d3+! 35 ♕f1 ♖h1+ 36 ♕g2 ♖e1 37 ♖a2 ♘c1 38 ♕f2 ♖xe2+ 39 ♖xe2 ♘xe2 40 ♕xe2 f5! −+ 41 gxf5 ♗h5+! 42 ♕e1 ♗xd1 43 ♕xd1 ♕f7 44 ♕e2 ♕f6 45 ♕f2 ♕xf5 46 ♕g3 ♕f6 47 ♔h3** 47 ♔g4 ♔g6 48 ♔g3 ♔h5 49 ♔h3 g4+ 50 ♔g3 ♔g5 51 ♔h2 ♔h4 52 ♔g2 g3 53 ♔g1 ♔g5! 54 ♔h1 ♔h5! 55 ♔g1 ♔h4 **♕g6 48 ♕g4 ♕h6 49 ♕f5 ♕h5 50 ♕e6 g4 51 ♕xd6 g3 52 ♕c7 g2 53 d6 g1♕ 54 d7 ♕g5 55 d8♕ ♕xd8+ 56 ♕xd8 ♕g4 57 ♕d7 ♕f3 58 ♕d6 ♕xe3 59 ♕xc5 ♕d3 60 ♕b5 e3 61 c5 e2 62 c6 e1♕ 63 ♕b6 ♕b1+ 64 ♕a7 ♕a2+ 65 ♕b8 ♕b3+ 66 ♕c8 ♕c4 67 c7 ♕d5 68 c4+ ♕c6 69 ♕d8 ♕d3+ 0-1 Ciamarra**

Bogoljubow Indian

121 Gheorghiu-Biyiasas USA 79
1 d4 ♘f6 2 c4 e6 3 ♘f3 ♗b4+ 4 ♘bd2 b6 5 g3 5 e3 ♗b7 6 ♗d3 0-0 7 a3 ♗xd2+ 8 ♗xd2 c5 9 ♗c3 += Gheorghiu-Tarjan, Lone Pine 79 **♗b7 6 ♗g2 0-0 7 0-0 ♗xd2 8 ♗xd2 d6 9 ♖c1** += **♘bd7 10 ♗c3 ♕e7** 10...♘e4! += **11 b3! ♖fe8 12 ♖e1 ♖ad8?!** 13 **♗b2 a5 14 d5!±** e5 14...exd5 15 ♘d4± **15 ♘d2 e4!?** 15...♘c5; 15... ♗c8!?± **16 ♗d4! c6 17 dxc6 ♗xc6 18 ♕c2 ♘g4 19 ♘f1!** 19 h3 ♘h6!∝ **♘c5 20 ♘e3! ♘xe3 21 ♗xe3 d5!?**

22 ♖ed1! dxc4 23 ♕xc4 ♖xd1+ 24 ♖xd1 h6 24...♖d8 25 ♖xd8+ ♕xd8 26 ♗xc5 +− **25 h4! ♗b7? 26 ♕b5!!** +− Zugzwang **♘e6 27 ♖d7!** +− **1-0 Gheorghiu**

122 Polugaevsky-Gipslis USSR 79
1 d4 ♘f6 2 c4 e6 3 ♘f3 ♗b4+ 4 ♗d2 ♕e7 5 g3 ♘c6 6 ♘c3! 6 ♗g2 ♗xd2+ 7 ♕xd2?! ♘e4 8 ♕c2 ♕b4+ =+; 7 ♘bxd2 d6 8 0-0 e5 9 d5 ♘b8 10 e4 a5 11 ♘e1 0-0 12 ♘d3 ♘a6 13 ♕e2? ♘b4!∓ Podgaets-Osnos, USSR 78; 13 ♕c2! += **♗xc3 7 ♗xc3 ♘e4 8 ♖c1 d6 9 d5! ♘xc3 10 ♖xc3 ♘b8 11 ♗g2 0-0** 11...e5!? **12 dxe6 fxe6 13 ♘d4 c6 14 0-0 e5 15 ♘c2 ♗e6 16 ♘e3!± ♘a6 17 ♕d2 ♖ad8 18 ♖a3! ♕f7?** 18...♕c7!? **19 b4 ♕b6 20 b5?!** ♘c5; 20 ♖b3!± **19 ♖d3! ♗xc4 20 ♘xc4 ♕xc4 21 ♖xd6 ♖xd6 22 ♕xd6 ♕xe2** 22...♕xa2 23 ♗h3! ♖f6 24 ♕d8+ ♖f8 25 ♕e7 +−; 24...♔f7 25 ♕d7+ ♔g6 26 ♕xb7 +− **23 ♗h3 ♕f3 24 ♕xe5 ♘b4 25 ♕d4! a5 26** a3 ♘d5 27 ♗g2 ♕b3 28 ♖e1 △ ♖e5 **♘f6 29 ♖e7 ♖e8 30 ♗f1! b5 31 ♖c7 ♖e6 32 ♕d8+ ♖e8 33 ♕d2! +−** △ ♕g5, ♖xc6 **♕e6 34 ♕c3** 34 ♕xa5 b4 35 axb4 axb4 36 ♕xc6 ♕xc6 37 ♖xc6 ♖e1 38 ♕g2 ♖b1 39 ♗c4+ ♕f8 40 b3 ♘g4 41 ♖c8+ ♕e7 42 ♖c7+ ♕f6 43 ♖f7+ ♕g6 44 ♖f4 ♘e5 45 ♗d5 ♖b2 46 ♖xb4 ♖xf2+ 47 ♕xf2 ♘d3+ 48 ♕e3 ♘xb4 49 ♗e4+ 1-0 Gufeld

123 Zaichik-Gipslis USSR 79
1 d4 ♘f6 2 c4 e6 3 g3 ♗b4+ 3...d5! **4 ♗d2 ♕e7 5 ♗g2** 5 ♘f3 ♘c6 6 ♘c3 ♗xc3 7 ♗xc3 ♘e4 8 ♖c1 d6 ∝/= **♘c6 6 ♘f3 ♗xd2+ 7 ♘bxd2 d6 8 0-0 a5 9 e4 0-0 10 ♕e2 e5 11 d5 ♘b8 12 ♘e1 ♘a6 13 ♘d3 c6!= 14 f4?** 14 ♖ae1 **exf4 15 gxf4** 15 ♘xf4 ♘c5 =+ **cxd5**

**16 cxd5 ♘xd5 17 ♕f2 ♘db4 18 ♘xb4
♘xb4 19 ♘c4 ♗e6∓ 20 ♘e3** 20 ♘b6
♖a6 21 f5 ♕c7! **♗xa2?!** 20...f6!∓
**21 e5! dxe5 22 ♘f5 ♕e6 23 fxe5
♖ae8** 23...♕xe5 24 ♖ae1∞

24 b3! ♕xe5 24...♗xb3? 25 ♘d4
♕c4 26 ♖fc1 ♕a6 27 ♘xb3 ♘d3
28 ♘c5 +−; 24...♕xb3? 25 ♘xg7!
25 ♖ae1 25 ♖xa2 ♘xa2 26 ♕xa2
b6 −+ ♕c7 25...♕f6 26 ♘h6+! ♔h8
27 ♘xf7+ ♔g8 28 ♘h6+ = **26 ♖xe8
♖xe8 27 ♘xg7!= ♕xg7 28 ♕f6+ ♔g8
29 ♕g5+ ♔f8 30 ♕h6+ ♔g8 ½-½** 30...
♔e7? 31 ♖xf7+! +− **Gufeld**

Queen's Indian

124 Petrosian-Harandi Rio 79
**1 d4 ♘f6 2 c4 e6 3 ♘f3 b6 4 a3 ♗b7
5 ♘c3 d5 6 cxd5 exd5 7 ♗f4 ♗d6?!**
7...c6?! 8 e3 ♗e7 9 ♗d3 0-0 10 ♕c2
c5 11 0-0 ♘bd7 12 ♘e5 g6?! 13
♗h6 ♖e8 14 f4 += Nijham-Hecht,
Wijk aan Zee 73; 7...♗e7!= **8 ♗g3
0-0 9 e3 ♘e4 10 ♕b3 c6** 10...♖e8 11
♗d3 c5 12 dxc5 ♘xc5 13 ♕c2± **
11 ♗d3 ♖e8 12 ♗xe4 dxe4 13 ♘e5
♗xe5 14 dxe5 ♘d7** 14...c5 15 ♖d1
♕c8 16 ♘b5± **15 ♘xe4!±** 15 ♖d1
♘c5!? 16 ♖xd8 ♖axd8! ∞/= 17
♕a2 ♗a6 18 ♘e2 ♘d3+ 19 ♔f1 ♘xb2;
17 ♕c2!? **♘xe5 16 ♖d1 ♕c7 17 ♘d6**

17...♗a6 17...♖e6 18 ♘c4! +− **18
♘xe8 ♖xe8 19 f3 ♕c8 20 ♗xe5 ♖xe5
21 ♔f2 h6 22 ♖d2 c5 23 ♖hd1 ♖e8
24 ♖d7 c4 25 ♕b4 1-0 Miles**

125 Gheorghiu-Adorjan Riga 79
**1 d4 ♘f6 2 c4 e6 3 ♘f3 b6 4 a3 ♗b7
5 ♘c3 d5 6 cxd5 exd5 7 g3 ♗e7 8
♗g2 0-0 9 0-0 ♘a6** 9...♘bd7; 9...a6±
**10 ♗f4 c5 11 ♘e5 ♖e8!? 12 dxc5!
♘xc5 13 ♘f3!** △ ♘d4± **♘fe4 14 ♘b5
a6 15 ♘bd4 ♗f6 16 ♖c1 g5!? 17 ♗e3
♕d7 18 ♘d2! ♖ac8 19 ♘xe4 dxe4
20 ♖c2!** △ ♖d2± **♘e6! 21 ♖d2 ♘xd4
22 ♗xd4 ♖ed8 23 e3! ♕e6?!** 23...
♗xd4 24 ♖xd4 ♕e7±

24 ♕h5!± 24 ♗h3?! ♕xh3 25 ♗xf6
♖d3!!∞ **♗xd4 25 ♕xg5+ ♕g6 26 ♕e7!!**
+− **♗c6** 26...♗f6 27 ♖xd8+ △ ♕xb7
+− **27 ♖xd4 ♖xd4 28 exd4 ♖e8 29**

♕c7 ♗b5 30 ♖e1 ♕f6 31 ♕c3! ♗d3
32 f3 ♕f5 33 fxe4 ♗xe4 34 ♕d2 ♖e6
35 ♕f4! ♕xf4 36 gxf4 f5 37 ♔f2 ♖h6
38 h3!? 38 ♗xe4 fxe4 39 ♔e3! ♖xh2
40 ♖e2!± ♗xg2 39 ♔xg2 ♖c6 40
♔f3 ♖h6 41 ♔g3 ♖d6 42 ♖d1! ♔f7
43 d5! a5 44 ♖d3! a4 45 ♔h4 h6
46 ♖d4! b5 47 ♖d2 ♔e7 48 ♖e2+!
+− ♔d7 48...♔f7 49 ♖e5! +− 49
♔h5 ♖xd5 50 ♔xh6 ♖d3 51 ♔g5!
+− ♖xh3 52 ♔xf5 b4 53 axb4 ♖b3
54 ♔g6 ♖xb4 55 f5 ♖g4+ 56 ♔f7 ♔d6
57 f6 1-0 Gheorghiu

126 Gheorghiu-B.Adam USA 79

1 d4 ♘f6 2 c4 e6 3 ♘f3 b6 4 a3 ♗b7
5 ♘c3 d5 6 cxd5 exd5 7 g3 ♗e7 8
♗g2 0-0 9 0-0 ♘bd7 10 ♗f4! ♘e4
11 ♖c1 ♗d6!? 11...c5± 12 ♗xd6
♘xd6 13 ♘e5! c6 14 ♘d3!± 14 e4
dxe4 15 ♘xe4 ♘xe4 16 ♗xe4 ♘xe5
17 dxe5 ♕e7! 18 ♕d6 ♖fe8∞ ♖e8
15 ♖e1 ♕f6!? 16 e3 ♖e7 17 b4! ♘e4
17...♗a6 18 a4± 18 b5! ♘xc3 18...c5±
19 ♖xc3 cxb5 20 ♕b3! ♕d6 21
♕xb5 ♖d8 22 ♖ec1 ♘b8 23 a4!
♔f8 24 a5 ♗a6 25 ♕b1! +− ♕g6 26
axb6 axb6 27 ♘f4! ♕xb1 28 ♖xb1
♗c4 29 ♖xb6 ♖a7 30 ♗xd5!! +−
1-0 Gheorghiu

127 Vaganian-Timman Rio 79

1 d4 ♘f6 2 c4 e6 3 ♘f3 b6 4 a3 ♗b7
5 ♘c3 d5 6 cxd5 ♘xd5 7 e3 ♗e7 8
♗b5+ c6 9 ♗d3 0-0 10 ♕c2!? 10 e4
♘xc3 11 bxc3 c5=; 10 0-0 ♘xc3 11
bxc3 c5 +=/= h6 11 ♗d2 ♘d7 12
e4?! 12 0-0 ♘xc3 13 bxc3 13 ♗xc3
c5= c5 14 0-0 ♖c8 =/=+ 15 ♕b1 ♕c7
16 a4 ♖fd8 17 ♖fc1 ♗c6 18 ♗e3 ♕b7
19 ♘d2 ♘b8 20 f3 ♗g5! 21 f4 21
♗xg5 hxg5 =+/∓ ♗e7 22 ♘c4 cxd4
23 cxd4 ♘a6! Δ ♘b4 24 ♘e5 ♘b4
25 ♘xc6 ♖xc6 26 ♕b3 ♖dc8 27

♖xc6 ♖xc6 28 ♗d2 ♕d7∓ 29 d5 29
♗e3 ♔c7∓ ♘xd3 29...exd5? 30 ♗b5
30 ♕xd3 30 dxc6? ♕d4+ −+ exd5
31 ♔h1 31 exd5 ♖d6 ∓/−+; 31
♕xd5 ♗c5+ 32 ♔h1 ♕xd5 33 exd5
♖d6 −+ ♖c4 32 exd5 ♖c5 33 ♗e3
♖xd5 34 ♕c2 ♖d3 −+ 35 ♗g1 ♕d5
36 ♖e1 ♖d2 37 ♕c8+ ♔h7 38 ♕g4
f5 39 ♕h3 ♗f6 40 ♖f1 ♕e4 41 a5
bxa5 42 ♗xa7 ♖d3 0-1 Miles

128 Gheorghiu-Browne
Novi Sad 79

1 d4 ♘f6 2 c4 e6 3 ♘f3 b6 4 a3
♗b7 5 ♘c3 d5 6 cxd5 ♘xd5 6...exd5
7 g3 g6!? 8 ♗g2 ♗g7 9 ♘e5! 0-0 10
♗g5 c6 11 e4!± Gheorghiu-Kurajica,
Novi Sad 79 7 e3 ♗e7 8 ♗b5+! c6
9 ♗d3 += 0-0 10 e4 ♘xc3 11 bxc3
c5 12 0-0 ♘d7!? 12...♘c6 += 13 ♕e2
♖c8 14 ♗b2 14 ♗f4 ♕c7 15 ♘d2 ♗g5
16 a4! ♖fd8 17 ♖fd1 g6 18 a5 ♗h6
19 axb6 axb6 20 f3± ♖a8! 21 e5!
Δ ♘e4± ♖xa1 22 ♗xa1 22 ♖xa1?
♗xd2! 23 ♕xd2 ♘xe5∓ ♖a8 23
♘e4 cxd4 24 cxd4 ♗d5 25 ♗c3 25
♗b2 ♖a2? 26 ♘c3!± ♖a2!∞ 26 ♕e1!
♗c4 27 ♕f1! ♗e3+ 27...♗xd3 28
♕xd3± 28 ♔h1 ♗d5 29 ♖a1! ♖xa1?!
30 ♕xa1 ♕c6 31 h4 h5 32 ♔h2 ♗h6
33 ♗b4! ♗f8 34 ♗xf8 ♔xf8 35 ♘d6!
♕c7 36 ♗b5 ♘b8 Zeitnot

**37 ♗e8! +− △ ♗xf7 ♕e7 38 ♔g3 g5
39 ♕c1!! gxh4+ 40 ♔h3 ♔g7 41 ♗xf7
♘c6 42 ♕f4 ♔h7 43 ♘e8! △ ♘f6+
+− 1-0 Gheorghiu**

---

129 Gheorghiu-Kudrin USA 79
**1 d4 ♘f6 2 c4 e6 3 ♘f3 b6 4 a3
♗b7 5 ♘c3 ♘e4!?** 5...d5; 5...♗e7?!
6 ♘xe4 ♗xe4 7 e3 7 ♗f4! Vaganian
♗e7 **8 ♗d3! ♗xd3 9 ♕xd3 d5 10
e4! dxc4** 10...dxe4 11 ♕xe4 ♘d7±
**11 ♕xc4 c5 12 dxc5! ♗xc5 13 0-0
0-0 14 ♗f4** 14 b4 ♗e7 15 ♗f4± ♕c8!
15 ♖ac1 15 b4?? ♗xf2+ −+ a5 **16
b4 axb4 17 axb4 ♖a4! 18 ♕c2!±**
18 ♗d2 ♕e8! 19 ♖fd1 ♘a6 20 ♖b1
b5!∞ ♖xb4 **19 ♗d2!± ♗xf2+!?** 19...
♘c6 20 ♗xb4 ♘xb4 21 ♕e2± **20
♖xf2 ♕xc2 21 ♖xc2 ♖xe4 22 ♘g5!!**
△ ♘xf7 +− ♖a4 **23 ♘xf7 ♖a1+ 24
♗c1 ♘d7 25 ♘g5 ♘c5! 26 ♖xf8+
♔xf8 27 ♖f2+! ♔e7 28 ♖f1 b5 29
♗b2 ♖xf1+** 29...♖a2 30 ♗xg7 +− **30
♔xf1 h6 31 ♗a3!! +−** hxg5 31...♔d6?
32 ♘e4+ +− **32 ♗xc5+ ♔f6 33 ♔e2
♔f5 34 ♔e3 g6 35 ♗d6 e5 36 ♗b4!**
Zugzwang **g4 37 g3 1-0 Gheorghiu**

---

130 Vaganian-Tompa
Kecskemet 79
**1 d4 ♘f6 2 c4 e6 3 ♘f3 b6 4 a3 c5
5 d5 ♗a6?! 6 ♕c2 ♕e7 7 ♗g5 h6?!**
N 7...exd5 8 ♘c3 ♗xc4 9 e4 +−;
8...♗b7 9 ♘xd5 ♗xd5 10 cxd5 g6∞
**8 ♗xf6 ♕xf6 9 e4 exd5 10 cxd5 ♗xf1
11 ♔xf1± d6 12 ♘c3 ♘d7 13 ♕a4**
△ e5 +− **♗e7 14 ♖d1?!** 14 e5!? dxe5
15 d6 ♗xd6 16 ♖d1 0-0-0 17 ♕a6+
♔b8 18 ♘b5 +−; 16...♕e6 17 ♕c6
+−; 15...♕xd6!? 16 ♖d1 ♕e6 17
♘xe5 ♕xe5 18 ♕xd7+ ♔f8 19 ♖e1

♕d6 20 ♕b7∞ **♕f4! 15 ♘d2** 15 ♘e2
b5! 16 ♕xb5 ♕xe4 17 ♘c3 ♕c2 △
♖b8∞ ♖d8 16 g3 ♕g4 17 ♔g2 0-0
18 ♘c4 ♕h5! △ f5; 19 ♘e3 ♕e5 **19
♖he1 f5! 20 exf5?!** 20 f4! += ♖xf5
**21 f4 ♖xf4! 22 gxf4 ♕g4+ 23 ♔h1
♕f3+ 24 ♔g1 ♕g4+ 25 ♔f2**

25...b5? 25...♗h4+ 26 ♔e3 ♖e8+
27 ♔d2 ♗xe1+ 28 ♖xe1 ♕xf4+ 29
♘e3 ♕d4+ 30 ♔c2 ♘f6=; 27 ♘e4
♗xe1 28 ♖xe1 ♕h3+ 29 ♔d2 ♕xh2+
30 ♔c3 ♕h3+ 31 ♔c2 ♖f8 += **26
♕xb5 ♖b8 27 ♕a4 ♗h4+ 28 ♔e3
♖e8+ 29 ♔d2 ♗xe1+ 30 ♖xe1 ♕xf4+
31 ♘e3 ♕d4+! 32 ♔c2 ♘f6 33 ♕xa7
♖xe3 34 ♕b8+ ♔h7? 34...♘e8!?
35 ♖xe3 ♕xe3 36 ♕xd6 ♘e4 37
♕c5 ♕d2+ 38 ♔b3 ♘xc3 39 bxc3
♕d1+ 40 ♔c4 ♕a4+ 41 ♔xc5 ♕a3+
42 ♔d4 1-0 Tompa**

---

131 Nogueiras-Tompa Kecskemet 79
**1 d4 ♘f6 2 ♘f3 e6 3 c4 b6 4 ♘c3
♗b7 5 a3 d5 6 cxd5 exd5 7 ♗g5 ♗e7
8 ♗xf6?!** ♗xf6 **9 g3** N 9 e3 0-0 10
♗e2 c5 11 ♖c1 cxd4 12 ♘xd4 ♘c6!?=
**0-0 10 ♗g2 ♖e8 11 ♕c2 a6 12 0-0
♕d6 13 ♖ad1?!** 13 ♖ac1 ♘d7 **14
♖fe1 ♖ad8 15 b4** 15 e4? dxe4 16
♘xe4 ♗xe4 17 ♖xe4 ♖xe4 18 ♕xe4
♘e5! 19 d5 ♘xf3+ 20 ♗xf3 ♗xb2∓
c5! 16 dxc5 ♘xc5! 16...bxc5? 17

95

♘xd5 ♗xd5 18 e4± **17 ♘h4** 17 bxc5
♕xc5 18 ♖c1 ♖c8∓; 18 ♖d3 d4 19
♘xd4 ♗xg2 20 ♘b3 ♕c6 −+; 17 ♘xd5
♗xd5 18 ♘g5 ♕e5!! 19 ♕xh7+ ♔f8 −+
♕e5 18 bxc5 ♕xc3 19 ♖c1 ♕xa3!?
19...♕xc2 20 ♖xc2 bxc5 21 ♖xc5
♖c8 22 ♖xc8 ♖xc8 23 ♖b1! ♗c6∞;
21...♗xh4 22 gxh4 ♖e7= **20 c6 ♗c8
21 c7 ♖d7 22 ♗h3 ♖xc7! 23 ♕xc7
♗xh3 24 ♕xb6 h6?** 24...♗xh4!? 25
gxh4 ♕a4=; 24...a5!∓ 25 ♕c5 ♕xc5
26 ♖xc5 ♖a8 27 ♖xd5 a4 −+ **25
♕c5 ♕b3 26 ♘g2 ♗b2?** 26...d4!?
**27 ♕c2! ♖b8 28 ♕xb3 ♖xb3 29 ♖c5
♗xg2?! 30 ♔xg2 ♗c3** Zeitnot **31
♖d1 d4 32 ♖d3 +− ♖b8 33 ♖c6 a5
34 ♖a6 ♖b1 35 h4 h5 36 e3 dxe3 37
♖xe3 ♗d2 38 ♖e8+ ♔h7 39 ♖e7 f5
40 ♖e5 1-0 Tompa**

132 Spragett-Browne USA 79
**1 d4 ♘f6 2 c4 e6 3 ♘f3 b6 4 ♘c3
♗b7 5 a3 d5 6 ♗g5** 6 cxd5 ♗e7 7 e3
**0-0 8 ♖c1 ♘bd7 9 cxd5 exd5 10
♗d3 c5 11 0-0 a6 12 ♗b1 ♖e8 13
♖e1 ♘e4! 14 ♗xe7 ♕xe7 15 dxc5
♘xc3! =+ 16 ♖xc3 bxc5 17 ♕d3**
g6 **18 ♖d1 ♖ad8 19 h3 d4! 20 exd4
♗xf3 21 ♕xf3 cxd4 22 ♖cc1 ♘e5!
23 ♕g3 ♕e6 24 ♗d3 ♕b3 25 ♗xa6**
d3 **26 f4 ♕xb2! 27 ♕f2** 27 fxe5 ♕b6+
∓ **♘f3+!! 28 gxf3** 28 ♕xf3 ♕b6+
Δ ♕xa6∓ **♖e2! −+ 0-1** 29 ♕c5 ♖g2+
30 ♔f1 ♕e2 mate **Gheorghiu**

133 Babev-Mechkarov Sofia 79
**1 ♘f3 ♘f6 2 c4 e6 3 d4 b6 4 ♘c3
♗b7 5 ♗g5 ♗b4 6 e3 h6 7 ♗h4 g5
8 ♗g3 ♘e4 9 ♕c2 ♗xc3+ 10 bxc3
d6 11 ♗d3 f5 12 0-0 ♘d7 13 ♘d2
♘xd2!?** N 13...♘df6 14 ♘xe4 ♗xe4
15 ♗xe4 ♘xe4 16 f3 ♘xg3 17 hxg3
♕e7= Gligoric-Taimanov, Zurich 53
14 ♕xd2 0-0 15 f3 ♕f6! 16 ♖ae1

e5= **17 ♕c2 ♗c6 18 ♗f2 ♖ae8 19
♕b3** 19 e4 f4 20 d5?! ♗b7 21 ♕a4
♕d8! 22 ♕xa7 ♕a8! 23 ♕xa8 ♖xa8
=+ e4! **20 ♗e2 ♔h8 21 ♕c2 ♕g6 22
d5 ♗b7 23 ♕d1 ♕g7 24 ♕d4 ♘c5
25 ♔h1 ♗c8 26 ♖g1 ♗d7 27 ♖ef1
♗a4 28 ♖c1 ♖e7 29 f4 g4 30 ♗h4
♖ee8 31 ♗gf1 ♔h7 32 ♔g1 ♕g6 33
♔h1 ♘d3 34 ♖a1 ♗c2! 35 a4 a5 36
♖a2 ♗b3 37 ♖a3 ♘c5 38 ♗d1** 38
♖fa1 ♗c2 Δ ♗d3! =+ **♗xd1 39 ♖xd1
♕h5 =+ 40 ♗g3 ♕f7 41 ♗h4 ♕d7 42
♖da1 ♘d3 43 ♖b1 ♖f7 44 ♔g1 ♖g8
45 ♔f1 ♕e8 46 ♔g1 ♖ff8 47 ♔f1?**
47 ♗e1!=

47...g3! −+ 48 hxg3 48 ♗xg3 ♕h5!
49 ♔g1 ♕e2! 50 ♖ba1! ♖xg3! 51
hxg3 ♕f2+ 52 ♔h1 ♕xg3 53 ♖aa2
♕h4+! 54 ♔g1 ♖g8 −+ **♕h5 49 ♔g1
♕e2 50 ♖aa1 ♖g4 51 ♔h2 ♖xh4+
52 gxh4 ♖g8 53 ♖g1 ♕f2! 0-1
Mechkarov**

134 Romanishin-Ribli Riga 79
**1 d4 ♘f6 2 ♘f3 e6 3 c4 b6 4 ♘c3
♗b7** 4...♗b4 **5 ♗g5 h6 6 ♗h4 g5 7
♗g3 ♘h5 8 e3 ♘xg3 9 fxg3!?** 9 hxg3
♗g7 **10 ♗d3 d6** 10...♘c6!? Δ ♕e7
**11 0-0 ♘d7 12 ♗c2! ♕e7 13 ♕d3
a6** Δ c5 **14 ♘d2 c5? Δ** f5 **15 ♘de4!
f5?!** 15...0-0-0? 16 ♖xf7; 15...
♖d8!±

16 dxc5! ♘xc5 16...fxe4 17 ♘xe4
♗xe4 18 ♕xe4± (△ ♕g6+) 18...0-0-0
19 ♕c6+ ♔b8 20 cxd6!; 17...♘xc5
18 ♘xc5 △ ♕g6+; 17...dxc5 18 ♘d6+
17 ♘xd6+ ♔f8 17...♔d7 18 ♘xf5+
♘xd3 19 ♘xe7 ♘b4 20 ♖f7!; 19...
♘xb2 **18 ♘xf5! exf5 19 ♕xf5+ ♔g8
20 ♘d5 ♕e8 21 ♖ad1! +−** 21 ♕g6?
♕xg6?? 22 ♘e7+ ♔h7 23 ♗xg6 mate;
21...♗xd5!; 21 ♘c7? ♕xe3+ 22 ♔h1
♖f8; 21 b4?! **♖c8** 21...♗xb2 22
♘c7 ♕f8 23 ♘xa8 ♕xf5 24 ♖xf5
♗xa8 25 ♖d8+ ♔g7 26 ♖xh8 ♔xh8
27 ♖f8+; 21...♖d8? 22 ♘e7+! ♕xe7
23 ♖xd8+ ♕xd8 24 ♕f7 mate **22
b4! ♘e6 23 ♘xb6 ♖c7 24 c5 h5 25
♖d6 ♖h6 26 ♖xe6! 1-0** 26...♖xe6
27 ♕h7 mate; 26...♕xe6 27 ♗b3 +−
Miles/Speelman

135 Kasparov-Butnorius USSR 79
**1 d4 ♘f6 2 c4 e6 3 ♘f3 ♗b4+ 4
♘bd2 0-0 5 e3 b6 6 ♗d3 ♗b7 7 0-0
d5 8 a3 ♗xd2 9 ♗xd2** 9 ♘xd2!?
♘bd7 10 cxd5 ♗xd5 10...exd5 11
b4 += **11 b4 c5 12 ♖c1! cxd4** 12...
♗xf3 13 ♕xf3 cxd4 14 exd4 +=/±
13 ♘xd4 ♘e5 14 ♗a6 14 ♗e2?! ♘e4
15 ♗e1 ♘d6!= **♘e4 15 ♗e1 ♕g5?!**
15...♘d6 16 ♕e2 += **16 f4! ♕g6 17
fxe5 ♘c5 18 ♗g3 ♘xa6** 18...♕e4?
19 ♕e2 ♘xa6 20 ♖f4 ♕xe5 21 ♖g4
+− **19 ♘f5!± ♖ae8 20 ♘d6 ♖e7 21**

**♖f4 h5 22 e4 ♗a8 23 ♗h4 ♖d7 24
♖c3 ♕h6** 24...♘c7 25 ♖g3 ♕h7 26
♖g5 g6 27 ♕a4 +− **25 ♕f1 ♘c7 26
♖cf3! +− f5 27 exf6 ♖xd6** 27...e5
28 ♕c4+ ♔h7 29 fxg7 exf4 30 ♘f5!
♖d1+ 31 ♖f1 +− **28 f7+ ♔h7 29
♗e7 e5 30 ♗xf8 exf4 31 ♗xd6 ♕xd6
32 ♕d3 ♕e7 33 ♕c4 ♔h6 34 ♖xf4**
34 f8♕! ♕xf8 35 ♕xc7 g5 36 ♖d3
**♘e6 35 ♕c8 ♕d6 36 ♕h8+ ♔g6 37
f8♘+ ♗xf8 8 ♕xf8 ♕d1+ 39 ♔f2
♕d2+ 40 ♔g3 ♕e1+ 41 ♔h3 1-0
Kasparov**

136 Spassky-Tal Montreal 79
**1 d4 ♘f6 2 c4 e6 3 ♘f3 b6 4 e3 ♗b7
5 ♗d3 d5 6 b3 ♗d6 7 0-0 0-0 8 ♗b2
♘bd7 9 ♘bd2?!** 9 ♘c3 a6 10 ♖c1
♕e7 11 ♘e2 ♘e4 12 ♘e5! += **♕e7 10
♖c1 ♖ad8** 10...♘e4!? 11 ♕c2 f5∝
11 ♕c2?! c5 12 cxd5 12 ♖fd1 exd5
**13 dxc5 bxc5 14 ♕c3?! ♖fe8 15
♖fd1 d4?! 16 exd4 cxd4 17 ♕a5?**
17 ♕xd4? ♘c5!; 17 ♘xd4! ♗xh2+
18 ♔xh2 ♘g4+ 19 ♔g3 ♕e5+ 20 f4
♕e3+ 21 ♘4f3 ♘df6 22 ♗xh7+! ♔xh7
23 ♕xe3 ♘xe3 24 ♖h1+ ♔g8 25
♗xf6 +=; 19 ♔g1 ♕h4 20 ♘4f3 ♕xf2+
21 ♔h1 ♖e5 22 ♗f5 ♘e3; 17...♕e5
18 ♘4f3 ♕h5 19 ♗e4!?; 19 ♘e4?
♗xe4! 20 ♗xe4 ♗f4!∓ **♘e5! −+ 18
♘xe5 ♗xe5 19 ♘c4** 19 ♘f1 ♘d5 20
♘g3 ♘f4 21 ♗f1 h5 **♖d5 20 ♕d2**
20 ♗a3 ♕e6 21 ♕d2 ♗xh2+ 22 ♔xh2
♖h5+ 23 ♔g1 ♖h1+ 24 ♔xh1 ♕h3+
−+ **♗xh2+ 21 ♔xh2 ♖h5+ 22 ♔g1
♘g4 0-1 Tal**

137 Lein-Miles
South Africa 79
**1 c4 b6 2 d4 e6 3 ♘f3 ♘f6 4 e3 ♗b7
5 ♗d3 ♘e4** 5...d5; 5...♗e7 **6 ♘c3 f5?!**
6...♗b4; 6...♘xc3 7 bxc3 ♗d6 8 e4
f6 △ ♘c6 **7 ♗xe4 fxe4 8 ♘d2 ♕g5?**

8...♗b4 9 ♕h5+ g6 10 ♕g4 ♗xc3 11
bxc3 ♕f6! 12 ♘xe4 ♕f5 13 f3 ♗xe4
14 ♕xe4 ♕xe4 15 fxe4 e5! +=/=
Hubner-Miles, Bugojno 78 **9 0-0 d5
10 f3! ♕xe3+ 11 ♔h1 ♕xd4 12 fxe4
♘a6** 12...dxe4 13 ♕h5+ g6 14 ♕g4
♕d7 15 ♘dxe4 +–; 12...dxc4 13 ♕f3
♕d7 14 ♘xc4 ♘c6 15 ♗g5 +–; 13...
♕f6!± **13 ♘b5 ♕e5** 13...♕c5? 14
♕h5+ g6 15 ♕e5 +–; 13...♕d3? 14
♖f3 **14 exd5 0-0-0 15 ♘f3** 15 ♖e1
♕h5 15...♕e4 **16 ♘g5! ♕xd1 17
♖xd1**

17...♖d7? 17...exd5! **18 ♘xe6 ♘c5**
18...c6 19 ♘xa7+ ♔b8 20 ♘xc6+
♗xc6 21 ♗f4+ +– **19 ♗f4 ♘e4 20
♖d4 ♘d6 21 ♘xa7+ ♔b8 22 ♘c6+
♗xc6 23 dxc6 ♖f7 24 ♖e1 h6 25**
c5 bxc5 26 ♘xc5 g6 27 ♘d7+ ♔c8
28 ♖a4 ♔d8 29 ♖a8+ 1-0 29...♔c8
30 ♖xc8+ ♔xc8 31 ♖e8 mate **Miles**

138 Ermolinsky-Polovedin
USSR 79
1 ♘f3 ♘f6 2 c4 b6 3 ♘c3 ♗b7 4 d4 e6
5 e3 ♗e7 5...♗b4 6 ♗d3 ♘e4 7 0-0∝
**6 ♗d3 d5 7 0-0 0-0 8 b3 c5 9 ♗b2
cxd4** 9...♘c6 10 ♕e2 cxd4 11 exd4
♘b4 12 ♗b1 ♗xf3∝; 10 cxd5!? **10
exd4 ♘c6 11 ♖c1** 11 ♕e2 ♖c8 **12
♖e1 ♘b4** 12...♖e8 13 ♘e5 dxc4 14
♘xc6 ♗xc6 15 bxc4 ♗f8 16 ♗c2 ♕d6

17 ♕d3 g6= **13 ♗e2?!** 13 ♗f1 dxc4
14 bxc4 ♗xf3 15 ♕xf3 ♕xd4 16 ♘d5
♕c5 17 ♗d4 ♕d6 18 ♘xf6+ ♗xf6
19 ♗xf6 gxf6 20 ♕xf6 ♕d8 21 ♕h6±;
17 ♘xf6+ ♗xf6 18 ♗xf6 gxf6 19 ♕xf6
♕f5 20 ♕xf5 exf5 21 a3± **♘e4 14
a3 ♘xc3** 14...♘c6 15 ♗d3 f5?! 16
cxd5 ♘xc3 17 ♖xc3 exd5 18 ♕c2
+= **15 ♖xc3 ♘c6 16 c5** N 16 cxd5
♕xd5 17 ♗c4 ♕h5∝ **bxc5** 16...e5!?
17 dxe5 bxc5 18 ♗d3 += **17 dxc5
♗f6** 17...e5 18 ♖c2! d4 19 b4 +=
18 ♖c2 18 b4!? ♗xc3 19 ♗xc3 a6 20
a4 ♘a7 21 ♗d3 ♗xb2 **19 ♖xb2 ♕a5
20 b4 ♕xa3 21 ♕a1! ♕xa1 22 ♖xa1**
a6 23 ♗xa6 ♖a8 24 b5 ♘b8 25 ♖ba1
♗xa6 26 bxa6 ♖c8 27 ♖a5 ♘c6
28 ♖b5 ♔f8 29 ♖b6 29 ♖b7 ♘d8
**♔e8 30 h4 ♖c7 31 ♖ab1 ♔d7 32
h5 f6 33 ♘e1 e5?!** 33...h6! += **34
f4 e4? 34**...h6 **35 ♘c2 ♘e7** 35...d4
36 ♘xd4 ♘xd4 37 ♖d1 **36 ♖d6+
♔e8** 36...♔c8 37 ♘d4 Δ ♘e6 +–
**37 ♖b7 ♖a7 38 ♖xa7 ♖xa7 39 ♘b4
+– ♖c7 40 c6 ♖c8 41 g4 d4 42
♖xd4 ♘xc6 43 ♖xe4+ ♔d7 44 ♘xc6
♖xc6 45 ♖a4 ♖c8 46 a7 ♖a8 47
♔f2 ♔c6 48 ♔f3 ♔b7 49 ♔e4 g6**
49...♖e8+ 50 ♔f5 ♖a8 51 h6 +–
50 hxg6 hxg6 51 ♔d5 1-0 Gufeld

139 Chechelian-Andrianov
USSR 79
1 ♘f3 ♘f6 2 c4 b6 3 d4 e6 4 e3 ♗b7
5 ♗d3 ♗e7 5...d5 6 0-0 ♘bd7 7 b3
♗d6= **6 0-0 0-0 7 ♘c3 d5 8 b3 c5
9 ♗b2 cxd4 10 exd4 ♘c6** 10...♘bd7
11 ♕e2 ♖c8!? N 11...dxc4 12 bxc4
♘b4 13 ♗b1 ♗xf3 14 gxf3 ♕xd4
15 ♘e4 ♕d8 16 ♖d1 ♕c7 17 ♘xf6+
♗xf6 18 ♗xf6? gxf6 19 ♗xh7+ ♔g7!∓;
18 ♗xh7+!± **12 ♖fd1 ♖e8 13 ♖ac1
♗f8 14 ♗b1 g6 15 ♘a4 dxc4 16
bxc4 ♗g7= 17 ♗a3 ♘a5 18 ♘e5 ♘d7**

19 f4 &xe5 20 dxe5 ♛c7 21 &d6
♛c6 22 &b2 &h6?! 22...&ed8 23
&d4 += &ed8 24 &cd1 &f8 25 ♛h1
♛e8 26 h4 &c6 27 &4d2 &e7 28
♛h2 &f5= 29 &xf5 exf5 30 &xf8
♛xf8 31 &d6 &xd6 32 &xd6 ♛e7
33 ♛h3 &d8 34 ♛d2 ♛e8 35 c5!
bxc5 36 &c4 &c8! 37 &xd8+ ♛xd8
38 &d6+ ♛f8 39 ♛d5 &e6 40 ♛xc5
♛b6 41 ♛a3 a5? 41...♛g1! 42 ♛f3!±
♛g1? 43 ♛a8+ ♛g7 44 ♛d8 +− ♛h1+
45 ♛g3 ♛e1+ 46 ♛h2 ♛h6 47 &e8
f6 48 ♛xf6 1-0 Gufeld

140 Spassky-Sigurjonsson
Munich 79

1 d4 &f6 2 c4 e6 3 &f3 b6 4 e3
&b7 5 &d3 &e7 6 0-0 0-0 7 b3 d5 8
&b2 &bd7 9 &c3 9 &bd2 c5 10 ♛e2
&e4! 11 &fd1 cxd4 12 exd4 &xd2
13 &xd2 &c8 14 &c2 &d6 15 &d1
♛e7 16 &c1 h6 Bondarevsky-Renter,
Pernau 47 c5 10 ♛e2 cxd4 10...dxc4?!
11 bxc4 ♛c7 12 &ad1 &ad8 13 d5!
a6 14 dxe6 fxe6 15 &g5! ♛c6 16
f4 h6 17 &f3 ♛c7 18 &h4!± Keres-
Spassky, Gothenburg 55; 10...&e4
11 &fd1 cxd4 12 &xd4 &xc3 13
&xc3 &f6 14 ♛f3 ♛c8 15 ♛h3 h6
16 &ac1 += Dely-Haag, Budapest
58; 10...&c8 11 &fd1 &d6 12 cxd5
exd5 13 &ac1 ♛e7 14 dxc5 bxc5
15 &a6 &xa6 16 ♛xa6± Grunfeld-
Nievergelt, Vienna 54 11 exd4 &e8
12 &ad1 &f8 13 &e5 g6 14 f4 &c8
15 &f2 &b8 16 ♛e3 &c6 17 &e2 &b4?!
17...&a5!? 18 &f3 &a5 19 cxd5
&xd5 20 &xd5 &xd5 21 &xd5 ♛xd5
22 &g4! &e7

Diagram

23 &a3! ♛h5 23...♛b7 24 &xe7
♛xe7 25 ♛e5 24 h3 &h4 25 &e2

f5 26 &e5 &c3 27 ♛xc3 ♛xe2 28
&c1 &d8 29 ♛c7 ♛f2+ 30 ♛h1 ♛xf4
31 ♛f7+ ♛h8 32 &f3 1-0 Samarian

141 Miles-Lein
South Africa 79

1 d4 &f6 2 c4 e6 3 &f3 b6 4 &f4
&b7 5 e3 &b4+ 6 &fd2 0-0 7 a3 &e7
8 &c3 c5 9 d5 exd5 10 cxd5 &xd5
11 &xd5 &xd5 12 ♛f3 &c7 13 ♛b7!
d6 14 &e4 ♛d7 15 0-0-0 &e6 15...
♛c6 16 &xd6 ♛xb7 17 &xb7 Miles-
Timman, Wijk aan Zee 79 16 ♛xd7
&xd7 17 &g3! d5 18 &xd5± &f6
19 &xf6+ &xf6 20 &a6 &ad8 21
&hd1 &xd5 22 &xd5 &d8 23 &xd8+
&xd8 24 &b8?! &c7? 24...&c7! 25
&xa7 &d8 (△ &c6) 26 &b5 ♛f8-
e7-e6, &c6=; 25 &xc7 += 25 &c4
a5 25...b5?! 26 &e2-f3-b7 26 a4
♛f8 27 ♛c2 ♛e7 28 ♛d3 &e8 28...f6
29 &g8 △ ♛e4-f5-g6 29 e4! &c7 30
&xc7 &xc7 31 e5 h6 31...f6 32 ♛e4
32 ♛e4 ♛f8 33 f4 ♛e7 34 g3 ♛f8
35 g4 ♛e8 36 h4 ♛f8 37 h5 ♛e7 38
g5 ♛f8 39 ♛f5 ♛e7 39...&e8 40
g6 f6 41 ♛e6 +− &c7+ 42 ♛d7 &e8
43 ♛d8 Zugzwang; 42...&a8 43
♛c6 40 g6 fxg6+ 41 ♛xg6 ♛f8 42
f5 b5 43 axb5 &a8 44 e6 &b6 45
e7+ ♛xe7 46 ♛xg7 &d7 47 b6 1-0
Miles

142 Spassky-Karpov
Montreal 79

1 d4 ♘f6 2 c4 e6 3 ♘f3 b6 4 ♗f4!? ♗b7 5 e3 ♗e7 6 ♘c3 6 h3 ♘h5 7 ♗g3 d6 8 ♗d3 8 ♘d2!? ♘d7 9 0-0 g6 10 h3? 10 ♗e4!?; 10 e4 f5 11 d5 f4 12 dxe6 ♘c5 Δ fxg3; 11 exf5 exf5! Δ f4 ♘xg3 11 fxg3 0-0∓ 12 ♖c1 ♗f6 13 ♖c2 ♗g7 14 ♖cf2 ♕e7 15 ♕h2 a6 16 ♕e2 ♖ae8 17 ♗b1 c6 17...f5 18 a3 18 e4 f5! 19 e4 c5! 20 exf5 exf5 21 ♕xe7 ♖xe7 22 dxc5 bxc5 23 ♖d1 23 ♘d5 ♗xd5 24 cxd5 ♖b8∓ ♗xc3 24 bxc3 ♖f6 25 ♖fd2 ♖e3 26 ♘g1 26 ♖xd6 ♖xd6 27 ♖xd6 ♗xf3 28 gxf3 ♘e5; 28 ♖xd7 ♖e2 ♔f8 27 ♖xd6 ♖xd6 28 ♖xd6 ♕e7 29 ♖d3 ♖e1 30 ♗a2 ♖c1 31 ♘f3 ♗xf3 32 ♖xf3 ♘e5 33 ♖e3 ♔f6 −+ 34 ♗b3 a5 35 ♗a4 ♘xc4 36 ♖e8 ♖xc3 37 ♖c8 ♘e3 38 ♗b5 c4 39 ♔g1 ♖c2 40 ♗c6 c3 41 ♗f3 g5 42 g4 f4 0-1
Keene

143 Miles-Lein
South Africa 79

1 c4 ♘f6 2 ♘f3 b6 3 d4 e6 4 ♗f4 ♗b7 5 e3 ♗e7 5...♗b4+ 6 ♘c3 0-0 7 h3 c5?! 8 d5 exd5 9 cxd5 d6 10 e4 ♘bd7 10...♘a6-c7 11 ♗c4 Δ 0-0, ♕d3, ♖ad1, ♖fe1, e5 a6 12 a4 ♘e8 13 0-0 ♗f6 14 ♕d2 ♘e5 15 ♘xe5 dxe5 16 ♗e3 ♘d6 17 ♗e2 ♖c8 18 ♖ab1! Δ b4 ♖e8 18...a5 19 b4 c4 20 b5 a5 21 ♖bc1 21 g3 h6 22 h4 h6 22 g3 22 ♘g4 ♖b8 23 ♖c2 ♗g5 24 ♖ec1 ♗c8∝ ♗g5 23 f4 ♗f6 23... exf4?! 24 gxf4 24 f5 ♗g5 25 ♗xg5? 25 h4 ♗xe3+ 26 ♕xe3 +− ♕xg5 25...hxg5 26 f6! 26 ♕xg5 hxg5 27 ♔f2 27 f6!? ♔f8 28 ♖f2 gxf6 29 ♖xf6 ♔e7∝ ♔f8 28 h4! 28 ♖h1 ♔e7 h4 gxh4 30 ♖xh4 ♖h8 31 ♖ch1 ♖xh4 32 ♖xh4 ♔f6= gxh4 29 gxh4

30 ♖g1 ♖h8 30...♖g8? 31 h5 ♖h7 32 ♖g2 ♖ch8 32...f6?! 33 ♖cg1 Δ h6; 32...♘e8! 33 ♖cg1 ♔f8 34 ♔e3 ♗c8 35 ♘b1 ♗d7 36 ♘a3 c3 37 ♖c1? 37 ♔d3 Δ ♗f3; 37...♘b7 38 ♘c4! ♘c5+ 39 ♔e3 ♘xa4 40 ♘xe5 ♗e8 41 d6; 39...f6 40 ♘xb6; 37 ♘b1 c2 38 ♘c3 ♔e7! 39 ♔d2 ♖c8 40 ♖c1 ♖xc3!?∝ ♖xh5! 38 ♗xh5 ♖xh5 39 ♖cg1 ♖h4 39...♖h3+!? 40 ♖g3 ♖xg3+ 41 ♖xg3 ♗xf5 40 ♖g4 ♖xg4 41 ♖xg4 g6 42 ♖g1 gxf5 43 exf5 ♗xf5! 43...♘xf5+ 44 ♔d3 ♘d4! (Δ c2) 45 ♔xc3?? ♘e2+; 45 ♘c4 ♗f5+ 46 ♔e3 c2 47 ♘xb6 ♘b3 48 ♘c4 c1♕+ 49 ♖xc1 ♘xc1 50 b5 ♗c8; 44 ♔e4 ♘d4 45 ♖c1!±; 44...f6 45 ♖c1 44 ♖c1 ♗g4? 44...♗e4? 45 ♘c4! +−; 44...c2! 45 ♘xc2 ♗e4! =+ 45 ♖xc3 f5 46 ♖c6 f4+ 47 ♔d3 ♗f5+ 48 ♔e2 ♗g4+ 49 ♔e1 ♔e7 49...♘e4 50 ♘c4 f3 51 ♘e3! f2+ 52 ♔f1 +− 50 ♘c4 50 ♖xb6?! e4 ♘xc4 51 ♖xc4

51...♗f3! 51 ♗d7 52 ♖c7 e4 53 ♖b7 e3 54 ♔e2! (54 ♖xb6? f3 55 ♖b7=) 54...♔d6 55 ♖xb6+ ♔e5 (55...♔xd5 ♖f6) 56 ♖g6 ♔e4 57 ♖e6+ ♔xd5 (57...♗xe6 58 dxe6 f3+ 59 ♔e1 Δ e7 +−) 58 ♖f6 ♗g4+ (58...♔e5 59 ♖f7) 59 ♔d3 ♔e5 60 ♖f7! ♗c8 (60...♗f5+ 61 ♖xf5+; 60...♗h3 61 b6 ♗f1+ 62 ♔c2 ♗a6 63 b7) 61 b6 ♗a6+ 62

100

♔c2 f3 (62...e2 63 ♔d2; 63 b7) 63
♖xf3 e2 64 ♔d2 ♔d6 65 ♖c3! ♔d5
66 ♖c7 ♔d6 67 ♖a7 ♗c4 (67...♗d3
68 ♖xa5 ♔c6 69 ♖e5) 68 ♖xa5
♔c6 69 ♖c5+! +– 52 ♖c7+ 52 ♖c6?!
♗xd5 53 ♖xb6 ♗b3 ♛d6 52...♔d8
53 d6; 53 ♖c6 53 ♖c6+ ♛xd5? 53...
♔d7!∞ 54 ♖xb6 ♗xd5 55 ♖a6 ♔c7 56
♖xa5? ♗b7=; 55 ♖f6 ♗b3; 54 ♖e6
♗xd5 55 ♖xe5 ♔d6 56 ♖f5 f3∞
54 ♖xb6 ♛c5 1-0 55 ♖e6 (1) 55...
♔d5 56 ♖c6 ♔d4 57 ♖c7 ♔d5 58
b6 ♔d6 59 ♖g7 △ b7 +–; (2) 55...♔d4
56 ♖e7! △ b6-b7; (3) 55...♔b4! 56
♖xe5 ♔xa4 57 b6 ♔b4 58 ♖e7 a4
59 b7 ♗xb7 60 ♖xb7+ ♔c3 61 ♖a7!
♔b3 62 ♔d2 a3 (62...f3 63 ♔c1)
63 ♖b7+! ♔c4 (63...♔a2 64 ♔c2;
63...♔a4 64 ♔c3) 64 ♔c2! ♔d4 65
♖a7 ♔e3 66 ♖xa3+ ♔e2 67 ♖a4 f3
68 ♖e4+ ♔f1 69 ♔d2 f2 70 ♖f4 ♔g2
71 ♔e2 +– **Miles**

144 Miles-Gheorghiu USA 79

1 d4 ♘f6 2 c4 e6 3 ♘f3 b6 4 ♗f4
♗b7 5 e3 ♗e7 6 h3! 6 ♘c3 ♘h5!=
c5! 6...♗b4+ 7 ♘fd2! 0-0 8 a3 ♗e7 9
♘c3 c5 10 d5!± 7 ♘c3 cxd4 8 ♘xd4
8 exd4 0-0 9 d5?! ♗b4!∓ a6 9 ♗e2
d6 10 ♘f3 0-0 11 0-0 ♛c7 12 ♖c1
♘bd7 13 b4 ♖ac8 14 ♛b3 h6!= 15
♖fd1 ♛b8 16 ♗g3 ♖fd8 17 ♘d4 ♛a8!
18 f3 d5!= 19 cxd5 ♘xd5 20 e4
♘xc3 21 ♖xc3 ♖xc3 22 ♛xc3 ♖c8
23 ♛b3 △ ♘xe6± ♘f8 24 ♔h1 ♛h8
25 a3 ♗f6 26 ♗f1 ♘g6! 27 ♘e2 ♗c6
28 ♛e3 ♛b7 29 ♗f2 b5 30 ♘d4 ♘e5!
30...♗e8 31 ♘b3 += 31 ♘xc6 ♛xc6
△ ♘c4= ½-½ **Gheorghiu**

145 Unzicker-Korchnoi
South Africa 79

1 d4 ♘f6 2 c4 e6 3 ♘f3 b6 4 g3 ♗a6
5 ♛a4 ♘e4?! 6 ♗g2 ♘d6 7 c5! bxc5

8 dxc5 ♘b7 9 c6! dxc6

10 ♘c3 ♗d6 11 0-0 0-0 12 ♖d1 ♛e8
13 ♘d4 ♘d8 14 ♗e3 ♗b7 15 ♘b3
♘d7 16 ♘e4 ♘b6 17 ♛a5 f5 18 ♘ec5
♗c8 19 ♖ac1 e5 20 ♗d2 e4 21 ♘d4
♘f7 22 ♗f4 g5 23 ♗xd6 cxd6 24 ♘a6
♛e5 25 ♛a3 c5 26 ♘c7 cxd4 27 ♘xa8
♘xa8 28 ♛xa7 ♗e6 29 ♖xd4 ♛b5
30 ♖d2 ♘b6 31 b3 ♘d5 32 ♛d4 ♘e5
33 ♖b2 ♛b7 34 b4 ♛g7 35 ♖d2
♛h6 36 ♖dc2 ♖b8 37 a3 ♘g4? 38
h3 ♘e5 39 ♛a7 ♛f8 40 ♛d4 ♖a8
41 b5 ♛b8 42 g4 fxg4 43 ♗xe4 ♘f4
44 e3 44 ♗xa8? ♛xa8 –+ ♘xh3+
45 ♔g2 ♛f8 46 ♗d5! ♗xd5 47 ♛xd5+
♔g7 48 ♖c7+ ♔h8 49 ♖1c2 ♖b8
50 ♛e4?! 50 a4! ♛h6 51 ♖c8+ ♖xc8
52 ♖xc8+ ♔g7 53 ♛g8+ ♔f6 54
♛f8+ +– ♛h6 △ 51...♘f4+ 52 exf4
♛h3+ 53 ♔g1 ♘f3+ 51 ♖c8+ ♖xc8
52 ♖xc8+ ♛g7 53 ♖c7+ ♛f6 54
♖xh7 ♛f8 55 b6 ♛e6 56 ♛c2 1-0
time **Miles**

146 Antoshin-Speelman
Frunze 79

1 d4 ♘f6 2 c4 e6 3 ♘f3 b6 4 g3
♗a6 5 ♛a4 ♗e7 6 ♘c3 0-0 7 e4 ♗b7
7...c6 8 e5!? ♘e8 9 ♗d3 d5 10 exd6
♘xd6 11 ♘e5∞; 10 ♛c2!? 8 ♗d3 d5
9 cxd5 exd5 10 e5 ♘e4 11 0-0 11
♛c2!? f5!? c5 12 ♛c2 c4 12...f5 13

exf6 ♘xf6 14 ♘g5∞; 13...♖xf6!?
14 ♘xe4 ♖xf3 15 ♘d2; 12...cxd4
13 ♘xd4!±; 13 ♘xe4?? dxe4 14
♗xe4 d3 −+ **13 ♗e2 ♞a6 14 a3** 14
♗e3 **♞c7 15 ♗e3 b5 16 ♞e1 a5?!**
16...♘xc3 **17 ♞g2** 17 ♘xe4! dxe4
18 a4! **♞xc3 18 bxc3 b4!?** 18...♘c8
19 axb4 axb4 20 ♖xa8 ♕xa8 21
cxb4 **♞e6?!** 21...♗xb4 22 f4 f5? 23
exf6 ♖xf6 24 f5±; 22...♞a3!∞; 22
♖b1∞ **22 ♖b1 ♕a7 23 ♗g4 ♖a8 24**
♗f5 g6 24...♘xd4? 25 ♕d1 ♘f3+ 26
♕xf3 d4 27 ♗e4! ♗xe4 28 ♕xe4 dxe3
29 ♘xe3 +−; 27 ♕h5 g6! **25 ♗xe6**
fxe6 26 ♞f4 ♞f7 27 h4 ♕a2 28 ♕d1
♖a3 29 ♖c1 29 b5!? c3? 30 ♖c1 ♕b2
31 ♕f3 +−; 29...♖b3!?∞ **♕b2 30**
h5!? g5 31 ♞xe6!? ♚xe6 32 ♕g4+
♞f7 33 ♖f1 ♖a1 34 ♕f5+! ♞e8 34...
♚g8? 35 e6 **35 ♕xh7 ♖xf1+ 36 ♞xf1**
c3 37 e6 ♞d8 38 ♗xg5 ♕xb4 39
♗f4 ♗c6 40 h6 ♕xd4

41 ♕b1 (a) 41 ♕g8+ ♗e8 42 h7 ♗f6
43 ♗g5 (1) 43...c2! 44 h8♕ c1♕+!
45 ♗xc1 ♗xh8 (2) 43...♗xg5 44
♕xg5+! ♚c7 45 ♕e7+ ♚b6 46 ♕xe8
♕d3+! 47 ♚g1 ♕b1+! 48 ♚g2 ♕e4+
49 f3 ♕c2+!=; 44...♚c8? 45 ♕g8;
44 h8♕?? ♕xh8 45 ♕xh8 c2 −+
(b) 41 ♚g2!! (1) 41...♕e4+ 42 ♕xe4
dxe4 43 h7 e3+ 44 f3 ♗f6 45 ♗g5
+−; (2) 41...♗e8 42 ♗c7+ ♚xc7 43

♕xe7+ ♚b6 44 ♕xe8 ∞/+−; (3) 41...
c2 42 ♕xc2 ♕c4 43 ♕b2! ♗b5 44
♚h2 △ h7 **♗c5??** 41...♗b4! 42 h7
c2! 43 ♕xb4 (a) 43...♕xb4? 44 h8♕+
♚e7 45 ♕g7+! ♚xe6 46 ♕e5+ ♞
♕c7+ +−; (b) 43...♕d1+? 44 ♚e1
♗b5+ 45 ♚g2 ♕xe1 46 h8♕+ ♚e7 47
♕g7+! ♚xe6 48 ♕g6+ ♚e7 49 ♕d6+
+−; 44 ♚g2?? d4+ −+; (c) 43...♕d3+!!
44 ♚g1 ♕d1+ 45 ♚h2 ♕h5+ = **42**
♕b8+ ♞e7 43 ♕c7+ ♞xe6 44 ♕xc6+
♞e7 45 ♕c7+ ♞e6 46 ♕c8+ 46 ♕e5+!
♞e7 47 ♕f5! ♕c4+ 48 ♚g2 ♗d4 49
h7 c2 50 ♗g5+ ♞d6 51 ♕f8+ ♞c7
52 h8♕ ♖xh8 53 ♕xh8 d4 53...c1♕
54 ♕d8+! ♚b7 55 ♗xc1 ♕xc1 56
♕xd5+ **1-0 Speelman**

147 Foiser-Troianescu
Baile Herculane 79

1 d4 ♞f6 2 c4 e6 3 ♞f3 b6 4 g3
♗a6 5 ♕a4 5 b3!? **♗e7** 5...c6 6 ♘c3!
6 ♗g2 c6 7 ♞c3 0-0 8 ♗f4! △ ♗xb8
+− **♗b7** (1) 8...b5?! 9 cxb5 cxb5
10 ♘xb5 ♘d5 11 ♘c3 ♘xf4 12 gxf4
d5 13 0-0 ♕b6 14 ♖ab1 ♘c6 15
♖fd1±; (2) 8...♕c8 9 ♖c1! d6 10
0-0 ♘bd7 11 ♖fd1 ♗b7 12 e4 d5
13 ♗e3!±; (3) 8...d6 9 ♖c1 ♕e8?!
10 0-0 b5 11 cxb5 cxb5 12 ♕b3!
d5 13 ♘e5 ♗d6 14 ♘d3! ♗xf4 15
gxf4 ♘bd7 16 ♕a3!± Ivkov-
Zuidema, Beverwijk 64 **9 0-0 ♞h5**
10 ♗d2 f5 11 ♞e5 11 e4? b5! 12
cxb5 cxb5 13 ♘xb5 fxe4 14 ♗a5
♕c8 15 ♖ac1 ♗c6 16 ♘e5 ♕a6 17
♘xc6 ♘xc6 Haik-Troianescu,
Manresa 75 **♕e8 12 d5!± ♗d6 13**
dxc6 dxc6 14 ♞d3 e5 15 c5! ♗c7
16 ♞b5! ♕f7 17 ♕b3 ♚h8 18 ♕xf7
♖xf7 19 ♞xc7 ♖xc7 20 cxb6 axb6
21 ♞xe5 +− c5 22 ♗xb7 ♖xb7 23
♖fd1 h6 24 ♗c3 ♞a6 25 a4 ♚h7
26 ♞c4 ♞c7 27 ♖d7 b5 28 ♞d6

♖ba7 29 ♘xf5 ♘e8 30 ♖xa7 ♖xa7
31 b3 b4 32 ♗e5 ♘hf6 33 h3 ♘d7
34 ♗b2 ♔g6 35 ♘e3 ♘d6 36 ♖d1
♖a6 37 ♗xg7! c4 37...♔xg7 38 ♖xd6!
38 ♘xc4 ♘xc4 39 ♖xd7 ♘a5 40
♗b2 ♘xb3 41 g4 △ ♖g7 mate ♔g5
42 ♖g7+ ♔h4 43 ♔g2 ♖e6 44 ♖e7!
1-0 44...♖xe7 45 ♗f6 mate **Vaisman**

148 Benjamin-Browne USA 79
1 d4 ♘f6 2 ♘f3 e6 3 c4 b6 4 g3 ♗a6
4...♗b7 5 b3 ♗b4+! 6 ♗d2 ♗e7 7 ♗g2
c6 8 ♘c3 d5 9 0-0 ♘bd7 10 cxd5
cxd5 =+ 11 a4 ♗b7 12 ♘e1?! 12 ♗f4
♖c8 13 ♘b5 0-0 13 ♘d3 ♘e4! 14
♖c1 ♖c8 15 ♘xe4 dxe4 16 ♘b2?!
16 ♘e5 ♘xe5 17 dxe5 ♕d5!∓ e5 17
♖xc8 ♕xc8 18 dxe5 ♘xe5 19 ♕b1
f5!∓ 20 ♖c1 ♕e6 21 ♖c7 ♗d5 22
b4 ♘c6 23 b5 ♘d4! 24 ♕e1 ♖c8
25 ♖xa7 25 ♖xc8+ ♕xc8∓ ♖c2 26
♘d1 ♘b3 27 ♗b4 ♗xb4 28 ♕xb4
♖c1 29 ♕e1 ♕d6! −+ 30 ♗h3 ♗e6
31 ♔g2 ♕xd1 32 ♕xd1 ♖xd1 33
♖b7 ♖d6 0-1 **Gheorghiu**

149 Georgadze-Kupreichik
USSR 79
1 d4 ♘f6 2 c4 e6 3 ♘f3 b6 4 g3 ♗a6
5 ♘bd2 5 b3 ♗b4+ 6 ♗d2 ♗e7 7
♗g2 d5 8 0-0 c6 9 ♘e5 +=; 5 ♕a4 c5
6 ♗g2 ♗b7 7 0-0 cxd4 8 ♘xd4 ♗xg2
9 ♔xg2 ♗e7 10 f3 0-0 11 ♖d1 ♕c8=
Trois-Polugaevsky, Riga 79 c5 6 ♗g2
♘c6 7 dxc5 ♗xc5 7...bxc5!? 8 0-0
0-0 9 a3! += ♗e7 10 b4 ♗b7 11 ♗b2
a5 11...♖c8 12 ♕b1! h6 13 ♖fd1
♕c7 14 ♘e4 ♘xe4 15 ♕xe4 f5 16
♕d3 += 12 b5 ♘b8 13 ♕c2 d6? 13...
h6 14 ♘g5 ♖a7 15 ♗xf6 hxg5 14
♘g5 ♗xg2 15 ♗xf6 g6 16 ♘xe6!
fxe6 17 ♗xe7 ♕xe7 18 ♔xg2 +− ♘d7
19 ♕e4 ♘c5 20 ♕d4 ♖ad8 21 ♖ad1
d5 22 ♘f3 ♘b3 23 ♕d3 a4 23...♕xa3

24 ♕e3! +− 24 ♘d4 dxc4 25 ♕xc4
♘xd4 26 ♖xd4 ♖xd4 27 ♕xd4 ♕xa3
28 ♖a1 ♕b3 29 ♕xa4 ♕d5+ 30 f3
♖d8 31 ♖a2 ♔g7 32 ♖c2 ♖d7 33
♖c6 ♕e5 34 ♕e4! ♕xe4 35 fxe4 ♔f6
36 ♖xb6 ♖d4 37 ♔f3 ♖b4 38 ♖b7
h5 38...♖b3+!? 39 ♔e3! ♔e5 40
♔d3 ♖d4+ 41 ♔c3 ♖xe4 42 ♖d7 ♖xe2
43 b6 ♖e1 44 ♖d2 ♖c1+ 1-0 45
♖c2 ♖d1 46 b7 ♖d8 47 ♖d2 ♖b8
48 ♖d7 ♔e4 49 ♔c4 **Gufeld**

150 Kuzmin-Larsen Riga 79
1 d4 ♘f6 2 c4 e6 3 ♘f3 b6 4 g3 ♗b4+
5 ♗d2 ♗xd2+ 6 ♘bxd2 ♗b7 7 ♗g2
d6 8 0-0 0-0 9 ♕c2 ♘bd7 10 e4 e5
11 ♖fe1 ♕e7 12 ♖ad1 ♖fd8 13 ♘b1
c5 14 dxe5 14 dxc5 ♘xc5?! 15 ♘c3
+=/±; 14...dxc5; 14...bxc5! ♘xe5!?
14...dxe5 15 ♘c3 += 15 ♘c3 ♘xf3+
16 ♗xf3 ♘d7 17 ♗g2 ♘e5 18 ♕e2
♘c6 19 ♘d5 ♕f8 20 ♕h5 ♖ab8 21 f4
♖e8 22 g4 ♘d4 23 e5! dxe5 24 fxe5
♖e6 25 ♖e3 ♖h6? 25...♖ae8 26 ♕g5
♕d8 27 ♕f4 27 ♘f6+ ♔h8!∓
Gheorghiu ♖e6 28 ♖f1 ♕d7

29 ♖f2 29 ♘f6+! gxf6 30 exf6 ♘e2+!
31 ♖xe2 ♕d4+ 32 ♕xd4 ♖xe2! 33
♕f2!± ♖be8 30 h3 △ ♗e4; 30 ♗e4!
♖xe5! 31 ♗xh7+ ♔xh7 32 ♖xe5 ♖xe5
33 ♕xe5 ♕xg4+ h6 31 ♗e4 b5 32 b3
bxc4 33 bxc4 ♗a6 34 ♗d3 ♔h8 35

♘f6! ♖xf6 36 exf6 g5 37 ♕d6! +−
♗c8 38 ♖e7 ♕a4 39 ♕e5 ♕d1+ 40
♔h2 ♖g8 41 ♕e4 ♗f5 42 ♖xf5! 1-0
Miles/Speelman

151 Shvedchikov-Chechelian
USSR 79
1 c4 e6 2 ♘f3 ♘f6 3 g3 b6 3...d5
4 ♗g2 ♗b7 5 0-0 ♗e7 6 ♘c3 0-0 7
d4 ♘e4 8 ♕c2 ♘xc3 9 ♕xc3 c5 10
♖d1 d6 11 ♗f4 11 b3 ♗f6 12 ♗b2
♕e7 13 ♕c2 ♘c6 14 e4 e5 15 d5 +=;
11 ♕c2∞ ♘c6 11...♕c7 12 b4!? **12
dxc5 bxc5 13 ♘e1?!** N ♕c7 14 ♖ac1
♖fd8 15 ♕d3 ♖ab8 =+ 16 ♘c2? 16
b3 g5! 17 ♗d2 ♘e5 18 ♕c3 ♗xg2
19 ♔xg2 ♕b7+ 20 ♔g1 ♕xb2 21
♘e3 ♕xc3 22 ♗xc3 f5 23 ♗xe5 dxe5
24 ♖xd8+ ♖xd8 25 ♖b1 ♖d2 26
♖b7 ♔f7 27 ♖xa7 ♖xe2 28 ♔f1 ♖b2
29 g4 f4∓ 30 ♘d1 ♖c2 31 f3 e4!
32 fxe4 ♖xc4 33 ♘f2 e5 34 ♔e1 ♖d4
35 a4 ♔e6 36 ♔e2 c4 37 a5 ♗b4 38
a6?! ♖d2+ Δ ♖xf2+, ♗c5+ −+ 0-1
Gufeld

152 Tal-Ubilava USSR 79
1 ♘f3 ♘f6 2 c4 b6 3 g3 ♗b7 4 d4
4 ♗g2 e5! e6 5 ♗g2 ♗e7 6 0-0 0-0
7 d5 N 7 ♘c3 **exd5** 8 ♘d4 c6?! 8...
♘a6! 9 ♘c3 c6 10 cxd5 ♘xd5 11
♘xd5 cxd5 12 ♘f5 ♗f6 13 ♘e3 ♘c7
14 ♘xd5 ♗xd5 15 ♗xd5 ♘xd5 16
♕xd5 ♖e8 =+ 9 cxd5 ♘xd5 10 e4
♘c7 11 ♘c3 g6?! 11...♘e8! **12 ♗h6±**
♖e8 13 e5 ♘e6 14 ♘e4 ♘xd4 15
♕xd4 c5 16 ♕c3 ♘c6 17 e6! ♘d4
18 exf7+ ♔xf7 19 ♘d6+ ♗xd6 20
♕c4+ ♘e6 21 ♗xb7 ♖b8 22 ♗e4 b5
23 ♕d5 ♗f8 24 ♗xf8 ♖xf8 25 f4 ♔g8
26 ♖ad1 26 f5 gxf5 27 ♗xf5 ♕f6
27 f5 gxf5 28 ♖xf5 ♕xb2 29 ♕xd7
♘g7 30 ♖h5! ♕f2+ 31 ♔h1 ♖f7 32
♕g4 ♖e8 33 ♖xh7 1-0 **Georgadze**

153 Tatai-Orso Budapest 79
1 d4 ♘f6 2 c4 b6 3 ♘c3 ♗b7 4 ♗g5!?
h6 5 ♗xf6 exf6 6 e3 f5 7 ♘f3 g6
8 ♗e2 ♗g7 9 0-0 d6 10 ♘d5± ♘d7
10...0-0 11 ♘d2 Δ ♗f3 **11 ♘d2 0-0
12 ♗f3 c6 13 ♘f4 ♖b8± 14 ♕c2 ♘f6
15 ♖ac1 ♖e8 16 b4 ♕d7** 16...c5 17
♗xb7 ♖xb7 18 dxc5 dxc5 12 ♖fd1
+= **17 a4 g5 18 ♘d3 ♘e4**

19 c5!± dxc5 20 bxc5 ♗a6 21 ♖fd1
g4? 21...♗xd3 22 ♕xd3 ♘xc5 23
♘c4± **22 ♗xe4 +− fxe4 23 ♘xe4
♗xd3 24 ♕xd3 b5 25 axb5 cxb5
26 c6 ♕d5 27 c7 1-0 B.Balogh**

Grunfeld

154 Botterill-Curtin Dublin 79
1 d4 ♘f6 2 c4 g6 3 ♘c3 d5 4 cxd5
♘xd5 5 e4 ♘xc3 6 bxc3 ♗g7 7 ♗c4
c5 8 ♘e2 ♘c6 9 ♗e3 0-0 10 0-0 ♕c7
11 ♖c1 ♖d8 12 ♗f4 ♕d7 13 dxc5 ♕e8
13...♘e5?! 14 ♗xe5 ♗xe5 15 ♕b3
♕e8 16 f4 ♗g7 17 f5 g5 18 f6! exf6
19 ♘d4± Botterill-Knott, London 78
14 ♗d5 ♗d7 14...e6? 15 ♗xc6 Δ ♗d6±
15 ♕c2 e5? 15...♖dc8! **16 ♗g5 ♖dc8
17 f4!± ♗e6** 17...♕f8 18 ♔h1 ♕xc5
19 ♗xf7+! ♔xf7 20 ♕b3+ +−; 17...h6
18 f5!± **18 f5 gxf5 19 ♗xe6 fxe6
20 exf5 exf5 21 ♕xf5 ♕g6 22 ♕xg6
hxg6 23 ♘g3 ♘d8 24 ♘e4 ♘e6 25**

♗e7 b6 26 ♖cd1 ♖c7 27 ♗d6 ♖c6 28
♘f6+ ♔h8 28...♗xf6 29 ♖xf6 ♘f4
30 ♗xe5 ♘e2+ 31 ♔f2 ♖xf6 32 ♗xf6
♖f8 33 ♔xe2 ♖xf6 34 ♖d6 +−; 31...
♖xc5 32 ♖xg6+ ♔f7 33 ♖g7+ ♔e6
34 ♗d4 ♘xd4 35 cxd4 +− 29 ♖d3!
♗xf6 30 ♖xf6 ♘f4 31 ♖f3! ♕g7 32
♗xe5 △ 32...♖xf6 33 ♖xf4 +− ♖xc5
33 ♖xb6+! ♖xe5 34 ♖b7+ ♔h6 35
♖xf4 +− ♖c8 36 ♖xa7 ♖xc3 37
h3 ♔g5? 38 ♖g4+ ♕f5 39 ♖f7+ ♔e6
40 ♖g7 ♖e1+ 41 ♔h2 ♖a3 42 ♖7xg6+
♔f5 43 ♖4g5+ ♔f4 44 g3+ ♔f3 45
♖f6+ ♔e2 46 ♖e5+ 1-0 Botterill

155 Polugaevsky-Bagirov
USSR Final 78

1 d4 ♘f6 2 c4 g6 3 ♘c3 d5 4 cxd5
♘xd5 5 e4 ♘xc3 6 bxc3 ♗g7 7 ♗c4
c5 8 ♘e2 ♘c6 9 ♗e3 cxd4 10 cxd4
b5!? 11 ♗d5! 11 ♗b3!? 0-0 12 ♖c1
♗d7 13 d5 ♘a5 14 ♗d4 ♘xb3 15
axb3 e5 16 ♗c5 += ♗d7 12 ♖c1 ♖c8
13 ♗xc6 13 0-0 e6 14 ♗xc6 ♖xc6
15 ♖xc6 ♗xc6 16 ♕c2 += ♖xc6 14
♖xc6 ♗xc6 15 d5 ♗d7 16 ♕d2! +=
16 0-0 ♕a5!= a5 17 0-0 0-0 18 ♖c1 b4
19 ♘d4 e6! 20 ♖c5! 20 d6!? ♕a8!
21 ♘b3! ♕xe4? 22 ♘c5 ♕c6 23
♘xe6 ♗c3 24 ♘xf8 ♗xd2 25 ♖xc6
♗xc6 26 d7 +−; 21...♗c6! exd5
21 exd5 ♖e8 22 ♘c6 ♕h4! 23 d6
23 ♘xa5?! ♗e5 24 h3 ♗xh3!; 23
♖xa5 ♕e4! ♗c3 24 ♕d3 h6 25 ♘e7+
♔h7 26 ♖xa5 ♕g4 27 ♖a7± ♖b8!
28 h3 ♕e6

Diagram

29 ♕d5?! 29 ♘d5! ♗b5 30 ♘c7 ♕c4!
31 ♕xc4 ♗xc4 32 ♘a6± ♕xd5 30
♘xd5 ♗e6 31 ♘e7 b3 32 axb3 ♖xb3
33 ♘c6 ♖b1+ 34 ♔h2 ♖d1!∝ 35
♗f4 g5 36 ♗g3 ♗f6 37 ♘e5 ♔g7 38

♘g4 ♗d4! 39 ♖a5 f5 40 ♘e3 ♗xe3
41 fxe3 ♕f7! 42 h4 ♖d3!= 43 ♖a7+
♔f6 44 ♖h7 ♔g6 45 ♖h8 ♗d7 45...
gxh4?! 46 ♗f4 46 ♖d8 ♗e6 47 ♖b8
♖xe3 48 ♖e8 f4 49 ♗f2 ♗f7! ½-½
Gufeld

156 Foigel-Sideifzade USSR 79
1 d4 ♘f6 2 c4 g6 3 ♘c3 d5 4 ♘f3
♗g7 5 cxd5 ♘xd5 6 e4 ♘xc3 7 bxc3
c5 8 ♗e2 ♘c6 9 d5 9 ♗e3?! ♗g4
♗xc3+ 10 ♗d2 ♗xa1 11 ♕xa1 ♘d4
12 ♘xd4 cxd4 13 ♕xd4 0-0! 13...f6
14 e5 0-0 15 ♗c4 b5 16 ♗b3 a5 17
d6+ e6 18 0-0 ♗d7 19 a3 ♖a6 20
♖c1± 14 ♗h6 ♕a5+ 15 ♔f1 f6 16
♗xf8 ♔xf8= 17 h4 17 ♕b2 ♗d7 △
♖c8 =+ ♕xa2 18 g4 18 h5 g5 ♗d7 19
g5 ♕a4! 20 ♕e3 f5! 21 exf5 ♗xf5
22 ♗f3 ♕a6+! 23 ♔g2 ♕d6∓ 24 h5
gxh5 25 ♖xh5 ♔g8 26 g6 26 ♖h6
♗g6 27 ♗e4 ♖f8 28 ♗xg6 hxg6 29
♕e4 ♖f5∓ hxg6 26...♗xg6 27 ♖e5
∝/=+ 27 ♖h1 ♖f8! 28 ♕h6 28 ♕xa7
♕f4!∓ ♔f7 29 ♕e3 ♔g8 30 ♕h6 ♔f7
31 ♕e3 b6 −+ 32 ♖h7+ ♔e8 33
♕c3 ♗d7 34 ♗e4 g5 35 ♖h8 ♕f4 36
♖xf8+ ♕xf8 37 ♕c7 ♕h6 38 ♕b8+
♔f7 39 ♕xa7 ♗h3+ 40 ♔g1 ♕h4 41
♖h1 ♕d4 42 ♕a2 ♗f5 43 ♗g2 ♕d1+
44 ♗f1 ♗d3 45 d6+ e6 46 ♔h2 ♕xf1
47 d7 ♔e7 48 d8♕+ ♔xd8 49 ♕a8+
♔e7 0-1 Gufeld

157 Foldi-Banner
Hungary 79

1 ♘f3 ♘f6 2 c4 g6 3 d4 ♗g7 4 ♘c3
d5 5 cxd5 ♘xd5 6 e4!? ♘xc3 6...
♘b6?! 7 ♗e2 += 7 bxc3 c5 8 ♗e3
♛a5!? 9 ♛d2 ♘c6 10 ♖c1 ♗g4 11
d5 ♖d8 12 ♗e2 0-0 13 0-0 ♗xf3!
13...f5? 14 ♘g5 14 ♗xf3 ♘e5 15
♗e2± ♘d7 16 c4! ♛xd2 16...♛c7?
17 f4 f6 18 ♘g4 17 ♗xd2 f5 17...
♗d4 18 ♔h1 △ f4 18 ♖b1 b6 19
exf5 gxf5 20 ♗g5 ♗f6 21 ♗h6 ♗g7
22 ♗xg7 ♔xg7 23 f4! ♘f6 24 ♗f3
♖d6 25 ♖fe1 ♘g8!? 26 a4 ♖ff6 27
a5 ♔f8 28 ♖a1 ♖d8 29 axb6 axb6
30 ♖a7 ♖b8 31 ♖b1 ♖d6 32 ♖c7?!
32 ♖b5! △ ♖a1-b1 ♖a8! 33 ♖b7
♖a4 34 ♗e2 ♖b4 35 ♖a1 ♖b3 36
♖a8+ ♔g7 37 ♔f2 ♖b2 38 h3 ♖g6
39 ♖a3 h5?! 40 g3 h4? 41 gxh4!
♔h6 42 h5 ♖d6 43 ♖g3 ♔h7 44
♔e1 ♖b1+ 45 ♔d2 ♖b2+ 46 ♔d1
♖d8 47 ♗d3 ♖a8 48 ♗xf5+ ♔h8 49
♔c1 ♖b4 50 ♗d3 ♖a1+ 51 ♔d2 ♖b2+
52 ♔c3 ♖f2 53 ♖xb6 ♖a3+ 54 ♖b3
♖xb3+ 54...♖a1 55 ♘b1! +- 55
♔xb3 ♖xf4 56 ♔a4! +- ♖f8 47 ♔b5
♖d8 57...♖c8 58 ♗f5 58 ♗f5 ♖f8
59 ♖g5 ♘f6 60 ♔xc5 ♘e8 61 ♗d3 ♖f3
62 ♔d4 ♘d6 63 c5 ♘b7 64 c6 ♘d6
65 c7 ♖f8 66 ♖e5 ♖e8 67 ♔c5 1-0
Foldi

158 Vaganian-Hubner
Rio 79

1 d4 ♘f6 2 c4 g6 3 ♘c3 d5 4 ♘f3
♗g7 5 ♛b3 dxc4 6 ♛xc4 0-0 7 e4
♗g4 8 ♗e3 ♘fd7 9 ♛b3 ♘b6 10 ♖d1
e6!? 10...♘c6 11 ♗e2 ♘c6 12 e5!?
12 ♘e5?! ♗xe2 13 ♘xc6? ♗xd1 -+
♘e7 13 h3 ♗xf3 14 ♗xf3 ♘f5 15
0-0 15 ♗xb7? ♖b8 △ ♘d5, ♘xe3
c6 16 ♘e4 ♘d5 17 ♗g5 ♛b6 18 ♛xb6
axb6 19 g4 19 a3 ♖a4∓

19...♘xd4! 19...♘e7 20 a3= 20 ♖xd4
♗xe5 21 ♖xd5 21 ♖d2 ♖xa2 =+/∓
exd5 22 ♘f6+ ♛g7 22...♗xf6 23
♗xf6 ♖xa2 24 ♖e1∝ 23 ♘d7 f6!
23...♖fe8 24 ♘xe5 ♖xe5 25 ♗d2
♖xa2! 26 ♗c3 f6!; 25 ♗e3 ♖xe3 26
fxe3 ♖xa2 =+/=; 25...♖xa2 26 ♗x
b6!?∝; 25 ♗f4! ♖e6 26 a3± ♖f6??
27 ♗e5 +- 24 ♘xf8 24 ♘xe5? fxg5
△ ♖ae8/♖xa2 -+; 24 ♗e3 ♖f7 25
♘xe5 fxe5∓ fxg5 24...♔xf8!? 25
♘d7 25 ♘e6+? ♔f6 -+ ♗xb2 26
♖e1! 26 ♘xb6 ♖xa2∓ ♖xa2 △ ♗d4
27 ♖e2! ♖a1+ 28 ♔g2 ♗d4 29 ♖e7+
♔g8 30 ♘b8!= ♖a2 31 ♖xb7 ♖xf2+
32 ♔g3 ♖c2 33 ♘xc6 ♗f2+ ½-½ 34
♔g2 ♗e3+ 35 ♔h1 ♖c1+ 36 ♔h2 ♖c2+
37 ♗g2 ♗f4+ 38 ♔g1 ♗e3+ 39 ♔h2
♗f4+ = **Miles**

159 Botterill-Birnboim
England 79

1 d4 ♘f6 2 c4 g6 3 ♘c3 d5 4 ♘f3
♗g7 5 ♛b3 dxc4 6 ♛xc4 0-0 7 e4
♗g4 8 ♗e3 ♘fd7 9 ♛b3 c5!? 9...♘b6
10 ♖d1 ♘c6 11 d5 ♘e5 12 ♗e2 ♘xf3+
13 gxf3 ♗h5 14 ♖g1! += 10 d5 ♘a6
10...♗xf3 11 gxf3 ♛b6 12 f4 ♘a6
13 h4!? Boleslavsky; 11...♘a6!? △
♖b8, ♛a5 11 ♘d2 11 ♗e2 ♖b8 12
0-0 ♛a5 13 ♗f4 ♗xf3 14 gxf3 ♘e5∝
Sapi-Filip, Budapest 54 f5!? 11...e6
12 h3 exd5 13 exd5 ♗f5 14 g4 c4!

15 &xc4 &ac5 16 ♕a3 &d3! 17 &xc5
&xc5 18 ♕xc5 ♖c8 19 ♕xf8+ ♔xf8
20 &xd3 &xc3 21 bxc3 ♕xd5 22 &e4
♖e8 23 0-0-0 ♖xe4 24 &xe4 ♕xe4 =+
|Judovich **12 f3 f4 13 &f2 &h5 14
g4!? fxg3 15 hxg3 &xf3 16 d6+ ♔h8
17 &xf3 ♖xf3 18 &e2 ♖f8** 18...♖f6!?
19 &e3 exd6 19...&d4!? **20 0-0-0 +=**
20...&f6? 21 e5 +–; 20...&xc3 21
♖xh7+! ♔xh7 22 ♖h1+ ♔g7 23
&h6+ ♔f6 24 ♕xc3+ &e5 25 ♖f1+
♔e7 26 &g5+ ♔d7 27 &b5+ ♔c8
28 &xd8 ♖xf1+ 29 &xf1 ♔xd8 30
&xa6 bxa6 31 ♕a5+ ♔d7 32 ♕xa6
♔c7 += ½-½ **Botterill**

160 Hausner-Roos
Iasi 79

**1 d4 &f6 2 c4 g6 3 &c3 d5 4 &f3
&g7 5 &f4 c5** 5...0-0!?; 5...c6 **6 dxc5
♕a5 7 cxd5 &xd5 8 ♕xd5 &xc3+
9 &d2 &xd2+?** 9...&e6! 10 ♕xb7
&xd2+ 11 &xd2 0-0 12 b4 ♕a4! 13
e4 &d7 14 ♕b5 ♕a3= Grigorian-
Tseshkovsky, Baku 77 **10 ♕xd2
♕xc5** 10...♕xd2+ 11 &xd2 0-0 12
e3 &e6 13 &b5!± A.Zaitsev-Szilagyi,
Albena 70 **11 ♖c1 ♕f5 12 &d4** 12
h4 &c6 13 h5 ♕f6 14 ♖c4 &f5 15
g4 ♖d8! 16 ♕c1 &d3! 17 ♖f4
Petrosian-Shamkovich, USSR Final
66 **♕d7 13 ♕h6 ♕xd4?!** N 13...&c6
14 &xc6 bxc6 15 ♕g7± Timman-
J.Littlewood, Netherlands-England 69
14 ♖xc8+ ♔d7 15 ♖c3! +– ♕g4 15...
♔e8 16 e3 ♕d7 17 &b5 &c6 18 0-0±;
16 ♕c1!; 15...♕e5 16 ♕d2+ ♔e6 17
♖e3; 15...♕f6 16 ♕d2+ ♔e6 17
♖e3+ ♔f5 18 ♖f3+ **16 g3! f5 17
♕d2+ ♔e6 18 ♖e3+ ♔f7 19 ♕d5+
♔f8 20 ♕xb7** 20 ♕d8+! ♔f7 21
♖xe7+ ♔f6 22 ♕d6+ ♔g5 23 f4+!
♔h6 24 ♕f6 ♖g8 25 ♕f7 ♕c4 **21
♕xe7+ ♔g8 22 ♖c3 1-0 Ciocaltea**

161 Gereben-Petran Budapest 79

**1 d4 &f6 2 c4 g6 3 &c3 d5 4 &f3
&g7 5 &f4 0-0 6 cxd5? &xd5 7 &xd5
♕xd5 8 &xc7?** 8 ♕b3 ♕a5+ 9 ♕c3
♕xc3+ 10 bxc3 c5= **&c6∓ 9 e3 &f5!
10 &e2 ♖ac8 11 &g3 ♕a5+ 12 ♔f1?
&b4 13 a3 &c2 14 ♖b1 &h6 15
♔g1 &xe3 16 fxe3 &xb1 0-1
B.Balogh**

162 Odendahl-Chandler USA 79

**1 d4 &f6 2 c4 g6 3 &c3 d5 4 &f3 &g7
5 &f4 0-0 6 e3 c5 7 dxc5 ♕a5 8
♖c1 ♖d8** 8...dxc4; 8...&e4 **9 ♕b3
&a6! 10 ♕b5 ♕xb5 11 &xb5 &e6
12 &fd4 &d7 13 &e5 dxc4 14 ♖xc4
♖dc8 15 &e2** 15 b4!? **♖xc5 16 ♖xc5
&xc5∓ 17 0-0 &fe4 18 &xg7 ♔xg7 19
♖c1 e5 20 &f3 &xb5 21 &xb5 ♔f6!∓
22 ♔f1 ♖d8 23 b4 &d3! 24 ♖c7
&b2 25 ♖xb7 ♖d1+ 26 &e1** 26 ♔e2
&c3 mate **&c3 27 &a6 e4 28 ♖c7
&d3! –+ 29 g3 ♖xe1+ 30 ♔g2 &e2
31 h4 ♖g1+ 32 ♔h2 ♖f1 –+ 0-1
Gheorghiu**

163 Farago-Kirov Lodz 79

**1 d4 &f6 2 c4 g6 3 &c3 d5 4 &f3
&g7 5 &f4 0-0 6 e3 c5 7 dxc5 &e4
7...&e6!? 8 ♖c1** 8 &xd5? &xb2!
9 &c7 ♕d7 10 ♖b1 &g7!∓; 8 &e5
&xe5 9 &xe5 &xc3 10 bxc3 ♕c7
11 ♕d4 f6 12 &d3 &c6 13 ♕xd5+
♔g7 14 &e2 &f5 15 &f4 e5!= **&xc3
9 bxc3 ♕a5?! 10 cxd5 &xc3+ 11
&d2 &f5** 11...&d7 12 ♕c2 &xd2+
13 ♕xd2± **12 e4! &xe4 13 ♕b3
&d4**

Diagram

14 ♕xb7!± N 14 ♕c4 &b2 15 ♖d1
&f5 16 &e2 += Farago-Ftacnik, Kiev
78 e5 **15 &g5 h6 16 &xh6 ♖d8 17**

♗c4 17 ♕xa8 ♗xd5 ♘d7 18 0-0 ♘xc5
19 ♕e7! ♗xd5 20 ♕f6! +− ♘e6 21
♘b3 ♕b6 22 ♘xd4 ♕xd4 23 ♖fd1
♕c5 24 ♗e2 ♕a5 25 ♗g4 ♕h7 26
♖d3! 26 ♗xe6 ♔xh6 ♖ac8 27 ♖h3
♕g8 27...♖xc1+ 28 ♗xc1+ ♔g8 29
♖h8 mate **28 ♖f1! 1-0 Pytel**

164 Portisch-Vadasz Hungary 78
1 ♘f3 ♘f6 2 c4 g6 3 ♘c3 d5 4 d4
♗g7 5 ♗f4 0-0 6 e3 c5 7 dxc5 ♘e4
8 ♖c1 ♘xc3 9 bxc3 dxc4! 10 ♕xd8
♖xd8 11 ♗xc4 ♘d7≈ 12 ♗g5 12
♘g5 ♖f8 13 ♘e4 ♘e5=; 12 ♗c7 ♖f8!
13 c6 bxc6 14 ♘d4 ♖e8! 15 0-0 ♘b6
16 ♗xb6 axb6 17 ♘xc6 ♗b7 18
♘b4 e6 19 ♗b3 ♖ec8 20 c4 ♖c7
21 ♘d2 ♖ac8 ½-½ Lukacs-Vadasz,
Hungary 78 **♖e8 13 ♗b5 a6 14 ♗a4**
h6 15 c6!? N 15 ♗h4 g5 16 c6?
♘c5! 17 cxb7 ♗xb7 18 ♗xe8 gxh4
19 ♗d7 ♘xd7 20 ♘xh4 ♘e5∓ Ribli-
Timman, Amsterdam 78 **♘c5 16 cxb7**
♗xb7 17 ♗xe8 hxg5 18 ♗xf7+ ♔xf7
19 ♘xg5+ ♔f6 20 ♘h7+ ♔f5! 21 g4+
♔xg4 22 ♖g1+ += ♔h4 23 ♔e2 ♘e4
24 f3 ♘xc3+ 25 ♔f2 ♖d8 25...♘b5??
26 ♖g3 **26 ♖xg6 ♖d2+ 27 ♔f1 ♖xh2**
28 ♖e1 ♗xf3 29 ♘g5 ♗h5 30 ♖xg7
♖h1+ 31 ♔f2 ♘d1+ 32 ♖xd1 ♖xd1
33 ♘f3+ ♗xf3 34 ♔xf3 ♖a1 35 ♖g4+
♔h5 36 ♖a4 ♔g5 37 ♔e4 ♔f6 38
♖xa6+ e6 39 ♖a7 ♖b1 40 a4 40 ♖d7!

♖b4+ 41 ♔f3 ♔f5 42 a5 ♖a4 43
♖a8 ♔e5 ½-½ Pytel

165 Marovic-Schmidt Rome 79
1 d4 ♘f6 2 c4 g6 3 ♘c3 d5 4 ♘f3
♗g7 5 ♗g5 ♘e4 6 cxd5 ♘xg5 7 ♘xg5
e6 7...c6 **8 ♕d2 exd5** 8...h6 **9 ♕e3+**
♔f8 10 ♕f4 ♗f6 11 h4 c6? 11...h6
12 ♘f3 ♔g7 13 0-0-0 ♗e6∞ **12 e4!**
h6 13 ♘f3 13 ♘xf7 ♔xf7 14 e5
dxe4 14 ♘xe4 ♕g7 15 ♗c4 ♕a5+!?
16 ♔f1 ♕f5 17 ♕xf5 ♗xf5 18 ♘d6
c5!? 19 dxc5 ♘d7 20 ♖d1 21 ♘xb7
♘xc5! 22 ♘xc5 ♖hc8 ♘xc5 21 ♘xf5+
gxf5 22 b4

22...♘e4?! 22...♖hd8! 23 ♖xd8 ♖xd8
24 bxc5 ♖d1+ 25 ♘e1 ♗c3 26 ♔e2
♖d2+ 27 ♔e3 ♖d1= **23 ♖d7 ♖hf8**
24 g3 ♖ad8 25 ♖xb7 ♘d6 26 ♖c7
♖c8 27 ♖xc8 ♖xc8 28 ♗b3 ♖b8 29
♔g2 ♖xb4 30 ♖d1 ♖b6 31 ♖d5 ♔f8
32 ♖a5 ♖b7 33 ♖d5 ♔e7 34 ♘e5
♖c7 35 ♘d3 ♖b7 36 ♘f4 ♗g7 37
♔f3 ♖b5 38 ♖d1 ♗e5 39 ♘d5+ ♔f8
40 ♔e2 ♖c5 41 ♖d3 41 ♘f6!? ♘b5
42 ♔e3 ♘c3 43 ♘xc3 ½-½ Schmidt

166 Inkiov-Honfi Trstenik 79
1 d4 ♘f6 2 c4 g6 3 ♘c3 d5 4 ♗f4
♗g7 5 e3 0-0 6 ♕b3 c5!? 7 cxd5
cxd4 8 exd4 e6 9 d6 9 dxe6 ♗xe6!?
10 ♕xb7 ♘d5∞ **♘c6 10 ♘f3 ♘h5 11**

♗e5 f6 12 ♘g3 ♘xg3 13 hxg3 ♕xd6
14 0-0-0 ♗d7 15 ♘e4 15 ♕xb7?!
♖ab8 16 ♕a6 ♖fc8∝ ♕c7 16 ♘b1
♘a5 17 ♕b4 ♗c6 18 ♗d3 ♖f7 19 g4
♘d5?! 19...♖d8! 20 ♘c3 ♘c6 21 ♕a4
♖d8 22 ♘xd5 exd5 23 ♖h3 ♗f8
24 ♖dh1 Δ ♗xg6 ♖g7 25 a3 ♖d6 26
♕c2 ♕d7 27 ♖h4 ♗e7 28 ♕d2 ♘d8
29 ♕h6 ♗f8 30 ♕e3 ♖e6 31 ♕d2
♘a2 ♗e7 35 g3 a6 36 ♖h6 ♕e6 37
♖6h4 ♗d8 38 ♕a1 ♕d7 39 ♗b1 ♖b5
40 ♕c2 ♕f7 41 ♖h6 ♕d7 42 ♕e2
♗e7 43 ♕d1 ♘a5! 43...♕xg4?! 44
♖1h4 Δ ♕h1± 44 ♖1h2 ♕c6 45
♗d3 ♘c4 46 ♕h1 46 ♗xc4 dxc4 47
♘e1 c3 48 b4 a5 −+ ♗xa3! 47 bxa3
47 ♖xh7 ♗xb2+ 48 ♔b1 ♗xd4+ 49
♔c1 ♘e3+ 50 ♔d2 ♖b2+ −+; 48 ♔a2
♖a5+ 49 ♔b1 ♖a1+ 50 ♔c2 ♕a4 mate
♖b3 47...♘d2! 48 ♔a2 ♕c3 −+ 48
♗b1 ♘d2 49 ♔a2 ♖xa3+ 49...♕c3!
50 ♔xa3 ♕c3+ 51 ♔a2 ♕b3+ 52
♔a1 ♕a3+ 0-1 53 ♗a2 ♕c3 mate
Honfi

167 Farago-Groszpeter Kecskemet 79
1 d4 ♘f6 2 c4 g6 3 ♘c3 d5 4 ♗f4
♗g7 5 ♘f3 0-0 6 e3 c5 7 dxc5 ♘e4
7...♕a5 8 ♖c1 ♘xc3 9 bxc3 ♕a5 10
♕b3 ♘bd7 10...dxc4!? 11 ♗xc4
♘d7 12 ♘g5 e6 13 ♕b4!± 11 cxd5
♘xc5 12 ♕b4! ♕xb4 13 cxb4 ♘e4
14 ♗c4! ♗c3+ 15 ♔e2 ♗xb4 16 ♖e5!
♗f5?! 16...♘d6!? 17 ♗b3 ♗d7 18
♘d4 ♖fc8 +=; 17 ♗d3 ♗g4 17 ♗d3
♘d6 18 e4! ♗g4 18...♘xe4? 19 ♗xe4
♘xe4 20 ♖c4 +−; 18...♘xe4 19 ♖c4
+− 19 ♗b2 ♖ac8 20 e5 ♘f5 21 h3
♗xf3+ 22 ♔xf3 ♖cd8? 22...♖fd8
23 ♗xf5! gxf5 24 ♖hd1 b6 25 ♖c7
a5 26 ♖c6 ♗c5 27 d6! ♖d7 28 ♗d4!
f6? 28...♗xd4 29 ♖xd4 exd6 30
exd6 ♖b8 31 ♔f4 +− 29 ♗xc5 bxc5

30 e6! ♖xd6 31 ♖dxd6 exd6 32
♕f4! d5 33 ♖xc5 1-0 Foldi

King's Indian

168 Guil.Garcia-Vaganian Rio 79
1 c4 e5 2 ♘c3 d6 3 e3 g6 4 d4 ♘d7
4...exd4 5 exd4 +=; 4...♗g7 5 dxe5
+= 5 ♘f3 ♘gf6 6 ♗e2 ♗g7 7 0-0 0-0
8 b3 ♖e8 9 ♕c2 e4 10 ♘d2 ♕e7
11 ♗a3 c6?! 11...c5!?; 11...♘f8 12
♖ae1 c5 13 f3! +=/± exf3 14 ♗xf3
♘f8 15 dxc5 dxc5 16 ♘d5 ♘xd5
16...♕d6? 17 ♘xf6+ Δ ♘e4 17 cxd5
♗f5!? 17...b6? 18 d6 +−; 17...♘d7
18 e4 18 ♕xc5 ♕xc5 19 ♗xc5 ♖ac8
Δ ♖c2 ♗d4+ 18...♗d7 19 e5!? ♗xe5
20 ♘c4 f6 21 d6± 19 ♕h1 ♖ac8 20
♖d1 20 exf5? ♕xe1 −+ ♗d7 21 ♘c4
♗g7 21...f6? 22 ♖xd4 +−

22 e5! ♗b5 22...♗xe5 23 d6±; 23
♘xe5 Δ ♗b2; 23 ♖de1± 23 ♖fe1
♗xc4 24 ♕xc4 ♗xe5 25 d6 ♕f6 25...
♕d7 26 ♗g4 +− 26 ♗xb7 ♗xd6 26...
♖cd8 27 ♖f1 ♕g7 28 ♗xc5 +−; 27...
♕e6 28 ♗d5 +− 27 ♖f1 ♕e7 28
♗xc8 1-0 28...♖xc8 29 ♖xd6 ♕xd6
30 ♕xf7+ ♔h8 31 ♗b2+ +− Miles

169 Portisch-Kavalek Montreal 79
1 ♘f3 g6 2 c4 ♗g7 3 d4 d6 4 ♘c3
♗g4 5 e3 e5?! 5...♘c6!?; 5...♘f6!?

Odendahl-Keene, Gausdal 79 **6 dxe5 dxe5 7 ♕xd8+ ♚xd8 8 ♘g5 ♞h6 9 ♗e2 ♗d7** 9...♗xe2 10 ♚xe2± **10 ♗d2 c6 11 0-0-0 ♞a6 12 ♖hg1** △ g4 **f6 13 ♞ge4 f5 14 ♘g5 ♕e7 15 e4** △ f4 **f4 16 g3!± fxg3 17 hxg3 ♞g4 18 ♗e1 ♗c8** 18...♘h6? 19 ♖xd7+ ♚xd7 20 ♗xg4+ +− **19 ♚b1 h6 20 ♞f3** △ ♘h4 **g5 21 ♞d2 ♖f8 22 f3 ♞f6** 22...♘e3 23 ♖c1 g4 24 f4! exf4 25 gxf4 ♖xf4 26 ♖g3 ♗d4 27 ♘b3 ♗b6 28 ♗d2 +−; 24 ♗f2 gxf3 △ ♘g4 **23 ♞f1** △ ♘e3-f5 g4 24 ♞e3 gxf3 25 ♗xf3 ♞e8 26 ♗e2 ♞d6 27 g4! ♗f6 28 ♗f2 ♗g5 29 ♞f5+ ♗xf5 30 exf5 b6 31 ♗g3 ♗f6 32 ♗f3 +− **♖ac8 33 ♖ge1 ♞f7 34 ♞e4 ♖fd8 35 ♞xf6 ♚xf6 36 a3** 36 ♖xd8 ♖xd8 37 ♗xc6 ♖d4 **♞c5 37 ♚c2 e4 38 ♗e2** 38 ♗xe4 ♖xd1+ 39 ♚xd1 ♖d8+ 40 ♚c2 ♘xe4 41 ♖xe4 ♘g5 (△ ♖d4) 42 ♘h4 ♖d6 43 c5! **a5 39 ♖xd8 ♖xd8 40 ♗c7 ♖d7 41 ♗xb6 ♞d3 42 ♖d1 ♞fe5 43 ♗e3** 43 ♗xa5 ♘xc4 44 ♗c3+ ♚g5 △ ♘e3+ **h5 44 gxh5 ♞xc4 45 ♗c1 ♞ce5 46 ♗xd3 ♞xd3 47 ♗e3!** 47 ♖f1 ♘xc1 48 ♚xc1 ♖h7= **♚xf5 48 ♖f1+ ♚e6 49 h6 c5 50 b3** △ ♖f8, ♚c3-c4 **♖f7 51 ♖xf7 ♚xf7 52 ♚c3** +− **♞e5 53 ♗xc5 ♞g4 54 h7 ♚g7 55 a4! ♚xh7 56 ♚d4 ♚g6 57 ♚xe4 ♞f6+ 58 ♚d4 ♞d7 59 ♗d6 ♚f5 60 ♗c7 ♚e6 61 ♗xa5?!** 61 ♚c4 +− **♚d6 62 b4??** 62 ♚c4! **♞b8!!=** △ ♘c6+ **63 ♚c4** 63 b5 ♘c6+!!= **♞c6 64 ♚b5 ♞xb4! 65 ♚b6 ♞d3 ½-½ Keene**

170 Odendahl-Keene Gausdal 79

1 d4 g6 2 c4 ♗g7 3 ♞c3 d6 4 ♞f3 ♗g4 5 e3 ♞f6 5...♘c6 6 ♗e2 e5 7 d5 ♘ce7 8 e4 ♗xf3 9 ♗xf3 ♗h6!?; 9...h5!? △ ♗h6 **6 ♗e2 0-0 7 ♕b3!? ♚c8 8 0-0 ♖e8** △ e5 **9 h3 ♗f5 10 d5** 10 ♘h4 ♗d7 11 f4 c5 12 d5 e6 13 e4? exd5 14 exd5 ♗xh3! 15 gxh3 ♕xh3∓ **♞a6 11 ♞d4 ♗d7 12 ♗f3 c6 13 ♕d1 e5 14 dxe6 fxe6 15 e4 e5 15...♕c7 16 e5!?** **16 ♞c2 ♚c7 17 b3 ♞c5 18 ♗a3 ♖ad8 19 ♚h2 a5 20 g3 ♗e6 21 ♕e2 ♗f7 22 ♖ad1 ♞fd7 23 ♞e3?! 23 ♕e3 ♘f8! 24 ♗xc5 dxc5 25 ♕xc5 ♘e6 26 ♕e3 ♘d4∓; 24 ♗g2 ♞fe6 25 f4 exf4 26 gxf4 g5!! 27 f5 d5+ 28 ♚h1 d4 29 fxe6 ♞xe6!; 25...♘d4? 26 ♘xd4 exd4 27 ♖xd4 ♗xd4 28 ♕xd4 △ ♗b2 +− ♞f8 24 ♗g2 ♞fe6 25 ♞c2 ♞d4 26 ♕d2 a4 27 b4 ♗xc4 28 bxc5 dxc5 29 ♕c1 ♗xf1 30 ♗xf1?** 30 ♖xf1 ♖f8!∓ **31 ♞e3 ♖xf2+ 32 ♚g1 ♖f3 33 ♗g2 ♖f7** 33...♖xg3 34 ♚h2 **34 ♚h1 ♕a5 35 ♗f1 ♚h8 36 ♞g4 ♖df8 37 ♞b1 b6 38 ♞d2 ♕a7 39 ♗d3? h5 −+ 40 ♞e3 ♕d7 41 ♗f1 ♖xf1+ 0-1** 42 ♖xf1 ♕xh3+ 43 ♚g1 ♘e2+; 42 ♘dxf1 ♕xh3+ 43 ♘h2 ♖f2 −+ **Keene**

171 Veingold-Kasparov USSR 79

1 d4 ♞f6 2 ♞f3 g6 3 c4 ♗g7 4 ♞c3 d6 5 e4 0-0 6 ♗e2 e5 7 d5 7 ♗e3 a5!? 7...♘bd7 8 ♗g5 h6 9 ♗h4 g5 10 ♗g3 ♞h5 11 h4 ♞xg3 12 fxg3∞ **8 ♗g5 h6** 8...♘a6 9 ♘d2 h6 10 ♗e3!? ♞e8 11 a3 f5 12 f3 ♗d7 13 ♖b1 ♘c5∞ **9 ♗h4 ♞a6 10 0-0 ♕e8 11 ♞d2 ♞h7?!** 11...♗d7!? 12 a3?! a4 13 ♘b5 c6! 14 dxc6 bxc6 15 ♘xd6 ♕b8 16 c5 ♘xc5 17 ♘dc4 ♗e6∓; 12 b3 ♘h7 13 a3 h5 14 f3 ♗h6 15 ♖b1 f5 16 b4 b6∞ **12 a3 f5?!** 12...h5!? **13 exf5 ♗xf5 14 g4! ♗d7 15 ♞de4 a4 16 f3 b6 17 ♗d3 ♗f6! 18 ♞xf6+ ♞xf6 19 ♕d2 ♞c5 20 ♗c2 ♚g7 21 ♖ae1** △ h3, f4 **♞b3 22 ♕d3 g5 23 ♗g3 ♞c5 24 ♕d2 ♕f7** 24...♘b3!? **25 h4 ♞h7 26 ♗xh7 gxh4 27 ♗xe5+! dxe5 28 ♗b1**

28...♕f4?? 28...♖ae8 29 ♔h2 ♕f6 30 ♕c2 ♖h8 31 ♘e4 ♕f4 32 ♔h1 ♘xe4 33 ♖xe4 ♕f6 34 c5± **29 ♕xf4 ♖xf4** 29...exf4 30 ♖e7+ ♖f7 31 ♖xf7+ ♔xf7 32 ♘e2 +− **30 ♖xe5 ♖af8** 30...♖xc4 31 ♖e7+ ♔f6 32 ♖h7 ♔g5 33 f4+ ♖xf4 34 ♖g7+ ♔f6 35 ♖g6+ ♔e5 36 ♖e1+ ♔d4 37 ♘e2+ +−; 31...♔g8 32 d6! +− **31 ♖e7+ ♖8f7 32 ♖xf7+ ♔xf7 33 ♘e4! ♘b3 34 ♔f2 ♗xg4 35 ♔e3** +− **♖f5 36 ♖f2 ♗h5 37 ♘d6+ cxd6 38 ♗xf5 ♔f6 39 ♗c2 ♘c5 40 ♖h2 ♔g5 41 ♗d1! 1-0 Gufeld**

172 Nejsis-Schislov corr. 79
1 d4 ♘f6 2 c4 g6 3 ♘c3 ♗g7 4 e4 d6 5 ♘f3 0-0 6 ♗e2 e5 7 0-0 ♘c6 8 d5 ♘e7 9 ♘d2 c5 10 dxc6! bxc6 11 b4 d5 11...♘e8 12 ♘b3 f5 13 ♗a3 fxe4 14 ♘xe4 ♗f5 15 ♘g3± Vaganian-Vukic, Odessa 75; 12 ♗a3 a6! 13 ♖e1 ♗e6 14 ♗f1; 11...♗e6 12 ♗a3 a6 13 ♘b3 ♘e8 14 ♘a5 f5 15 ♕d2? ♖a7!∝ Pytel-Gralka, Poland 77 **12 cxd5** N 12 ♗a3 d4 13 ♘a4 ♗h6 14 ♘c5 ♕c7 15 ♘db3 ♘e8 16 ♗c1! ♗g7 17 ♗d2 f5 18 ♖c1 ♘d6 19 f3 ♔h8 20 b5 +− Smejkal-Ciocaltea, Sandomierz 76 **cxd5 13 b5 dxe4 14 ♘dxe4 ♘xe4 15 ♘xe4 ♘f5 16 ♗a3 ♖e8 17 ♘d6 ♘xd6 18 ♕xd6 ♗e6 19 ♗f3 e4?! 20 ♗xe4 ♗xa1 21 ♗xa8**

♕xa8 **22 ♖xa1 ♗xa2! 23 ♗b2! ♕e4 24 h3 ♗d5 25 f3 ♕e3+ 26 ♔h2± ♕g5 27 ♖e1! ♗e6** 27...♖xe1? 28 ♕b8+ +− **28 ♕d4 f6 29 f4 ♕h4?** 29...♕f5 **30 ♖e4!** +− △ f5 **♕h6 31 ♕xf6 ♗d7 32 ♖xe8+ ♗xe8 33 ♕e6+! ♗f7 34 ♕e5! 1-0** 34...♘b3 35 ♗a3! Pytel

173 Fedorowicz-J.Meyer USA 79
1 c4 g6 2 d4 ♘f6 3 ♘c3 ♗g7 4 e4 d6 5 ♘f3 0-0 6 ♗e2 e5 7 0-0 ♘c6 8 d5 ♘e7 9 ♘e1 ♘d7 10 ♘d3 f5 11 ♗d2 11 exf5 gxf5 12 f4 ♘g6 13 ♗e3 ♘f6 14 ♕c2?! N ♖e8 15 ♖ae1 exf4! 16 ♖xf4 ♘e5 17 g3 ♕f6∓ Brandts-E.Meyer, USA 79; 14 c5 += ♘f6 11...fxe4?! 12 ♘xe4 ♘f5 13 f3! += Ligterink-Westerinen, Jurmala 78; 11...c5!? 12 f4 exf4 (12...a6) 13 ♘xf4!? ♘f6 14 ♘e6! ♗xe6 15 dxe6 ♘xe4 16 ♘xe4 fxe4 17 ♗f4 ♗d4+ 18 ♔h1 ♘f5 19 ♕c2 g5 20 ♕xe4! gxf4 21 ♖xf4± J.Meyer-P.Whitehead, USA 79; 13 ♗xf4 ♗xc3 14 bxc3 fxe4 15 ♘e1 ♘f6 16 g4 ∝/+= **12 f3 f4** 12...♔h8 13 c5 +=; 12...c5 13 b4 cxb4 14 ♘xb4 ♕b6+ 15 ♔h1 ♕xb4 16 ♘a4 ♕a3 17 ♗c1 ♕b4 18 ♗d2 ♕a3 ½-½ Ree-Biyiasas, Lone Pine 78; 13 g4! += **13 c5 g5 14 cxd6** 14 ♖c1 ♘g6 15 cxd6 cxd6 16 ♘f2 ♖f7 (16...a6!) 17 a4 h5 18 h3 ♗f8 19 ♘b5 ♖g7 20 ♕c2± J.Meyer-Grant, USA 79; 16 ♘b5! Miles-Vukic, Bugojno 78; 14 a4!? J.Fernandez-Villareal, Mexico 78 **cxd6 15 ♘f2 ♖f7** 15...♔h8!?; 15...h5 **16 ♕c2 ♘g6 17 ♖fc1!? h5** 17...a6 18 a4 h5 19 h3 b6 20 ♖a3 ♗f8 21 ♘a2 ♘h4 22 ♕d1 ♖g7 23 ♗e1 ♕e8! 24 ♘b4 ♕g6 25 ♘c6 g4! 26 fxg4 hxg4 27 hxg4 ♗xg4 28 ♘xg4 ♘xg4 29 ♗xg4 ♕xg4 30 ♕xg4 ♖xg4= Ree-Browne, Lone Pine 78 **18 ♘b5 ♘e8** 18...g4 19 ♘c7

111

△ ♘e6 +– **19 a4** 19 ♘xa7 ♗d7 20 ♘b5 g4 ∝/= **♞h4** 19...a6 20 ♘a3; 19...♗f8 20 ♖a3 a6 21 ♘c3 b6 22 h3±; 19...♗d7!? **20 ♞xa7** 20 h3 ♕f6!? 21 ♕xc8 ♖xc8 22 ♖xc8 ♖f8 23 ♘xa7∝ **♗d7 21 ♞b5 g4 22 fxg4**

22...f3! 23 gxf3 ♞xf3+? 23...hxg4! 24 ♘xg4? ♗xg4 25 fxg4 ♕b6+ 26 ♔h1 ♕f2 27 ♗f1 ♘f3 –+; 24 fxg4 ♕b6 25 ♖f1 ♗xb5 26 ♗xb5 ♘f3+ 27 ♔h1 ♘d4 ∝/+=; 26 axb5 ♖xa1 –+; 25 ♗e1 ♗h6 △ ♗e3 =+ **24 ♗xf3 ♖xf3 25 g5!± ♕b6 26 ♗e1 ♖f4 27 ♖a3 ♖c8?!** 27...♕d8 28 ♖g3 ♖c8 **28 ♕xc8! ♗xc8 29 ♖xc8 ♖xe4** 29...♔f7 30 ♖b3 △ a5± **30 ♖xe8+ ♔h7** 30... ♔f7? 31 ♗a5! ♖g4+ 32 ♔f1 ♕xa5 33 ♘xd6+ ♔g6 34 ♖e6+ ♔xg5 35 ♘h3+ ♔h4 36 ♘f5 mate **31 g6+ +– ♔xg6 32 ♖e6+ ♔h7 33 ♕f1 ♖xa4 34 ♞xd6** 34 ♖xa4? ♕xb5+ **♖f4 35 ♖g3 ♕a6+?** Zeitnot; 35...♗f8 36 ♘de4 ♕b5+; 35...♕xb2? 36 ♖e7 **36 ♔g2 ♗f8 37 ♞de4 ♕c4 38 ♖xe5 h4 39 ♖h5+ ♗h6 40 ♖xh4! ♕xd5** 40...♖xh4 41 ♘f6+ ♔g8 42 ♖g8 mate **41 ♖xh6+ 1-0** 41...♔xh6 42 ♗d2 **Ciamarra/A.Smith**

174 Chechelian-Geller
USSR 79

1 ♞f3 ♞f6 2 c4 g6 3 ♞c3 ♗g7 4 e4 d6 5 d4 0-0 6 ♗e2 e5 7 0-0 ♞c6 8

♗e3!? ♖e8! 9 d5 9 dxe5 ♘xe5 10 ♘xe5 dxe5 11 c5!? **♞d4 10 ♞xd4 exd4 11 ♗xd4 ♞xe4 12 ♗xg7 ♕xg7 13 ♞xe4 ♖xe4 14 ♗d3 ♖e8** 14...♖d4!? **15 ♕b3 b6 16 ♖fe1 ♖xe1+ 17 ♖xe1 ♗d7 18 ♕c3+ ♕f6 19 ♕xf6+ ♔xf6 20 f4 h6 21 ♕f2 a5 22 ♕f3 g5! =+ 23 h3 ♖g8 24 ♗h7!? ♖b8?!** 24...♖g7 25 ♗e4 gxf4 26 ♔xf4 h5 ∝/=+ **25 ♖e2 ♖h8 26 ♗e4 ♖g8 27 ♖e3** 27 ♗h7 g4+! **h5 28 fxg5+ ♖xg5 29 h4! += ♖e5 30 ♕f4 ♗f5 31 b3 b5! 32 cxb5 ♗xe4 33 ♖xe4 ♖xd5 34 a4 ♖d3 35 ♖e3 ♖d4+ 36 ♖e4** 36 ♔g3!? **½-½ Gufeld**

175 Gralka-Hazai
Sofia 79

1 d4 ♞f6 2 c4 g6 3 ♞c3 ♗g7 4 e4 d6 5 ♞f3 0-0 6 ♗e2 e5 7 0-0 7 ♗g5!? h6 8 ♗h4 g5 9 dxe5!? gxh4 10 exf6 ♕xf6 11 ♕d2 ♗e6 12 ♖d1 ♘d7 13 ♕e3 ♘e5? 14 ♘xe5 dxe5 15 ♘d5 ♗xd5 16 cxd5 += Korchnoi-Kavalek, Buenos Aires 78; 13...♘b6!= **♞bd7 8 ♖e1** 8 ♗e3 a5 9 ♖e1 ♘g4 10 ♗g5 f6 11 ♗c1 c6 12 h3 ♘h6 13 b3 exd4 14 ♘xd4 ♘c5 15 ♗f4 f5 16 ♕d2 ♕f6 17 ♖ad1 fxe4! –+ Hort-Vogt, Halle 78; 15 ♗e3! **c6 9 ♗f1 a5 10 ♗e3** 10 dxe5!? dxe5 11 ♘a4 ♕e7 12 ♕c2 ♖e8 13 h3 ♘c5 14 ♘xc5 ♕xc5 15 ♗e3 ♕e7 16 ♖ad1 ♗e6! 17 c5 a4!= Malich-Vogt, Halle 78 **♞g4 11 ♗g5 f6 12 ♗d2?** 12 ♗c1; 12 ♗h4 **exd4 13 ♞xd4 f5 14 ♞f3 f4 –+ 15 h3 ♞ge5 16 ♞xe5 ♞xe5 17 ♕c2?** 17 f3 ♕h4 –+ **♕h4 18 ♞e2 f3 19 g3 ♕h5 20 g4** 20 ♘f4 ♖xf4!

Diagram

20...♗xg4 21 ♞f4 ♖xf4! 22 ♗xf4 ♗xh3 0-1 Mechkarov

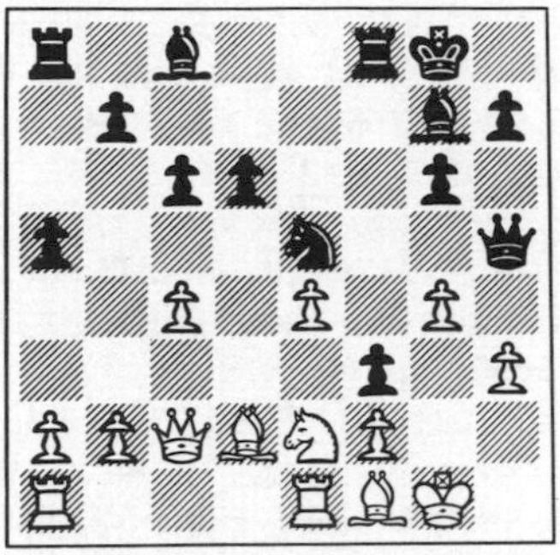

176 Luczak-Vogt Naleczow 79

1 d4 ♞f6 2 c4 g6 3 ♞c3 ♝g7 4 e4 d6 5 ♝e2 0-0 6 ♞f3 e5 7 0-0 ♞bd7 8 ♜e1 c6 9 ♝f1 exd4 9...a5 **10 ♞xd4 ♜e8 11 ♞c2 ♞e5 12 h3 ♝e6 13 ♞e3** 13 b3 **♞h5 14 g3 ♛f6 15 f4 ♞xg3** 15...♘xf4?! 16 gxf4 ♕xf4 17 ♘f5 ♘f3+ 18 ♔f2± **16 fxe5 ♛h4 17 exd6 ♞xf1 18 ♜xf1 ♝xh3 19 ♞g2 ♝xg2! 20 ♚xg2 ♝xc3?!** 20...♗e5 21 ♖f3 ♕h2+ 22 ♔f1 ♗xd6∓ **21 ♜f4!** 21 bxc3 ♖xe4 –+ **♛e1** 21...♕g5+? 22 ♖g4 **22 ♛xe1 ♝xe1 23 ♝e3 ♝b4??** 23...♗a5∞ **24 c5 b6 25 ♜af1 ♜f8 26 e5 ♝xc5 27 ♝xc5 bxc5 28 d7!! +– Δ e6!! f5 29 e6 ♜fd8 30 ♜e1 ♚g7 31 e7 ♜xd7 32 e8♛ ♜xe8 33 ♜xe8 ♜b7 34 b3 ♚f6 35 ♜c4 ♜d7 36 ♜e2 ♚g5 37 ♜xc5 ♚g4 38 ♜xo6 f4 39 ♜c4 g5 40 ♜ec2 h5 41 ♜c7 ♜d3 42 ♜7c3!** 42 ♖xa7 f3+! 43 ♔f2 ♔h4 Δ g4 **♜d1 43 ♚h2** Δ ♖g2+ **♚f5 44 ♜c5+ 1-0 Vogt**

177 Zilberstein-Rashkovsky
USSR 79

1 d4 ♞f6 2 c4 g6 3 ♞c3 ♝g7 4 e4 d6 5 ♞f3 0-0 6 ♝e2 ♞bd7 6...e5 7 **0-0** 7 e5!? ♘e8 8 ♗f4 += **e5 8 ♜e1** 8 ♗e3 a5!? **c6 9 ♝f1 exd4** 9...a5 10 dxe5!? dxe5 11 ♘a4 ♕e7 12 ♕c2 += **10 ♞xd4 ♜e8 11 ♝g5** N 11 ♗f4 += **h6! 12 ♝h4 ♞c5 13 ♛c2 g5 14 ♝g3 ♞h5 15 ♜ad1 ♞xg3** 15...a5? 16 ♘f5± **16 hxg3 a5 17 b3** 17 ♖e3 f5!? 18 ♘xf5 ♗xf5 19 exf5 ♖xe3 20 fxe3 ∞/= **♝e5 =+ 18 ♜e3 ♛f6 19 ♞ce2 h5 20 f3 ♛g6 21 a3** 21 f4 ♗g7! **♝g7 22 ♞f5?** 22 b4 axb4 23 axb4 ♘a6 =+ **♝xf5 23 exf5 ♛f6∓ 24 ♛d2 ♛xf5 25 b4 axb4 26 axb4 ♜xe3 27 ♛xe3 ♞e6 –+ 28 g4** Zeitnot 28 ♖xd6 ♗f8 –+ **hxg4 29 fxg4 ♛xg4 0-1 Gufeld**

178 Gereben-B.Balogh
Budapest 79

1 d4 ♞f6 2 c4 g6 3 ♞c3 ♝g7 4 e4 d6 5 ♝e2 ♞bd7 6 ♞f3 e5 7 0-0 0-0 8 ♝e3 ♞g4 9 ♝g5 f6 10 ♝c1! c6 11 dxe5 dxe5 12 b3 ♛e7! 12...♕a5 13 ♗d2± **13 a4 ♜d8 14 ♝a3 ♛e8 15 ♛c2** 15 ♘d5?? cxd5 16 ♕xd5+ ♕f7 17 ♕xf7+ ♔xf7 18 ♖fd1 ♖e8 –+ **♞f8= 16 ♜ad1 ♝e6 17 c5 ♞h6 18 ♞d2 ♞f7 19 ♞c4 ♝xc4 20 ♝xc4 ♞e6 21 ♞e2 ♝h6 22 g3 ♚g7 23 ♚g2** 23 b4 Δ ♗c1 **♝g5 24 ♛c3 h5 25 b4**

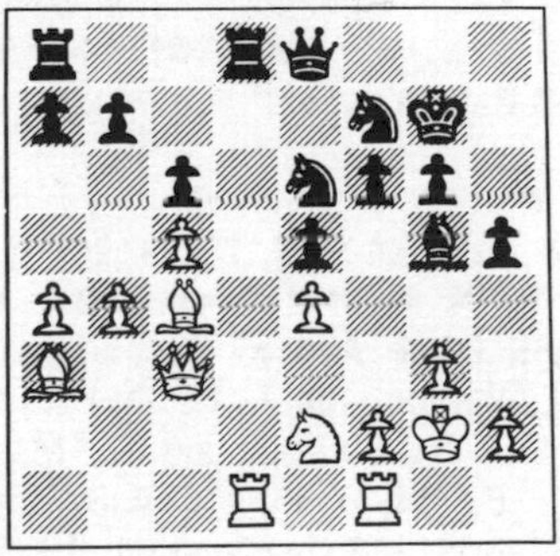

♜xd1? 25...♖d7= **26 ♜xd1 ♜d8 27 ♜xd8 ♞fxd8 28 ♛d3 += ♞f7 29 a5 ♝h6** 29...♕d8?? 30 ♕b3 +– **30 ♝b2 g5 31 h3 g4 32 h4 ♚f8 33 ♛b3 ♞fd8 34 ♛d3 ♛e7 35 f3 ♚e8 36 ♝c3 ♛d7 37 ♛xd7+ ♚xd7 38 fxg4 hxg4 39 ♚f2 ♚e7 ½-½ B.Balogh**

179 Petran-B.Balogh
Budapest 79
**1 d4 ♘f6 2 c4 g6 3 ♘c3 ♗g7 4 e4 d6
5 ♗e2 ♘bd7!?** 5...0-0 **6 ♘f3 e5 7 0-0
0-0 8 ♗e3 ♘g4 9 ♗g5 f6 10 ♗h4!?**
10 ♗c1! **♘h6** 10...c6 **11 ♕c2 c6
12 dxe5!** 12 ♖ad1 ♕c7 13 ♖fe1 ♖e8
14 b4 ♘f8 15 d5 ♘f7= **dxe5 13
b4 ♕e7! 14 c5 ♘f7 15 ♖fd1 a5!**
15...♖d8 16 ♗c4 ♘f8 17 ♖xd8 ♕xd8
18 ♖d1 ♕e7 19 ♘a4 += **16 a3 ♖d8
20 ♘d2 ♘f8 21 ♘b3 axb4 22 axb4
♖xd1+ 23 ♖xd1** 23 ♕xd1 ♖xa1 24
♕xa1 ♗e6 25 ♘a5 ♕d7= Δ ♗h6-d2
♗h6 21 ♕b2 ♔g7!? 21...♗e6 **22 ♗g3
♔g8 23 h3 ♗g5 24 ♘a5 ♗e6 25 ♘a4
h5! 26 h4 ♗h6 27 ♘b6 ♖d8 28 ♖xd8
♘xd8 29 ♕c2 ♗f7 30 ♕d1** 30 ♘c8
♕e6 31 ♘d6 ♕a2 32 ♕d1 ♕d2 33
♘xb7 ♘xb7 34 ♘xb7 ♕xb4=; 32
♕xa2 ♗xa2 33 ♘xb7 ♘xb7 34 ♘xb7
♗d2= **♘fe6 31 ♘ac4 ♘d4 32 ♘d6
♘xe2+! 33 ♕xe2 ♕e6 34 ♘bc4 ♕g4
35 ♕d3 ♗xc4 36 ♘xc4 ♘f7= 37 ♘a5
g5! =+ 38 ♘xb7 gxh4 39 ♗h2 h3 40
♕g3 ♘g5 41 ♕xg4** 41 f3! hxg4 42
♘d8 ♘xe4 43 ♘xc6 ♕f7 44 ♗xe5!
½-½ **B.Balogh**

180 Foldi-Marosi Hungary 79
**1 c4 g6 2 d4 ♘f6 3 ♘f3 ♗g7 4 ♘c3
0-0 5 e4 d6 6 ♗e2 e5 7 0-0 ♘bd7
8 ♗g5 h6 9 ♗h4 g5** 9...c6 10 dxe5?
dxe5 11 ♕c2 ♕c7 12 ♘e1 ♘c5 13
f3 ♘e6 =+ Armas-Najdorf, Mar del
Plata 67 **10 dxe5!** 10 ♗g3 ♘h5 11
♘d5 ♘xg3 12 hxg3 exd4 13 ♘xd4
♘f6 14 ♕d3 ♖e8 15 ♖fe1 c6=
Taimanov-Kots, USSR 61 **dxe5 11
♗g3 ♘h5 12 ♗xe5! ♘xe5 13 ♘xe5
♘f4! +=** 13...♗xe5 14 ♗xh5± **14
♘d3 ♘xe2+ 15 ♘xe2?** 15 ♕xe2!
♗e6 16 ♘c5 ♗xc3 17 bxc3 f5 18 e5
f5! ½-½ Foldi

181 Tal-Spassky Montreal 79
**1 ♘f3 ♘f6 2 c4 g6 3 ♘c3 ♗g7 4 e4
d6 5 d4 0-0 6 ♗e2 e5 7 0-0 exd4!?
8 ♘xd4 ♖e8 9 f3 c6 10 ♔h1** 10 ♘c2
d5?! 10...♘bd7 11 ♗g5 h6 12 ♗h4
♕b6 13 ♘b3 ♕c7 14 ♕d2 ♘e5 15
♗xf6?! ♗xf6 16 ♕xh6 ♗e6 17 f4 ♕d8
18 fxe5? ♗g5 −+; 18 f5!±; 16...♕e7
17 f4? ♗e6=+; 17...♗g7; 17 ♕d2; 15
♘d4!? +=; 12...♘c5 13 ♕c2 a5 14
♘b3! += **11 cxd5 cxd5 12 ♗g5** 12
♗b5 ♘bd7 13 exd5 a6 14 ♗a4 b5
15 ♗b3 ♗b7 Korchnoi-Ghitescu, Bath
73 **dxe4** 12...♘c6 13 exd5 ♘xd4
14 ♕xd4 h6 15 ♗xf6 ♗xf6 16 ♕d2±
**13 fxe4! ♘bd7 14 ♘db5 ♖e5 15
♗f4 ♘xe4 16 ♗xe5 ♗xe5 17 ♘xe4
♕h4 18 h3 ♕xe4 19 ♕b3?** 19 ♘d6!!
♗xd6 20 ♕xd6 ♕xe2 21 ♖ae1 ♕c4 22
b3 ♕c5 23 ♖e8+ ♔g7 24 ♕xc5 ♘xc5
25 ♖c1 Δ b4 +− **♘f6!** 19...♕xe2 20
♕xf7+ ♔h8 21 ♕e8+ ♔g7 22 ♘d6 +−
20 ♗c4 ♕h4 20...♗xh3? 21 ♗xf7+
♔g7 22 ♕xh3 ♔xf7 23 ♕xh7+ +−
21 ♗xf7+ ♔h8 21...♔g7 22 ♖ae1
♕g3 23 ♕xg3 ♗xg3 24 ♖e7 ♔f8
25 ♖e3 +− **22 ♖f3 ♗f5** 22...♗g4
23 ♖e3 ♗f4 24 ♖f1 ♗xe3 25 ♕xe3±
Δ ♘d6/♕e5; 24 ♖e7 ♖c8; 24...♖d8!?
23 ♘c3 ♘e4 23...♘h5 24 ♘e2 ♗g4
25 ♕c4 +−; 24...♖f8!? **24 ♘xe4
♗xe4** Zeitnot **25 ♕c4**

25...♖d8? 25...g5! 26 ♕e2 ♗d6 27 ♕d2 ♗e5 28 ♖e1! ♗xf3 29 ♖xe5 ♕xh3+ 30 ♔g1 +−; 28...♖f8 29 ♖xe4 ♕xe4 30 ♗d5 ♖xf3! Δ ♖f1 mate; 29 ♕e3! +−; 26 ♕c5 ♗xb2 27 ♖c3 ♗xg2+! 28 ♔xg2 ♕e4+ Δ ♗xa1 −+; 26 ♖e3 ♕f4! −+ **26 ♖af1 ♕g7 27 ♗e6 ♖d2 28 ♕c5 ♗xf3 29 ♕xe5+ ♕f6 30 ♕xf6+ ♔xf6 31 ♗g4 ♖xb2 32 ♖xf3+ 1-0 Keene**

181 Pribyl-M.Tseitlin Trnava 79
1 d4 ♘f6 2 c4 g6 3 ♘c3 ♗g7 4 e4 d6 5 ♘f3 0-0 6 ♗e2 ♗g4 7 ♗e3 ♘fd7 8 ♖c1! += 8 0-0 ♘c6 9 d5 ♗xf3 10 ♗xf3 ♘a5 11 ♗e2 ♗xc3 12 bxc3 c6 ∝/= **e5 9 d5 a5** 9...♗xf3 10 ♗xf3 f5 11 b4! += **10 0-0 ♘c5 11 a3** 11 ♘d2 ♘ba6 12 ♘d2 ♗d7 Δ a4 **13 b3 f5 14 f3 ♗f6!** Δ ♗g5 **15 ♖b1 ♗g5 16 ♗f2 ♗f4 17 ♖e1** 17 b4 axb4 18 axb4 ♕g5! ♕f6!? **18 b4 axb4 19 axb4 ♘a4 20 ♘xa4 ♗xa4 21 ♕xa4 ♗xd2 22 ♖ed1 ♕g5** 22...♘xb4 23 ♕b3 ♖a2 24 ♖b2± **23 exf5 gxf5** 23...♘xb4!? **24 c5! ♗xb4** 24...♘xc5? 25 ♕c2 +− **25 ♕b3 ♘a6 26 cxd6 cxd6 27 ♕xb7 ♘c5=** 28 ♗xc5 dxc5 29 d6 ♔h8 30 ♕e7! ½-½ Gufeld

183 Plachetka-Basagic Sofia 79
1 d4 ♘f6 2 c4 g6 3 ♘c3 ♗g7 4 e4 d6 5 ♘f3 0-0 6 ♗e2 ♗g4 7 0-0 ♘fd7 8 ♗e3 ♘c6 8...♗xf3 9 ♗xf3 e5 10 d5 f5 11 ♖b1 (Δ b4) += Simagin-Gufeld, USSR 60 **9 d5** 9 ♘e1 ♗xe2 10 ♘xe2 e5 11 d5 ♘e7 12 ♘d3 f5 13 f3 ♘f6 14 ♘c3 f4 15 ♗f2 g5 16 c5 ♘g6 17 ♖c1 ♖f7 18 ♕b3 += Kagan-Szabo 67 **♗xf3 10 gxf3!?** N 10 ♗xf3 ♘a5 11 ♗e2! =+ ♗xc3 12 bxc3 e5 13 dxe6! fxe6 14 f4 ♕e7 15 ♕a4 b6 16 ♖ae1 ♘b7 17 ♗f3 ♘bc5 18 ♕c2 ♖ae8 =+ Cuellar-Tal,

Leningrad 73; 13 g3 ♖e8 14 ♕a4 b6 15 ♖ae1 ♘c5 16 ♕c2 ♕d7 17 ♗g5 ♕a4 =+ Mack-Kochiev, Manila 74; 11 ♕a4? ♗xc3! 12 bxc3 b6 13 ♗e2 e5 14 g3 ♘c5 15 ♕c2 ♕d7 =+ Hamman-Geller 60 **♘cb8 11 f4 ♗h6** 11...e6!? Δ ♕h4/♘f6! **12 ♔h1 e5 13 ♕d2 f6 14 ♖g1 a5 15 ♖g3 ♖f7 16 ♖ag1 ♘f8 17 ♗g4 exf4 18 ♗xf4 ♗xf4 19 ♕xf4 ♕e7 20 ♘b5 ♘a6 21 ♘d4 ♘c5 22 f3 ♕e5 23 ♕e3 ♖g7 24 b3 ♖a6?** 24...♖e8!=

25 ♘f5! +− gxf5 26 ♗xf5 ♖xg3 27 ♖xg3+ ♕f7 28 ♕h6! ♘d3 29 ♕h5+! ♕e7 30 ♖g7+ ♔d8 31 ♕f7 ♕a1+ 32 ♖g1 **1-0 Mechkarov**

104 Benko-Savage Philadelphia 79
1 c4 g6 2 ♘c3 ♗g7 3 d4 ♘f6 4 e4 d6 5 ♗e2 0-0 6 ♗g5 ♘bd7 7 ♕d2 e5 7...c5 8 d5 a6 9 ♘f3 ♕a5 10 0-0 b5! 11 cxb5 axb5 12 ♗xb5 ♗a6 13 ♗xa6 ♖xa6 14 ♖fe1 ♖b8∝ Ginsburg-E. Meyer, USA 79 **8 ♘f3!?** 8 d5 ♘c5 9 ♗f3!? a5 10 ♘ge2 c6 11 ♘g3 cxd5 12 ♘xd5 ♘e6= Olafsson-Petrosian, Moscow 71 **c6** 8...♕e8 9 0-0 exd4 10 ♘xd4 ♘xe4 11 ♘xe4 ♕xe4 12 ♘b5 ♕c6 13 ♖ac1 a6 14 ♘c3 ♘b6 15 b3 Δ ♗f3 += Polugaevsky; 8... exd4 9 ♘xd4 ♘c5 10 f3 h6 11 ♗e3 ♘fd7 12 0-0-0 += Gufeld/Ciamarra

9 0-0 exd4 9...♖e8!?; 9...♛b6?!; 9...
♛a5 **10 ♘xd4 ♖e8** 10...♘c5! **11 f3**
♛c7? 11...♘c5 12 ♖fd1? ♘fxe4 13
♘xe4 ♘xe4 14 fxe4 ♗xd4+ 15 ♛xd4
♛xg5 −+; 12 ♛f4!? ♛e7 +=; 12 ♔h1
+= **12 ♖fd1± ♘c5 13 ♔h1 a5 14 ♘c2!
♖e6 15 ♗f4 ♗f8 16 ♘d4 ♖e8 17
♘b3! ♘xb3 18 axb3 ♛b6 19 ♛d4?!**
19 ♘a4! ♛xb3? 20 ♖a3 ♛b4 21
♛d4 Δ ♛xf6/♗d2 +− **♛xb3! 20 ♛xf6?**
20 ♗xd6 ♗xd6 21 ♛xd6 ♗e6 =+ **♗g7
21 ♛xd6 ♛xb2 22 ♘a4?** 24 ♗d2
♗xc3 25 ♖ab1 ♗e5∓ **♛xe2 23 ♖ac1**
Δ ♖d2 **♗h3! −+ 24 gxh3** 24 ♖d2
♗xg2+ 25 ♔g1 ♛xf3 26 ♖xg2 ♖xe4
−+; 24 ♖g1 ♖ad8 25 ♛c7 ♗d4 −+
**♛xf3+ 25 ♔g1 ♖xe4 26 ♖f1 ♛xh3
27 ♛d2 ♖ae8 28 ♛g2** 28 ♖ce1 ♗d4+
29 ♔h1 ♖xe1 30 ♖xe1 ♛f3+; 29 ♛xd4
♖xe1 **♛a3! 29 ♘c3 ♗xc3 30 ♔h1 ♗g7**
30...♖xf4 **31 ♗c7? ♛xc1 0-1 Ciamarra/
A.Smith**

185 Portisch-Torre Rio 79
**1 d4 ♘f6 2 c4 g6 3 ♘c3 ♗g7 4 e4
d6 5 f3 c5 6 dxc5 dxc5 7 ♛xd8+
♔xd8 8 ♗e3 ♘fd7 9 ♘ge2 ♘c6 10
0-0-0 b6 11 f4 ♗b7 12 g3 ♘a5 13
b3 e6 14 ♗h3 ♔e7 15 f5! ♗e5** N
15...gxf5 16 ♖hf1 f4 17 gxf4 ♖ad8
18 ♗f2 f6 19 ♗h4± Karpov-Barle,
Ljubljana 75 **16 fxe6 fxe6 17 ♗f4
♘c6 18 ♘b5** 18 ♖he1!? Δ ♘d5+
♘f6

Diagram

**19 ♖d6!± ♗xd6 20 ♗xd6+ ♔f7
21 ♖f1 e5! 22 ♗d7?** 22 ♘ec3 Δ
♘d5± **♘b4 23 ♘c7** 23 ♗xe5? ♘d3+
♖ad8 **24 ♗e6+ ♔g7 25 ♗e7 ♘xe4∓
26 ♗d5 ♗xd5 27 cxd5 ♖xd5! 28
g4 ♖c8 29 ♘xd5 ♘xd5 30 ♗h4 c4
31 ♔b2 c3+ 32 ♔a3 ♘e3 33 ♖g1**

♘c2+ 34 ♔a4 ♘d4 0-1 Miles

186 Gheorghiu-Hertan USA 79
**1 d4 ♘f6 2 c4 g6 3 ♘c3 ♗g7 4 e4
d6 5 f3 c6** 5...♘c6; 5...e5; 5...0-0
6 ♗e3 a6 7 a4 7 ♛d2 b5 8 0-0-0±;
7 c5!? **a5 8 ♗d3 ♘a6 9 ♖c1** 9 ♛d2
♘b4 10 ♖d1 += **0-0 10 ♘ge2 e5 11
♛d2 ♘d7 12 0-0** 12 ♖d1! exd4 13
♘xd4 ♘dc5 14 ♗b1± **exd4 13 ♘xd4
♘dc5 14 ♗c2 ♘b4 15 ♖cd1 ♛c7
16 ♗b1 +=** b6! **17 ♗h6! ♗xh6 18
♛xh6 ♗a6 19 b3** 19 ♘f5 gxf5 20
♛g5+ = d5 **20 exd5 cxd5 21 ♘db5**
21 ♘f5 f6!!∓ **♗xb5 22 ♘xb5 ♛c6!**∝
22...♛e5 23 ♖fe1! ♛g7 24 ♛xg7+
♔xg7 25 cxd5 ♘xb3 26 d6± **23 f4!
f5! 24 h4 ♖ad8!** 24...dxc4 25 ♖d6!
**25 h5 ♛f6 26 hxg6 hxg6 27 ♖de1
♖f7** Δ ♖h7∓ **28 ♛h3 dxc4 29 bxc4
♖fd7 30 g4! ♖h7** 30...fxg4 31 ♛xg4±
**31 ♛g2 ♔h8 32 ♖e3!± Δ ♖fe1/♛h3±
♛c6 33 ♛xc6 ♘xc6 34 gxf5 gxf5
♗xf5 ♖g8+ 36 ♔f2 ♖h2+ 37 ♔f3!
♘xa4 38 ♗e6! ♖f8 39 ♔g3 ♖h5
40 ♗g4! ♘d8!!** 40...♘c5 41 ♖g6 ♔h7
42 f5! +− **41 ♗xh5 ♘xe6 42 f5! ♘b2
43 ♖h1!** 43 fxe6? ♖xf1 44 e7 ♖e1=
**♘c5 44 ♘d6 a4 45 ♔f4 ♘bd3+ 46
♔g5 ♔g8 47 ♗f3 ♔g7?** Zeitnot 47...
♘b4! 48 f6± **48 f6+! 1-0** 48...♖xf6
49 ♘e8+ **Gheorghiu**

187 Weinstein-Odendahl
USA 79

1 d4 ♘f6 2 c4 g6 3 ♘c3 ♗g7 4 e4 d6 5 f3 0-0 6 ♗e3 b6 6...♘c6 7 ♘ge2 a6 **7 ♗d3 ♗b7** 7...a6 8 ♘ge2 c5 9 e5! ♘e8 10 ♗e4 ♖a7 11 dxc5 bxc5 12 ♗xc5 ♖d7 13 ♗e3!±; 9...♘fd7 10 exd6 exd6 11 ♗e4 ♖a7 12 0-0 ♘f6 13 ♗c2 ♘c6 14 ♕d2 ♘b4!? ∝/+= **8 ♘ge2 c5 9 d5 e6?!** 9...♘bd7! 10 ♗c2 ♘e5 11 b3 e6 += **10 ♕d2** 10 ♗g5!? exd5 11 exd5 ♘bd7 12 f4±; 10 g4!? exd5 11 cxd5 ♖e8 12 ♔f2∝; 10 0-0 exd5 11 cxd5 ♗a6 12 ♗xa6 ♘xa6 13 ♖b1 ♘d7 14 a3 ♘e5 15 b4± Pachman **exd5 11 exd5 11** cxd5! **♘fd7?!** N 11...♘bd7! 12 ♗h6 ♗xh6 13 ♕xh6 ♘e5 14 ♖d1 a6 15 0-0 b5= **12 0-0± ♖e8** 12...♘a6!? 13 ♗f4±; 12...♘e5 13 ♘g3 (13 ♗f4 ♘bd7) ♖e8 14 ♘ge4 ♘a6!?± **13 ♗g5 f6 14 ♗h4 ♕e7 15 ♖ae1 ♕e3+ 16 ♕xe3 ♖xe3 17 ♗c2 ♗a6?** 17...♘a6 (Δ ♘c7) 18 ♘e4 ♘b4 (18...♗f8 19 ♗g3) 19 ♗b1 +−; 17...♘e5 18 b3! (Δ ♗f2) ♘d3? 19 ♗xd3 ♖xd3 20 ♘e4 +−; 17... ♖e8!? **18 ♗f2 ♖e8 19 ♘f4** Δ ♘e6 **♖e5 20 b3 f5?** 20...♘f8 Δ ♘bd7 **21 ♘e6 ♖xe6 22 dxe6 ♗xc3 23 e7 +− ♘f6 24 e8♕+ ♘xe8 25 ♖xe8+ ♔f7 26 ♖d8 ♗e5 27 ♗g3 ♘c6!? 28 ♖xa8 ♗b7 29 ♗xe5 dxe5 30 ♖h8 ♔g7 31 ♖d1! ♔xh8 32 ♖d7 1-0** 32...♗c8 33 ♖c7; 32...♗a6 33 ♖c7 ♘b4 31 ♗b1 Δ a3, ♖xa7 +− **Ciamarra**

188 Ivkov-Petrosian
Rio 79

1 d4 ♘f6 2 c4 g6 3 ♘c3 ♗g7 4 e4 d6 5 f3 0-0 6 ♗e3 c6!? 7 ♕d2 a6 8 a4!? 8 ♗d3 b5 9 ♘ge2∝ e5 8...a5 Δ ♘a6, e5 **9 dxe5** 9 d5 +=; 9 ♘ge2?! a5 Δ ♘a6= **dxe5 10 ♕xd8 ♖xd8 11 a5 ♗e6 12 ♘a4 ♘bd7 13 b4** 13

♖a3!? ♗f8 14 ♖b3 +=; 13...♘e8! 14 ♖b3 ♘d6 =+ **♗f8 14 c5 ♘e8** Δ ♘c7-b5-d4 **15 ♘b6 ♘xb6** 15...♖b8!? **16 axb6∝ ♘f6 17 ♘h3** 17 ♖a5!? ♘d7!? (Δ ♘xb6) 18 ♗d2!∝ **a5** 17...♖d7 18 ♘g5±; 17...h6?! **18 ♖xa5 ♖xa5 19 bxa5 ♘d7** 19...♖a8?! 20 a6 +=/± **20 ♘g5 ♗b3** 20...♗a2!? **21 ♕d2! h6** 21...♗xc5 22 ♗xc5 ♘xc5+ 23 ♔c3 ∝/± ♖d1? 24 a6! +−; 21...♖a8? 22 ♔c3 Δ ♔b4± **22 ♕c3 ♗a2 23 ♔b2 ♖a8** 23...♗xc5 24 ♗xc5 ♘xc5 25 ♔xa2 hxg5 26 ♗c4! ♖a8 27 ♔a3!± ♖xa5+? 28 ♔b4 +− **24 a6?** 24 ♗d2! += **hxg5 25 axb7!** 25 ♔xa2 ♗xc5∓ **♖b8** 25... ♖a4 26 ♗b5! cxb5 27 c6 ♖b4+ 28 ♔a1! +−; 27 ♖d1 ♘b8 28 ♖d8 ♘c6 29 ♖c8 +−; 26...♖b4+ 27 ♔xa2 ♖xb5 28 ♖d1 +−; 25...♖a5 26 ♗e2 Δ ♖d1 +−; 26 ♗c4!? ♗xc4 2̅7̅ ♖d1 **26 ♕xa2 ♗xc5 27 ♗xc5 ♘xc5 28 ♗e2 ♖xb7** 28...♘d7? 29 ♗a6± **29 ♖c1 ♘d7 30 ♖xc6 ♘xb6 =/=+ 31 ♗a6 ♖b8 32 ♔b1** 32 ♔b3? ♘d5+; 32 ♔b2 ♘d5+ **33 ♔c1 ♘f4 34 g3** 34 ♗c4 ♔g7 35 ♖c7 ♖f8 36 g3; 34...♘xg2 35 ♖xg6+ **♘e6 35 ♗c4 ♘d4**

36 ♖c7?? 36 ♖xg6+ ♔f8 37 ♗xf7! ♔xf7 38 ♖xg5= **♖f8 −+ 37 f4 gxf4 38 gxf4 exf4 39 ♔d1 ♘f3 40 ♔e2 ♘e5 41 ♖c5 ♖e8 42 ♗b5 ♖e7 0-1 Miles**

189 Gheorghiu-Ginsburg USA 79
**1 d4 ♞f6 2 c4 g6 3 ♞c3 ♝g7 4 e4 d6
5 f3 0-0 6 ♝e3 e5 7 d5 c6 8 ♝d3 cxd5
8...b5?!∝ 9 cxd5 ♞a6 10 ♞ge2 ♝d7
11 0-0 ♞c5 12 ♝c2** 12 ♝b5!? ♝xb5
13 ♞xb5 ♛b6 14 b4! ♛xb5 15 bxc5
dxc5 16 ♖b1∝ **a5 13 a3 b5** 13...♛b6
14 ♖b1± **14 b4 ♞a6! 15 ♖b1 a4 16
♝d3 ♛b8 17 ♛d2 ♞c7 18 ♖bc1 ♛b7
19 h3! ♞fe8** 19...♞h5 20 g4± **20
f4! f5 21 fxe5 dxe5 22 ♝c5 ♖f7 23
exf5! gxf5 24 ♝b1** △ ♝a2 ♖a6 **25 d6
♞e6 26 ♝a2! ♔h8 27 ♞g3 ♞xc5 28
bxc5!** +− 28 ♝xf7 ♞b3!∝ **♖f6 29
♛d5!** +− 29 ♞d5! ♝h6 30 ♛e2! +−
♛xd5 **30 ♞xd5 ♝h6 31 c6!! ♖xc6
32 ♖xc6 ♝xc6 33 ♞xf6 ♞xf6 34
♞xf5 ♝f4 35 g3 ♝g5 36 h4! ♝d2 37
♞e7 ♝e3+ 38 ♔h2 ♞g4+ 39 ♔h3
♝d7 40 ♖f8+ ♔g7 41 ♖f7+ ♔h8 42
♞g6+ 1-0** 42...hxg6 43 ♖xd7 +−
Gheorghiu

190 Tiltins-Savage
Philadelphia 79
**1 d4 ♞f6 2 c4 g6 3 ♞c3 ♝g7 4 e4
d6 5 f3 0-0 6 ♝g5 c5** 6...♞bd7
Beljavsky-Ermenkov, Alicante 78;
6...c6?! 7 ♛d2 ♖e8 8 ♞ge2 a6 9 a4
c5 10 d5 += Korchnoi-Ghitescu,
Bucharest 66 **7 d5 e6! 8 ♛d2 exd5**
8...♛a5 9 ♞b5 ♛b6 10 a4 a6 11 a5
axb5!? 12 axb6 ♖xa1+ 13 ♔f2 exd5∝
Pachman **9 exd5** 9 ♞xd5 ♝e6 10
♞e2 ♝xd5 11 cxd5 ♞bd7 12 ♞c3 a6
13 a4= Gulko-Dvoretsky, USSR 74
♖e8+ 10 ♞ge2 ♞bd7 N 10...a6 11 a4
♛a5 =+ **11 0-0-0** 11 ♞b5 ♞e5∓;
11...♛b6!? 12 ♝f4 ♞e5∓; 12 a4 a6
13 a5 axb5! 14 axb6 ♖xa1+ 15 ♔f2
♞xb6 −+ **a6 =+ 12 ♔b1 b5! 13 cxb5
♛a5 14 ♞c1 ♝e5 15 ♞e4** 15 bxa6
♝xa6 16 ♞e4 ♛xd2 17 ♞xf6+ ♝xf6
18 ♝xd2 ♝xf1 19 ♖hxf1 ♞c4∓;

15 ♞b3 ♛b6 16 ♞a4 ♛b8! 17 b6
♝d7∓ **♛xd2 16 ♞xf6+** 16 ♞xd2 ♝f5+
17 ♔a1 axb5 18 ♝xb5 ♖eb8∓ **♝xf6
17 ♝xd2 ♝f5+ 18 ♔a1 axb5 19 ♝c3**
19 ♝xb5? ♖eb8 −+; 19 ♝f4 ♞c4 20
♝xc4 bxc4 21 ♝xd6 c3 −+; 21 ♝d2
♖eb8 −+ **b4 20 ♝xe5 ♖xe5 21 ♝b5
♖a7!∓ 22 ♖he1 ♖ae7 23 ♖xe5?**
23 ♞d3 ♖xe1 24 ♞xe1 ♝d4∓; 24
♖xe1 ♖xe1+ 25 ♞xe1 ♝d4∓; 25...g5!?;
23...♝xd3 24 ♖xe5 ♖xe5 25 ♝xd3
♖xd5 26 ♝c2 =+ ♝d4?! 27 f4! **♖xe5
24 ♞e2?** 24 g4 ♝c8∓ h5! **25 ♝c4**
25 ♞g3 ♝c2 26 ♖c1 ♖xd5 h4 **26
♞c1 ♔f8 27 ♞b3 ♖e3 28 ♞d2 ♔g7
29 ♞f1 ♖e7?** Zeitnot **30 ♞d2 ♖e3
31 ♞f1 ♖c3! −+ 32 ♞b3** 32 ♝b5 ♖c2
33 ♖b1 ♖xg2 −+ **c4 33 ♝a4** 33 ♖b1
cxb3 34 bxc3 bxc3 −+ **♖a3 34 ♞d2** 34
♝b5 b3 **♖xa4 35 ♞xc4 b3 0-1
Ciamarra/A.Smith**

191 Romanishin-Grunfeld
Riga 79
**1 c4 ♞f6 2 g3 g6 3 ♝g2 ♝g7 4 d4
0-0 5 ♞f3 d6 6 0-0 ♞c6 7 ♞c3 a6
8 b3!?** 8 ♞d5!? ♞d7 9 ♝e3 b5 10
cxb5 axb5 11 ♖c1 ♝b7 12 ♞xc7!
♛xc7 13 d5 ♞db8 14 dxc6 ♞xc6
15 ♞d4 ♝xd4 16 ♛xd4! ♞xd4 17
♖xc7 ♝xg2 18 ♔xg2 ♞f5 19 ♝a7!∓
Romanishin-Adorjan, IBM 78; 8...
♝g4! 9 ♞e3! ♝xf3 10 ♝xf3 ♞d7 11
d5 ♞d4 Portisch-Timman, Montreal
79; 8...e6!?; 8 h3; 8 d5 **♖b8 9 ♝b2
b5 10 cxb5 axb5 11 ♖c1** 11 ♞e1?!
♞a5 12 ♖c1 c5 13 e4 ♞d7 14 ♞c2
e6 15 ♝a1 b4∓ Romanishin-
Tseshkovsky, USSR Final 78; 13...
cxd4! **♞a5 12 ♛c2** 12 d5 e5= **♝b7
13 ♖fd1** 13 ♖fe1!? ♛d7 13...♛e8!?
14 e4! b4

Diagram

15 e5! bxc3 15...♘e8 16 d5!? **16 ♗xc3 ♗h6?!** 16...♘d5 17 ♗xa5± **17 exf6 ♗xc1 18 ♕xc1 ♗xf3 19 ♗xf3 ♕f5 20 fxe7 ♖fe8 21 ♕e3 ♖b6** 21...♘b7 22 d5± **22 d5 ♘b7 23 g4 1-0 Miles**

192 Botterill-P.Delaney
Dublin 79
1 c4 ♘f6 2 ♘c3 g6 3 d4 ♗g7 4 ♘f3 0-0 5 g3 d6 6 ♗g2 ♘c6 7 0-0 a6 8 d5 ♘a5 9 ♘d2 c5 10 ♕c2 ♖b8 11 b3 11 ♖b1 e6∞ Botterill-Taulbut, Hastings 78/9; 11 ♖b1 b5! 12 cxb5 axb5 13 b4 cxb4 14 ♖xb4 ♕c7 15 ♕d3 ♗a6!∓ Δ 16 ♘xb5 ♕c5 **b5 12 ♗b2 bxc4 13 bxc4 ♗h6! 14 f4 e5 15 dxe6** 15 ♖ae1 exf4 16 gxf4 ♘h5 17 e3 ♗g7 18 ♘d1 ♗f5! 19 ♗e4 = Boleslavsky ♗xb2 20 ♘xb2 ♖xb2! 21 ♕xb2 ♘xc4 22 ♘xc4 ♗xe4 =+ **fxe6** 15...♗xe6?! 16 ♘d5 ♗xd5 17 cxd5 ♗g7 18 ♗c3± Portisch-Timman, Bugojno 78 **16 ♘ce4** 16 ♖ab1!? **♘xe4!** 16...♘g4? 17 ♘b3! ♘xb3 18 axb3 ♗g7 19 ♗xg7 ♔xg7 20 ♕c3+ ♔g8 21 ♖fd1 +— Portisch-van der Sterren, Wijk aan Zee 78 **17 ♘xe4?** 17 ♗xe4 d5 18 ♗e5 ♖b7 ∞/=+ **♗xb2 18 ♕xb2 ♘xc4 19 ♕c1 d5∓ 20 ♘f2 ♗g7 21 ♖b1 ♕a5 22 ♖d1 ♗d4 23 ♖d3 ♕xa2 24 ♗f3** 24 e3 ♘xe3 —+ **♗d7** 24...a5! —+ **25 ♖b7 ♗b5 26 ♖e7**

♘e5??! 26...♖e8∓ **27 fxe5 ♗xf2+** 27...♕xd3? 28 ♕h6 +— **28 ♔g2** 28 ♔xf2? ♗xd3 29 ♕h6 ♕xe2+ —+ **♗d4! 29 ♕h6 ♖f7 30 ♖xf7 ♕xf7 31 ♖d2** Zeitnot 31 ♕xh7+ ♔f8 32 ♕h8+ ♔e7 33 ♕f6+ ♔d7 34 ♕f7+ ♔d8 35 ♕f8+ ♔c7 36 ♕d6+ ♔b7 37 ♕xe6! ♔a7! += **♕b1 32 ♕xh7+ ♔e8 33 ♕g8+ ♔e7 34 ♕g7+ ♔e8 35 ♕g8+ ♔e7 36 ♕g7+ ♔e8 ½-½ Botterill**

193 Tukmakov-Tseshkovsky
USSR Final 78
1 d4 ♘f6 2 ♘f3 g6 3 c4 ♗g7 4 g3 0-0 5 ♗g2 d6 6 0-0 ♘c6 7 ♘c3 a6 8 d5 ♘b8 9 ♘b2 b5 10 cxb5 axb5 11 d5 ♘xd5 12 ♘d4∞ ♘a5 9 ♘d2 c5 10 ♕c2 10 a3∞ e5!? 10...♗f5 11 e4 ♗d7 12 b3 += **11 b3** 11 a3!? b6 12 b4 ♘b7 13 ♖b1 ♗d7 += **♘h5!?** 11...♘g4 12 e4 f5 13 exf5 gxf5 14 ♘d1 b5∞ **12 e4 f5 13 exf5 gxf5 14 ♖b1 ♗d7 15 a4 ♖c8∞ 16 ♗b2 ♖f7! 17 ♖fe1 b6 18 ♘e2 ♕g5!? 19 ♗c3 ♕h6 =+ 20 b4 ♘b7 21 bxc5! ♘xc5 22 ♖xb6 ♘xa4 23 ♖xa6 ♘xc3 24 ♘xc3 e4∞ 25 ♗f1 ♗e5**

26 c5! ♖xc5 27 ♘c4 ♗xc3 28 ♕xc3 ♗b5 29 ♖a5 ♖fc7 30 ♖a8+ ♖c8 31 ♖xc8+ ♖xc8 32 ♕e3!= ♕xe3 33 ♘xe3 ½-½ Gufeld

194 Portisch-Adorjan
Hungary 79
**1 d4 ♘f6 2 c4 g6 3 ♘f3 ♗g7 4 g3
0-0 5 ♗g2 d6 6 ♘c3 ♘c6 7 0-0 a6 8
♘d5 △ ♘e4?!** 8...♗g4! 9 ♘e3 ♗xf3
10 ♗xf3 ♘d7 11 d5 ♘d4 12 ♗g2 c5
13 ♗d2 b5 14 ♖c1 a5!? 15 cxb5 a4
16 ♘c4 ♘xb5 17 f4 ♕c7 18 e3 ♖a6
19 ♖f2 ♕a7 20 ♗f1 ♖b8 21 ♗e1 ♕a8
22 ♖d2 ♖a7 23 ♕f3 ♘c7∝ Portisch-
Timman, Montreal 79 **9 ♘e3 f5 10
d5 ♘a5** 10...♘e5 **11 ♘d2 ♘g5** 11...
♘f6? 12 b4 +− **12 ♖b1 c5 13 a3 f4!?**
13...b6 14 b4 ♘b7 15 f4± ; 13...b5
14 cxb5 axb5 15 b4 cxb4 16 axb4
♘b7 17 ♘b3± **14 gxf4 ♘h3+ 15 ♔h1!
b5** 15...♖xf4 16 b4 ♘xf2+ 17 ♖xf2
♖xf2 18 bxa5 +− **16 f5! ♘f4** 16...
gxf5? 17 ♗xh3 f4 18 ♗xc8 fxe3 19
♗e6+ +− **17 fxg6 ♘xg2 18 gxh7+
♔h8 19 ♘xg2 e6** 19...♘h3 **20 b4
cxb4** 20...♘xc4 21 ♘xc4 bxc4 22
♘f4! ♕f6 23 ♖g1± **21 ♖xb4 bxc4
22 ♘xc4 ♘xc4 23 ♖xc4 exd5 24
♖h4! ♖b8 25 ♗h6 ♕f6 26 ♗xg7+
♕xg7 27 ♘f4 ♗f5 28 ♖g1 ♕e5 29 ♘d3!
♕f6** 29...♗xd3 30 ♕xd3 ♖xf2 31
♕g6 △ ♕g8+ **30 ♖f4 ♖f7 31 ♖g3
♖bf8 32 f3 ♖xh7 33 ♕g1 ♕h6?**
Zeitnot **34 ♖xf5! 1-0 Meleghegyi**

195 Dorfman-Tukmakov
USSR Final 78
**1 c4 ♘f6 2 g3 g6 3 ♗g2 ♗g7 4 d4
0-0 5 ♘c3 d6 6 ♘f3 ♘c6 7 0-0 ♗f5!?**
7...a6 **8 d5** 8 h3 ♘e4∝; 8...♖e1!?
♘e4 9 ♘d5 ♖e8 10 ♘e3 += **♘a5 9
♘d4 ♗d7** 9...♘xc4? 10 ♘xf5 gxf5
11 ♕d3 **10 b3** 10 ♕d3!? c5 11 ♘b3
+= **c5 11 dxc6 bxc6 12 ♗b2 ♖b8=
13 ♖b1 c5 14 ♘c2 ♘c6 15 ♕d2 ♕a5!
16 ♖fd1 ♖fd8 17 ♗a1 ♘b4 =+ 18
♘xb4 ♕xb4 19 h3 ♕b6** 19...a5 =+
20 g4!? ♗c6 21 e4= e5 21...♘d7 22

♘d5 += **22 ♗f3 ♘e8 23 ♗g2 ♘f6 24
♗f3 ♘e8 25 ♗g2 ♘f6 ½-½ Gufeld**

196 Browne-Knaak
Novi Sad 79
**1 d4 ♘f6 2 ♘f3 g6 3 c4 ♗g7 4 ♘c3
d6 5 g3 0-0 6 ♗g2 ♘bd7 7 0-0 e5 8
e4 a6!? 9 ♖e1** 9 d5 b5 10 cxb5 axb5
11 b4! ♘b6 12 ♖e1 ♗d7 13 ♗f1 +=
exd4 **10 ♘xd4 ♘e5** 10...♘c5 **11 b3
c5 12 ♘c2 ♖b8?!** 12...b5!? **13 ♗b2
b5 14 f4! ♗g4 15 ♕d2 ♘f3+ 16 ♗xf3
♗xf3 17 ♕d3 ♗g4 18 ♘e3! += ♗h3**
18...bxc4? 19 ♘xc4 ♘e8 20 ♘d5± **
19 cxb5!** 19 ♖ad1? ♘g4! **♘g4** 19...
axb5 20 ♘xb5 ♘xe4 21 ♗xg7 ♔xg7
22 ♘d5! ♘f6? 23 ♕c3! ♗e6 24 ♘bc7!
+−; 22...f5 23 ♘bc3 ♘f6 24 ♖e7+± **
20 ♘xg4 ♗xg4 21 bxa6 ♕a5** 21...
♗d4+ 22 ♔g2 ♕a5 23 ♘a4 ♕xa4 25
bxa4 ♖xb2+ 26 ♔h1 ♖f2! −+; 22
♔h1∝ **22 ♕c2!** 22 ♘a4! c4 23 ♕xc4
♖b4 24 ♕d3 ♖xa4 25 ♗xg7 ♖xa2 26
♗c3 +− **♗d4+ 23 ♔g2 ♗e6 24 f5! gxf5
25 exf5 ♗d7** 25...♗xf5 26 ♕xf5 ♗xc3
27 ♖e4! ♗xb2 28 ♖g4+ ♔h8 29
♖h4 ♕d2+ 30 ♔h3 h6 31 ♖d1 ♕e3
32 ♖xd6? f6 33 ♖d7; 32...♗g7; 32
♖e1! ♕d2 33 ♖e2 ♕c1 34 ♖xb2 +−**
26 ♘e4! ♗xf5 27 ♗xd4 cxd4 28 ♕f2
♕d5 29 ♕f3! ♗g7 30 ♘d2! 30 ♘xd6??
♗h3+! −+ ♕xf3+ 31 ♔xf3? 31 ♘xf3
d3 32 ♘h4! ♗c8 33 a7! ♖a8 34 ♖e7±;
32...♗g4 33 ♖e4 ♗e2 34 ♘f5+ ♔f6
35 ♘d4 +− ♖b4?? 36 ♖f4+ ♖a8 32
♖ec1 ♖xa6 33 ♖c4 d3 34 ♖d4 ♖e8
35 ♘c4?? 35 g4 d5 36 ♔f4?? 36 ♘e3
♖f6 37 ♘b2 ♗h3+ 38 ♔g5 ♖e5+ 39
♔h4 ♖h6 mate 0-1 Browne**

197 Portisch-Meleghegyi
Hungary 79
**1 c4 g6 2 d4 ♗g7 3 e4 d6 4 ♘c3
♘d7 5 ♘f3 c6 6 ♗e2 e5 7 0-0 ♘h6!?**

8 ♖b1 8 c5!? dxc5 9 dxe5 0-0 10 h3 ♔h8 11 ♗f4! ♘g8 12 ♕d6 ♕e8 13 a4 h6 14 ♖fd1 g5 15 ♗g3 ♘e7 16 a5 ♘g6 17 a6± Uhlmann-Ciocaltea, Bucharest 78 **0-0 9 b4 exd4 10 ♘xd4 ♘e5 11 b5** 11 h3?! ♕h4 12 ♖b3 g5!? 13 ♘f3 ♘xf3+ 14 ♗xf3 g4! 15 hxg4 ♘xg4∓ Donner-Ljubojevic, Nice 74 **♕h4 12 bxc6 bxc6 13 ♖b3 ♗g4 14 f3 ♗e6!? 15 ♘xe6 fxe6 16 ♕xd6?!** 16 f4! ♘ef7 17 ♗e3 +=

16...♘hg4!? **17 fxg4** 17 h3 ♕g3!! 18 ♕xe6+ ♔h8 19 fxg4 ♖xf1+ 20 ♔xf1 ♖f8+ 21 ♔g1 ♘f3+! 22 ♗xf3 ♗d4+ 23 ♔h1 ♕e1+ 24 ♔h2 ♗g1+ −+; 20 ♗xf1 ♘f3+; 19 hxg4 ♖ae8 **♖xf1+ 18 ♗xf1?** 18 ♔xf1 ♖f8+ 19 ♗f3 ♘xf3 20 gxf3 ♖xf3+ 21 ♔e2 ♖f2+ 22 ♔e3 ♗h6+ 23 ♔d4 ♗xc1; 23...e5+!? 24 ♔c5 ♗f8 25 ♖b8∞; 22 ♔d3? ♕h3+! 23 ♗e3 ♕f1+ −+; 21...♕f2+!? 22 ♔d1 ♕f1+ 23 ♔c2 ♕xc4; 20 ♕xe6+? ♔h8 21 gxf3 ♖xf3+ 22 ♔e2 ♕f2+ 23 ♔d1 ♖d3+ −+ **♖f8 19 ♘d1** 19 ♕d2 ♘xg4 20 g3 ♗d4+; 20 h3 ♗e5 **♕e1!** **20 ♕xe6+ ♔h8 21 ♗f4 ♕xd1 22 ♕e7 ♘xg4?** 22...♕d4+ 23 ♗e3 ♕xe4 24 ♕h4 ♘xg4 Δ ♖xf1+! −+ **23 ♖f3 h5** 23...♕d4+ 24 ♗e3 ♖xf3 25 ♕e8+! +− **24 ♗e5!! ♖g8 25 ♗xg7+ ♖xg7 26 ♕c5 ♕a1! 27 h3 ♘e5 28 ♖f2 ♔h7 29 ♔h2 ♖f7 30 ♖xf7+ ♘xf7 31 ♗e2**

31 ♔g1 ♕xa2 32 ♗f3 ♕b2 33 ♕xa7 33 ♕xc6 ♕e5+ ♕e5+ 34 g3 ♕f6 35 ♗g2 ♔h6 36 ♕e3+ ♔g7 37 c5 ♘e5 ½-½ **Meleghegyi**

198 Portisch-Kagan Rio 79

1 ♘f3 d6 3 d4 g6 3 c4 ♗g7 4 ♘c3 ♘d7 5 e4 e5 6 ♗e2 ♘e7 6...♘gf6 **7 dxe5?! dxe5** =/=+ **8 b3 0-0 9 0-0 b6 10 ♗a3 ♖e8 11 h4?** 11 ♘d5; 11 ♕c2 ♗b7 **12 ♘g5?! h6 13 ♘f3 ♘c6 14 h5 g5** =+/∓ **15 ♘h2 ♘d4 16 ♘g4 ♘f6 17 ♘xf6+ ♕xf6 18 ♗g4** 18 ♘d5 **♗f8 19 ♗b2 c6 20 ♘e2 ♖ad8 21 ♘xd4 exd4 22 ♕d3 c5 23 ♖ae1 ♗d6 24 g3 ♖e7 25 ♖e2 ♖de8 26 ♖fe1 a6 27 ♗f5 ♕g7 28 ♔h2 ♗c8! 29 ♗xc8 ♖xc8 30 ♗c1 ♖e5 31 ♔g2** 31 f4? gxf4 Δ ♖xh5+ ♖ce8 32 ♗d2? 32 f4! g4! 33 ♗f4 33 f4!? ♖xh5 34 e5; 33...gxf3+ 34 ♕xf3 **♖5e6 34 ♕d2 ♗e5 35 ♕d3** 35 ♗xe5 ♕xe5 Δ ♖f6-f3 −+ **♕f6 36 ♗d2 ♕g7 37 ♖h1 ♖f6 −+** Δ ♖f3 **38 b4 ♖f3 39 ♕b1 d3 40 ♖e1 ♗d4 41 ♖hf1 ♕e5 42 ♗e3 ♗xe3 0-1 Miles**

199 Keene-Yap Manila 79

1 ♘f3 g6 2 c4 ♗g7 3 d4 d6 4 g3 ♘d7 5 ♗g2 e5 6 ♘c3 ♘e7 7 0-0 0-0 8 e4 ♘c6 9 ♗g5 9 d5 ♘e7 **f6 10 ♗e3 exd4 11 ♘xd4 ♘de5 12 ♘de2 ♗e6?** 12...f5!∞ **13 b3 f5 14 ♘f4!± ♗d7 15 exf5 ♗xf5 16 h3 ♘f3+?!** 16...h5!? **17 ♕xf3 ♗xc3 18 ♖ac1 ♗g7 19 ♕d5+ ♔h8 20 ♘e6 ♗xe6 21 ♕xe6 ♘e5 22 ♕d5** 22 ♗xb7 ♖b8 Δ c6 **♖b8 23 ♖c2** 23 ♗xa7 ♖a8 24 ♕xb7 c6! **♘c6 24 ♕d1 ♕c8 25 ♔h2 a5 26 ♖e2 ♕d7 27 c5! +− ♖bd8 28 cxd6 ♕f5 29 ♖d2 cxd6 30 ♖xd6 ♖xd6 31 ♕xd6 ♖d8 32 ♕c7 ♗e5 33 ♕xb7 ♘b4 34 ♕e7 ♕f6** 34...♗f6 35 ♗d4! ♖xd4 36 ♕f8 mate **35 ♕xf6+**

♗xf6 36 ♗b6 ♖b8 37 ♗c7 ♖c8 38
♗xa5 ♘xa2 39 ♖d1 ♘c1 40 b4 ♘b3
41 ♖d6 ♗c3 42 ♖d8+ 1-0 42...♖xd8
43 ♗xd8 ♗xb4 44 ♗f6+ ♔g8 45
♗d5+ +− Keene

200 Keene-R.Rodriguez
Manila 79
1 c4 g6 2 d4 ♗g7 3 e4 d6 4 ♘c3 e5
5 dxe5 dxe5 6 ♕xd8+ ♔xd8 7 f4!
♘d7 7...f6 Gheorghiu-Dzindzihashvili,
Buenos Aires 2 78; 7...♘c6!?; 7...
♗e6!? 8 ♘f3 c6 9 ♗e2 f6 10 fxe5
♘xe5 11 ♘xe5 fxe5 12 0-0 ♗e6 13
♗g5+ ♔e8 13...♔c7 14 ♗g4! ♗xg4
♖f7+± 14 ♖ad1 ♗h6! 15 ♖d6 ♗xg5
15...♗d7 16 h4 ♗xg5 17 hxg5 ♘e7
18 ♖df6 += 16 ♖xe6+ ♘e7 17 ♖xe5
♗e3+ 18 ♔h1 ♗d4 19 ♖g5 ♗xc3 20
bxc3 ♖d8 21 ♖a5 a6 22 ♖b1 ♖f8
23 ♔g1 23 ♖xb7?? ♖d1+ 24 ♗xd1
♖f1 mate ♖d7 24 ♗g4 ♖c7 25 ♖f1
♖xf1+ 26 ♔xf1 ♔f7 27 ♔e2 c5 28
♔e3 ♔f6 29 ♖a3 ♘c6 30 ♗e2 ♘e5
31 ♖b3 ♔e6 32 ♖b1 ♖d7 33 ♖b6+
♔f7 34 ♔f4 ♘c6 35 ♗g4 ♖e7 36 h4
h6 37 ♗f3

37...♔f6? Zeitnot 37...♘e5! 38 e5+
♖xe5 39 ♗xc6 ♖e6 40 ♖xb7 g5+?
40...♖xc6 41 a4± 41 hxg5+ hxg5+
42 ♔g4 ♖xc6 43 ♖h7 +− ♖c8 44
♖h6+ ♔e5 45 ♖xa6 ♔e4 46 ♖d6 ♖a8

47 ♖d5 ♖xa2 48 g3 ♖c2 49 ♖xg5
♖xc3 50 ♖xc5 ♔d4 51 ♖c8 ♔e5 52
♔h4 ♔d6 53 ♔g4 ♔d7 54 ♖c5 ♔d6
55 ♖d5+ ♔e6 56 ♖d4 ♔e5 57 ♖f4
♔e6 58 ♖e4+ ♔f6 59 ♔f4 ♖c1 60
g4 ♖c3 61 g5+ ♔f7 62 ♔f5 ♖f3+
63 ♖f4 ♖e3 64 c5 ♖c3 65 ♔e5+ ♔g6
66 ♔d6 ♔xg5 67 ♖f1 1-0 Keene

2 b3

201 Gurgenidze-Zaichik USSR 79
1 e4 c5 2 b3 ♘c6 2...d6 3 ♗b5+ ♗d7
4 c4 ♗xb5 5 cxb5 a6! 6 ♘c3 ♘f6 7
♘f3 g6∞ Lein-Polugaevsky, Buenos
Aires 78 3 ♗b2 d6 3...♘f6 4 e5 ♘d5
5 ♘f3 d6 6 ♗c4 += 4 ♗b5 ♗d7 5 ♘e2
e6 6 0-0 ♘f6 7 d3 ♗e7 8 ♘d2 0-0 9
♘g3 d5 10 f4 △ e5 a6 11 ♗xc6 ♗xc6
12 ♕e2 b5 13 f5 d4 △ e5 =+ 14
♘f3 ♗d7 15 b4?! e5 16 bxc5 f6 17
c3 dxc3 18 ♗xc3 ♗xc5+ 19 ♔h1
b4! 20 ♗b2 ♗b5 21 ♖fd1 ♘b6 22
♖ac1 ♘a4 23 ♗a1 ♖a7∓ △ ♖d7 −+
24 a3 b3 25 ♖b1 b2 26 ♖xb2 ♖d7
27 ♘e1 ♔h8 28 ♗a1 ♗xa3 29 ♕a2
♗c5 30 ♘e2 ♗a7 −+ 31 d4 ♗xd4 32
♘xd4 exd4 33 ♕a3 ♖e8 34 ♘f3 ♘c3
35 ♗xc3 dxc3 36 ♖xd7 ♕xd7 36...c2!
−+ 37 ♕xc3 ♖xe4 Zeitnot 0-1 Gufeld

202 Zaichik-Mik.Tseitlin USSR 79
1 e4 c5 2 b3 ♘c6 3 ♗b2 d6 3...e6 4
♘f3 ♘f6 5 e5 ♘d5 6 ♗b5 ♗e7 7 0-0
0-0∞ 4 ♗b5 ♘f6 4...a6!?; 4...♗d7
5 ♗xf6!? gxf6 5...exf6!? 6 ♕h5 ♗g7
7 ♘c3 0-0 8 ♗xc6 bxc6 9 ♘ge2 +=
e6 10 0-0 d5 11 d3 ♕a5 △ f5! 12
f4 f5 13 ♖f3 fxe4 13...♗xc3 14 ♖g3+!
+− 14 dxe4 dxe4

Diagram

15 ♘xe4! f5 15...♗xa1 16 ♖g3+ ♔h8

17 c3± **16 ⟨h3** 16 ⟨d6? ⟨xa1 17 c3
⟨c7! **h6?** 16...fxe4! 17 ⟨xh7+ ⟨f7
18 ⟨g3 ⟨g8 19 f5 exf5 20 ⟨f4∞
17 ⟨d6!± ⟨a6 17...⟨xa1 18 c3! +−
Georgadze ⟨c7 19 ⟨xh6! **18 ⟨g3**
⟨xe2 19 ⟨xe2 ⟨h8 20 ⟨xe6 ⟨d2
21 c3 ⟨ad8 22 ⟨f7+ ⟨xf7 23 ⟨xf7
⟨xc3 24 ⟨f1 ⟨d4+ 25 ⟨h1 ⟨e2
26 ⟨c4! +− ⟨e4 27 ⟨g6 ⟨g7 28
⟨f7 ⟨d4 29 ⟨xf5 c4 30 bxc4 ⟨xc4
31 ⟨b1 ⟨d2 32 f5 ⟨b2 33 ⟨d1 ⟨d2
34 ⟨f3 1-0 Gufeld

203 Franzen-Banas Prievidza 79
1 e4 c5 2 b3 ⟨c6 3 ⟨b2 e6 4 ⟨f3
⟨f6 5 e5 ⟨d5 6 ⟨c3 6 ⟨b5 ⟨xc3 7
⟨xc3 ⟨e7 8 ⟨d3 f5! N 8...b6 9 ⟨e2
⟨b7 10 h4 ⟨c7 11 ⟨h3 g6 12 ⟨g5
⟨d4 13 ⟨xd4 cxd4 14 f4 h6=
Schweber-Mecking, Buenos Aires 70;
9 ⟨e4 ⟨b7 10 d4!? **9 0-0 0-0 10**
⟨e1 b6 11 ⟨c4 ⟨b7 12 d4 cxd4 13
⟨xd4 ⟨xd4 14 ⟨xd4 ⟨c7= 15 ⟨h5?!
g6 16 ⟨e2 ⟨f7 17 a4? 17 ⟨a6 ⟨xa6
18 ⟨xa6 d5! 19 exd6 ⟨xd6 20 ⟨xe6=
g5!∓ **18 f3 g4 19 f4 h5 20 ⟨ec1 h4
21 ⟨f2 ⟨g7 22 ⟨g1 ⟨f7?** 22...g3+∓
**23 ⟨e1!= ⟨c8 24 ⟨e3 ⟨e4 25 c3
⟨gg8 26 ⟨a2 ⟨gd8 27 ⟨d2 ⟨c6
28 ⟨a6 ⟨b7 29 ⟨c4 ⟨c6= 30 ⟨a6
⟨b8?! 31 ⟨e2 ⟨g8 32 h3! += ⟨bf8
33 hxg4 fxg4 34 ⟨d3 ⟨e8 35 ⟨d1
⟨g7 36 ⟨c2 ⟨b7 37 ⟨b2 ⟨d8 38**

a5 bxa5 39 ⟨xa7 a4 40 b4 ⟨c8 41
⟨a3 ⟨gf7 42 ⟨c5 ⟨xc5 43 ⟨xc5
⟨c7 44 f5? 44 ⟨a6+ += exf5 45
⟨c4 ⟨e4! 46 ⟨xc7+ ⟨xc7 47 ⟨xf7
⟨xf7 48 g3 h3∓ 49 b5 ⟨h7 50 ⟨h2
⟨e7 51 c4? 51 ⟨xa4 ⟨xe5 52 ⟨b4 d6
53 ⟨c3 ⟨g2 −+ 54 ⟨hxg2 hxg2 55
⟨d3 ⟨b6 56 ⟨xg2 ⟨c5 57 ⟨b2 d5
58 b6 dxc4+ 59 ⟨d2 ⟨e8 60 b7
⟨b8 61 ⟨c3 a3 62 ⟨f2 ⟨xb7 63
⟨xf5+ ⟨d6 64 ⟨a5 ⟨b3+ 65 ⟨xc4
⟨xg3 66 ⟨d4 ⟨f3 67 ⟨a6+ ⟨e7 68
⟨e4 ⟨b3 69 ⟨g6 g3 0-1 Banas

204 Gurgenidze-Chechelian
USSR 79
1 e4 c5 2 b3 d6! 3 ⟨b2 e5!? 4 f4?!
4 ⟨b5+ exf4 5 ⟨f3 ⟨f6 6 ⟨b5+
⟨d7 7 ⟨xd7+ ⟨bxd7 8 0-0 ⟨e7 =+
9 ⟨h4 g6 10 ⟨a3 0-0 11 ⟨xf4 ⟨e5
△ ⟨h5∓ **12 ⟨f3 ⟨h5∓ 13 ⟨xe5 dxe5
14 ⟨g4 ⟨h8** △ f5! **15 ⟨e2? f5! 16
exf5 gxf5 17 ⟨xe5+ ⟨f6 18 ⟨xf5
⟨g7!** −+ **19 ⟨e4 ⟨xa1 20 c3 ⟨d7
21 ⟨h4 ⟨f5 22 ⟨e1 ⟨b2 23 ⟨c4
⟨c2 24 h3 ⟨ae8** 24...⟨c1? 25 ⟨xb2
⟨xb2 26 ⟨g5 **25 ⟨f2 ⟨c1 26 ⟨h2
b5 27 ⟨d6 ⟨d8 28 ⟨e4 ⟨xd2! 29
⟨exd2 ⟨xf3 30 ⟨xf3 ⟨xd2 31 ⟨e4
⟨d6+ 32 ⟨h1 h5 33 ⟨e2 ⟨e8 34
⟨e4 ⟨xe4 35 ⟨xe4 a6 36 g4 hxg4
37 hxg4 ⟨e6 38 ⟨f5 ⟨g7 39 a4 b4
40 cxb4 cxb4 41 ⟨f3 ⟨d4 0-1 Gufeld**

2 c3

205 Nunn-Pedersen Cleveland 79
1 e4 c6 2 c4 d5 3 exd5 cxd5 4 cxd5
⟨xd5 5 ⟨c3 ⟨d6! N 5...⟨a5; 5...⟨d8
6 d4 ⟨f6 7 ⟨f3 e6 1 e4 c5 2 c3 d5 3
exd5 ⟨xd5 4 d4 e6 5 ⟨f3 cxd4 6 cxd4
⟨f6 7 ⟨c3 ⟨d6 8 ⟨d3 ⟨e7 9 0-0
⟨c6 10 ⟨g5?!= 10 ⟨e1 0-0 11 ⟨c1
⟨b4? 11...⟨d8! 12 ⟨b5 ⟨d7 13

♘e5! ♘xe5 14 ♖c7! ♘xd3! 15 ♖xd7
♗xd7 16 ♕xd3 ♗c6 Δ ♖d7, ♖ad8=;
14...♕d5 15 dxe5 ♕xe5 16 ♖xe7
♕xg5 17 ♗xh7+ +− **12 ♗b1 ♘bd5**
13 ♘e5 ♗d7 14 ♕d3 += g6 15 ♖fe1
15 ♕f3 ♗c6 16 ♘xc6 bxc6= ♗c6
16 ♕h3 ♘xc3!? 17 bxc3 ♖ac8 18
♖cd1 Δ c4; 18 ♕h4 ♘d5 **b5**

19 d5!! ♗xd5 19...♘xd5? 20 ♗xe7
♕xe7 21 ♘xc6 ♖xc6 22 ♖xd5 +−;
19...exd5 20 ♘g4 Δ ♖xe7; 20 ♘g4
♗d7 21 ♗xf6 ♗xg4 22 ♗xe7 +−;
20...♘e4 21 ♘h6+ ♔g7 22 ♗xe4
♗xg5 23 ♘xf7! +−; 20...♗d8 21
♘h6+ ♔g7 22 ♕xc8 **20 ♕h4 ♔g7**
20...♕d8 21 ♘g4 ♔g7 22 ♗h6+ ♔g8
23 ♗xf8 ♔xf8 24 ♘xf6 ♗xf6 25
♕xh7± **21 ♘g4??** 21 ♗h6+? ♔g8 22
♗xf8 ♖xf8∞; 21 ♕h6+! ♔g8 22
♘xg6 fxg6 23 ♗xg6 ♖c7 24 ♗f4 ♕c5
25 ♗xc7 ♕xc7∞; 24 ♖e3 ♗d8∞; 22
♖d3! (Δ ♖h3, ♗xf6) ♘h5 23 ♗xe7
♕xe7 24 g4 ♘f6 25 ♖h3 +− Δ 26 g5
♘h5 27 ♖xh5 ♘g8!∓ **22 ♖xd5** 22
♗xe7 ♕xe7 **exd5** 22...♕xd5 23 ♗xe7∞
23 ♖xe7 ♖xc3? 23...h5! 24 ♘e3 d4!
−+ **24 ♖e1 d4 25 ♗h6?** 25 ♗d2!
♖cc8 26 ♘h6∞; 25...♖c5? 26 ♗b4
d3 26 ♗d2 ♖c4 27 ♕h3 ♖d8 28 ♖e3?!
28 ♘xf7 ♔xf7 29 ♕xh7+ ♔f8 30
♕h8! g5! −+; 28 a3∓ **♕a3?!** 28...
♖c2! −+ 29 ♘xf7 ♖xd2; 28...♘xh6?

29 ♖xd3 **29 ♖e1 ♕b2 ½-½(!)** 30
♕e3∓ **Nunn**

206 Chandler-Gheorghiu USA 79

1 e4 c5 2 c3 d5 2...♘f6 **3 exd5 ♕xd5**
4 d4 ♘f6 5 ♘f3 e6 6 ♗d3 cxd4 7
cxd4 ♘c6 8 0-0 ♗e7 9 ♘c3 ♕d8
9...♕d6∞ **10 ♗e3!? 0-0 11 ♖c1 b6!**
12 ♘e4 ♗b4! 12...♗b7?! 13 ♘xf6+
♗xf6 14 ♗e4± **13 ♘xf6+ ♗xf6 14**
♖b1 14 ♗e4 ♗a6! =+ **♗b7 15 a3 ♘d5**
16 ♕d3 g6 17 ♗h6 ♗g7 17...♖e8! =+
18 ♗xg7 ♔xg7 19 ♕d2 ♕e7 20 ♖fe1
♖fd8 21 h4! ♕d6! 22 h5 ♖ad8 23
h6+ ♔g8 24 ♘e5! f6! =+ 24...♘f6?!
25 ♕g5! ♖xd4? 26 ♖c7!! +− **25**
♘g4 ♔f7! 26 ♗a2 ♖6d7 27 ♘e3
♕d6 28 ♕e2 ♖e7 29 ♘g4 ♕f4!∓ 30
♕xf4 30 ♕h3 ♘xe3 31 fxe3 ♕g5 =+;
30...♕g5∓ **♗xf4 31 ♖cd1 ♖ed7 32**
♘c2 32 g3 ♘h3+! ♗xg2 33 ♗xe6+
♗xe6 34 ♔xg2 ♘xd4 35 ♘e3 ♗e6!
36 ♖xd7+ 36 ♖c1 ♘f4+ Δ ♘d3 −+
♖xd7 37 ♖c1 ♘f4+ 38 ♔f1 f5! 38...
g5? 39 ♖c8! ♔g6? 40 ♖g8+ ♔xh6?
41 ♘g4+ +−; 40...♔h5 41 ♖g7! **39**
♖c4 ♘d3 40 b3 ♘e5 41 ♖b4 ♔f6
−+ Δ ♔g5 **42 a4 ♘d3 43 ♖b5 ♔g5**
44 b4 ♔xh6 45 a5 bxa5 46 bxa5
♔g5 47 ♔e2 ♘f4+ 48 ♔f3 ♘e6 49
♖e5 ♔f6 0-1 Gheorghiu

207 Garner-Gheorghiu USA 79

1 e4 c5 2 c3 d5 2...♘f6 **3 exd5 ♕xd5**
4 d4 ♘f6 5 ♘f3 e6 5...♗g4= **6 ♗e2**
♗e7 7 0-0 0-0 8 ♘a3 ♘c6 9 dxc5
♗xc5 10 ♘b5 ♕d8 11 ♗f4 11 ♕xd8
♖xd8 =+ **a6 12 ♘bd4 ♗d7= 13 ♘b3**
♗e7 14 ♘e5 ♘xe5 15 ♗xe5 ♕c8!
16 ♗f3 ♗b5! =+ **17 ♖e1** 17 ♘a5!∞
♖d8 18 ♘d4 ♗c4! 19 b3 ♗d5 20
c4 ♗xf3 21 ♕xf3 ♖d7! 21...♘d7 =+
22 ♖ad1 ♕c5!∓ 23 ♘c2 ♖xd1 24
♕xd1 ♖d8 25 ♗d4 ♕a5 26 ♕a1 ♕d2!

27 ♕d1! 27 ♕b1 ♖xd4 −+ ♕a5 27...
♕xd1 28 ♖xd1 e5 29 ♖e1!! exd4
30 ♖xe7 d3 31 ♘e3= **28 ♕a1 b5 29
♗c3 ♕c7 30 ♘e3 bxc4 31 ♘xc4 ♘g4!
32 g3 ♕c5 33 ♘e3 ♖d3!! 34 ♘xg4**
34 ♗xg7 ♘xe3 35 fxe3 ♖xe3 −+
**♖xc3 35 ♕d1 ♖c2 36 ♕b1 ♗g5 37 h4
♗d2 38 ♖f1 h5 39 ♘h2**

39...♗e3!! −+ **40 ♕e1** 40 fxe3 ♕xe3+
41 ♔h1 ♕e2 −+ **♗xf2+ 41 ♖xf2 ♖c1
42 ♕xc1 ♕xc1+ 43 ♔g2 e5 44 ♘f1
♕e1 45 ♖f3 e4 46 ♖e3 ♕d1! 47
♔f2** 47 ♖xe4 ♕c2+ ♕d4 **48 ♔e2 f5
49 ♘d2 ♔h7 50 a4 g5 51 hxg5 ♔g6
52 ♘f1 ♔xg5 53 ♘d2 ♔g4 54 ♘f1
h4 55 gxh4 f4 −+ 0-1 Gheorghiu**

208 Sveshnikov-Hartston Sochi 79
**1 e4 c5 2 c3 ♘f6 3 e5 ♘d5 4 d4 cxd4
5 ♘f3 ♘c6 6 cxd4 d6 7 ♗c4 dxe5!?**
7...e6; 7...♘b6 **8 dxe5** 8 ♗xd5 ♕xd5
9 ♘c3 ♕d6! 10 d5 ♘d4 11 ♘xd4
exd4 **12 ♕xd4 e5=** ♘db4 **9 0-0!?**
9 ♕b3 e6 10 0-0 ♗d7∝ ♕xd1 **10
♖xd1 ♗g4!** N 10...♘c2? 11 ♘c3
♘xa1 12 ♘b5± **11 e6! fxe6 12 ♘c3 g6
13 ♘b5** 13 ♘e4!? **♖c8 14 ♗f4 ♗xf3
15 gxf3** 15 ♗xe6 ♗xd1 16 ♖xd1
a6! −+ **♘d5! 15**...e5? 16 ♗e6! +−
16 ♖xd5! exd5 17 ♗xd5 e5! 18 ♗e6
18 ♖e1!? ♗e7! 19 ♗e6 ♖b8= **♖b8!
19 ♗g5** Δ ♘c7 mate **♗f6 ♗e7 20 ♗e3**

♗f6! 20...a6 21 ♘c7+ ♔d8 22 ♗b6
21 ♗c5 ♗e7 22 ♗e3 ♗f6 22...h5?! ∝/+=
23 ♗c5 ♗e7 24 ♗e3 ½-½ Hartston

209 Preissmann-Ungureanu
Satu Mare 79
**1 e4 c5 2 c3 ♘f6 3 e5 ♘d5 4 d4
cxd4 5 cxd4 d6 6 ♘f3 ♘c6 7 ♗c4 e6
8 0-0 ♘c7 9 ♕e2 b6 10 ♘c3** 10 a3!?
d5 11 ♗d3 ♘b4 12 ♗g5 ♕d7 12...♗e7
13 ♗b5+ ♘xb5 14 ♗xe7 ♕xe7 15
♕xb5+ ♗d7 16 ♕e2 +=; 13...♗d7 14
♗xe7 ♕xe7 15 a3 ♘c6 16 ♖ac1±
13 ♘b5! 13 ♖fc1 ♘xd3 14 ♕xd3 h6
15 ♗h4· ♗a6 16 ♕e3 g5 17 ♗g3 ♗e7
18 ♖c2 0-0-0 19 ♖ac1 ♔b8 20 ♘e4?
dxe4 21 ♖xc7 ♕xc7 22 ♖xc7 ♔xc7
23 ♘d2 ♗b7∓ Novak-Cvetkovic,
Stary Smokovec 77 **♘xd3 14 ♘xc7+
♕xc7 15 ♕xd3 += ♕c4 16 ♕e3 h6 17
♗h4 g5 18 ♗g3 ♗e7 19 h4?** 19 ♖fc1
♕b5 20 ♖c2 += **♗a6!= 20 ♖fd1?!** 20
hxg5 ♕d3! 21 ♖fe1= **♕e2 21 hxg5
hxg5?!** 21...♕xe3 22 fxe3 hxg5
♔d7 =+ **22 ♖ac1?** 22 ♖e1= ♕xb2?
23 ♘xg5 ♗xg5 24 ♕xg5 ♕xd4 25
♕f6± **♕d7! =+ 23 ♖d2 ♕xe3 24 fxe3
♖ac8 25 ♖dc2 ♖xc2 26 ♖xc2 ♗d3!
27 ♖c1 ♖c8 28 ♖xc8 ♔xc8 29 ♔f2?**
29 ♗e1 Δ ♗c3, ♘d2 =; 29...g4 30
♘h2 ♗f5 31 ♘f1 =+ **♗b1!∓ 30 a3
♔d7 31 ♘d2 ♗c2 32 e4?** −+ 32 ♔e2
Δ ♗e1∓ **dxe4 33 ♔e3 ♔c6 34 ♘xe4
♕d5 35 ♘d2 b5 36 ♘f3 ♗e4 37 ♗e1
g4 38 ♘h2 ♗xg2 39 ♘xg4 ♔c4 40
♔f4 ♔b3! 41 ♘h6 ♔xb2 42 ♘xf7
♔xa3 43 ♘d6 a6 44 ♘e4 b4 0-1
Banas**

210 Zhuravlev-Gufeld USSR 79
1 e4 c5 2 c3 ♘f6 2...d5 **3 e5 ♘d5
4 d4 cxd4 5 ♘f3** 5 ♕xd4 ♘c6 **6
cxd4 d6 7 ♗c4 e6** 7...dxe5 8 ♗xd5
♕xd5 9 ♘c3∝; 7...♘b6 8 ♗b5 dxe5

9 ♘xe5 ♗d7 10 ♘c3 e6 11 ♗xc6=
**8 0-0 ♗e7 9 ♕e2 0-0 10 ♘c3 dxe5
11 dxe5 ♘xc3 12 bxc3 b6** 12...♕c7!?
13 ♗d3 ♖d8 14 ♕e4 g6 15 ♗h6 ♗d7
△ ♗e8= **13 ♗d3 ♗b7** 13...♕c7!? 14
♕e4 g6 **14 ♕e4 g6 15 ♗h6 ♘a5 16
♕e3 ♖e8 17 ♗b5?! ♗c6 18 ♖fd1**
18 ♖ad1!? **♕c7 19 ♘d4 ♖ed8!= 20
♗f1** 20 ♘xc6 ♘xc6 =+

20...♗a4?? 20...♖d5!? 21 ♕g3!? ♕xe5
22 ♗f4 ♕g7 23 ♘xc6 ♘xc6 24 ♖xd5
exd5∝ **21 ♖e1 += ♖d5 22 ♕f4** △
♘xe6 **♗e8 23 ♖e3± ♖c8** 23...♖c5
24 ♘xe6! fxe6 25 ♖f3 +− **24 h4 ♘c4
25 ♗xc4 ♕xc4 26 h5 ♖cd8? 27 hxg6**
27 ♘f5! ♖d1+ 28 ♖e1 ♖xe1+ 29
♖xe1 ♕c5 30 ♘xe7+ 31 ♗g5 +− **hxg6
28 ♖h3** 28 ♘f5 +− **♖xd4 29 cxd4
♖xd4 30 ♕c1 ♗a4 31 ♕xc4** 31 ♖c3
♖d1+! **♖xc4 32 ♖c1 ♗c2!? 33 ♗d2!
♕g7** 33...b5!? **34 ♖c3 ♖xc3 35 ♗xc3
♗e4 36 ♗d4! ♗a3 37 ♖c7 b5 38
♖xa7 b4 39 ♗c5 g5?!** 39...♗d5!?
40 ♗e7 40 ♗xb4 △ ♖a4 **♗g6 41
♗xb4 ♗xb4 42 ♖a4 ♗d5 43 ♖xb4
♗xa2 44 f3 ♗d5?!** 44...f6 45 ♖b8
♗c4 46 ♔h2 ♗d3 47 ♔g3 ♗f5 48
♖g8+ ♔h6 49 ♔f2 +− **♗h7 50 ♖d8
♗c2 51 ♔e3 ♗f5 52 ♔d4 ♗g6 53 ♖b8
♗f5 54 ♔c5 g4** 54...♗g6 55 ♔d6
♗f5 56 ♔e7 +− **55 f4 ♗e4 56 ♖g8
♗xg2 57 ♖xg4 ♗e4 58 ♔d6 1-0 Gufeld**

211 Buljovcic-Browne
Novi Sad 79
**1 e4 c5 2 c3 ♘f6 3 e5 ♘d5 4 d4
cxd4 5 ♕xd4** 5 cxd4 ♘c6 6 ♘f3 d6
7 ♗c4 ♘b6 9 ♗b5 dxe5 10 ♘xe5 ♗d7
11 ♘c3 e6 12 ♗xc6 ♗xc6 12 ♘xc6
bxc6 13 ♕g4 h5! 14 ♕f3 ♖c8 15
0-0 ♕xd4!?∝ Sveshnikov-Browne,
Novi Sad 79 **e6 6 ♘f3 ♘c6 7 ♕e4
d6 8 ♘bd2 ♗d7!?** 8...dxe5 **9 ♘c4
♘xc3! 10 bxc3 d5 11 ♕f4** 11 ♕g4!?
dxc4 12 ♗xc4 ♕a5 **dxc4 12 ♗xc4 ♗e7**
12...♕a5 13 ♖b1! **13 ♗d3?!** 13 0-0
0-0 14 ♗d3 ♕a5 15 ♕g3 ♖fd8
Sveshnikov-Beljavsky, USSR Final 78
♕a5! 14 ♗d2 g5! 15 ♘xg5 15 ♕g3
g4! 16 ♕xg4 ♘xe5 17 ♘xe5 ♕xe5+
18 ♕e4 ♗d6!; 18 ♕e2 ♕xe2+ 19
♔xe2 ♗c6 =+ **♘xe5** 15...♕xe5+ 16
♕xe5 ♘xe5 17 ♗e4! ♘c4!∓ **16 ♗e2!**
16 ♗e4? f5!; 16 ♗c2? ♗c6 17 0-0
0-0-0∓ **♗c6?!** 16...0-0-0! 17 c4 ♗b4
18 ♗xb4 ♕xb4+ 19 ♔f1 ♕b2 20 ♖e1
f6!? 21 ♕xf6? ♖df8 22 ♕e7 ♘d3 −+
17 c4! 17 0-0? 0-0-0 18 ♘xf7 ♕d5
19 f3 ♗c5+ −+ **♗b4 18 ♗xb4 ♕xb4+
19 ♔f1 ♕b2** 19...♕c5!? **20 ♖e1 ♖g8**
20...♔e7 21 ♘e4! ♗xe4 22 ♕xe4
♘d7! 23 ♖b1 ♕xa2 24 ♖xb7 ♖ab8−
=+ **21 ♗f3!** 21 ♘h5 0-0-0! 22 ♕xe5
♕xe5 23 ♖xe5 f6 24 ♖xe6 ♖xg5
25 ♗f3 ♗xf3 26 gxf3 ♖d1+; 22 ♖xe5
♖xg5!! 23 ♕xg5 f6! 24 ♕xf6 ♕a1+
25 ♔e2 ♕xa2+ 26 ♔e1 ♕b1+ 27
♔e2 ♕c2+ 28 ♔e1 ♕c1+ −+ **♖xg5!
22 ♕xg5 ♘d3 23 ♖xe6+!= ♔f8!** 23...
fxe6 24 ♕g8+ +− **24 ♕h6+ ♔g8 25
♕g5+ ♔f8 26 ♕h6+ ♔g8 27 ♕g5+
½-½ Browne**

212 Maric-Cvetkovic Ochrid 79
**1 e4 c5 2 c3 ♘f6 3 e5 ♘d5 4 d4
e6 5 ♘f3 cxd4 6 ♕xd4 ♘c6 7 ♕e4
d6?!** 7...f5 8 ♕e2!? △ g3∝ **8 ♘bd2**

f5 9 exf6! ♘xf6 10 ♕h4 ♗e7 11 ♗d3!
♗d7 11...0-0?! 12 ♘e4 ♘xe4 13 ♕xe4
g6 14 ♗h6 △ h4 12 ♗g6+ ♔f8 13
♗c2± ♕a5 14 0-0 ♘d5 15 ♕g3 15
♕e4 ♘f6 16 ♕e2± ♘xc3!? 16 bxc3
♕xc3 17 ♖b1 ♕xc2 18 ♖xb7 ♖d8
19 ♗b2 e5 20 ♖c1 ♕a4 21 ♘g5! ♔e8
21...♕f4? 22 ♖xd7! ♕xg3 23 ♘e6+!
+− 22 ♘ge4 g6 23 ♘c4 ♗e6

24 ♖xe7+! +− ♔xe7 24...♘xe7 25
♘cxd6+ ♔d7 26 ♘f6+ +− 25 ♕h4+!
g5 25...♔d7 26 ♘c5+ dxc5 27 ♘xe5+
+− 26 ♕xg5+ ♔e8 26...♔d7 27 ♕g7+
♘e7 28 ♘b6 +− 27 ♕g7 1-0 Maric

213 Vasjukov-Gufeld USSR 79
1 e4 c5 2 c3 ♘f6 3 e5 ♘d5 4 d4 cxd4
5 ♕xd4 5 ♘f3; 5 cxd4 b6!? 6 ♘f3
e6 7 a3 ♗e7 8 ♗d3 ♗b7 9 0-0 ♘a6∞
Sanz-Miles, Amsterdam 78 e6 6 ♘f3
6 ♗c4!? ♘c6 7 ♕e4 d6 8 exd6!? +=
♘c6 7 ♕e4 ♘de7?! 7...d6! 8 ♘a3!
+= d5 9 exd6 ♘f5 10 ♗f4 10 ♘b5
♘xd6 11 ♘xd6+ ♗xd6 12 ♗c4=
Vorotnikov-Vitolins, USSR 79 ♗xd6
11 0-0-0 ♗xf4+ 12 ♕xf4 ♕f6? 12...♕e7
13 ♗b5 0-0? 13...♘fe7 14 ♕xf6 gxf6
15 ♘c4 0-0 16 ♖d2± 14 ♗xc6 bxc6
15 ♘e5 c5 16 ♘ac4 ♕e7 17 g4 ♘h4
18 ♘c6 ♕f6 18...♕b7 19 ♕d6 +−
19 ♕xf6 gxf6 20 ♘e7+! ♔g7 21
♘xc8 ♖fxc8 22 ♖d7 +− ♖d8 23

♖hd1 ♖xd7 24 ♖xd7 ♘f3 25 h3 h5!?
25...♘g1 26 h4 ♘f3 27 h5! +− 26
gxh5 ♘e5 27 h6+! 27 ♘xe5 fxe5
28 ♖c7 ♖h8 29 ♖xc5 ♖xh5 ♔g6 28
♘xe5+ fxe5 29 ♖c7 ♖h8 30 ♖xc5
♔f6 30...e4 31 ♖e5! +−; 30...♔f5
31 ♖c7 +− 31 ♖a5 31 ♖c7 a6!?
♖xh6 32 ♔d2 ♖xh3 33 ♖xa7 1-0
Gufeld

2 ♘c3/2 d3

214 Balashov-Timman Rio 79
1 e4 c5 2 ♘c3 ♘c6 3 g3 g6 4 ♗g2
♗g7 5 d3 e6 6 ♗e3 d6 7 ♕d2 ♘ge7
8 ♘h3 0-0 9 ♗h6 ♗xh6 10 ♕xh6 f6
11 0-0 ♘d4 12 ♕d2 e5 13 f4 ♕b6!
14 ♖ab1 c4 15 ♔h1 cxd3 16 cxd3
♗e6 =/=+ 17 ♖f2 ♔g7 18 ♖bf1 ♖ac8
19 ♘g1 ♕c5 20 ♘f3 ♗xf3 21 ♖xf3
b5 22 a3 a5 23 ♖3f2 b4 24 axb4
axb4 25 ♘d1 ♗d7 26 ♘e3= ♕d4 26...
♗b5 27 fxe5 dxe5 28 ♘g4 ♘g8!∞;
27 ♗h3!? ♖cd8 28 ♗e6 △ ♘g4±
27 ♘c4 ♕c5 27...♗b5? 28 fxe5 dxe5
29 ♕xb4 △ ♕xe7+ 28 ♖c1 ♖c7 29
♖ff1 ♖fc8 30 h4 ♕d4?

31 fxe5± dxe5 31...fxe5 32 ♕xb4
♕xd3 33 ♘xe5 +− 32 ♕xb4 ♗e6
33 ♖c3 ♘g8 34 ♖fc1 ♖d8 35 ♕b6
♖xc4 36 ♕xe6 ♖xc3 37 ♖xc3 ♕a7
38 ♔h2 ♘e7 39 ♖a3 ♕d7 40 ♗h3 ♕c7

**41 ♖a6 ♞g8 42 ♕c4 ♕xc4 43 dxc4
♖d2+ 44 ♔g1 ♖xb2 45 ♖a7+ ♔f8
46 ♖xh7 ♖b6 47 c5 ♖c6 48 ♗d7
♖xc5 49 ♗e6 △ ♖h8 ♖c6 50 ♗d5
♖c1+ 51 ♔g2 ♖c2+ 52 ♔f1 ♞h6!
53 h5!** 53 ♖xh6?? **♔g7 ♞g4 54 ♖f7+
♔e8 55 hxg6 ♞e3+ 56 ♔g1 ♖g2+
57 ♔h1 ♖xg3 58 ♗c6+ ♔d8 59 g7
♖g6 60 ♗d7 ♖g5 61 ♗h3 ♞d1 62
♔h2 1-0 Miles**

215 Erlebacher-Gheorghiu
Chicago 79

**1 e4 c5 2 ♘c3 ♘c6 3 g3 g6 4 ♗g2
♗g7 5 d3 d6 6 f4** 6 ♗e3; 6 ♘ge2
e5! **7 ♞h3 exf4!** 7...♘ge7 8 0-0 0-0?
9 f5!± **8 ♞xf4 ♞ge7 9 0-0 0-0 10
♞fd5 ♞xd5 11 ♞xd5 b5!** =+ **12 c3
b4 13 ♗f4** 13 ♗e3 bxc3 14 bxc3
♘e5!∓ **bxc3 14 bxc3 ♗e6 15 ♕d2
♗xd5!∓ 16 exd5 ♞e5 17 ♖ad1** 17
d4? ♘c4∓ **♕a5 18 c4 ♕a3! 19 ♗xe5
♗xe5 20 ♖b1 ♖ab8 21 ♔h1 a5** 21...
♖b6!? **22 ♖xb6 axb6 23 ♖b1 ♖a8
24 ♖xb6 ♕xa2 25 ♕xa2 ♖xa2** △ h5∓
**22 ♞h3 f5! 23 g4 f4 24 g5 ♖b4 25
♗e6+ ♔g7 26 ♖xb4 axb4** 26...♔xb4∓;
26...cxb4?! 27 d4 ♕e3! 28 ♖d1!∞
27 ♖f3 ♕c3! 28 ♕f2 28 ♕xc3 bxc3
−+ **♕a1+ 29 ♔g2 ♖a8 30 ♕h4 ♕xa2+
31 ♖f2 b3! −+ 0-1** 32 ♕h6+ ♔h8 33
♗f7 ♕a7 34 ♗xg6 ♕g7! −+ **Gheorghiu**

216 Savage-Gheorghiu USA 79

**1 e4 c5 2 ♘c3 ♘c6 3 g3 g6 4 ♗g2
♗g7 5 d3 d6 6 f4 e5!** Botvinnik **7
♞h3 exf4 8 ♞xf4 8** gxf4?? ♗xh3 △
♕h4+ −+ **♞ge7 9 0-0 0-0 10 ♗e3 b5!**
N 10...♖b8∞ △ b5 **11 a3 ♞e5! 12
h3 ♖b8 13 ♕d2 a5 14 ♖f2 b4 15
axb4 axb4 16 ♞cd5 ♗b7!∓** 16...
♘xd5?? **17 ♘xd5 ♗b7** 18 ♗g5! **17 g4
♞xd5 18 ♞xd5 ♗xd5 19 exd5 c4!∓**
19...♖a8 20 ♖xa8 ♕xa8 21 b3! =+

20 ♖a6 20 d4 c3!∓ **b3! 21 d4 ♕c8!!**
−+ △ c3 **22 ♖a1 c3 23 ♕xc3 ♕xc3
24 bxc3 b2 25 ♖b1 ♞c4 26 ♗f4
♞a3 27 ♖ff1 ♞xb1 28 ♖xb1 ♖b6!**
−+ △ ♖a8 **29 ♗xd6 ♖a8 30 ♖xb2
♖xb2 −+ 0-1 Gheorghiu**

217 Romanishin-Sturua USSR 79

**1 e4 c5 2 ♞c3 ♞c6 3 g3 g6 4 ♗g2
♗g7 5 d3 d6 6 ♗g5** N 6 f4 e5 7 ♘h3!?;
6...e6 7 ♘f3 ♘ge7 8 0-0 0-0 9 ♗e3
♘d4 10 ♖b1 Romanishin-Timoshenko,
USSR 78 **♞f6 7 ♞ge2 0-0 8 0-0 ♖b8=
9 ♞d5** 9 a4 a6 **♞xd5 10 exd5 ♞e5**
10...♘d4 11 ♘xd4 ♗xd4 12 c3 +=
**11 d4 cxd4 12 ♞xd4 h6 13 ♗c1 ♗g4
14 f3 ♗d7 15 c3 ♕b6 16 ♖e1 ♗b5!
17 ♗e3! ♞c4 18 ♗f2** 18 ♗c1! (△ b3,
♗e3) 18...♘e5!= **♞xb2 19 ♕c2** 19
♕d2!? ♘d3 20 ♖eb1 ♘xf2 21 ♖xb5
♘e4! 22 ♕b2 ♘xc3! 23 ♖xb6 ♗xd4+
24 ♔h1 axb6 ∞/=+; 20 ♖ab1 ♘xe1!
♞d3 20 ♖eb1 ♞xf2 21 ♖xb5 ♞h3+!
21...♗xd4 22 ♖xb6 ♗xb6 23 ♔f1 +=
22 ♔h1 ♕a6 22...♘f2+? 23 ♕xf2
♗xd4 24 ♕e2 +− **23 ♖ab1 ♞g5?!**
23...♗xd4!? 24 ♗xh3 ♗f6= **24 ♞c6
bxc6 25 ♖xb8 cxd5 26 f4 ♞e4** +=
27 ♗xe4?! 27 c4! += dxe4 28 ♕xe4
♗xc3= **29 h4!** 29 ♕xe7? ♕c6+ −+
♖xb8 30 ♖xb8+ ♔g7 31 a4 31 ♕xe7
♕f1+ = **♕f1+ 32 ♔h2 h5 33 ♕e3!
♗f6 34 ♖c8?** Zeitnot 34 ♕xa7 ♕e2+ =
½-½ 34...d5! =+ **Gufeld**

218 Dorfman-Magerramov USSR 79

**1 g3 g6 2 ♗g2 ♗g7 3 e4 c5 4 ♞e2
♞c6 5 c3 e5!=** 6 0-0 **♞ge7 7 d3** 7 b4!?
cxb4 8 d4 bxc3 9 dxe5 d6!! 10 exd6!?
c2 11 ♕xc2 ♗xa1 12 dxe7 ♕xe7 13
♗a3∞ **0-0 8 a3 d5!** 9 exd5 **♞xd5 10
c4!? ♞c7** 10...♘de7 11 ♗e3 b6 12
b4 += **11 ♞bc3 ♗f5 12 ♞e4 ♞e6 13
♗e3 ♞cd4?!** 13...b6 14 ♘xc5 bxc5

15 &xc6 &b8 16 &d5 &xb2∝ **14
&xd4 exd4** 14...cxd4 15 &d2 += **15
&d2 h5 16 b4** += **b6 17 &b1** 17 bxc5
&xc5! 18 &xc5 bxc5 19 &xa8 ♕xa8
=+; 17 a4!? **&c8 18 h3** 18 bxc5
&xe4!? 19 &xe4 &xc5= **&e8 19 f4**
19 g4 hxg4 20 hxg4 &xe4 21 &xe4
♕h4 ∝/+=

19...b5! 19...a6 20 g4!± **20 cxb5 c4
21 dxc4** 21 ♕f3!? c3 22 &c1∝ **d3!**
21...&xc4? 22 ♕b3± **22 &f2** 22 &c5
&xc5 23 bxc5 &xc5∝ **&d4**∝ **23 c5
&e2 24 &c1?** 24 g4? hxg4 25 hxg4
♕h4 26 gxf5 ♕g3 −+; 24 a4!? &c2∝
&e6! △ &b3/&d5 **25 &c3?!** 25 &c3!
=+ **&xd2 26 ♕xd2 &e2+ 27 ♔h2
&xc3 28 ♕xd3 ♕xd3 29 &xd3 &c4
30 &f3 &xb5** −+ **31 &e5 &xe5 32
fxe5 &c7 33 &f4 &b5 34 &f6 &e8
35 &c6 &e6 36 &xe6** 36 &xb5 &xf6
37 exf6 &xb5 −+ **fxe6 37 &e4 ♔f7
38 ♔g2 &e8 39 &c2 &b5 40 a4 &d4
41 &d1 &c6 41 b5 &xe5 42 &e2
&d7 0-1 Gufeld**

3 &b5

219 Arkhipov-Filipenko USSR 79
1 e4 c5 2 &f3 &c6 3 &b5 e6 4 &xc6!?
4 0-0 &ge7 5 b3 ∝/+= **bxc6 5 d3
&e7 6 b3 &g6 7 &b2 f6 8 0-0 &e7
9 &c3 e5** 9...0-0!? **10 &e2 0-0 11**

♔g3 d6 12 &f5 &e6 !3 &c1 ♕d7 14
g4?! 14 &xe7+ △ &d2 ♔h8 15 ♔h1
&f7 16 &g1 &g8 =+ 17 &g3 &f8 18
&e3 &e7 19 &3h4 g6 20 ♕f3 ♕d8!
20...gxf5? 20 gxf5 += **21 &h3 gxf5
22 gxf5 &d7 23 ♕h5 &e8** △ &fg7
24 &g6+ &xg6 24...&xg6? 25 fxg6
+− **25 fxg6 &g7 26 &h6 &xg6 27
&xg7+ &xg7∓ 28 ♕h4 &g8 29 &g1
&h6 30 &hg3** △ &xg6! ♕e8 **31 ♕h3
d5 32 ♕g2 &e7 33 h4 ♕f7 34 f3
&e3! 35 h5** 35 &f1 &f4 −+ **&xh5
36 &g7 ♕f8 37 &xe7 &xg1 −+ 38
&c7 &e3 39 ♕h3 ♕g8! 40 &c8 &xf3+!
41 ♕xf3 ♕xc8 42 ♕xe3 0-1 Gufeld**

220 P.Whitehead-Lindsay USA 79
1 e4 c5 2 &f3 &c6 3 &b5 g6 3...&d4!?
Glek-Shirjaev, USSR 78 **4 0-0 &g7
5 c3 &f6** 5...e5 6 d3 &ge7 7 &e3 d6
8 d4 exd4 9 cxd4 0-0 10 &c3 +=
6 d4!? 6 &e1 0-0 7 d4! cxd4 8 cxd4
d5 9 e5 &e4 10 &c3 &xc3 11 bxc3
&g4 12 h3 &xf3 13 ♕xf3 &c8 +=
Barendregt-Gunsberger, Polanica 63;
10...&e8!? △ &g4, &c7-e6=; 10 &xc6
bxc6 11 &c3 &xc3 12 bxc3±
Georgadze; 7 h3 ♔c7! Hardicsay-
Mednis, Budapest 78 **cxd4** 6...&xe4
7 d5 &b8 8 &e1 &d6 9 &d3 0-0 10
♕a4 f6 11 &f4 e5 12 dxe6 dxe6
13 &a3 e5 14 &e3 ♕c7∝ Keres-
Smejkal, Luhacovice 69; 9 &f4!?
&xb5 10 a4 0-0 11 axb5 d6 12 ♕e2
+= Lutikov-Silva, Odessa 76 **7 cxd4**
7 e5 &d5 8 cxd4 0-0 9 &c3 &c7
10 &c4 d6= **&xe4 8 d5 &d6!** N 8...&b8
9 ♕e2 &d6 10 &d3 += **9 a4!?** 9 &a4
b5 10 dxc6 bxa4 11 ♕xa4 dxc6 12
♕xc6+ &d7 =+; 10 &c2 &a5 **a6 10
dxc6 axb5 =+ 11 c7!** 11 cxd7+ &xd7;
11 cxb7 &xb7 ♕xc7 **12 &c3 &xc3!**
12...0-0 13 &d5 ♕d8 14 &e1 e6 15
&f4 exd5 16 &xd6 &e8 17 ♕xd5±;

14...♖e8 15 ♗f4 ♘xb2 16 ♖b1 ♗g7
17 ♘xd6 exd6 18 ♖xe8+ ♕xe8 19
♘c7 +− **13 bxc3 ♖xa4** 13...♕xc3?!
14 ♗g5 f6 15 ♖e1 fxg5 16 ♕xd6 +−
14 ♖xa4 bxa4 15 ♗f4 15 ♕xa4??
0-0 −+ ♕**c6** 15...0-0 16 ♖e1 ♕c6
17 ♖xe7 ♘f5 =+ **16 ♖e1 ♘f5 17
♘d4!∞ ♕d5** 17...♘xd4? 18 ♕xd4±;
17...♕xc3? 18 ♘xf5 gxf5 19 ♗e5 +−
18 ♗e5 ♖g8 18...0-0?? 19 ♘xf5
♕xd1 20 ♘xe7 mate **19 c4 ♕xc4
20 ♘xf5 gxf5 21 ♗d6 e6 22 ♕d2
b6 23 ♖c1** 23 ♕h6? ♗b7 **♖xg2+!
24 ♕xg2** 24 ♔h1? ♗b7 **♗b7+ 25 f3**
25 ♔g1? ♕g4+ 26 ♔f1 ♗a6+ 27 ♔e1
♕g1 mate **♕g4+ 26 ♗g3 ♕xf3+ 27
♔g1 ♕h1+ 28 ♔f2 ♕g2+ 29 ♔e1
♕h1+ 30 ♔e2 ♕f3+ ½-½ Ciamarra/
A.Smith**

221 Faibisovich-Loginov ·
USSR 79

1 e4 c5 2 ♘f3 ♘c6 3 ♗b5 g6 4 0-0
♗g7 5 c3 ♘f6 5...d5 6 ♕a4 ♕d6!
7 exd5 ♕xd5 8 d4 cxd4 9 ♘xd4 ♗d7=;
9 cxd4 +=; 5...a6 6 ♖e1 6 ♕e2 0-0
7 ♖d1 ♕c7 8 d4 cxd4 9 cxd4 d5 10
e5 ♘e4? 11 ♘e1 △ f3±; 7...a6 8 ♗xc6
dxc6 9 h3 += **0-0 7 d4** 7 h3 a6! 8
♗f1 e5 9 d4 exd4 10 cxd4 d5= **cxd4
8 cxd4 d5 9 e5 ♘e4 10 ♘c3** 10 ♗xc6
bxc6 11 ♘c3 ♘xc3 12 bxc3 ♕a5!
13 ♕b3 ♗g4= **♘xc3 11 bxc3 ♘a5
12 a4** 12 ♕a4 a6 13 ♗f1 ♗g4 +=
a6 13 ♗d3 ♗g4 14 ♗a3 ♖c8= 15
♗c5? 15 ♖b1 ♗xf3 16 gxf3 b6 17
♗b4 ♘c4 △ a5 **18 ♗xc4 ♖xc4 19
a5 b5 =+ 20 ♕d2 ♕d7 21 ♕g5 ♖e8
22 e6?** 22 h4 e6 23 h5 ♗f8 24 ♗xf8
♖xf8 25 ♖e3 **fxe6 23 ♖ad1**

Diagram

23...♖f8! 24 ♖d3 ♖f5 25 ♕xe7 ♕xe7

26 ♗xe7 ♖c6∓ 27 ♔g2 ♔f7 28 ♗d8?!
28 ♗b4 ♖c8 29 ♗b6 ♗f8 30 ♖de3
♖f6 31 h3 ♗d6 32 ♔f1 ♔e7 33 ♔e2
♔d7 34 ♖g1 ♖c4 35 ♖a1 ♗f4 36
♖d3 ♖f5 37 ♔f1 ♖g5 38 ♗c5 ♗h2!
39 ♔e2 ♖h5 40 f4 40 ♖h1 ♖xh3 41
f4! ♖h5 42 ♔f3 ♖a4 43 ♗b4 ♖a2
44 ♔g2 ♗xf4 45 ♖xh5; 40...♗d6! −+
**♗xf4 41 ♖f3 ♖f5 42 ♔d3? e5 0-1
Gufeld**

222 van Riemsdyk-Mednis
Riga 79

1 e4 c5 2 ♘f3 ♘c6 3 ♗b5 g6 4 0-0
♗g7 5 c3 ♘f6 6 e5 6 ♖e1! ♘d5 7 d4
cxd4 8 cxd4 0-0 9 ♘c3 ♘c7 10 ♗f4
♘xb5! 11 ♘xb5 a6 12 ♕a4!? N 12
♘c3 d6 13 exd6 ♗g4!= Klovsky-
Korsunsky, USSR 78 **d6! 13 exd6
♗g4! 14 ♘c7 ♗xf3 15 ♘xa8 exd6!?**
15...♗e2! 16 dxe7 (16 ♖fe1 ♗b5 17
dxe7 ♘xe7 18 ♕a3 ♘d5 19 ♗d6 ♕xa3
20 ♗xf8 ♕xf8 =+) 16...♕xe7 17
♘c7 (17 d5? ♘d4 18 ♘b6 ♗h5! −+;
17 ♘b6 ♗xf1 18 ♔xf1 ♘xd4 =+
19 ♖e1? ♕d8! −+) 17...♗xf1 18
♔xf1 ♘xd4 19 ♖e1 ♕c5 =/=+ **16
gxf3 ♘xd4 17 ♗e3 ♘xf3+ 18 ♔g2?**
18 ♔h1!∞ **♘h4+ 19 ♔h1 ♘f5 20
♗b6! ♕xa8∓ △ ♗d4! 21 ♖ad1 ♕c8**
21...♗xb2!? **22 ♖fe1?!** 22 b3!∓
**♗xb2 −+ 23 ♖d3 ♗f6 24 ♔g1 ♗e5
25 ♔h1 ♔g7 26 ♖a3 h5 27 ♕e4**

♗f6 28 ♔g1 ♕d7 △ d5 29 ♕a4! ♕xa4?!
29...♕c8! 30 ♔e4 h4 △ ♖h8-h5 30
♖xa4 ♖c8 31 ♖b1 ♖c6 32 ♔f1 ♗e7?!
32...♗e5! 33 h3 ♘e7 −+ 33 ♗d4!
b5 34 ♗xf6+ ♔xf6 35 ♖f4+ ♔f5
35...♔g7! 36 a4! bxa4 37 ♖xa4 ♔g5
37...d5! 38 ♖ba1 d4 39 ♖xa6 ♗e6!∓
38 ♗ba1 ♔f6 39 ♖xa6 ♖xa6 40
♖xa6 ♔e6 =+ 41 ♔e2 ♔e5 42 ♖a7 f6
43 ♖a8 ♘d4+ 44 ♔e3 ♘e6 45 ♖e8
g5 46 ♖e7 h4 47 f4+?? 47 f3! =+
gxf4+ 48 ♔e2 h3! −+ 49 ♖a7 ♘g5
50 ♖a3 d5 51 ♖a5! ♔e4 52 ♖a6 ♔e5
53 ♖a5 ♔e4 54 ♖a6 ♗f3? 54...f5!
55 ♖g6 ♘f3 56 ♖e6+ ♘e5 −+ 57
♖h6 f3+ 58 ♔d2 d4! 59 ♖xh3 d3
△ f2 55 ♖xf6 ♗xh2 56 ♖e6+! 56
♖h6? f3+ 57 ♔e1 f2+! −+ ♔f5 57
♖d6! ♔e5 58 ♖d8! d4 59 ♖h8!= f3+
60 ♔f2 ♔f4 60...d3 61 ♔e3 d2! 62
♖e8+! ♔d6 63 ♖d8+ ♔e7 69 ♖xd2!
♘f1+ 65 ♔xf3 ♘xd2+ 66 ♔g3 61
♖f8+! ♔e4 62 ♖e8+ ♔f4 63 ♖f8+
♔e4 64 ♖e8+ ♔d5 65 ♖d8+ ♔c4 66
♖c8+ ♔b3 67 ♖d8 ♔c3 68 ♖c8+
♔d2 69 ♖h8! ♗g4+ 70 ♔xf3 ♘e3 71
♖xh3 ♔d3 72 ♖h4 ♘c4 73 ♖xd4+
½-½ Mednis

223 Toth-Hardicsay
Salgotarjan 79
1 e4 c5 2 ♘f3 ♘c6 3 ♗b5 g6 4 0-0
♗g7 5 ♖e1 ♘f6 6 ♘c3 0-0 7 h3 7
e5!; 7 ♗xc6= ♘d4! 7...d6= 8 ♗c4
8 ♗f1 d6 △ ♘xf3+, ♘d7-e5-c6-d4=
d6 9 a4?! 9 d3; 9 a3!? ♘xf3+ 10
♕xf3 ♘d7! 11 ♕g3 ♘e5 12 ♗a2 ♘c6
13 ♘d5! e6 14 ♘e3 ♘b4∓ 15 ♗b1
d5 16 e5 16 c3 ♘c6 −+ ♘c6 17
f4 f6! 18 ♘g4! fxe5 19...f5? 19
♘h2 △ ♘f3= 19 fxe5 ♘d4! 20 c3
♘b3 21 ♖a3 ♗xc1 22 ♖xc1 ♕g5
23 h4 23 ♖d1? h5 −+ ♕xd2 23...
♕f4!? 24 ♖e1 c4! 25 b4 ♕f4 26 ♔h2

♕xg3+ 27 ♔xg3 ♗d7 28 ♖a1 a6 29
♗c2 ♖ad8 30 ♖ad1 ♗c6 31 ♘h2!
♗h6 32 ♖d4 ♖d7 33 ♗d1 ♖df7 34
♗g4 ♖e8 35 a5 ♗a4 −+ 36 ♖e2 ♔f8
Zeitnot 37 h5 ♔e7 38 hxg6 hxg6 39
♘f3 ♖ef8 40 ♘h4 ♖g7 41 ♘f3 ♖ff7
42 ♗h3 ♖gg8 43 ♖h4 ♗c1 44 ♘d4
♗d7 45 ♘f3 ♖gf8 46 ♖g4 ♗f4+ 47
♔f2 ♖g7 48 g3 ♗h6 49 ♖h4 ♗c1 50
♗g4 △ ♖h1 +− d4!! 51 cxd4 ♗c6
52 ♖c2 52 ♔g2 c3 −+ ♗g5 53 ♖h2
♖gf7 54 ♖xc4 54 ♖c3 ♗d2 −+ ♖xf3+!
55 ♗xf3 ♖xf3+ 56 ♔e2 ♖xg3 57
♖h7+ ♔f8 0-1 Hardicsay

5...e5

224 Tal-Tseshkovsky Riga 79
1 e4 c5 2 ♘f3 ♘c6 3 d4 cxd4 4 ♘xd4
♘f6 5 ♘c3 e5 6 ♘db5 d6 7 ♘d5!?
♘xd5 8 exd5 ♘b8 8...♘e7 += 9 c4
a6 10 ♘c3 ♗e7 11 ♗e2 0-0 12 0-0
f5 13 f4! ♗f6 14 ♕c2 ♘d7 15 ♔h1
15 ♕xf5? exf4! 16 ♕e6+ ♔h8 17
♗xf4 ♘e5! −+ g6 16 g3 ♖e8 17
♗d2 b6 18 ♖ae1 ♗g7. 19 b3 ♖a7 20
a4 ♖c7 21 ♗d1!? ♗b7?! 21...h5!∞

22 g4!± e4!? 22...fxg4 23 ♗xg4
exf4 ±/∞ 23 gxf5 gxf5 24 ♗e3 ♘c5
25 ♖g1 ♘d3 26 ♖ef1 26 ♖e2?! ♕h4!;
26 ♗xb6? ♘xe1 27 ♖xe1 ♕h4∓ ♕h4
27 ♖g3 ♔h8 28 ♗xb6± ♖f7 29 ♗e3

♖f6 30 ♕g2 △ ♖h3 +− ♖g6 31 ♖xg6 hxg6 32 ♕xg6 ♖g8 33 ♖g1 ♘xf4 34 ♕g5! ♕xg5 35 ♖xg5 ♗xc3 36 ♖xg8+ ♔xg8 37 ♗xf4 ♗e5 38 ♗xe5 dxe5 39 ♔g2 ♔g7 40 ♗c2 ♔g6 41 ♔f2 ♔g5 42 ♔e3! 1-0 Gheorghiu

225 Ljubojevic-Adorjan Riga 79
1 e4 c5 2 ♘f3 ♘c6 3 d4 cxd4 4 ♘xd4 ♘f6 5 ♘c3 e6 6 ♘db5 d6 7 ♗f4 e5 8 ♗g5 a6 9 ♘a3 b5 10 ♘d5 ♗e7 11 ♘xe7 ♘xe7 12 ♗xf6 gxf6 13 c4 13 ♕f3 f5 14 exf5 ♗xf5 15 ♗d3 += ♗b7 14 cxb5?! 14 ♗d3 bxc4 15 ♘xc4 d5 16 exd5 ♕xd5 17 ♘d6+ ♔f8 18 ♗e4 ♕a5+ 20 ♕d2 ♕xd2+ 21 ♔xd2 ♖d8!= ♗xe4 15 ♕a4 d5! =+ Gheorghiu 16 bxa6+ ♔f8 17 ♕b4 17 f3 ♗f5 18 g4 ♗c8 △ ♕b6, ♗xa6; 17 h4?! ♖g8 18 f3 ♗f5 19 g4 ♗c8 20 0-0-0 ♕b6 21 ♔b1 ♔g7 22 ♘c2 ♗xa6 23 ♕b4 ♕e6 24 ♗xa6 ♖xa6 25 g5 d4 26 gxf6+ ♔xf6!∓ Izvozchikov-Sveshnikov, Riga 75 ♖g8!? N 17...♔g7 △ ♘c6, d4 18 f3 ♗f5 19 g4 ♗c8!∓ Gheorghiu 20 0-0-0 ♗xa6 21 ♔b1 ♔g7 22 ♘b5?! 22 f4 ♘g6 23 fxe5 fxe5 24 ♗xa6 ♖xa6 25 ♖hf1 ♕d7∝ ♘c6!? 22...d4 △ ♘d5 23 ♔c5?? 23 ♕b3 ♗xb5 24 ♗xb5 ♘d4 25 ♖xd4! exd4 26 ♖d1∝; 24 ♖xd5 ♗a4 −+; 23...d4 △ ♕d7, ♖gb8 =+ ♕a5! −+ 24 a4 24 ♕xc6 ♗xb5 25 ♕xb5 ♕xa2+ 26 ♔c1 ♖gb8 −+ ♘d4 25 b3 ♘xb3 26 ♕xd5 ♕b4 0-1 Adorjan

226 Ostaszewski-Stankovic
Bialystok 79
1 e4 c5 2 ♘f3 e6 3 d4 cxd4 4 ♘xd4 ♘f6 5 ♘c3 ♘c6 6 ♘db5 d6 7 ♗f4 e5 8 ♗g5 a6 9 ♘a3 b5 10 ♘d5 ♗e7 11 ♗xf6 11 ♘xe7 ♗xf6 12 c3 12 h4!? 0-0 13 ♘c2 ♖b8 13...♗g5 14

a4 bxa4 15 ♖xa4 a5 16 ♗c4 ♗d7 17 ♕a1 ♘e7= 14 ♗e2 ♗g5 15 0-0 ♔h8! 16 a4 bxa4 17 ♘cb4 ♗xb4 18 ♘xb4 ♗b7 19 ♕xa4?! ♗xe4! 20 ♘xa6? 20 f3

20...♗xg2!! 21 ♘xb8 21 ♔xg2 ♗f4 △ ♕g5+ ♗f4! 22 ♔xg2 ♕g5+ 23 ♔h1 ♕h4 24 ♕xf4 ♕xf4 25 ♘d7 25 ♘a6!? ♖d8 △ ♕e4+ 26 ♗b5 ♕f3+ 27 ♔g1 h5! △ h4-h3 −+ 28 ♖fe1 ♕g4+ 29 ♔f1 ♕h3+ 30 ♔e2 30 ♔g1 e4! △ 31...♖xd7 32 ♗xd7 ♕d3 mate 31 ♖ad1 e3!! 32 fxe3 ♕g2+ 0-1 33 ♔d3 ♕d5+ Vaisman

227 Nunn-Wirthensohn
Cleveland 79
1 e4 c5 2 ♘f3 e6 3 d4 cxd4 4 ♘xd4 ♘f6 5 ♘c3 ♘c6 6 ♘db5 6 g3 d6 6...♗b4 7 ♗f4 e5 8 ♗g5 a6 9 ♘a3 b5 10 ♘d5 10 ♗xf6 gxf6 11 ♘d5 f5 12 ♗xb5!? ♗e7 11 ♗xf6 ♗xf6 12 c3 0-0 12...♗g5 13 ♘c2 ♖b8 14 a4! bxa4 15 ♘cb4 += 13 ♘c2 ♖b8 13...♗g5 14 a4 bxa4 15 ♖xa4 a5 16 ♗c4 ♖b8 17 b3 += 14 h4!? g6 15 g3 15 ♕d2 ♗g7 16 h5 ♗e6 17 hxg6 hxg6 18 ♘ce3 ♗e6 += ♗e6 16 ♘ce3 ♗g7 17 h5 ♘e7 18 hxg6 hxg6 18...fxg6 19 ♘h3 ♗f7 += 19 ♘xe7+ 19 ♘h3 ♗xd5 20 ♘xd5 ♘h6 △ ♔g7= ♕xe7 20 ♕f3 20 ♘h3 ♗h6 21 ♗xe6

Âxe3 22 Âd5 Âg5 23 ♕g4 ♔g7 24
f4 exf4 25 gxf4 Âf6 26 0-0-0 ♖h8=
b4 21 c4 Âf6!= 22 Âh3 ♕g7 22...
Âg5!= **23 0-0-0 Âg5 24 ♔b1! ♔c7** 24...
Âxe3 25 ♕xe3 Âxc4 26 Âf1! Âxf1
27 ♕h6+ ♔f6 28 ♕h4+? ♔e6 29 ♕g4+
f5 30 ♕xg6+ ♖f6 31 exf5+ ♔d7 −+;
28 ♖hxf1! ♖h8 29 ♕d2 ♔g7 30 ♕xd6
=/+=; 29...♖b6 30 f4∞ **25 b3 a5?**
25...♖h8 26 Âxe6 fxe6 27 ♘c2 +=
a5? 28 ♕g4 ♕e7 29 f4 exf4 30 ♘d4±
26 Âf5+! Âxf5 26...gxf5 27 exf5
Âd7 28 ♕h5 ♕d8 29 ♖xd6±; 27...Âc8
28 f6+! Âxf6 29 Âxc8 ♕xc8 30
♖xd6 Âg5 31 ♖h7+! ♔g8 32 ♖h5!
+− f6 33 ♖xg5+ **27 exf5 e4?!** 27...a4
28 ♕g4 Âf6 29 fxg6 fxg6 30 Âg2!
Δ Âe4±; 28...axb3 29 ♕xg5! bxa2+
30 ♔b2 ♕xc4 31 f6+ ♔g8 32 ♕d2!
+− Δ Âd7, ♖h8+ **28 ♕g4!± ♕e7**
28...Âf6 29 fxg6 fxg6 30 Âg2± **29
♖he1 a4** 29...♖be8 30 Âg2; 29...e3
30 ♕d4+ **30 ♖xe4??** 30 ♕xe4± ♕f6∓
31 ♖ed4?! 31 f4 axb3 32 axb3 ♕c3;
31 ♖dd4 d5 32 cxd5 ♕a6 **axb3 32
axb3 ♖a8 33 f4 ♕d8??** 33...♕e7!
34 ♕xg5 ♕a7 −+ 35 f6+ ♔g8 36
♔c2 ♕a2+ 37 ♔d3 ♖fe8 **34 ♕xg5
1-0** 34...♕a5 35 f6+ ♔g8 36 ♕xa5
Nunn

228 Vrabec-Hardicsay Prague 79
**1 e4 c5 2 Âf3 Âc6 3 d4 cxd4 4 Âxd4
Âf6 5 Âc3 e6 6 Âdb5** 6 ♘xc6 bxc6
7 e5∞ d6 **7 Âf4 e5 8 Âg5 a6 9 Âxf6
gxf6 10 Âa3 b5 11 Âd5 f5 12 Âxb5!?
axb5 13 Âxb5 ♕g5** 13...♖a4!? 14
♘bc7+ ♔d7 15 0-0 ♖xe4 16 ♕h5
♘d4!? (16...♘e7∞) 17 ♕xf7+ Âe7 18
♘a8 ♕f8!! 19 ♘db6+ ♔d8 20 ♕d5
♕h6! −+ Petronic-Porubszky,
Zalaegerszeg 79 **14 Âdc7+ ♔d8 15
♕d5! Âb7 16 ♕xf7 ♕e7 17 ♕xe7+
Âxe7 18 Âxa8 Âxa8 19 exf5 ♖g8**

N 19...♖f8 20 g4 Âb4 21 a3 =+
Szalanczy-Hardicsay, Hungary 78 **20
0-0-0 ♕d7 21 f6** 21 ♖he1 ♖xg2 −+;
21 g3 Âd4 22 Âxd4 Âxh1 23 ♖xh1
exd4= **Âf8 22 f7 ♖g6! 23 c4** 23
Âxd6 ♖xd6 24 ♖xd6+ ♔xd6! =+;
24...Âxd6? 25 ♖d1 +−

23...Âd8!∓ 24 f3 24 c5 d5∓ **Âxf7
25 Âc3** 25 ♖hg1 e4!?∓; 25...Âh6+
26 ♔b1 Âe3 −+ **♖xg2 26 Âd5 Âh6+!
27 ♔b1 Âxd5 28 ♖xd5** 28 cxd5!?
Âe3 29 a4 Âd4 30 ♖b5 Âg5 −+ **31
♖f1** 31 f4 exf4 32 ♖d1 Âe3 −+
Âe6! 32 a5 ♔c6 33 ♖d1 Zeitnot
**Âc7 34 ♖b8 Âa6 35 ♖b5 Âc5 36
♖f1 ♖xh2 37 f4 e4 38 f5 e3 39 f6
♖f2! 40 ♖e1 ♖xf6 41 ♖xc5+ ♔xc5
42 ♖xe3 ♔xc4 43 ♖h3 h6 44 ♔a2
♔b4! 0-1 Hardicsay**

**229 Capello-Goldenberg
Reggio Emilia 78/79**
**1 e4 c5 2 Âf3 e6 3 d4 cxd4 4 Âxd4
Âf6 5 Âc3 Âc6 6 Âdb5 d6 7 Âf4 e5
8 Âg5 a6 9 Âxf6 gxf6 10 Âa3 b5 11
Âd5 f5 12 Âxb5?! axb5 13 Âxb5
♕g5!?** 13...Âa7; 13...♖a4!? **14 0-0**
14 Âdc7+ ♔d8 15 Âxa8 ♕xg2 16
♖f1 ♕xe4+ 17 ♕e2 ♕a4! 18 Âac7
Âd4! 19 Âxd4 exd4 20 ♕b5 ♕xc2!
21 Âd5 Âh6 −+ Honfi-Horvath,
Subotica 78; 20 cxd5 ♕a5+ ♖b8

15 f4! exf4 16 ♕e2 fxe4 17 ♕xe4+
♗e6 18 ♘bc7+ ♔d7 19 ♖xf4 ♗e7
20 ♖d1 ♖xb2 −+ 21 ♘xe6 fxe6 22
♘xe7 ♕c5+! 22...♔xe7 23 ♕xc6
♕xf4 24 ♕c7+ +=; 22...♘xe7? 23
♕d4 +− 23 ♔h1 ♔xe7 24 ♕f3 ♘e5
25 ♕g3 ♘g6 26 ♖af1 ♔d7? 26...
♖xc2! (Δ ♖c1) 27 ♖f7+ ♔d8! −+;
27...♔e8? 28 ♖xh7! +− 27 ♖f7+
♔d8 28 ♕f3 ♔c8 29 ♕a8+ ♖b8 30
♕a6+ ♔d8 31 ♕a4 ♘e5 31...♕b5 32
♕a7 ♖c8 33 a4 ♕c6 34 ♖b1 ♖a8 35
♖b8+ ♖xb8 36 ♕xb8+ ♕c8 37 ♕xd6+
♔e8 38 ♖c7 ♕d8 39 ♕c6+ ♔f8 40
♖c8 +− 32 ♕h4+ ♔c8 33 ♖g7 ♕c4
34 ♕f6 ♖e8 35 ♕f8! ♕c6 36 ♖e7
♖d8 37 ♕f6 ♕c4 38 h3 ♖b2? Zeitnot
38...♖b7!? 39 ♕xe6+ ♕xe6 40 ♖xe6
♔d7 41 ♖h6 ♔c6 −+; 39 ♖xe6??
♖f7 −+; 39 ♖xb7 ♔xb7 40 ♖f4
♕xc2! 41 ♕xd8 ♕c1+ −+; 41 ♖b4+
♔c7 42 ♕xe6 ♕c1+ 43 ♔h2 ♘f3+!
44 gxf3 ♕d2+; 44 ♔g3 ♕e1+ −+;
39 ♖f4 ♕xf4! −+ 39 ♖xh7 ♖xc2??
40 ♕xd8+ 1-0 Paoli

230 Marcovici-Kertesz Iasi 78
1 e4 c5 2 ♘f3 ♘c6 3 d4 cxd4 4 ♘xd4
♘f6 5 ♘c3 e5 6 ♘db5 d6 7 ♗g5 a6
8 ♘a3 b5 9 ♗xf6 gxf6 10 ♘d5 f5 11
c4?! 11 ♗d3; 11 exf5; 11 ♗xb5!?
♕a5+ 12 ♕d2 ♕xd2+ 13 ♔xd2 ♗h6+!
13...♔d8 14 ♔d1 0-0 15 cxb5 axb5
16 ♗xb5 16 ♘xb5!? ♘d4 17 ♗d3
♗a6! 18 ♗xa6 ♖xa6 19 ♘e7+ ♔h8
20 ♖e1 ♖b8! 21 ♘xf5 21 ♘c4 ♖b4!∓
♘xf5 22 exf5 ♖xb2 23 ♘c2 23 ♘c4
♖xf2 −+ ♖a5! Δ ♖d5+ 24 ♖e2 ♖axa2!
−+ 25 f6 25 ♖xa2 ♖b1 mate ♖xa1+
26 ♘xa1 ♖b1+ 0-1 Vaisman

231 Rigo-van der Wiel Rotterdam 79
1 e4 c5 2 ♘f3 e6 3 d4 cxd4 4 ♘xd4
♘f6 5 ♘c3 ♘c6 6 ♘db5 d6 7 ♗f4

e5 8 ♗g5 a6 9 ♗xf6 9 ♘a3! gxf6 10
♘a3 b5 10...f5 11 ♘d5 f5 12 ♗d3
♗e6 13 c3?! 13 ♕h5; 13 0-0 ♗xd5!?
13...♕g7= 14 exd5 ♘e7 15 ♘xb5
♗g7 16 ♘a3 0-0 17 0-0 e4∝ 18 ♗c2
♘g6 18...♕a5! 19 ♕h5 ♕c8 19...♕f6
20 f4± 20 f3 ♖b8 21 ♖ab1 ♖fe8
22 ♔h1 ♖e5 23 f4 ♖e7?! 23...♖e8!∝
24 g4! e3! 25 gxf5 e2 26 ♖fe1 ♗xf4
27 ♕f3 ♕c5?! 27...♗h6∝ 28 ♕xf4
♕xd5+ 29 ♔g1 ♔h8

30 ♕c4?? 30 f6!? ♗h6 31 ♕xh6
♖g8+ 32 ♗g6!!=; 30...♖g8 31 ♗g6!;
30 ♗b3! ♕c6 31 ♗a4! ♕d5 32 ♕c4±
♕f3! 31 ♖f1 exf1♕+ 32 ♖xf1 ♖g8!
0-1 33 ♖xf3 ♗d4+ −+ Haag

232 van Riemsdyk-Adorjan Riga 79
1 e4 c5 2 ♘f3 e6 3 d4 cxd4 4 ♘xd4
♘f6 5 ♘c3 ♘c6 6 ♘db5 d6 7 ♗f4
e5 8 ♗g5 a6 9 ♘a3 b5 10 ♗xf6 gxf6
11 ♘d5 f5 12 ♗d3 ♗e6 13 c4 ♕a5+
14 ♔f1 fxe4! 14...b4 15 exf5!! ♗xd5
16 cxd5 ♕xd5 17 ♘c4 ♖g8 18 ♘e3
♕d4 19 ♖c1± Ljubojevic-van Riems-
dyk, Riga 79 15 ♗xe4 ♗g7 16 ♕f3
♘d4 17 ♕g3 ♔f8!∝ 18 ♖d1 ♕d8
19 ♘e3 ♖c8 20 ♘ac2 bxc4 21 ♘xd4
exd4 22 ♘f5 ♗xf5 23 ♗xf5 ♖c5!∓
24 ♕f3 ♖e5 25 g4 h5 26 h3 hxg4
27 hxg4 ♖xh1+ 28 ♕xh1 d5! 29 b3
d3 −+ 30 bxc4 dxc4 31 ♕c6 ♕d5

32 ♕xd5 ♖xd5 33 ♗e4 ♖d4 0-1 Gheorghiu

233 Klovan-Gurgenidze
USSR 79
1 e4 c5 2 ♘f3 ♘c6 3 d4 cxd4 4 ♘xd4 ♘f6 5 ♘c3 e5 6 ♘db5 d6 7 ♗g5 a6 8 ♘a3 b5 9 ♗xf6 9 ♘d5 gxf6 10 ♘d5 f5 11 ♗d3 ♗e6 12 ♕h5 ♗g7 13 0-0 ♘b8 N 13...f4 14 c4 bxc4 15 ♗xc4 0-0 16 ♖ac1 ♖b8 17 b3 ♕d7 18 h3 ♔h8 19 ♖fd1 ♘d4 20 ♘c2 ♘xc2 21 ♖xc2 f5 22 exf5 ♗xf5 =+ Tukmakov-Sveshnikov, USSR Final 78 **14 c4 ♘d7 15 exf5 ♗xd5 16 cxd5 ♘f6 17 ♕f3 0-0 18 ♘c2 ♖e8≈** 18... ♔h8!? △ ♗h6, ♖g8 **19 ♗e4 ♕b6 20 ♖ad1 ♖ac8 21 ♘e3 ♕a5 22 ♗b1 ♕b4 23 ♕e2 ♗h6 24 ♖d3 ♔h8 25 ♖a3 ♖g8 26 ♖xa6 ♗xe3 27 fxe3 ♖g5 28 g3 ♖cg8 29 e4 ♖g4 30 a3 ♕d4+ 31 ♕f2 ♕c4 32 ♖c6 ♕b3** △ ♖xg3+ **33 ♖c3 ♕a4 34 ♗c2** 34 b4!? ♘xe4? 35 ♗xe4 ♖xe4 36 ♕b6 +−; 34...h5! =+ **♕a5 35 b4 ♕d8 36 ♖e1 ♕f8! 37 ♕d2 h5 38 ♔h1 h4 39 ♕g2 ♕h6 40 ♗d1 ♖f4! 41 ♔g1 hxg3 42 ♖xg3** 42 hxg3 **♖h4 43 ♖xg8+ ♘xg8 44 ♔h1 ♘f6 45 ♗f3 ♔h7 46 ♗e2** 46 ♖g1 ♘g5! **♘g5 47 ♗xb5 ♘f3! 48 ♕xf3 ♖xh2+ 49 ♔g1 ♖h3 =+ 50 ♕g2 ♕h4 51 ♗f1 ♖g3 52 ♖e2 ♖xg2+ 53 ♗xg2 ♕g3 54 a4 ♕b3 55 b5 ♕xa4 56 ♗f1 ♔g7 57 ♗g2 ♕xb5 58 ♖e1 ♔f6 59 ♔h2 ♕d3 60 ♖f1 ♕e2 61 ♖a1 ♕h5+ 62 ♔g1 ♔g5 63 ♖a3 ♔f4 64 ♖h3 ♕g4 65 ♔h2 f6 66 ♔g1 ♕xh3 67 ♗xh3 ♕xe4 68 ♔f2 ♔xd5 69 ♔e2 ♔c5 70 ♔d3 d5 ½-½ Georgadze**

234 Zuckerman-Day Canada 79
1 e4 c5 2 ♘f3 ♘c6 3 d4 cxd4 4 ♘xd4 ♘f6 5 ♘c3 e5 6 ♘db5 d6 6...h6?! **7 ♘d6+ ♗xd6 8 ♕xd6 ♕e7 9 ♘b5 ♕xd6 10 ♘xd6+ ♔e7 11 ♘f5+ ♔f8 12 b3! d5 13 ♗a3+ ♔g8 14 exd5 ♘xd5 15 ♘d6±** Spassky-Gheorghiu, Bath 73; 12...♘xe4 13 ♗a3+! ♔g8 14 f3! △ ♘d6± Acers **7 ♗g5 a6 8 ♘a3 b5 9 ♗xf6 gxf6 10 ♘d5 f5 11 ♗d3 ♗e6 12 ♕h5 ♖g8!?** N 12...f4?! 13 g3 f3 14 c3 ♗g7 15 ♘c2 ♘e7 16 ♘ce3 ♘xd5 17 exd5 ♗d7 18 ♕xf3± Blatny-Radojevic, Sombor 66; 12...♗g7 13 0-0 f4 14 ♔h1!? (△ g4) ♖b8 15 ♘b1 h6 16 ♘d2 += Wedberg-Bouaziz, Gausdal 78; 14 c4 bxc4 15 ♗xc4 0-0 16 ♖ac1 ♘e7 17 ♖fd1 ♖c8 18 ♕e2!± Paolozzi-Kudrin, New York 79 **13 0-0?** 13 c4! bxc4 14 ♘xc4 ♗xd5 15 exd5±; 13...b4 14 ♘c2±; 13... ♖xg2 14 ♕f3±; 13 c3!? **f4! 14 c3?** 14 h3 ♖g6! △ ♖h6 −+; 14 ♗e2 ♘d4 15 ♗d1∓

14...♗g4 −+ **15 ♕xh7 ♖g6 16 f3 ♗e6 17 ♖f2** 17 ♔f2 ♖h6 **♖h6 18 ♕g8 ♖c8 19 ♗xb5 f5 20 ♕xe6+ ♖xe6 21 exf5 ♖h6 22 ♗xa6 ♘e7 23 ♗xc8 ♕xc8 24 ♖d1 ♘xd5 25 ♖xd5 ♕xf5 26 b4 ♕h7 27 h3 ♖xh3 28 ♖xe5+ dxe5 29 gxh3 ♕d3 0-1 Ciamarra/Diesen**

235 Collier-Winslow USA 79
1 e4 c5 2 ♘f3 ♘c6 3 d4 cxd4 4 ♘xd4 ♘f6 5 ♘c3 e5 6 ♘db5 d6 7 ♗g5 7 ♘d5!? ♘xd5 8 exd5 ♘b8 9 c4 ♗e7

10 ♗d3 0-0 11 0-0 f5!? 12 f4 a6 13
♘c3 ♘d7 =+ Collier-Greenlaw, USA 79
a6 8 ♘a3 ♗e6!? 9 ♘c4 ♖c8 9...♘d4?!
10 ♗xf6 gxf6 11 ♘b6 ♖b8 12 ♘cd5
♕d8 13 c3 ♘c6 14 ♕a4±; 10...♕xf6
11 ♘b6! **10 ♘e3** 10 ♗xf6 gxf6 11
♘e3 △ ♘cd5 +=; 10...♕xf6! 11 ♘xd6+
♗xd6 12 ♕xd6 ♘d4 13 ♗d3 ♕g5 14
♔f1 h5! 15 h4 ♕f4 △ ♖h6∓; 13
0-0-0 ♕h6+; 11 ♘b6 +=; 10 ♘d5
♗xd5 11 ♗xf6 gxf6 12 ♕xd5 ♘b4
13 ♕d2 d5 14 exd5 ♕xd5= Larsen
♗e7 11 ♗xf6 ♗xf6 12 ♘cd5 12 ♗c4!?
+= **♗g5! 13 c3** 13 ♘f5 ♗xf5 14 exf5
♘d4 15 c3 ♕a5!; 13 ♗e2 ♘d4! **0-0
14 ♗e2** 14 g3 △ h4 g6 **15 0-0 f5=
16 exf5 gxf5 17 ♔h1** 17 f4?! ♗h6 =+
♕h8 18 f4 ♗h6 19 ♗d3 ♗e7 19...e4
20 ♗e2 ♘e7 ∝/+= **20 ♘xe7 ♕xe7 21
♕h5 ♗xf4! 22 ♘xf5 ♕g5 23 ♕xg5
♗xg5 24 h4** 24 ♘xd6 ♖xf1+ 25 ♗xf1
♖c7≈ **♗f4 25 g3 ♗xf5 26 ♗xf5 ♖xf5
27 gxf4 ♖c4** 27...♖cf8 28 ♖ad1 ♖8f6
29 ♔g2 exf4 30 ♖f3= **28 ♖ad1 ♖fxf4
29 ♖xf4 ♖xf4 30 ♖xd6 ♖xh4+ 31
♔g2 ♖g4+ 32 ♔f3 ♖f4+ 33 ♔e3
♔g7 ½-½ Ciamarra**

3 ♗b5+

236 Ciocaltea-Banas
Satu Mare 79
1 e4 c5 2 ♘f3 ♘c6 3 ♗b5 d6 4 0-0
4 c3 ♘f6 5 ♕e2 ♗d7 6 0-0 a6 7 ♗a4
b5 8 ♗c2 ♗g4! Pollard-Browne, USA
77 **a6** 4...♗d7!? 5 ♖e1 ♘f6 6 c3 a6
7 ♗f1 ♗g4 8 h3 ♗xf3 9 ♕xf3 g6 10
♕d1 ♗h6!= Lein-Browne, USA Final
77; 7 ♗xc6 ♗xc6 8 d4!? ♗xe4 9 ♗g5
♗d5! 10 ♘bd2 e6 11 c4 ♗xf3 12
♕xf3 cxd4 13 ♕xb7 ♕c8=
Timoshenko-Kupreichik, USSR 78;
9...♗xb1?! 10 ♖xb1 e6 11 ♗xf6!
gxf6 12 d5 ♕d7 13 b4 0-0-0 14

♕d3 += Jusupov-Timoshenko, USSR
78; 9...d5?! 10 ♘bd2 ♗xf3 11 ♕xf3
e6 12 ♗xf6! ♕xf6 13 ♕xd5±
Georgadze-Tal, USSR Final 78; 5
♕e2 g6 6 e5?! dxe5 7 ♘xe5 ♘xe5 8
♕xe5 ♗b5 9 ♕xh8 ♗xf1 10 ♕xg8
Kuzmin-Dorfman, Lvov 78; 5 c3
♘f6 6 ♖e1 a6 7 ♗a4 c4?! 8 ♗c2
♗g4 9 h3= Suetin-Balashov, USSR 69
5 ♗xc6+ bxc6 6 h3! N 6 d4 **e5 7 c3
♘f6 8 ♖e1 ♗e7 9 d4 ♔c7?!** 9...cxd4
10 cxd4 exd4 11 ♘xd4 += **10 dxe5
dxe5 11 ♘a3 ♘d7 12 ♘c4 f6** +=
13 ♘h4! g6 13...0-0 14 ♘f5 ♖e8
15 ♕g4 ♗f8?! 16 ♘cd6! +− **14 ♘h6
♗b6 15 ♕e2! ♗e6 16 ♘xb6 ♕xb6
17 f4! exf4 18 ♘f5! ♕b5 19 ♘g7+
♔f7 20 ♕f3 ♖hd8 21 ♘xe6± ♔xe6
22 e5 f5 23 ♕xf4 c4 24 ♗g5 ♕c5+
25 ♔h1 ♗xg5?!** 25...♖a7!± **26 ♕xg5
♕e7 27 ♕f4 ♕c5 28 ♕h4! +− ♕e7
29 ♕xc4+ ♔d7 30 ♖ad1+ ♔c7 31
♖xd8 ♕xd8 32 ♕f4! ♕e7 33 ♖d1
♖d8 34 e6+ ♔c8** 34...♖d6 35 ♖e1!
**35 ♖xd8+ ♕xd8 36 ♕e5 ♕e7 37
c4! ♕c7 38 ♕c5 ♕b7 39 e7 ♕d7 40
♕e5 ♕e8 41 b4 g5 42 ♕d6 1-0
Ciocaltea**

237 Gaprindashvili-Semenova
Piotrkow 79
**1 e4 c5 2 ♘f3 ♘c6 3 ♗b5 d6 4 0-0
♗d7 5 c3 a6 6 ♗xc6 ♗xc6 7 ♖e1
♘f6 8 d4!? ♗xe4 9 ♗g5 ♗xb1?!** N
9...d5 10 ♘bd2 ♗g6 11 dxc5 e6 12
♕a4+ ♕d7 13 ♕d4 ♖c8 14 b4! ♗e7
15 a4 0-0 16 ♘c4 dxc4 17 ♕xd7 ♘xd7
18 ♗xe7± Gaprindashvili-Dzindzihash-
vili, Wijk aan Zee 79; 10...♗xf3 11
♕xf3 e6 12 ♗xf6 ♕xf6 13 ♕xd5
♕e7 14 ♕e5 cxd5 15 cxd4 ♕d6 16
♕e4± Georgadze-Tal, USSR 79 **10
♖xb1 e6 11 ♗xf6 gxf6?** 11...♕xf6
11 dxc5 ♕d8!∝ **12 d5 e5 13 b4! ♕d7**

14 ♘d2± ♖g8 15 ♘e4 ♖g6 16 bxc5 dxc5 17 ♖b6! +− 0-0-0 18 d6 ♕h3 19 ♘g3 ♕e6 19...♕d7 20 ♕f3 ♖d7 21 ♘e4 ♗xd6 22 ♖d1! 1-0 Pytel

238 Zaichik-Romanishin USSR 79

1 e4 c5 2 ♘f3 d6 3 ♗b5+ ♘c6 4 0-0 e5?! N 4...♗d7; 4...♗g4 5 c3 a6 6 ♗xc6+ bxc6 7 ♖e1 7 d4!? ♗e7 8 d4 ♕c7 9 dxe5 += dxe5 10 ♘a3 10 ♕a4!? += f6 11 ♘c4 ♗e6 12 ♕a4! g5!? 13 ♗e3 13 ♘e3!± ♘h6 14 ♘a5 ♘g4!? 14...♗d7 15 ♘b3 +− 15 ♕xc6+ ♕xc6 16 ♘xc6 ♘xe3 17 ♖xe3 ♗d6 17...c4!? 18 ♖d3?! 18 ♘a5± ♗c7 19 ♖ad1 c4 20 ♖3d2 △ ♘b4-d5 a5! 21 ♖d5! ♖g8 21...♗xd5 22 exd5 △ ♘d2 +− 22 ♖b5?! 22 ♖c5! ♖a6!∝ 23 ♘b8 ♖a8 24 ♘c6 ½-½ Gufeld

239 van Riemsdyk-Gheorghiu Riga 79

1 e4 c5 2 ♘f3 d6 3 ♗b5+ ♗d7 4 a4 ♘c6!= 5 0-0 ♘f6 6 ♕e2 e6 7 ♖d1 ♗e7 8 d4 cxd4 9 ♘xd4 ♕c7! 10 ♘c3 0-0 11 ♗xc6?! bxc6! =+ 12 b3 e5! 13 ♘f3 △ ♗g5 h6! 14 ♗a3 ♗e6 15 ♘d2 ♖fd8 16 ♘c4 ♖ac8 17 a5 ♗f8 18 a6 ♖b8! △ ♗c8!∓ 19 ♗b2 ♗g4! 20 f3 ♗c8 21 ♔h1 ♘d7 22 ♘b1?! ♘c5 23 ♗c3 ♕e7 24 ♘e3 ♕g5 25 ♘f1 ♖d7 26 ♗d2 ♕f6 27 b4 ♘e6 28 c3

28...d5!∓ 29 exd5 cxd5 30 ♕f2 d4 31 ♘g3 ♕d8! 32 ♖e1 dxc3 33 ♗xc3 f6!∓ 34 ♕a2 ♖d6 35 ♘d2 ♖xa6 36 ♕b3 ♖xa1 37 ♖xa1 ♕c7 38 h3 ♔h8 39 ♘de4 a6 40 ♘f5 ♘f4! 41 ♘xh6?! gxh6 42 ♘xf6 ♕g7!! −+ 43 ♕b2 ♘d3! 44 ♕e2 ♕xf6 45 ♕xd3 ♗g7 46 ♖e1 ♗f5 47 ♕d5 ♖b5! 48 ♕a8+ ♔h7 49 f4 ♕g6 50 ♖e3 ♗d7! △ ♗c6 −+ 51 ♕e4 ♕xe4 52 ♖xe4 ♔g6 53 fxe5 ♗e6 54 ♖e1 ♔f5!? 55 g4+ ♔g6 56 ♔g2 ♗f8! 57 ♖d1 ♗e7 58 ♖a1 ♗c8 59 ♖a5 ♖b6 60 ♖a4 ♖c6 61 ♖a3 a5!! −+ 0-1 Gheorghiu

Najdorf

241 Hardicsay-Stull Prague 79

1 e4 c5 2 ♘f3 d6 3 d4 cxd4 4 ♘xd4 ♘f6 5 ♘c3 a6 6 ♗e2 e5 7 ♘b3 ♗e7 8 f4!? 8 0-0 b5?! 9 a4 b4 10 ♘d5 ♗b7! 11 ♗f3 ♘bd7 12 ♘xb4 ♘xe4 12...♗xe4 13 ♘c6!± 13 ♘d5! ♘dc5 14 ♘xc5 ♘xc5 15 0-0 15 ♘xe7? ♕xe7 16 ♗xb7 ♕xb7!∓ 0-0 16 ♗e3 e4 17 ♗e2 ♘d7 18 c3 ♗xd5!? 19 ♕xd5 ♘f6 20 ♕d2 d5 21 ♗d4 ♕c7 22 ♔h1 ♕b7 23 b4 ♖fc8 24 ♖fb1 24 ♖fd1! ♘e8 25 ♖d1 ♗f6! 26 ♗c5 ♘c7 27 f5! ♕c6 28 ♕e3 h6 28...a5! 29 ♗d4!± 29 ♖a3! ♘e8 30 h3 ♘d6 31 ♕f4 △ c4 ♘b7 32 ♗d4 ♗xd4 33 ♖xd4 +− ♘d6 33...♖d8 34 c4 +−

34 ♕e5 a5!

35 c4!! 35 ♖xd5 ♘c4 36 ♗xc4 ♕xc4
+= ♘xc4 36 ♗xc4 dxc4 37 ♖g3 f6
38 ♕e7 g5 39 ♖d7 ♕xd7 40 ♕xd7
axb4 41 ♕e6+ 1-0 Hardicsay

242 Mednis-Ljubojevic Riga 79
1 e4 c5 2 ♘f3 d6 3 d4 cxd4 4 ♘xd4
♘f6 5 ♘c3 a6 6 ♗e2 e5 7 ♘b3 ♗e7
8 0-0 ♗e6 9 a4 0-0 10 ♗e3 10 f4!
♘c6! 10...♘bd7 11 a5 ♖c8 12 ♕d2
♕c7 13 ♖fc1! ♕c6 14 ♗f3 ♖fd8?
15 ♘d5! ♗xd5 16 exd5 ♕c4 17 ♕d3!±
Mednis-Bouaziz, Riga 79; 14...♗c4!∞
Mestel-Browne, Lone Pine 78 **11
♔h1 ♖c8 12 f4 ♘b4!?** 12...exf4=
13 ♗f3 13 f5?! ♗c4 14 ♗xc4 ♖xc4
15 ♘d2 ♖c6 Δ d5 =+ **d5! 14 fxe5
♘xe4= 15 ♗d4 ♘c6! 16 ♕d3 ♘g5
17 ♗e2 ♘b4 18 ♕d1** 18 ♕d2?! ♘e4!
19 ♘xe4?! dxe4!∓ **♕d7 19 ♗d3**
19 a5! ♗f5 20 ♗d3= **♗g4 20 ♕d2
♘e6 21 ♗e2?** 21 a5= **♗g5 22 ♕d1
♗xe2 23 ♕xe2 ♖c4∓ 24 ♖ad1 ♕c7
25 ♖fe1 ♖e8 26 a5 ♗f4 27 ♗b6!
♕c6 28 ♕f2 ♘f8 29 ♖f1?** 29 ♘d4
♕h6 30 ♘f3! =+ **♕g6! 30 ♗c5 ♕xc2!
31 ♗xf8 ♕xf2 32 ♖xf2 ♔xf8?** 32...
♖xf8! 33 ♘xd5 ♗xe5 −+ **33 ♖df1
♗xe5 34 ♖xf7+ ♔g8 35 ♖xb7= ♖h4
36 h3 ♖c4 37 ♘d2 ♖f4 38 ♖xf4 ♗xf4
39 ♘f3 ♗d6?!** 39...♖b8 40 ♖d7=

**40 ♖d7 ♖e6 41 ♖d8+ ♗f8 42 ♘xd5
♘xd5 43 ♖xd5 ♖d6! 44 ♖d4** 44
♖xd6= **♕f7!** 44...♖xd4? 45 ♘xd4
♔f7 46 ♘c6 ♗d6 47 b4 ♔e6 48 b5
♔d5 49 ♘a7!± **45 ♖f4+ ♔g8!** 45...
♔e8? 46 ♖e4+± **46 ♖d4 ♔f7 47
♖f4+ ♔g8 ½-½ Mednis**

243 Ljubojevic-Ribli Riga 79
1 e4 c5 2 ♘f3 d6 3 d4 cxd4 4 ♘xd4
♘f6 5 ♘c3 a6 6 ♗e2 e5 7 ♘b3 ♗e7
8 0-0 ♗e6 9 f4 ♕c7 10 ♔h1 ♘bd7
11 a4 0-0 12 f5 ♗c4 13 ♗g5! h6 14
♗h4 ♖fc8 15 ♗d3?! 15 ♖f3!± **d5!=**
16 exd5 ♗xd5 17 ♘xd5 ♘xd5 18
♗xe7 ♘xe7 19 ♕f3 ♘f6 20 ♘d2
♘ed5 21 ♘e4 ♖e8! 22 ♖ae1 ♖ad8
23 c4?! ♘xe4 24 ♗xe4 ♘f6! =+ 25
♗xb7?

25...e4!∓ 26 ♗xe4 ♕xc4? 26...♕e5!!
−+ **27 b3?? ♕b4!** + 0-1 Gheorghiu

244 Vogt-Fedorowicz
Naleczow 79
1 e4 c5 2 ♘f3 d6 3 d4 cxd4 4 ♘xd4
♘f6 5 ♘c3 a6 6 ♗e2 e5 7 ♘b3 ♗e7
8 0-0 0-0 9 a4 ♘c6!? 9...♗e6 **10 ♗g5**
10 f4 ♗e6 **11 ♗xf6 ♗xf6 12 ♘d5 ♗g5
13 a5 ♖c8** Δ 14...♗xd5 15 ♕xd5 ♘b4
14 c4 ♘e7 14...g6 15 ♕d3 f5 16
♗f3 ♖f7 17 ♘b6 ♖b8 18 ♖ad1 ♗e7
19 exf5 gxf5 20 ♗d5 += Vogt-

Nicevski, Naleczow 79 **15 ♘b6 ♖c6 16
♘d2 ♘g6 17 g3 ♔h8 18 ♖a3! ♖e8
19 ♖e1 ♘f8 20 b4 g6 21 ♘f1 f5 22
exf5 gxf5 23 ♘e3 ♘g6 24 ♘ed5 ♗h6
25 ♗f1 ♖f8 26 ♕h5 ♗g7** 26...♕g5 +=
27 ♗g2 e4 28 g4!? ♘e5 28...fxg4
**29 ♗xe4 ♕h4 30 ♕xh4 ♘xh4 31
♘f4±** 29 **♖h3 ♗g8?** 29...h6 30 ♘f4±
**30 gxf5 ♘xc4 31 ♗xe4 +− ♘xb6
32 axb6 ♗d4 33 ♘f4** 33 f6! +− **d5
34 ♗xd5 ♖cf6 35 ♗xg8 ♖xg8+ 36
♘g6+ ♖gxg6+ 37 fxg6 ♗xf2+ 38
♔h1 ♕g8 39 ♕xh7+ ♕xh7 1-0 Vogt**

245 Larsen-Romanishin Riga 79
**1 e4 c5 2 ♘f3 d6 3 d4 cxd4 4 ♘xd4
♘f6 5 ♘c3 a6 6 ♗e2 e5 7 ♘b3 ♗e7
8 0-0 0-0 9 f4 b5** 9...♗e6 **10 a4** 10 a3
♗b7 11 ♗d3 ♘bd7 12 ♔h1 ♖c8 13
fxe5 ♘xe5 14 ♗f4 ♘c4!∓ **b4 11 ♘d5
♘xd5 12 ♕xd5 ♕b6+ 13 ♔h1 ♗b7
14 a5** 14 ♕d3 ♘bd7 15 a5 ♕c6!
**♕c7 15 ♕d3 ♘d7 16 ♗d2 ♘c5 17
♘xc5 dxc5 18 ♕f3** 18 ♕g3! ♗xe4
19 fxe5 ♗xc2 20 ♖ac1∞ **♖ad8 19
♗e3**

19...**f5! 20 ♕g3?** 20 ♗c4+ ♔h8 21
♗d5! =+ **♗xe4 21 ♗xa6** 21 fxe5
♗xc2 22 ♗h6! ♖f7 23 e6 **♖d6! 22
♗d3! ♗a8!** 22...♖g6? 23 ♗xe4 ♖xg3
24 ♗d5+ ♔h8 25 hxg3∞ **23 ♕f2
♖g6 24 ♖g1 ♗d6 25 ♖af1 ♕xa5**

246 Ambarzjuman-Novikov
USSR 79
**1 e4 c5 2 ♘f3 d6 3 d4 cxd4 4 ♘xd4
♘f6 5 ♘c3 a6 6 ♗e2 e5 7 ♘b3 ♗e7
8 0-0 0-0 9 f4 ♕c7 10 a4 ♗e6 11
♔h1 ♘bd7 12 ♗e3 ♖fc8** 12...exf4!
13 ♖xf4 ♖ad8!= **13 f5 ♗c4 14 a5
♗b5!?** 14...b5 **15 ♖e1!?** 15 ♘xb5
axb5 16 ♗xb5 ♕xc2 **♗c6 16 ♗f3 b5
17 axb6 ♘xb6 18 ♕e2 ♗b7**∞ 19
g4?! 19 ♘a5 ♘c4!; 19 ♗xb6!? **♘c4
20 ♗c1 d5! 21 ♘xd5 ♘xd5 22 exd5
♘b6?** 22...♖d8! 23 ♖d1 ♘b6 **23 ♖d1?**
23 ♕xe5 ♗d6∓; 23 ♘a5! ♗xd5 24
♗xd5 ♘xd5 25 ♕xe5 ♗b4 26 ♕xc7
♖xc7 27 c3 ♘xc3 28 bxc3 ♗xc3 29
♗f4 ♖c5 30 ♘b3± **♖d8 24 ♕g2 ♘xd5!!
25 ♖xd5 ♖xd5 26 ♗xd5 ♖d8 27
♗f3** 27 c4 ♕xc4!! 28 ♗xc4 ♖d1+;
27 ♖a5 ♕xa5! **e4 28 ♗e2** 28 ♗e3
exf3 29 ♕f2 ♗h4!! **e3 29 ♗f3 ♖d1+
30 ♗xd1 ♕f4! 31 ♔g1 ♗xg2 32 ♗xe3
♕f1 mate 0-1 Pytel**

247 Adorjan-Ribli (4) 79
**1 e4 c5 2 ♘f3 d6 3 d4 cxd4 4 ♘xd4
♘f6 5 ♘c3 a6 6 ♗e3!? e5 7 ♘b3 ♗e6
8 ♕d2 ♘bd7 9 f3 ♖c8 10 g4 ♗e7
11 0-0-0 ♘b6?! 12 h4!** 12 g5 ♘h5
0-0 **13 h5! ♘c4** 13...d5 14 ♗xb6
♕xb6 15 g5 d4 16 ♘a4 ♕c6 17 gxf6
gxf6 18 ♘ac5! ♗xc5 19 ♖g1+ ♔h8
20 ♕h6 +−; 17...♗xf6 18 ♘ac5 +−
14 ♗xc4 ♖xc4 15 g5 ♘d7 16 ♖dg1!±

♕c7 17 g6 ♖fc8 17...♘f6 18 ♗h6!
♘e8 19 ♗xg7 ♔xg7 20 h6+ ♔g8 21
g7 +−; 19...♘xg7 20 ♕h6 +−; 17...
♗f6 18 ♗h6! +− 18 ♗h6! ♗f6 19
gxh7+ ♚xh7 20 ♗xg7! ♗xg7 21
h6!! 21 ♖xg7+? ♔xg7 22 ♕g5+ ♔f8
23 h6 ♖xc3? 24 h7 ♖xc2+ 25 ♔b1
♖xb2+ 26 ♔xb2 ♕c3+ 27 ♔a3 +−;
23...♕d8! −+ ♗f6 21...♗h8 22 ♖g7+
+−; 21...♗f8 22 ♕g5 f6 23 ♕g6+ ♔h8
24 h7 Δ ♕g8+ 22 ♕g2! Δ ♕g7+
1-0 Adorjan

248 Mik.Tseitlin-Zaichik USSR 79
1 e4 c5 2 ♘f3 d6 3 d4 cxd4 4 ♘xd4
♘f6 5 ♘c3 a6 6 f4 ♕c7 7 ♗d3 g6
8 0-0 ♗g7 9 ♔h1 0-0 10 ♘f3 ♘bd7
11 ♕e1 ♘c5 11...b5!? 12 e5 dxe5
13 fxe5 ♘g4 14 ♕e4 ♘dxe5 15 ♕xa8
♘xf3; 14 e6 ♘de5 15 ♘xe5 ♗xe5
16 ♘d5 ♕d6 17 exf7+ ♖xf7 18 ♖xf7
♔xf7 19 ♕h4 ♔g7 =+ 12 ♕h4 12
e5!± e6 13 ♗e3 b5 14 ♗d4 ♘h5 15
♗xg7 ♚xg7 16 f5 b4 17 g4?! 17 ♘e2
(Δ ♘f4, ♕d8) 18 ♕f2∞

17...♕d8!∓ 18 ♕f2 ♘f6 19 e5 19 g5
bxc3 20 gxf6+ ♕xf6 −+ ♘xg4 19...
bxc3? 20 exf6+ ♕xf6 21 g5 ♕d8 22
f6+ 20 f6+ ♔h8 21 ♕h4 bxc3 22 ♘g5
22 ♕xg4 dxe5 −+ h5 23 ♘xf7+ ♖xf7
24 ♗xg6 ♗b7+ 25 ♔g1 ♖h7! −+ 26
♗xh7 ♕b6 26...♔xh7 27 ♕xh5+

♘h6 −+ 27 ♖f2 27 ♕xh5 ♘d3+ −+
cxb2 28 ♖af1 ♕c6! 28...b1♕ 29
♕xh5 ♕xf1+ 30 ♔xf1 ♕b1+ 31 ♔e2
♕c1! 32 ♕xg4 ♕h6 29 ♗e4 ♕xe4
30 ♕xh5+ ♕h7 31 ♕xh7+ ♚xh7
32 ♖f4 ♘xe5 33 ♖b1 ♘f3+ 34 ♔f2
♘e4+ 35 ♚e3 ♘c3 0-1 Georgadze

249 Penrose-Nunn
British Final 79
1 e4 c5 2 ♘f3 d6 3 d4 ♘f6 4 ♘c3
cxd4 5 ♘xd4 a6 6 ♗e2 ♘bd7 6...e5
7 f4 e5 8 ♘f5 ♘c5 9 ♘g3 ♕b6 10
f5 10 ♖b1 ♗e7 11 ♗e3 exf4 12 ♗xf4
♘cxe4! 13 ♘gxe4 ♘xe4 14 ♘xe4
♕b4+ 15 ♕d2 ♕xe4= Karpov-Browne,
Amsterdam 76 ♗d7 11 ♖b1 11 a4
♗c6 12 ♗f3 a5 13 b3 ♗e7 14 ♗e3
♕b4 15 ♗d2 ♕b6 16 ♗e3 ♕b4 17
♗d2 ½-½ Adorjan-Tal, Hastings 72/73
♗c6 12 ♗e3!? 12 ♗f3 ♗e7 13 ♗e3
♕c7 14 0-0 b5 15 ♗g5?! ♘d7 16
b3   a5   =+   Olafsson-Quinteros,
Lanzarote 74 ♕c7 13 ♘d5 ♗xd5 14
exd5 b5 15 0-0 ♗e7 16 ♕d2 0-0?!
16...♖b8!= 17 c4 b4 17 c4! += bxc4
18 ♖fc1 18 ♗xc4? ♘g4 ♕b7! 19 ♗xc4
♖fc8 19...♘g4 20 ♗xc5 dxc5 21
♕e2 += 20 h3?! 20 b4 += ♘cd7
21 ♗b3 Δ ♗a4-c6; 22 b4 ♘b6 ♕b5!=
21...♘b6? 22 ♕b4; 21...♗d8 22 ♗a4!
♕xd5 23 ♕xd5 ♘xd5 24 ♗xd7 ♖xc1+
25 ♗xc1; 22...♘xd5 23 ♖xc8+ ♖xc8
24 ♗xd7 ♘xe3 25 ♗xc8; 22...♖xc1+
23 ♖xc1 ♕xd5 24 ♕xd5 ♘xd5 25
♗c6 +− 22 ♘e2 ♘b6 23 ♘c3 ♕b4 24
♗xb6 =/=+ ♕xb6+ 25 ♔h2 h6 26
♕d3 ♕f2 27 ♖f1 ♕h4 28 g3?! 28
♖be1 Δ ♘e4 ♕b4 29 ♖fe1 ♖c7 30
♘c2?! 30 ♘e4 ♖ac8 =+ ♖c4! 31 ♗b3
♖d4 32 ♕e2 h5!? 33 ♖bd1 h4 34
♖xd4?! 34 g4 hxg3+ 35 ♚xg3 ♕xd4
36 ♕e3 ♕b4 37 ♘e4 ♖c8 38 ♘xf6+
♗xf6 39 ♖e2 a5?! 39...♗d8 40 ♕e4

♕b6 41 ♗c4! △ b3 ♕g1+ 42 ♖g2
♖xc4!? 42...♕c1 43 ♖c2 =+ 43 ♕xc4
♕e3+ 42...♕e1+?! 43 ♖f2 e4 44 ♕f1
♕e3+ 45 ♔g2∞ 44 ♚h2 44 ♔g4? e4
−+ e4 45 ♖e2? −+ 45 ♖g4? ♗e5+ 46
♔g2 ♕f3+ 47 ♔g1 ♗g3 48 ♕c2 e3 −+;
45 ♕b3! ♗e5+ 46 ♔h1 ♕e1+ 47 ♖g1
♕f2 48 ♖g2 ♕f1+ 49 ♖g1 ♕xf5 50
♕e3!∞ ♗f4 51 ♕c3 ♗e5+ 46 ♚g2
♕f3+ 47 ♚g1 ♗d4+! 48 ♕xd4 48
♔h2 ♗f2 −+ ♕xe2 49 a3 ♕e1+! 49...
e3 50 ♕h4 50 ♚g2 e3 51 ♕f4 51
♔f3 ♕f2+?? 52 ♔e4; 51...e2 52 ♕f2
♕f1 −+ e2 0-1 Nunn

250 Kupreichik-Zilberstein
USSR 79
1 e4 c5 2 ♘f3 d6 3 d4 cxd4 4 ♘xd4
♘f6 5 ♘c3 a6 6 f4 ♕c7 7 ♕f3 N
7 ♗d3; 7 a4 e6 8 ♗e3 b5 9 g4 ♘fd7!?
10 ♗d3 ♗b7 11 0-0-0 b4 12 ♘ce2
♘c5 13 ♔b1 ♘bd7 14 ♖hf1∞ g6!?
△ e5 15 f5?! 0-0-0! 16 fxe6 ♘e5 17
♕h3 17 ♕f6 ♗e7∓ fxe6 18 g5 ♕d7=
19 ♘f3 ♗xf3 20 ♕xf3 20 ♖xf3 ♘xe4
♗g7 21 ♘f4 ♖f8 22 ♗xc5? dxc5
23 ♗c4 ♕c7 24 ♖xd8+ ♕xd8 =+
25 ♕d3 25 ♗xe6+ ♔b8 △ ♕d4∓
♕xd3 26 ♗xd3 ♔d7 27 ♗c4 ♔e7
28 ♘h3 ♖xf1+ 29 ♗xf1 ♗e5 −+ 30
♘f2 ♗xh2 31 ♗g2 ♗f4 32 ♘d3 ♗e3
0-1 Gufeld

251 Rogobete-Buzbuchi
Poiana Brasov 78
1 e4 c5 2 ♘f3 d6 3 d4 cxd4 4 ♘xd4
♘f6 5 ♘c3 a6 6 ♗g5 e6 7 f4 b5 8 e5
dxe5 9 fxe5 ♕c7 10 ♕e2 ♘fd7 11
0-0-0 ♗b7 12 ♕g4 ♕b6 12...♕xe5
13 ♗e2 ♘c5!? 14 ♖hf1! △ ♗f4!± 13
♗e2 13 ♗d3 ♘xe5?! 13...h6 14 ♕h3
♘xe5 15 ♖he1 ♘bd7 16 ♗h4 g5
17 ♗xg5 ♖g8!∞ Kavalek-Polugaevsky,
Manila 75 14 ♕h3!? 14 ♕g3 ♘bd7 15

♗f4 f6 16 ♗g4!± ♘bd7 15 ♖he1
♗c5? 15...g6?! 16 ♗g4 h5 17 ♗xe6!
fxe6 18 ♘xe6 ♖h7 19 ♘c7+! ♕xc7
20 ♕e6+; 15...♗e7 16 ♘xe6! fxe6
16...♕xe6 17 ♗g4! +− 17 ♗h5+
♔f8 17...g6 18 ♗xg6+ 18 ♖f1+ ♘f6
18...♔g8 19 ♖xd7! 19 ♗xf6 gxf6 20
♖xf6+ ♔g7 20...♔e7 21 ♕h4! 21
♖xe6 ♗e3+ 22 ♔b1 +− ♖hd8 22...
♕c5 23 ♕g3+ 23 ♖xb6 ♗xb6 24 ♕e6
1-0 Vaisman

252 Harandi-Portisch Rio 79
1 e4 c5 2 ♘f3 d6 3 d4 cxd4 4 ♘xd4
♘f6 5 ♘c3 a6 6 ♗g5 e6 7 f4 ♕b6 8
♕d2 ♕xb2 9 ♖b1 9 ♘b3 ♕a3 10 ♗xf6
gxf6 11 ♗e2 ♘c6 12 0-0 ♗d7 13 f5
♘e5 14 fxe6 fxe6 15 ♗h5+∞
Suradiradja-Minic, Plovdiv 77 ♕a3
10 f5 ♘c6 11 fxe6 fxe6 12 ♘xc6 bxc6
13 e5 dxe5 13...♘d5?! 14 ♗xf6 gxf6
15 ♘e4 ♗e7 16 ♗e2 h5 17 ♖b3 ♕a4
18 c4 18 ♘xf6+ ♗xf6 19 c4 ♗h4+
20 g3 ♗e7 21 0-0 ♗d7 22 ♖b7 ♖d8?±
Timman-Ribli, Niksic 78; 21...♖a7 22
♖b8 ♖c7 23 ♕d3 ♗c5+ 24 ♔h1 ♔e7∞
Vitolins-Gavrikov, USSR 77; 23 ♗d3!?
Hund-Fischdick, Rio 79 f5 19 0-0
fxe4 20 ♔h1?! 20 ♕e3∞ Kavalek-
Fischer, Sousse 67

20...♖a7 21 ♕c2 ♕a5 22 ♕xe4 ♕c5
23 ♗xh5+ ♔d8 ∓/−+ 24 ♗g4 ♖f8

25 ♖d1+ ♚c7 26 h3 ♖b7 27 ♖xb7+
♚xb7 28 ♖b1+ ♚a8 −+ 29 ♕c2 ♗d6
0-1 Miles

253 Nunn-Macaulay
British Final 79
1 e4 c5 2 ♘f3 d6 3 d4 ♘f6 4 ♘c3
cxd4 5 ♘xd4 a6 6 ♗g5 e6 7 f4 ♕b6
8 ♕d2 ♕xb2 9 ♖b1 ♕a3 10 f5 ♘c6
11 fxe6 fxe6 12 ♘xc6 bxc6 13 e5
dxe5 13...♘d5; 13...♘d7?! 14 ♗xf6
gxf6 15 ♘e4 ♗e7 16 ♗e2 h5 17 ♖b3
♕a4 18 ♘xf6+!? ♗xf6 19 c4 ♗h4+
19...♗e7; 19...♖a7 20 g3 ♗e7 21
0-0 ♗d7?! 21...♖a7 22 ♖b8 ♖c7 23
♕d3 ♗c5+ 24 ♔h1= Vitolins-Gavrikov,
USSR 77; 23 ♗d3!? ♗c5+ 24 ♔h1
♖f8! 25 ♗g6+ ♔e7 26 ♖xf8 ♔xf8 27
♕h6+ ♔e7 28 ♕g7+ ♔d6 29 ♕f8+ =
22 ♖b7 c5 22...♖d8 23 ♗d3 ♗c5+
24 ♔h1 ♖g8 25 ♗e2! ♔e7 26 ♗xh5
♖g7 27 ♕h6! +− Timman-Ribli,
Niksic 78 23 ♗d1!± 23 ♕d3?! 0-0-0
♕c6 24 ♗f3 ♕d6 24...♕c8 25 ♕e2 Δ
♕xe5, ♗xh5+ 25 ♕c2 e4 25...♕d4+
26 ♔h1 (Δ ♖d1) 0-0-0 27 ♕b3 ♗d6
28 ♖b8+ 26 ♖d1 26 ♗xe4 ♗g5 27
♖d1 ♗e3+ 28 ♔h1 ♗d4∞ ♗c6? 26...
exf3 27 ♖xd6 ♗xd6 28 ♕g6+ ♔d8 29
♕g7 +−; 26...♕e5! 27 ♖dxd7 0-0
28 ♕xe4! ♕xe4 29 ♗xe4 ♗f6 30 ♗g6!
♗d4+ 31 ♔g2 ♖f2+ 32 ♔h3 ♖b2 33
♗f7+ ♔f8 34 ♖xb2 ♗xb2 35 ♗xe6 +−
27 ♖xd6 ♗xd6 28 ♖b6 +− exf3 29
♖xc6 ♔e7 29...♔d7 30 ♖b6 30 ♕d3
♗e5? 30...♖ad8 31 ♕xf3 31 ♕e4!
♗d4+ 32 ♔f1 e5 33 ♖c7+ ♔d6 34
♕c6 mate Nunn

254 Kuzmin-Gheorghiu Riga 79
1 e4 c5 2 ♘f3 d6 3 d4 cxd4 4 ♘xd4
♘f6 5 ♘c3 a6 6 ♗g5 e6 7 f4 ♗e7 8
♕f3 ♕c7 9 0-0-0 ♘bd7 10 ♗e2!?
10 ♗d3; 10 g4 b5! 11 e5!? 11 ♗xf6

♘xf6 12 e5 ♗b7 13 exf6 ♗xf3 14
♗xf3 ♗xf6 15 ♗xa8 d5!∞ Keres-
Fischer, Jugoslavia 59 ♗b7 12 ♕g3
dxe5 13 fxe5 ♕xe5! 14 ♗f4 ♕c5!
15 ♗e3 ♕e5 16 ♗f4 ♕c5 17 ♗e3 ♕c8!∓
18 ♖hf1 0-0 19 ♗d3 ♘c5! 20 ♗g5!?
20 ♗h6 ♘e8∓

20...♘fe4!∓ 21 ♘xe4 ♘xe4 22 ♗xe4
♗xg5+ 23 ♕xg5 ♗xe4 24 ♕e5 ♗g6!
−+ 25 h4 ♖d8! Δ ♖xd4! −+ 26
♕e2 ♕c5 27 ♘b3 ♕c6 28 g4 h6 29
h5 ♗h7 30 ♕f2 f6 31 ♖fe1 e5 32
♘c5 ♖d5! −+ 33 ♖xd5 ♕xd5 34
♕e3 ♖c8 35 ♖d1 ♕xc5 36 ♖d8+
♔f7 37 ♕b3+ ♔e7 0-1 Gheorghiu

255 Shakarov-Nasybullin
USSR 79
1 e4 c5 2 ♘f3 d6 3 d4 cxd4 4 ♘xd4
♘f6 5 ♘c3 a6 6 ♗g5 e6 7 f4 ♗e7 8
♕f3 h6 9 ♗h4 g5 10 fxg5 ♘fd7 11
♕h5 11 ♘xe6?! fxe6 12 ♕h5+ ♔f8
13 ♗b5 ♖h7! 14 0-0+ ♔g8 15 g6 ♖g7
16 ♖f7 ♗xh4 17 ♕xh6 ♕f6! 18 ♖xf6
♗xf6 =+ ♘e5 12 ♗g3 ♗xg5 13 ♗e2
13 ♘f3!? ♕b6 14 ♗xe5 dxe5 15 ♘f3
♕xb2 16 ♘d1 ♕b4+ 16...♕xa1?!
17 ♘xg5 ♖f8 18 ♘xf7 += 17 c3 ♕e7
18 0-0 ♖h7! N 19 ♘f2 ♘d7 20 ♘g4
♘f6 21 ♘xf6+ ♕xf6?! 21...♗xf6!∓
22 ♔h1 ♗d7 23 ♘xe5 0-0-0 24 ♘xf7
♗e8 25 e5 ♗g5 26 ♘d6+ ♔xd6≈

22 ♖ad1?! 22 ♖ab1! += **♗d7 23 ♘d2 ♕e7 24 ♘c4 ♗c6** 24...0-0-0? 25 ♖xf7; 25...♗a4!? **25 ♔h1 ♖d8 26 ♖xd8+ ♕xd8?!** 26...♔xd8!? 27 ♘xe5 ♗e8 **27 ♘xe5 ♕c7 28 ♘xc6 ♕xc6 29 ♕h3 +=** ½-½ Shakarov

Sozin

256 Ivanovic-Prevoznik
Naleczow 79
1 e4 c5 2 ♘f3 ♘c6 3 d4 cxd4 4 ♘xd4 ♘f6 5 ♘c3 d6 6 ♗c4 ♕b6 7 ♘b3 7 ♘de2?! e6 8 0-0 ♗e7 9 ♔h1 0-0 10 ♗e3 ♕c7 11 f4 a6 12 a3!? ♖d8∞ **e6 8 0-0** 8 ♗e3 ♕c7 9 ♗d3 a6 10 f4 ♗e7 11 ♕e2 b5!∞ **♗e7** 8...a6 9 ♗e3?! ♕c7 10 f4 b5 11 ♗d3 ♗e7 12 ♕f3 0-0 13 a4 b4 14 ♘e2 ♗b7∞ Tisdall-Hort, Hastings 77/78 **9 ♔h1! 0-0 10 f4 ♕c7 11 a3!?** a6 **12 ♘d2 b5 13 ♗a2 b4?!** 13...♗b7 **14 axb4 ♘xb4 15 ♗b3 ♗b7 16 f5 e5 17 ♘c4! d5** 17...♗xe4 18 ♘xe4 ♘xe4 19 c3 ♘c6 20 ♘e3 ♘f6 21 g4!∞; 17...♗xe4 18 ♘xe4 ♗xe4 19 ♕g4 d5 20 ♗h6! ♗f6 21 ♘d2 ♔h8 22 ♘xe4 dxe4 23 ♗d2 ♕b7 24 ♖fe1±; 17...♖fd8 18 ♘e3 **18 exd5 ♘bxd5 19 ♘xd5 ♗xd5** 19... ♘xd5 20 ♘a5 **20 ♕e2!± ♗c5** 20... ♖fb8!? **21 ♗g5 ♖fe8** 21...♘e4 22 ♗h4 **22 ♖ad1 ♗c6 23 ♖d3** 23 ♗xf6? gxf6 24 ♕g4+ ♔h8 25 ♕h4 ♕e7 26 ♖d3 ♖g8∓ **♘d5 24 ♖g3 ♘f4**

Diagram

25 ♕g4! 25 ♗f6?? ♘xe2 26 ♖xg7+ ♔f8 27 ♖xh7 ♗xg2+! −+ **h5 26 ♕h4 ♘e2 27 ♗f6! ♘xg3+ 28 ♕xg3 ♗f8 29 ♗xg7 ♔h7 30 f6 ♕d7 31 ♘e3 1-0 Ivanovic**

257 Guseinov-Uusi USSR 79
1 e4 c5 2 ♘f3 ♘c6 3 d4 cxd4 4 ♘xd4 ♘f6 5 ♘c3 d6 6 ♗c4 e6 7 ♗e3 ♗e7 7...a6 **8 ♕e2 a6 9 0-0-0 ♕c7 10 ♗b3 0-0 11 g4** 11 ♖hg1 ♘a5 12 g4 b5 13 g5 ♘xb3+ 14 axb3 ♘d7 15 f4 b4 16 ♘f5∞ **♘d7** 11...♘xd4 12 ♖xd4 b5 13 g5 ♘d7 14 h4 ♘c5 15 f4!?∞ **12 ♖hg1 ♘c5 13 g5 ♗d7 14 ♕h5** ∆ ♖g3-h3 **♖fc8 15 ♖g3 g6 16 ♕h6 ♗f8 17 ♕h4 ♗e7 18 ♗c4?! h5∓ 19 ♘f5!? b5!** 19...exf5 20 ♘d5 ♕a5 21 ♘f6+ ♗xf6 22 gxf6 ♗e6 23 ♕xh5 +− **20 ♘h6+ ♔g7 21 ♗f1 b4∓ 22 ♗xc5 bxc3 23 ♗a3 cxb2+ 24 ♗xb2+ e5 25 ♖d2** 25 f4 ♘b4 **♖ab8 26 ♗c4 ♖xb2! 27 ♔xb2 ♕a5 28 ♖d5 ♕b4+ 29 ♗b3 ♗e6 30 a3 ♕b6 31 ♖e3 a5 32 a4 ♗xd5 33 exd5 ♘a7?** 33...♘d4 ∆ ♖xc2+ −+! **34 ♖f3 ♖f8 35 ♖e3 ♘c8 36 ♖e4** 36 ♕g3 ♕d8 37 h4 ♕d8 −+ **37 f4 exf4 0-1 Gufeld**

258 Nunn-Large
British Final 79
1 e4 c5 2 ♘f3 ♘c6 3 d4 cxd4 4 ♘xd4 ♘f6 5 ♘c3 d6 6 ♗c4 e6 7 ♗e3 ♗e7 8 ♕e2 0-0 9 0-0-0 a6 10 ♗b3 ♕e8 10...♕c7 **11 f4** 11 ♖hg1 **b5!?** 11... ♘d7 12 g4 ♘c5 13 ♔b1 b5 14 f5 ♗f6?! 15 fxe6 fxe6 16 ♘f5! += Velimirovic-Spassov, Porec 74; 11...

♗d8?! 12 ♘xc6 ♕xc6 13 e5 dxe5
14 fxe5 ♘e4 15 ♕g4!± Stean-
Beljavsky, Teesside 73 **12 f5** 12 ♘xc6
♕xc6 13 e5 dxe5 14 fxe5 ♘d7 15
♘d5?! ♗d8∓; 12 e5!? dxe5 13 fxe5
♘xe5 14 ♗g5∞ **♗xd4** 12...b4 13
♘a4 ♘xd4 14 ♖xd4 += **13 ♖xd4!** 13
♗xd4? b4 14 ♘a4 e5 15 ♗f2 ♗b7
16 ♘b6 ♗xe4! 17 ♘xa8 ♕xa8∓ **exf5**
14 ♖f1 ♗xe4 15 ♗xe4 fxe4 16 ♖xe4
16 ♗d5? ♗e6! 17 ♗xa8 ♕xa8∓

16...♗b7? 16...♗e6! 17 ♗xe6 fxe6 18
♖xe6 ♖xf1+ 19 ♕xf1 ♕f7!=; 17 ♗d4
d5! 18 ♗xd5 ♗xd5 19 ♖xe7 ♕c6 20
♗xg7! ♗c4! 21 ♕g4 ♕g6 22 ♕xg6
hxg6 23 ♗xf8 ♗xf1 =; 21 ♕f2 ♗xg7!
22 ♕d4+ ♔g8 23 ♖f3? ♕h6+ 24 ♔b1
f6 25 ♖h3 ♖ad8! −+; 23 ♖f4 ♕h6
24 b3!?∞; 21 ♕e5? ♗xf1 22 ♗f6 ♗d3
−+; 20...♔xg7? 21 ♕e5+ ♔g8 22
♖f5±; 20 ♕e5 ♕h6+ 21 ♔b1 ♖ad8=
17 ♖g4 d5 17...♔h8 18 ♖xg7? ♔xg7
19 ♕g4+ ♔h8 20 ♗h6 ♗f6! 21 ♗xf8
♕e3+ 22 ♔b1 ♖xf8 −+; 18 ♗d4! f6
19 ♗e6 △ ♗f5, ♖h4 **18 ♗d4 f6?** 18...
♗g5+? 19 ♖xg5 ♕xe2 20 ♖xg7+ +−;
18...g6! 19 ♕e5 f6 20 ♗xd5+ =; 20
♕f5! += **19 c3!± ♕d7?** 19...♗d6 20
♕f3 ♕e6 21 ♗xf6 ♖xf6 22 ♕xf6 ♕xg4
23 ♕f7+ ♔h8 24 ♕xb7 ♖e8 25 ♕xd5±
20 ♗c2 +− △ ♕d3, ♖h4 **g6 21 ♗xg6!**
hxg6 22 ♖xg6+ ♔f7 23 ♖gxf6+

♗xf6 24 ♖xf6+ ♔g8 25 ♖g6+ 1-0
Nunn

259 Honfi-Blubaum
Baden-Baden 79

1 e4 c5 2 ♘f3 d6 3 d4 cxd4 4 ♘xd4
♘f6 5 ♘c3 e6 6 ♗c4 a6 7 ♗b3 ♗e7
8 f4 0-0 9 ♕f3 ♕c7 10 f5 ♘c6 11
♗e3 ♘xd4 12 ♗xd4 e5 13 ♗e3 13 ♗f2
d5!? 14 ♘xd5 ♘xd5 15 exd5 ♗b4+
16 c3 e4∞ **b5 14 a3 ♗b7 15 0-0**
15 ♖d1!? **♗c6 16 ♗g5 ♘xe4!?** 16...a5
17 ♗xf6 ♗xf6 18 ♗d5 b4 19 ♗xc6
♕xc6 20 ♘d5 ♕xc2 21 ♘xf6+± **17**
♗xe7 ♘f6 17...♘xc3? 18 ♕xc3 +−;
17...♘d2? 18 ♕g4 △ f6 +− **18 ♘d5!**
18 ♗xd6= **♘xd5 19 ♗xf8 ♘f4 20**
♕g4 ♕b6+ 21 ♖f2 ♗xf8 22 g3! h5
23 ♕h4 ♕e3 23...♘e2+ 24 ♔f1 ♘d4
25 ♕xh5 +− **24 gxf4 ♕e4 25 ♔f1**
♕h1+ 26 ♔e2 ♕xa1 27 ♕xh5 ♖a7 28
♕h8+ ♔e7 29 ♕xg7 ♔d8 30 ♕f6+
♔c8 30...♔c7 31 fxe5 dxe5 32 ♕xe5+
♔b6 33 ♖f1 +− **31 ♕xd6 ♖c7 32**
fxe5 ♕xb2 33 e6 ♕f6 34 ♖f4 ♕g5
35 exf7 ♕g2+ 36 ♔e1 ♕g1+ 37 ♔d2
1-0 Honfi

Richter-Rauzer

260 Plaskett-Lombardy
New York 1979

1 e4 c5 2 ♘f3 ♘c6 3 d4 cxd4 4 ♘xd4
♘f6 5 ♘c3 d6 6 ♗g5 ♗d7 7 ♗xf6!?
7 ♕d2 ♖c8 8 ♘b3 += **gxf6 8 ♘f5**
♕a5 9 ♗b5 a6 10 ♗xc6 bxc6 10...♗xc6
11 ♕h5 ♕e5 12 0-0-0 e6 13 ♖he1
0-0-0 14 ♘g3 ♕g5+ 15 ♔b1 +=; 11...
♗xe4?? 12 ♘xd6+ +− **11 ♕d3 ♖b8!?**
11...♖g8 12 0-0 ♖g5 △ ♖xf5∞; 11...
d5 12 exd5 cxd5 13 0-0 e6 14 ♖fe1
+=; 11...♗xf5?! 12 exf5 +=/± **12**
0-0 += ♖g8 12...♖xb2? 13 ♖ab1 ♖xb1
14 ♖xb1± **13 b4! ♕c7 14 ♖fd1 ♖xb4**

15 ℤab1 ℤxb1 16 ℤxb1 += ♗c8 16...
e6? 17 ♕xa6! exf5 18 ♕a8+ ♔e7 19
exf5 ℤg5 20 ℤe1+ ♗e6 21 fxe6 △ ℤb1
+−; 19...d5 20 ℤe1+ ♔d6 21 ♕a3+
c5 22 ♕a6+ ♗c6 23 ♘b5+ +−; 20...
♕e5 21 ℤxe5+ fxe5 22 a4 +−; 18...
♗c8 19 ℤb8 ♔d8 20 ♘a4 △ ♘b6 +−
17 ♕c4 e6 18 ♘d4 ℤg5 19 ♘b3
19 ♕xc6+? ♕xc6 20 ♘xc6 ℤc5 −+
f5?! 19...♗e7 20 f4 ℤg4 21 exf5 ♗g7

22 ♘d5! ℤxg2+?! 22...exd5? 23
♕e2+ +−; 22...♕a7+ 23 ♔h1 ♗d7 24
♕e2 ℤh4 25 ♕e1 ℤh5 26 ♘e3 △ ♗a5,
ℤb7±; 22...♕b7 23 ♕e2 ℤh4 24
♕e1 ℤh5 25 ♘a5 ♕a7+ 26 ♘b6 ℤxf5
27 ♔h1±; 24 ♕xa6? ♕xa6 25 ♘c7+
♔e7 26 ♘xa6 ℤxf4 ∓/−+ **23 ♔xg2
exd5 24 ℤe1+ ♔f8 25 ♕e2 +− ♕d8
26 ♘a5 ♗d7** 26...c5?! 27 ♘c6 ♕d7
28 ♘b8 ♕d8 29 ♘xa6 +−; 26...♕d7?
27 ♘xc6! ♕xc6 28 ♕e7+ ♔g8 29
♕d8+ ♗f8 30 ℤe8 +− **27 ♕xa6 ♗c3
28 ♘b7 ♕f6** 28...♕h4 29 ℤe3 ♗xf4
30 ♕a8+ ♔g7 31 ℤg3+ +− **29 ℤe3
♗xf5 30 ♕xc6 ♗d2** 30...♗e4+ 31
ℤxe4! +− **31 ℤe8+ ♔g7 32 ♕xd6
♗e4+ 33 ℤxe4! ♕xd6 34 ♘xd6 dxe4
35 ♔g3 e3 36 ♘f5+ ♔f6 37 ♘d4 ♔e7
38 ♔f3 ♔d6 39 ♘f5+ ♔d5 40 ♘xe3+
♔d4 41 ♘f5+ ♔c3 42 ♘d6 ♔xc2 43
♘xf6 ♔b2 44 ♘g5 h6 45 ♘h7 1-0
Ciamarra/A.Smith**

261 Tarjan-Mednis Riga 79
1 e4 c5 2 ♘f3 ♘c6 3 d4 cxd4 4 ♘xd4
♘f6 5 ♘c3 d6 6 ♗g5 e6 7 ♕d2 a6 8
0-0-0 ♗d7 9 f3 ♗e7 10 ♗e3 0-0 10...
b5 Shamkovich-Peters, USA Final 77
**11 g4 ♘xd4 12 ♗xd4 ♗c6 13 g5
♘h5?!** 13...♘d7 += **14 ♗e3** 14 f4??
♘xf4! **♕c7?!** 14...b5! **15 ♖h3! b5 16
♗g4 g6 17 ♗xh5 gxh5 18 ℤhg1± b4**
18...ℤfc8!? **19 ♘e2 d5 20 e5!!** 20
♘f4? dxe4 21 ♘xh5 ℤfd8∞ **ℤfc8?**
20...d4! 21 ♘xd4 ♗d5± △ a5, a4
21 ♘d4! 21 f4?! d4! 22 ♘xd4 ♗e4 +=
♕xe5 22 f4 ♕e4 23 f5! +− e5 23...
exf5 24 ℤde1 ♗d6 25 g6! hxg6 26
♗g5 **24 ℤde1 exd4 25 ♗xd4 ♕xf5
26 ℤxe7 ♘b5** 26...♘a4 27 b3 ℤxc2+
28 ♕xc2 ℤc8 29 ♕xc8+ ♕xc8+ 30
♔b2 +− **27 g6!! hxg6 28 ℤe5 ♕f3**
28...♕d3 29 ℤe8+! ♔h7 30 ℤh8+
29 ♕h6 △ ℤe8+ **♗xc2+ 30 ♔b1**
30 ♔xc2?? ♕d3+ 31 ♔c1 ℤc8+ 32
♗c3 ℤxc3+! −+ **ℤc1+ 31 ♔xc1 ℤc8+
32 ♔b1 ♕d3+ 33 ♔a1 ♕xd4 34
ℤxg6+! fxg6 35 ♕xg6+ ♔f8 36 ♕f6+
♔g8 37 ℤg5+ ♔h7 38 ℤxh5+ 1-0
Mednis**

262 Gufeld-Filipenko USSR 79
1 e4 c5 2 ♘f3 ♘c6 3 d4 cxd4 4 ♘xd4
♘f6 5 ♘c3 d6 6 ♗g5 e6 7 ♕d2 a6
7...♕b6 8 ♗xf6 gxf6 9 ♘b3 += **8 0-0-0
♗d7** 8...h6 9 ♗e3 ♗d7 10 f4 b5 11
♗xb5!? **9 f4** 9 f3!? ♗e7 10 h4 ♕c7
11 g4 += **b5 10 ♘xc6** 10 ♗xf6 gxf6
11 ♔b1!? +=; 10 e5!? dxe5 11 fxe5
♘xe5 12 ♕e1! += **♗xc6 11 ♗d3** 11
♕e3 ♗e7 12 ♗xf6 ♗xf6!= Gufeld-
Ermenkov, Jurmala 78 **♗e7 12 ℤde1?!**
12 e5 dxe5 13 fxe5 ♘d7 14 ♗xe7
♕xe7 15 ♗e4!?∞ Kasparov-Panchenko,
USSR 78; 12 ℤhe1 0-0 13 e5 dxe5
14 ♕f2 h6 15 ♗xb5∞ **0-0 13 h3?!
b4 14 ♘d1 a5 15 ♘f2 ♘d7 16 ♗xe7**

♕xe7 =+ 17 ♗e2 a4?! 17...♘c5 =+ 18 ♕xb4! a3 19 b3 ♕h4 19...♕f6 20 ♕xd6 ♕b2+ 21 ♔d2 Δ ♘d3 20 ♘d3 ♘c5! 21 e5!= 21 ♘xc5? ♕xf4+ 22 ♕d2 ♕e5∓ ♘xd3+ 22 ♗xd3 dxe5 23 ♖xe5 ♗xg2 24 ♖g1! ♕f2 25 ♖ge1 ♖fb8 25...♗xh3!? 26 ♕d2 ♕xd2+ 27 ♔xd2 ♗xh3 28 c4! ∝/+= g6 29 ♔c3 ♕f8?! 30 b4 ♗g2 31 b5 ♔e7 32 ♔b4± ♖d8 33 ♗e4 ♗xe4 34 ♖5x e4± Zeitnot h5 35 b6 h4 36 c5 ♖d2 37 ♖4e2 ♖b2+ 38 ♖xb2 axb2 39 ♖b1! +− ♔d7 40 ♖xb2 ♔c6 41 ♖d2 1-0 Gufeld

263 Timman-Torre Rio 79
1 e4 c5 2 ♘f3 ♘c6 3 d4 cxd4 4 ♘xd4 ♘f6 5 ♘c3 d6 6 ♗g5 e6 7 ♕d2 a6 8 0-0-0 ♗d7 9 f4 b5 10 ♗xf6 gxf6 11 ♔b1 ♕b6 12 ♘ce2 0-0-0 12...♘xd4 13 ♘xd4 Δ g3, ♗h3 13 g3 h5 14 ♗g2 14 ♗h3 h4 15 f5 ♖e8 ♔b8 15 ♖hf1 ♘e7? 15...♗e7 += 16 ♘b3 ♗c6 17 ♘ed4 ♗a8 18 ♕e2 d5? 19 e5 f5 19... ♗g7!? 20 ♘f3± 20 ♘f3± ♗h6 21 ♘bd4 ♘g6 22 h4 ♖c8 23 ♕e3 ♕a7 23...♖c7? 24 ♘xf5 +− 24 ♖d3 ♕d7 25 ♖fd1 ♖c7 26 ♗f1 ♖f8 27 ♘g5 ♗c5 28 ♗e2 ♗b7 29 ♕d2 ♗b6 30 ♖c1! ♕e7 31 ♕d1! +− ♖c4?! 32 ♖d2 ♖a4 33 c3 ♖c8 34 b3 ♖a5 35 b4 ♖a4 36 ♕b3 ♗c6 37 a3 ♗e8 38 ♗xh5 ♘f8 39 ♕b2 a5 40 ♗e2 axb4 41 cxb4 ♖xc1+ 42 ♕xc1 ♕a7

Diagram

43 ♕c6! ♗d7 44 ♕d6+ ♔b7 45 ♗xb5 ♖xa3 46 ♗c6+ ♗xc6 47 ♕xc6+ ♔b8 48 ♕e8+ ♔b7 49 ♕xf7+ ♗c7 50 ♕xc7+ ♔xc7 51 ♘b5+ ♔d7 52 ♘xa7 ♖xa7 53 ♖a2 ♖b7 54 ♖c2 ♔e7 55 h5 ♖xb4+ 1-0 56 ♖b2 ♖c4 57 ♖b7+ ♔e8 58 h6 +−; 56...♖d4? 57 ♖b7+

♔e8 58 ♖b8+ ♔e7 59 ♖xf8 +−; 56... ♖xb2+ 57 ♔xb2 +− Miles

264 Prandstetter-Ivanovic
Naleczow 79
1 e4 c5 2 ♘f3 ♘c6 3 d4 cxd4 4 ♘xd4 ♘f6 5 ♘c3 d6 6 ♗g5 e6 7 ♕d2 a6 8 0-0-0 h6 9 ♗f4 9 ♗e3 ♗d7 10 ♘xc6 ♗xc6 11 ♕e3 11 ♕e1 ♗e7! 12 e5 ♘h5 13 ♗e3 ♕c7 14 ♗e2 g6∝ e5!? 12 ♗g3 ♗e7 13 ♗e2 ♕c7 14 ♔b1 0-0?! 14...♖ac8! 15 f4 ♖ac8 16 ♖hf1 b5 17 fxe5 dxe5 18 ♖f5 ♕b7! 18...♘d7= 19 ♖xe5 b4 20 ♘d5 ♗xd5 21 exd5 ♗d6 22 ♖f5 ♖fe8 23 ♕f3 ♘e4∝ 24 ♗xd6 ♘c3+?! 24...♘xd6 25 ♖f4 a5 25 ♔a1 ♘xd1 26 ♗xd1 ♖e1 27 ♖e5 ♖xc2 28 ♖e8+! ♖xe8 29 ♗xc2 ♖e1+? 29...♖d8= 30 ♗b1 ♕b5 31 ♗g3 ♖f1 32 ♕e4 g6 33 ♗e1! a5 34 d6 ♕d7? 34...♔h7 35 ♗g3 a4 36 ♕e7 ♕e6 36...♕g4 37 ♗e1 +− 37 ♕xe6 fxe6 38 b3 a3? 38...axb3= 39 d7 ♖d1 40 ♗e1 +− e5 41 ♗xb4 e4 42 ♗a5 ♖xd7 43 ♗xe4 ♖d1+ 44 ♗b1 ♖g1 45 g3 ♖g2 46 ♗b4 ♖xh2 47 ♗xa3 ♔f7 48 ♗b2 ♖g2 49 a4 1-0 Ivanovic

265 Perenyi-Bielczyk Zamardi 79
1 e4 c5 2 ♘f3 ♘c6 3 d4 cxd4 4 ♘xd4 ♘f6 5 ♘c3 d6 6 ♗g5 e6 7 ♕d2 a6 8 0-0-0 h6 9 ♗f4 ♗d7 10 ♘xc6 ♗xc6

**11 f3 d5 12 ♕e1 ♗b4 13 a3 ♗a5
14 ♗d2!?** N ♕e7 14...0-0 15 exd5
♘xd5 16 ♘xd5 ♗xd2+ 17 ♖xd2 ♗xd5
18 ♗c4 +=; 15...exd5 16 ♗d3±; 14...
d4? 15 ♘e2 ♗xd2+ 16 ♖xd2 e5 17
♕g3± **15 ♔b1 ♗c7** 15...dxe4 16 fxe4
0-0 17 e5?! ♘d7 △ ♗c7; 17 ♗d3 ♗c7
18 g4!; 16...0-0-0 17 ♘d5! **16 exd5
♘xd5** 16...exd5 17 ♗d3± **17 ♘xd5
exd5** 17...♗xd5 18 ♗c3!± **18 ♗c4 ♗e5**
18...dxc4 19 ♗b4 ♕e6 20 ♕f2 ♖d8
21 ♖de1 ♗e5 22 f4±; 22 ♖xe5; 18...
♕e6!? **19 ♗b4 ♕e6 20 f4! 0-0-0** 20...
♗xf4 21 ♗xd5 ♗xd5 22 ♖xd5± **21
♗xa6 ♗xf4 22 ♗d3 ♖he8?** 22...♕xe1±
**23 ♕f1! ♕f6 24 ♕f2 ♗e5 25 ♕a7
♗b8 26 ♕a8 g6 27 ♖hf1 ♕e6 28
♗a5 ♖d6** 28...♖d7 29 ♖de1 +− **29
♗b6 ♖d7 30 ♗f2 +− b6 31 ♕a6+
♗b7 32 ♕b5 ♕c6 33 ♗xb6 ♖e6 34
♗g1 ♗e5 35 ♕xc6+ ♗xc6 36 c3 ♔c7
37 ♖de1 ♔d6 38 g3 f5 39 ♗e3 ♗g7?**
Zeitnot **1-0** 40 ♗c5+ **Adorjan**

6 g3

266 Filipenko-Anikaev USSR 79
**1 e4 c5 2 ♘f3 ♘c6 3 d4 cxd4 4 ♘xd4
♘f6 5 ♘c3 d6 6 g3 ♗g4** 6...e5! **7 f3
♗d7 8 ♗e3 e6 9 ♕d2 a6 10 g4 h6?!**
10...♗e7∞ **11 h4 b5 12 0-0-0!** +=
b4 13 ♘ce2 d5?! 14 ♘xc6 ♗xc6 15
e5 ♘d7 16 ♘d4 ♗b7 17 f4± ♕a5?!
17...♘c5 **18 ♔b1 ♘c5 19 ♗g2 0-0-0
20 ♘b3! ♘xb3** 20...♕b6 21 ♘xc5
♗xc5 22 ♗xc5 ♕xc5 23 ♖h3± **21
cxb3! ♔d7 22 ♕d4** △ ♕a7 ♖a8 **23
f5± ♗e7 24 g5 hxg5 25 fxe6+ fxe6
26 ♕g4!** △ ♗h3 ♖ae8 26...♖xh4 27
♖xh4 gxh4 28 ♗h3 +− **27 ♗xd5!
♗xd5 28 ♖xd5+ ♕xd5 29 ♖d1** +−
♕xd1+ 29...♔c6!? **30 ♕xd1+ ♔c6
31 ♕g4! hxg4 32 ♕xe6+ ♔b7 33 ♕b6+
♔c8 34 ♕xa6+ ♔b8 35 ♕b6+ ♔c8**

36 e6 ♖hf8 37 ♕a6+ 37 ♗f4! ♖xf4
38 ♕c6+ +− ♔b8 38 ♕b5+ 1-0 Gufeld

Scheveningen

267 Rohde-Gheorghiu USA 79
**1 e4 c5 2 ♘f3 e6 3 d4 cxd4 4 ♘xd4
a6 5 ♗d3 ♘f6 6 0-0 d6 7 ♘c3 ♗e7
8 f4 ♘bd7! 9 ♔h1 0-0 10 ♕f3 ♘c5!=
11 ♕g3 ♘xd3 12 cxd3 ♘d7! 13 ♗e3**
13 f5 ♗f6! 14 ♕xd6? ♗e5! 15 ♕b4
a5! 16 ♕c4 ♘b6 −+; 14 fxe6 ♗xd4
15 exd7∞ ♗h4! 13...♗f6 14 ♘f3! +=
14 ♕h3 ♗f6 15 ♖ac1 ♘c5!∓ 16 e5!?
16 ♗g1? ♗xd4! 17 ♗xd4 e5 −+;
16 ♖fd1 ♗xd4 −+ **dxe5 17 ♘c6!
bxc6 18 ♗xc5 ♖e8!** 18...exf4? 19
♗xf8 ♕xf8 20 ♕f3± **19 fxe5** 19 ♘e4
exf4∓ ♗xe5 20 **♖xf7!?** 20 ♕h5 f5∓;
20...f6 **♕xf7 21 ♕h5+** 21 ♕xh7
♗xc3∓ ♕g8 22 ♕xe5 ♕f6! 22...♕xd3
23 ♘e4 **23 ♕c7 e5 24 ♘e4 ♕d8! 25
♕xc6 ♗d7 26 ♕d5+ ♗e6 27 ♕xe5
♗d5?!** 27...♗xa2! 28 ♕g3 ♖e6! △ ♖g6
−+ **28 ♕f4! ♗xe4 29 dxe4 ♖c8 30
b4 ♕f6! 31 ♕g4? ♕e6! 32 ♕xe6+
♖xe6 33 h3 ♖xe4 34 ♖d1 ♖e2 35
♖d7 ♖xa2 36 ♗d4 g6! −+ 37 ♖g7+
♔f8 38 ♖xh7 ♖cc2 39 ♖a7! ♖xg2
40 ♖xa6 ♖h2+** 40...♖xa6? 41 ♔xg2=
**41 ♔g1 ♖ag2+ 42 ♔f1 ♖c2 43 ♔g1
♖hd2! 44 ♗c5+ ♔f7 45 ♖a1 ♖g2+
46 ♔f1 ♖h2 47 ♖b1 ♖xh3 48 ♗b6
g5 49 ♔g1 ♖hc3! 50 ♗d4 ♖c1+ 51
♖xc1 ♖xc1+ 52 ♔g2 ♖b1 53 ♗c5
♖b3! −+ 54 ♔f2 ♔e6 55 ♔e2 ♔e5
56 ♔f2 ♔f4 57 ♗d6+ ♔g4 58 ♔e2
♔h3! 59 ♔d2 g4 60 ♔c2 ♖f3 61
b5 ♖f5! 62 b6 ♖b5 63 ♗c7 g3 −+
0-1 Gheorghiu**

268 Kasparov-Polugaevsky USSR 79
**1 e4 c5 2 ♘f3 d6 3 d4 cxd4 4 ♘xd4
♘f6 5 ♘c3 e6 6 ♗e3 a6 7 g4 ♘c6 8**

g5 ♘d7 9 ♖g1 ♗e7 10 h4 0-0 11 h5!?
N ♘de5 12 ♘xc6?! 12 f4 ♘xc6?!
12...bxc6! **13 f4 b5 14 ♕f3?!** 14 ♗d3!
♗b7 15 ♕g4 +=; 14...b4 15 ♘e2 +=
♗b7 15 ♗d3 ♘b4! 15...b4?! 16 ♘d5!
exd5 17 exd5 ♘a7 18 ♕e4 g6 19 hxg6
hxg6 20 0-0-0± **16 f5! exf5** 16...
♘xd3+ 17 cxd3 b4 18 h6! g6! 19 f6
bxc3 20 fxe7 ♕xe7 21 bxc3 d5?
22 ♗c5! ♕xc5 23 ♕f6 +–; 21...♖fc8∞
17 ♕xf5 ♘xd3+ 17...d5? 18 exd5
♘xd3+ 19 ♕xd3 b4 20 ♘e4 ♕xd5
21 ♘f6+± **18 cxd3 ♕c8! 19 h6!**
19 ♕xc8 ♖axc8 20 ♔d2 f5 =+ ♖e8!
19...g6 20 ♘d5! **20 hxg7** 20 ♕f4 g6
=+ ♕xf5 20...d5 21 ♕f4!∞ **21 exf5**
♗xg5 22 ♖xg5 ♖xe3+ 23 ♔d2 ♖f3
24 ♘e4 ♗xe4 25 dxe4 ♖e8?! 26 ♖c1
d5?! Zeitnot 26...f6 27 ♖h5 ♖e7 28
♖c6= **27 e5! h6 28 ♖h5 ♖xe5?** 28...
♔xg7 29 ♖g1+ ♔h7 30 f6 ♖g8 31
♖xh6+ +=

29 f6! +– ♖f2+ 30 ♔d3 ♖f3+ 31
♔d4 ♖e4+ 32 ♔xd5 ♖e8 33 ♖xh6
♖f5+ 34 ♔d4 ♖f4+ 35 ♔c5 ♖e5+
36 ♔b6 ♖e6+ 37 ♖c6 1-0 Kasparov

269 Velimirovic-Hubner Rio 79
1 e4 c5 2 ♘f3 d6 3 d4 cxd4 4 ♘xd4
♘f6 5 ♘c3 e6 6 ♗e3 ♗e7 7 g4 h6
8 ♖g1 a6 9 ♕f3!? ♕c7 10 h4 ♘fd7
11 g5 ♘e5 12 ♕g3 hxg5 13 ♗xg5

13 hxg5 += ♗xg5 **14 hxg5** 14 ♕xg5!?
♕e7!∞; 14...g6 15 ♕f6 ♖h7 16 f4
♘fd7 17 ♘xe6! **♘bc6 15 ♘b3 ♗d7**
16 0-0-0 0-0-0 17 f4 ♘g6 18 ♗e2
♘ce7 Δ d5! **19 ♖d4?! ♘xf4 20 ♕xf4**
e5 21 ♕xf7 exd4 22 ♘xd4 ♘c6 23
♘f5 23 ♘d5 ♘xd4! **♗xf5 24 ♕xc7+**
♔xc7 25 ♘d5+ ♔d7 26 exf5 ♘e5
27 g6 ♖h2 28 ♗f1 ♖e8 29 ♗g2 ♘c4
Δ ♖xg2 **30 c3 ♖e2 31 ♘f4** 31 f6?
♖hxg2 32 ♖xg2 ♖xg2 33 fxg7 ♖xg6
34 g8♕ ♖xg8 35 ♘f6+ ♔e6 36 ♘xg8
♘e5! 37 ♔d2 ♔f7 38 ♘h6+ ♔g6 39
♘g8 ♘c6! Δ ♔g7 –+ **♖hxg2 32 ♘xg2**
32 ♖xg2? ♖e1+ 33 ♔e2 ♘e3+ **♖f2**
33 b3 ♘e5 34 ♘e3 ♘d3+ 35 ♔b1
♖f3 36 ♔c2? 36 ♘d5 ♖xf5 37 c4 =+
♖xe3 37 f6 ♘c5 38 f7 ♗f3? 38...
♘e6 Δ ♔e7, ♘f8 –+ **39 ♖h1! ♖f2+**
40 ♔d1 ♘e6 41 ♖h8 ♖f6 42 ♖e8!=
d5 42...♖xg6 43 ♖xe6! **43 a4 ♔d6 44**
a5 ♔e5 45 c4 dxc4 46 bxc4 ♔f5 47
c5 ♔xg6 48 ♖xe6 ♔xf7 49 ♖b6 ♖c6
50 ♖xb7+ ♔e6 ½-½ Miles

270 Lutikov-Chechelian USSR 79
1 e4 c5 2 ♘f3 e6 3 d4 cxd4 4 ♘xd4
♘c6 5 ♘c3 d6 6 ♗e3 ♘f6 7 f4 ♗e7 8
♕d2?! 8 ♕f3; 8 ♗c4; 8 ♗e2 a6 9 0-0-0
0-0 10 ♗c4? ♕c7 =+ **11 ♗b3 ♘a5**
12 ♕e2 b5 13 a3 ♘xb3 14 ♘xb3 ♗b7
15 ♗d2 15 ♗d4 e5 ♖ac8∓ Δ ♘xe4
16 ♘d4 ♕c4 17 ♕e3 ♖fe8! Δ e5 18
♗e1 e5 –+ **19 fxe5 dxe5 20 ♘f3 ♘xe4**
21 ♖d7 ♗c5 22 ♕d3 ♕xd3 23 ♖xd3
♘xc3 24 ♖xc3 e4 25 ♘d2 f5 26 ♖f1
g6 27 g3 e3 28 ♘b3 e2 0-1 Gufeld

271 Velimirovic-Cvetkovic
Ochrid 79
1 e4 c5 2 ♘f3 e6 3 d4 cxd4 4 ♘xd4
♘f6 5 ♘c3 d6 6 f4 a6 7 ♕f3 ♕b6
8 ♘b3 ♘c6 9 ♗d3 ♗e7 10 ♗e3 ♕c7
11 a4! ♘a5 12 0-0 0-0 13 ♘d2 ♖b8

14 ♔h1 ♞c6 15 ♞c4 b6 15...b5 16 axb5 axb5 17 ♘a3 b4 18 ♘ab5 ♕d8 19 ♘e2± **16 e5!** ♞e8 16...dxe5 17 fxe5 ♘xe5? 18 ♘xe5 △ ♗f4 +– **17 ♕h3 f5** 17...g6 18 ♕h6! △ ♖f3-h3 **18 exf6 ♞xf6 19 f5!** e5 20 ♗g5± ♞b4 **21 ♞e3 ♗b7 22 ♗c4+ ♔h8 23 ♗b3 ♖bd8 24 ♕h4!** a5 25 ♖ae1 ♕c5 25... d5 26 ♘g4 e4 27 ♖e3 ♘xg4 28 ♖h3 ♘h6 29 ♗xe7 +–; 26...d4 27 ♘xe5! **26 ♞g4 ♕d4?! 27 ♞b5 ♕c5 28 ♖e3! ♕c6** 28...♘xg4 29 ♖h3 +– **29 ♖g3 ♖de8 30 ♞xf6 gxf6**

30 ♕xh7+! 1-0 30...♔xh7 31 ♖h3+ ♔g7 32 ♗h6+ ♔h8 33 ♗xf8 mate
Maric

272 Sideifzade-Panchenko
USSR 79

1 e4 c5 2 ♞f3 e6 3 d4 cxd4 4 ♞xd4 ♞f6 5 ♞c3 d6 6 f4 a6 6...♗e7 7 ♗e3 0-0 8 ♕f3 e5 9 ♘f5∞ **7 ♕f3** 7 ♘f3 ♕c7 8 ♗d3 ♘c6 9 0-0 ♗e7 10 ♔h1 b5 11 a3∞ **♕b6!? 8 ♞b3 ♕c7 9 g4 9** ♗d3 b5 10 g4! += **b5** 9...♘c6 10 g5 ♘fd7 11 ♗d3 += **10 g5 ♞fd7 11 ♗e3 b4 12 ♞e2 ♗b7 13 0-0-0 ♞c5 14 ♞g3 ♞bd7 15 ♗xc5!?** 15 f5!? ♘e5 16 ♕f4 += **♞xc5 16 f5 exf5** 16...0-0-0 17 fxe6 fxe6 18 ♗h3!± **17 ♕xf5 ♖c8 18 ♖d2 ♕e7?!** 18...♗e7 19 ♗c4 0-0 20 ♗d5 +=; 18...♘e6 19

♘h5!? **19 ♗h3! ♞xb3+?! 20 axb3 ♖c5 21 ♕f2± g6 22 ♕d4 ♕e5 23 ♕xb4 ♖b5 24 ♕a4 ♕c5! 25 ♔b1!** 25 ♗f1? ♗g7 26 ♗xb5+ axb5 27 ♕a5 0-0 ∞/∓ **♕b4 26 ♕xb4 ♖xb4 27 ♗f1 ♗e7 28 ♗c4! ♗xg5 29 ♖xd6 ♗e7 30 ♖d2?** 30 ♖dd1 f5 31 ♖hf1 +– f5 31 ♖f1 f4 32 ♞e2 g5 += **33 ♞d4 ♖b6 34 ♞e6** Zeitnot **♗c8** Zeitnot **35 ♞g7+ ♔f8 36 ♞f5 ♖f6 37 ♗d3 a5 38 ♖g2 ♗xf5 39 exf5 ♖g8 40 ♗e4 ♗d6 41 h3 ♖g7!= 42 ♖d1 ♖e7 43 ♖e2 ♖e5 44 c3 ♔e7 45 ♖d5 ♖h6 46 ♗d3 ♖xe2 47 ♗xe2 ♗c7 48 ♗b5 ♔f6 49 ♖d7 ♗e5 50 ♗c4 ♔xf5 51 ♗d3+ ½-½ Gufeld**

273 Hardicsay-Jankovec
Prievidza 79

1 e4 c5 2 ♞f3 d6 3 d4 cxd4 4 ♞xd4 ♞f6 5 ♞c3 a6 6 ♗e2 e6 7 f4 ♕c7 8 ♗f3 ♞c6 9 ♗e3 ♗d7 9...♘a5?! 10 ♕d3 ♘c4 11 0-0-0 += **10 ♞b3 ♞a5? 10**... b5?! 11 ♕e2 △ ♘d5, g4-g5 +–; 10... ♗e7 **11 ♞xa5 ♕xa5 12 0-0 ♗c6 13 ♕e1! +–** ♗e7 **14 ♖d1** 14 ♕g3!? 0-0 15 e5! ♘e8 16 ♗xc6 +– **♖c8 15 ♕g3 0-0 16 ♔h1 ♞d7** 16...♖fd8! 17 ♗d4 +– **17 e5! +–** ♗xf3 17...dxe5? 18 ♗xc6 ♖xc6 19 ♖xd7 +–; 17...d5 18 f5 +– **18 ♖xf3 ♖fd8 19 exd6 ♗f6 20 f5! ♗xc3** 20...exf5 21 ♘d5! +– **21 bxc3 exf5 22 ♗d4 g6 23 ♖df1 ♕xa2 24 ♖xf5 f6 25 h4 ♕xc2 26 h5 ♔f7** 26...g5 27 ♖xg5+ +– **27 hxg6+ hxg6 28 ♖xf6+! 1-0 Hardicsay**

274 Bouaziz-Ribli Riga 79

1 e4 c5 2 ♞f3 d6 3 d4 cxd4 4 ♞xd4 ♞f6 5 ♞c3 a6 6 ♗e2 e6 7 0-0 ♗e7 8 f4 0-0 9 ♔h1 ♕c7 10 a4 ♞c6 11 ♞b3!? 11 ♗e3 ♗d7 12 ♘b3 += **b6 12 ♗f3 ♗b7 13 ♕e1 ♖ac8 14 ♗e3 ♖fe8 15 ♖c1 ♞d7 16 g4 ♞a5! 17 ♞xa5 bxa5**

18 ♗d2 ♘c5 19 b3 ♕b8 20 ♕e2 ♕a8! 21 g5

21...d5!∓ 22 exd5 exd5 23 ♕g2 ♘e4! 24 ♘b1 ♘xd2 25 ♕xd2 ♗b4 26 c3 d4! 27 cxb4 ♗xf3+ 28 ♔g1 ♖e2 29 ♖xf3 ♖xd2 30 ♖xc8+ ♕xc8 31 ♘xd2 ♕c1+ 32 ♘f1 axb4 −+ 33 ♔g2 ♕c2+ 34 ♔g3 ♔f8 0-1 Gheorghiu

275 Tseshkovsky-Polugaevsky Riga 79

1 e4 c5 2 ♘f3 d6 3 d4 cxd4 4 ♘xd4 ♘f6 5 ♘c3 a6 6 ♗e2 e6 7 f4 ♗e7 8 0-0 0-0 9 ♔h1 ♘c6 10 ♗f3 ♕c7 11 a4 ♖e8 11...♖d8!∞ 12 g4 ♘xd4 13 ♕xd4 ♘d7 14 g5 b6 15 ♕f2 ♗b7 16 ♗g2 ♗f8 17 ♗e3 ♗c6 18 f5! exf5 19 exf5 ♘e5 20 ♗d4± ♖ac8 21 ♖ad1 ♕b7 22 ♗xc6 ♕xc6+ 23 ♕g2 ♕xg2+ 24 ♔xg2 ♘c4

25 ♘d5!± ♖e2+ 26 ♖f2 ♖xf2+ 27 ♔xf2 ♘xb2 28 ♗xb2 ♖xc2+ 29 ♔e3 ♖xb2 30 ♖c1!!± △ ♖c8 +− ♖b3+ 31 ♔e2 ♖b2+ 32 ♔e1 f6 33 g6! ♖a2 34 ♖c8 ♖a1+ 35 ♔d2 ♖a2+ 36 ♔d3 ♖a3+ 37 ♔c2 ♖a2+ 38 ♔c3 hxg6 39 ♘e7+! ♔h7 39...♔f7 40 ♘xg6 +− 40 fxg6+ ♔h6 41 ♖xf8 ♖e2 42 ♖h8+ ♔g5 43 h4+ ♔g4 44 ♘d5 ♖h2 45 ♖h7! +− ♖h3+ 46 ♔d4 ♔f5 47 ♖h5+ ♔g4 48 ♖h7 ♔f5 49 ♘e7+ ♔e6 50 ♖xg7 ♖xh4+ 51 ♔e3 1-0 Gheorghiu

276 Urzica-Suba Rumania 79

1 e4 c5 2 ♘f3 d6 3 d4 ♘f6 4 ♘c3 cxd4 5 ♘xd4 e6 6 ♗e2 ♗e7 7 0-0 a6 7...♘c6 8 f4 ♕c7 9 ♕e1 0-0 10 ♔h1 b5?! 10...♘c6 11 ♗f3 ♗b7 12 e5!± ♘e8 13 ♕g3 ♘d7 14 a3 ♔h8 15 ♗e3 ♘b6 16 ♗xb7 ♕xb7 17 ♖ae1 ♖d8 18 f5! dxe5 19 ♕xe5 ♘c4 20 ♕g3 e5 21 ♘f3 ♘xb2 21...f6 22 ♘h4! △ ♘g6+ 22 ♘xe5 ♘f6 23 ♗g5 ♖c8 24 ♘g4! ♖c4 25 ♖xe7! ♕xe7 26 ♘xf6 h6 26... gxf6 27 ♘d5! 27 ♘cd5 ♕e2 28 ♖e1 ♕xc2 29 ♗xh6 gxh6 30 ♘h5 1-0 30...♖g8 31 ♕e5+ Vaisman

277 Panchenko-Klovsky USSR 79

1 e4 c5 2 ♘f3 e6 3 d4 cxd4 4 ♘xd4 ♘f6 5 ♘c3 d6 6 ♗e2 ♗e7 7 0-0 0-0 7...♘c6 8 ♗e3 a6 9 f4 ♗d7 10 ♕e1 += 8 f4 ♘c6 9 ♔h1 9 ♗e3 e5!? 10 ♘b3 exf4 11 ♗xf4 ♘d7!= a6 10 ♗e3 ♕c7 11 ♕e1 ♘xd4 12 ♗xd4 b5 13 a3 13 ♕g3!? ♗b7 14 ♕g3 g6 14...♖fd8!? 15 f5 e5 16 ♗e3 ♔h8!? 17 ♗g5?! 17 ♗d3!? += ♘xe4 18 ♘xe4 ♗xe4 19 f6 ♗d8 20 ♕h4 ♕c6 21 ♗f3 ♗xf3 22 ♖xf3 h5! 23 ♗h6 23 ♖af1 ♕c4 ♖g8 24 ♕g5 △ ♗f8! ♔h7 25 ♖af1 ♕xc2 26 ♕e3 ♕c5 27 ♕d2 e4!∓ 28 ♗e3 ♕c4 29 ♖f4 ♖c8 30 g4 ♕d3 31 gxh5 ♕xd2 32 ♗xd2 d5 33 ♗c3 ♗b6

−+ **34 Rd1 gxh5! 35 h3 d4 36 Bxd4 Bxd4 37 Rxd4 Rc1+ 38 Kh2 Rc2+ 39 Kh1 e3 40 Rd1 Rgg2 0-1 Gufeld**

278 Telesijevic-Honfi Trstenik 79
1 e4 c5 2 Nf3 e6 3 d4 cxd4 4 Nxd4 a6 5 Be2 Nf6 6 Nc3 d6 7 0-0 Be7 8 Kh1 Nc6 9 f4 Qc7 10 Bf3 Bd7 10... 0-0 11 Nxc6 bxc6 12 e5!? **11 Be3 0-0 12 Qe1 Rac8 13 Rd1 b5 14 a3 Na5 15 Qg3?!** 15 Rd3!? Nc4 16 Bc1 **Nc4 16 Bc1 Nxa3 17 e5 Ne8 18 Ne4** 18 Nf5? exf5 19 Nd5 Qd8 20 Nxe7+ Qxe7 21 bxa3 Rxc2 −+ **Nc4! 19 b3 dxe5 20 fxe5 Nxe5 21 Bf4 f6 22 Bh5** Δ Nf3

22...Qb7! 23 Bh6 Nf7! −+ 24 Nxf6+ Bxf6 25 Rxf6 Nxh6 26 Rxh6 Nf6! 27 Bf3 Qc7 28 Qg5 e5 29 Ne2 Qxc2 30 Ng1 Qxd1!! 31 Rxh7 31 Bxd1 Ne4 32 Qe3 Nf2+ −+ **Nxh7 32 Qxe5 Rxf3 0-1 Honfi**

279 Ivanovic-Moisejev
Naleczow 79
1 e4 c5 2 Nf3 e6 3 d4 cxd4 4 Nxd4 Nc6 5 Nc3 Qc7 6 Be2 a6 7 0-0 d6 8 Be3 Nf6 9 f4 Be7 10 Kh1 0-0 11 Qe1 Bd7 12 Qg3 Qh8 13 Rad1 Rac8 14 a3 b5 15 Bd3 Nxd4 16 Bxd4 Ne8 16...Nh5? 17 Qe1! **17 e5 dxe5 17...** f5!? **18 Bxe5 Bd6 19 Bxh7! Kxh7**

19...Bxe5 20 Rxd7! Qxd7 21 Qh3 Nf6 22 Bd3+ Kg8 23 fxe5 **20 Rxd6 Qc4 21 Rfd1 Bc6 22 R6d4 Qc5 23** f5 f6 24 fxe6! fxe5 25 Rh4+ Kg8 26 **Qh3 Bxg2+ 27 Kxg2 Qf2+ 28 Kh1 Qf3+ 29 Qxf3 Rxf3 30 Nd5! +−** g5 **31 Rg1 Rf5 32 Rh5 Kf8 33 h4 e4 34 Rhxg5 Rxg5 35 Rxg5 Rxc2 36 h5 e3 37 Nxe3 Rxb2 38 Rf5+ Kg7 39 Rf7+ Kh6 40 Rf8 Nd6 41 e7 Re2 42 Nd5 Kg5 43 Rd8 1-0 Ivanovic**

Dragon

280 Nikolic-Kovacs
Reggio Emilia 78/79
1 e4 c5 2 Nf3 d6 3 Nc3 Nf6 4 d4 cxd4 5 Nxd4 g6 6 Be2 Bg7 7 Be3 Nc6 8 h3 0-0 9 Qd2 Bd7 10 Nb3 Rc8 11 0-0 a6 12 f4 Be6 13 Rad1 Qc7 14 Bf3 b5? 15 Nd5! Bxd5? 15...Qb7? 16 Nxf6+ Bxf6 17 e5! dxe5 18 Na5 +−; 15...Qb8 **16 exd5 Nb8 17 Nd4 Rfe8 18 Qf2 b4 19 Rd3 Nfd7 20 Rd2 Qa5 21 Ra1 Nc5 22 a3 bxa3 23 Rxa3 Qb6 24 c3** Δ b4, Ne6 **Qb7 25 b4 Ncd7 26 Nc6 += Nf6 27 Bd4 Nfd7 28 Re2 Bxd4 29 Qxd4 Nf6**

30 Ra1! Zugzwang Δ 31 b5! axb5 32 Ra7 Nxc6 33 dxc6 Qb8 34 Rexe7 Rxe7 35 Rxe7 Nh5 36 Bd5 Rf8 37

g4 ♘g7 38 c7! ♔c8 39 ♕f6 +−; 35...
♔g7 36 ♗d5 ♖f8 37 c7! ♔c8 38 ♗e6
+−; 31...♕xb5 32 ♘a7 ♕c7 30...h6
31 g4 **31 ♘xb8 ♖xb8 32 ♖xa6 ♖b7
33 g4 ♖eb8 34 ♖ea2 ♘d7 35 ♖c6
♕d8 36 g5 ♘b6 37 c4 ♘d7 38 b5 ♘c5
39 ♗g4! ♕f8** 39...♖a8?? 40 ♖xa8
♕xa8 41 ♖xc8+ +− **40 h4 h5 41 ♗h3
♖e8 42 f5 ♔h7 43 ♖f2! +− ♕g7 44
fxg6+ fxg6 45 ♕xg7+ ♔xg7 46 ♗e6
♘xe6** 46...♖f8 47 ♖xf8 ♔xf8 48 ♗c8!
♖a7 49 ♗a6 **47 dxe6 ♖a8 48 ♖f7+
♔g8 49 ♖xd6 ♖xb5 50 cxb5 exd6
51 ♖d7 1-0 Paoli**

281 Zaltsman-Chandler USA 79
**1 ♘f3 ♘f6 2 c4 g6 3 ♘c3 ♗g7 4 e4
c5 5 d4 0-0 6 ♗e2 cxd4 7 ♘xd4 d6
8 0-0 a6 9 ♗e3 ♘c6 10 ♕d2 ♘g4 11
♗xg4 ♗xg4 12 ♘d5** 12 f4 +=; 12 f3
**♗d7! 13 ♖ac1 e6 14 ♘c3 ♖c8 15
♘de2 ♘e5 16 b3 b5! 17 cxb5 axb5
18 a3?!** 18 ♕xd6 b4 19 ♕xb4 ♘d3∓
**♕a5 19 ♕xd6 ♗c6 20 ♕b4 ♕xb4
21 axb4 ♘d3 22 ♖cd1 ♖fd8= 23
f3 ♘xb4 24 ♗d4 ♘c2 ½-½ Gheorghiu**

282 Gavrikov-Kimmelfeld USSR 79
**1 ♘f3 c5 2 c4 g6 3 d4 cxd4 4 ♘xd4
♗g7 5 e4 ♘c6 6 ♗e3 d6 7 ♘c3 ♘f6
8 ♗e2 ♘d7 9 ♕d2 ♘c5 10 ♖d1 ♘e6
11 ♘b3 0-0 12 0-0 b6 13 f4 ♗b7 14
♕e1! += Δ e5 ♕e8 15 f5?! ♘c5 16
♘d5 ♘xe4!? 17 ♘c7 ♕c8 18 ♘xa8
♗xa8 19 fxg6 hxg6 20 ♘d2 ♕e6 21
♘xe4 ♕xe4 22 ♗d3 ♕e6 23 b3 ♘e5
24 ♗e2 f5! 25 ♗f4 ♔h7** 25...♔f7!?
Δ ♖h8 **26 ♕d2 ♗f6 27 ♖c1 ♖h8 28
♗g5 ♕g7 29 ♖c3 ♘f7 30 ♗xf6+ ♕xf6
31 ♗f3 ♕h4?!** 31...♗xf3 32 ♖cxf3
♘e5!∞ **32 g3 ♕f6 33 ♗xa8 ♖xa8 34
g4! += ♘g5** 34...e6!? **35 gxf5 exf5 +=
35 gxf5 ♘e4 36 ♕d5 ♕xc3** 36...♘xc3
37 ♕xa8 d5! ∞/+= **37 ♕xe4!± ♖f8**

38 **♕xe7+ ♖f7 39 f6+ ♕xf6! 40
♖xf6 ♖xe7 41 ♖xd6 ♔h6 42 ♖d2
♕g5 43 ♔f2 ♔f4 44 h4! ♖f7! 45
♖d4+ ♕e5 46 ♔e3 ♖f1 47 ♖d7 ♖e1+
47...a5 48 ♖d5+ Δ ♖b5 48 ♔f3 ♖f1+
49 ♔g2 ♖a1 50 ♖xa7 +− ♔f4 51
♖a4! ♔e3 52 ♖a6 ♔f4 53 ♖xb6 ♖xa2+
54 ♔h3 1-0 Gufeld**

283 Ljubojevic-Miles Riga 79
**1 e4 c5 2 ♘f3 d6 3 d4 cxd4 4 ♘xd4
♘f6 5 ♘c3 g6 6 f3 ♗g7 7 ♗e3 0-0 8
♗c4 ♗d7 9 ♕d2 ♘c6 10 h4 ♖c8 11
♗b3 h5 12 0-0-0 ♘e5 13 ♗g5 ♖c5 14
f4 ♘c4 15 ♕d3 b5 16 e5 ♘g4** N
16...dxe5?! 17 ♗xf6 ♗xf6 18 ♘dxb5
Klovan-Gufeld, USSR 78 **17 ♘e4 ♖d5**
17...♖c8!? 18 exd6 f6; 18 ♘xd6 ♘f2
18 ♘xd6! ♘gxe5 18...♘f2 19 ♕f3
♘xd1 20 ♕xd5 ∞/±; 20 ♖xd1!?
19 fxe5 ♘xe5 20 ♗xd5! 20 ♕e4!?
♖xd6 21 ♗f4 ♕a8! 22 ♖he1 ♕xe4
23 ♖xe4 ♗g4 24 ♖d2∞; 20 ♕g3!?
♖xd6 21 ♗f4 ♖xd4! 22 ♖xd4 ♘g4
23 ♖dd1 ♕c8∞ **♘xd3+ 21 ♖xd3 ♕b6**
21...♗xd4 22 ♘xf7! ♖xf7 23 ♗e6
♗xe6 24 ♕xd4 ♖f1 +−; 23 ♖xd4
♗g4 24 ♗xf7+±; 22...♕b6 23 ♘e5+;
22 ♖xd4 ♕b6 **22 ♗xe7! ♗xd4 23
♖f1! ♕c5!**

24 **♗xf8??** 24 ♗b3! ♗xb2+ 25 ♔b1
♕e5 26 ♗xf8 ♗a1 27 ♔c1! ♗b2+ 28

♔d2 +−; 27 c3? ♕e2! −+; 26...♗a3
27 ♗xf7+ ♔xf8 28 ♖xa3 ♕xd6±;
25 ♔d2! ±/+−; 24 ♗xf7+± ♕xd5
25 ♖xf7 ♗f5!∓ 26 ♘xf5 26 ♖g3
♕e5 −+ ♔xf7 27 ♘xd4 ♔xf8 28 g3
♕xa2 29 c3 a5 30 ♘c2 ♕c4 31 ♔d2
♕e4 32 ♘d4 ♔g7 33 ♔c2 a4 34 ♘f3
♕e2+ 35 ♘d2 ♔f6 36 ♖d5 ♔f7 37
♖d4 37 ♖g5! =+ g5! 38 hxg5 ♔g6
39 ♖d5 ♕g2 40 ♖d3 ♔xg5 41 ♖e3
♔g4 −+ 42 ♖e7 42 ♖d3 ♔e2
Zugzwang ♕f2 43 ♖g7+ ♔h3 44 ♔d3
44 ♖g7 ♔g2 45 ♖g8 ♔e2 46 ♖g7
♔f2 46 ♖g5 ♔e1 47 ♖e5!; 46...♔e8!
(Δ ♔e2, ♕e3) 47 ♔d1 ♔e6! Zugzwang
45 ♖b7 ♕f5+ 46 ♔e2 ♕g4+ 47 ♕d3
♕xg3+ 48 ♔c2 ♔e5 49 c4 bxc4 50
♖b4 ♕f5+ 51 ♔c1 h4 52 ♖xc4 ♔g3
53 ♘e4+ ♔g2 54 ♖c2+ ♔g1 55 ♖e2
h3 56 ♔d2 ♕f4+ 57 ♔d3 h2 58 ♖e1+
♔g2 59 ♖e2+ ♔f1 60 ♖e3 h1♕ 0-1
Miles

5 f3

284 Wolf-Quinteros
USA 79
**1 e4 c5 2 ♘f3 d6 3 d4 cxd4 4 ♘xd4
♘f6 5 f3!?** 5 ♘c3 e6 6 c4 ♗e7 7 ♘c3
0-0 8 ♗e2 b6! 9 0-0 ♗b7 10 ♗g5
♘bd7 11 ♕d2 a6 12 ♔h1 ♖c8 =+ 13
♖fd1 ♕c7 14 ♕e3 ♘e5 15 b3 h6!?
16 ♗xh6 gxh6 17 ♕xh6 ♘g6 18
♘xe6 fxe6 19 ♕xg6+ ♔h8 20 ♕h6+
♔h7 21 ♕xe6 ♗f6!∓ 22 ♖ac1 ♗g5
23 ♖c2 ♖f6 24 ♕g4 ♖g8 25 ♘d5
♗xd5 26 ♖xd5 ♗e3! 27 ♕h3 ♖h6
28 ♖h5 ♕g7! −+ Δ ♕a1+/♖xh5
29 g4 ♕a1+ 30 ♕f1 ♕xf1+ 31 ♗xf1
♖xh5 32 ♖e2 32 gxh5 ♖g1 mate
♗d4 0-1 **Gheorghiu**

4 ♕xd4

285 Chase-A.Smith USA 79
**1 e4 c5 2 ♘f3 d6 3 d4 cxd4 4 ♕xd4
♗d7** 4...a6 5 ♗e3 ♘f6 6 ♘c3 ♗g4 7
e5! +=; 5 c4 ♘c6 6 ♕d2 g6 7 ♘c3
♗h6!? **5 c4 ♘c6 6 ♕d2 g6 7 ♘c3 ♘f6**
7...♗h6 8 ♕d1 ♗g7 9 ♗e2 ♗xc3+!?
10 bxc3 ♘f6 ∞/+= **8 b3 ♗g7 9 ♗b2
0-0 10 h3** 10 ♗d3 ♕a5 11 0-0 ♖ac8
Δ ♗g4≈ **♕a5** Δ ♘xe4 **11 ♗d3 ♘h5
12 a3!?** N 12 0-0 ♘f4 13 ♕xf4 ♗xc3=;
12 ♖c1!? **♘f4 13 ♗c2?** 13 b4 ♘xd3+
14 ♕xd3 ♕h5 15 0-0-0 f5∞; 14...♘e5
15 ♘xe5 ♕xe5 16 ♖b1 +=; 13 0-0?!
♗h6∓ **♗h6!** 13...♘xg2+!? 14 ♔f1
♘f4 15 ♕xf4 ♗xc3 16 b4 ♗xb4 17
♕h6 f6 18 axb4 ♕xb4 19 ♘g5! ♖f7!
20 ♘xf7 ♕xb2∓; 19...♕xc4+ 20 ♔g1±;
16...♘xb4? 17 ♗xc3; 15 b4? ♗xb4
16 axb4 ♕xb4 −+ **14 ♔f1 ♕h5 15
♘b5** 15 ♕d1 ♗g4 **♘xg2 16 ♔c3**

16...♘e3+! −+ **17 ♔e2** 17 ♔g1 f6
18 ♗d1 ♘xd1 19 ♖xd1 ♗xh3 ♘e5 **18
♘bd4 ♘xc2 19 ♕xc2 f5! 20 ♖ab1**
fxe4 21 ♕xe4 ♖xf3 22 ♘xf3 ♗c6
0-1 Ciamarra

2...e6, 4...a6

286 Arnold-Honfi
Baden-Baden 79
**1 e4 c5 2 ♘f3 e6 3 ♘c3 a6 4 d4 cxd4
5 ♘xd4 ♕c7 6 g3 ♗b4 7 ♗d2 ♘f6 8**

♗g2 ♞c6 9 ♞b3 0-0 10 0-0 ♗e7 11
f4 d6 12 a4 b6 13 g4 ♖b8 14 g5
♞d7 15 f5?! 15 ♕h5!? ♖e8 16 ♕h5
g6 17 ♕h3 ♞de5! 17...♞c5? 18 fxg6
fxg6 20 ♖f7! +− 18 f6 ♗f8 19 ♖ad1
19 ♖f4? ♞c4 20 ♖h4 e5 −+; 19 ♕g3!?
Δ h4-h5 b5 20 axb5 axb5 21 ♞e2?!
♞c4 22 ♗c1 d5! 23 ♕g3 23 exd5
exd5 24 ♕f3 ♗f5! −+ ♗d6 24 ♕h4
dxe4 25 ♗xe4 ♞6e5 26 ♗f4 ♗b7 27
♗xb7 ♖xb7 28 ♖d4 ♕b6 29 ♞a5
♞xa5 30 ♗xe5 ♗f8 31 ♚g2 ♞c4
31...♞c6!? 32 ♕e4 ♗c5 33 b4 ♗xb4
34 ♖b1 ♞d2 35 ♖xd2 ♗xd2 36 ♗d4
♕c7 37 ♗e5 ♕c8 38 ♕h4 ♕c6+ 39
♚f2 ♕c5+ 40 ♞d4 ♕xe5 41 ♕h6
♕xd4+ 42 ♚f1 ♕f4+ 0-1 Honfi

287 Varasdy-Zichichi Athens 79

1 e4 c5 2 ♞f3 e6 3 ♞c3 a6 4 g3 ♞c6
5 ♗g2 d6 6 0-0 ♞ge7!? 6...♗e7 7 d4
7 d4 cxd4 8 ♞xd4 ♞xd4 9 ♕xd4 ♞c6
10 ♕d3 ♗e7 11 b3 ♕c7 12 ♗b2 0-0
13 ♞d1 ♗d7 Δ ♖fd8, ♗f8, ♗e8 14 ♞e3
♖fd8 15 ♕e2 ♗f8 16 ♚h1 ♞e7 17 f4
d5!? 18 exd5 18 f5?! dxe4 19 f6
♞g6 20 fxg7 ♗xg7 21 ♗xg7 ♚xg7
22 ♞g4 f5∓ ♞xd5 19 ♞g4 Δ ♞h6+!;
19 ♞xd5 exd5 20 ♗xd5 ♗b5! 21 c4
♖xd5 22 cxb5 ♖xb5; 22...axb5 =+;
20 ♗e5 ♕c5 21 ♖ad1 ♗f5! 22 ♖d2
f6 23 ♗d4 ♕a5 24 c4 ♗e4! 25 ♗xe4
dxe4 26 f5?! ♗c5! 27 ♗e3 ♗xe3 28
♖xd8+ ♖xd8 29 ♕xe3 ♕e5! =+; 23
♗b2 ♖e8 24 ♕d1 ♗e4 25 ♗xe4 dxe4
26 ♖d5 ♕c6 27 c4 e3! =+ ♞e7?! 19...
♗e8 20 f5; 19...♞c3? 20 ♕e5! ♕xe5
21 fxe5 ♞d5 22 c4 += 20 ♞e5? 20
♕e5! ♕xe5 21 ♞xe5 ♞c6 22 ♞xd7
♖xd7 23 ♖ad1 ♖ad8 24 ♗f3 +=;
20...♖ac8?? 21 ♞h6+! +− ♗e8 21
♖ad1 ♖ac8 22 c4 b5 23 ♖c1 ♕b6
24 ♖fd1 ♞f5 25 ♖xd8 ♖xd8 26
cxb5 axb5 27 ♗e4 ♕a5 =+ 28 ♗c3

b4 29 ♗e1 ♕a3 30 ♖b1 ♖c8 31 ♗f2
♞d6! 32 ♞c4 32 ♗g2 ♗b5 33 ♕d2
♖c3 34 ♗d4 f6!∓ ♞xc4 33 bxc4 ♗c6
34 ♗xc6 ♖xc6 35 ♗d4 ♕a8?! 35...
♕a6! 36 ♖c1 h5! 37 ♕c2 h4 36 ♚g1
36 ♕g2 ♕c8 37 c5 ♗xc5 38 ♖c1 ♖c7
39 ♗e5 ♖d7 −+; 39 ♗xc5 ♖xc5 40
♖xc5 ♕xc5 41 ♕a8+ ♕f8 42 ♕b7
h5 =+ ♖d6! 37 ♗c5 37 ♗f2 ♖a6
38 ♖b2 b3! 39 axb3 ♖a1+ 40 ♚f2
♖h1 −+; 37 ♗e3 ♕e4 38 ♖xb4?
♖d1+ −+; 38 ♖b3 ♖d4 Δ ♖xc4 −+;
38 ♖e1 ♖d3! 39 c5 ♖c3 40 ♗f2
♕c6 −+ ♖a6 38 ♗xb4 ♖xa2 39 ♖b2
39 ♕f1 ♕e4 40 ♗xf8 ♕c2 −+ ♗xb4!
40 ♖xa2 ♗c5+ 0-1 Paoli

288 Beljavsky-Gheorghiu
Novi Sad 79

1 e4 c5 2 ♞f3 e6 3 d4 cxd4 4 ♞xd4
a6 5 ♗d3 ♞f6 6 0-0 d6 7 c4 g6 7...e6
8 ♞c3 ♗g7 9 ♖e1 0-0 10 ♗f1! N 10
♗e3 ♞bd7 11 ♗f1 += b6 11 ♗g5!±
♗b7 12 ♕d2 ♕c7 13 ♖ad1 ♖c8!
13...♖d8?? 14 e5! dxe5 15 ♞xe6! +−
14 ♞c2 ♞e8 15 ♗h6! ♗h8!∞ 15...
♗xh6?! 16 ♕xh6± 16 ♞e3 ♞d7
17 ♚h1?! 17 f3! += ♗xc3! 18 ♕xc3
♗xe4 19 ♗g5 e5! 20 ♞g4 f5! 21
♗h6+ 21 ♖xe4!? ♚g7 22 f3 ♗b7 23
b4 ♞ef6 24 ♕b2 ♖e8 25 ♖d2 ♖e6!∓
Δ ♖ae8 26 ♖ed1 ♖ae8 27 a3 e4!∓
28 f4 e3! 29 ♖c2 ♕c6!! Δ e2∓ 30
♖e1 e2! 31 ♖exe2 ♖xe2 32 ♖xe2
♕xc4 33 h3 33 ♖e7+?? ♖xe7 −+
♖xe2 34 ♗xe2 ♕e4 35 ♗f1 35 ♗f3
♕e1+ ♕e1 36 ♚g1 ♗d5! 37 ♕c2 ♞e4
38 ♕b2+ ♞ef6?! 38...♞c3 −+ 39
♕c2 b5 40 ♕c7

Diagram

40...♗e6!! −+ 41 a4!? 41 g4?! ♞e4!
−+; 41 ♕a7 ♗c4 42 ♗xf6+ ♚xf6 43

♕xd7 ♕xf1+ 44 ♔h2 ♕xf4+ Δ ♕xh6
−+; 41 ♕d8 ♗c4! −+; 41 ♕xd6 ♗c4!
−+; 41 h4!! ♕e3+! 42 ♔h2 ♕b6 −+
0-1 Gheorghiu

2...e6, 4...♘c6

289 Widera-Kruszynski Poland 79
1 e4 c5 2 ♘f3 e6 3 d4 cxd4 4 ♘xd4
♘c6 5 ♘b5 d6 5...♘f6! 6 ♘1c3 d6 7
♗f4 e5∞ **6 c4 ♘f6 7 ♘1c3** 7 ♘5c3
♗e7 8 ♗e2 0-0 9 0-0 b6 10 ♗f4 ♗b7
11 ♘d2 ♖c8 12 ♖e1 a6 13 ♖c1 ♘e5
14 a3 ♖e8 15 b4 += Ljubojevic-
Polugaevsky, Las Palmas 74; 13...
♖e8!?∞ Polugaevsky **a6 8 ♘a3 ♗e7**
9 ♗e2 0-0 10 0-0 b6 10...♖b8 11
♗e3 ♕a5 12 ♖c1 ♖d8 13 ♕b3 ♘d7
14 ♖fd1 ♘c5 15 ♕c2 ♗d7 16 ♕b1
♗e8= Vasyukov-Korchnoi, USSR Final
66/67; 10...♗d7!? 11 ♕b3 ♖b8 12
f4 ♕a5 13 ♘c2 b5 14 cxb5 axb5 15
a3 += Boleslavsky **11 ♗e3 ♗b7 12**
♕b3 12 ♖c1 ♖b8 13 ♕d2 ♘e5 14
f3 d5!= Karpov-Olafsson, Moscow 71
♘d7 13 ♖fd1 13 ♖ac1 ♖e8 14 ♖fd1
♘c5 15 ♕c2 ♗f6 16 ♘ab1 ♕c7 17 a3!±
♘e5 18 f4 ♘g6 19 b4 ♘d7 20 ♕d2
♗e7 21 e5 ♘h4 22 exd6 ♕c6 23
♗f1! +− Georgadze-Polugaevsky,
USSR 79 **♘c5 14 ♕c2** 14 ♗xc5?!
bxc5 15 ♕xb7?? ♘a5 −+ **♘b4?!** 14...
♗f6 15 ♖ac1! ♗e5 16 ♘ab1 ♕h4

17 g3 ♕f6 18 f4 ♗d4 19 ♕d2 e5 20
♘d5 ♕d8 21 ♘1c3 ♔h8 22 f5 ♘d7
23 ♗f3 ♗c5 24 ♔g2 f6 25 ♘e2 a5 26
♘dc3 ♖f7 27 ♘b5 +− Karpov-Olafsson,
Amsterdam 76 **15 ♕d2 ♕c7 16 f3**
♖ad8?! 16...♘c6 **17 ♘cb5! axb5 18**
♘xb5 ♕b8 19 ♕xb4± d5 20 cxd5
exd5 21 exd5 ♗xd5 22 ♕f4! ♕b7 23
♕c7 ♗f6 24 ♕xb7 ♗xb7 25 ♗d4 ♗xd4
26 ♖xd4 ♖xd4 27 ♘xd4 ♖d8 28 ♖d1
g6 29 b3! ♖a8 30 ♖d2 ♖d8 31 ♔f2
♖a8 32 ♗c4 ♔f8 33 b4!? ♘a6 33...
♘d7 **34 ♘c2 ♖c8 35 ♗b3 ♔e7 36**
♔e3 ♖c7 37 ♔f4 Δ ♔g5 **h6 38 h4!**
b5 39 ♖e2+ ♔f6 39...♔d6 40 h5
40 ♖e5 ♗c6 41 g4 ♖d7 42 g5+ hxg5
43 hxg5+ ♔g7 44 ♔e3 ♔f8 45 ♘d4
♘xb4 46 a3!? ♘d5 47 ♗xd5 ♗xd5 48
♘xb5 ♗b7 49 ♖c5 ♖e7+ 50 ♔f4 ♖e2
51 ♘d6 ♖e7 52 ♖b5 ♗c6 53 ♖b8+
♔g7 54 ♖c8 ♗a4 54...♗d7 55 ♖c7
♔f8 56 ♘e4! **55 ♘e4! ♖e8 56 ♖xe8**
♗xe8 57 ♔e5 ♗a4 58 ♘c5 ♗d1 59
f4 ♗f3 60 a4 ♔f8 61 ♔f6 1-0 Pytel

290 Shamkovich-Timman Rio 79
1 e4 c5 2 ♘c3 ♘c6 3 ♘f3 e6 4 d4 cxd4
5 ♘xd4 a6 6 g3 ♕c7 7 ♗g2 ♘f6 8
0-0 ♗e7 9 ♖e1 ♘xd4 10 ♕xd4 ♗c5
11 ♕d1 d6 12 h3 12 ♗f4!? **♘d7 13**
♗e3 0-0 14 ♕d2 ♘e5 15 ♗xc5 ♕xc5=
16 ♖ad1 ♘c4 17 ♘a4 17 ♕c1 ♗d7 =+
♕c7 17...♘xd2 18 ♘xc5 dxc5 19
♖xd2 b5 += **18 ♕c3** 18 ♕c1 ♗d7 =+
♗d7 19 b3?! 19 ♘b6!? ♕xb6 20
♕xc4 ♕xb2 21 ♖xd6 =/=+; 20...♖fc8
21 ♕d4 ♕xd4 22 ♖xd4 ♖xc2 23 ♖xd6
♗e8 24 ♖b6=; 23...♗c6 24 ♖ed1
♔f8 25 ♖6d2= **♗xa4 20 ♗f1 ♗b5**
21 bxc4 ♖fc8 22 ♕b4 ♗xc4 23 ♗xc4
♕xc4 24 ♕xb7 ♕c6 =+ 25 ♕e7!?
25 ♕xc6 ♕xc2 26 ♖xd6 ♕xa2 27
♖d7 ♖f8∓ 28 ♖e3 ♖ac8 29 ♖f3
♕e2 30 ♖f4 30 ♖xf7? ♖c1+ 31 ♔g2

♕xe4+ 32 f3 ♕e2 mate; 32 ♔h2 ♖h1 mate; 31 ♔h2 ♕xf2+! 32 ♖xf2 ♖xf2 mate **e5** 30...♖c1+ 31 ♔g2 ♕f1+ 32 ♔f3 ♖c2?? 33 ♕xf7+! +−; 30...h6 31 ♔g2∞; 30...♖c1+ 31 ♔g2 h6? 32 ♕xf8+!= **31 ♕xe5 ♖c1+ 32 ♔g2 ♕f1+** 32...h6!? 33 ♖dxf7 ♕f1+ 34 ♔f3 ♕d1+! 35 ♔e3 ♖xf7 36 ♕e8+ ♔h7 37 ♖xf7 ♖c3+ 38 ♔f4 ♕d6+ 39 e5 ♖c4+ 40 ♔f3 ♕d5+ 41 ♔e2 ♖c2+ 42 ♔e3 ♖c3+ 43 ♔e2 ♕d3+ 44 ♔e1 ♖c1 mate; 39 ♕e5 ♖f3+; 39 ♔g4 ♕g6+; 33 ♕e7! Δ ♕xf8+ **33 ♔f3 ♖c2 34 ♔g4 ♖xf2 35 ♖dxf7! ♕d1+ 36 ♖f3!=** 36 ♔h4? ♕d8+

36...h5+ 36...♕xf3+ 37 ♖xf3 ♖2xf3 38 ♕e6+ = **37 ♔g5** 37 ♔xh5? ♖xf7 38 ♕e8+ ♔h7 −+; 37 ♕xh5 ♖xf3 −+; 37 ♔h4 ♕d8+ **♕d8+ 38 ♖e7 ♖f7 39 ♖xf2** 39 ♖xf7?? ♖xf7 −+ **♖xe7 40 ♕d5+ ♕xd5+ 41 exd5 ♖e5+ 42 ♔g6 ♖xd5 43 ♖c2 ½-½ Miles**

291 Paoli-Bruno Catanzaro 79
1 e4 c5 2 ♘f3 e6 3 ♘c3 ♘c6 4 d4 cxd4 5 ♘xd4 a6 6 g3 ♘ge7 7 ♘de2?! 7 ♗g2; 7 ♘b3! ♘a5 8 ♕h5! ♘xb3 9 axb3 ♘c6 10 ♗g5! ♗e7 11 ♗xe7 ♕xe7 12 ♗g2 0-0-0 += Timman-Radev, Tbilisi 71 **♘g6 8 ♗g2 ♗c5 9 0-0 0-0** 9...b5 10 ♘f4 ♗b7 11 ♘d3 ♗b6 12 a4 b4 13 ♘a2 a5 14 c4? =+

Kapengut-Taimanov, USSR 71, 14 ♘d2! **10 a3 b5 11 h3 ♗b7 12 ♔h2 ♘ge5 13 f4 ♘c4 14 ♕d3 ♗e7 15 ♘d1** 15 b3? ♘xa3! Δ b4 **♕c7 16 b3 ♘b6 17 ♗b2 ♖fd8 18 ♘e3 ♖ac8 19 ♖ac1 ♘a5?! 20 c4!? bxc4 21 ♕c3± ♗f6 22 e5 ♗xg2 23 ♔xg2** 23 ♘xg2? ♘d5 −+ **♘xb3 24 exf6 ♘a4 25 ♕c2 ♘xb2 26 ♕xb2 ♘xc1 27 ♖xc1 d5 28 ♕d4?!** 28 fxg7! (Δ ♘g4) d4? 28 ♖xc4 +− **♕c5 29 fxg7 ♕xd4 30 ♘xd4 ♔xg7 31 ♔f3 ♗f6 32 g4 h6 33 h4 ♖d6 34 ♖b1 ♖c7 35 ♖b8?!** 35 g5+! hxg5? 36 fxg5+ ♔e5?? 37 ♖d1 f5 38 ♘ec2 Δ ♖e1 mate; 36...♔g6 37 ♘g4 +− **♔g6 36 h5+ ♔h7 37 g5 hxg5 38 fxg5 c3 39 ♘g4?!** Zeitnot 39 ♔f4!± **e5 40 ♘c2?** 40 ♘xe5 c2 41 ♘xc2 ♖xc2 42 ♖b7 ♔g8 43 ♖b8+ ♔h7 44 ♖b7= **d4 −+ 41 ♘xe5 d3 0-1 Paoli**

4 ♘

292 Vitolins-Georgadze USSR 79
1 e4 c5 2 ♘f3 ♘c6 3 d4 cxd4 4 ♘xd4 ♘f6 5 ♘c3 e6 6 ♘xc6 6 ♘db5 bxc6 **7 e5 ♘d5 8 ♘e4 ♕c7 9 ♘d6+** 9 f4 ♕b6 10 ♗d3 ♗a6 11 a3 ♗e7 12 ♕e2 ♗xd3 13 ♕xd3 f5 14 ♘f2 ♗c5 15 0-0 a5 16 c4 ♘e3 17 b4!≈ Tseshkovsky-Sveshnikov, USSR Final 78 **♗xd6 10 exd6 ♕xd6 11 ♗e2 ♕c7** 11...♕e7!? **12 0-0 c5 13 c4 ♘e7 14 ♗g5 ♘c6?!** 14...h6!? 15 ♗d2 ♗b7 16 ♗d3 ♕c6 17 ♕g4 f5 =+; 14...♗b7 15 ♗d3 ♕c6! =+ **15 ♗d3 ♗b7 16 f4! ♕d6?** 16...f6 17 ♗h4 f5 18 ♕h5+ g6 19 ♕h6 ♔f7 19 ♕g5 **17 a3 f6 18 ♗h4 f5?**

Diagram

19 ♗xf5!! ♕xd1 19...♕d4+ 20 ♕xd4 ♘xd4 21 ♗d3 +− **20 ♖axd1 exf5**

21 ♖fe1+ ♔f8 22 ♖xd7 ♖b8 23 b4 cxb4 24 axb4 a6? 24...♘xb4 25 ♖ee7 ♗e4 26 ♖f7+ ♔g8 27 ♖xg7+ ♔f8 28 ♖df7+ ♔e8=; 25 ♗e7+ ♔e8 26 ♖c7 ♗e4 27 ♗xb4 ♖xb4 28 ♖c8+ ♔f7 29 ♖xh8 ♖xc4 30 ♖a1 += **25 b5 +− axb5 26 cxb5 h6 27 ♖c1!** 27 ♖e6!? ♗c8 28 bxc6 ♗xd7 29 cxd7 ♔f7 30 ♖e5! +− **♗c8 28 ♖c7 ♘d4 29 ♖xc8+ ♔f7 30 ♖1f7+ ♔e6 31 ♖xh8 ♖xh8 32 b6 ♖a8 33 h3 ♖a1+ 34 ♔h2 ♖a2 35 b7 ♖b2 36 ♗f2 1-0** Georgadze

2...e6, 4...♘f6

293 Martorelli-Vujovic Naples 79
1 e4 c5 2 ♘f3 e6 3 d4 cxd4 4 ♘xd4 ♘f6 5 ♘c3 ♗b4?! 6 e5! ♘e4 6...♘d5 **7 ♕g4 ♘xc3 8 ♕xg7 ♖f8 9 a3 ♗a5** 9...♕a6? **10 ♘b3! +− 10 ♗h6 ♕e7 11 ♘b3 ♗c7 12 bxc3 ♘c6 13 f4 f6 14 ♕xe7+ ♔xe7 15 ♗xf8+ ♔xf8 16 ♗d3 fxe5 17 fxe5 ♗xe5 18 0-0 ♔g7 19 ♖f3 d6 20 ♖af1 ♘d8 21 ♖h3 h6 22 ♖h4 ♘f7 23 ♖g4+ +− ♘g5 24 h4 ♗f6 25 ♖gf4! ♗e5 26 ♖f8 1-0** Paoli

294 Tarjan-Tal Riga 79
1 e4 c5 2 ♘f3 d6 3 d4 cxd4 4 ♘xd4 ♘f6 5 ♘c3 e6 6 g3 ♗e7 7 ♗g2 0-0 8 0-0 ♘c6 9 b3 9 ♘ce2! ♗d7 10 c4 ♖c8 11 b3 a6 12 ♗b2 b5 13 cxb5

♘xd4 14 ♘xd4 axb5 15 ♕d2 ♕b6 16 ♖ac1 ♖fd8= Gligoric-Boleslavsky, Zurich 53; 9 ♘xc6 bxc6 10 e5 dxe5 11 ♕xd8 ♖xd8 12 ♗xc6 ♖b8= **♗d7 10 ♗b2 ♖c8 11 ♘de2** 11 ♘ce2 (△ c4) ♘xd4 12 ♘xd4 b5! =+ **♕a5 12 h3 ♖fd8 13 ♔h1?!** Kapengut **♗e8** △ d5∓ Gheorghiu **14 ♕e1 b5 =+ 15 a3 ♕b6 16 ♖d1 b4!∓** Gheorghiu; 16...a5!? **17 axb4 ♘xb4 18 ♖d2 a5 19 ♘d4 ♖c5! =+** Kapengut **20 ♘d1?! d5! 21 exd5** 21 e5 ♘e4 22 ♗xe4? dxe4 23 ♕xe4 ♘xc2! 24 ♖xc2 ♖xd4! 25 ♕xd4 ♕b7+ 26 ♔g1 ♖xc2 −+; 22 ♖e2 ♖c7! 23 f3 ♘c5 24 f4 ♘c6 =+; 22...♖cc8∓; 21 c3!? **♘bxd5 22 ♗a3 ♖cc8 23 ♗xe7 ♘xe7 24 ♘f3 ♗b5! 25 c4 ♗c6 26 ♘e3 ♘e4 27 ♖a2**

27...♖d1!∓ 27...♕xb3 28 ♕xa5? ♖a8; 28 ♖xa5 ♖d3∓ Kapengut **28 ♕xa5** 28 ♘e5 ♘xg3+ 29 fxg3 ♖xe3 30 ♘xc6! ♖xe1 31 ♘xe7+ ♔f8 32 ♘xc8 ♖xf1+ 33 ♗xf1 ♕xb3! 34 ♖xa5 ♕d1 35 ♔g1 ♕d4+ 36 ♔h1 ♕e4 37 ♔g1 ♕e3+ 38 ♔h1 ♕e1 −+; 37 ♔h2 ♕e1; 34 ♖a1 a4 △ a3 −+; 33...♕b7+?! 34 ♗g2 ♕xc8 35 ♖xa5= **♘xg3+ 29 fxg3 ♕xe3∓** Gheorghiu **30 ♘e5** 30 b4 ♘f5 31 ♔h2 ♘d4 **♗xg2+ 31 ♖xg2 ♖xb3! 32 ♔h2** 32 ♖xf7 ♘g6 33 ♘g4 ♖b1+ 34 ♔h2 ♕c1 35 ♖xg7+ ♔xg7 36 ♕a7+ ♔h8 37 ♕d4+ e5 −+; 33

♕a6 ♘xe5 34 ♕xe6 ♖b1+ 35 ♔h2
♘f3+; 33 ♖c7 ♖xc7 34 ♕xc7 ♘xe5;
32 ♘xf7 ♘f5? 33 ♖xf5! exf5 34
♕d5 +−; 32...♖f8! 33 ♕c7 ♘f5 −+
f6! Gheorghiu 33 ♘d7 ♕d4! △ ♔g6
34 ♖d2 ♖b2 35 ♖ff2 ♖xd2 36 ♖xd2
♕xc4 37 ♘b6 ♕c5! −+ Kapengut
38 ♖d8+ ♔f7! Gheorghiu 39 ♖f8+
♔g6! Gheorghiu 40 ♕xc5 ♖xc5 0-1
Miles/Speelman

2 f4

295 Wibe-Keene Gausdal 79

1 e4 g6 2 ♘c3 c5 3 f4 ♗g7 4 ♘f3
♘c6 5 ♗c4?! e6! 6 f5?! ♘ge7! 7
fxe6 fxe6 8 d3 d5 9 ♗b3 b5! 10
exd5 10 a3 ♘d4 11 ♘xd4 cxd4 12
♘e2 0-0∓; 10 ♘xb5 ♕a5+ 11 ♘c3
d4 12 0-0 dxc3 13 bxc3 ♕xc3 14
♖b1∞; 13...h6!?∓; 11...c4 12 dxc4
dxc4 13 ♗xc4 ♗xc3+∓ exd5 11
♘xd5!? ♘xd5 12 ♕e2+ ♘de7 13 0-0
♗f5 14 a4 b4 15 ♗e3 ♘a5!! 16 ♗e6?
16 ♗xc5 ♘xb3 17 cxb3 ♗xd3 18
♕e6 ♗xf1 19 ♖d1 ♕c7 20 ♗xe7 ♕b6+
−+; 16 ♗g5 ♘xb3 17 ♖ae1 ♘d4!
♗xe6 17 ♗xc5 ♗f5 18 ♖ae1 ♘ac6
19 g4 ♗xg4 20 ♕e4 ♗xf3 21 ♕xf3
♗d4+ 22 ♔g2 ♖c8 0-1 time 23 ♕f7+
♔d7 24 ♕e6+ ♔c7 25 ♗xe7 ♘xe7
26 ♕xe7+ ♕xe7 27 ♖xe7+ ♔b6 −+
Keene

296 Day-Angantjsson USA 79

1 e4 c5 2 f4 g6 3 d3 ♗g7 4 g3 d5 5
e5 f6 6 exf6 exf6 7 ♗g2 ♘e7 8 ♘f3
♘bc6 9 0-0 ♗e6 10 ♖e1 ♕d7 11
d4! cxd4 12 ♘xd4 ♘xd4 12...♗g4
13 ♘xc6 ♗xd1 14 ♖xe7+ +− ♕xe7
15 ♘xe7 ♔xe7 16 ♘c3∞; 13 ♕d2∞
13 ♕xd4 0-0 14 ♘c3 ♗f7 15 ♕c5
♖fe8 16 ♗e3 ♖ec8 17 ♕a3 d4 18
♖ad1 f5 19 ♗f2 ♘c6 20 ♘b5 ♗d5

21 ♕d6!± ♕xd6 22 ♘xd6 ♗xg2
23 ♘xc8 ♗f3 24 ♖e8+! ♗f8 24...
♔f7? 25 ♘d6+ 25 ♖d3 ♗e4 26 ♘e7+
♔f7 27 ♖xa8 ♗xe7 28 ♖xd4 +−
1-0 28...♘xd4 29 ♗xd4 △ ♖xa7
Gheorghiu

1 e4 c6

297 Mednis-Larsen Riga 79

1 e4 c6 2 ♘c3 d5 3 ♘f3 ♗g4 4 h3
♗xf3 5 ♕xf3 e6 6 d3 ♘f6 7 ♗d2
♘bd7 8 g4 g6! 9 ♗g2 9 0-0-0 ♗d6!?
♗d6! 10 exd5!? 10 ♕e2 d4 11 ♘d1
e5= cxd5 11 ♕e2! ♕b6?! 11...0-0
12 f4 ♕b6 13 0-0-0∞ 12 g5 d4?!
12...♘h5 13 ♘xd5 ♕xb2 14 ♗c3
♗b4 15 ♗xb4 ♕xa1+ 16 ♔d2 ♕e5
17 ♕xe5 ♘xe5 18 ♘c7+ ♔d7 19 ♘xa8
♖xa8 20 ♗c3 ♘c6 21 ♖b1 b6 22 ♗e5!
+= 13 gxf6 dxc3 14 ♗xc3 ♗b4 15
♗xb4 ♕xb4+ 16 c3 ♕b6 17 0-0-0
♘xf6 17...0-0-0 18 ♕f3 e5 19 d4!
♖he8 20 ♕d5!± 18 ♕e5 ♕e7 19 d4
♖hd8 20 d5?! 20 ♖d3!± △ ♖f3 ♗d6!=
21 dxe6 ♖xe6 22 ♕d4 ♕xd4 23 ♖xd4
♖b8 24 ♖hd1 b6

25 ♗f1?? 25 ♖c4 ♘e8 26 h4= ♖c8∓
26 ♗d3 ♖c5 27 ♔c2 ♖ee5 28 ♖f4
♖c7 29 ♖d4 ♘h5 30 h4?! 30 b4∓
♘g7 31 ♖g1 ♘e6 32 ♖e4 ♖xe4 33

♗xe4 ♖c5 34 ♗d3 ♞f4 35 ♗e4?!
35 ♖g4∓ ♖e5 36 ♗f3 30 ♗d3 ♘h3 −+
♞h3 −+ 37 ♖g4 ♞xf2 38 ♖c4 ♖f5
39 ♗b7 ♕d6 40 ♕d2 0-1 time **Mednis**

298 Wells-Kotov (1) 79
1 e4 c6 2 d4 d5 3 ♞c3 dxe4 4 ♞xe4
♞d7 5 ♞f3 ♞gf6 6 ♞g3 e6 7 ♗d3
♗e7 8 0-0 0-0 9 c3 c5 10 ♖e1 b6 11
♕e2 ♗b7 += 12 ♗e3 cxd4 13 ♗xd4
♗c5 14 ♖ad1? 14 ♗xc5 ♘xc5 15
♗b1 += ♗xf3! 15 ♕xf3 ♗xd4 16 cxd4
♖c8= 17 ♗b1?! 17 ♘e4! ♘xe4 18
♗xe4 ♘f6 19 d5!= ♖e8 18 h3 ♖c7
=+ 19 ♕d3 g6 20 ♞e2 ♞d5 21 ♞c3
♞7f6 22 ♞b5? 22 ♖d2 △ ♖ed1 =+
♖d7 23 ♕f3 ♔g7 24 ♞a3 △ ♘c4 -
e5 ♞e7! 25 ♕c3 ♕c8 26 ♖c1 26
♕xc8 ♖xc8 27 ♘c2 ♘f5 −+ ♔b8!
△ ♖c8 27 ♗c2 b5! 28 ♗b3? 28 b4
♕b6 29 ♖cd1 ♘c6 −+ b4 0-1 **Kotov**

299 Wells-Kotov, (3) 79
1 e4 c6 2 d4 d5 3 ♞c3 dxe4 4 ♞xe4
♗f5 5 ♞g3 ♗g6 6 ♞f3 ♞d7 7 ♗d3
♞gf6 8 0-0 e6 9 ♖e1 ♗d6 10 ♞f5
♗xf5 11 ♗xf5 0-0 12 ♗d3 c5= 13 c3
cxd4 14 ♞xd4 ♞e5 15 ♗c2 ♕b6=
16 ♕e2 ♞g6 17 ♗g5 ♞d5 18 h4?!
18 g3= ♗f4?! 18...h6! 19 h5 ♘e5
20 ♗c1 ♖ae8 =+; 20 ♗h4− 19 ♗xf4
♞gxf4? 19...♘dxf4 20 ♕f3 e5=
20 ♕e4 f5 21 ♕f3 ♕xb2 22 g3!± e5
22...♘h3+ 23 ♔h2 +−; 22...♘g6
23 h5!± 23 gxf4 e4 24 ♕e2! 24 ♕g3
♖f6 △ ♖g6 ♕xc3 24...♘xf4? 25 ♗b3
+ △ ♕xb2 25 ♞e6 ♕f6 25...♖f6 26
♗b3 +− 26 ♞xf8 ♞xf4 27 ♕e3 ♕xh4
28 ♗b3+! ♔h8 28...♔xf8 29 ♕c5+!
+− 29 ♞e6 ♞h3+ 30 ♔g2 f4 31 ♕xh3
f3+ 32 ♔h2 ♕xf2+ 33 ♔h1 1-0 **Kotov**

300 Klovsky-Bobolovich USSR 79
1 e4 c6 2 d4 d5 3 ♞c3 dxe4 4 ♞xe4

♞f6 5 ♞xf6+ gxf6 5...exf6 6 ♘f3
♗d6 7 ♗e2 ♘a6!?∞ Torre-Korchnoi,
Buenos Aires 78 6 ♗e2 6 ♗e3!? +=
♗f5 7 ♞f3 ♕c7 8 0-0 ♞d7 9 c4 +=
e6 10 d5! N 10 ♗e3 △ ♕a4, b4−b5
+= ♗d6

11 ♞d4! ♗xh2+ 12 ♔h1 ♗e5 13 dxc6
bxc6 14 ♞xf5 exf5 15 f4± ♗d6 16
♕c2 ♕f8 16...c5 17 ♕xf5 ♖e8 18
♗g4 ♖e7 19 ♗d2 +− h5 20 ♗h3 ♖g8
21 ♗a5 ♕b8 22 ♖ad1 △ ♗d8! ♞c5 23
♖xd6! ♕xd6 24 ♗b4 ♕d3 25 ♗xc5
♕xf1+ 26 ♔h2 ♕e2 27 ♕d7 ♕e4 28
♕d8+ ♔g7 29 ♕xe7 ♕xf4+ 30 ♔h1
♕f1+ 31 ♗g1 1-0 **Gufeld**

301 Unzicker-Lein South Africa 79
1 e4 c6 2 d4 d5 3 ♞c3 dxe4 4 ♞xe4
♞f6 5 ♞g3 5 ♘xf6+ ♗g4 6 ♗e2 6
♘f3?! ♗xf3 7 ♕xf3; 6 f3?! ♗e6 ♗xe2
7 ♞1xe2 e6 8 ♕d3 ♞bd7 9 0-0 ♗e7
10 c4 0-0 11 b3 ♖e8 12 ♗b2 ♕a5
13 ♕f3 ♖ad8 14 ♖fd1 ♗f8= 15 ♞e4
♞xe4 16 ♕xe4 ♕g5 17 ♕f3 ♞f6 18
h3 ♖d7 19 ♖d3 ♖ed8 20 ♖ad1 ♗d6
21 ♞g3 ♗xg3 22 fxg3!? 22 ♕xg3
♕xg3 23 ♖xg3 e5= ♕g6 23 ♖e1 h6
24 ♖de3 ♖c8 25 ♖e5 b6 26 ♔h2
♔h7 27 g4 c5 28 dxc5 bxc5 29 ♕f2
♖dc7 30 ♖5e2 a5? 30...♞d7= 31
♗c3 ♖a7 31...♖a8 32 ♗xf6 gxf6 33
♖f1 ♔g7 34 ♕f3! △ ♖ef2 32 ♗xf6

♛xf6 32...gxf6 33 ♖f1 ♔g7 34 ♖e3 (Δ
♖f3) e5± **33 ♛xf6 gxf6 34 ♖f1 ♔g7
35 ♖ef2 a4 36 ♖xf6 axb3 37 axb3
♖d8 38 ♖6f3 ♖d2 39 ♖1f2 ♖xf2
40 ♖xf2 ♖d7 41 ♖a2 ♔f6 42 ♖a5
♖d3 43 ♖b5 ♔g6 44 ♔g1 f5 45 gxf5+
exf5 46 ♔f2 f4 47 ♖xc5 ♖xb3 48
♖c8 ♖c3 49 c5 ♔h7 50 c6 ♔g7 51
♔e2 ♔g6 52 ♔d2 ♖c5 53 ♔d3 ♔g7
54 ♔e4 ♖g5 55 ♔xf4 ♖xg2 56 ♔e5
♖e2+ 57 ♔d6 ♖d2+ 58 ♔c7 ♖h2
59 ♖d8 ♖xh3 60 ♖d5 1-0 Miles**

302 Sax-Guil.Garcia Rio 79

**1 e4 c6 2 d4 d5 3 ♘d2 g6 4 h3 ♗g7
5 ♘gf3 ♘h6!?** 5...dxe4 += **6 ♗d3 f6
7 0-0 0-0 8 ♖e1 ♘f7 9 c4!?** += 9 e5!?
♘a6! **10 ♗f1** 10 cxd5 cxd5 11 exd5
♘c7=; 10 b3!?; 10 ♘b1!? ♘b4!?
♘c7 **11 b3 dxe4 12 ♘xe4 f5!? 13 ♘eg5
c5! 14 ♘xf7 ♖xf7 15 ♘e5** 15 ♗b2
♘e6 **♗xe5 16 ♖xe5** 16 dxe5 ♘e6!?
17 ♛xd8+ ♘xd8 18 ♖d1 ♘c6! Δ ♗e6
+=/= ♛xd4 **17 ♛xd4 cxd4 18 ♗b2
♘e6 19 c5?!** 19 ♖ae1± ♖f6 20 c5!
Δ ♗c4 ♘d8 **20 ♗c4** 20 ♗xd4? ♘c6
21 ♖d5 ♗e6 −+ **e6 21 ♖d1 ♘c6 22
♖e2 ♔f8 23 ♖ed2** 23 ♗xe6? +=;
23 ♗xd4 ♖d7 24 ♖ed2 ♘xd4 25 ♖xd4
♖xd4 26 ♖xd4 ♔e7 +=/± **♖c7 24
♗xd4 ♘xd4 25 ♖xd4 ♖xc5 26 ♖d8+
♔e7 27 ♖h8** 27 a4!? **b5** =+ **28 ♖xh7+
♔f6 29 ♗e2 a5 30 ♖d8 ♗b7 31 ♖dd7
♗c6 32 ♖c7 ♖c1+ 33 ♔h2 ♖e1∞
34 ♗d3 ♗e8 35 ♖h8 ♗c6 36 ♖hh7
♗e8 37 f4** Δ g4-g5 mate; 37 ♖b7!?
b4 38 f4! e5? 39 ♖b6+ +−; 38...g5;
37...♖e5!? **e5 38 ♖ce7 ♖e3** =/=+
39 fxe5+ ♖xe5

Diagram

**40 ♖b7?? ♖d8! −+ 41 ♖b6+ ♔g5
42 ♗f1** 42 ♗b1 ♖d1 43 ♗c2 ♖d2 −+

♖d1 **43 ♔g3 f4+** 43...♖xf1?? 44 h4
mate **44 ♔f2 ♖d2+ 0-1** 45 ♔f3 ♖e3
mate; 45 ♔g1 ♖e1 Δ ♖dd1 −+ **Miles**

303 Velimirovic-Maric Ochrid 79

**1 e4 d5 2 exd5 ♘f6 3 c4 c6 4 d4
cxd5 5 ♘c3 g6 6 cxd5 ♗g7 7 ♗b5+
7 ♕b3 ♗d7 8 d6! exd6 9 ♕e2+ ♕e7
10 ♗f4 ♕xe2+ 11 ♗xe2 d5 12 ♘b5!
♗xb5 13 ♗xb5+ ♘c6 14 ♗xc6+ bxc6
15 ♖c1** += **♘h5?! 16 ♗e3 ♔d7 17
♘f3 ♖he8 18 ♔d2 f5 19 ♔d3 ♖e4?!
20 ♖c3 f4 21 ♗d2 ♖b8 22 ♖hc1 ♖b6
23 ♖a3 a6 24 ♖cc3 ♖e8! 25 ♖cb3
♖eb8 26 ♖xb6** 26 ♖xa6 ♖xb3+ 27
axb3 ♖xb3+ 28 ♗c3 ♖b7 29 ♖a8
♗f6 += **♖xb6 27 b3 ♗f6! 28 ♖a4 g5=
29 g4?!** 29 g3 fxg3 30 hxg3 h6 ♘g7
30 ♗a5 ♖b5 31 ♗c3 ♖b6 32 ♘e1
32 ♗a5= ♘e6 **33 ♔c2? c5!∓ 34 ♘f3
34 dxc5 ♘xc5 35 ♖a5 ♖c6! −+
cxd4 35 ♘xd4 ♘xd4+ 36 ♗xd4 ♗xd4
37 ♖xd4 ♔e6 38 ♖d3 ♔e5 39 ♖h3
♔e4! 40 ♔d2! h6 41 ♖c3 f3! 42
♖c8 ♖f6? 42...♖e6! 43 ♖f8 h5! 44
h3 hxg4 45 hxg4 ♖h6 Δ ♖h2∓; 44
gxh5 g4 45 ♖g8 ♔f4 46 ♖f8+ ♔g5
47 ♖g8+ ♔h4!! 48 ♖h8 ♖e2+ 49
♔d3 ♖xf2 50 h6 ♖xh2 −+ 43 ♖h8
♔d4 44 ♖e8 ♖f4 45 h3 h5 46 gxh5
♖h4 47 ♖a8!= ♖xh3 48 ♖xa6 ♔e4
49 ♖e6+ ♔d4 50 ♖a6 ♔e4 ½-½ Maric**

1 e4 d5

304 Karpov-Larsen Montreal 79
**1 e4 d5 2 exd5 ♕xd5!? 3 ♘c3 ♕a5
4 d4 ♘f6 5 ♗d2?! ♗g4 6 ♗e2 ♗xe2
7 ♘cxe2!?** 7 ♕xe2 ♕b6 8 ♘f3 ♘bd7
8...♕xb2 9 ♖b1 ♕xa2 10 ♖xb7± **
9 0-0 e6 10 c4 ♗e7** 10...♕xb2? 11
♘c3 Δ ♖b1/d5/♘b5 **11 b4 0-0 12
a4 c6** 12...♗xb4? 13 a5 ♕d6 14 c5
+−; 12...a6 13 ♕b3 ♘e4 14 c5 ♕c6
15 b5± **13 ♕c2 ♕c7 14 ♖fe1 b6 15
a5 ♖fb8 16 a6!?** 16 ♘g3 bxa5 17
bxa5 ♗d6=; 16 axb6 axb6 17 ♗f4
♗d6= **b5 17 c5 ♘d5 18 ♘c1 ♖e8 19
♘d3 ♖ad8 20 g3 ♗f6 21 ♖e4 ♘f8 22
h4 ♖d7 23 ♕g2 ♖ed8 24 g4** 24 h5
♖e8 **25 g5** 25 h5 ♗d8 26 ♘fe5 ♖de7
**27 ♗f4 ♕c8 28 ♗g3 f6 29 ♘f3 ♖f7
30 ♕d2 fxg5! 31 ♘xg5?** 31 hxg5
♖f5 32 ♘de5 ♗c7 **♖f5 32 ♖a3 ♘g6∓
33 ♘f3 ♖ef8 34 ♘fe5 ♘xe5 35 ♖xe5**
35 ♘xe5 ♗c7 Δ ♗xe5 ♖f3 36 ♖a1?
36 ♕e2 ♖3f6 37 ♖e4 ♗c7 38 ♗xc7
♕xc7 39 ♖xe6 ♖xf2+ 40 ♘xf2 ♘f4+
−+

36...♗xh4! 37 ♕e2 37 ♗xh4 ♖xd3
38 ♕xd3 ♘f4+ −+; 37 ♖xd5 exd5
38 ♗xh4 ♕h3+ −+ **♗xg3 38 fxg3
♕d7 39 ♕xf3 ♖xf3 40 ♔xf3 ♘xb4
41 ♖d1 ♕xd4 42 ♖e4 ♕d5 43 ♔f2
♕h5+** 43...♕xc5 **44 ♔g2 ♘d5 45**

**♖xe6 h6 46 ♖d3 ♕h7 47 ♖f3 b4 48
g4** 48 ♖xc6 ♘e3+ ♕g5 49 ♕g3 ♕c1
**50 ♘h3 ♕c4 51 g5 h5 52 ♖e8 h4+
53 ♕g2 b3 54 ♖b8 ♕e2+ 55 ♘f2 ♘e3+
0-1 Keene**

305 Spassky-Larsen Montreal 79
**1 e4 d5 2 exd5 ♕xd5 3 ♘c3 ♕a5 4
d4 ♘f6 5 ♘f3 ♗f5?!** 5...♗g4 6 h3
♗h5 7 g4 ♗g6 8 ♘e5 e6 9 ♘c4 ♕a6
10 h4 ♕c6 11 ♖h3 ♗b4 12 h5 ♗e4
13 ♗d2 ♗xc3 14 ♖xc3 ♘d5 15 ♖b3
h6; 10 ♘e5 Bellin-Bohm, Erbeek 78
6 ♗d2 ♘bd7 7 ♗c4 Δ ♘d5 **c6 8 ♕e2
e6** 8...♗xc2? 9 ♘b5 Δ ♘d6+ +− **9
d5! cxd5 10 ♘xd5 ♕c5** 10...♕d8 11
♘xf6+± **11 b4 ♕c8 12 ♘xf6+ gxf6**
12...♘xf6? 13 ♗b5+ +− **13 ♘d4 ♗g6
14 h4 h5 15 f4** Δ f5 ♗e7 **16 ♖h3!
♕c7 17 0-0-0 ♕b6 18 ♗e1 0-0-0**
18...♗xb4? 19 ♖b3 +− **19 ♘b5 ♘b8
20 ♖xd8+ ♕xd8** 20...♖xd8 21 ♗f2
+− **21 ♗f2 ♕c6 22 ♗xa7 ♘d7 23 a3
♕e4 24 ♗e3 ♗f5 25 ♖g3 ♕c6 26 ♘d4
♕a4 27 ♘xf5 ♕xa3+ 28 ♔d1 ♕a1+
29 ♗c1 ♗xb4** 29...exf5 30 ♖d3 Δ ♗b5
**30 ♗b5 ♘b6 31 ♕e4 ♕a5 32 ♕xb7
1-0 Keene**

**306 Banas-Biriescu
Satu Mare 79**
**1 e4 d5 2 exd5 ♕xd5 3 ♘c3 ♕a5 4
d4 ♘f6 5 ♘f3 ♗g4** 5...♗f5 Larsen
6 h3 ♗h5 7 g4 ♗g6 8 ♘e5 e6! 8...c6
9 h4 ♘bd7 10 ♘c4 ♕c7 11 h5 ♗e4
12 ♘xe4 ♘xe4 13 ♕f3± **9 ♘c4** 9
♘xg6 hxg6 10 ♗g2 += **♕a6 10 ♗f4?!**
10 h4 ♕c6 11 ♖h3! ♗b4 12 h5 ♗e4
13 ♗d2 += **♕c6**

Diagram

11 ♘d6+? 11 ♘b5? ♕xh1 12 ♘xc7+
♔d8 13 ♘xa8 ♕e4+ 14 ♗e3 b6 −+;

11 Rg1 Bb4 12 Bd2 De4 =+ Bxd6!
11...Kd8 12 d5 Dxd5 13 Bb5 Wb6
(13...Dxc3 14 Dxb7+) 14 Da 4 Wa5+
15 Bd2 +– ; 11...Ke7 12 d5 Dxd5
13 Bb5 Wc5 14 Dxb7 Wb4 15 Bg5+
f6 16 a3 +– **12 Bb5 Bxf4 13 Bxc6+
Bxc6 14 Wf3 Bd6 15 0-0-0 0-0-0∓ 16
a3 h5! 17 g5 Bd5 18 Dxd5?** –+ 18
De4 Bxe4 19 Wxe4 Bf4+ 20 Kb1
Bxg5 21 c4∓ **exd5 19 h4 Rhe8 20
Wh3+ Re6!** 20...Kb8?! 21 Rhe1 Rxe1
22 Rxe1∓ Dxd4?? 23 Wd7 +– **21
Rhe1 Rde8 22 Rxe6 Rxe6 23 f3
Kb8 24 Wg2 De7 25 Wf2 Df5 26 Re1
Bg3 27 Rxe6 fxe6 28 Wd2 Dxh4 29
We3 Bf7 30 Kd1 Df5 31 Wg1 h4 0-1
Banas**

307 Short-Botterill British Final 79
**1 e4 e5 2 Df3 Dc6 3 Bb5 a6 4 Ba4
Df6 5 d4 exd4 6 0-0 Be7 7 Re1 0-0 8
e5 Dd5 9 Dxd4 Dxd4** 9...Db6!? 10
Bb3 d5 11 exd6 Bxd6 12 Dxc6 bxc6
13 Wh5! += **10 Wxd4 Db6 11 Bb3 d5
12 exd6 Bxd6** 12...Wxd6 13 We4±
13 Bf4 Wh4 14 g3 Wg4 15 h3 Wd7
15...Wf3!? 16 Re3! Wc6 17 Rc3!± **
16 Bxd6 Wxd6 17 Wxd6 cxd6 18
Kh2?!** 18 Re7!± **Be6 19 Dd2 a5 20
f4?! d5 21 a3 Dc4 22 Dxc4 dxc4 23
Ba4 Ra6?** 23...Rad8 24 Rad1 h5! =+ **
24 Bb5 Rd6 25 Rad1 Rxd1 25...**

Rfd8?? 26 Rxd6 Rxd6 27 f5 +–
**26 Rxd1 g6= 27 c3 Rc8 28 a4 Wf8
29 g4 We7 30 Wg3 h5 31 Rd4 ½-½
Botterill**

308   Arnlind-Haag   corr   77/79
**1 e4 e5 2 Df3 Dc6 3 Bb5 a6 4 Ba4
Df6 5 0-0 Dxe4 6 d4 b5 7 Bb3 d5
8 dxe5 Be6 9 c3 Bc5 10 Dbd2 0-0
11 Bc2 Bf5 12 Db3 Bg4 13 Dxc5
Dxc5 14 Re1 Re8 15 Bf4 De6? 16
Wd3! g6 17 Bg3 Bf5 18 We2 De7 19
Bh4! Bxc2 20 Wxc2 c5 21 Rad1 Ra7
21...Wa5!? 22 Wc1 Rd7 23 Bf6 d4
23...Wa5 24 cxd4 cxd4 25 Rd3 Wa5 26
g4 Dd5 27 Wh6 Rc8? 27...b4± 28
Red1! Dxf6 29 exf6 Rc5 30 Dxd4
Rcd5 31 Rh3 1-0 Haag**

309 Haag-Weiner corr 77/79
**1 e4 e5 2 Df3 Dc6 3 Bb5 a6 4 Ba4
Df6 5 0-0 Dxe4 6 d4 b5 7 Bb3 d5 8
dxe5 Be6 9 c3 Bc5 10 Dbd2 0-0 11
Bc2 Bf5 12 Db3 Bg4 13 Dxc5 Dxc5
14 Re1 Re8 15 Bf4 De6?** 15...d4
16 Bg3? 16 Wd3! **De7 17 Wd2 Bf5 18
Bxf5 Dxf5 19 Rad1 c6 20 Dd4!
Dexd4** 20...Dfxd4 21 cxd4 c5!? **21
cxd4 Dxg3?** 21...Re6 += **22 hxg3 Re6
23 Rc1 a5 24 Rc5 g6 25 Rec1 Ra6**

26 g4!± Wh4 27 g5 h6 28 gxh6 g5

29 ♖5c3 ♛xh6 30 ♖h3 ♛g7 31 g4!
♖h6 32 ♖xh6 ♚xh6 33 ♚g2 ♛g7
34 ♛d3 ♛h6 35 ♛f5 ♖a8 36 ♛d7
♛e6 37 ♛xe6 fxe6 38 ♖xc6 ♛f7 39
♖c7+ ♚g6 40 ♖e7 ♖a6 41 ♚g3 ♖c6
42 f4 gxf4+ 43 ♚xf4 b4 44 b3 ♖a6
45 g5 ♖c6 46 ♚g4 ♖a6 47 ♖d7 ♖a8
48 ♖d6 ♚f7 49 g6+ ♚xg6 50 ♖xe6+
♚f7 51 ♖d6 a4 52 ♚f5 axb3 53
axb3 ♖a3 54 e6+ ♚e8 55 ♖b6 ♖xb3
56 ♚e5 1-0 Haag

310 Ciric Velimirovic Ochrid 79

1 e4 e5 2 ♘f3 ♘c6 3 ♗b5 a6 4 ♗a4
♘f6 5 0-0 ♘xe4 6 d4 b5 7 ♗b3 d5
8 dxe5 ♗e6 9 ♘bd2 ♘c5 10 c3 d4 11
♗xe6 ♘xe6 12 cxd4 ♘cxd4 13 ♘xd4
♛xd4 14 ♛c2 14 ♛f3 ♖d8 15 a4
♗b4!= c5 15 ♘f3 ♛d5 16 ♖d1 ♛c6
17 a4 ♗e7 18 axb5 axb5 19 ♖xa8+
♛xa8 20 ♛d3?! 20 ♛f5 0-0 21 ♘g5
g6 22 ♛g4 =+ ♛b7! 21 h3 0-0 22
♛d7 ♖b8! 23 ♛xb7 ♖xb7 24 ♗e3 f5!∓
25 exf6 ♗xf6 26 b3 ♚f7 27 ♚f1 ♚e7
28 ♖d5 28 ♖c1 c4 29 bxc4 bxc4
30 ♖d2 c3 31 ♖c2 ♖b2 32 ♖c1 ♚d6
33 ♘e1 ♛d5 34 ♘d3 ♖b8 35 ♖a1
♚c4 36 ♘c1 ♘c5! −+ 37 ♚e2 37 ♗xc5
♚xc5 △ ♗d4, ♖b2 ♗d4 38 ♗xd4 ♚xd4
39 ♚f3 ♖f8+ 40 ♚e2 ♚c4 41 ♖a7
♖e8+ 42 ♚f3 42 ♚d1 ♖d8+ 43 ♚e1
c2 44 ♚e2 ♖d1 45 ♖a1 ♘d3! 46
♖a4+ ♚b5 47 ♘xd3 ♚xa4 48 ♘b2+
♚b3 49 ♘xd1 c1♛ ♖e1 43 ♘a2 c2
44 ♖a3 ♘b3 45 ♖a4+ ♚c5 46 ♖a7
♖a1 0-1 Maric

311 Sax-Ivkov Rio 79

1 e4 e5 2 ♘f3 ♘c6 3 ♗b5 a6 4 ♗a4
♘f6 5 0-0 ♗e7 6 ♗xc6 dxc6 7 ♘c3
♗g4!? 7...♘d7 8 h3 ♗h5 9 g4 ♗g6
10 ♛e2 10 ♘xe5!? ♘d7 11 d4 exd4
12 ♘xd4 h5 13 ♘f5 hxg4 14 hxg4
♗d6 15 f4?! 15 ♘xd6+ cxd6 16

f3 ♛h4 17 ♛g2∝ ♗xf5 16 exf5+
♚f8 17 g5 ♘c5 18 b4 18 ♗e3 ♛d7∓

18...♛d7! 19 bxc5 19 ♛g4!? ♖e8 (△
♘e4) 20 bxc5 ♗xc5+ 21 ♚g2 ♛d4
22 ♛f3 ♗b4 23 ♗b2! ♖e3 24 ♛d1!
♖hh3!? 25 ♛xd4 ♖hg3+ =; 24...
♛c4 25 ♛d8+ ♖e8 26 ♛d3∝ ♗xc5+
20 ♗e3 ♛xf5∓ 21 ♘e4! 21 ♗xc5+?
♛xc5+ −+; 21 ♛f3 ♗xe3+ 22 ♛xe3
♛g4+ 23 ♚f2 ♖h2+ 24 ♚e1 ♖e8 25
♘e4 ♛g2 −+ ♗xe3+ 22 ♛xe3 ♛h7 23
♚f2 ♛h2+ 24 ♚e1 ♖e8 25 ♛a3+ ♚g8
26 ♛e3 ♚f8? 27 ♛a3+ ♚g8 28 ♛e3
♚f8? 28...f5! 29 gxf6 ♛xc2 −+; 29
♘f6+ ♚f7 −+ ½-½ Miles

312 Panchenko-Podgaets USSR 79

1 e4 e5 2 ♘f3 ♘c6 3 ♗b5 a6 4 ♗a4
♘f6 5 0-0 ♗e7 6 ♖e1 b5 7 ♗b3 d6 8
c3 0-0 9 d4 ♗g4 10 a4!? 10 ♗e3;
10 d5 ♘a5 11 ♗c2 c6 12 h3 ♗xf3
13 ♛xf3 cxd5 14 exd5 ♘c4 15 ♘d2
♘b6= ♘a5 10...♛d7! 11 axb5 axb5
12 ♗xf7+ ♚xf7 13 ♛b3+ d5! =+
Panchenko-Suetin, Dubna 79; 13...
♚g6?? 14 ♘h4+ ♚h5 15 ♖xa8 ♖xa8
16 ♛f7+ ♚xh4 17 ♛xg7 +− 11 ♗c2
d5?! 11...c5 12 dxe5 ♗xf3 13 ♛xf3
dxe5 14 ♘d2 c4 ∝/+= 12 exd5 e4
13 axb5! 13 ♗xe4 ♘xe4 14 ♖xe4
♗xf3 15 gxf3 ♗f6 += axb5?! 13...
exf3 14 ♖xa5 fxg2 15 ♛d3± 14

♗xe4 ♘xe4 15 ♖xe4 f5?! 15...♗f5!?
16 ♖e5 ♗g6 17 b4 ♘c4 18 ♖xa8
♕xa8 19 ♖xe7 ♗xb1± **16 ♖e1 ♗d6**
16...♗f6 17 ♗f4! +− **17 ♕d3!** +−
♘b3 18 ♗g5! ♕c8 19 ♖xa8 ♕xa8 20
♕xb5 ♖b8 21 ♕d7 ♗xf3 22 gxf3 f4 23
♗e7 h6 1-0 Gufeld

313 Chiburdanidze-Psahis USSR 79
1 e4 e5 2 ♘f3 ♘c6 3 ♗b5 a6 4 ♗a4
♘f6 5 0-0 ♗e7 6 ♖e1 b5 7 ♗b3 0-0
8 d4 d6 8...♘xd4 9 ♗xf7+ ♖xf7 10
♘xe5 ♖f8∞ **9 c3 ♗g4 10 d5** 10 ♗e3
♘a5 11 ♗c2 c6 11...♕c8!? 12 h3 ♗d7
13 ♘bd2 c6 14 b4 ♘b7 15 dxc6
♕xc6 16 ♗b2 ♘d8 17 ♗d3 ♘e6 18 c4
♕b7 19 a3 ♘f4 20 ♗f1 ♖ec8 =+
Tseshkovsky-Romanishin, Tallinn 79,
12 a4!? c6 13 ♗g5 h6 14 ♗xf6 ♗xf6
15 dxc6 ♖d8 16 axb5 axb5 17 ♕d5
♕xc6 18 ♗d3! += Tseshkovsky-
Romanishin, Tallinn 79 **12 h3 ♗xf3**
13 ♕xf3 cxd5 15 exd5 ♘c4 15 ♘d2
♖c8!? N 15...♘b6 16 ♘f1∞ **16 ♘f1?!**
♘e8 17 a4 g6 18 ♘e3 ♗g5! =+ **19**
axb5 axb5 20 ♘xc4 bxc4 21 ♗xg5
♕xg5 22 ♗a4 ♖c5 23 ♗c6?! 23 ♗xe8
f5 24 ♖a8 ♘f6∓ 25 ♖xf8+ ♔xf8 26
♖a1 ♕d2 27 ♕g3

g5 28 ♖a8+ ♔g7 29 ♖d8 h6! 30 ♕e3
30 ♖xd6? f4 31 ♕f3 e4 ♕d1+ **31 ♔h2**
f4 32 ♕f3 ♕d2 33 g3 e4 34 ♕g2 f3

35 ♕f1 e3 36 ♖xd6 ♕xf2+! 0-1 Pytel

314 Sellos-Honfi Trstenik 79
1 e4 e5 2 ♘f3 ♘c6 3 ♗b5 a6 4 ♗a4
♘f6 5 0-0 ♗e7 6 ♖e1 b5 7 ♗b3 d6
8 c3 0-0 9 h3 ♘a5 10 ♗c2 c5 11 d4
♕c7 12 ♘bd2 cxd4 13 cxd4 ♗b7
14 ♘f1 ♖ac8 15 ♗d3 d5 16 dxe5
♘xe4 17 ♘g3 f5 18 exf6 ♗xf6 19
♘xe4 dxe4 20 ♗xe4 ♖fd8 21 ♕e2 ♖e8
22 ♕d3?! N 22 ♘d2 ♖e7 23 ♕f3 ♕d6∞
Nowak **♖xe4! 23 ♖xe4 ♖d8 24 ♖d4!**
24 ♕e2? ♗xe4 ♕xe4 ♖d1+ 26 ♘e1
♕e7 27 ♕xe7 ♗xe7 28 ♔f1 ♗b4 −+
♗xd4 25 ♘xd4 ♕d6?! 25...♕e5! 26
♗e3 (26 ♘f3 ♕f6) ♘c4 27 b3?!
♘xe3 28 fxe3 ♕g3 29 ♕e2 ♗xg2! 30
♕xg2 ♕xe3+∓ **26 ♗d2! ♘c6 27 ♕b3+**
♔h8 28 ♘f3 ♕g6 29 ♗g5! ♖f8 29...
♖d3? 30 ♘h4! ♕xg5 31 ♕xd3 ♕xh4
32 ♕d7 ♕e7 33 ♖d1 +−; 29...♘d4?
30 ♘e5 +− **30 ♕e3 h6 31 ♗h4 ♘a5**
32 ♗g3 ♗xf3 33 ♕a3 ♕f6 34 ♕xa5
♕xb2 35 ♖e1 ♗d5 36 a3 ♕f6 37 ♕d2
♗b7 38 ♕b4 ♕g8 39 f3 ♕g6 40 ♔h2
♖e8 41 ♕b3+ ♔h7 ½-½ Honfi

315 Brodhuhn-Honfi Baden 79
1 e4 e5 2 ♘f3 ♘c6 3 ♗b5 a6 4 ♗a4
♘f6 5 0-0 ♗e7 6 ♖e1 b5 7 ♗b3 d6
8 c3 0-0 9 h3 ♘a5 10 ♗c2 c5 11 d4
♕c7 12 ♘bd2 cxd4 13 cxd4 ♗b7 14
♘f1 ♖ac8 15 ♖e2 d5 16 ♘xe5?! N
dxe4 17 ♘g3 ♖fd8! 18 ♘f5 18 ♘xe4?
♕xe5! 19 dxe5 ♖xd1+ 20 ♗xd1 ♘xe4
−+ **♗c5! 19 ♕d2?!** 19 ♗g5? ♗xd4
20 ♘xd4 ♕xe5 −+; 19 ♗e3!? ♘c6 =+
h6 20 ♕f4 20 ♘xh6+? gxh6 21 ♕xh6
♗xd4 22 ♕g5+ ♔f8 23 ♕xf6 ♕xe5 24
♗h6+ ♔g8 25 ♕h4 f5 −+ **♗xd4 21**
♘xd4 ♖xd4 22 b3 ♘d5 23 ♕g3 ♕c3 24
♕xc3 ♘xc3 25 ♖e1 f6 26 ♘g6 ♔f7 27
♘f4 ♘c6 28 a3 ♖dd8 29 b4 ♘d4 30 ♗b1
g5 31 ♘h5 ♘ce2+ 32 ♔h2 ♘xc1 33

Ξxc1 Ξxc1 34 ♗a2+ Ξc4! 0-1 Honfi

316 Tal-Romanishin Riga 79

1 e4 e5 2 ♘f3 ♘c6 3 ♗b5 a6 4 ♗a4
♘f6 5 0-0 ♗e7 6 Ξe1 b5 7 ♗b3 d6 8
c3 0-0 9 h3 ♗b7 10 d4 Ξe8 11 ♘bd2
11 ♘g5 Ξf8 12 f4?! exf4 13 ♗xf4 ♘a5
14 ♗c2 ♘d5! =∓ 15 exd5 ♗xg5 16 ♕h5
h6 17 ♗g3 g6!∓ Ljubojevic-Gligoric
(5) 79; 15 ♘h7 ♘xf4; 15 ♕h5 h6; 12
♘f3 ♗f8 12 a3!? Kapengut N 12 ♗c2
h6 13 ♗c2 ♘b8 14 b4 ♘bd7 15 ♗b2
c5!? Gheorghiu 15...♕b8 Kapengut 16
bxc5 dxc5 16...exd4 17 ♗xd4 dxe5 18
d5!± 17 dxe5?! 17 ♘xe5!± Kapengut
♘h5!∞ Kapengut, 17...♘xe5 18 ♘xe5
Ξxe5 19 c4± 18 c4! Gheorghiu ♘f4
19 cxb5 axb5 20 a4± Gheorghiu
♕b6 21 axb5 Ξad8

22 ♗c3 22 ♗a4 ♕g6! 23 ♘h4 ♘xh3+
24 ♔f1 ♕g5 25 ♘df3 ♕g4 26 gxh3
♕xh3+ 27 ♔e2 ♘xe5∞; 24 ♔h2 ♘xf2
25 ♘xg6 ♘xd1 26 ♘xf8 ♘xb2 −+ ;
22...♘d3 23 ♘c4 ♘xb2 24 ♘xb6 ♘xd1
25 ♘xd7 Ξxd7 26 b6! +− ; 22 Ξa3!
♕g6 23 ♘h4 ♕g5 24 ♘df3 ♘xh3+ 25
♔f1 ♕g4 26 gxh3 ♕xh3+ 27 ♘g2
♘xe5 28 ♘xe5! ♕h1+ 29 ♔e2 Ξxd1 30
Ξxh1 Ξxh1 31 Ξa7 +− Kapengut
♕g6 23 ♘h4 ♕g5 24 ♕g4! Gheorghiu
♕xg4 ! Gheorghiu; ?! 24...♘xe5 25
♕xg5 hxg5 26 ♘hf3 ♘xf3+! 27 ♘xf3
♘d3 28 Ξe3 c4 29 ♗d4 Ξxe4 30

♗xd3 Ξxe3= Kapengut 25 hxg4
♘xe5 26 Ξa7 ♗c8 27 ♗b3 Ξd7?!±
27...c4!? 28 ♗xe5! Ξxe5 29 ♗xc4+
Kapengut 28 b6 Ξb7 28...c4!
Romanishin 29 ♘xe5!±/ +− Ξxe5 30
♘c4 Ξee7 31 ♘d6 Ξxa7 32 bxa7
Ξxa7 33 ♘xc8 Ξc7 34 ♘b6 Ξb7
35 Ξb1! c4 36 ♘xc4 ♘e2+ 37 ♔f1
♘c3 38 Ξb2 1-0 Miles/Speelman

317 Gufeld-Kakageldiev USSR 79

1 e4 e5 2 ♘f3 ♘c6 3 ♗b5 a6 4 ♗a4
♘f6 5 0-0 ♗e7 6 Ξe1 b5 7 ♗b3 d6 8
c3 0-0 9 h3 ♘a5 9...♗b7!? 10 ♗c2
c5 11 d4 ♕c7 12 ♘bd2 cxd4 13 cxd4
♘c6 13...♗d7 14 ♘f1 Ξac8 15 ♘e3
Δ b3, d5 += 14 ♘b3 14 a3 exd4 15
♘b3 += Razuvaev-Kakageldiev,
USSR ½-Final 78 a5 15 ♗e3 a4 16
♘bd2 ♗e6?! 16...♘b4 17 ♗b1 ♗d7 18
a3 ♘c6 19 ♗d3 ♘a5∞ 17 a3 ♘a5 18
Ξc1 ♕b8 19 ♘g5! += ♗d7 20 f4 ♗d8?
20...♘c6 21 fxe5 dxe5 20 dxe5± ♘e8
22...♕xe5 23 ♘df3 ♕xb2 24 e5 +−
23 ♘df3 ♗c6 24 e6 f6

25 ♘xh7! ♘c4 25...♔xh7 26 ♘g5+
fxg5 27 ♕h5+ ♔g8 28 e5 +− 26 ♘xf8
26 ♗d4 ♔xh7!; 26 ♗c5 ♗b6! ♘xe3 27
Ξxe3 27 ♘d7! +− ♗b6 28 ♕d2 28
♕e2 ♕a7!?± ♘d6! 28...♕a7 29 Ξe1
♔xf8 30 ♔h1 ♗xe3 31 Ξxe3 +− 29
♘d7! 29 ♗d3 ♕a7 30 Ξe1 Ξxf8±

♘c4 29...♗xd7 30 exd7 ♘c4 ♕d5+
+− **30 ♘xb8 ♘xd2 31 ♖ce1** 31 ♘xc6
♗xe3+ ♔h1 ♘xf3 33 ♖d1 +− **♘xf3+ 32
gxf3 ♖xb8 33 ♔g2 ♗xe3 34 ♖xe3 ♔f8
35 ♖c3 ♖b6 36 ♗b1 ♔e7 37 ♗a2 b4
38 axb4 ♖xb4 39 ♖c2 ♔d6 40 ♔f2 g5
41 ♖d2+ ♔e7 42 ♔g3 1-0 Gufeld**

318 Strenzwilk-Shapiro USA 79
**1 e4 e5 2 ♘f3 ♘c6 3 ♗b5 a6 4 ♗a4
♘f6 5 0-0 ♗e7 6 ♖e1 b5 7 ♗b3 d6 8
c3 0-0 9 h3 h6 10 d4 ♖e8 11 ♘bd2**
11 ♗e3 ♗f8 12 ♘bd2 ♘a5 13 ♗c2
c5 14 d5 ♗d7 15 b4 += Ghinda-
Ciocaltea, Rumania Final 78; 12...♗b7
13 dxe5 ♘xe5 14 ♘xe5 dxe5 15 ♕f3
c5= Smyslov-Tal, USSR 62; 13 ♕b1!?
♗f8 12 ♘f1 12 ♗c2 ♗d7 13 ♗d3! ♕b8
14 b3 g6 15 ♗b2 ♗g7 16 d5 ♘d8
17 c4 ♘h5 18 ♗f1 ♘f4 19 ♕c2 +=
Savon-Geller, Lvov 78; 12 d5 ♘e7 13
a4 ♗d7 14 c4 ♘g6 15 axb5 axb5 16
♖xa8 ♕xa8 17 cxb5 ♗xb5 18 ♘b1
♖b8 19 ♘c3 ♗d7= Gligoric-Spassky,
Havana 62 **♗b7** 12...♗d7 13 ♘g3 ♘a5
14 ♗c2 ♘c4 15 ♘h2 c5 16 b3 ♘b6 17
f4 cxd4 18 cxd4 ♕c8!?≈ Geller
13 ♘g3 ♘a5 13...g6 14 ♘h4! d5 15
exd5 ♘a5 16 dxe5 ♘xb3 17 axb3
♘xd5 18 ♘f3 ♗g7 19 ♘e4 ♘b6 20 ♗f4
+= Gufeld-Tukmakov, USSR 75 **14
♗c2 g6!?** 14...c5 15 d5 ♗c8 16 b3 g6
17 ♗e3 ♗g7 18 ♕d2 ♔h7 19 ♖f1±
Shamkovich-Liberzon, USSR 64; 14...
♘c4 15 ♗d3 ♘b6 16 ♗d2 c5 17 d5
♗c8! 18 ♘h2 ♘h7! 19 ♖f1 ♗e7 20 f4
exf4 21 ♗xf4 ♗g5 22 ♕f3 ♖a7!=
Hecht-Gligoric, Busum 69 **15 b3** 15
a4 ♘c4 16 ♗d3 d5!∞; 15...♕d7 16 b3
♗g7= **c5 16 dxe5** 16 d5! ♖c8 17 ♗e3±
dxe5 17 ♕e2 c4 18 b4 ♘c6 19 ♗e3 a5
19...♕c7!? Δ ♖ad8 **20 a3 axb4 21 ax
b4 ♕c7 22 ♘h2** += Δ ♘g4 ♖xa1 **23 ♖x
a1 ♖a8 24 ♖xa8** 24 ♖d1 ♖a2 ♗xa8 **25**

♗g4 ♘xg4 26 ♕xg4 ♗b7 27 ♘f5 h5
27...♗c8? 28 ♕g3 ♔h7 29 ♘xh6 ♗xh6
30 ♕h4 +−; 28...h5 29 ♕g5 +− **28 ♕g3
♔h7 29 ♘h4!** ♗g7 Δ ♘e6; 30 ♘f3
♗g7 +=; 30...f6!? 31 ♘h4 ♕f7 +=/±
**30 ♘f3 ♗c8 31 ♕h4 ♕e7 32 ♗g5 f6
33 ♗d2** 33 ♗e3?! ♘xb4 34 cxb4 ♕xb4
35 ♗d2 c4 ∓/−+ **♔g8?** 33...♗h6!=
34 ♗xh6 ♔xh6 35 g4 ♗e6 **34 ♕g3!** g5
35 h4 g4 36 ♘e1 ♕d6 37 ♕e3 ∓/+=
♘d8 38 ♕e2 ♘e6 39 g3 ♗d7 39...♗b7
40 ♘g2 (Δ ♘e3−f5) f5? 41 exf5
♕d5 42 ♗e4! ♕xe4 43 ♕xe4 ♗xe4
44 fxe6 ♗f5 45 e7 ♔f7 46 ♗g5 +−
40 ♘g2 ♗c6 41 ♘e3 ♗h6?? 41...♕d7±
**42 ♘xc4 bxc4 43 ♗xh6 ♗b5 44 f3
1-0 Ciamarra**

319 Kagan-Harandi Rio 79
**1 e4 e5 2 ♘f3 ♘c6 3 ♗b5 a6 4 ♗xc6
dxc6 5 0-0 f6 6 d4 ♗g4 7 c3!?** 7
dxe5 +=/= **♗d6** 7...exd4 8 cxd4
♗xf3 9 ♕xf3 ♕xd4 10 ♘c3∞ **8 ♗e3
♗e7 9 ♘bd2 ♕d7 10 h3 ♗e6 11 dxe5
fxe5 12 ♘g5 ♗g8 13 ♕h5+ ♗g6 14
♖fd1 0-0-0 15 ♘f1 ♕e8 16 ♘g3 h6
17 ♘f3 ♗f7 18 ♘f5 ♖g8 19 ♖d2 ♔b8
20 ♘3h4** 20 ♘h2!? **♗e7 21 ♕d1 ♘c8
22 ♕a4 ♗f8 23 ♖xd8 ♕xd8 24 ♘f3
♕f6 25 ♕a5 c5** 25...♗d6 +=/± **26 b4**
26 ♗xc5? b6 **♗h5**

27 bxc5!? 27 ♘d2 ♗xf3 **28 gxf3 g6 29 ♘g3 h5** 29...♕xf3? 30 c6± **30 ♖b1 ♕c6 31 ♖b4 ♗e7 32 ♕g2± ♖d8 33 ♕b3 ♗h4 34 ♘f1 g5?! 35 ♘h2 ♘e7 36 ♖d1?** 36 ♕f7± **♖f8 37 ♕c4 ♕f6 38 ♕e2 ♘g6 39 c6?∓** 39 ♔h1 ♘f4∞ **♕xc6 40 ♕d3 ♘f4+ 41 ♗xf4 gxf4 42 ♖b1 ♖d8 0-1** 43 ♕c2 ♖g8+ 44 ♔h1 ♕g6 −+; 44 ♔f1 ♕c4+; 43 ♕e2 ♖g8+ 44 ♔h1 ♕e6; 44 ♔f1 ♕g6 −+ **Miles**

Ponziani

320 Velimirovic-Harandi
Rio 79
1 e4 e5 2 ♘f3 ♘c6 3 c3 ♘f6 4 d4 d6 4...♘xe4 5 d5 ♘e7 6 ♘xe5 ♘g6 7 ♕d4 ♘f6 8 ♕xe4 ♕xe5= Velimirovic-Smejkal, Rio 79 **5 h3** 5 ♗b5 **g6** 5...♘xe4?? 6 d5 △ ♕a4+ +− **6 ♗e3 ♗g7 7 dxe5 dxe5 8 ♕xd8+ ♘xd8 9 ♘bd2 0-0** 9...♘d7 △ ♘e6= **10 ♘xe5 ♖e8 11 f4!?** ♘h5 **12 0-0-0 ♗h6** △ ♖xe5 **13 ♘ef3 ♗xf4 14 ♗xf4 ♘xf4 15 e5 ♗f5 16 g4! ♗d3** 16...♘d3+ 17 ♔c2? ♘f2+? 18 gxf5 ♘xh1 19 ♘e4±; 17...♘b4+! 18 ♔b3 ♗c2+ −+; 18 ♔c1 ♘xa2 mate; 17 ♗xd3 ♗xd3 18 ♖he1 △ ♘e4 += **17 ♖h2 ♗xf1 18 ♖xf1 +=** ♘c6 **19 ♔c2 h6 20 g5 h5 21 ♘e4 ♕g7 22 ♘f6 ♖ed8 23 h4 ♘e6 24 ♖hf2 a5 25 ♖e2 a4 26 ♘e1 ♘c5 27 ♘e4 ♘xe4 28 ♖xe4 ♖e8 29 ♘d3 ♖a5 30 ♖fe1 ♘d8?!** 30...♘e6 31 ♔b1!? △ b4, c4 **31 ♖b4 b5?!** 31...b6 **32 ♘c5 ♘c6 33 ♖be4 b4 34 ♘d3 bxc3 35 ♔xc3± ♖e6 36 ♔c4** △ ♘c5, e6 **♘d8 37 ♕b4 ♖d5** 37...♘c6+ 38 ♔a3 +− **38 ♖1e3 ♖b6+ 39 ♔xa4 ♘e6 40 b4 +− c5 1-0** time **Miles**

4 ♘

321 Kallai-L.Kovacs Hungary 79
1 e4 e5 2 ♘f3 ♘c6 3 ♘c3 ♘f6 4 d4 exd4 4...♗b4 5 ♘xe5 ♕e7 6 ♕d3 ♘xe5 7 dxe5 ♕xe5 8 ♗d2 0-0 9 0-0-0 ♗xc3 10 ♗xc3 ♕xe4?! 11 ♕g3 ♘e8 12 ♗d3 ♕e6 13 ♖he1 ♕h6+ 14 ♗d2 ♕h5 15 ♖e5 f5 16 ♖de1 ♘d6 17 ♗c3 ♕h6+ 18 f4 b5 19 ♖e7 ♖f7 20 ♖xf7 ♔xf7 21 ♕e3 +− Vegh-Florian, Hungary 79 **5 ♘d5 ♘xd5** 5...♗b4!? **6 exd5 ♗b4+?!** 6...♘b4 7 ♗c4 ♕e7+ 8 ♔d2 g6 9 ♕e1 +=; 8 ♔f1!? **7 ♗d2 ♕e7+ 8 ♕e2 ♗xd2+ 9 ♕xd2 ♕xe2+ 10 ♗xe2 ♘e7 11 d6! cxd6 12 ♘xd4 a6** 12...0-0 13 ♘b5 d5 14 ♗f3± **13 ♖he1 g6** 13...0-0 14 ♗f3 ♘c6 15 ♘f5±; 14 ♗xa6? ♘c6!= **14 ♗f3 ♖d8 15 ♖ad1 ♖b8** 15...♘c6 **16 ♔c1 b5 17 ♘e2 ♖e8?** 17...♖b6 **18 ♖xd6 ♘f5 19 ♖f6! ♖e7** 19...♔e7 20 ♘c3+± **20 ♔d2 ♘g7 21 ♗d5 ♘e6?** 21...♔e8 **22 ♘c3 ♖b6 23 ♘e4 ♔c7 24 f4! ♗b7** 24...♘d8 **25 ♖xb6 ♔xb6 26 ♘d6 ♖xe1 27 ♔xe1 ♔c5 28 ♘xf7! ♔xd5 29 ♘xd8 ♔e4 30 ♘f7! +− 25 ♗xb7 ♕xb7 26 f5 gxf5 27 ♖xf5 ♔c7 28 ♘f6! ♖d6+ 29 ♖d5 ♔c6 30 ♖xd6+ ♔xc6 31 g4 +− ♔c6 32 h4 h6 33 h5! ♔d6 34 g5 ♘xg5 35 ♘e8+ ♖xe8 36 ♖xe8 f5 37 ♔e3 ♘e6 38 ♖h8 ♔e5 39 ♖xh6 f4+ 40 ♔f2 a5 41 ♖h7 ♘c5 42 ♖f7 ♘e4+ 43 ♔e1 d5 44 h6 1-0 Vegh**

1 e4 e5 2 ♘f3 ♘c6 3 ♗c4

322 Gipslis-Ruderfer USSR 79
1 e4 e5 2 ♘f3 ♘c6 3 ♗c4 ♗c5 4 c3 ♘f6 5 d3 d6 5...d5? 6 exd5 ♘xd5 7 ♕b3 +− **6 ♘bd2 a6 7 ♗b3!** 7 0-0 ♘a5 **0-0 8 0-0 ♗a7** 8...♗e6 9 ♘c4 += **9 ♖e1 ♘e7** 9...♘g4 10 ♖e2± **10 h3 ♘g6 11 ♘f1 h6 12 ♘g3 c6 13 d4± ♕c7 14 ♗e3 b5 15 ♕d2** △ ♗xh6

♕h7 16 ♖ad1 ♗b7 17 ♘f5! ♘xe4
17...♘g8 18 dxe5!± 18 ♕c1 ♗c8

19 ♘xg7! f5 19...♔xg7 20 ♗xh6+ +−
20 ♗xh6 f4 21 ♖xe4 21 ♘e6 ♗xe6
22 ♗xf8± ♕xh6 22 ♘e6 ♗xe6 23
♗xe6 d5 24 ♖xe5± ♘xe5 25 ♘xe5
♕d6 25...♖ae8 26 ♖e1! 26 ♖e1
♕g7 26...♕xe6?? 27 ♘g4+ +− 27
♗d7 c5 28 ♕d1 f3 29 ♖e3! cxd4
30 cxd4 ♖ad8 31 ♖xf3! ♖xf3 31
♖xd7 32 ♖g3+ ♔h7 33 ♘xd7 +−
32 ♕xf3 ♕f6 32...♖xd7 33 ♕g4+ +−
33 ♕g4+ ♕f8 34 g3 +− ♗b6 35 ♕g2
♖b8 36 ♗xb5 1-0 Gipslis

323 Miles-Korchnoi
South Africa 79
1 e4 e5 2 ♘f3 ♘c6 3 ♗c4 ♗c5 4 c3
♘f6 5 d4 exd4 6 cxd4 ♗b4+ 7 ♗d2
♗xd2+ 8 ♘bxd2 d5 9 exd5 ♘xd5 10
♕b3 ♘ce7?! 10...♘a5! 11 0-0 0-0 12
♘e5 12 ♖fe1 c6 13 ♘e4 ♕b6 14
♖ad1 ♕xb3 15 ♗xb3 ♖d8 16 ♖fe1
♕f8 17 f3 f6 18 ♘c4 18 ♘d3?! ♘f5
b6 19 ♕f2 ♗a6 20 g4 ♖d7 21 g5?!
♗xc4! 21...f5 22 ♘e5; 21...fxg5 22
♘xg5; 22 ♘e5 22 ♗xc4 f5! 23 ♘c3
22 ♘g3 f4; 22 ♗xd5 ♘xd5 23 ♘c3
♘f4 ♘f4 24 ♘e2 24 ♕g3 ♘h5+ 25
♔h4 g6 ♘xe2 24...♘h3+ 25 ♔g3 ♘xg5
26 ♘f4; 26 h4 ♘f7 27 ♘f4 25 ♖xe2
♖ad8 26 ♕e3 26 ♖ed2 f4 △ ♖d6

♘f5-e3 b5! 27 ♗e6 27 ♗b3 c5 28 ♖ed2
c4 −+ ♖d6 28 ♕f4 ♖xd4+ 29 ♖xd4
♖xd4+ 30 ♕e5 c5 31 ♗b3 31 ♖c2
♘g6+ 32 ♔xf5 ♖f4 mate ♖d8 32 ♗e6
♘c6+ 33 ♕f4 ♘d4 33...♖d4+ 34
♔xf5? g6+ 35 ♔f6 ♖f4+ −+ 34 ♖e5
g6 35 ♗d5 a5 36 b3 ♖d7 37 a4 c4!
38 bxc4 bxa4 39 ♖e3 39 c5 a3 40 c6
♖e7 41 ♖xe7 ♔xe7 42 ♔e5 ♘xc6+
−+ ♖e7! 40 ♖xe7 40 ♖a3 ♘e2 mate
♕xe7 41 ♕e3 a3 42 c5 ♘c2+ 0-1
Miles

324 Levitt-Botterill England 79
1 e4 e5 2 ♘f3 ♘c6 3 ♗c4 ♘f6 4 ♘g5
d5 5 exd5 ♘a5 6 ♗b5+ c6 7 dxc6 bxc6
8 ♗e2 h6 9 ♘f3 9 ♘h3!? g5!? 10 d3
g4 11 ♘g1 ♗c5 12 ♘c3 ♕b6 13 ♘a4±
Estrin, 13...♗xf2+ 14 ♔f1 ♕d8!∞
e4 10 ♘e5 ♗d6 11 d4 exd3 12 ♘xd3
♕c7 13 ♘d2 0-0 14 b4!? ♘d5! 15
♗b2 ♘xb4 16 ♘xb4 ♗xb4 17 0-0
♗d6?! 17...♖d8 18 ♗d3 ♕f4! 19 ♘f3
♘c4 20 ♗c1 ♕f6∓ Spielmann-Cohn,
Stockholm 09 18 ♘f3 ♖d8 19 ♕e1!
19 ♗d3 c5, △ ♗b7∓ c5?! 19...♗g4!≈
Speelman 20 ♕c3 ♗f8 21 ♘e5± ♖b8
22 ♖ad1 ♖e8 23 ♗h5 ♗e6 24 ♖d7!?
24 f4! △ f5 ♕b6! 24...♗xd7? 25
♗xf7+ ♔h7 26 ♕d3+ 25 ♗a1? 25
♕f3!=

25...f6! 26 ♗f7+ 26 ♗xe8 ♖xe8∓

♗xf7 27 ♘xf7 ♖e7 28 ♖d6 ♕b5
△ ♕xf1+ 29 ♘xh6+ gxh6 30 ♖fd1
♗g7 31 ♕g3 ♖be8 32 f4 ♖e3 33 ♕h4
♘c4 34 ♖xf6 ♕b4 35 c3 ♕a4 36 ♖d7?
♖e1+ 37 ♔f2 ♖8e2+ 38 ♔g3 ♖e3+
39 ♔g4 ♕xd7+ 0-1 Botterill

Scotch

325 Biriescu-Ciocaltea
Satu Mare 79
1 e4 e5 2 ♘f3 ♘c6 3 d4 exd4 4 ♘xd4
♗c5 4...♘f6 5 ♘xc6 bxc6 6 e5 ♕e7 7
♕e2 ♘d5 8 c4 ♕b4+ 9 ♘d2 ♘f4 10
♕e4 ♘e6 11 ♗e2 +=; 8 ♘d2 ♘b4 9
♘f3 ♗a6 10 c4 d5? 11 a3 ♗xc4 12
♕d1 ♗xf1 13 ♔xf1 ♘a6 14 ♕a4
♘b8 15 ♗g5± Tatai-Adorjan, Amsterdam 77; 4...♕h4 5 ♘b5 ♗b4+ 6 ♘d2?!
♕xe4+ 7 ♗e2 ♕xg2! 8 ♗f3 ♕h3 9
♘xc7+ ♔d8 10 ♘xa8 ♘f6 11 c3 ♖e8+
12 ♗e2 ♘e5! 13 ♕a4 ♘d3+∓ Brajovic-
Perovic, Jugoslavia 78 5 ♘b3 ♗b4+
6 ♗d2 6 c3 ♗e7 7 c4 ♘f6 8 ♘c3 0-0
9 ♗e2 ♖e8 10 f3 a5! 11 a4 d6 12 0-0
♘d7 13 ♗e3 ♗f6 14 ♕d2 b6= Ivanovic-
Petrosian, Tallinn 79; 10 0-0 a5 11
a4 d6 12 ♗e3 ♘d7 13 ♘b5! ♗f6 14
♕c2 ♘b4 15 ♕d2 b6 += Ljubojevic-
Gligoric, Niksic 78 ♗xd2+ 7 ♕xd2
♘f6 8 ♘c3 0-0 0 0-0-0 ♖e8! 9...d6
10 f3 ♗e6 11 ♘d4 ♘xd4 12 ♕xd4 ♘d7
13 f4 ♘b6= Petrosian-Trifunovic,
Belgrade 54 10 f3 d6 11 g4 ♗e6 12
g5 ♘d7 13 h4 a5! 14 ♗b5 ♘b4! 15
♗xd7 15 a3 c6! 16 axb4 axb4 =+;
16 ♗e2 ♗xb3! 17 cxb3 ♘c5 ♗xd7?!
15...♕xd7! 16 ♘c5 ♕c6 17 ♘xe6
fxe6 18 f4 b5! 19 f5 b4!∓ 16 a3
♘c6 16...♘a6 17 ♘xa5 ♘c5 18 b4
17 f4 b5! 18 h5! b4 19 ♘d5 ♘e7 20
♘f6+?! 20 h6 ♘xd5 21 ♕d4 ♘f6 22
hxg7 ♖xe4 23 ♕xf6 ♖e6; 21 ♕xd5!
+= gxf6 21 gxf6

21...♘f5! 22 e5?! 22 exf5 ♕xf6 =+
♔h8 23 ♖hg1 ♖g8 24 axb4 axb4
25 ♕xb4 ♖xg1! −+ 26 ♖xg1 ♖a4!
27 ♕d2 ♕a8 28 ♔b1 ♗e6 29 ♖e1
♖a1+! 0-1 Ciocaltea

326 Honfi-B.Lengyel Budapest 79
1 e4 e5 2 ♘f3 ♘c6 3 d4 exd4 4 ♘xd4
♗c5 5 ♗e3 ♕f6 6 c3 ♘ge7 7 g3 d6 8
♗g2 0-0?! 8...♘e5!? 9 0-0 ♘e5 10
♘c2! ♗b6 11 ♘d2 ♕g6 12 ♗xb6 axb6
13 ♘e3 ♘g4 14 ♕e2 ♘xe3 15 ♕xe3
+= ♕h5 16 ♖fe1 ♗d7 17 a3 ♖fe8 18
♕d3 ♘c6 19 f4 ♗h3 19...♗e7 △ ♖ae8,
f6, g5 20 ♗xh3 ♕xh3 21 ♖e3 ♖e6?!
22 ♖ae1 ♖a5?! 23 ♘f3 ♖h5?! 24
♖1e2 h6 25 ♖g2 ♕g4 26 b4 ♖g6??
26...♖h3 27 b5 ♘a5 28 f5 ♖f6 29
h4 1-0 29...♕h3 30 g4 +−; 29...♘b3
30 ♘h2 ♕h3 31 g4 +− Honfi

Petroff

327 Ardijansah-Handoko
Jakarta 79
1 e4 e5 2 ♘f3 ♘f6 3 ♘xe5 d6 4 ♘f3
♘xe4 5 d3?! ♘f6 6 ♗e2 ♗e7= 7 0-0
0-0 8 b3?! 8 d4 ♘c6 9 ♗b2 ♘d5 △
♘f4 10 ♕d2 ♗f6 11 d4 ♖e8 12 c4
♘f4 13 ♕xf4 ♖xe2 14 ♘bd2 14 ♘c3
♖xb2 15 ♕c1 ♗g4! 16 ♕xb2 ♗xf3
△ ♘xd4 h5 15 ♖ae1 15 h4 ♗g4 g5!

169

16 ♛xf6 16 ♛g3 h4 17 ᐨxh4 ♖xd2
–+ **♛xf6 17 ♖xe2 ♗f5** –+ **18 ᐨe4
♗xe4 19 ♖xe4 ᐨb4 20 ♗c3 ♛f5 21
♖e2 ᐨd3 22 ♖e3 0-1 Keene**

1 e4 e6

328 Kagan-Vaganian Rio 79

**1 e4 e6 2 d3 d5 3 ᐨd2 ᐨf6 4 ᐨgf3
ᐨc6 5 g3** 5 e5!? ᐨfd7 6 d4; 5 c3
**♗c5!= 6 ♗g2 dxe4 7 dxe4 e5 8 0-0
0-0 9 c3 a5 10 a4 b6 11 ♛e2? ♗a6
12 ᐨc4 ᐨe8 13 b3 ᐨd6∓ 14 ᐨh4
♛f6 15 ᐨf5 ᐨxc4 16 bxc4 ᐨe7 17
♗e3 ♗xe3 18 ᐨxe3 ♛c6 19 ♖fe1
♛c5 20 ♗f1 ♖ad8 21 ♛a2 ♖d6 22
♖ed1 ♖fd8 23 ♛b3 ᐨc8?! 24 ♖d5!
♖xd5 25 cxd5 ♗xf1 26 ♖xf1 ᐨd6
27 ♛c2 b5 28 axb5 ᐨxb5 29 ♖c1
♖a8 30 ᐨg4?** 30 ♛a4!? ᐨxc3 31 ♛c2
ᐨe2+ 32 ♔f1 ♛xc2 33 ♖xc2 ᐨd4
34 ♖xc7 **f6 31 ᐨe3 a4** ∓/–+ **32 ♔g2
0-1** time **Miles**

329 Mark.Tseitlin-Vilela
Trnava 79

**1 e4 e6 2 d4 d5 3 ᐨc3 ♗b4 4 ᐨge2
dxe4 5 a3 ♗e7 6 ᐨxe4 ᐨf6 7 ᐨ2g3
7 ♛d3!?** Bronstein **ᐨc6 8 c3 e5?!**
8...0-0 9 f4! b6 10 ♗d3 +=; 8...ᐨxe4!
9 ᐨxe4 ♛d5 10 ♛f3 b6 11 ᐨg5=; 11
♗f4 ♗b7 12 ᐨd2 ♛d7 =+ **9 ᐨxf6+
♗xf6 10 d5 ᐨe7 11 c4 += ᐨf5?** 11...
ᐨg6!? **12 ♗d3 ᐨxg3 13 hxg3± b6 14
♗e3 e4?** 14...♗b7 15 ♛d2 c6; 15 ♗e4
♗g5 **15 ♗xe4 ♗xb2 16 ♖a2 ♗c3+
17 ♔f1 ♗e5**

Diagram

**18 c5! +– ♔f8 19 ♖h5 ♗f6 20 d6 g6
21 ♗xa8 gxh5 22 ♗d5 ♗f5 23 ♛f3
♗d3+ 24 ♔g1 ♔g7 25 dxc7 ♛d7**
25...♛xc7 26 ♗f4 +– **26 ♗h6+ ♔g6**

27 ♖d2 ♗e5 28 ♛xd3+ 1-0 Banas

330 Honfi-Stajcic
Baden-Baden 79

**1 e4 e6 2 d4 d5 3 ᐨc3 ♗b4 4 ᐨge2
ᐨf6 5 e5 ᐨfd7 6 a3 ♗e7 7 f4 f5 8
exf6 ᐨxf6** 8...gxf6? 9 f5± **9 ♗e3
b6 10 ♛d2 c5 11 g3 ᐨc6 12 ♗g2
12 ♗h3!? 0-0 13 0-0!** 13 0-0-0? ᐨa5∓;
13 h3? ᐨh5 Δ cxd4∓ **ᐨg4 14 ᐨd1!**
14 ♔h1? ᐨxe3 15 ♛xe3 ♗f6 16
dxc5 d4 17 ♛f2 dxc3 18 ♗xc6 cxb2∓
**ᐨxe3 15 ᐨxe3 ᐨxd4 16 ᐨxd4 cxd4
17 ♛xd4 ♗c5** 17...♗f6 18 ♛b4 a5
19 ♛b3 ♗a6 20 ♖fe1± **18 ♛d3 a5 19
♖fe1 ♗a6 20 ♛d2 ♛f6** 20...d4? 21 ᐨg4
d3+ 22 ♔h1 dxc2 23 ♛xc2 +– **21
c3 a4** 21...d4?! 22 cxd4 ♗xd4 23
♗xa8 ♖xa8 24 ♖ad1 ♖d8 25 ♛f2 +–
**22 ♔h1 ♖ad8 23 ᐨg4 ♛f5 24 ᐨe5
g5?** 24...d4?! 25 c4± ; 24...♗b5!? +=
25 ᐨc6! Δ ♖e5 gxf4 26 ᐨxd8 ♗e3
26...f3 27 ᐨxe6 fxg2+ 28 ♛xg2 +–
**27 ♖xe3 fxe3 28 ♛xe3 ♖xd8 29
♛xb6 ♖a8 30 ♖e1?!** 30 ♛c6!? ♖a7
31 ♛xa4 +– **♗c4 31 h4!** 31 ♛xe6+?!
♛xe6 32 ♖xe6 ♖b8 += **♖e8 32 ♔h2 e5
33 ♛c6 ♛f7 34 ♛xa4 e4 35 b3 ♗d3
36 ♛d4 ♖b8 37 ♖e3 ♗c2** 37...♖xb3
38 ♖xd3! **38 b4 ♗b3 39 ♖e2 ♛g7
40 ♛c5 ♗c4 41 ♖f2! ♛xc3 42 ♛d6
♖e8 43 ♖f5! e3 44 ♛d7 ♖b8 1-0**

45 ♕e6+ ♔h8 46 ♖e5 △ ♕f6+ +– **Honfi**

331 Jansson-Botterill London 79
1 e4 e6 2 d4 d5 3 ♘c3 ♗b4 4 e5 c5
5 a3 ♗xc3+ 6 bxc3 ♘e7 7 ♕g4 ♕c7
8 ♕xg7 ♖g8 9 ♕xh7 cxd4 10 ♔d1
dxc3 10...♘bc6 11 ♘f3 dxc3; 10...
♕xc3!? 11 ♖b1 ♘d7; 10...♘d7 11
♘f3 ♘xe5 12 ♗f4 ♕xc3 13 ♘xe5
♕xa1+ 14 ♗c1 ♖f8 15 ♗d3 +=; 10...
♘d7 11 ♘f3 dxc3!?; 11...♘f8!? **11**
♘f3 ♘bc6 12 ♗f4 12 ♘g5!? ♘xe5
13 ♗f4 (13 f4 ♖xg5 14 fxg5 ♘5g6
15 h4 ∝/=+) 13...♕b6?! 14 ♗xe5
♖xg5 15 ♗xc3! ♕xf2 16 ♗b5+ ♔d8
17 ♖f1 ♕c5 18 ♖xf7! ♕xb5 19 ♖f8+
♔d7 20 ♗b4!± ; 12 ♘g5 ♘xe5 13 ♗f4
♕c5! =+ **♕b6!** 12...♘d7 13 ♘g5 0-0-0
14 ♘xf7 ♕b6∝ Moe-Holm, Denmark
70; 12...♗d7 13 ♗g3 0-0-0 14 ♗d3
0-0-0 15 ♔e2 += Kuijpers-Padevsky,
Moscow 63 **13 ♔e1** 13 ♗g3 ♕b2!?
14 ♖c1 ♕xa3 **♗d7 14 ♘g5 ♘xe5 15**
♗xe5 ♖xg5 16 ♗f6 ♖g6 17 ♕h4 ♘g8
18 ♗e5! 18 ♗xc3 e5!∓ **f6! 19 ♗d3**
19 ♕h5? 0-0-0 20 ♕xg6 fxe5∓ **♖h6**
20 ♕g3 0-0-0 21 ♗xc3 d4 22 ♗d2
♖h5 23 ♕g6 ♖e5+ 24 ♔f1 ♕b2 24...
♗b5!? **25 ♖d1 ♕xa3 26 f4 ♖d5 27 ♔f2**
♕f8 28 ♖a1 ♗e7 29 ♕e4 ♘c6 30 ♖hb1
♕h6?! 30...♕d6! =+ **31 ♗c4 f5 32**
♕f3 ♘e5

33 ♗xd5! 33 fxe5 ♕xd2+ 34 ♔g1
♘c6 35 ♗xd5 ♖xd5∝ **♘xf3 34 ♗xb7+**
♔c7 35 ♗a5+ ♕d6 36 ♗xf3? 36 ♗b4+!
♔c7 37 ♗xf3 ♖b8 38 ♖xa7+ ♔c8 39
♗d6! +– **♕e7! 37 ♗xd8+ ♕xd8 38**
♖b8+ ♕e7 39 ♖xa7 ♕xf4 40 ♖bb7
½-½ Botterill

332 Vitolins-Holmov USSR 79
1 e4 e6 2 d4 d5 3 ♘c3 dxe4 4 ♘xe4
♗d7!? 5 ♘f3 ♗c6 6 ♕e2!? 6 ♗d3 ♗xe4
7 ♗xe4 c6 8 0-0 ♘f6 9 ♗d3 +=; 6...
♘d7 += **♘f6 7 ♘xf6 gxf6** 7...♕xf6 8
♘e5± **8 ♗f4 ♗d6 9 ♗g3 ♘d7 10 0-0-0**
♕e7 11 c4 += **♘f8 12 ♗xd6 ♕xd6**
13 d5 ♗a4 14 b3 ♗d7 15 dxe6 ♕xe6
16 ♘d4 16 ♕c2!?; 16 ♕d2 += **♕xe2**
17 ♘xe2!? 17 ♗xe2 ♘e6 += **0-0-0**
18 ♘f4 ♗c6 19 ♖xd8+ 19 ♘h5!?
♖xd1+ 20 ♔xd1 ♘d7 21 f3 ♖g8 22
h4!± **♕xd8 20 ♗e2 ♘e6 21 ♖d1+**
♕e7 22 ♘d5+ ♗xd5 23 ♖xd5 ♘f4 +=
24 ♖d2 f5 25 ♗f3 c6 26 b4 a5! 27 b5
27 a3 axb4 28 axb4 ♖a8 29 ♔b2
♖a4 30 ♔b3 ♖a1 += **cxb5 28 cxb5**
♖c8+ 29 ♔d1 b6= 30 ♗c6 ♖d8 31
♖xd8 ♕xd8 32 ♔d2 ♕e7 33 ♔e3 ♘e6
34 ♗f3 ♕f6 35 ♗h5 h6 36 h4 ♘g7
37 ♗d1 ♕e5 38 f4+ ♕d6 39 ♗b3 ♘e6
40 ♗c2 ♘g7 41 ♗b3 ♘e6 ½-½ 42
♗xe6 ♔xe6!= **Gufeld**

333 Klovsky-Gutop USSR 79
1 e4 e6 2 d4 d5 3 ♘c3 ♘f6 4 ♗g5
♗b4 5 e5 h6 6 ♗e3 ♘e4 7 ♕g4 ♕f8 8
a3!? ♗xc3+ 9 bxc3 c5 9...♘xc3 10 ♗d3
c5 11 dxc5 ♕a5 12 ♗d2 ♕a4 13 ♕b4!?
10 ♗d3 ♕a5 11 ♘e2 cxd4 12 ♗xd4
♘c6 13 0-0± △ f4-f5 **♘c5 14 c4!**
△ ♗c3 **♘xd3 15 cxd3 ♘xd4 16 ♕xd4**
16 ♘xd4± **♗d7 17 ♘f4 ♗c6 18 cxd5**
♗xd5 19 ♘xd5 ♕xd5 20 ♕xd5 exd5
21 ♖ac1 ♔e7 22 ♖c7+ ♔e6 23 d4
♖hc8 24 ♖xb7 ♖ab8 25 ♖xa7 ♖c4

26 f4 g6 27 a4 ♖xd4 28 g3! ♖d8 29
♕g2 ♖d2+ 30 ♔f2 ♖d1 31 ♖e2! △
♖a6+ ♖d4 32 ♔f2 h5 33 ♖a6+ ♔e7
34 e6 +− ♖e4 35 ♖xe4 dxe4 36 exf7
♔xf7 37 ♔e3 h4 38 ♖a7+ ♔f6 39
g4 1-0 39...♖d3+ 40 ♔xe4 ♖h3 41
g5+ ♔e6 42 ♖g7 +− **Gufeld**

334 Sax-Vaganian Rio 79
1 e4 e6 2 d4 d5 3 ♘d2 c5 4 exd5
exd5 5 ♗b5+ ♘c6 6 ♕e2+ ♗e7 7 dxc5
♘f6 8 ♘b3 0-0 9 ♗e3 ♘a5? N 9...a6
10 ♗xc6!? 10 ♘f3 a6 11 ♗d3 ♖e8
12 ♘fd4 ♗g4? 12...♘xb3 13 ♘xb3 d4
14 ♘xd4 ♗xc5 15 c3 ♕c7!? 16 ♘c2?
♗g4 17 ♕d2 ♖ad8∓; 16 h3! △ 0-0±;
15...♗g4!? 16 0-0-0!± ; 15 ♘f3 ♕b6
+=/=; 12...♘g4! 13 0-0?! ♘xb3 14
♘xb3 d4 15 ♘xd4 ♗xc5∞; 12...♕c7!?;
13 0-0-0 ♘xe3 14 fxe3 ♗g5 15 ♔b1
+= 13 f3 ♘xb3 14 ♘xb3 d4 15 fxg4
15 ♘xd4? ♗xc5 16 c3 ♘d5 −+ ♗xc5
15...dxe3? 16 0-0± 16 0-0 ♖xe3 17
♕f2± △ g5/♘xc5 ♕d5 18 ♕h4 ♖ae8
18...h6 19 ♖xf6 gxf6 20 ♕xh6 +−
19 ♖f5? 19 ♖xf6!? gxf6 20 ♕h6 (1)
20...♖8e4! 21 ♘xc5 ♕xc5 22 ♕xf6
♖e1+ 23 ♖xe1 ♖xe1+ 24 ♔f2 ♕e5∓;
22 ♖f1 ♖e1∓; 22 ♗xe4 ♖xe4 ∞/∓;
21 ♘d2!? f5! 22 ♕g5+ ♔f8 23 gxf5∞;
21 ♗xe4 ♕xe4∓ 22 ♖f1 ♖e2; 22
♘xc5? ♖e1+ −+; (2) 20...f5 21 ♗xf5
d3!? 22 ♗xh7+ ♔h8 23 ♗xd3+ ♔g8
24 ♗h7+ ♔h8 25 ♗e4+ ♔g8 26 ♘xc5!
+−; 21...♖e1+ 22 ♖xe1 +−; (3) 20...
♖e1+ 21 ♖xe1 ♖xe1+ 22 ♔f2 ♖e2+
23 ♔xe2 +−; 21 ♔f2? ♖1e2+! −+;
19 ♘xc5! ♕xc5 20 g5 ♘e4 21 ♖f4!
♖e5 22 ♖af1 ±/+−; 21...♘xg5 22
♖f5; 21...♕xg5 22 ♖xe4 +− ♖8e5
20 ♖af1 ♗e7! 20...♖xf5? 21 ♖xf5
♖e5 22 ♖xe5 ♕xe5 23 g5 +−; 20...
h6? 21 ♖xf6 +− 21 g5 ♘e4

22 ♖xf7? 22 ♗c4! ♕xc4 23 ♖xe5
♘g3 24 ♘d2 (1) 24...♕e2 25 ♖xe7!
♘xf1 26 ♘e4!! ♔f8 27 g6! hxg6 28
♖xb7 +−; 27...fxg6 28 ♖e5 +−;
25...♖xe7 26 ♕xg3 ♕xd2 27 ♕b8+
+−; (2) 24...♕c8 25 ♖xe7! ♘xf1 26
g6! △ ♗xf1/♘e4! +−; (3) 24...♕xc2?
25 ♖xe7! ♖xe7 26 g6! +−; (4) 24...
♕c7 25 ♖xe3; 22...♖xf5 23 ♗xd5
♖xd5 24 ♕f4 +− ♘xg5 22...♕xf7
23 ♖xf7 ♔xf7 24 ♕f4+ ♔e6 25 ♘xd4+
+− 23 ♖7f4! 23 ♖7f2 ♘h3+! 24 gxh3
♖g5+ −+ b5?? (1) 23...♘f3+ 24 ♖1xf3
♖e1+ 25 ♗f1 ♕xf3 26 gxf3 ♗xh4 27
♖xh4 ♖5e2 28 ♖xd4 ♖xc2 29 ♖d2±;
24...♖xd3 25 ♕xe7? ♖d1+ 26 ♔f2
♕xf3+ −+; 25 cxd3! ♕xf3 26 gxf3
+−; 24 ♖4xf3 ♖xd3 25 cxd3 ♕xf3
26 ♕xd4 ♕e3+ 27 ♕xe3 ♖xe3 28
♖d1±; 25 ♕xe7? ♖xf3 −+; (2) 23...
h5?! (△ ♘h3+) 24 ♖xd4 ♘f3+ 25
gxf3 ♗xh4 26 ♖xd5 ♖xd5 27 ♗c4
+−; 24 ♔h1? ♘h3 25 ♕xe7 ♘xf4 −+;
24 ♕f2? ♘h3+ −+; (3) 23...♘h3+?
24 gxh3 ♖g5+ 25 ♖g4 +−; (4) 23...
♖f3?! 24 gxf3! +−; (5) 23...h6 24
♕f2 +−; (6) 23...♖xd3! 24 cxd3 ♘e6!
≈ 24 ♕f2± 24 ♖xd4? ♘f3+! −+
♗f6 25 ♖xd4 ♕e6? 25...♕a8± 26
♖d8+ ♔f7 27 ♗f5 ♕b6 28 ♖d7+ ♔e8
29 ♖d3 ♘f7 30 ♗xh7 +− ♘d6 31
♗g6+ ♔f8 32 ♘d4 ♖xd3? 32...♔g8

33 ♘e6+ ♖xe6 34 ♛xb6 ♖d2 35 ♛d8+ 1-0 Miles

335 Sax-Petrosian Rio 79
1 e4 e6 2 d4 d5 3 ♘d2 c5 4 exd5 exd5 5 ♗b5+ ♘c6 6 ♛e2+ ♗e7 7 dxc5 ♘f6 8 ♘b3 0-0 9 ♘f3 ♖e8 10 ♗e3 10 0-0 ♗xc5 11 ♛d3 ♗b6 12 ♗g5 += Keres **a6!** 11 **♗a4** 11 ♗xc6 bxc6 12 0-0 a5 =+ Δ ♗a6, a4 **♘e4 12 0-0-0 ♗xc5** =+ 13 **♘fd4 ♗d7 14 ♘xc6 bxc6 15 ♖he1 ♗b4 16 ♖f1** 16 c3? ♗xc3 **♛c7 17 ♛d3?! ♛xh2!∓ 18 ♖h1 ♛e5** 18...♛xg2? 19 ♖dg1 ♛f3 20 ♖xg7+ ♔xg7 21 ♗h6+ Δ ♛xf3 +− **19 ♘d4 ♖ac8 20 c3 ♗d6 21 ♗c2 g6 22 ♛xa6 ♖a8 23 ♛d3** 23 ♛xb7 ♘c5 **♖xa2 24 ♗b1 ♖a1 25 ♘c2 ♖aa8 26 ♘d4 ♛f6! 27 ♘f3** 27 ♖df1 c5 28 ♘f3 ♗f5∓ **♖a1 28 ♛c2 ♗f5 29 ♘d4 ♖xb1+ 30 ♛xb1 ♘xc3 31 ♘xf5 ♘xb1 32 ♘h6+ ♔f8 33 ♔xb1 ♖b8 34 ♖d2 ♗f4 35 ♖h3 ♗xe3 36 ♖xe3 ♔g7 37 ♖f3 ♛xf3 0-1 Miles**

336 Tal-Portisch Montreal 79
1 e4 e6 2 d4 d5 3 ♘d2 c5 4 exd5 exd5 5 ♗b5+ ♗d7 6 ♛e2+ ♗e7 6...♛e7 **7** ♗xd7+ ♘xd7 8 dxc5 ♘xc5 9 ♘b3 ♛xe2+ 10 ♘xe2 += Karpov-Korchnoi, (16) 78 **7 dxc5 ♘f6 8 ♘b3 0-0 9 ♘f3 ♖e8 10 ♗e3 a6 11 ♗d3 ♗a4 12 ♘fd4!?** += **♘bd7 13 0-0-0** N 13 0-0= Larsen-Portisch, Tilburg 78 **♘xc5 14 ♘f5 ♗f8 15 ♘xc5** 15 ♛f3 ♘ce4! **♗xc5 16 ♛f3 ♗xe3+ 17 ♘xe3** 17 fxe3?! ♗d7= **♖c8** 17...♗c6 18 ♘f5 += **18 ♗f5!? ♖c5 19 ♖d4!?** 19 ♛f4!? ♗c6 20 b4 +−; 19...♗d7!? **♗c6** 19...♗d7 20 ♗xd7 ♛xd7 21 ♖hd1± **20 b4 ♖b5** 20...♖c3?? 21 ♔b2 +− **21 a4 ♖b6** 21...♛b6 22 c3; 21...♖xb4! 22 ♖xb4 d4 23 ♛d1 dxe3 24 ♛xd8 ♖xd8 25 fxe3 ♗xg2 26 ♖d1 ♖e8 27 ♗d7!

♖xe3 28 ♗c8±; 27...♖b8!? **22 a5 ♖b5** 22...♖xb4!?

23 ♛f4! += 23 ♗d3? ♖xb4! 24 ♖xb4 d3∓ **b6** 23...♘e4 24 ♗xe4 ♖xe4 25 ♛xe4 +− **24 ♗d3 bxa5 25 ♗xb5 axb5** 25...♗xb5!? **26 ♖hd1!** axb4 **27 ♔b2** 27 ♖xb4?! ♛a5 **♛c8 28 ♖xb4 ♘e4 29 ♖d3** 29 ♘f5 ♗d7 30 ♖xe4 ♖xe4 31 ♛xe4 ♗xf5 32 ♛e2 b4!!= 33 ♛d2 d4! 34 ♖a1 h6= **♘c5 30 ♖a3 ♘a4+** 30...♘e6 31 ♛d6 ♖d8 32 ♛e5 f6 33 ♛f5 += **31 ♔c1 ♗d7** 31...h6!? **32 ♛d6 ♗c6** 32...♗f5 33 ♖xb5 ♖xe3 34 ♖b8 +− **33 ♖d3 h6** Δ ♛e6 **34 ♖f4!** Δ ♘f5 **♛e6?** 34...♖e6 **35 ♛xe6 fxe6 36 ♘g4!±** e5 **37 ♖f5 ♘c5** 37...e4 **38 ♖g3 +− 38 ♖c3 ♗d7 39 ♖xe5 1-0 Tal**

337 Westerinen-Botterill
England 79
1 e4 e6 2 d4 d5 3 ♘d2 c5 4 exd5 exd5 5 ♗b5+ ♘c6 6 ♘gf3 ♗d6 7 0-0 ♘ge7 8 dxc5 ♗xc5 9 ♘b3 ♗d6 10 ♘bd4 0-0 11 b3!? N 11 c3 ♗g4 12 ♗b2 ♛b6 13 ♗e2 ♗c5 14 ♘xc6 bxc6 15 ♘g5** 15 ♘e5!? ♗f5 16 ♗d3 f6!? 17 ♗xf5 fxe5 18 ♗e6+ ♔h8 19 ♗xe5 ♗xf2+ 20 ♔h1 ♘g6 **♗f5 16 ♗d3 f6 17 ♗xf5 ♘xf5** 17...fxg5 18 ♗e6+ ♔h8∞ **18 ♘e6 ♖fe8 19 ♘xc5 ♛xc5 20 ♛d3 ♖e4 21 c4 ♖ae8 22 cxd5**

♕xd5 23 ♕xd5+ cxd5 24 ♖ad1 ♖e2
25 ♗c3?! 25 ♗a1= ♖c8 Δ ♖cc2, ♘e3
26 ♖xd5 ♘e3 27 fxe3 ♖xc3 28 ♖d4
♖xa2 28...h5 29 ♖c4 ♖d3 30 ♖d4
29 ♖f2 ♖c1+ 30 ♖f1 ♖cc2 31 ♖g4
h5 32 ♖g3 ♔f7 33 h4! Δ ♖d1=; 32
♖g3 h4 33 ♖g4 h3 34 gxh3 ♖xh2 35
♖xf6= ½-½ **Botterill**

338 Barry-Botterill Dublin 79
1 e4 e6 2 d4 d5 3 ♘d2 c5 4 exd5
exd5 5 ♘gf3 ♘c6 6 ♗b5 ♗d6 7 0-0
♘ge7 8 dxc5 ♗xc5 9 ♘b3 ♗d6 10
♘bd4 0-0 11 c3 ♕c7!? N 11...♗g4
12 ♕a4 ♗h5≈; 11...♕d7 12 h3 a6 13
♗d3 ♘g6 14 ♕c2 ♖e8 15 ♗e3 ♘a5
16 ♘f5?! 16 ♖ad1 Δ 16...♘c4 17
♗c1 += ♗xf5 17 ♗xf5 ♘c4 18 ♗d4
♖e7 19 ♖fe1 ♖ae8 20 ♖xe7 ♖xe7
21 ♖e1? 21 ♗d3

21...♖xe1+? 21...♘h4! −+ 22 ♗xe1
♕e7 Δ 23 ♘f3 ♘h4! −+ 23 ♔f1 ♗f4
24 ♘d3? 24 ♘f3! ♘h4 25 ♗xh7+
♔h8 26 ♕e2! += ♘d2+ 25 ♔g1 ♕e2!
26 ♘xf4 ♕e1+ 0-1 27 ♔h2 ♘f1+ 28
♔g1 ♘e3+ **Botterill**

339 Hubner-Larsen Montreal 79
1 d4 e6 2 e4 d5 3 ♘d2 ♘c6!? 4 ♘gf3
♘f6 5 e5 ♘d7 6 ♘b3 6 ♗e2!? a5 7
a4 b6 8 c3 8 ♗b5 ♘cb8!? Δ ♗a6
♗e7 9 ♗d3 9 h4!? ♗a6 10 ♗xa6 ♖xa6

11 0-0 ♖a8 12 ♖e1 ♘f8 13 ♘bd2
♘g6 14 ♘f1 ♕d7 Δ f6 15 ♕e2 0-0
16 ♘g3 ♖ae8 17 ♘h5 f6 18 ♘f4
18 exf6 ♗xf6 19 ♘xf6+ ♖xf6= ♗xf4
19 ♗xf4 f5 20 ♖eb1 ♖a8= 21 ♕b5
♖fc8 22 ♗g5 ♗f8 23 ♗d2 h6 24 b4
g5?! 24...♘b8 25 ♕xd7 ♘xd7 26
bxa5 ♖xa5 27 c4 ♖a7 28 cxd5 exd5
29 ♖b5±; 24...♕e8!= 25 h4! += g4
26 ♘e1 Δ ♘d3-f4 ♕e8 27 ♕d3 axb4
28 cxb4 ♖a7 29 ♗c3 ♖ca8 30 ♕d1
♘d8 31 b5! c5 32 dxc5 ♗xc5 32...
bxc5? 33 ♘d3 ♘b7 33...g3 34 ♘xc5
gxf2+ 35 ♔xf2 bxc5 36 a5 34 g3
d4?! 34...h5 35 ♘f4 ♗f8 (Δ ♗h6)
36 ♗d4± 35 ♗d2 ♗f8 36 ♕b3 ♖c8
37 ♖c1 ♖aa8 38 ♖a2 ♖xc1+ 39 ♗xc1
♘a5 40 ♕b1 ♖c8 41 ♖c2 ♖c3 42
♖xc3 dxc3 43 ♕c2 ♕c8 44 ♗e3 Δ
♗d4 ♕c4 45 ♗xb6 ♘b3 46 ♗e3 ♘a1
46...♕xa4 47 b6 +− 47 ♕e2 ♕xa4
48 b6 ♘b3 49 ♕c2! +− ♕c4 50 ♕a2!
50 b7? ♕b5! ♕d5 51 ♘f4 ♕d1+ 52
♔h2 c2 53 ♕xb3 1-0 **Keene**

340 Grunfeld-Mednis Riga 79
1 e4 e6 2 d4 d5 3 ♘d2 ♘f6 4 e5 ♘fd7
5 c3 c5 6 ♗d3 b6 7 ♘h3! ♗a6 8 ♗xa6
♘xa6 9 0-0 += ♘c7 10 ♕g4! N 10 ♖e1
Ivanovic-Andersson, Niksic 78 ♕c8?
10...♘b8!? 11 dxc5! (11 ♘f3 ♕d7 12
♘f4 g6) 11...bxc5 12 c4! +=; 10...c4!?
11 ♘f3 ♘b8 11 ♘f3 ♕a6 12 ♘f4 g6
13 ♘g5 ♗e7 14 h4!± ♘f8?! 14...h5
15 ♕g3 ♘f8 16 ♘fh3!± Δ ♕f3 15 h5
♕a4 16 dxc5! bxc5 17 b3 ♕c6 18
♗d2 ♖g8? 18...♖d8± 19 h6! +− ♖d8
20 ♖fe1 ♖d7 21 ♘fh3! ♘a8 22 ♕f4
♗d8 23 ♖e3 ♘b6 24 ♖f3 ♕c7 25
♖d1 ♕b7 26 ♗c1! ♘c8 27 ♗a3 ♖c7?
27...♗b6 28 ♕a4+! ♕c6 29 ♕xc6+
♖xc6 30 ♖xf7 ♖h8 31 ♖g7 ♘d7 32
♖e1 ♖a6 33 ♗c1 ♖xa2 34 ♘xe6 ♗a5
35 ♘hg5! ♗xc3 36 ♘c7+ 1-0 **Mednis**

341 Finlayson-Botterill England 79
**1 e4 e6 2 d4 d5 3 e5 c5 4 c3 ♞c6 5
♞f3 ♛b6 6 a3 c4 7 g3 f6!? 8 exf6
♞xf6 9 ♝g2 ♝d6 10 0-0 0-0 11 ♕e2
♞a5 12 ♞bd2 ♚h8 13 ♚h1** 13 ♘e5
♝xe5 14 ♕xe5! += **♝d7 14 ♞e1 ♝e8
15 f4 ♝g6 16 ♖g1** 16 ♕xe6 ♖ae8
17 ♕h3 ♝d3! **♖ae8 17 ♝f3 ♛c6** 17...
e5!? 18 fxe5 ♝xe5 19 dxe5 ♘c6∞
18 h4 h6 19 ♞g2 ♝d3 20 ♕e3

20...♛c8∓ Δ e5, ♕h3 mate **21 ♕h2
♞c6 22 b4 e5! 23 ♕f2** 23 fxe5 ♝xe5
24 dxe5 ♘xe5 −+ **exd4 24 cxd4
♞g4+ 25 ♝xg4 ♛xg4 26 ♕f3 ♝f5 27
♛xg4 ♝xg4 28 ♝b2 ♖e2 29 ♝c3 ♞xd4
30 ♝xd4 ♖xd2 31 ♝e3 ♖d3 32 ♖gc1
d4 33 ♝f2 ♖d2 34 ♕g1 b5 35 ♖e1
c3 36 ♖ec1 ♝c7 37 ♝e1 ♖b2 38
♝f2 ♝b6 39 f5 ♖xf2 40 ♛xf2 d3+
0-1 Botterill**

**342 Speelman-Botterill
British Final 79**
**1 e4 e6 2 ♕e2 c5 3 ♞f3 ♞c6 4 g3 g6
5 ♝g2 ♝g7 6 0-0 d6 7 c3 e5** 7...♘ge7
8 d4!± **8 ♞a3 ♞ge7 9 d4?! cxd4 10
cxd4 exd4 11 h3 0-0 12 ♖d1** 12
♝f4 h6! =+ **a6 13 ♞c2 ♛b6 14 ♕d2
d5 15 exd5 ♞xd5 16 ♞fxd4 ♞xd4**
16...♖d8! 17 ♘xc6 bxc6 =+ **17 ♞xd4
♖d8 18 ♞b3 ♝e6 19 ♛a5 ♛xa5 20
♞xa5 ♞c3= 21 ♖xd8+ ♖xd8 22 ♝g5**

**22 bxc3? ♖d1+ 23 ♚h2 ♝xc3∓ ♖d1+
23 ♖xd1 ♞xd1 24 ♝f3= ½-½ Botterill**

1 e4 ♞f6

343 La Rota-Valvo USA 79
1 e4 ♞f6 2 ♞c3 d5 3 exd5 3 e5 d4 4
exf6 dxc3 5 fxg7 cxd2+ 6 ♛xd2
♕xd2+ 7 ♝xd2 ♝xg7 8 0-0-0 ♞c6
(8...0-0=) 9 ♝b5! ♝d7 10 ♞f3 (10
♞e2!?) h6 11 ♖he1 e6 12 ♖e3 a6 13
♝a4 0-0-0 14 ♝c3 ♝xc3 15 ♖xc3 +=
Nogueiras-Popov, Kecskemet 79; 3...
♞d7 4 ♞xd5 ♞xe5 5 ♞e3 c5 6 b3
♞ec6! 7 ♝b2 e5 8 g3 ♝d6 9 ♝g2 0-0
10 ♞e2 f5 11 ♞c4 ♝c7 12 d3 ♝e6
13 ♛d2 ♝d5= Groszpeter-Suba,
Kecskemet 79; 5...♞bc6 6 b3?! (6
♞f3) e6 7 ♝b2 ♝e7 8 f4 ♞g6 9 ♝xg7
♖g8 10 ♝b2 ♞xf4 11 g3 ♞d5 12 ♝g2
♞xe3 13 dxe3 ♝d7 14 ♕f3 ♝b4+!
15 c3 ♝c5∓ Nimzovich-Reti, Baden-
Baden 25 **♞xd5 4 ♝c4 4** ♛f3 e6 5
♝c4 ♞b4 6 ♝b3 ♞8c6 7 ♞ge2 ♝e7!
8 a3 ♞e5 9 ♛g3 ♞bc6 10 d4 ♞g6
11 d5 exd5 12 ♞xd5 ♝d6= Bellon-
Alburt, Bucharest 78; 4 ♞xd5 ♛xd5
5 d4 ♞c6 6 ♞f3 e5 7 ♝e3 exd4 8 ♞xd4
♝c5= **e6 5 ♞f3 ♝e7** 5...c5 6 0-0 ♝e7 7
d4 ♞xc3 8 bxc3 0-0 9 ♕e2 ♞c6 10
♖d1 ♛c7! Δ b6, ♝d7≈ **6 0-0 0-0**
6...♞xc3 7 bxc3 0-0 8 ♞e5?! c5 9
f4 ♛c7 10 ♕e2 ♝d6 11 d4 ♞c6 12
♝e3 cxd4 13 cxd4 ♞e7= Rosselli-
Grunfeld, Baden-Baden 25 **7 ♖e1**
Δ ♞xd5 **♞f6** 7...♞xc3 8 bxc3 ♝d7 Δ
b6, ♝b7; 7...♞b6!? **8 d4 ♞bd7 9 ♝f4!
+= c5** 9...a6!? 10 a4 c5 **10 ♞b5!? ♞e8**
10...a6? 11 ♝c7 ♛e8 12 ♞d6 ♝xd6
13 ♝xd6 +− **11 d5! ♞b6** 11...exd5
12 ♛xd5 ♞b6 13 ♛xd8 ♝xd8 14
♞e5! +=

175

12 dxe6! ♘xc4! 12...♕xd1? 13 exf7+
+−; 12...♖xe6!? 13 ♗xe6 fxe6 14
♕xd8 ♗xd8∞; 14 ♕e2 ♖xf4 15 ♕xe6+
♖f7 16 ♘e5 ♕d5 17 ♘xf7 ♕xe6 18
♖xe6 ♔xf7 19 ♖ae1 ♘c8! (19...♗f6?
20 ♖xe8 +−) 20 ♖6e3∞ **13 exf7+
♖xf7 14 ♕e2 +=/∞ ♘ed6?** 14...♘xb2!
15 ♖ab1 ♗f6 16 ♘e5+ ♗xe5 17 ♗xe5
a6 18 ♘c3 ♕b6≈; 15 ♘e5+?! ♔g8!∓
15 ♖ad1! +− ♗f5 15...♔g8 16 ♘xd6!
+− **16 ♘e5+ ♗xe5 17 ♗xe5 ♕d7 18
♗xd6 ♗xd6 19 ♖xd6 1-0** 19...♘c8
20 ♕c4+ ♗e6 21 ♖dxe6 +− **Ciamarra**

344 Bellon-Kovacevic Karlovac 79
1 e4 ♘f6 2 ♘c3 d5 3 e5 3 exd5 ♘xd5
4 ♗c4 ♘b6 5 ♗b3 c5 6 ♕h5 e6 7 d3
♘c6 8 ♘ge2 += **♘fd7?!** 3...d4 4 exf6
dxc3 5 fxg7 cxd2+ 6 ♕xd2 ♕xd2+
7 ♗xd2 ♗xg7 8 0-0-0 0-0 +=; 3...
♘e4!? 4 ♕f3 ♘xc3 5 dxc3 g6 6 ♗f4
♗g7 7 0-0-0 c6 8 h4 h5= Dolmadian-
Donchev, Bulgaria Final 78 **4 e6!**
4 ♘xd5 ♘xe5 5 ♘e3 c5 6 b3!? ♘ec6!
7 ♗b2 e5= **fxe6 5 d4 g6?!** 5...e5 6
dxe5! e6 7 ♗d3!±; 5...c5 6 ♘f3 ♘c6
7 dxc5 g6 (7...♘xc5 8 ♗b5 ♗d7 9
♗e3 +=) 8 h4 ♘f6 9 ♗b5 ♗d7 10 h5!?
♘xh5? 11 ♖xh5! gxh5 12 ♗xc6 ♗xc6
13 ♘e5 +−; 10...gxh5!?; 10 ♗e3 ♗g7∞
6 h4!± ♘f6 6...♗g7 7 h5 ♘f8 8 ♘f3!
7 h5! ♘xh5?! 7...gxh5? 8 ♗e2 ♕d6
9 ♗xh5+ ♔d8 10 ♘f3 ♘bd7 11 ♘g5
+− Voellmy-Staehelin, Geneva 38
8 ♖xh5 gxh5 9 ♕xh5+ ♔d7 10 ♘f3!
Δ 11 ♘e5+ ♔d6 12 ♘b5 mate **♗g7
11 ♗h6! ♗f6 12 ♘xd5!!± exd5** 12...
♕e8 13 ♘e5+ ♔d8 14 ♘f7+ ♔d7 15
♗c4! +−; 13...♗xe5 14 ♕xe5 ♕d8
15 ♘xc7! +−; 12...♘c6± Hort **13
♕xd5+ ♕e8 14 ♕h5+ ♕d7 15 0-0-0
+− c6 16 ♗f4 ♕g8 17 ♘e5+ ♕d8**
17...♗xe5 18 dxe5+ ♔c7 18 e6+ ♔b6
19 ♗e3+ c5 20 ♕xc5 mate; 18...♔e6?

19 ♗c4 mate **18 ♗f7+! ♕d7 19 ♕f5+
♕e8 20 ♕xc8+ ♕xf7 21 ♗c4+ 1-0**
21...♔g6 22 ♕g4+ ♗g5 23 ♕xg5 mate;
21...♔g7 22 ♕g4+! ♔f8 23 ♗h6+
♔g7 24 ♕c8 mate **Ciamarra**

345 Bohm-Bagirov
Burevestnik v Volmac 79
**1 e4 ♘f6 2 e5 ♘d5 3 d4 d6 4 ♘f3
♗g4 4...♘b6 5 ♗e2 e6 6 0-0 ♗e7 7
h3 ♗h5 8 c4 ♘b6 9 ♘c3 0-0 10 ♗e3
d5 11 c5 ♗xf3 12 ♗xf3** 12 gxf3!?
**♘c4 13 ♗f4! ♘c6 14 b3 ♘4a5 15
♗g4!** N 15 ♖c1; 15 ♕d2 **b6** 15...f5
16 exf6 ♗xf6 17 ♗xe6+ +− **16 ♘a4
bxc5 17 ♘xc5 ♗xc5 18 dxc5 += ♘e7
19 ♕d2 ♘ac6 20 b4 ♘g6 21 ♖fe1
♗xf4 22 ♕xf4 a6 23 a3?!** 23 ♖ab1;
23 a4± **♕d7 24 ♕e3 ♘e7 25 ♖ab1
♖fb8 26 ♗e2 ♘f5 27 ♕d2 h6 ½-½
Georgadze**

1 e4 g6

346 Gipslis-Avate Calcutta 79
**1 e4 d6 2 d4 ♘f6 3 ♘c3 g6 4 ♘f3
♗g7 5 ♗e2 0-0 6 0-0 c6 7 h3 b5 8 e5**
8 a3 ♘bd7 9 ♗e3 ♕c7 10 ♕d2 a6 11
♗h6 c5= Kuzmin-Timman, Sombor
72 **♘e8 9 a4!** 9 ♗f4 ♘d7 10 ♖e1
♗b7 11 ♗f1 b4 12 ♘e4 c5 Smyslov-
Lange 61; 13 exd6!?± **b4 10 ♘e4 ♗f5**
10...f5? 11 ♘ed2 ♘c7 12 ♖e1 h6 13
h4!± Vasyukov-Gurgenidze, USSR 61
11 ♘g3 ♗e6 12 c4 12 a5 ♘d7 13 ♗f4
dxe5 14 dxe5 ♘c7∞ Averbakh-Kotov,
Moscow 63 **bxc3 13 bxc3 ♘d7** 13...
♗d5 14 ♖e1 ♘d7 15 ♗f4 dxe5 Karpov-
Hort, Nice 74; 14 a5!? **14 exd6 ♘xd6**
14...exd6 15 a5!± **15 a5 ♖b8 16
♗a3 ♘b5** 16...♘c4 17 ♗b4± **17 c4
♘c3** 17...♘xa3 18 ♖xa3 c5 19 d5 ♗f5
20 ♘xf5 gxf5 21 ♗d3 e6 22 ♖e1 ♖e8
23 ♗c2±; 18...♘f6 19 ♘e5!± **18**

♕d2 ♘xe2+ 19 ♕xe2 ♖e8 20 ♖fd1±
♖b3 21 d5! cxd5 21...♗xa1 22 dxe6±
22 cxd5

22...♗xa1 22...♗xd5 23 ♖xd5 ♗xa1
24 ♕a2!± 23 dxe6! +− ♖xa3 24 exf7+
♔h8 24...♔xf7 25 ♘g5+ ♔g8 26
♕e6+ ♔g7 27 h4! +−; 25...♔f6 26
♘3e4+ +−; 25...♔g7 26 ♘e6+ +−
25 fxe8♕+ ♕xe8 26 ♕b5! 1-0 26...♘f6
27 ♕xe8+ ♘xe8 28 ♖d8 +− Gipslis

347 Psahis-Gufeld USSR 79
1 ♘g3 g6 2 e4 d6 3 d4 ♘f6 4 ♘c3 ♗g7
5 ♗e2 0-0 6 0-0 ♗g4 7 ♗e3 7 ♗g5!?
♘c6 8 d5 ♗xf3 9 ♗xf3 ♘e5 10 ♗e2 +=
♘c6 8 ♕d2 8 ♕d3 ♘d7! 9 ♘d2 ♘b4
10 ♕c4 ♗xe2 11 ♘xe2 c5! 12 dxc5=
Polugaevsky-Sax, Buenos Aires 78
e5 9 d5 9 dxe5!? dxe5 10 ♖ad1 ♘e7
10 ♖ad1 ♗d7!? 10...♘d7 11 ♘e1?!
♗xe2 12 ♕xe2 f5 13 f4 exf4 14 ♗xf4
♗xc3! 15 bxc3 fxe4 16 ♕xe4 ♘c5
17 ♕c4 ♕d7 18 ♘d3 ♕a4 =+ Geller-
Kuzmin, USSR 78; 10...♘c8 11 ♘e1
♗d7 12 f4∞ 11 ♘e1 11 h3 b5! b5!?
11...♘g4 12 ♗xg4 ♗xg4 13 f3 ♗d7
14 f4 ♗g4 15 ♘f3 f5 16 fxe5 dxe5 17
h3= 12 ♘d3 a5 13 b4!? c6 14 dxc6
♗xc6 14...♘xc6 15 ♗g5!? 15 f3 ♕c7=
16 bxa5 ♕xa5 17 ♖b1 d5! 18 ♘xe5
18 ♗c5 dxe4 19 fxe4 ♖fe8∞ ♘xe4 19
fxe4 19 ♘xc6? ♘xd2 20 ♘xa5 ♘xf1∓

♗xe5 20 ♗d4 ½-½ 20...♗xd4+ 21 ♕xd4
dxe4 22 ♘xe4 ♕a7 23 ♕xa7 ♖xa7 24
♘c3= Gufeld

348 Zhidkov-Sher USSR 79
1 ♘f3 g6 2 e4 ♗g7 3 d4 d6 4 ♘c3 ♘f6
5 ♗e2 0-0 6 0-0 ♗g4 7 ♗e3 ♘c6 8 ♕d2
e5 9 dxe5 dxe5 10 ♖ad1 ♕c8?!
10...♕xd2 11 ♖xd2 a6! 12 ♖fd1
♗xf3 13 ♗xf3 ♖fd8 +=; 10...♕e7 11
♘d5 ♘xd5 12 exd5 ♗xf3 13 ♗xf3
♘d4 14 ♗g4 f5 15 ♗h3 += 11 h3 ♗xf3
12 ♗xf3 ♖d8 13 ♘d5 ♘xd5 14 exd5
♘d4 15 ♗e4 ♘f5 16 c4?! 16 ♗xf5
♕xf5 17 c4 Δ c5, ♕b4 += ♘xe3 17
♕xe3 f5 18 ♗c2 e4 19 c5! ♔h8 19...
♗xb2 20 d6 ♔h8 21 ♗a4 += 20 ♗a4
♗xb2 21 f3?! 21 d6! += exf3 22
♖d4! b6! 22...♗xd4 23 ♕xd4+ ♔g8
24 ♖e1± 23 ♖b1 23 ♕e5+ ♔g8 24
d6 h5? 25 ♗b3+ ♔h7 26 ♕e7+ ♔h6
27 ♖d2±; 24...♗xd4+! 25 ♕xd4
cxd6 26 cxd6? ♕c5 =+; 26 ♗b3+
d5 27 ♗xd5+ ♖xd5 28 ♕xd5+ ♔g7
29 ♕e5+ = bxc5!= 24 ♖xb2 cxd4
25 ♕xd4+ ♔g8 26 d6 cxd6 27 ♗b3+
d5 28 ♗xd5+ ♖xd5 29 ♕xd5+ ♔h8
30 ♕e5+ ½-½ Gufeld

349 Vorotnikov-Sturua USSR 79
1 e4 d6 2 d4 ♘f6 3 ♘c3 g6 4 ♘f3
♗g7 5 ♗f4!? c6 5...♘c6 6 ♗e2 0-0 7
h3 ♘bd7 8 e5 += ♘e8 9 exd6 ♘xd6
9...exd6± 10 0-0 ♘f6 11 ♕d2 ♘d5
12 ♗e5 ♗f5 13 ♗xg7 ♔xg7 14 a3
♕b6= 15 ♘h4?! 15 b3 ♕xb2 16 ♘xd5
cxd5 17 g4 ♗e4 18 f3 ♖ac8! 19
♖ac1 ♖xc2 20 ♖xc2 ♗xc2 20...♕xc2?
21 ♕e3 21 ♖c1 ♖c8 22 ♗d1

Diagram

22...♘b5!! 23 ♖xc2 ♖xc2 24 ♕xc2
♕xd4+ 25 ♔g2 ♘xa3∓ 26 ♕c7 ♕d2+

27 ♔g3 ♕e1+ 28 ♔h2 ♕xh4 29 ♕c3+
d4! −+ 30 ♕xd4+ ♕f6 31 ♕xa7 ♕d6+
32 ♔g2 ♕d2+ 0-1 Gufeld

350 Timman-Kagan Rio 79
1 d4 d6 2 e4 g6 3 f4 ♗g7 4 ♘c3 a6?!
5 ♘f3 b5 6 ♗d3 ♗b7 7 0-0 ♘d7 8 e5
c5 9 ♗e4 ♗xe4 10 ♘xe4 cxd4 11 e6!
11 exd6 ♘h6!?∞; 11 ♕xd4? dxe5
12 fxe5 ♘xe5∓ fxe6 12 ♘eg5 ♘f8
13 ♘xd4∞ ♗xd4+ 13...♕d7? 14
♘dxe6! ♘xe6 15 ♕d5! +−; 13...♕c8
14 c3!? Δ a4∞; 14 ♖e1 e5 15 fxe5
♗xe5 16 ♘df3± ♗g7 17 ♕xd6 14
♕xd4 ♘f6 15 ♖e1 ♕c8 16 a4!± b4
16...bxa4 17 ♕xa4+ ♕d7 18 ♘xe6±
17 ♕xb4 ♕xc2 18 ♗e3 ♕c8 19 ♖ac1
♕b8 20 ♕c4 ♕b7 21 ♗d4 +− d5 22
♕c3 ♘8d7 23 ♘xe6 ♘e4 24 ♖xe4
dxe4 25 ♘c7+ ♔f7 26 ♕c4+ 1-0 Miles

351 Denman-Goodman
Brighton 79
1 e4 g6 2 d4 d6 3 ♘c3 ♗g7 4 f4 ♘c6
5 ♗b5 5 ♗e3 ♘f6 6 ♗e2 0-0 7 ♘f3
a6 6 ♗xc6+ bxc6 7 ♘f3 ♗g4 8 0-0
♕b8!? 8...♘f6 9 ♕d3 ♘f6 10 ♕c4
♕b7! 10...♕b6?! 11 e5 ♗e6 12 ♕d3∞
11 e5 ♘d5 12 ♘e4 12 ♘xd5 cxd5 =+
0-0 13 h3 ♗xf3 13...♗f5!? 14 ♘g3
♕b5 =+ 14 ♖xf3 ♕b5! 15 ♕b3 15
♕xb5?! cxb5 =+ ♖fb8 16 c4 ♕xb3

17 ♖xb3 17 axb3 ♘b4! Δ ♘c2∓
♗b4 17...♖xb3!? 18 axb3 ♘b4 18 ♖c3

18...c5!∓ 19 d5 dxe5 20 a3 exf4
21 axb4 ♗xc3 22 bxc3 cxb4 23
♗xf4 23 cxb4 ♖xb4 24 ♘d2 b3!
24 c5 Δ ♗xc7; 24 ♗xc7 ♖c8 ♖a7
25 c6 a5 Δ a4, a3 −+ 26 ♘c5 ♖b5
27 ♘a4 ♖xd5 28 c4 ♖f5 29 ♗e3 ♖a6
−+ 30 ♖b1 ♖xc6 31 c5 31 ♖xb3
♖xc4 32 ♘c3 a4 ♖e6 32 ♖xb3 ♖e4
33 ♘b2 ♖b4 34 ♖xb4 34 ♖d3 f6!
axb4 35 ♗f2 f6 36 c6 ♔f7 37 ♘d3
b3 38 ♗g3 e5 39 ♘b2 ♔e6 Δ ♔d6,
♔xc6 0-1 Fedorowicz

352 Morris-Keene Sydney 79
1 e4 g6 2 d4 ♗g7 3 ♘c3 d6 4 f4 ♘c6
5 ♗e3 ♘f6 6 ♗e2 0-0 7 ♘f3 a6!?
7...♗g4?! 8 e5! R.Byrne-Keene,
Hastings 71/72 8 0-0? 8 e5! ♘g4 9
♗g1 b5 10 ♘g5 f6!; 10...♘h6?!
Bednarski-Keene, Hanover 76 b5 9
e5 ♘g4 10 ♗c1 ♗b7 11 d5?! ♘a5
12 e6 f5! 13 a4? 13 a3 c6 =+ b4 14
♘a2 c6∓ Δ ♕b6+ 15 ♔h1 ♕b6 16
♕e1 b3 17 h3 ♘f6 18 ♗d2 bxa2 19
♗xa5 ♕xb2 20 dxc6 ♗xc6 21 ♗c3
♕a3 22 ♗c4 ♕xa4 23 ♗xa2 ♕xf4
24 ♘d4 ♕e4 24...♗xg2+ 25 ♔xg2
♕g5+ 26 ♔h1 ♘e4 27 ♘f3!∞ 25
♕f2 ♖ac8 26 ♗b2 ♗a8 27 ♗b3 ♕b7 28
♖g1 ♘e4 29 ♕f3 ♗e5 30 ♖gb1 ♘g3+

178

31 ♔g1 ♗xd4+ 32 ♗xd4 ♕xf3 33 gxf3 ♘e2+ 0-1 Keene

353 A.Smith-Diesen
USA 79
1 e4 d6 2 d4 ♘f6 3 ♘c3 g6 4 f4 ♗g7 5 ♘f3 c5! 6 ♗b5+ 6 e5!; 6 dxc5∞
♗d7 7 e5 ♘g4 8 ♗xd7+ ♕xd7 8...
♘xd7? 9 e6 △ ♘g5 **9 d5 dxe5** 9...
♘a6!? (△ 0-0-0, ♘c7) 10 h3 ♘h6
11 g4!? 0-0-0 12 ♗e3 e6 13 ♕e2! f5
14 0-0-0!± Filipowicz-Heiberg 77;
11 ♗e3!? **10 h3 e4 11 ♘xe4 ♘f6
12 ♘e5** 12 ♘xc5 ♕xd5 13 ♕xd5 ♘xd5
14 ♘xb7 ♘c6 =+; 12 ♘xf6+ ♗xf6
13 0-0 0-0 14 c4 e6 15 ♘e5 ♕d6 16
♕b3 b6= **♕d8** 12...♕a4!? **13 ♘xf6+
exf6** 13...♗xf6 14 0-0 0-0 15 c4 +=
14 ♘f3?! 14 ♘c4!? △ 0-0, c3, ♗e3
+= **0-0 15 0-0 f5 16 c4** 16 c3 +=
♘d7 △ ♘f6-e4 **17 ♕c2?** 17 ♗e3 +=
**♘f6 18 ♗e3 ♕d6!∓ 19 ♖ad1 ♖fe8
20 ♖fe1 ♖e4! 21 b4?!** 21 g3 ♖ae8
22 ♗f2 **♘d7 22 bxc5 ♘xc5 23 ♗c1
♖ae8 24 ♖xe4** 24 g3 fxe4 25 ♖e1
♖e7 26 ♘g5 ♗d4+ 27 ♔h1 f5! −+
27...♘d3 28 ♖xe4! ♘f2+ 29 ♔h2 ♘xe4
30 ♘xe4∞ **28 ♗a3 ♕xf4! 29 ♘e6
♘xe6 30 ♗xe7** 30 dxe6 ♗e5 31 g4
♕g3 −+ **♗e5 31 g4 ♕g3 32 ♖f1** 32
dxe6 ♕xe1+ 33 ♔g2 f4; 32 ♖d1 ♕f3+
33 ♔g1 ♘f4 **♕xh3+ 0-1 Ciamarra**

354 Balashov-Diesen
Karlovac 79
**1 e4 d6 2 d4 ♘f6 3 ♘c3 g6 4 f4 ♗g7
5 ♘f3 c5 6 dxc5 ♕a5 7 ♗d3 ♕xc5
8 ♕e2 0-0 9 ♗e3 ♕a5 10 0-0 ♗g4 11
h3 ♗xf3 12 ♕xf3** 12 ♖xf3 ♘c6 13
♖af1 ♘d7 14 ♖g3 ♕b4 15 ♘d1 ♖ac8=
Haikin-Inkev, USSR 73 **♘c6 13 a3**
13 ♖ad1 ♘d7 14 ♗c4 ♘c5 15 e5!?
dxe5 16 f5∞ **♘d7 14 ♗d2** 14 b4!?
♕d8 15 ♘e2 ♗xa1 16 ♖xa1 e6 17

♖d1 a6 18 c3 ♕e7 19 ♗c2 ∞/+=
Ljubojevic-Torre, Manila 75; 18...b5!?
♕b6+ 14...♖ac8 15 ♔h1 ♕d8 16
♖ab1 += **15 ♔h1 ♘c5 16 ♖ab1** 16 b4
♘xd3 17 ♕xd3 ♕d4= **♘xd3 17 cxd3
f5?!** N 17...e6 18 f5! exf5 19 exf5
♘d4 20 ♕g3 ♘xf5 21 ♖xf5! gxf5
22 ♘d5 f4! 23 ♕g4 f5 24 ♘xb6 fxg4
$\frac{1}{2}$-$\frac{1}{2}$ S.Szabo-Antoskiewicz, corr 75;
23 ♘f6+?! ♔h8 24 ♕h4 h6 25 ♗c3
♕b5! ∞/=+; 18 ♗e3 ♕a5 $\frac{1}{2}$-$\frac{1}{2}$! Spassky-
Bronstein, Tallinn 73 17...♕b3? 18
f5! ♕c2 19 ♗g5 ♘e5 20 ♕g3 f6 21
♗f5! Nunn-Torre, London 77 **18
♘d5 ♕d8 19 exf5 gxf5** 19...♘d4 20
♕e4 ♘xf5 21 ♗e1± **20 ♗c3 +=/± e6
21 ♘b4 ♖c8 22 ♖bc1** 22 ♕g3 ♕d7
♕d7 23 ♗xg7 ♔xg7 24 ♕e3!

24...♕f7?! 24...♘xb4 25 ♕d4+ ♔f7 26
♕xb4 ♖c6 27 ♕b5 ♕c7 +=; 25 ♖xc8
♖xc8 26 axb4 b6 += **25 ♘c2! ♖g8
26 ♘d4 ♘xd4 27 ♕xd4** 27 ♖xc8
♕xc8 28 ♕xd4 ♕c5∞ **b6?!** 27...♖xc1
28 ♖xc1 b6 += **28 ♖xc8 ♖xc8 29
♖e1 ♕c6** 29...♕e7!? △ ♖c6, ♕f6 **30
♕e3 ♕d5 31 ♕e2! ♕f6 32 ♕h5 ♖g8
33 ♕h6+ ♔f7 34 ♖e2! ♖g7 35 ♖c2
♕b7 36 ♕h5+ ♔f8?? Zeitnot** 36...
♔e7± **37 ♕h4 +− ♖e7 38 ♕f6+
♔g8 39 ♖e2 ♕d7 40 ♖e3 e5 41 ♖g3+
♖g7 42 ♖xg7+ ♕xg7 43 ♕xd6 1-0
Ciamarra**

355 Vegh-Puskas Hungary 79
1 e4 d6 2 d4 ♘f6 3 ♘c3 g6 4 f4 ♗g7
5 ♘f3 0-0 6 ♗d3 c5?! 6...♘a6; 6...♘c6
7 dxc5 dxc5 8 ♕e2 ♘c6 9 e5 ♘d5 10
♘xd5 ♕xd5 11 ♗e4 ♕d7 11...♕d8
12 ♗e3 ♕a5+ 13 c3± 12 ♗e3 b6 12...
♕c7 13 ♕b5! 13 h4! f5? 13...♗b7
14 ♗d3 h5 15 0-0-0 ♕c7 16 ♘g5 e6
17 g4! +− hxg4 17...fxg4 18 ♗xg6 +−
18 h5 ♗h6 18...♘xe5 19 fxe5 ♕xe5
20 c3 f4 21 h6! ♗f6 22 ♘e4 fxe3 23
♕xg4 ♔h7 24 ♖h5!! ♕c7 25 ♖g1 +−;
23...g5 24 ♕h5 ♔h8 25 ♘xf6 ♕xf6
26 ♖df1 +−; 25...e2 26 ♕g6!; 23...
♕f5 24 ♕g2 +− 19 hxg6 ♔g7 19...
♗xg5 20 ♖h7 +− 20 ♖xh6! ♔xh6 21
♖h1+ ♔xg6 22 ♕h2 1-0 Vegh

356 Morris-Chandler USA 79
1 e4 d6 2 d4 ♘f6 3 ♘c3 g6 4 f4
♗g7 5 ♘f3 0-0 6 ♗d3 ♘c6 7 e5 dxe5
8 fxe5 ♘g4! 8...♘d5!? 9 ♘xd5 ♕xd5
10 c3± 9 ♗e4 f6 10 h3 ♘h6 11 exf6
exf6 12 ♗e3 ♘f5 13 ♗f2 ♗h6! 14
♕d3 ♘d6!∓ 15 0-0 ♘b4 16 ♕d1 ♗xe4
17 ♘xe4 ♗f5 18 a3 18 ♖e1 ♖e8∓
♗xe4 19 axb4 ♕d6 20 c3 a6 21 ♖e1
♖fe8 22 ♗e3 ♗g7 23 ♘d2 f5 24
♘xe4 ♖xe4 25 ♗f2 ♖ae8 26 ♖xe4
♖xe4 27 ♕d3 c6 28 ♖d1 ♗f6 29 b3
♗d8 30 ♖e1 ♖xe1+ 31 ♗xe1 ♕e6∓
32 ♕d1 ♕e3+ 33 ♔f1 ♕f7 34 ♕e2
♕xe2+ 35 ♔xe2 g5 36 ♔d3 h5 37
c4 ♔e6 38 ♗f2 ♗c7 39 ♗e1 ♗f4 40
♗f2 g4 41 ♗e1 ♗g5 42 ♗f2 ♗e7 43
♗e1 ♗g5 44 hxg4 fxg4 45 ♔e4 b5!
46 g3 ♗d8 47 ♗f2 ♗e7 48 ♗e1 ♗d6!
Zugzwang 49 ♔e3 ♕f5! −+ 50 ♔d3
h4 51 gxh4 g3 52 c5 g2 53 ♗f2 ♗g3
54 ♗g1 ♗xh4 55 ♗e3 −+ 0-1
Gheorghiu

357 Sax-Torre Rio 79
1 e4 d6 2 d4 ♘f6 3 ♘c3 g6 4 f4 ♗g7

5 ♘f3 0-0 6 ♗d3 ♘c6 7 0-0 e5 8 dxe5
dxe5 9 f5 ♘b4 10 ♗g5 ♕d6 11 ♔h1
♘xd3 12 ♕xd3 ♕xd3 13 cxd3 c6=
14 ♖ad1 ♘d7?! 14...b6 △ ♗a6 15
♗e3 gxf5?! 15...b6 16 exf5 += △ ♘e4
♘b6 17 ♘d2 17 ♗c5!? ♖d8?! 18 ♗e7!
♖e8 19 f6 ♗f8 20 ♗xf8 ♔xf8 21
♖de1± 17...♖e8! 18 ♘e4 ♘d5∞
♖d8 18 ♘de4 f6 19 g4± ♘d5 20
♗c1 b6 21 g5 ♗b7 22 h4 c5 23 ♔h2
♘xc3 24 bxc3 c4 25 gxf6 ♗xe4

26 ♖g1 ♗xf5 27 ♖xg7+ ♔h8 28 ♖e7
♖e8? 28...♖xd3 29 ♖xd3 cxd3 30 ♗h6
(△ f7) ♗g6 31 f7 d2 32 ♗xd2 ♖f8
33 ♗h6 ♖xf7 34 ♖e8+ +−; 32...♔h7
33 ♖e8 +−; 28...♗g6 29 ♗h6 cxd3 30
f7 e4∞ 29 dxc4 +− ♖xe7 30 fxe7
♖e8 31 ♖f1 1-0 time 31...♗g6 32 ♗h6
Miles

358 Prokopovic-Verus Ochrid 79
1 e4 d6 2 d4 ♘f6 3 ♘c3 g6 4 f4 ♗g7
5 ♘f3 0-0 6 ♗e2 c5 7 d5 e6 8 dxe6
♗xe6 9 ♘g5?! d5! 10 e5 ♘e8 11 ♗f3
♘c7 12 ♘e2 ♘c6 13 c3 ♗c8! △ f6
14 g4?! f6 15 exf6 ♗xf6 16 h4 d4
17 ♕b3+ ♔h8 18 ♗d2 h6 19 ♘e4
♗xh4+ 20 ♔d1 ♗e6 21 ♕a3 21 ♕c2
d3 −+; 21 ♕xb7? ♘a5 −+ d3 22 ♘g1
♗e7∓ 23 f5 c4! 24 ♗xh6 ♔g8 25
b4 gxf5! 26 gxf5 26 ♗xf8 fxe4 27
♗xe7 ♕xe7 28 ♗g2 ♗xg4 −+ ♖xf5

27 ♕b2

27...d2!! 28 ♕c2 28 ♕xd2? ♖d5 −+
♘e5 **29 ♘xd2 ♗g5!** 29...♘xf3 30 ♘xf3
♖xf3? 31 ♕g6+ +− **30 ♗xg5 ♕xg5**
31 ♘h3 ♕e3 −+ **32 ♕e4** 32 ♗e2
♖d8 −+ **♖xf3 33 ♖g1+ ♔f8 34 ♕h7**
♖xh3 **35 ♕g7+ ♔e8 36 ♖e1 ♗g4+**
37 ♔c2 ♕xc3+ 38 ♔b1 ♗f5+ 0-1
Maric

359 J.Delaney-Botterill Dublin 79
1 e4 d6 2 d4 g6 3 ♘c3 ♗g7 4 f4
♘f6 5 ♘f3 0-0 6 ♗e3(!) ♘a6!? 6...b6!?;
6...c5 7 e5 ♘g4 8 ♗g1 c5 9 h3 cxd4
10 ♕xd4 ♘h6 11 g4 11 0-0-0 △ 11...
♘f5 12 ♕f2 △ g4; 11 0-0-0 ♗d7 12
g4 ♗d7 **12 0-0-0** 12 ♗c4 ♗c6 13 ♗d5
+= Byrne-Botterill, Haifa 76; 12 ♗c4
b5!?∝ **♗c6 13 ♕e3 ♕a5 14 ♖h2 ♖fc8**
15 ♗f2!? 15 ♔b1! ♘b4 16 ♔b1 ♘d5
16...♗xf3 17 ♕xf3 dxe5 18 a3? ♘xc2!
19 ♔xc2 e4 20 ♕e3 ♕a4+ 21 ♔c1
♖xc3+ 22 bxc3 ♕xa3+ 23 ♔c2 ♕a2+
24 ♔c1 ♖c8 −+; 18 ♗e1! e4 19 ♕e3!;
19 ♕xe4? ♗xc3 20 ♗xc3 ♖xc3 21
bxc3 ♘xa2∓; 19...♗xc3 20 ♗xc3
♖xc3 21 bxc3 ♕xa2+ 22 ♔c1± **17**
♘xd5 ♗xd5 18 a3 ♗xf3 19 ♕xf3 dxe5
20 ♖d5 ♕a4 21 ♗e3! e4 21...e6 22
♖xe5!± **22 ♕d1 e6 23 ♖d7 b5 24**
♖hd2 ♕a5 25 ♖b7?? 25 b4 ♕xa3
26 ♖d8+ ♗f8 27 ♘c5 ♖xc5=; 25 c3!±

♖cb8?? 25...♗xb2! −+ **26 b4! +−**
♕xa3 **27 ♖xb8+ ♖xb8 28 ♖d8+ ♗f8**
29 ♘c5 1-0 Botterill

360 Botterill-Chandler
British Final 79
1 e4 d6 2 d4 ♘f6 3 ♘c3 g6 4 f4 ♗g7
5 ♘f3 0-0 6 ♗e3 c5 7 dxc5 ♕a5 8
♗d3 dxc5 8...♘g4 9 ♗d2 ♕xc5 10
♕e2 ♘f6 11 ♗e3 ≈/+= **9 e5 ♘d5 10**
♗d2 ♘xc3 11 ♗xc3 ♕a4!? N 11...♕c7
12 ♕e2 ♘c6 13 h4! h5 14 ♗e4 ♗g4
15 ♕c4 b6 16 0-0-0± Kurajica-Eising,
Wijk aan Zee 2 74; 13...♗g4 14 h5!±
Kurajica-Cvetkovic, Jugoslavia 74;
11...♕b6 12 ♕e2 ♘c6 13 0-0-0 ♗e6
14 ♗c4 ♘b4 Radulov-Vadasz, Ulnja
76 15 a3!± **12 ♕d2 ♕c6 13 ♕e3 ♘a6**
14 ♗e4 ♕c7 15 0-0 15 h4!? ♗d7 **16**
♖fd1 ♖ad8 17 ♗e1! ♗c8 18 ♗h4
♖xd1+ 19 ♖xd1 ♖d8 20 ♖xd8+ ♕xd8
21 ♕d3 ♕c7 21...♕xd3 22 ♗xd3± △
♗xe7/♗xa6, ♗f2 **22 ♕b5 ♗f8 23**
♕e8 ♗d7 23...h6? 24 ♗xg6! fxg6
25 ♕xg6+ ♗g7 26 f5±; 25...♔h8 26
f5± **24 ♕a8 ♗c8 25 ♕xa7 e6 26 c4!**
♗h6 27 g3 ♗f8 28 a3 h6 29 ♕a8 ♕d7
30 ♔f2 ♔h7 31 ♗f6 ♕g8±

½-½? 32 g4 ♔h7 33 ♔g3 ♔g8 34
h3 ♔h7 35 ♗d8! ♔g8 (35...♕xd8
36 ♗xb7 +−) 36 ♗a5 ♗e7 37 ♕a7
♗d8! 38 b4!±; 38 ♗xd8 ♕xd8 39

♗xb7?! ♕d7 40 ♕xa6 ♗xb7 ∝ Botterill

361 Gutman-Zaichik USSR 79
1 d4 d6 2 e4 ♘f6 3 ♘c3 g6 4 f4 ♗g7
5 ♘f3 0-0 6 e5 dxe5 7 dxe5 7 fxe5!?
♕xd1+ 8 ♘xd1 8 ♔xd1 ♘h5! 9 ♗c4
♘c6 10 ♖f1 ♔h8∝ ♘d5 9 g3 ♘c6!
10 c3 10 ♗g2 ♘cb4 11 ♘d4 c5 −+
♗f5 11 ♘e3 ♗e4 12 ♔f2 g5 13 ♖g1
gxf4 14 ♘xd5 ♗xd5 14...fxg3+ 15
♖xg3 ♗xd5 16 ♗h6 +− 15 gxf4 ♕h8
16 ♗h3 e6 17 ♘d2 17 ♘g5 h6 18
♘f3 f6 19 ♘h4 ♗e7! ♘e7 18 c4 ♗c6
19 ♘f3 f6 =+ 20 ♗d2 20 ♘d4 ♗d7
21 ♗xe6 fxe5∓ ♗xf3 21 ♕xf3 fxe5
22 ♗xe6 ♗h6∓ 23 ♖g4 ♗xf4 24
♖xf4 ♖xf4+ 25 ♗xf4 ♖f8 26 ♖e1
♘g6 27 ♕g3 exf4+ 28 ♕f3 ♕g7 29
♗g4 ♕f6 30 ♖d1 ♖e8 31 ♗h5 ♖e3+
32 ♕g4 ♘e5+ 33 ♕xf4 ♖h3 34 ♗e2
♖xh2 35 ♕e3 ♖h3+ 36 ♕d4 ♖h4+
37 ♕d5 c6+ 38 ♕c5 ♖e4 39 ♗f1
♕e7 40 b3 b6+ 41 ♕b4 h5 42 ♗h3
a5+ 43 ♕a4 ♖e2 44 a3 ♖e3 45 ♗f1
h4 46 ♖d4 ♘f3 47 ♖f4 ♘d2 48 b4
♘b1 49 bxa5 ♘c3+ 0-1 Georgadze

362 Gufeld-Karasev USSR 79
1 e4 d6 2 d4 ♘f6 3 ♘c3 g6 4 g3!?
♗g7 5 ♗g2 0-0 6 ♘ge2 6 ♘f3?! ♗g4
7 ♗e3 ♘c6 8 h3 ♗xf3 9 ♕xf3 e5 10
dxe5 dxe5= e5 6...♘bd7 7 0-0 c5
8 h3 a6 9 ♗e3 ♕c7= 7 0-0 7 h3!?
♘c6 8 dxe5 dxe5 9 ♗g5 ♕xd1 9...♗e6;
9...♘d4!? 10 ♖axd1 h6 11 ♗e3 b6!
12 ♘b5!? 12 ♘d5 ♗a6! ♗a6 13 c4
13 a4 ♘a5!? ♘b4! 14 b3!? 14 ♖d2
♖ad8! 15 ♖fd1 ♖xd2 16 ♖xd2 ♘g4!
=+ ♗xb5 15 cxb5 ♘xa2 16 ♖a1 ♘b4
17 ♖fc1= ♖fd8! 17...♘e8?! 18 h3?!
♘e8 19 ♘c3 Δ ♗f1± a6? 19...a5!
20 ♘d5!± ♘xd5 21 exd5 e4 22
♖xa6 f5 23 ♗f1 23 f3 ♘f6!?; 23
♗f4 ♖ab8 24 ♖a7 ♖a8 25 ♖xa8 ♖xa8

26 d6! cxd6 27 ♗xb6? 27 ♗c4+!
♔f8 28 ♗xb6± d5! 28 ♖d1 d4 29
♗c4+ 29 ♗xd4 ♖d8 30 ♗xg7 ♖xd1
31 ♗xh6 ♖b1 ♕h7 30 ♗d5 ♖b8 31
♗xd4 ♗xd4 32 ♖xd4 ♖xb5 33 ♗c6
♖b8 34 ♖d7+ ♘g7 35 ♗d5 g5?!
35...h5 36 h4±

36 g4 +− ♕g6 37 ♖d6+ ♕h7 38
gxf5 ♘h5 39 ♗xe4 ♕g7 40 ♖g6+
♕f7 41 ♗d5+ ♕e7 42 ♖e6+ ♕d7 43
♖xh6 1-0 Gufeld

363 Izvozchikov-Chikovani
USSR 79
1 e4 d6 2 d4 g6 3 g3 ♗g7 4 ♗g2 ♘f6
4...♘c6!? Δ e5 5 ♘e2 0-0 6 0-0 e5
6...♘bd7 7 ♘bc3 c5!? 7 ♘bc3 ♘c6
8 ♖e1!? 8 dxe5=; 8 d5 ♘e7 9 f4 +=
exd4 8...♖e8 9 ♘xd4 ♘xd4?! 9...♗d7
10 ♕xd4 ♖e8 11 ♕d3 += ♗d7 12 h3
♗c6 13 ♗g5 h6 14 ♗e3 ♘d7 15 ♕d2
♕h7 16 ♖ad1 ♘c5 16...♘e5 17 b3?!
♕f6; 17 ♕e2 += 17 ♗d4 a5 18 f4
♗xd4+ 18...♘e6 19 ♗xg7 Δ f5±
19 ♕xd4± ♖e6 Δ ♕f6 20 e5! ♕e7
21 ♗d5! dxe5 22 fxe5 ♖e8 22...♖d8
23 ♕f4± 23 ♕h2 23 ♗xe6 ♘xe6∝
♖d8 24 ♕f2 f5 25 exf6 +− ♕xf6
26 ♕xc5 ♗xd5 27 ♘xd5 ♖xd5 28
♖xe6 1-0 Gufeld

364 Crouch-Botterill England 79
**1 g3 ♘f6 2 ♗g2 g6 3 e4 d6 4 d4 ♗g7
5 ♘e2 0-0** 5...c5 **6 0-0 e5 7 ♘bc3
♘bd7** 7...c6 8 a4! ♘bd7?! 9 a5! exd4
10 ♘xd4 ♘c5 11 h3 ♖e8 12 ♖e1
♘fd7 13 ♗e3 ♕c7 14 f4± Benko-
Fischer, Curacao 62 **8 a4! a5 9 dxe5
♘xe5** 9...dxe5 10 ♘b5 += **10 h3
♖e8 11 g4 h5?!** 12 g5 ♘h7 13 f4
♘c6 14 ♖a3! ♘b4 15 ♘b5 ♗f8 △ c6,
d5 16 f5! c6 17 ♘bd4 d5!? 17...♘xg5?
18 ♖g3 +− **18 fxg6** 18 exd5! ♘xd5
19 ♖d3±; 18...cxd5 19 ♖af3± △ c3
**fxg6 19 ♘f4 dxe4!∝ 20 ♘xg6 ♗c5 21
c3 ♘d3 22 ♗e3! ♕d6! 23 ♕xh5 ♕g3
24 ♗f4** 24 ♖f7? ♕xe3+ 25 ♔h1 ♕c1+
−+; 24 ♗d2 e3 25 ♖f7! +− **♘xf4
25 ♘xf4 ♖e5!** 25...♗f5? 26 g6 ♘g5
27 h4 +− **26 h4!** 26 ♕g6+ ♔h8 27
♘h5? ♕xg5∓ **♗g4 27 ♕g6+ ♔h8 28
♕h6!** 28 ♕f7 ♖g8 29 ♘g6+ ♖xg6
30 ♕xg6 ♗f3 31 ♖f2 ♗xg2? 32 ♖xg2
♕e1+ 33 ♔h2 ♕xh4+ =; 31...♕xh4
=+/∓; 28 ♘h5 ♕e3+ 29 ♔h1 ♖g8 30
♕h6 ♗f3! (△ ♗f8 −+) 31 ♘f6 ♗xg2+
32 ♔xg2 ♖exg5+! 33 hxg5 ♖xg5+
−+ **♗f3! 29 g6 ♖e7 30 gxh7 ♖g7
31 ♖f2 ♖f8** 31...e3? 32 ♖xf3 e2 33
♖a1 +− **32 ♘fe6 ♖g6**

33 ♕xf8+? 33 ♕xg6! ♕xg6 32 ♘xc5
∝/± **♗xf8 34 ♘xf8 ♖f6 35 ♘d7
♗xg2! −+ 36 ♖xg2 ♕e1+ 37 ♔h2**
♕xh4+ **38 ♔g1 ♕e1+ 39 ♔h2 ♖h6
mate 0-1 Botterill**

365 Tseitlin-Karasev USSR 79
**1 e4 d6 2 d4 ♘f6 3 ♘c3 g6 4 ♗g5!?
c6 5 ♕d2 b5?!** 5...♘bd7 **6 ♗d3 ♘bd7**
6...h6 7 ♗e3 ♘g4 8 ♗f4 e5 9 dxe5
dxe5 10 ♗g3 h5 11 ♘f3 +=; 7 ♗f4!?
△ e5 **7 f4 +=** ♘b6 7...e5?! 8 dxe5
dxe5 9 ♘f3; 7...h6 8 ♗h4 e5?! 9 dxe5
dxe5 10 ♘f3 **8 ♘f3 ♗g7 9 e5 ♘fd5
10 0-0 ♘c4?** 10...0-0 11 f5! ♗xf5 12
♗xf5 ♘c4 13 ♕c1 △ ♗h6; 11...f6
12 fxg6! fxg5 13 ♘xg5±; 10...f6!?
11 exf6 exf6 12 ♖ae1+ ♔f8 += **11
♗xc4 bxc4 12 ♖ae1! ♘xc3 13 ♕xc3
d5** 13...♗e6 14 b3 cxb3 15 ♕xc6+
♗d7 16 ♕a6± **14 ♕a3± ♗e6 15 ♕c5
♕d7?** 15...♕d7 16 b3 cxb3 17 axb3
♖c8! △ ♖c7, 0-0; 17...f6? 18 exf6
exf6 19 ♖xe6! +− **16 b3 cxb3 17 axb3
♖e8 18 ♖a1 f6** 18...♕c7 19 ♖a6 f6
20 ♖fa1 +− **19 exf6 ♗xf6 20 ♖a6
♕c7 21 ♖fa1 +− ♖eb8 22 ♘e5+
1-0 Gufeld**

366 Klaman-Karasev USSR 79
**1 e4 d6 2 d4 ♘f6 3 ♘c3 g6 4 h4 ♗g7
5 ♗e2 c5** 5...♘c6!? **6 dxc5 ♕a5 7
♔f1 ♕xc5 8 ♗e3 ♕a5 9 h5 gxh5
10 ♘h3** N 10 ♗xh5 ♘c6 11 ♗e2
♗e6 △ 0-0-0, d5 =+; 10 f3 ♘c6 11
♘h3 ♗e6∝ **♘c6** 10...♘g4 11 ♗d4
♗xd4 12 ♕xd4 ♖g8∝ **11 ♘f4 ♗g4?**
11...♘g4 12 ♗d2 ♕b6 13 ♗e1 ♗e5
14 ♘xh5 ♖g8 =+ **12 ♘xh5 ♗xh5 13
♗xh5 ♕b4 14 ♘d5 ♘xd5 15 ♕xd5**
15 exd5 ♘e5 16 ♗d4 ♕c4+ 17 ♗e2
♕xd5 18 f4 ♘c4 19 ♗xg7! ♘e3+
20 ♔f2 ♘xd1+ 21 ♖axd1 ♕c5+ 22
♗d4 ♕xc2 23 ♗xh8 f6∝ **♘d8** 15...
♕xb2?! 16 ♗xf7+ ♔d8 17 ♖d1 ♕xc2
18 g3!; 15...♘e5 16 ♗d4 0-0!=; 16 f4!
♕c4+ 17 ♗e2 ♕xd5 16 exd5 **16 ♕b3?!**

16 ♖b1 ♖c8 17 ♗d1 += ♕xe4 17 ♖e1 ♕f5 18 ♗e2 a6 18...h6 19 ♗d3 ♕d7 20 c3 20 ♖xh7 ♖xh7 21 ♗xh7 ♕b5+! =+ h6 21 ♖h3 ♞c6 22 ♗e4? 22 ♗f4 e6 23 a4∞ e6 23 ♖g3 ♗e5 24 ♖h3 d5! 25 ♗xd5? 25 ♗d3 h5 =+ ♕xd5 26 ♕xd5 exd5 27 ♗d4 f6 28 f4 0-0!∓ 29 fxe5 fxe5+ 30 ♗f2 ♖f6 31 ♔g1 ♖af8 Zeitnot 32 ♗c5 ♖d8 33 ♖d1 ♔f7 34 ♗e3 ♖dd6 35 ♗c5 ♖d7 36 ♗e3 ♔g7 37 ♗c5 ♔f7 38 ♗e3 ♖dd6 39 ♗c5 ♖d8 40 ♗e3 ♔g7 41 ♗c5 ♖f5! 42 ♗b6 ♖d7 43 ♖dd3 43 ♖hd3 h5 44 ♖h4 ♔g6 45 ♖g3+ ♖g5 46 ♖gh3 d4 47 ♖d3 ♖g4 48 ♖xg4+ hxg4 −+ 49 cxd4 exd4 50 ♔f2 ♔f5 51 ♔e2 ♔e4 52 ♖d1 ♞b4 53 ♗a5 ♞d5 54 ♗d2 ♖c7 0-1 Gufeld

367 Rostovtsev-Foigel
USSR 79
1 e4 g6 2 d4 ♗g7 3 ♞f3 d6 4 ♗c4 e6 5 ♕e2 ♞e7 6 ♞c3 a6 7 a4 b6 8 ♗g5 h6 9 ♗h4 ♞d7 10 0-0 0-0 11 ♖ad1 ♗b7 12 ♖fe1 ♕e8 13 ♗g3 ♞c8 14 h4?! c5! 15 dxc5 ♞xc5 16 ♗xd6 ♞xd6 17 ♖xd6 ♕e7 18 ♖ed1 18 ♖xb6 ♗xc3 19 bxc3 ♕c7 ♗xc3 19 bxc3 ♗xe4∞ 20 ♖6d4 ♗xf3 21 ♕xf3 h5!? 22 g3 ♔g7 23 ♕e3 ♖ac8 24 ♖d6 ♕f6 25 ♖1d4 ♞xa4 26 ♗xa6 ♖xc3 27

♕d2 ♖a3! 28 ♕c1 ♖a2 29 ♗c4 ♞c3 30 ♔g2 ♖a4 31 ♕d2 ♖c8 32 ♖f4 ♞e4!∓ 32 ♕e3 ♖axc4 33 ♖xf6 ♞xf6 34 ♕e5? 34 ♖d2∓ ♖8c5 35 ♕a1 ♖xc2 −+ 36 ♖xb6 ♖f5 0-1 Gufeld

368 Polgar-Ujtelky Budapest 79
1 e4 g6 2 d4 ♗g7 3 ♞f3 e6 4 h4 h6 5 c4 ♞e7 6 ♞c3 d5 7 ♗e3 dxe4 8 ♞xe4 b6? 8...♞bd7 9 ♗d3 ♞f6 10 ♞e5 ♞xe4 11 ♗xe4 0-0 12 0-0 c5 13 ♕d3 cxd4 14 ♗xd4 ♞f5 15 ♗c3 ♕xd3 16 ♗xd3 ♖d8 17 ♖ad1 ♗d7 += 9 ♞e5 ♗b7 10 ♕f3± △ ♞f6+

10...♗xe5?? 10...♞f5 11 g4 ♕c8 += 11 dxe5 ♔f8 13 ♖d1 +− ♕e8 14 ♕f4 ♞d7?? 15 ♖xd7 ♕xd7 16 ♞f6 1-0 16...♕c6 17 ♕xh6+ ♖xh6 18 ♗xh6 mate B.Balogh

184

Games Index